THE RISE AND FALL
OF THE
HOLY ROMAN EMPIRE

From Charlemagne to Napoleon

David Criswell

FORTRESS

ADONAI
PRESS

Dallas, TX

i

THE RISE AND FALL

OF THE

HOLY ROMAN EMPIRE

From Charlemagne to Napoleon

ISBN NUMBER 978-0692476550

Cover Design by David Criswell

David Criswell

FORTRESS

ADONAI
PRESS

Dallas, TX

Printed in the United States of America

Preface

When I began to write my dissertation in theology at Tyndale Seminary in Fort Worth, Texas I realized that I needed to study medieval history. This then led me to another more disturbing revelation. I found that there was not a single solitary book currently in print on the whole history of the Holy Roman Empire. Certainly a few books existed on the Middle Ages and a few dealing with individuals from the Holy Roman Empire but none that gave a comprehensive survey of its history. Even worse, I found that what books I was able to ferret out, whether from out–of–print book shops or lesser histories, yielded to the philosophy of separating Church history from secular history. I could read about one or the other but they were always treated separately as if they had no relation to one another, and this in the Middle Ages!

As a result I found myself writing not one but two books; my dissertation and this history book before you. My goal was twofold. First, I wanted to provide a comprehensive history of the empire from its foundation in 800 A.D. to its demise at the time of Napoleon. I wished for this to be more than a simple survey but I did not want it to be a series of multiple volumes. It was to be comprehensive but not exhaustive and to be no more than two volumes. My second goal was to merge Church history with secular history. Because the two are so intertwined in medieval history one would not normally think this would be such a hard task but the biases and prejudices of other authors made this a far more difficult task than I ever could have imagined.

The book you have before you is therefore the compilation of the history of the Holy Roman Emperors and their counterparts, the popes. Nevertheless, there is one other aspect of this book that differs from traditional histories. I have chosen not to treat the empire as a Germanic one. As I hope to prove this is a myth perpetrated not only by the proud Germanic people but also by its enemies. I include not merely Germany and Italy in my history but, where necessary, France, England, Normandy, Spain, and even the Latin States of Palestine, Byzantium, and America as they, at various times, remained under the sovereign authority of the papacy, even when the emperor's authority was in check in those countries. The Holy Roman Empire has been called an "empire of many nations." Any history which ignores this, ignores history. This history is, therefore, the history of many nations under the banner of ancient Rome, but also of an empire in transition. It is the history of world during its puberty. It was the beginning of the civilizations we know today.

iv

Table of Contents

†   †   †

1

Introduction

In the last hundred years Europe has seen two World Wars and countless conflicts between nations. The continent, once home of the greatest empire on earth, has been divided and beset by discord. Adolph Hitler claimed to restore Germany to its former glory. He arrogantly claimed he would restore that great "reich." This first Reich was the Holy Roman Empire and according to Hitler his Third Reich was to last a thousand years even as the Firsrt Reich had lasted a thousand years. Indeed, for just over one thousand years the Holy Roman Empire reigned over Europe, and in fact, touched the whole of the world. Since its fall, however, Europe has been constantly at war with itself. Despite this, and even because of this, modern historians often treat the history of the Europe as the history of separate nations. Yet from this single empire emerged all these separate nations. It is, therefore, ironic that there is not a single book currently in print that deals with the entire history of the Holy Roman Empire. Each book either deals with the history of individual nations, ignoring the larger empire to a great extent, or takes a brief period of the empire's history. Still other books examine the middle ages without a clear picture of the empire that engulfed it. Yet it is this great empire that has shaped the course of modern history.

What Was the Holy Roman Empire?

The Holy Roman Empire is unique in history. In many ways it was a continuation of the ancient Roman Empire, but in many other ways it was the forerunner of modern states and governments. Indeed, while this era is popularly, and erroneously, referred to as the "dark ages," the appropriate term, preferred by historians, is "middle ages." It is so called because it was an age of progression between the barbarism of the ancient empires and the arts, literature, sciences, and freedoms of the modern. The "dark ages" were not, by and large, as dark as the ancient world. Many advancements were made. Many new ideas of freedom and justice arose. The old barbarianism remained, but veiled with a new cloak of respectability. Paganism now bore the nominal title of Christianity, and it is for this reason that the middle ages are so despised: not because they were truly worse than the ancient Romans but because of their hypocrisy. Few have even heard of the heinous crimes of Augustus Caesar or Marcus Aurelius, so glamorized by historians and recent film makers, but all have heard of the atrocities committed by the Crusaders.

To be sure the Holy Roman Empire was far from Holy, as Voltaire once flippantly remarked, but neither was it truly barbaric. Indeed, most might be shocked to learn that the most barbaric age that the world has ever seen was

1

not the 12th Century nor the 13th Century but the 20th Century. Never before in history had so much butchery and depravity plagued the earth. In Europe two world wars threatened the peace of the entire earth, Communism executed and slaughtered countless tens of millions of people, and Hitler tried to exterminate the Jewish people from the face of the planet. With the acquisition of nuclear weapons terrorism became the new tool of weaker nations, as the attack on the World Trade Center proved.

The simple truth is that the Holy Roman Empire was a mixture of good and evil, and was the seed of everything good and evil that has since encompassed the globe. Revisionists historians have remarked that history is tainted by white male European bias, but true history is based on those people, places, and events that effect the lives of people *today*. There is nowhere on earth today, whether China or Africa or South America, which is not indelibly influenced by European history, and by the Holy Roman Empire. Whether for good or evil there is no modern world without the Holy Roman Empire. The very concept of human rights for which we struggle today emerged from a Christian perception of "rights" that were unheard of in ancient times, and grew out of a response to medieval oppression.

History is not simply a series of unrelated accidents of happenstance. True history is a link of chains which all connect to one another and forge a link to the modern world. Without the Holy Roman Empire, there are no middle ages; without the middle ages, there is no Reformation and no Renaissance; without the Reformation, there are no Puritans; without the Puritans, there is no modern democracy; without modern democracy, there is no modern world. Science, art, literature, and even modern democracy are all products of the Reformation and Renaissance yet without the middles ages, these would never have existed. Indeed, without the evils of the Holy Roman Empire there would have been no reaction against those evils, and no security of the liberties we enjoy today. Had there never been an Inquisition there could be no freedom of religion. Yes, the Holy Roman Empire is the seed for everything good and bad that has happened since that time.

But what exactly is the Holy Roman Empire? This question will probably be debated for centuries, but the following facts prevail. In the course of time the ancient Roman Empire had grown so large that one man could no longer control it all. From the time of Constantine two emperors ruled over the Roman Empire as alleged equals; one in Constantinople and one in Rome. As the years passed the western half of this empire deteriorated and fell into the hands of Germanic barbarians who claimed allegiance to the emperor of Constantinople and set themselves up as Romans, but who were in reality a new group of rulers. The eastern emperors retained nominal authority over the west but their negligence inspired the people of Rome to restore the western emperors in the person of Charlemagne. With the rise of Charlemagne the eastern and western Roman empires split but maintained good relations.

The Holy Roman Empire is that western Roman Empire from the time of that split. Many consider it to be Charlemagne's empire alone but others see Charlemagne's dynasty merely as the shining star of the Holy Roman Empire. The empire itself came to be made of many different states, or countries, with semi–autonomous rule. It was called the "empire of many nations." This empire also came to be the property of the Papacy. Three ruling entities emerged; the imperial authority, the papal authority, and the authority of local kings and countries. Together these maintained an uneasy alliance until Napoleon's failed attempt to revive the shattered remains of what was once the greatest empire on earth.

If this does not clearly answer the question then the reader should begin to see the dilemma that plagues historians. Exactly what the empire "was" was perhaps unclear even to its own vassals. In reality, it was an empire in transition. The Holy Roman Empire was indeed the legitimate remnant of the Roman Empire but it was in a crucial transitional stage. The old ideas about empires were vanishing and the new ideas were slowly emerging; transforming the empire. Ancient Rome had once been a Republic which transformed into Imperialism. Throughout the middle ages the Roman Empire was now swinging back in the other direction. Amid the power struggles, power plays, and Crusades notions of individual rights, stemming from the Bible, as well as older, but improved, ideas about Republics garnered more support. Countries maintained the facade of the old empire while embracing new ideas. Eventually it became clear that the two could not coexists. Sooner or later either the empire had to die, or modern freedoms had to die. The Reformation split the empire and left it in its deathrows. Yet to this very day Europeans cling to the hope that it may yet be resurrected and save them from their own folly.

Our own forefathers in America spoke of the Holy Roman Empire and the French were in rebellion against it. Napoleon sought to restore it under his leadership, although it was he who destroyed it. Yet its absence had left a void that many have endeavored to fill ever since. Kaiser Wilhelm and Adolph Hitler sought to restore it. The United Nations sought to replace it. Theologians predict its revival. The Holy Roman is *the* legacy of Europe and it is the reason for everything that is in the modern world; good and evil, just and unjust, right and wrong.

When Did it Fall?

Many assume that the Holy Roman Empire fell with the Reformation. Even some scholars have debated as to exactly how long the Holy Roman Empire may be said to have existed. Nevertheless, most historians date the fall of the Holy Roman Empire with the German Emperor Francis II's "retirement" of the title of Emperor in 1806 when Napoleon invaded Germany. Ironically, Napoleon had himself been crowned emperor by papal approval, which, by charter, had crowned the Holy Roman Emperors for centuries, only ceasing after the Reformation. Indeed, how could Francis retire a title that he had no right to bestow? The fact is that Francis "retired" the title because he realized that he had already been stripped of the title by the pope who had given the crown to his rival Napoleon just a few years earlier. Napoleon wanted the title for himself and Francis was forced to oblige, but he had no desire to see the crown pass to the hated French so he opted to reject the validity of the title by declaring that the emperor was dissolved of its allegiance. For the Germans of the 19th Century the Imperial title could be bestowed only on those of Germanic blood but now a Frenchman was claiming the title again.

Regardless of whether Francis II or Napoleon should be deemed the last emperor, Napoleon's failure at Waterloo was the fatal blow to the empire. Germany no longer yielded to the pope's authority and France had crumbled as an empire. Democracies and Republics were cropping up everywhere, leaving the authority of the pope challenged by even the uneducated masses. Soon even Italy would declare its dependence from the papacy and the pope would be left in control only of Vatican City. For the first time since Charlemagne, Europe had no one vying for the title of "emperor." The once great empire had consisted of Imperial authority, papal authority, and local authority. The demise of the Imperial authority led to the segregation and independence of the local authorities but the papal authority, though greatly diminished, has not yet completely died. The empire went comatose after Napoleon but some say it still lives, awaiting its revival.

Was It an Empire?

Cynical historians have opted not to call the Holy Roman Empire a true empire at all. They have scoffed at the notion that it is a continuation of ancient Rome and suggested that its German Emperors were merely kings with a greater title. Nevertheless, this is too simplistic an approach and ignores both the facts and the very thoughts of the European people. True, the later Holy Roman Emperors did not wield vast authority of Europe as had Charlemagne but neither were they mere kings. Even Richard the Lionhearted, the greatest king of Europe, accepted the emperor's authority and even paid tribute. Can we deny the imperial authority of the emperor if Richard the Lionhearted did not? More importantly, can we restrict the empire to its imperial boundaries? This is the real challenge of defining the Holy Roman Empire. Ancient empires were usually the property of one man. The ancient Roman Emperors were both *pontifex maximus* and Caesar. In the Holy Roman Empire the two were allegedly separate but equal entities. By the late Middle Ages the papacy wielded vast political control in countries that the emperor had no authority over. Can we restrict the empire to older definitions that no longer apply? Some scholars will belittle the empire, some will revere it. Some call it Rome's successor, some call it a mockery of Rome. Some call it an age of progression, others an age of ignorance. Such controversy is perhaps to be expected for the Holy Roman Empire is unlike any empire that has preceded it or will follow it. It is, therefore, necessary to explain my own presuppositions in regard to it.

In order to understand the empire a parallel must be made to other empires. Such a parallel is, however, virtually impossible. The Holy Roman Empire differed from every other empire in history. For one thing, the power of the empire did not rest in Imperial authority alone but, as aforementioned, was divided between the papacy and the emperor, as well as local kings. These three entities maintained an uneasy balance throughout history with one or the other gaining marginal superiority throughout various ages and generations. A poor man's analogy might be a comparison to the United States balance of the three branches of the government; Executive, Judicial, and Legislative. At times the Supreme Court and the Judicial system has made laws, struck down laws made by the people, and dispensed justice (or lack thereof) at their own leisure. Likewise, there have been times when a strong President was virtually a king and could do anything he wanted, with or without Congressional approval. At other times, the President was merely a puppet to the Legislature with no real power himself. The administration of General Grant is an example of the later. In the Holy Roman Empire, the emperor might be compared to the President, the papacy to the Supreme Court, and the local kings to Congress, although they really acted more as Governors (sometimes rebellious ones). This uneasy alliance was maintained to insure Europe's unity and survival against aggressors. Had this institution not existed it is very likely that the Saracens would have overrun Europe and conquered the known world.

Thus the Holy Roman Empire as it emerged late in history was a conglomeration of nations under the protection and authority of both the emperor and pope. At times that authority was nominal while at other times it was real and pronounced. Always, however, the Europeans *considered themselves* to be of one Christian Empire, headed by the pope and unified by the kings of Europe under the nominal, if not real, authority of the emperor of Rome.

Was It Roman?

"The emperor of Rome," as he was properly called throughout the Middle Ages, rarely resided in Rome. Usually they resided in Germany where many of the emperors were born. Voltaire once said that the Holy Roman Empire was neither; it was neither holy nor Roman. Historians have argued ever since that the Holy Roman Empire was an unholy Germanic Empire but such an argument ignores history. While the Kaiser and Hitler thought that the authority of the once great empire resided in Germanic blood, the facts of history prove otherwise. It may be admitted that the Holy Roman Empire was far from Holy, but it was most certainly *Roman.*

First, any survey of the empire will show that, save Charlemagne himself, those emperors who ruled from Rome or subjected Rome to themselves were great emperors but those who ruled from the faraway lands or never set foot in Rome were quickly forgotten and of little consequence. As the emperors moved their capitol out of and away from Rome their power and authority shrank proportionally. In coincidence this is so with the papacy as well for when they resided in Rome they gained more and more authority as the emperors' diminished but that authority diminished when they moved to Avignon. Thus while some historians consider the Holy Roman Empire a German Empire it was most decidedly still a *Roman* one. Indeed, virtually all the great emperors took up residence in Rome. When the emperors took up residence elsewhere they quickly found Italy in rebellion and the Empire in disobedience. Otto the Great, for example, tried on numerous occasions to rule from Germany but each time he left Italy the Italians were plotting and conspiring against him. He was forced to finally take up residence in Rome where his Empire and his legacy became complete.

When the emperors were absent from Rome it was the Pope who exercised great authority over the empire, enforcing his will as supreme, even over the emperor's. So also, when the papacy left Rome for Avignon, in France, the power of the papacy diminished and faith in the Vatican's authority dissipated, giving rise to the Reformation movement which was growing long before Luther. So great was the authority of Rome, and its Church, that one historian said "the Holy Roman Church and the Holy Roman Empire are one and the same."

One might rightfully asks why this is so. What made Rome the seat of power, rather than individuals. The answer may never be known completely but there is no doubt that the Italians themselves were a proud, and even arrogant, people. The Roman Empire was the greatest empire in history. If the Holy Roman Empire was truly the legitimate successor of Rome, then Rome would have to continue to be its seat of power and the Italians were determined to keep it that way. Indeed, the very existence of Charlemagne, great though he was, is owed to Rome and its leader, the pope. Constantinople and Rome had long been in contests with each other over power. When the western emperors disappeared in Rome it was the popes who took their place. As Constantinople continued to ignore the plight of Rome, the pope was forced to look elsewhere for military strength and aid. The Romans would have to find a *western* emperor. Charlemagne was that man. He owes his legacy to Rome, not Germany. The annals of history show Charlemagne as Constantine VI's successor (the Byzantine emperor), not Romulus Augustulus's (the last of the old "Roman" emperors). Charlemagne was wise enough to see this. He did not seek to overthrow Rome but to restore it. He did not conquer Rome but liberated it. He was for Rome a deliverer, not a conqueror. That he was of German blood no longer mattered. While the Italians had once abhorred the Germans, they now abhorred the Greek emperors.

If the emperors were now predominantly German, does this not make the empire German? Such an argument cannot be valid for it ignores both the power of the papacy in Rome, the heritage of the ancient emperors, and the heritage of the Holy Roman emperors. The ancient Roman Emperors were not all Italians. Philip the Arab was born in Africa and Constantine the Great was the son of a native English woman. Despite this no one considers Constantine to have been an "English Emperor" yet he never set foot in Italy until many years later. The Roman Empire had grown beyond the borders of Italy. To be a Roman meant to be a part of the Roman Empire, not just a native of Italy. Charlemagne, of German blood, was more Roman than the Greek Emperors of Constantinople, and the Romans knew this. Truly the empire's seat of authority was still Rome. Moreover, it is a myth that all the emperors of the Holy Roman Empire were German. Even if the French claim that the early emperors were French is ignored there remained emperors from England, Spain, Italy, Sicily, Bohemia, Burgundy, and even Holland. It must be concluded that the Holy Roman Empire stands unique among the empires of history. Neither the pure domain of emperors nor of pontiffs but always the pure domain of *Rome*.

What Were Its Boundaries?

The boundaries for the empires of old were easily defined. The emperors wielded direct control over certain regions often through a regional governor or even kings who would pay tribute to the emperor. In its early days under Charlemagne and Louis the Pious this was the case but as the High Middle Ages emerged the emperor had not the military might or strength to extract tribute even from those countries who readily acknowledged his rule. Such well defined borders, therefore, again defy the Holy Roman Empire. So then, how can the boundaries of the empire be defined?

It is readily acknowledged that empire was a compact between the emperors and popes. The pope, in theory, was only a spiritual leader, not a political one but none doubt that the popes would one day wield far greater political power than many of the emperors. Were all Catholic countries are part of the empire then? Not necessarily for Ireland, at one time, followed the pope but the pope's authority did not extend to political power until many years later. Popes often used their powers to garner control of the kings or archbishops but if the pope's word was ignored, and the emperor had neither the will nor ability to enforce his word, then those countries remained Catholic, but not Roman. In other words, I have divided the Holy Roman Empire into two separate parts. For lack of better words, I have dubbed these the Imperial Empire and the Papal Empire, both equal portions of the Holy Roman Empire. The Imperial Empire is defined as the ancient empires were. The Papal Empire, however, is defined as any portion of the empire, nominally under the authority of the emperor and pope, whose king's succumbed to papal will in issues of politics as opposed to religion. Thus Spain, loyal to the papacy, became a part of the empire in the late Middle Ages and became the pope's most ardent supporter, even being the birthplace of one Holy Roman Emperor. So also England, never under the *direct* authority of the emperor, was an important part of the Holy Roman Empire and medieval history.

The History of Holy Rome Defined

The Holy Roman Empire is then the story of both emperors and popes. Any history which ignores one ignores the whole. This book will discuss each and every emperor *and* pope. It will tell the story of Italy, Germany, France, and the Kingdom of Jerusalem. It will recount the later history of England and Spain as well as those countries that at one time or another were a part of the "empire of nations." The history of the Holy Roman Empire will engulf not only the conquests of emperors and the politics of the papacy but the Crusades, the Inquisition, and even the Conquistadors as they sought to enlarge the Papal Empire to the shores of the New World. The story of the Holy Roman Empire will take us from Charlemagne's coronation to the Reign of Terror and Napoleon's snatching of the crown from Pope Pius VII's hands. It will stretch from the thrusting of a crown upon an unsuspecting Charlemagne to the self coronation of a man who thought himself supreme. It will, in fact, engulf the whole of European history and the emergence of the modern world.

8

2
—
Rome Before Charlemagne

When Edward Gibbon wrote his classic *Decline and Fall of the Roman Empire* he immediately found himself in somewhat of a quandary. Historians like to compact history into small easily manageable segments. The history of Rome, however, extends over twenty five hundred years. Gibbon really wanted to write about *ancient* Rome but after writing three volumes (in the form it is presently published), he found that he had not only failed to reach the fall of Rome but that the division of the empire under Charlemagne into two seperate bodies complicated matters, especially since one branch of that empire, the western or "Holy Roman" empire still existed in his day. Gibbon admitted that he had no desire to write a history of the Middle Ages and had no love for the Catholic Church which was so intertwined with the western Roman empire. He, therefore, decided to follow the eastern emperors through to the fall of Constantinople in 1453 with only occasional references to the western empire. It is Gibbon, perhaps more than any other, who propagated the erroneous myth that the fall of Rome occurred is 476 A.D. when Germanic barbarians sacked the city; something he readily admits is inaccurate. Nevertheless, the events of 476 did serve to create a somewhat arbitrary line which permitted historians to divide history into smaller fragments.

The actual division of the Roman empire did not take place until Charlemagne, but it can be traced back to Constantine who moved the capital of the empire from Rome to Constantinople. Rome then became the residence of a "Caesar" or co–emperor whose authority lay just beneath that of the emperor of Constantinople. After Charlemagne, however, it is clear that the Holy Roman Empire was a continuation of the Roman empire, and not just in that it supplanted it but in that it is truly its offspring and progeny. Indeed, the Holy Roman Empire can easily be said to be far more the progeny of Rome than the Byzantine Empire of the east. Moreover, its legacy is still felt today. The Byzantine Empire, however, can truly be said to have fallen when the Muslim Turks finally captured and conquered its capital in Constantinople. Only Russian and the Greek Orthodox who live throughout eastern Europe and the middle east still feel the weight of Byzantium, but all the world feels the burden of Holy Rome. It is ironic, therefore, that of the countless books on the Roman Empire and even the middle ages, not a single book currently in print expressly deals with the complete history of the Holy Roman Empire.

An ancient Bible prophecy, interpreted by both Jews and Christians long before Charlemagne's birth, or even the birth of the Frankish Empire, states that the last great empire of the world would be divided in two. This empire, universally held to be Rome by Jews and Christians alike, would one day be crushed by the Messiah/Christ, but several things would have to happen first. First it would divide in two, and then it would break into ten pieces. Finally, the anti–Christ would put the pieces back together again, but his empire would only last seven years before the Messiah/Christ crushes it once and for all. Such a prophecy is mentioned for it echoes the history of Rome, although the later prophecy has yet to be seen. The great Roman Empire was indeed divided in two separate halves, and later fell into many more pieces.

Historians recognize that these two pieces of Rome are the eastern and western Roman empires, or as modern historians have dubbed them, the Byzantine Empire and the Holy Roman Empire. They do, however, mislead the public with their terminology for the split between east and west had been long in the making. The Roman Empire was divided between the westerners who held Rome sacred and the eastern Greeks who resided in Constantinople. It was not, however, until Charlemagne that the two halves parted ways. Therefore, when historians date Byzantium back to Constantine, they are doing so for expediency, not accuracy. Constantine was clearly a Roman Emperor, and one of the greatest. Likewise, the sack of Rome in 476 A.D. did nothing to alter Rome except remove a weak and decadent line of Caesars, or junior emperors, who acted as a co–regents to the emperor of Constantinople. In a way the Italians were relived to have gotten rid of them. When the Emperor Justinian reasserted his authority over Italy a hundred years later he was hailed as a hero and a savior. Historians themselves often call Justinian the last true *Roman* Emperor, despite his residence in Constantinople. Ever since Justinian the east and west drifted further apart, securing the rise of Charlemagne two hundred years later.

Before we can fully understand the impact that Charlemagne had upon the restoration of the Roman Empire in the west, we must first understand how the empire came to decline. The great empire which had once ruled over the "whole earth" had deteriorated to near disintegration when Charles the Great came to liberate the city and restore its old imperial dignity, but if, indeed, Charlemagne restored the Roman Empire then what happened between the so–called "fall of Rome" in 476 and 800 A.D. when Charlemagne took the crown? I will endeavor to recount this laborious task as briefly as possible.

The "Ostrogothic Kingdom"

Following the sack of Rome in 476 by Germanic barbarians, the "Ostrogothic Kingdom" would arise in Italy. Although erroneously referred to as a "kingdom," the Ostrogothic Kingdom was nothing of the sort. Italy was still a part of the Roman Empire and under the sovereignty of the emperor in Constantinople. Nevertheless, the political turmoil of the day, as well as the ever increasing weakness and inability of Rome to protect itself, caused the emperor and the Italians to come to terms with their Germanic invaders. Odoacer, the leader of the revolt, had served in the Roman army many years earlier. He expressly made known that he did not wish the destruction of the Roman Empire, but its protection and acceptance. The barbarians war with Rome was a racial one. They did not seek to supplant Rome but to become a part of it. Not more than a week after sacking and pillaging Rome Odoacer stood before the Roman Senate with his demands. The Roman Senate proclaimed him Patrician (the highest office behind the emperor and the now extinct office of "Caesar") and sent messengers to Emperor Zeno. Soon Zeno himself acknowledged Odoacer and made him a sort of co–regent. In most every respect, save the title of the office, he was co–emperor, or Caesar, even as Romulus Augustulus, whom he had exiled, had been. Rome had not truly changed.

Back in 475 A.D., a year earlier, the region of Gaul (mainly the region of modern France, as well as part of Germany) had seceded from Rome and a German King named Euric (who had murdered his own brother to assume the throne) created the Toulouse Kingdom. This kingdom would not last but was the beginning of a long series of conflicts and wars that would lead to the creation of the Frankish Kingdom, later destined to merge with the Holy Roman Empire. It soon came into conflict with the west and Odoacer who did not take long to begin acting like the Roman Emperors of old. He sought to reclaim the once precious land of Gaul and expand the empire. However, he had no real loyalty to the true Emperor Zeno. Zeno was consumed with a war against Persia in the east and often neglected the west, but Odoacer made the mistake of underestimating Zeno's occupation with the east. While engaged in war with Euric Odoacer made a dreadful mistake. When he attacked a region of the eastern empire, hoping to take it under his "protection," he found the emperor Zeno was unwilling to forgive this trespass. Zeno enlisted the aid of Theodoric, King of the Ostrogoths. Under the agreement Theodoric could secure a home for his people (the Ostrogoths) in Italy as Zeno's subjects, just as the Italians were his subjects.

Theodoric took to the field and a war ensued. By 493 A.D. it was obvious that Odoacar's cause was lost, but he could easily hold out for a much longer time and possibly deplete the army of Theodoric or even hope for some other disaster to force Theodoric's retreat. Theodoric was well aware of this and began negotiations with Odoacar. That same year a compromise was reached. Odoacar agreed to surrender in return for the consulship (an ancient Roman office below that of the Patrician). A banquet was then held in honor of Theodoric, but Theodoric was not a nobleman; he was a true barbarian. As a barbarian, the agreement as nothing more than a means to an end and at the banquet he pulled his sword and literally cut Odoacar in half, laughing about it afterwards.

Despite the traitorous and barbaric rise to power, Theodoric's reign was a long one of peace and prosperity. For the first time in over a hundred years Rome was free from invasions and wars. It was a time of peace and it was a time when the medieval papacy was beginning to rise. The vacuum created by the absence of the old emperors was filled by the Church. The pope himself rose to prominence in many of the duties and honors of the old emperors. Theodoric, as a barbarian heretic who denied the Trinity, could not fill this void, nor did he try. The term "Caesaropapism" has often been used to describe this merger between the duties of the old Caesar and those of the papacy. It was initially a merger taken by necessity rather than conspiracy and went largely unnoticed for hundreds of years.

All seemed well in Italy. Rome was finally at peace but the Romans were a proud people. Racism is not new. The people of Italy resented having a German "barbarian" as ruler, and particularly a heretical one. The Germans were "Arians," a heretical sect that denied the Trinity. For many years disputes, and even open persecution, occurred throughout the empire between Trinitarians and Arians. Though Theodoric was tolerant his religion was still seen as that of a barbarian and the Romans' distaste for their Ostrogothic Patricians would eventually culminate in the reclamation of Italy by the great Emperor Justinian not long after the death of Theodoric.

The Frankish Kingdom Emerges

After Euric broke away from Rome his kingdom became engulfed in war. Euric sought to expand his kingdom but other Germanic tribes also had their sights on what was once Gaul. By the time of his death the Burgundian Kingdom, which laid to the south (between Italy and Toulouse), was the most prominent rival of the Toulouse Kingdom. Alaric II succeeded Euric as king. He reduced, but did not eliminate, the fierce persecution that the Arian Euric had installed against Niceaen, or Trinitarian, Christians. Alaric II also wrote a code of law that was based on Roman law, showing the influence that the Roman civilization still had on Gaul. He was, however, hampered by wars from the Burgundians, but more importantly from the pagan Franks to the east.

The Franks were a particularly brutal tribe of pagans. They had emerged from out of the forests of Germany only a few generations previous. The tribal chieftain, Merovig, had passed the throne down to his son, and by him to Merovig's grandson, a man named Clovis. This Clovis was rapidly conquering much of the Toulouse Kingdom and turning it into a Frankish one but, barbarian and pagan that he was, he also knew and learned the advantages of politics. He arranged a political marriage with the daughter of the former Burgundian King. This woman was named Clotilda and although the Burgundians were Arians she had converted to the true Christian faith. She, therefore, brought the gospel with her to Clovis. His conversion was not immediate but a product of many years of Clotilda's persuasion. She was a devout and faithful woman. Although some doubt the sincerity of Clovis's conversion, none doubt her own. Her Christian character and devotion were evident to all.

It was not until a critical battle in the year 507 that Clovis finally gave in to the Christian faith. He felt that all was lost. The tides of war can change with but a single battle and Clovis was losing it. It is then that he called out to the Christian God and promised his devotion if the tide of battle would change. It did, and he did. For this Clovis has been called a "second Constantine." Like Constantine it was on the battlefield that he converted to Christ. Later Clovis was baptized with thousands of his own soldiers. The scene was significant for it created new alliances with Rome. The Germanic barbarians tribes had been a constant threat to the remnants of the western Roman Empire but now, in the new Frankish kingdom, there was a new political power emerging who looked to the same faith as that of the Roman pontiff and Rome. Rome now had a strong ally on whom they would lean in the years to come. The Frankish kingdom was made a "Federate" of the Roman Empire and Clovis himself was given the title of Consul.

Justinian The Great

The emperors who resided at Constantinople are generally referred to as Byzantine Emperors. Although the empire was still one and the same Roman Empire at that time historians have become accustomed to referring to eastern emperors as Greek or Byzantine Emperors. Justinian, however, is also called the last of the true *Roman* Emperors. He is universally hailed as the greatest of the Byzantine Emperors. This is perhaps a strange contradiction but it reflects the desire to show Justinian the respect he deserves. In comparison to Augustus or Constantine Justinian falls far short, but it is to them, and not the later Greek Emperors, that Justinian owed his legacy. Like the former, he sought to reunify the empire and he had a far greater respect for Rome and Italy than would his successors. He sought to establish the papacy over the east and west alike and secure the political unity of the two sections of the empire without the need of an untrustworthy co–regent in Italy. In these respects he fell short of his goals, but he did restore a brief moment of glory to the quickly fading, and once great, Roman Empire. It is with his death that division between the Holy Roman Empire and the Byzantine Empire slowly began to take form. It would not happen for another two hundred years, but the events that ensued following Justinian's reign would insure that the two could not remain together forever.

Justinian may legitimately be said to have kept the two portions of Rome together. Had Justinian never lived it is far more likely that the east and west would have split a hundred years earlier than it really did. Like the Italians, Justinian could not tolerate the thought of heretical barbarians ruling

Italy in his name. Like the Romans, he also believed that the churches in the east and west should be united together under the sovereignty of the pope.

Since the death of Theodoric the Great the Ostrogothic leadership of Italy had become weak and Justinian soon found a perfect excuse to "rescue" Italy from their grips. Upon Theodoric's death, his eight year old grandson, Athalaric, ruled the kingdom. However, Athalaric's mother, Amalasuntha, desired the seat of power for herself. Eventually she had allegedly reached a secret agreement with Justinian to stage a coup in which he could come and "rescue" her, thus securing the emperor's direct control over Italy, with her acting on his behalf. However, by Athalaric's sixteenth birthday he had become a drunkard and succumbed to debauchery from which he died that very year. This left the west under the leadership of Theodahad who quickly reached his own agreement with Amalasuntha, naming her co–regent. Such an agreement was far more preferable to her than the nominal authority that Justinian would have bestowed her, so she took Theodahad's offer. Nevertheless, in less than a year Theodahad turned on Amalasuntha and arrested her. She was then found murdered shortly afterwards. This was an act of usurpation and the signal for Justinian to invade and restore the old glory that was once Rome.

Justinian sent the great general Belisarius to handle the occupation of Italy. He began by taking Sicily with barely a fight and then Naples fell after only three weeks. The Ostrogoths, seeing the dangers imminent, deposed Theodahad and appointed Vitiges as new king. The people of Italy, however, were not appeased. They viewed Justinian's army as liberators, not invaders, and in 536 the pope invited Belisarius to march into the city of Rome and claim it for the empire. It was then the Goths became the aggressors and besieged the great city. For the next sixteen years the Goths fought in some fashion. Although the empire claimed Italy as its own it was not until 552 that Justinian could clearly say that the Gothic "invaders" had been quelled.

Despite this, and the fact that Justinian was hailed as a hero by many in Italy, several factors actually contributed to the eventual split between east and west. Higher taxation and oppressive Byzantine officials hurt but perhaps nothing struck the west so much as the actions of Justinian toward Pope Vigilus. In 546 the Goths gained temporary control of Rome and, the pope had fled to Constantinople, never to see Rome again. Justinian, far from being a generous host, treated the pope like a prisoner. This had stemmed from a theological dispute between Justinian and the Patriarch of Constantinople. Justinian naturally sought the pope to take a stand in defense of him, but when the pope condemned the treatise of Justinian in favor of the Patriarch, Justinian sought his arrest. Imperial guards literally tried to drag the pope out of church, but the people, upon seeing this display, became angry. Justinian backed down but placed the pope under unofficial house arrest and called a General Council of his own condemning the pope until such time as the pope should repent. Pope

Vigilus later died on his return journey to Rome in 555, leaving a bitter strife between east and west that would only grow greater over time.

The Lombard Conquest

Not five years after Justinian's death another invasion of Germanic barbarians began in Italy. The Lombards were a tribe that had broken away from another clan back in 508. They had been granted permission to live in Dacia (roughly corresponding to Austria) where they dwelled for many years. Under Justinian they had become federates and allies of the empire, but like the emperor Theodosius and the Goths of a century earlier, the alliance was broken upon the death of the emperor and those tribes turned on the empire, invading Italy. History was repeating itself. In 568 they sought to take land from Italy and establish their own country. Unlike the Goths of Theodosius' time, the Lombards did not show respect for the empire or the church. They were cruel and barbaric. They burned churches to the ground, murdered priest, and raped nuns. The barrage was quick and incisive. By the time Albuin, king of the Lombards, died in 572, much of northern Italy was in Lombard possession and rule. With his death the invasion halted but the oppression did not. As long as the Lombards did not take further aggression deeper into Italy there was an unofficial truce as the emperor in Constantinople had his hand full in the east.

This was one reason that the western Romans would find themselves turning to their allies, the now Christian Franks. The eastern emperors who followed Justinian were by and large (with a few exceptions) weak and feeble. In the east the war with Persia raged, not to mention the arrival of the Muslim invaders fifty years later. By the time of Charlemagne, the once great eastern empire had shrunk dramatically. By the time the Holy Roman Empire was in its heyday, the Byzantine Empire encompassed a small portion of modern Turkey and Greece; hardly enough to be called an empire at all. Obviously, with the east experiencing the difficulties that had once plagued the west, they sent no help to deal with Italy's problems and were content to ignore the Lombards so long as sacred Rome remained unharmed and a part of the empire.

It was not until the Emperor Maurice, more than a decade after the invasion began, that any legitimate help arrived. Maurice established "exarchates" which would field garrisons for the protection of the remaining areas of Italy. Throughout the next two centuries the Lombards and Romans would live together in mutual hatred. Occasional conflicts and fighting occurred throughout this time but the Lombards usually avoided out and out war. Perhaps because the Lombards knew of Rome's importance to the empire, and did not wish to incur the wrath of the emperor, the Lombards with few exceptions skirted around Rome. Even whey they attempted to seize central and southern Italy they ignored Rome. They did not wish open war with the Roman Empire of the east but they sought to conquer what lands they could. They oppressed the people of Italy for two hundred years, until Charlemagne crushed the threat once and for all, but they rarely engaged in all out war and left Rome untouched. The uniqueness of this invasion can be seen more clearly by examining a map of Italy during this time. The domain of the Lombards and the Roman (or Byzantine) Empire were not split evenly but with different territories cutting through one another. Obviously, rights of way were ignored and crimes often occurred when the Lombards passed though Roman territory.

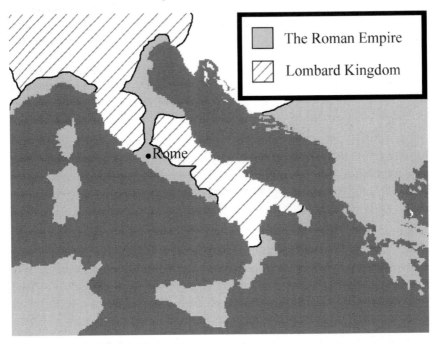

The importance of the Lombard invasion is that the reluctance of the eastern emperor to help the western states during this difficult time not only bred hostility and mistrust but forced the Italians to seek help from the Franks. The first of these Frankish rulers to become involved in this conflict was Charles Martel.

The Frankish Kingdom Rises

The descendants of Clovis were largely weak and degenerate kings who did little to enhance or strengthen the Frankish Empire. Of Clovis's sons some were said to have buried men alive in punishment. Under Clovis, however, the empire had adopted certain Roman laws and customs that placed local provinces under Mayors, who were themselves like regional governors of the kings. This would be advantageous to the Franks for when the kings became weak and incompetent, good Mayors were able to build up what the kings were tearing down.

By the seventh century several Mayors were clearly stronger and better respected than the Frankish kings. Charles Martel, dubbed "the Hammer," was the illegitimate son of one of these Mayors in the Eastern Frankish Kingdom. It was for this reason, or more likely this excuse, that his hereditary right to the Mayor's office was challenged. Martel was forced to defend his position by war against his enemies, including King Chilperic II and Ratbod. In 719 King Chilperic was defeated and Charles Martel was accepted as Mayor of the eastern Franks.

The king was now incompetent to do anything against Martel whose power grew steadily. Martel reunified much of the Frankish kingdom that had fallen into disarray. Despite Martel's successes in the Frankish Empire, it was his intervention against the Muslim threat from Spain that first significantly drew the attention of the Roman Pontiff.

For many years the Islamic invaders had tried desperately to get a foothold in Europe. If the Muslims were to conquer Europe as they hoped then they had to have a solid base of operations on the continent to which they could retreat, regroup, fortify, and rally. Nonetheless, Europe seemed a fortress. The second Roman capitol of Constantinople blocked the eastern passage to Europe and was perhaps the greatest fortress ever built. The Muslims were never able to conquer it until the fifteenth century. It might have been possible to travel the long route up through modern Russia, but in order to pass through there they needed to pass between the Black Sea and the Caspian Sea which was dominated by the Khazar Empire. This left only Italy and Spain as a possible base. The Muslims would try for many centuries to gain a sufficient base in Italy but they were never able to hold one for long. Spain was their best chance.

The Muslims had crossed into Europe via Spain and established their base of operations, but it was not as solid a base as they had once hoped. To the north of Spain lay the Pyrenees mountains which effectively cut Spain off from the rest of Europe. The Muslim Saracens decided to march their massive army across the Pyrenees and move into Italy. If successful the Saracens could have gained a true foothold in Europe and, so all historians say, conquered the entire continent. This was the backdrop to Charles Martel's intervention. When he had heard that the Muslims were moving toward Italy he decided act, despite the fact that they never attacked Frankish territory. Martel would meet the army at the battle of Portiers in 732 and forever halt the expansion of Islam into Europe.

The victory by Charles Martel cannot be underestimated and certainly no one in Rome underestimated it. Had Martel not been victorious the Muslims would most assuredly have taken all Italy. Martel had saved the Roman Empire, and Europe with it. Never again would the Muslims reach as far into Europe. The popes in particular took notice. The Franks had done what the emperor could not. While Rome and Italy were plagued by Lombards Charles Martel was crushing the army of the greatest empire on earth at that time. The Islamic Dynasty of that day was in the golden age of Islam. It was the day when Baghdad reigned and the tales of Arabian Knights fancied the imagination. Europe, by contrast, was little more than half civilized barbarians, but Martel proved that this was about to change.

The previous year Pope Gregory II had died and Pope Gregory III now decided that the emperor was not reliable. The Lombards had conquered the Ravenna exarchate and again threatened Rome. Gregory sent an embassy to Charles Martel and offered him both the title of Patrician and Consul of Rome if he would liberate Italy from the Lombards. Ironically, both men died the same year shortly before they were able to reach a final agreement. It was two years later when Pope Zacharias resumed negotiations with Charles Martlel's son and father to Charlemagne, Pepin the Short.

Pepin the Short

In 737 the Merovigian king of the Franks had died leaving no heirs. Since the kings had been so unpopular no attempt was made to find an immediate replacement and the Mayors, led by Charles Martel, continued to function as the effective government of the Franks. When Martel died his kingdom was divided between his two sons, Pepin the Short and Carloman. After the death of Martel and the division of land, the politicians finally decided upon a new king and Childeric III was named that king, but he was a king with no true authority. Like the modern day Queen of England, Childeric was little more than a figurehead. Then in 747 Carloman grew tired of politics and retired as Mayor to become a monk. This left Pepin the Short as Mayor of all that had been his father's.

In Italy the death of Charles Martel forced the new Pope Zacharias to negotiate with the Lombards. Temporary peace had been established, but when the king of the Lombards died in 743 the new king resumed its policy of aggression. Expecting no help from Rome's own emperor in Constantinople Zacharias began to negotiate with Pepin. Politics and the long distance between countries kept the final terms from being agreed upon until many years later but finally Zacharias agreed to depose Childeric III and sanction Pepin's ascension to the Frankish throne. Although Pepin was already king in all but name he wanted the name just the same. In 751 Pepin was coronated by Boniface, the "apostle to Germany," with the pope's blessing the last of the Merovigian kings was replaced by a new line of Carolingians, from the name Carolos or Charles.

With the coronation over, Pepin kept his promise to Zacharias and rode out to Italy. The Lombards were beaten into submission and backed off of their aggressive stance. No real conquest was made but the Lombards learned that Pepin was now Rome's protector and promised no further hostilities. Despite this it was no more than a year later before the Lombards recovered from their defeat and again brutalized the Roman subjects. Pope Stephen IV (Zacharias died in 752) urged Pepin to make another campaign and even dared to promise Pepin salvation if he would help. While Pepin did not take the promise of salvation literally he was a loyal Christian who viewed the pope with respect. He again took the field, even though Stephen had promised him nothing except salvation which was not his to give. This time Pepin conquered a large section of Northern Italy.

This conquest brought the immediate attention of the Emperor Constantine V who had been so quiet throughout the years of Lombard oppression. He objected that Pepin had invaded the Roman Empire and demanded an explanation. Pepin's response is significant. He declared to the Emperor that he did not invade the land but liberated it out of love for the Church. Pepin promised that none of the conquered land would be kept by the Franks but he would instead donate all the territory to the Church.

To this Constantinople offered no objections and the land was passed from Pepin to Pope Stephen IV. It has been alleged that this "Donation of Pepin" was inspired by the forged document "the Donation of Constantine." This "Donation of Constantine" alleges that Constantine the Great had himself bequeathed virtually all the land of Italy to the Church and was accepted as genuine for centuries despite the fact that its first appearance in history occurred at this convenient time. Whether or not Pepin was truly fooled by the document is unknown, as is whether or not the document truly even existed at the time, but Pepin's motives should not be doubted.

Pepin received the Roman title of Patrician, signifying the Franks importance to Rome. The Frankish Empire was already a federate of the Roman Empire and its king was now Patrician. After seeing Pepin's generosity in Italy, and with the east preoccupied, even the emperor of Constantinople had no objections. The Franks were the Lord Protectors of Italy and its king was already a virtual emperor of the west. Not fifty years later Pepin's son, Charlemagne, would become the first western emperor since Romulus Augustulus. Not more than five decades from this time, history would change forever.

Theodor Friedrich Kaulbach – The Coronation of Charlemagne – 1861

3
―

The Age of Charlemagne

With the ever increasing gulf between the emperors of Constantinople and the Roman subjects of Italy the Franks had already become the protectors of the Roman See. Its kingdom was a federate of the Roman Empire and its king was both Patrician and Consul. The events of the east, coupled with the increasing hostilities of the Lombards, all but insured that the Roman Empire would divide.

Contrary to the views put forth by some the Roman Empire was not to become a Frankish one, but rather the Frankish Empire was to become a Roman one. The Franks had long since adopted Roman customs, laws, and religion. Under Clovis, centuries earlier, Roman laws replaced the older order. Clovis's conversion not only made the Franks Christians but Roman as well. They were still barbarians at heart, but so were the ancient Romans. No great emperor of the ancient Roman Empire could ever truly claim to be more just than the Franks. The butchery and brutality of the ancient Romans is often forgiven because they were pagans while the hypocrisy of the Franks is touted by virtue of their Christian faith, but as a historian, it is prudent to simply relate the facts and the fact is that the Franks were little different than the Romans they *became*.

Italy before Charlemagne

In 768 Pope Paul I lay dying. The papal office had become the temporal throne of Rome, as well as its spiritual one. The appearance of the Papal States awarded by Pepin further enhanced the political power of the papacy and many a politician was aware of this. With Paul's death imminent the election of a new pope could hold significant advantage. A certain Duke Toto was particularly interested in securing a papal puppet and so upon Paul's death he proclaimed his brother, Constantine, pope and backed it up with armed soldiers who secured the Lateran (the first papal palace).

Immediately, the Lombards saw their opportunity to exploit the situation to retake much of the land lost when Pepin had seized it, but they would do this through political savvy rather than military prowess. The people were furious that a pope could be appointed and installed by military troops so the chief notary, eager to oust Constantine, agreed to a pact with the Duke of Spoleto and the Lombard King Desiderius. Having no doubt heard of the pact Constantine wrote to Pepin and begged him to help, but Pepin appears to have been silent. There is little doubt that Pepin would have had sympathies with the detractors of Constantine for he had clearly usurped the papal throne and had no right to sit there, but even if Pepin had planned to protect Constantine only a month had passed since the pope's ascension before the Lombards would intervene. Had Pepin desired to enter the fray he would not have had the time to arrive. Pepin's death that same year would cause Rome to wait.

At the end of July 768, less than a month after Constantine had taken the throne, Lombard troops entered Rome and a battle raged. Duke Toto died in the battle and Constantine fled only to be caught and imprisoned. Constantine's eyes were later put out by a mob at the monastery where he was to remain a prisoner for the rest of his life. The Lombards now sought to establish their own puppet pope, named Philip. Now a certain Christopher, who had made the pact with the Lombards, protested that this was never a part of the deal and left Rome refusing allegiance. The people of Rome again became furious, but Philip protested that he had been forced to take the post and had no true desire to maintain it. He quietly retired to a monastery to appease the public.

With Philip removed, Christopher and the bishops then conducted a proper election which placed Stephen III (sometimes considered the IV) on the throne, but he too was supposed to be a puppet. Christopher had become the champion of the people in his desire to install a duly elected pope, but he secretly harbored the desire to make this new pope his own pawn. In the meantime it was necessary to secure Stephen's claims to the throne. A papal legate was immediately sent to Charlemagne and his brother Carloman, who had become co–regents after their father Pepin's death. The purpose was not only to secure Frankish support but also to accept the appointment of Frankish bishops that would further create ties to the Franks and insure the mutual friendship of the two.

This alliance would only further disturb the Lombard King Desiderius. The political situation in Rome demanded action. He had hoped to secure more power in Rome but knew his limitations. Charlemagne was well aware of the Lombard position and suggested that a marriage alliance would benefit them both. Desiderius agreed to surrender certain lands to the pope and in exchange his daughter, Bertrada, was given to Charlemagne as his wife in 770. At the same time, however, Desiderius was negotiating a secret pact with Pope Stephen. Stephen had become agitated with his advisor Christopher, who had tried to turn him into his mouthpiece, while Desiderius was seeking more control in Rome. It was, therefore, agreed that Desiderius' chamberlain, Afiarta, would become Stephen's chief aide and advisor if Christopher was put out of the way.

Christopher's murder quickly reached the ears of Charlemagne and Stephen was equally quick to write to him that Christopher had plotted against his life. Charlemagne, however, was an intelligent man and not easily fooled. He sent men to ascertain exactly what had happened and when it was found that Afiarta was now Stephen's advisor he renounced his new Lombard bride, Bertrada, and perpetual enmity between the Lombards and Franks was ensured.

The Fall of Desiderius

Upon the death of Pepin the Short the lands of the Franks were divided between his two sons, Carloman and Charles, later known as Charlemagne or Carolus Magnus, both meaning Charles the Great. The two had shared power until Carloman died in 771, less than three years after their coronation. Carloman's widow demanded that his heirs take the throne but Charlemagne ignored those demands, preferring to keep the Frankish kingdom united under his sole authority. Carloman's widow, however, was not to be denied easily. She found an ally in Charlemagne's enemy, Desiderius. The separation of Bertrada from Charlemagne created more enmity between the two kingdoms and Desiderius was more than pleased to assist in setting up rivals to Charlemagne's rule. After reaching a pact with Carloman's heirs, Desiderius was prepared to order the pope to coronate Carloman's heirs, thus usurping Charlemagne's authority, but Stephen died before this could occur. In January of 772 Pope Stephen III (IV) was dead and the newly elected Pope Hadrian I was not willing to bow to Desiderius' will, as Stephen had.

After Hadrian's consecration he granted amnesty to the many oppressed people of Rome whom Afiarta had victimized and he even succeeded in having Afiarta arrested. These events aggravated Desiderius, but he was not in a position to make Hadrian his enemy. He made it known that he was willing to overlook the transgressions if Hadrian would help set up rivals to Charlemagne's throne. In the meantime, the Lombards were tightening their grip on cities throughout Italy and further oppressing its people. Hadrian was well aware of the subtle threats, but was unwavering in his stance. He refused to coronate Charlemagne's rivals and continued to speak out against the brutality of the Lombards. Hadrian also dispatched messengers to Charlemagne requesting his assistance.

When it became obvious that Hadrian would not cede to Desiderius's plans, he besieged the city of Rome. It was not long after, however, when he heard that Charlemagne had received Hadrian's message and was marching toward Italy. Desiderius immediately abandoned his siege of Rome and retreated to Pavia, the Lombard capitol, where he prepared to become the besieged. In September 773 Charlemagne arrived and the siege of Pavia began. The siege, like most in the Middle Ages, promised to last a year or more so Charlemagne, during the interim, went to Rome for Easter where he met Pope Hadrian and promised to grant more land to the Papal States. In all, almost three quarters of Italy was promised to the pope, although Spoleto and a few other regions would soon be lost. In June 774 the fate of Pavia was assured and Desiderius surrendered. The siege was lifted and Desirderius was banished while Charlemagne was crowned King of the Lombards. He was now King of the Franks and the Lombards, as well as Patrician of Rome. He was not yet, however, emperor of Rome. What Charlemagne was, was the master of Europe. Only the Saxons and Muslim Spain eluded Charles' grip, but his reign was just beginning.

Charlemagne's Character & Administration

To understand history one needs to understand not only the circumstances and situations of historical figures but also their character and motives. Alexander the Great was a conqueror, but he was never a leader. His death, while still in his thirties, made it impossible to tell exactly what kind of ruler he might have been. So also Julius Caesar was assassinated before he could prove what kind of world he would truly have made. Both men, famed in history, were conquerors who laid the groundwork for others, but had no true part in what was built on their foundation.

Charlemagne was far more than a conqueror. He stands as one of the few true indispensable men of history. Other men are as much beneficiaries of circumstances as they are molders of history. It has been said that Constantine was inevitable. The course of history was determined before he ever took the throne and had he never lived, another emperor would have followed in his path. Had Abraham Lincoln never lived, slavery would still have ended, and a civil war would still have occurred. These events were centuries in the making and the heroes of these earth changing events, great though they were, could easily have been replaced other men of stature. On rare occasions, however, men arise that history cannot replace. As James Bryce said:

> "The assassins of Julius Caesar thought that they had saved Rome from monarchy, but monarchy came inevitable in the next generation. The conversion of Constantine changed the face of the world, but Christianity was spreading fast, and its ultimate triumph was only a question of time. Had Columbus never spread his sails, the secret of the western sea would yet have been pierced by some later voyager : had Charles V broken his safe–conduct to Luther, the voice silenced at Wittenberg would have been taken up by echoes elsewhere. But if the Roman Empire had not been restored in the West in the person of Charles, it would never have been restored at all."[1]

Charlemagne, like George Washington, was one of very few people who were truly indispensable to history. True, the division between the eastern and western Roman Empire had been brewing for centuries, but how that division would take place is the critical question, and more importantly, what direction would the empires take after their division. So who was this man who was destined to restore the Roman Empire? What was his motivation?

Charlemagne was first and foremost a devout Christian. It must be understood, however, he was devout in the context of his barbarian culture and society. Charlemagne was far from perfect. Societies do not change overnight; cultures take a thousand years to change. The Jews that Moses led out of Egypt could never truly grasp what monotheism meant for nearly a thousand years. When Moses parted the Red Sea the former slaves feared that Ra might be stronger than their God and failed to appreciate the great miracle occurring before their very eyes. The disobedient kings of Israel engaged in idolatry and worship of pagan gods for centuries. It was not until the Babylonian exile that the Jews finally understood; the LORD was not *their* God, He was the *only* God. So also, it would take a thousand years to change the barbarians of Europe into the founders of democracy and freedom. This is the epic of the Middle Ages. This is what makes medieval history so beautiful. It is the saga of barbarians and savages slowly transforming into the harbingers of science, freedom, and education, and it was that tiny Jewish sect, called Christianity, that sparked that change.

To Charlemagne's eyes, all these things were possible, but only through conquest. In one sense he was right. Christ might change an individual's heart, but cultures do not change overnight. The barbarian Saxons persecuted Christian missionaries and brutalized all who professed Christ. Military conquest seemed the only way to insure the freedom of missionaries, but in Charlemagne's mind it was also a prophetic event. He was a well learned king who loved Augustine and took his *City of God* at its face value. Ironically, *City of God* was actually a highly allegorical treatment of the prophecies of the Bible. Augustine took the literal Kingdom of God and placed it, symbolically, in their very midst. Charlemagne then took *City of God* and made it his guidebook to rule. Augustine had once declared that we must "compel them to come to Christ" and, therefore, the Saxons were to be compelled to accept the faith or die! This was a barbarian's interpretation of the *City of God*, and it would prove to be the guide for the medieval kingdom to come.

Despite this brutal interpretation of missions, Charlemagne was a wise statesman. He was not unwilling to compromise with enemies or ally himself with Muslims. In Charlemagne's kingdom, vassal states and people could retain their own laws and chiefs under certain provisions. Subjects were required to pledge an oath of loyalty not only to him but also to the "holy service of God" and they were sworn never to do harm to their neighbors. Most of the laws of the Frankish Kingdom were modeled after the Old Testament laws and the nation of Israel. It is little wonder then that Charlemagne had a profound respect for the Jews. He allowed them to set up their own duchies where they could live in peace. Jews from all over the world flocked to Germany in hopes of finding a home where they could find rest. Germanic anti–Semitism was all but unheard of until many centuries later, for Charlemagne profoundly respected the Jews who had produced the Bible and Christ.

Charlemagne also knew that education was the best tool for the long term acceptance of Christendom. He would create many schools and Churches and further advanced the cause of education wherever possible. It is said that he once gave a boy lashes with a whip for misconjugating a Latin verb. Interestingly enough, Charlemagne was educated in his own schools. As a youth he did not learn Greek, Hebrew, or Latin but learned these later in life at the very schools that he established, for each of those languages were required to be taught. This emphasis on education, art, and religion was called the Carolingian Renaissance after Charles (Carolos) himself. It lasted for nearly a century before the degradation of his descendants allowed literacy and education to diminish. The so–called ignorance of the Middle Ages would not come into existence for hundreds of years.

In addition to education, Charlemagne brought many just laws to Europe molded from the Old Testament. As Constantine had done before him, he found the Bible to filled with moral principles and justice that had never been known in ancient Rome, nor pagan Europe. Concepts that would one day give rise to freedom first began to find their ways into his laws. He may even be considered the father of the code of chivalry. He also instituted reformation of certain aspects of the government ranging from the correction of abuses to laws designed to stimulate the economy. Among these, as aforementioned, education was required by law.

As with all men, Charlemagne had a sinful side to his nature. This is particularly true with men of power, and Charlemagne had much power. Despite Charlemagne's devotion to Christianity and the Church, he never seemed to have a great respect for the sanctity of marriage. He was extremely promiscuous and fathered numerous illegitimate children. He had divorced several times (though the Church and pope were conspicuously silent) and did not hesitate to commits acts of infidelity with other men's wives. Wherever he went women were eager to be pleased by him, and he was eager to please.

In an age of barbarity and savagery his sexual licentiousness might seem the least of possible vices, and the occurrence of marriage alliances in what was now a monogamous society was doubtless the cause of many a king's unfaithfulness. Nevertheless, all in all, only the old Roman Emperor Theodosius exceeded Charlemagne in his devotion to God. He was constantly in Church and at prayer, and earnestly sought to enlarge the faith as he believed it should be done. He resided over councils and usually took what might be considered Protestant stances on some critical issues. He was by all rights a *Christian barbarian*.

The Expansion of Charlemagne's Kingdom

With Italy seemingly secured and at peace Charlemagne sought to subjugate the savage pagan tribe known as the Saxons. They had centuries earlier invaded England and driven Christianity from the island. Among the Saxons, to even speak of Christ was a crime punishable by death. Churches were burned, nuns raped, and missionaries were martyred. In 772 when Charlemagne was preparing to leave for Italy they had launched an unprovoked attack on the lower Rhine region of his kingdom. Now, thought Charlemagne, was the time for the Saxons to learn the fear of God. Beginning in 775 Charles descended on the Saxon tribes in a way that the old Romans had never imagined.

Part of the success of the barbarian tribes against the Roman Empire was the fact that the old Romans had fought tribes as if they were an empire. Against an empire, an army could be dispatched or a leader killed and the rest would flee. Submission of a king meant submission of the country, but in tribes there was no central unity. Various tribes might have a king, but for the most part it was every man for himself. The Romans would take out a vast army and then be hit by another tribe. There seemed no way to stop them. If they killed the tribal king, a new king was elected and the war continued. Charlemagne did not seek the subjugation of a king, but all the Saxons.

For two years defeated armies were given the choice of baptism or death. For pagans, who had little loyalty to cruel gods, the choice was an easy one. In many cases hundreds, and even thousands, of soldiers would descend into rivers for baptism. Religious leaders criticized Charlemagne for this, but politically it was savvy. It must be remembered that ancient paganism and Christianity simply could not coexist. History had proven this. The pagan gods of Germany were vengeful gods who could never accept the idea of monotheism. Charlemagne was not so foolish as to believe that he was truly changing the hearts of those who were baptized but he knew that the act of baptism was a blasphemy that the pagan gods could not forgive. In essence, he was not forcing them to truly believe the gospel but to accept it and to teach it to their children. Charlemagne was driving paganism from Germany by force.

The ultimate victory over the Saxons would never be completed until 805, five years after the establishment of the Holy Roman Empire, but in 777 Charlemagne was able to secure a diet at Paderborn in which the Saxons officially acceded and granted certain religious freedom to missionaries, as well as the founding of many Churches and schools in what was Saxon lands. A large number of Saxons agreed to accept baptism and Charlemagne was contented.

Among those present at the diet were emissaries from the Emir of Saragossa Spain who were soliciting his aid against the Umayyad Emir of Cordoba; a man who had seized Saragossa and threatened all Spain. Charlemagne showed that he was tolerant and was willing to work with others against a common foe. While Charlemagne has been accused of hypocrisy for his service to Islamic allies, even against nominal Christian enemies, the truth is that Charlemagne was a wise and, for the age in which lived, a fair man who did not force conversions with the sword unless he was at war. So long as Christian missionaries were free to work and certain laws were obeyed Charlemagne was more than willing to accept freedom of non–Christian religions. The Emir knew this.

Charlemagne agreed to liberate northern Spain and set out to reconquer Spain. In this he was only partially successful. He was able to restore much of the Emir's land and would eventually, years later, establish the famed Spanish March to protect the lands in his absence. The Spanish March consisted of overlords who served Charlemagne, but cooperated with the Emir. It would also serve as a "buffer zone" against any future aggression by Muslims that might turn north towards Christian Europe.

Having achieved much success, Charles now besieged the city of Saragossa. Nonetheless, as with all men, Charlemagne had to face defeat sooner or later. He was unable to take the fortress and was forced to retreat. The enemies pursued Charlemagne all the way across the Pyrenees mountains where Charlemagne's army took many casualties. Further compounding Charlemagne's failure was news that the Saxons were in rebellion. The rebel leader Widukind had burned Churches and monasteries almost immediately after Charlemagne had left for Spain. Saxony was again in the hands of pagan rebels.

The defeat and rebellion made Charlemagne realize that it was time to consolidate his conquest. Too often conquerors become consumed with pride and take too much too quickly. Charles was wise and sage. The defeat convinced him that he was not unbeatable and if his empire was to survive he would need to strengthen it from within.

The Consolidation of Charlemagne's Kingdom

Charles began to concentrate on the building of new schools and churches. Laws were made requiring a certain amount of education and correcting abuses that had occurred in the past. Over the next decade the Frankish Kingdom was to rise to the heights of Europe's civilization.

In 781, Charlemagne returned to Rome where Pope Hadrian crowned his sons, Louis and Pepin, as kings. It was at this time that Irene, regent for emperor Constantine VI, officially recognized Charlemagne as Patrician of Rome, and therefore regent of the western Roman Empire, but this momentous occasion was to be short–lived for news of more Saxon rebellions reached Charlemagne's ears not long after. In 782, Charlemagne marched into Saxony to crush the rebellious Saxons, but his severity has drawn severe criticism throughout the ages. Over forty–five hundred Saxons were executed for treason in retaliation for the deaths of many nobles and counts but the deed was revenged by the Saxon slaughter of many priest and nuns as well as the burning of Churches which had recently been built. These atrocities made Charlemagne more determined than ever to drive the pagan spirit from the Saxons. For the next two decades he would undertake at least eighteen expeditions against Saxon rebels and force the conversion of the vanquished. So harsh was Charlemagne that Alcuin, his prime minister, attempted to chastise the king.

Alcuin was born in Britain, where he was trained at the famed cathedral school of York. Under the archbishop of York, Alcuin became a celebrated teacher, deacon, and master of the school. In 780, he had been sent on a diplomatic mission to Charlemagne whom he befriended. Charlemagne soon asked Alcuin to become master of the School of the Palace, which was Charles's school for the nobles and knights of his court. Over the next few decades Alcuin would become Charlemagne's tutor as well as his friend. There can be observed a direct relationship between many of Charlemagne's theological stances from this time forward and those of Alcuin, which, incidentally, echo the sentiments of later Protestants. There was, however, one major theological notion upon which they disagreed: the conversion of the Saxons.

Alcuin quietly chastised Charles for his brutal use of force in converting Saxons. He told the king that Christ must change their hearts. Education and evangelism were to be the tools of conversion, not the sword. In this, Charlemagne did not fully listen. Ideally Charles may have agreed but he was a politician as well as a Christian. The Saxons were not willing to allow the freedom of the gospel, except where compelled. How could the gospel be taught to the Saxons' children if the ministers of the gospel are not free to do so? The real debate was over the severity of the law. Charles used fear to ensure that the Saxons would harm no Church, nor persecute missionaries. It is doubtful that he really believed that all those he had forced to be baptized were true believers, but he knew that it put them in the Church, and under his dominion. They would be forced to obey and raise their children to learn the gospel, or there would be consequences.

To an extent, they were both right. Alcuin's views were Biblical but Charlemagne's were practical from a political perspective. The old paganism was intolerant and though Charles may be accused of equal intolerance this would be an overstatement. Had the Saxons allowed Christian missions they might well have expected to find as much freedom as Muslims and Jews enjoyed under him, but then the similarity of Islam and Judaism to Christianity may also have been a point in their favor. Christianity was once viewed as a Jewish sect and clearly arose from Judaism. Charlemagne had the deepest respect for them. Islam too shared a common root. It was once considered a Christian cult and, while a deviant and heretical sect, it had much in common with the Jews and Christians. Nevertheless, Charlemagne waged a full spiritual war with the temporal sword. The Saxons were forced to accept baptism and to obey Christian laws. Rebellions were crushed rigorously.

In 782, and again in 785, it appeared as if the Saxon problem had been solved, but it was not to be. In 782, the First Saxon Capitulatory was made.

This agreement instituted many laws such as prohibitions against human sacrifice, cannibalism, burning Churches, and murdering priest. All these things were punishable by death, but critics have noted that equally punishable were crimes such as praying to sacred trees, cremation of the dead, and even eating meat on lent. An interesting law, which indicates Charlemagne did not fall into the modern stereotype of the medieval man, was the prohibition against burning those accused of being witches. Overall, the laws were an attempt to bring justice and morals to the pagan world yet, in contrast to the currently held view that Charlemagne was wholly intolerant, certain pagan practices were still tolerated. There is reason to believe that the practice of sacrificing animals continued, and the burying of animals alive, a kind of sacrifice, certainly continued. Despite this the pagan Widukind stirred up another revolt as soon as Charlemagne's army had left the region.

Charlemagne was again forced to return to Saxony. He set out not only to quell the rebels but to make life so miserable for the Saxon peasants that they would never again follow the rebels. Crops and fields were burned so that the Saxons might suffer through the winter with little food. By 785 even Widukind was ready to acquiesce. Despite the pleas of many of Charlemagne's advisors, Charles showed great mercy to Widukind. The rebel general agreed to accept baptism and Charlemagne made himself Widukind's godfather. This move showed again that Charlemagne could be amazingly merciful when he wished, and it is of interest to note that most Franks were offended by the mercy. Indeed, a conspiracy to assassinate Charlemagne was uncovered shortly after this time and the conspirators were blinded and exiled.

This last act of capitulation by Widukind would settle the Saxon problem temporarily. For a number of years the Saxons appeared content and Charlemagne was free to undertake expeditions elsewhere. In 787, Charles first began to engage in expeditions into southern Italy and, in 788, he took Bavaria directly under his control while beginning expeditions into what was the Avar Empire. This included much of what is today Hungary and Austria. In addition, his expansion also served to create many of the Slavic states, which nominally accepted Charlemagne's authority and weakened the Avars. By the time of Pope Hadrian's death in 795 Charlemagne's kingdom stretched from the Atlantic Ocean to beyond the Rhine river. It took in what is today the northernmost part of Spain, all of France, Switzerland, Belgium, the Netherlands, Germany, the Czech republic, and part of Austria, Poland, Hungary, Slovakia, and Croasia. The only part of the once great Roman Empire that remained in Europe was Greece and Italy, of which Charlemagne was Patrician.

Charlemagne and Theology

Among the great loves of Charlemagne was theology. His tutor, Alcuin, was a well educated and knowledgeable teacher who was well versed in the Bible. His tutelage of the King showed through at various time. Among the most momentous of Charlemagne's theological achievements was a council he convened at Frankfort in 794. The council was convened with the purpose of doing what the council of Nicaea (and other councils convened by the pope) had done. Charlemagne hoped to resolve certain theological disputes, some of which threatened the security and peace of many cities. Among the issues were iconoclasm and the doctrine of "adoptionism."

Iconoclasm had been a controversy since the days of Emperor Leo "the Isaurian," decades earlier. Leo had been a devout Christian but he was also an emperor and had inherited their arrogance. Over the centuries Christians, borrowing from their pagan ancestors, had made many statues, icons, idols, and paintings of the various saints of the Bible. As time went on many Christians actually prayed to the saints, and their idols. This was Biblically the sin of idolatry and forbidden in the Ten Commandments themselves. The Muslims hurled accusations of idolatry, as did more educated Christians, and the embarrassment of Leo was too much for him to endure. Leo decided to rid Christianity of idolatry, but his arrogance in so doing ensured that icons and/or idols would remain a part of both the later Catholic and Eastern Orthodox Church, for Leo was not content to rid himself of idols, but to force the general populous to accept this as well.

The controversy began in the early eighth century when Leo nobly decided to make an example of himself. Adorning the Imperial Palace itself was a large statue. He felt he would show the people his devotion by destroying this idol: a statue of Jesus Christ. Obviously, the people saw the act as blasphemy. The emperor had torn down a memorial to the Savior and rioting enveloped the city. Pope Gregory II condemned the act as well but rather than learning from his actions Leo became more determined than ever.

Leo bided his time and in five years time he acted again. This time soldiers were given orders to break into homes and search for icons. All icons were to be destroyed and smashed, hence the name "iconoclasm" (meaning to smash icons). This act was far worse than the first and again brought condemnation from Pope Gregory. Pride, however, feeds pride and Gregory's defiance of Leo made the emperor determined to make the pope submit. He ordered Gregory's arrest, but Gregory died before the arrest could occur.

He was succeeded by Gregory III who almost immediately held a synod condemning Leo and excommunicated the emperor himself. The breach did not permanently divide east and west, but it did put the popes at enmity with the emperors. The emperor's failure to defend the west against the Lombards was compounded by the seeming blasphemy of Leo. For the next half century the "Iconoclast" and the supporters of icons fought with one another, sometimes violently.

Officially the pope and the Catholic Church held that icons were not idols and may be revered. Ironically, Charles the Great took the stance that favored Leo but without militant enforcement. He declared, with Alcuin, that image worship was idolatry and should not be permitted by believers. This view was in direct contrast to that presented by Pope Hadrian at the second council of Nicaea in 787, which had declared iconoclasm a heresy and restored the veneration of images. The pope, however, was able to argue that Charlemagne had a faulty translation of the edict and the Church only permitted "adoration" of images. The fact that the pope was so eager to make Charlemagne's edict compatible with his own illustrates the esteem which Charles held in Italy, as well as his own kingdom.

The second issue of note is that of "adoptionism." This doctrine teaches that Christ was an ordinary man "adopted" by God and was not His only *begotten* son. Along with Protestants and modern Catholics, Charlemagne justly condemned this heresy. Its significance is in the fact that it took a stance which not only put it at odds with the Spanish Church, where adoptionism flourished, but that several popes had also taught the doctrine as well. Pope Hadrian, nevertheless, was not among its adherents and was delighted at the decision. Hadrian likewise condemned the view and the Catholic Church officially distanced itself from this doctrine, despite its adherents that continue in the minority to this very day. Indeed, Martin Scorsese's controversial movie *The Last Temptation of Christ* is based on adoptionists' theology.

The council was only one of many that Charlemagne held but it shows his concern for doctrine and truth as well as his skill in diplomacy. The end result of Charlemagne's condemnation of icons was negligible, but it stands in stark contrast to Leo's which had resulted in riots, death, and persecution. Even the pope danced around Charlemagne's views and pretended that they were compatible with his own.

Among those who had attended the Council of Frankfort was Claudius the Bishop of Turin. Claudius has often been called the "Protestant of the Ninth Century" because of his strong stances against traditionally Catholic views. In fairness, however, most of these controversial beliefs were not yet formally established as Church doctrine. They were, nevertheless, gaining prominence among the people and the clergy, and Claudius was quick to condemn them. He criticized the worship of relics, prayer for the dead, too much emphasis on tradition, and held that the Lord's supper was a memorial, not an actual sacrifice of Mass. He is significant for he, with the support of the Archbishop of Lyons and other Milanese, advocated independence from Rome. He and his allies in northern Italy near Milan often disregarded and even ignored the pope. This independent minded attitude continued in that region for centuries and produced the first forerunners of the Reformation. It is the place from whence the Waldenses blossomed and where John Calvin would follow in Martin Luther's steps. It is also where Charlemagne's best supporters came from.

The Last Days of the United Roman Empire

The east and west had been distancing themselves for centuries. The controversy with Leo "the Isaurian," who had once tried to arrest the pope, and the inability, or desire, of the emperors to protect Rome from the Lombards had strained the relations between the two to their breaking point. Now the Roman emperors of Constantinople seemed as bad as the old pagan emperors. One was even openly a bisexual who flaunted his disrespect for Biblical Christianity. By the end of the eighth century Constantine VI had become emperor, as a child. His mother Irene, a beautiful but vile woman, was the one who held the real power of the Empire. When Constantine VI had become of age Irene refused to turn the reigns of the government over to him, and after seeing that he was determined she had her own son arrested and imprisoned. Nevertheless, this act did nothing to win support for her. The army refused allegiance to her and she was placed under house arrest. Constantine VI was proclaimed sole ruler of the Roman Empire in 790.

In 795 Pope Hadrian I died. Charlemagne is said to have mourned his death as one who had lost a son. The papal election then decided between Hadrian's nephew, the chief notary, Paschalis, and Leo. The later was preferred and Pope Leo III was proclaimed the new pontiff. He promptly sent notice of his ascension not to Constantine VI but to Charlemagne. Charles in turn recognized the pope, but the act shows that it was really the pope who recognized Charlemagne, and his importance. No such courtesy or respect was ever offered to the eastern emperor who was to be assassinated by his own mother in eighteen months time.

For seven years Constantine VI reigned as emperor, but, in 797, Irene secretly ordered the assassination of her own son. Constantine's eyes were gouged out and he died shortly afterwards. Irene became the first true empress of Rome. She was a vile and corrupt woman who alienated both her own subjects and the western empire. She quickly bankrupted the empire and was both unwilling and unable to come to the west's defense against its enemies, and it was in 799 that Rome needed help. Irene was to be the first and last empress of the United Roman Empire.

Paschalis had not forgotten his humiliation in losing the election to Leo and he accused Leo of adultery. At his instigation, while Pope Leo was riding in a procession at Mass, a riot ensued and Leo was attacked by a gang of Paschalis's supporters. In the mass confusion they attempted to gouge out his eyes and cut off his tongue. Legend says that they succeeded and that his tongue miraculously grew back, but regardless of the legend he was temporarily blinded and severely wounded. Leo was brought before some bishops and formally deposed. They then imprisoned him in a monastery but with the help of friends he made his escape from Rome and set off to the one place where he knew help could come. That was place was not Constantinople but the Frankish empire.

The Founding of the Holy Roman Empire

By the time Leo arrived in Charlemagne's kingdom Paschalis had realized what was happening and sent agents of his own to formally charge Leo with adultery and perjury. Charlemagne was in a difficult situation. Supposedly a pope could not be judged by a mortal man yet the pope stood before him demanding justice while his accosters stood accusing. Charlemagne, whose adulterous affairs were many, probably did not care that greatly for the charges to start with. The brutal attack could hardly have been justified over sexual sin but was obviously a power play by Paschalis, who hoped to become pope himself. Charlemagne was well aware of the political situation and decided to defer judgment until after his agents had investigated the charges. In the meantime Charles would come to Rome itself.

Upon Charlemagne's arrival in Rome a grand ceremony was thrown, as if the emperor himself had arrived. It was December 800. Christmas was near and Charlemagne hoped to have the predicament resolved before Christmas Mass. His agents had finished their investigation and informed Charlemagne quietly of their opinions. They believed that Leo might be guilty of adultery but could not prove it. That the attack upon Leo was instigated by Paschalis seemed undeniable. Charles was ready for his verdict. On December 23 those who had conspired against the pope were sentenced to death, but Leo, in an act of nobility, pleaded that their sentence be commuted to exile. This was agreed to and the traitors were banished.

Christmas was now two days away and Leo's gratitude to Charlemagne was boundless. They had spoken at length over how Leo might reward Charlemagne but what happened is said to have shocked him. At Christmas Mass Charles the Great kneeled to pray and when he arose he found the pope over him with a crown in hand. Carolos Magnus, Charles the Great, was crowned Emperor of the Roman Empire and Pope Leo himself knelt before Charles in homage. This was the first and last act of obedience by a pope, but then there was never to be another Charlemagne.

Much debate had ensued about whether or not Charlemagne knew of the coronation before hand. According to Einhard, a contemporary historian and witness, Charlemagne later protested that he would never have set foot in Church had he known what was to happen. More cynical historians have doubted this, arguing that negotiations had already occurred, but the results of those negotiations are unknown. Certainly, Charlemagne expected to be rewarded, and he may even have entertained a hope of achieving the Imperial Diadem, but he was not so egocentric as to be blinded by reality. Leo had made Charlemagne a rival usurper to the Roman Empress Irene. There is no doubt that Charles would have accepted the crown if it were offered, but he would have wanted it on his terms. Leo's bestowal was truly a shock to the king and a monument to history. Charles the Great could truly say that the throne was thrust upon him.

While Charles was doubtless glad to be emperor he knew now that he had to deal with Irene. As emperor he was no longer Patrician, regent of Irene, but a rival to the throne. The Roman Senate had given their full support to Leo in his coronation of Charlemagne and even if he did not know of the plans before hand, they probably did. This was no accident. The Romans no longer wanted to be a part Constantinople's government. The east, upon hearing of Charlemagne's coronation, quaked in fear. Did Charles plan to invade Constantinople and take the throne? Did he expect them to swear fealty? Irene, already hated and despised by her own people, was no less expectant. To her delight, however, Charlemagne had no intention of invading the east. In fact, Charles wisely offered a marriage alliance. Irene was a widow and unmarried. He asked for her hand in marriage.

Such a move, if it had occurred, would have united the empires and vastly increased the already great kingdom of Charlemagne. Alas, it was not to be. Though Irene joyfully accepted, the people of Contantinople were not thrilled. They still considered the Germans to be barbarians and the revulsion that the people had for Irene, murderer of her own son, was overpowering. In 802 Irene was deposed by her subjects and the east and west would forever more be divided into two separate empires. Historians would henceforth call the east the Byzantine Empire, after Byzantium where Constantinople was built, and the west has been dubbed the Holy Roman Empire. The famed quotation of Hobbes was that the Holy Roman Empire "was the ghost of the deceased Roman Empire, sitting crowned upon the grave thereof."

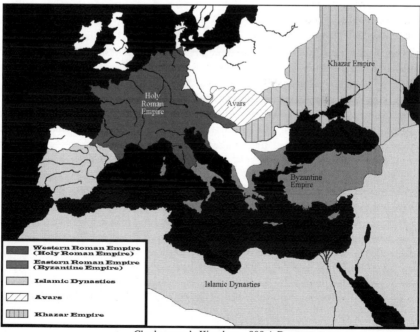

Charlemagne's Kingdom – 800 A.D.

The Holy Roman Empire

Hobbes was only partially correct. His statement acknowledges that the Holy Roman Empire is more than a Frankish empire. Its haunting imagery of ghosts and graves illustrates the fact that Rome still haunts the land. In 812 even the Byzantine Emperor Michael II reluctantly granted recognition to Charlemagne as emperor, though he deliberatly avoided using the title Roman Emperor. To the Byzantines it was they who were still the Roman Emperors, but to history it is clear that there were now *two* Roman Empires. Anncient historians even refer to the Byzantines as the "eastern Roman Empire" as opposed to the "western Roman Empire." It is merely the clumsiness of the terms that led historians to prefer "Byzantine" and "Frankish."

Voltaire's flippant remark "the Holy Roman Empire was neither," is untrue. Certainly, the empire was far from Holy but that it was Roman should never be doubted. Its laws, customs, and religion were Roman. While its emperor was German its true authority proceeded from Rome. Charlemagne was to be the first and last emperor who truly wielded supreme authority from Germany. Thereafter, as the pages of history will prove, the great emperors were forced to take up residence in Rome or at least march on the city to secure the pope's submission. It was Rome where the emperors were to be coronated, and Rome where the sovereign pontiff would one day usurp the authority of the emperors. The Holy Roman Empire was Roman in every possible way. Even the appearance of Germanic emperors was not truly new. Several ancient emperors had been of Germanic blood and many had been born in faraway Roman lands. Emperor Philip was called "the Arabian." Constantine himself was the son of a native British woman and it was there in Briton that he lived his childhood.

The Holy Roman Empire was to last a thousand years. It began with Charlemagne and ended no less dramatically with its last emperor, Napoleon. It was an empire which saw the world change. The pagan barbarity of ancient Rome would slowly, and haphazardly, change into a world of freedom and science, spawned by a once tiny religion centering around a man the Romans themselves had crucified.

Church and State Under Charlemagne

It had been popularly, and inaccurately, reported by many careless historians that the Church and State were one and the same in Charlemagne's reign. These same inattentive scholars maintain that it was Constantine who first merged Church and State and made Christianity the official state religion. Nevertheless, if man is to learn from history then it is important to look at history objectively and not read twenty–first century ideas of Church and State into medieval concepts. The first thing that must be understood is that *all* the ancient empires saw no distinction between *religion and government*, which must be differentiated from *Church and State*. In Egypt the Pharaoh was god incarnate. In Babylon the king was also a god, although later kings merely became the gods' voice. In ancient Rome, the emperor was also the High Priest or *Pontifex Maximus*. Religion and government were inexorably intertwined long before Constantine. What Constantine did was to make Christianity a *legal* religion. As such it enjoyed many of the liberties that the pagan religions enjoyed, and continued to enjoy. Christianity was now a *legally sanctioned religion* but it was not *the only* state sanctioned religion. Paganism would continue to be practiced for many decades, and the Senators of Rome continued to offer sacrifices to the gods in the senate itself.

The major effect of Christianity upon the old government of Rome was in that the laws were impacted by the Christian faith which had done much to make those laws more just. Constantine had established a measure of religious freedom previously unknown, he abolished cruel forms of execution including crucifixion, he outlawed the branding of prisoners, the murder of slaves, and the gladiatorial games, although the later would be reenacted after his death. These *moral* laws proceeded from religion, but so do *immoral* laws. The idea that laws should be *amoral* is an absurdity of modern philosophy and its failures are obvious from Communism. Law, by its very nature, is either just or unjust, and justice proceeds from religious notions.

If anything, it was Constantine's intrusion into Church affairs that was the most detrimental, not his religious impact upon Roman law. Before Constantine the Christian Church was preserved and shielded from the debasing influences of politics and power. Christianity was truly an innocent religion devoid of the corruption that power wrought. The close alliance between Church and State which *the Roman government* established degraded the Church, not vice versa. Between the time of Constantine and Charlemagne much would change in the Church, but the government remained largely the same. Over the centuries the powers of the government and the church (which were once many centuries before one and the same) *diverged*, yet they both wielded great power. The nature of the Christian Church spoke against the emperor being its high priest and under the emperor Gratian the title *Pontifex Maximus* was dropped from the Imperial office. The duties of the Church were then held to be separate from those of the emperor. Eventually the Bishop of Rome picked up the title, but in so doing he assumed many of the powers of the emperor. When the western emperors disappeared from the Italian landscape it was the popes who slowly emerged as the political leader of the west. Much of this was an accident of fate, not a conspiracy. When Attila the Hun stood outside Rome's gates it was Pope Leo the Great who negotiated peace, not the emperor. By the time of Charlemagne, there were two separate leaders of Rome; the temporal leader and the spiritual leader.

The idea that the Church and State were one and the same under Charlemagne is a false stereotype which proceeds, in part, from the happenings of the later Middle Ages, but it also proceeds from our own political ideas and the desire to shape history as we see fit. The fact is that Charlemagne had clearly asserted that the two were separate spheres. He created a mild form of separation of Church and State wherein the Pope would be the sovereign of the spiritual but Charlemagne was to be the sovereign of the temporal. In former governments, the two had never truly been separated, nor could they have. This very concept is one with which we struggle to this very day. Communism has proven that a truly secular state has never existed and never will exist. In Communism atheism becomes the state religion and all those with views held contrary to the state accepted doctrine are imprisoned, tortured, or sent to psychiatric hospitals. Atheism has butchered more people than all the religions of human history combined. Religious freedom and secularism are adversaries, not companions.

The very nature of government itself speaks to religious principles. Those who argue "you cannot legislate morality" ignore the fact that all just laws, such as prohibition against murder, rape, and slavery, are inherently moral and religious. Does not the United States' Declaration of Independence tout the notion of being "endowed by our Creator with certain inalienable rights"? Does not the very concept of "rights" itself come from religion? If not, how can we declare inalienable what we ourselves created? In ancient empires the king, as a god, bestowed rights and therefore it was his right to take those rights away. "I am the law," said the ancient kings. Later medieval kings adopted a similar stance by arguing for a "divine right of kings" but were unable to defend it against their critics. In Charlemagne's domain the Church was not to be inferior to the State, but it was not to control the State.

Charlemagne's theory of government accepted a distinction between the duties of the Church and the duties of a king. However, as a Christian he knew that government could not be secular and such a thought would never have occurred to him, but Charlemagne's enforcement of religious law was not based upon Church control. All to the contrary, Alcuin had beseeched Charlemagne not to force the Saxons to convert. The stance of the Church was missionary work at that time. Charles, however, took a *political* view that the forced baptism and enforcement of Christianity upon the pagan Saxons was essential to secure freedom for Christian schools and Churches. If we are to understand Charlemagne then we must think as he thought, not as a twenty–first century philosopher.

In Charlemagne's government the Church and State were to work together, but not necessarily as one. Although the Church would slowly gain increasing authority over the State, and eventually win out over the emperor, thus merging Church and State to an extent, this was not the case in the ninth century. The influence, however, that Christianity held over the new empire should not be underestimated, nor should it be derided. On the whole it was beneficial, for it was Christianity which brought principles to the once pagan empire that, when they blossomed a millennium later, would change the world. For the first time in history Christianity had secured the belief that the emperor was not above the law. God was supreme. Even later medieval kings, who attempted to argue for a "divine right" of kings, could not openly declare themselves to be above the law. This was the very justification that the Puritan Oliver Cromwell used when he legally executed the king of England and created the first Democratic Republic since ancient Rome. Kings and emperors would desperately try to cling to their authority for as long as they could but when Charlemagne, the greatest of all emperors, was crowned by the pope the world saw at once that his authority came not from himself but from above. Later popes would argue the authority was the Church rather than God Himself for they argued the Church represented God on earth, but to the men of Charlemagne's day this was not so. This was itself evident when Pope Leo knelt before the emperor; the only pope to ever do so.

The Last Days of Charlemagne

The average reign of kings and emperors over the centuries was only about a decade. Charlemagne reigned for over forty–five years. Of those years only thirteen were after the foundation of the Holy Roman Empire and thirty two of them were in anticipation of that historic event. His last years were good and peaceful. The Saxons had finally submitted and only the occasional Norman raid from the Vikings disturbed what would become the golden age of the Holy Roman Empire. Schools and Churches were erected practically everywhere where once savage barbarians could neither read nor write.

Charlemagne's health remained good, although he began to drag one foot in his last few years. The fact is, Charlemagne would outlive two of his own children. Pepin was a hunchback who died from his degenerate condition in relative youth. Charlemagne had forgiven him for a feeble usurpation attempt he had made in 792, and he had hoped to divide his vast empire amongst his children. Perhaps it is best that he did outlive most of his legitimate children for the age old Frankish practice of dividing lands, while it guaranteed all children an inheritance, was destined to divide the empire. When Charles's heir, Louis, himself died decades later the lands of the empire would be forever divided. France and Germany represent the remnants of that division made years later by Charlemagne's grandchildren, but for now the entire empire would be bequeathed to his only surviving son, Louis the Pious. Toward the end of the year 813, realizing that he was dying, Charles the Great personally crowned Louis co–emperor and heir to the throne. Louis was much like his father in devotion to God, minus the sexual habits. In many ways he was the perfect man to inherit his father's kingdom but he had not the brutal strength that

Charlemagne is so criticized. Without that, he was unable to truly carry on his father's legacy.

In January 814 Charlemagne died. His legacy did not.

The Legacy of Charlemagne

Charlemagne is universally recognized as one of the greatest men of history. He has been called the "Moses of the Middle Ages" and the very Arthurian legends which so captured the imagination of England were actually based more on Charlemagne than the real Arturius. Indeed, most consider that the Arthur of legend is really just an Anglicization of the great emperor. Chivalry might also be considered the invention of Charlemagne as well, for although he could be fierce, his army was disciplined and they were not, as so many before them, want to rape and pillage. In Czechoslavokia the word they use for king was derived from their pronunciation of Charlemagne's name, *kral*. The same is also true of Poland; *krol*. Yet Charlemagne's fame did not rise from his conquest as so many others in history have. It was the country he made, not the country he conquered.

This was perhaps what made Charlemagne greater than all those before or after him. He was far more than a conqueror. Indeed, Gibbon who is want to grant recognition to any Christian, reluctantly admitted Charlemagne's greatness yet pointed out less than charitably that Charlemagne never faced great odds or showed military genius. The greatness of Charlemagne was not in his conquest but in his building up of European civilization. Where once paganism, ignorance, and brutality reigned civilization and learning was beginning to take root.

If Constantine was the beginning of the Christianization of Rome, then Charlemagne was the beginning of the Christianization of Europe, and the world. Nevertheless, this process was not to be achieved overnight as he might have hoped. The Middle Ages had been called the era of "baptized paganism." It is ironic then that Charlemagne did literally just that. He baptized pagans but they were still pagans in their hearts. Europe was still barbarian, but it was slowly learning that barbarianism was not compatible with its new religion. The Holy Roman Empire was to become a mixture of Christian virtue and pagan vices. Magic was merged with science, mysticism with religion, and justice with savagery. Charlemagne was truly the founder of everything good and bad that would happen for the next thousand years.

4

The Fall of the Carolingian Dynasty

If ever there was an empire that was the product of one man it was Charlemagne's Holy Roman Empire. True, he owed some credit to his forefathers and to the pope, but in most every other sense of the word, the Holy Roman Empire was *his* empire. Julius Caesar built upon Pompey's conquest and those of his predecessors, Nebuchadnezzar restored Babylon to its greatness but he did not create it; Napoleon's kingdom did not even survive to his own death. Only Alexander the Great comes close to Charlemagne, and Alexander only so in conquest. Alexander was a conqueror, not a ruler. He left no great marks upon science or education or law or administration. All this Charlemagne did. When Charlemagne died, it was only a matter of time before the dynasty he created would crumble to the ground. Perhaps this is Charlemagne's great weakness; he did not, as the forefathers of America, build a kingdom that could survive without a strong leader. The Holy Roman Empire required such a leader to survive and the history of the middle ages is a history of searching for that leader.

Despite protests from some scholars, it is clear that the Holy Roman Empire did survive, but not as a United Kingdom. The unity of Europe and the empire depended on the emperor and the pope. At various times the individual states of the empire were virtually independent in everything but name. At other times, the emperor and/or the pope held a tight grip upon each individual country and state. Charlemagne's immediate successors, however, were not among the later. Save for Louis the Pious, Charlemagne's successors would vie with each other for power, and eventually crumble their own dynasty by their own hands. During the reign of the Carolingian dynasty it can be fairly said that the empire as a whole was in good shape and suffered little from outside invaders, economic crises, or plagues, but within the empire its leaders were constantly engaged in civil war and civil strife. The interest of the people was rarely evident and a cursory reading of history shows that these emperors did little of consequence for the people. Theirs was the tale of a struggle for self glory and pride. Theirs was the tale of the fall of the Carolingian Dynasty.

Louis the Pious

It is ironic that the tale of the Carolingian's dynasty begins with Louis the Pious for in many respects Louis was, or at least could have been, a great emperor : if only he had been impotent. Like King David of Israel, Louis loved his children to his own detriment. He spoiled them in their youth, crowning one king at six years of age. They soon found that they were not willing to wait for their father to pass away and one or more of his sons attempted to usurp his throne no less than five times. Each time, however, he forgave his sons and took no further steps to punish them. By the time Louis died, the empire was engaged in a civil war as the brothers fought each other over the throne.

In many respects Louis was a good king. During his reign there was very little threat from invasion or outside perils. The economy and society was far greater than it would be in the middle ages to come. The Carolingian Renaissance had not yet died. By and large the people were at peace. It was the conflicts within the empire, and particularly that of Louis's own children that caused the empire to be in disarray at his death.

In terms of character Louis the Pious passed even Charlemagne. He had most of Charlemagne's virtues but lacked the sexual vices of Charlemagne. He was devout, gave generously to the Church, cared for the clergy and people, and was said to have been courageous in battle, but to his credit he seldom entered the battlefield save when it was truly necessary. He even turned the great palace into a monastery. One might generously say that he was too Christian for a society that was still pagan in spirit. Another might more cynically say that his virtue and religion could not compensate for his naïveté. Although he did give orders to blind a rebellious step–son as punishment, the step–son died as a result of his injuries and Louis never again issued such orders. Instead, he ignored the treason and sedition of his sons and turned a blind eye towards their ambitions. He simply did not have to stomach to punish his children.

Although Charlemagne had crowned Louis, Stephen IV (V) {so reckoned because of an "antipope" years earlier also called Stephen} did anoint the new emperor in 816 to show his approval. At this anointing Pope Stephen IV (V) presented Louis with the "crown of Constantine." This symbol was meant to show the support of the papacy for Louis, but it also set the tone for future emperors' coronations. No sooner had the young empire started than the struggle between emperor and pope began, but in these early days the struggle was largely a peaceful one with each side granting certain concessions. After Stephen's death, Paschal ascended to the Lateran throne. Louis the Pious assured Paschal and Rome of his trust and faithfulness to the Church. He passed a statute guaranteeing that the emperor would never intervene in papal affairs except when asked or when the voices of the oppressed demanded it. The only thing that was required of the papacy was a renewal of a treaty of friendship with the emperor whenever a new pope ascended. Henceforth, all emperors were also supposed to be crowned in Rome by the pope.

In theory the Church governed spiritual matters and the Imperial Palace controlled temporal matters. Consequently, the Church and State were technically separate. As symbol of the emperor's temporal authority Pope Paschal I gave a sword (as well as a crown) to the young Lothair when he was made co–emperor. Such an arrangement is noble, and is the very thing that many argue should be true today, but this was a naïve presupposition. The very nature of government deals with fundamentally religious issues such as "human rights." It was inevitable that the Church and State would come into eventual conflict, just as they have ever since, down to this very day. A government can no more be secular than it can, or should, be controlled by the Church. The proper balance between these two would be fought over for the next thousand years.

When Louis first took the throne in 814 Charlemagne had left the most glorious kingdom since ancient Rome, from which his kingdom justly took its name. Louis had no need of conquests and was not interested in such. He sought merely to render justice throughout the kingdom. These early years were still a continuation of Charlemagne's kingdom and glory. He appointed his two sons, Lothair and Pepin, kings over specific regions of the empire, as sort of regional governors, and gave Italy to his step–son Bernard. In 817, Bernard showed his appreciation by revolting against Louis. Louis quickly put down the revolt and issued orders for an ancient punishment. The rebel's eyes were to be put out. As cruel as this punishment seems, it was actually an act of mercy for execution usually followed. In this case, Louis showed mercy in an age where mercy was rare. Nevertheless, whether by accident or intent, the soldiers performed the deed with such savagery that Bernard died of the injuries. This would be the last time that Louis ever ordered such a punishment. His conscience troubled him so severely that he would henceforth refuse to punish rebellious sons no matter what their sins.

Louis did not want to die without having named an heir so he had his son Lothair crowned co–emperor by Pope Paschal I in 823. Later he would crown his two youngest sons kings in 829. Louis ("the German") would be but eleven years old and Charles ("the Bald") would be a mere child of six years of age. Although he gave his children the best education possible, such power placed upon mere children could only guarantee their pride and arrogance. Even before their rebellion the young Lothair first precipitated conflict between Church and State by asserting the right of interference in Church decisions and policy. In response, Paschal had two Frankish supporters of Lothair executed in the Lateran Palace itself. Such an act outraged the people and the emperor but Paschal assured the emperor that they were lawfully executed for treason.

Further scandal occurred when Paschal became the first pope to issue papal indulgences. Such indulgences had originated about a century earlier in England where repentant sinners might donate money to show remorse for their sins. As time proceeded the indulgences were like "fines" levied for sins. Naturally, this practice would lead to the corruption of papal indulgences where the rich could merely buy salvation.

Upon Paschal's death the people of Rome celebrated his demise and Pope Eugene II was quickly promoted. The Emperor sought to clarify the role of the pope and his relation to the Imperial office so a constitution was written in 824 that guaranteed the right of the people, as well as the clergy, to vote in the Papal elections. This policy had existed in the past but had been suspended in recent years. With a constitution it was hoped that the policy would become law, but alas the constitution itself would eventually be forgotten and by the time of Pope Gregory VII no one would be allowed to vote for the pope except specific members of the clergy. Pope Eugene, however, was elected by all the people. He acknowledged the sovereignty of the emperor and swore an oath of loyalty to Louis the Pious.

Eugene II and Louis the Pious were often in contact with each other through the years. At one time Louis sought Eugene's help in condemning the worship of relics and idols but Eugene maintained that there was nothing harmful in images. Despite their differences Louis did not assert his authority in this matter but allowed Eugene to render his decision as he saw fit. The two were to become friends and idealized the proper relationship between Church and State. Unfortunately, Eugene died in 827. He successor, Valentine, was unanimously elected but died less than a month after his election. Gregory IV was then elected in his place and with his election the short lived era of peace between emperor and pope seemed to fade. The problems began when imperial judges permitted certain abbeys to be exempt from tribute to the papal see.

In the meantime Louis had his two younger sons crowned co–emperors. This was the year 829. With three young brothers, two still children, holding such power in their hands it was perhaps inevitable that they would rebel. It was not a year later when Lothair, with the support of his brothers, declared his father deposed. Nevertheless, this did not sit well with the people or the Frankish bishops. A general assembly gathered and restored Louis the Pious to the throne in 830. Louis forgave his sons and did little to punish them beyond changing some of the political boundaries of their kingdoms.

Despite such generosity by their father, Lothair again usurped the throne, this time with the support of Pope Gregory IV. The support of Gregory was indeed ironic, for it was Lothair who had originally granted exemption from papal tribute, but Gregory was willing to forgive this if Lothair reversed his position. Gregory most probably sought money and power through the support of Louis' rebellious children. Such actions, however, did not endear the pope to the people or the clergy at large. Indeed, rarely had the Church had an ally of Louis the Pious's stature. The clergy was outraged and not only condemned Gregory for his actions but the local bishops actually threatened to *excommunicate the pope* if he did not repent! Despite the threats, Gregory marched together with Lothair's army in 833 where they prepared to meet Louis on the battlefield. Lothair and his younger brothers then asked the pope to negotiate a peaceful settlement with their father. Gregory agreed and met with Louis only to realize that he was being used as a puppet. While Gregory negotiated with Louis, the army of Louis was deserting. The entire negotiation had been little more than a distraction technique. Lothair and his men won over the support of many of Louis's soldiers with bribery, or other measures, and Louis was forced to surrender unconditionally. He was deposed shortly thereafter.

Despite the support of Gregory IV, Lothair's actions brought anger from the Frankish bishops. Gregory IV had himself been threatened with excommunication and did little to help Lothair. Perhaps Gregory finally realized that he had been Lothair's puppet or perhaps he had bowed to the bishops whose support he had clearly lost. In either case, he reversed his position and refused to support Lothair. Without the Church's support Lothair could not hope to rule so Louis was again restored to the throne in 834. Once more, he did nothing to punish his sons, nor alter his will. Lothair was still heir to the throne and retained his possessions.

Louis's refusal to punish Lothair proved him weak in Lothair's eyes. Lothair was still determined to seize the throne before his father's natural death. That very same year Lothair revolted for a third time. This time Louis's army drove Lothair deep into Italy where they retreated. Believing Lothair no longer posed a threat, Louis's army departed, leaving Lothair intact. This would actually be the last time that Lothair would revolt but his brother Louis the German had other ideas.

In 839 Louis the German also tried to seize the throne and depose his father. Like Lothair, Louis the German was defeated and driven back by Louis the Pious. Like Lothair, Louis the German escaped punishment. By this time, it was obvious that Louis had left no sons worthy of the throne and when Louis died in 840 it was destined that civil war would erupt.

The Civil War and Lothair

Despite his character, integrity, and charity Louis the Pious left the Empire in chaos and turmoil. Upon his death his spoiled and corrupt children immediately fought for the vacant throne. Lothair had been named Louis's heir but his two surviving brothers, Charles the Bald and Louis the German (Pepin had died earlier), refused to accept his authority. For three years a civil war raged as the three fought for power. The pope, Gregory IV, was now but a feeble ruler who was unable to negotiate any peace between the three and seemed more preoccupied in glorifying himself than in the empire. Gregory's time was spent commissioning mosaics of himself as well as constructing a formidable fortress, named Gregoriopolis, to help defend Rome against the new Muslim threat from the south.

By 843 none of the claimants had made any sufficient gains. Tiring of the war, they consented to meet and ratify a treaty. The treaty of Verdun agreed to accept Lothair nominally as emperor but Charles and Louis would each rule their own respective kingdoms as they saw fit. Charles the Bald received

Western Franconia (or France), Louis the German received Eastern Franconia or Germany (hence the nickname), and Lothair acquired Italy as his true domain.

Although Lothair was the recognized emperor of the Holy Roman Empire in name, the empire was now effectively divided into three smaller kingdoms; Eastern Franconia (Germany), Western Franconia (France), and Italy (which did not then include the southern portion). Burgundy and other smaller kingdoms fell into one of these three domains. Each had its own king who was supposedly under the authority of the emperor, much like state governors are under the authority of the President of the United States. Local states elect governors and make laws as they see fit, so long as these do not conflict with the authority of the federal government and the President. Like the U.S., the Holy Roman Empire had its periods of strong federal government, and its periods of weak federal government. The President, and the emperor, have only as much authority as the other members of government allot him. Strong Presidents do as they wish with no fear of Congress while weak ones are impeached, ignored, or are puppets of advisors. So also, strong emperors kept the Holy Roman Empire together and unified the kingdoms. Weak emperors held the title of emperor but wielded no true authority. Such was the era of the Holy Roman Emperors from Lothair until Otto the Great restored the Empire to a glimmer of its former glory.

Lothair left his brothers alone for a time. Italy was problem enough. Unlike his father Lothair was not initially a true ally of the Church. When Gregory IV died a faction was created. The common people favored a Pope John whom they installed after storming the Lateran Palace, while the nobility elected Sergius II as pope. The nobility then used their political might to forcibly quell all opposition. John's life was spared, at Sergius's request, but he was ordained without waiting for approval from Lothair. This angered Lothair who sent his son, Louis II, to investigate. While en route to the Papal Palace Louis II and his men stopped to pillage several cities within the Papal territories. When Louis finally arrived Sergius was able to pacify him and to convince him to accept his ascension. Despite his mercy toward John and his political victory, Sergius was far from innocent. He treated the papacy as if it were a money laundering racket. Church offices were sold to the highest bidders and bribery was common.

In addition to the Church matters, Lothair had the more pronounced threat of the Arab Saracens who had been harassing Italy for some time and were seeking a foothold in Europe. They had conquered much of Spain but been unable to penetrate into Europe's mainland since Charles Martel had thwarted their attempt a hundred years before. The Byzantine Empire obstinately held its own ground against the Islamic invaders at the south–eastern edge of Europe and the Khazar Empire (south of modern day Russia) kept the Muslims from entering Europe by way of the east. Italy was now the focal point of the Saracen's attack.

In 846 disaster struck. The Muslim Saracens had reached Rome and stormed the city. While they did not break Aurelian's wall, they were able to sack and plunder St. Peter's and St. Paul's, both of which had lain outside the walls. When Pope Sergius died the next year it was up to the new pope, Leo IV, to rebuild the destruction caused by the Saracens. Leo constructed a new wall on the Tiber which would enclose St. Peter's and St. Paul's within its walls and he created new fortifications. One might criticize Lothair for letting the pope do what he ought to have done himself but it was not the only time that Leo would make him look bad. Years later Leo IV asserted such authority that he had three of Lothair's agents executed for the murder of a papal legate. This same Leo is said to have hallowed the young Englishman Alfred, who would become Alfred the Great of England.

Whether from remorse for his sins, or from fatigue of trying to rule an empire in decay, Lothair voluntarily abdicated his throne to become a monk in 855. Perhaps this was his one bright spot, for as an emperor he left no stamp upon history save as the son who tried three times to usurp his righteous father's throne and went to war with his brothers to insure it remained his. One thing is for sure, whatever the reasons for his abdication, health was not an issue. He lived fourteen more years as a monk before dying and never again tried to regain the throne. Perhaps it is best to assume that Lothair repented of his sins and tried to make amends in the monastery.

The Reign of Louis II

Lothair left the empire to his son, Louis II. Like his father, however, Louis II was an emperor in name, but not in power. He was the authority of Italy, but even that would be contested. Indeed, one of his first acts resulted in his humiliation. Pope Leo IV had died and a new pope was needed. Although the people had elected Pope Benedict III, Louis II wanted a colleague of his to become pope. The Imperial party tried fruitlessly to make Anastasius the new pope, but the people resisted him. Using the law which required Imperial consent Louis refused to recognize Benedict and his troops forcibly entered the Papal Palace, arrested Benedict, and placed Anastasius on the throne. Despite this, and because of it, the people and the clergy refused to accept him. Threats of torture were even made against the bishops who refused to consecrate him but they would not back down. Louis had to admit defeat. He made arrangements for Benedict to resume the papal throne on the condition that Anastasius be treated with leniency. Benedict agreed and Anastasius eventually even rose to become the Church Librarian or Bibliothecarius. In the meantime, Louis had lost to the will of the people.

Far worse than this humiliation, Louis II inherited an empire that was seeing invasions on all sides. The Vikings and Britons had begun to invade France, which Charles the Bald ruled, while Louis the German saw the pagan

Magyars from the east sacking and pillaging his territory. In Italy the Saracens had secured southern Italy, which had formerly remained a part of the Byzantine Empire. Perhaps it was for the best that Charles the Bald and Louis the German sought no help from the emperor, for Louis's hands were full in Italy. Fearing the presence of Muslim invaders in Italy, Louis II joined forces with the Byzantine Empire and with their combined armies and drove the Saracens back.

Despite this success, Louis II merely inherited more problems. This included a pope that would overshadow him in both respect and political power. Pope Nicholas I reigned during the tenure of Louis II, from 858–867. During this time Nicholas came into conflict with both kings and the emperor, but always Nicholas prevailed.

One problem with historians of the Holy Roman Empire is that they get in the routine of seeing an empire entirely as the domain of the emperors, but it is clear that by the High Middle Ages, the emperor was subservient to the papacy. Countries over which the emperor had no direct control were thoroughly under the dominion of the pope and the emperor could not intervene with those countries without the pope's permission. When did this ascension of papal power occur? In truth, over a great many years. At this time, the empire may truly be defined as a loose confederation of states nominally ruled by the emperor. Pope Nicholas I, however, made no small effort to enhance his supremacy over the temporal domains of Europe. Although his vision would not be realized until centuries later, his reign would serve as an archetype for later popes. His arrogance demanded complete submission and failed to acknowledge even the possibility of error on his part. For Nicholas, the pope reigned for God on earth and was His sole voice.

It is perhaps poetic justice that the same pope who sought to assert his unity over the whole of Christianity was also the pope under whom the final break between east and west occurred. For some time the eastern church (today referred to as eastern Orthodox) had been distancing itself from the west. Conflicts over the power and authority of the papacy, as well as doctrinal debates concerning the nature of Christ (whether or not He had two natures – one divine and one human – or one nature both human and divine), had increasingly placed a strain on relations between the two. The Eastern Patriarch was the head of the eastern church, just as the Pope was the head of the west. During the reign of Byzantine Emperor Michael III, Patriarch Ignatius had publicly rebuked the "Caesar" Bardas (who was the real ruler behind the throne of Byzantium) for immorality. Bardas was excommunicated when he married his own daughter–in–law. He exacted his revenge, however, by having Ignatius deposed and banished. He was then replaced by Patriarch Photius. Ignatius excommunicated Photius who likewise cast the anathema at Ignatius. Photius then wrote to the pope informing him of his ascension and asking for recognition. Nicholas sent dignitaries to investigate the issue but when they were in Constantinople they were never permitted to speak to or see Ignatius, who had been imprisoned and beaten. The dignitaries were threatened and bribed into deciding in favor of Photius. Nicholas, however, angrily refused to accept their decision. He promptly reversed the rulings of his commissioners and decided in favor of Ignatius. Photius and the emperor refused to accept to the judgment and the breach was complete. Ever since this time (863) the Eastern Orthodox Church and the Roman Catholic Church, as they are called today, have been two separate entities which even to this day continue to debate over reunification. Indeed, Photius and Nicholas would continue to war with one another over the years.

One such battle was fought over Bulgaria. In the 860s the Khan Boris of Bulgaria had become a Christian. He had forged an alliance with the Holy Roman Empire years earlier and was now seeking Christian missionaries to come and convert his nation. Since Constantinople was far closer to his country than Rome, he naturally sent emissaries to the Patriarch Photius. Photius deviously promised to send the missionaries but only if he would renounce his allegiance to the Holy Roman Empire of which his kingdom was officially a part. Boris agreed to this and the great Christian Missionary Cyril was wisely chosen to lead many missionaries into Bulgaria. It was Cyril who even gave the Slavic people their alphabet (Cyrillic), for they had no written language before.

All was well until Boris wrote Photius and requested native bishops as well as lenience in customs. The eastern Church had been quite rigorous in enforcing the rituals of Greek customs in the Church. Even little things such as whether or not women could wear pants were stringently enforced by Photius. When Boris wrote Photius requesting the exact theological reasoning for each of these conflicting customs, Photius simply ignored them and refused to accept Bulgarian bishops. Boris then decided to appeal to Pope Nicholas. He was already well aware that a split had occurred between east and west and hoped that Nicholas would be more reasonable. Nicholas was. He allowed certain customs of the Bulgarians to stand but meticulously explained the theological reasonings for each and every stance which conflicted with Bulgarian customs. He also allowed Bulgarians to become bishops if they showed proper credentials. Boris was well pleased with the decision, which gave Bulgarians more freedom, and he promptly kicked the eastern missionaries out of the country. Bulgaria now belonged to the papal Church and was again allies with the Holy Roman Empire.

It was not, however, the struggles between east and west for which Nicholas I is known. Indeed, the breach had been brewing for some time, and the Nicholas I was right to have ruled for Ignatius and Boris. It is in relations with the western temporal powers that Nicholas I is best known. The first incident involved the late Emperor Lothair's despicable son. Lothair II had abused his wife and lived with a mistress, who was well known to the people. He falsely accused his wife in an attempt to gain a divorce but when her "champion" survived being boiled in oil, he persuaded the archbishops to grant his divorce anyway. After the divorce he then married his mistress, whom he publicly paraded as a Queen. This scandal angered both the people and pope who deposed the archbishops and threatened Lothair II with excommunication if he did not leave his mistress and return to his lawful wife. In defense of Lothair II the emperor threatened Rome with military troops if the pope did not back down. Nicholas hid out in St. Peter's but held firm to his pronouncements.

Seeing an opportunity to wreak revenge, the eastern Patriarch Photius sent emissaries to Louis II and a plot was contrived. Photius would call a Council and have the pope deposed as a heretic. The grounds for heresy was nothing more than the Catholic view of "double Procession" meaning that the Holy Spirit proceeded from both the Father *and* the Son. Photius maintained that the Holy Spirit proceeded only from the Father. In any case, the deposition of Nicholas was the real purpose. After this Council was held Louis II could then legitimately use military force to flush Nicholas from St. Peter's and restore Lothair II. This plot almost succeeded but for the assassination of Byzantine Emperor Michael III. Basil the Macedonian became the new emperor of Constantinople and deposed Photius in favor of Ignatius, the man whom Nicholas had fought so hard for years earlier. Louis II and Lothair II were forced to back down. Nicholas had won again.

While Nicholas I was in the right, and other popes had threatened excommunication for sins, the pope's use of spiritual powers to bring an unrepentant member of royalty into submission helped to pave the way for later popes who would clearly abuse this power for their own aims. It was obvious that the pope could wield powerful control over even the Emperor's will. In yet another instance Nicholas I came into conflict with Hincmar, the archbishop of Rheims, who was notorious for defying the authority of the papacy, yet declared his own sovereignty over all France. When Rothad, the local bishop of Soissons, defied the authority of Hincmar, Hincmar had Rothad deposed and falsely imprisoned with the help of Charles the Bald, whom Hincmar had crowned king. Nicholas I, however, came to the aid of Rothad and after much debate, protests, and politicking Nicholas I had Rothad reinstated.

During this controversy, Nicholas I unmistakably asserted his authority over the domain of France as well as Italy. Despite the fact that Nicholas I was generally in the right in these matters, his assertion of authority and his use of spiritual powers over civil and temporal ones would eventually become the common abuses of later popes. He is generally considered one of the greatest of the early medieval popes in an generation of notoriously bad popes. Indeed, within fifty years the papacy would fall into the era commonly called the "papal pornocracy."

When Pope Nicholas died an immediate and heated debate occurred over who would be the next pope. The Imperial party did not want another Nicholas. His interference with the emperor and kings left a sour taste in their mouth and was but a foreshadowing of future generations. On the other side, the clergy, and even many of the people, distrusted the politicians and preferred a pope that was not afraid to stand up to them. In the end a compromise was reached. A certain Hadrian had twice been nominated pope in preceding elections but Hadrian did not have the desire for the office. Twice Hadrian had declined to become pope, a sign of humility that only made him more popular. This time he accepted.

Pope Hadrian II showed promise in terms of character. He appeared to be an honest Christian who was devoted to God and his family (priestly marriage was permitted in these days) but in a day of corruption he did not have the stomach to stand up against it. Hadrian's reign would begin ingloriously as the Duke Lambert would pillage Rome in defiance of the emperor. This same Lambert was the ancestor to Guy and another Lambert who would many decades later usurp the throne. Doubtless this escapade was an early attempt to increase the power of Spoleto, of which he was Duke. Again, this showed the weakness of the emperor, as well as the new pope, who could do nothing and, from all extant accounts, did not attempt to rebuke or excommunicate the Duke.

Even worse for Hadrian II was the agony he had to endure at the hands of the brother of the former antipope Anastasius. Hadrian's daughter was raped and murdered, and his own wife also fell to the assassin. Although Louis II had the perpetrator apprehended and executed Hadrian's loss was but a foreshadowing of the political strife that the papacy would soon endure. Anastasius was quietly excommunicated for his suspected participation, but Hadrian himself later reinstated Anastasius.

With neither a strong emperor nor a strong pope to bring order Charles the Bald annexed land from Louis the German who promptly invaded France in 869. The next year a treaty was concluded that allowed Charles the Bald to keep the territory that he had annexed. That same year Louis II decided to act on his authority as Holy Roman Emperor. He invaded Germany in an attempt to bring it under subjugation. This brief war concluded with a treaty that divided some land between Louis the German and Louis II. Louis II doubtless saw this as a first step in restoring the power of the emperor, but others were not as willing to be subjected to the emperor's law. In 871 Louis II found himself unexpectedly captured as a prisoner of Duke Adelchis, ruler of southern Italy. After Louis's joint victory over the Saracens, the Duke had feared that his domain was to be added to the emperors so he held Louis II prisoner until he promised, with the backing of a papal dispensation, not to intervene in the Duke's right to rule over southern Italy. This was reluctantly granted and Louis II was released.

Because of the humiliation that Louis II faced at the hands of the Duke, Pope Hadrian II solemnly recrowned the emperor on Pentecost of 872 in order to show his support. It was, however, too little and too late. Hadrian II would die later that same year and Louis II's reign would last but a few more years. During this time one of Louis the German's own sons revolted against him (873) as the other had done years earlier (861). This irony is perhaps just punishment for a man who had himself attempted to usurp his father Louis the Pious. In the end, Louis the German never would get the emperor's crown although his youngest son, Charles the Fat did attain the title for a short time.

The Decay of the Empire

With the death of Pope Hardian II, John VIII took the tiara. John VIII hoped to follow in the paths of Gregory the Great and Nicholas I and he was, in some ways, quite successful. John VIII asserted himself into political matters and made himself an emperor maker. In order to secure his own position he excommunicated and expunged all whom he thought aspired to become, or control, the pope. This list included Formosus who would become pope almost fifteen years later. With the threat of Saracens from the south John VIII created his own Papal Navy and built new fortifications to protect the Papal States. Then Louis II died in 875. John VIII did not believe that Louis the German would be a trustworthy ally so on Christmas that same year Pope John VIII placed the emperor's crown upon Charles the Bald's bald head. In return Charles the Bald increased the boundaries of the Papal States and renounced the Emperor's right to have Imperial emissaries at papal elections.

The imperial reign of Charles the Bald would last but a few short years. In the meantime, Louis the German died shortly after Charles's ascension, and Charles immediately tried to bring Germany under his authority. Nevertheless, Louis the Younger (Louis the German's son) repelled Charles's army. Later, Louis the Younger was aided by his brother Carloman who marched against Charles. Carloman was ready to take the crown for his own. He marched into Italy but even Charles's own vassals tired of the conflict and incompetence. Charles the Bald did not meet Carloman on the battle field but instead retreated across the Alps where he died.

Carloman now demanded that Pope John VIII crown him emperor. This event passes quietly among historians but it is significant for it shows that even usurpers acknowledged that the emperor had to receive his royal diadem from the pope. John VIII, however, stalled. Fortunately, Carloman fell ill and was forced to return to Germany, but his supporters entered Rome on his behalf. Along with those excommunicated by John VIII, Duke Lambert of Spoleto and Adalbert of Tuscia had John imprisoned when he refused to crown Carloman. This was the same Lambert who had sacked Rome years earlier and the same Duke whose descendants would usurp the Imperial crown in less than two decades. Despite many threats John VIII repeatedly refused to coronate Carloman. The Dukes and Carloman were in a precarious predicament. Murdering a pope would not help their aspirations and the empire now knew that the pope was defying them even while he was in prison. When Carloman died a short time later they reluctantly released him. Carloman's only son,

Arnulf, was illegitimate and therefore could not be recognized for succession. John VIII, therefore, set out to find a worthy emperor.

John VIII first sought out Louis the Stammerer of France. In fact he was coronated king by the pope in 878, but Louis the Stammerer was reluctant to accept the Imperial office. He may not have wanted to become the target of other power seeking dukes or he may have realized that his time was already short for he died eight months later without having come to terms with the pope. John VIII then sought out several other candidates but settled on Charles the Fat. In 879 Charles the Fat was named King of Italy and in February 881 he received the crown of the Holy Roman Emperor.

Charles the Fat showed no more aptitude for leadership than most of his predecessors. While his domain increased from that of his predecessors this acquisition was merely because of the natural deaths of his relatives. As the kings died, many left no heirs forcing the people to turn to Charles the Fat for leadership. In one country, however, Boso usurped Charles's authority and defected from the empire. This seems ironic since Boso was, in fact, one of the men that John VIII had approached about the possibility of becoming emperor. Nevertheless, Boso's territory was relatively small and Charles's actual authority was becoming far greater than the emperors before him. He was the closest thing to a real emperor since Louis the Pious. Still, he was not a good emperor, but a weak and feeble emperor. In regard to the Viking threat from the north he merely paid large sums of ransom and bribe money to keep them in line.

The year following his coronation Charles lost one of his strongest allies. The very pope that had helped him to attain the crown had become the first papal victim of assassination. For reason's unknown John VIII's own men are said to have poisoned him and beat him to death with clubs. He was followed by Pope Marinus I (sometimes referred to as Martin II) who came to an agreement with Charles the Fat that Formosus, and the others accused of conspiracies by John VIII should be reinstated. Their banishment was lifted by the emperor and Marinus lifted their excommunications.

During this time political pressure from Charles's enemies increased. With the backing and encouragement of Marinus Charles deposed one of his chief rivals, Guy of Spoleto. Another rival was Arnulf, the illegitimate son of Carloman. Arnulf was gaining more support throughout the realm but he did nothing at this time to antagonize the emperor. Charles's chief security came from the support of the papacy, but that support was threatened when Marinus died after a reign of only a year and half.

Hadrian III replaced Marinus, and Charles now needed to secure his support, not only for himself, but also for his son whom he hoped would succeed him as emperor. This was compounded by the fact that Charles's only son, Bernard, was illegitimate and could not normally claim to be an heir to the throne. Only with the backing of the new pope could Bernard hope to succeed his father. Hadrian seemed agreeable but before he could formalize a deal he died under mysterious circumstances. Although Hadrian had ruled only a little over a year he had made many enemies with whom he dealt severely. In one case he ordered a high official's eyes to be put out and is even alleged to have had a noble woman stripped naked and flogged in public. It is, therefore, little surprise that Hadrian's death occurred suddenly after so short a reign, despite the fact that historians have been unable to ascertain the exact cause of death.

Charles the Fat had now seen three different popes die in just under three years. With increasing dissatisfaction over Charles's rule, and the inability to secure the right of succession for his son Bernard, Charles hopes now rested with Pope Stephen V (VI). If Charles was to maintain his throne and earn young Bernard's right to succeed him he would have to have Stephen's blessing. He did not, however, start off on the right foot for when he had heard that a new pope was elected without his consultation he sent a chancellor to depose the new pope. Still, when the chancellor saw that the pope had the full support of the clergy and the people, he too supported Stephen and advised Charles to accept him as well. Despite this initial encounter, Charles might still have found favor with the new pope had he answered the pope's call for assistance.

In 886 Pope Stephen V (VI) had called on Charles the Fat to come and protect the Holy See from Saracens invasions. The Muslims had increasingly stepped up their efforts to gain a solid foothold in Italy and were staging more raids on Rome and the Papal States. Charles was at first obligued to obey but when he heard of disturbances in his homeland he thought them to be more important and ignored Stephen's plea. Angry at the incompetence and unwillingness to protect the Church, Stephen V (VI) deposed Charles the Fat the following year. Charles would die a beggar less than two months later and with him the Carolingian dynasty is said to have died as well.

Despite such eulogies the Carolingians had not passed away. Following the brief interlude of two counterfeit emperors the Carolingians would see two illegitimate descendants sit briefly and ingloriously upon the throne. In the meantime, Rome was again without an emperor and Stephen V (VI) needed someone who would protect the Papal States. Arnulf may have been illegitimate but his birth was by no fault of his own. Arnulf was a Carolingian, albeit illegitimate, and he was growing in military power and strength. In 887, after deposing Charles the Fat, Stephen called upon Arnulf to come and liberate Italy. Despite Arnulf's desire to help, not to mention attain the Imperial diadem, he was unable to respond because of his own troubles. The western Franks and Burgundy refused allegiance to him. Arnulf was not yet strong enough. He became king of the eastern Franks but would have to consolidate his strength through the submission of the western Franks as well as defend his own realm against Viking raids.

The First Usurper

Pope Stephen V (VI) was in a bind. The situation in the empire required the pope to seek help but he had deposed the emperor who alone was able to protect him. He soon found an unlikely ally in Guy, sometimes called Guido III, of Spoleto. Spoleto was a major province of central Italy and it had never been a great supporter of the papacy or Rome. Guy had been deposed by Charles at a former pope's instigation and his father Lambert had twice entered Rome in defiance of the pope, having imprisoned Pope John VIII a decade earlier. Guy, however, did have the staunch support of the Archbishop of Rheims. Moreover, Guy had recently secured the throne of Italy as king. He had been engaged in a war with Berengar, the previous king of Italy, when he dealt Berengar a decisive blow and secured for himself a major victory in 889. That same year Guy became the King of Italy and Pope Stephen V (VI) adopted Guy as his son. Despite this, he stalled when it came to offering the imperial crown to him. No doubt Stephen was well aware that Guy was not a true protector of the Church or the pope but for the time being he would have to suffice.

By 891 it was obvious that Stephen was right about Guy's allegiances. Guy did not care for the Church but for the throne. Guy had grown tired of waiting for his adopted father, the pope, to crown him emperor so he compelled the pope to do it by threats of force. In 991 the Empire again had an emperor. Nevertheless, such methods of gaining the crown, particularly while Arnulf remained king in Germany, did nothing to earn him loyal subjects. Although he had been coronated by the pope, all knew that the pope did so under duress. Guy was a usurper, not a true emperor. When Pope Stephen V (VI) died, he was succeeded by Pope Formosus. Like his predecessor, he too was forced to crown Guy. This time the coronation was not only to show his support for Guy but also to crown Guy's son Lambert co–emperor. This occurred in 892, only a year from the original coronation. Nevertheless, Formosus was not content to be the emperor's puppet. Even before Guy died, Formosus had spirited legates out of Rome to urge Arnulf to come and reclaim the crown from the usurpers. Arnulf made his first attempt in 894 but he was driven back by superior forces. When Guy died, Lambert ascended the throne, but Formosus again pleaded with Arnulf to come and liberate Italy. This time, with the assistance and backing of Berengar, the old enemy of the Dukes of Spoleto, Arnulf succeeded. Rome was captured in late 895 and Lambert was deposed. In February 896 Pope Formosus then crowned Arnulf Emperor of the Holy Roman Empire.

It might have seemed the Carolingian Dynasty was resurrected from the dead but, alas, Arnulf fell violently ill, suffering paralysis, and returned to Germany. Lambert then seized the opportunity to return to Rome and reclaim the crown. He exacted revenge against Formosus who was murdered. This murder was not, however, to be the final act of revenge for eight months later

Lambert and his new puppet pope, Stephen VI (VII), would enact one of the most despicable, macabre, and bizarre acts of vindictiveness in history.

The Cadaver Synod

In January of 897 Pope Stephen VI (VII) had the body of Formosus exhumed. The body was attired in royal vestments and sat upon the throne whereupon a mock trial occurred. The dead body was tried on such ludicrous charges as perjury and coveting the papal throne. Nearby a deacon spoke for the deceased body, doubtless making it far easier to be convicted of perjury. Upon the body's conviction its two consecrated fingers were cut off and the body was thrown into the Tiber river. It should not go without noting that the Lateran was shaken and severely damaged by an earthquake at the very hour that this sham trial occurred. This event became known as the "Cadaver Synod." Lambert finally had a puppet pope. What Lambert did not have was the respect of the people. The earthquake had justly been seen by the people as a sign of God's wrath and the vile act so enraged the populous that within seven months a rioting mob of citizens stormed the Lateran and threw Pope Stephen VI (VII) in prison were he was soon found strangled to death. The body of Formosus had been recovered from the Tiber but would still find no rest as it would be again exhumed years later for further humiliation.

Over the next year turbulent forces would vie for power. Within fourteen months three different popes, and one antipope, would sit in the Lateran and Lambert's reign would be at an end. Romanus became the first of these popes but after less than three months the people were angered that he did little to restore Formosus or condemn Stephen. They then forced him to retire to a monastery and elected Theodore II. Theodore II looked as if he would please the people inasmuch as he convened a synod to condemn the "Cadaver Synod." Lamentably, the very month of his ascension Theodore met his death at an early age, historians know not how. One thing is certain, there were many who wanted Theodore dead.

No sooner had Theodore II died then a power struggle ensued between pro–Formosan and anti–Formosan parties. Sergius III represented the anti–Formosan party but John IX, supported by the people and the Formosans, won out. Sergius III contested the election declaring victory for himself. With the help of his colleagues, Sergius III entered the Lateran and seated himself upon the throne. John IX promptly excommunicated Sergius III who repaid the favor. Popular support for John IX, duly elected, drove Sergius III from the throne where he proceeded to set himself up as antipope under the protection of the Spoleto region. Sergius III would remain the wings of history until 904 when he would usurp the papal crown again with the backing of one of Italy's most notorious vixens. In the meantime John IX held a council in which Pope Formosus was reinstated and which condemned the Cadaver Synod. The acts of

Pope Stephen VI (VII) were likewise condemned and the clergy he had deposed were restored. Finally, the council ratified Lothair I's *Constitution Romana* which required Imperial emissaries at all papal elections.

Jean Paul Laurens – The Cadaver Synod – 1870

Although Lambert had been behind the "Cadaver Synod" he knew that his Imperial authority rested with the support of the pope and the people. Moreover, it was Formosus who had crowned Lambert Emperor. If Formosus's excommunication was allowed to stand then all his acts, including Lambert's coronation, would be void.   Since he was not an *active* participant in the "Cadaver Synod" he gave his support to John IX and the new Synod. Ironically, the one concession that was made at this Synod was that Formosus's coronation of Arnulf was invalidated on the grounds that it had been forced by threats of violence. This was contrary to every piece of evidence, including Formosus himself, who maintained the opposite.   Lambert had usurped the throne by threats, not Arnulf whom the late pope had sought for deliverance. Nevertheless, the concession secured Lambert's position and cleared him of bad press for his involvement in the "Cadaver Synod." The concession, however, did not appease Lambert's enemies who were many. There was more than one man who sought the Imperial Diadem and in late 898 Lambert died in a hunting "accident." Most historians call it an assassination but whomever ordered the assassination is uncertain.

In Search of an Emperor

Arnulf was now, finally, the uncontested emperor but he too would die, in 899, leaving behind a divided and crumbling empire. Arnulf had lost virtually all true authority in both France and Italy. The empire had not seen competent leadership in decades. In fact, the strongest leader that the Holy Roman Empire had seen since Charlemagne was a pontiff. With Arnulf now dead only the pope remained but John IX would follow Arnulf to the grave upon the new year. Amid the continuing controversy caused by the anti–Formosans Benedict IV, a supporter of Formosus, was elected the new pope and entrusted with the job of finding the empire a new emperor.

Even before Benedict IV became pope the struggle for the Imperial Crown had already begun. Louis the Child officially assumed the title but, as he as a mere child, the real power was Hatto, archbishop of Mayence. With such a farce evident to all, it was clear that a new emperor was waiting the wings, awaiting a pope who would anoint him. The lead contender at this time was Berengar, but in 899 he had been brutally defeated by the Magyars leaving his army a shambles. At this same time, another Louis (who later came to be called "the Blind") entered Italian territory seeking the throne and war erupted between he and Berengar.

Benedict IV was quick to seek out a real emperor in place of Louis the Child. Louis the Blind was the grandson of Emperor Louis II and therefore of noble blood. Moreover, he was already the king of Provence (west of Italy and south of Burgundy and France). His expeditions against Berengar proved himself capable of commanding an army and Benedict IV needed a strong emperor to survive the increasing invasions and anarchy of Rome. Benedict believed he had found his man. He crowned Louis the Blind emperor in February 901, but Louis did not prove to be as strong a leader as Benedict had hoped for. Almost immediately after the crowning of Louis the Blind, Berengar began plotting his own rise to power. The very next year Berengar's soldiers captured Louis and forced him to leave Italy under threat of death. Despite this, Louis did return in 904 with an army and succeeded in conquering the northern regions of Italy until he was captured a second time by Berengar. This time Louis's eyes were gouged out as punishment, hence his nickname. Berengar, after nearly fifteen years of struggles, had now secured total control of Italy and its regions. He had seen five emperors sit in the chair he desired for himself, but he still could not claim that seat for himself. Louis the Blind remained emperor in name but without authority. He was merely a namesake whose authority rested solely in Provence. Although there were no other claimants to the throne Berengar would have to wait over ten more years before his wish could ultimately be granted. During this time Rome, and Italy, would decay into virtual anarchy, France would be largely independent, and the kingdoms were divided. Only Germany showed any signs of hope.

Like most of the other kingdoms in the Holy Roman Empire, Germany was divided. The Saxons, eastern and western Franks, Bavarians, and Swabians were all vying for power. A bitter power struggle raged for decades but from this would eventually emerge the man who would restore the Holy Roman Empire to a glimmer of its former glory. Two kings would precede him, however. The first was Conrad I. Although some historians prefer to list Conrad I of Germany as an emperor during this time, this is naïve. Conrad I never claimed the title for himself nor did he ever truly receive the credit due him even in Germany. Most of his life was spent in war against the various Dukes. The inclusion of him in a few modern Imperial lists does, nevertheless, show that he was the strongest leader of his day. His rule was mainly a military one concerned with securing his right to rule, but he also showed wisdom and tolerance by striking a deal with his enemy, Henry the Fowler, guaranteeing him the right to succeed him in exchange for peace and loyalty. Fowler agreed and the rise of the House of Saxony in Germany was assured.

Conversely in Italy the papacy, in the absence of an emperor, had sunk into one of its darkest eras. Benedict IV died in 903, some suggests the victim of Berengar's assassins. The ensuing struggle over his successor would lead to the era known as the Papal Pornocracy or Hetaerocracy. This era could be traced back to Formosus posthumous trial but most start it from the rise of Sergius III. This same Sergius III had been an active participant in the infamous "Cadaver Synod" and had become the antipope of John IX. He had fled to Spoleto where he soon earned the support of Alberic I, the Duke of Spoleto at that time. There he sat patiently awaiting his opportunity to return to Rome and seize the throne. That day was about to come.

The Last Carolingian & the Papal Pornocracy

After Benedict's death a simple Parish priest was selected from a region outside Rome. Historians think this odd since at this time Rome was extremely proud and arrogant, considering all non–Romans to be outsiders. For them being Italian was not enough. Still, the near anarchy which had encompassed Rome probably convinced many that a man from the outside was necessary. Leo V was elected in the fall of 903, but only thirty days later one of his own men headed a palace revolt and Christopher seized the pontificate for himself. He threw Leo V in prison and had himself consecrated, although he had never been elected. This was Sergius III's signal.

With an obvious antipope sitting in the Lateran Sergius III made his move. With the assistance of Alberic and his Tusculum soldiers he entered Rome and took the tiara from Christopher. Christopher was thrown in prison alongside Leo V and together the two of them were later strangled to death at Sergius's orders. Sergius further had Formosus's body once again exhumed and this time the head was cut off before being tossed in the Tiber, only to be

59

rescued again from the river by Formosus's supporters. Sergius III was now the pope and with him one of the most notorious vixens in history would soon arrive on the scene; Marozia.

Sergius III had won the support of Alberic I, the Count of Tusculum and Duke of Spoleto. Together they were allied with the powerful Consul and Commander of the Militia, Theophylactus. This same Theophylactus was married to an equally powerful and ambitious senator (she preferred the term "Senatrix") named Theodora. Her daughter, but a teenager at the time, was Marozia. Marozia, only fifteen years old, would become the forty five year old pope's lover. Later she would become the wife of Alberic I. She would also become the most famous Jezebel since Jezebel.

Marozia learned well from her mother. She too sought power and she was better at it than her mother. She would one day rise to be a senator, or Senatrix, and marry two other men whom she thought would become emperor. In addition, both her son and grandson would rise to the papacy while another son became her own dreaded enemy. Despite her "noble" upbringing she could neither read nor write and her signature is found on records today as a simple "+" mark.

With such a powerful alliance Sergius III, Theophylatus, Theodora, and Alberic achieved a virtual dictatorship of Rome. This happened the very same year that Berengar has deposed Louis the Blind. For a time Berengar too would forge an alliance with these leaders and together the history of the empire would be the story of their debauchery until Otto the Great entered Rome and cleansed the filth from the Lateran and Senate.

Sergius III, who had participated in the Cadaver Synod, not surprisingly reversed the previous synods that had cleared Formosus of all charges and which had condemned Stephen VI (VII). Members of the clergy had been forced under threats of torture and death to attend a new synod and to vote as told. Throughout his administration his rule was enforced with military power whenever necessary. He began to completely rebuild the Lateran which had fallen prey to an earthquake during the Cadaver Synod and printed money with the his own likeness upon it. Through the teenage Marozia he fathered a future pope before mercifully dying in 911.

Still under the control of Theophylactus and Theodora two puppet popes were appointed in the years following his death. Then in 914 when the office again became vacant Theodora now had her own former lover appointed to the papacy. Pope John X reigned from 914 to 928, making him the longest surviving pope since Gregory IV (827–844). Together Theodora and John discussed the possibility of a further alliance with any possible future emperors. They decided that Marozia should marry Alberic whom many thought would be the next emperor of Rome, but it was not to be. Threats from the Muslim Saracens pressed Italy hard and a decision had to be made. Pope John X became the first pope to wield a sword in battle and was true to the legacy of the era.

For years the Saracens had plagued the Mediterranean and particularly southern Italy. Without an emperor Italy was exposed and helpless to protect itself adequately. Local Dukes scarcely had enough military troops or prowess to defeat the massive armies of the Saracens. For many years the Byzantine Empire had been trying to negotiate a military treaty between themselves and the western Roman Empire, but the quick passing of emperors had left this largely a dream. In 915 an agreement was finally reached that would allow them to unite their forces and deal the Saracens a crushing blow. The Byzantine Emperor Constantine IV, King Berengar of Italy, Alberic I of Spoleto, Theophylactus, and Pope John X himself all rode out into battle and secured a major victory for Europe. The Saracens had lost what little foothold they had been able to create in southern Italy.

That very year, in exchange for his support in the battle, Berengar was finally granted his desire. In 915 Pope John X crowned Berengar Holy Roman Emperor. His reign was longer than his predecessors but ended the same way. By 920 Theophylactus and Theodora had died leaving Berengar with Alberic I and his new wife, the powerful Marozia, as his allies. It was not enough. The other countries had never given Berengar much credence to start with and in 922 King Rudolf II of Burgundy and several Italian nobles revolted against him. Berengar was driven deep into Italy and, in 924, Berengar was murdered by one of his own men.

The Carolingian dynasty (the descendants of Charles the Great) had begun in glory and ended in infamy. Although the Carolingians would continue to reign as kings in France for a short time (until Louis the Lazy's reign), there were to be no more Carolingian emperors. For the next four decades the House of Saxony in Germany would slowly rise to prominence. Each country continued to rule itself under its own king but the vacuum created by the Carolingian's downfall would not last long. Henry the Fowler, sometimes considered a true emperor, paved the way for Otto the Great who would restore some of the glory to the Holy Roman Empire and reform the corruption that was already encompassing the Holy Church of Rome.

Emperor – Papacy Chart (800–924 A.D.)

<u>Holy Roman Emperor</u>	<u>Pope</u>	*<u>AntiPope (if any)</u>*

—————————— 800 ——————————

Charlemagne (Charles I)   Leo III

—————————— 814 ——————————

—————————— 816 ——————————

Stephen IV (V)

—————————— 817 ——————————

Paschal I

Louis the Pious (Louis I)

—————————— 824 ——————————

Eugenius II

—————————— 827 ——————————

Valentine

—————————— 827 ——————————

—————————— 840 ——————————

Civil War   Gregory IV

—————————— 843 ——————————

—————————— 844 ——————————

Sergius II   *John*

Lothair I   ———— 847 ————   *– 844 –*

Leo IV

—————————— 855 ——————————

—————————— 855 ——————————

Benedict III   *Anastasius*

                         – 855 –

—————————— 858 ——————————

Louis II   Nicholas I

—————————— 867 ——————————

Adrian II

—————————— 872 ——————————

—————————— 875 ——————————

Charles the Bald (Charles II)

—————————— 877 ——————————

Interregnum   John VIII

(Charles the Stammerer – 878 – rejected crown)

—————————— 881 ——————————

—————————— 882 ——————————

Marinus I

—————————— 884 ——————————

Charles the Fat (Charles III)

Adrian III

—————————— 885 ——————————

—————————— 887 ——————————

Holy Roman Emperor	Pope	AntiPope (if any)
	——— 885 ———	
——— 887 ———	Stephen V (VI)	
Second Interregnum (Arnulf – not anointed until 896)		
——— 891 ———	——— 891 ———	
Guy of Spoleto (Usurper)		
——— 894 ———	Formosus	
Lambert (Usurper)		
——— 896 ———	——— 896 ———	
	Boniface VI	
	——— 896 ———	
	Stephen VI (VII)	
	——— 896 ———	
Arnulf	Romanus	
	——— 897 ———	
	Theodore II	
	——— 897 ———	
	——— 898 ———	
——— 899 ———	John IX	
	——— 900 ———	
Louis the Child	Benedict IV	
(was too young to be anointed)	——— 900 ———	
——— 901 ———	*Interregnum*	
	——— 903 ———	
Louis the Blind (Louis III)	Leo V	*Christopher*
	——— 904 ———	
——— 905 ———	Sergius III	
	——— 911 ———	
Third Interregnum	Anastasius III	
(Louis remained Emperor in name)	——— 913 ———	
	Lando	
	——— 914 ———	
——— 915 ———		
Berengar	John X	
——— 924 ———		
	——— 928 ———	

King's List

King of England	King of France (Western Frankonia)	King of Burgundy	King of Provence
	800		
	Charlemagne (Emperor)		
	814		
	Louis the Pious (Emperor)		
	843		
	Charles II (later Emperor)		
	877		
	Louis II		
871	879	879	
Alfred the Great	Louis III & Carloman	Boso	
	882		
	Carloman (alone)		
	884		
	Charles (III) (later Emperor)		
	887		888
	888	888	Boso (same king as Burgundy)
	Hugh (Eudes)	Rudolf I	890
	889		Louis the Blind (III) (Emperor)
899	Charles III	911	
Edward the Elder	923	Rudolf II	928
	Robert I		Hugh of Arles (also King of Italy)
924	923		934
Athelstan	Rudolf		Kingdom ceded to Burgundy
	936	937	
939	Louis IV		
Edmund	954		
946			
Eadred			
955			

64

5

The Coming of Otto

The era of the Haeterocracy did not end with the collapse of the Carolingian Dynasty. Far from it; it was but the beginning. From the Cadaver Synod and Sergius III to the coming of Otto (also called Otho) remained an era of corruption and decadence in Italy, but of unification and consolidation in Germany. While Italy sunk into utter depravity and folly, Germany's rise found true leaders where Italy had none.

With the assassination of Emperor Berengar a new power struggle immediately ensued as petty kings, counts, dukes, and popes strove for the precious title. John X was not quick to anoint a new emperor. The throne had become more of a title in recent years than a true office and for whatever reason, John X waited. The following year Marozia convinced Alberic I to take Rome by force and compel John to crown him as emperor. Alberic did as advised but he failed. Alberic was killed in the battle and John X forced Marozia to look upon her husband's dead body to show her what she had wrought. His death left Hugh of Provence (variously called, Hugh or Hugo or Burgundy, Italy, Provence, Arles, or Lusignan) and Guido (or Guy), the marquis of Tuscany, as the two primary contenders. Marozia, now a senator and Patrician, or "Patricia," chose Guido as the most likely successor and married him, aspiring to add Empress to her already impressive list of titles. The following year, however, John X gave his support to Hugh of Provence who was now the king of Italy. He signed a pact with Hugh but did not yet offer him the crown. He would never have the chance. Marozia was enraged by John's actions. Her mother was now dead and Marozia had no allegiance to her mother's former lover, John X. She and Guido stirred up accusations and slander, eventually leading to full revolt. John X's own brother, Peter, would be slain before his very eyes in the Lateran itself, and by 928 he was deposed and cast in the dungeon of the Castle St. Angelo at Marozia's orders. The very next year she silently ordered his murder and he was suffocated to death in his cell.

Marozia made sure that the next two popes were but puppets of her will. If Guido was not to be emperor, neither would Hugh of Provence. In 931 Marozia's bastard son, by Sergius III, was now old enough to take office and Pope Stephen VII (VIII) was conveniently assassinated, leaving Marozia free to force the election of her son, Pope John XI. Still better luck was the passing away of Guido. This left Marozia a widow again and free to marry Hugh of Provence, the likely new emperor. Unfortunately, Hugh was still married himself. This inconvenience was quickly erased when Hugh murdered his wife and had his own brother's eyes put out for objecting to his marriage with

Marozia. Then Marozia's legitimate son by Alberic, who possessed the same name, became resentful. Alberic II was sickened to see his mother marrying a vile man for the sole purpose of attaining more power. Alberic made his displeasure known and at the ceremony, which he was obliged to attend, Hugh is said to have turned and slapped him before all. King Hugh and Marozia had made a bitter enemy that they would live to regret having disgraced.

Within months Alberic II incited a revolt. He reminded the people of Rome that they were once the masters of the world and said that they were now but slaves to the Burgundians who sat as King of Italy. The people too were angry at the marriage. Indeed, debased as Italy had become they were still nominally Christian and yet a bastard Pope officiated the wedding of his own mother to her brother–in–law, through another political marriage. It was too much. In December 932 Alberic II and an armed mob stormed the Castle St. Angelo. King Hugh managed to escape with the help of his men but Marozia was captured and imprisoned by her own son in the St. Angelo dungeon. The macabre irony was that Marozia would spend the last fifty four years of her life in the very dungeon where she had imprisoned so many innocent herself.

Alberic II was now the supreme authority in Rome. He had himself proclaimed the prince of Rome, senator, count, and Patrician. He spared John XI's life but kept him a prisoner in the Lateran, a personal slave to Alberic's will. Naturally, a public war ensued between him and Marozia's husband, Hugh the King of Italy. The very streets of Rome sometimes ran with blood but life bustled on as usual. For nearly thirty years Italy, and the Holy Roman Empire, would exist without a true crowned Emperor until Otto rode into Rome much as Charlemagne had before him, and liberated Rome from its own folly.

The Empire in Germany

Charles Dickens's "A Tale of Two Cities" might have been a medieval story had he chosen to write about Germany and Italy, rather than England and France, for like Dickens's novel the two countries were headed in different directions. In Germany Conrad, Henry the Fowler, and Otto were unifying Germany and securing its borders from foreign invaders. In Italy power struggles, corruption, and debauchery continued to make a mockery of the once great city of Rome.

Ancient Germany had been a huge forest of differing tribes. There was only national pride to hold the tribes together, but when they had no foreign enemy they were at each other's throats. With the fall of the Carolingian Dynasty, and the death of Louis the Blind, the Germanic peoples were now reluctant to accept anyone but their fellow tribesmen as king. Nevertheless, the tribes elected another Frank, the tribe from which Charlemagne had sprang. The new king was Conrad I and no sooner was he elected than tribes began to rebel against him. The Saxons, Barvarians, and Swabian Dukes all refused allegiance to him.

Much of Conrad's relatively short reign was spent in war with the Dukes. He tired of fighting his own brethren and soon hoped to secure peace through compromise. In 912 Henry the Fowler had become Duke of Saxony. Henry had been at war with Conrad for three years when Conrad I reached an agreement in principle with him. In exchange for Henry's support and loyalty Henry the Fowler would become heir to the throne. In 918 Conrad died and Henry was ready to assume the throne. He would be the first Saxon King of Charlemagne's Eastern Kingdom (Germany) and he faced the same rebellion as Conrad had. In 919 Henry officially became king, despite protests, and immediately he had to defend that title. The other dukes refused to acknowledge him and Henry's entire reign, from 919 to 936, was spent at war, either with his kinsmen or with foreign invaders who now began to plague Germany.

From the east came pagan warriors named the Magyars. The Swabians and Bavarians also continued their aggression. With the loyalty of the Franks and Saxons, however, Henry was able to protect the borders from the new invaders as he continued war with the neighboring dukes. By the time of Henry's death Otto, son and heir to Henry, inherited a country at war. Nevertheless, Henry the Fowler had started the job that Otto would finish and Henry's conquest and wars did much to consolidate and secure what would become modern Germany. Under no circumstances can Henry the Fowler's reign be considered a failure for in other hands Germany might have fallen apart. Indeed, some historians wrongly list Conrad I and Henry the Fowler as Holy Roman Emperors. This is going too far for they never even claimed such a title for themselves, but it is a testament to the fact they were the strongest kings in the Holy Roman Empire, at a time when strong kings were lacking.

In 936 Otto (also called Otho), soon to be Otto the Great, became king. He had married the granddaughter of the great Christian King of England, Alfred the Great, and secured with it the trust and respect of England, a new ally that would one day become a part of the great Empire. In Germany, however, respect was not as easily attained. Henry, his father, had done much to consolidate Germany but Otto would have to prove himself a worthy heir, and prove to the rival dukes that the Saxons were the rightful kings. To add to Otto's problems, his own younger brother sought the throne and rebelled. This younger Henry was forced to capitulate, only to plot Otto's assassination in 941. When the plot was discovered Otto punished all those responsible save young Henry whom he again forgave. One might at first glimpse think that Otto was repeating Louis the Pious's error, but Henry seems to have been moved by Otto's mercy and never again rebelled although many such opportunities arose.

By the 940s Otto had secured most of the borders of Germany from invaders, forced the dukes into submission, erected a monastery and several bishoprics. His career was achieving fame for himself not only in Germany but throughout the empire where he was respected. At one point Western Franconia (France), in the absence of an emperor, would even ask him to negotiate a peace treaty between two warring parties. In Italy too his fame was heard of, so that he would soon be asked to come and liberate Italy from themselves.

The Empire in Italy

Since Alberic II's rise to power King Hugh naturally sought to regain his authority in Rome. War ensued for a number of years. At one point King Hugh even laid siege to Rome itself but a peace treaty was negotiated by Pope Agepetus II. When Hugh died his son, Lothair II, assumed the royal crown. At this same time Berengar's grandson, surnamed Berengar the Younger, was rising to prominence in hopes of filling his grandfather's ignoble shoes.

The uneasy peace ended soon after Lothair II died. Berengar II was then crowned King of Italy and Italy again had two despots ruling over her, for Alberic II and Berengar II both exceeded their forefathers in tyranny. Berengar sought to solidify his position by marrying his son, Adalbert, to the widow of Hugh of Italy (who was also the daughter of Rudolf, the King of Burgundy). However, Adalbert was sternly rejected by her. This woman Adelaide (also called Adelheid), was imprisoned for her scorn of Berengar II but soon escaped. She fled to Germany in 951 and, with the Pope's support, begged King Otto of Germany to come deliver Italy from the hands of the tyrant.

Otto's First Expedition into Italy

Otto, whose first wife had passed away, married Adelaide and set out to force Berengar into subservience. This first expedition into Italy was successful as Berengar was easily subjected and forced to render an insincere oath of loyalty to Otto. By this time it had become obvious that the Empire was in desperate need of a good leader to fill the vacuum created by the fall of the Carolingian Dynasty. Pope Agepetus II, with the backing of the people, offered to make Otto the emperor. Of all Rome only Alberic II objected. Doubtless still aspiring to become Emperor himself, Alberic II virulently opposed the coronation of Otto. The point became mute, however, when Otto heard that his own son, Liudolf, was trying to usurp the German throne. Otto graciously accepted the title "King of the Lombards" and left for Germany without accepting the Imperial title.

Upon his return to Germany Otto took up arms to crush his now defiant son. The war continued for some years until the Magyars again invaded Germany in 954. Liudolf was overwhelmed and acquiesced to his father who was now able to do what Liudolf could not. Otto concentrated his forces on the Magyars and at the battle of Lechfeld the Magyars were vanquished. So severe was their defeat that the Magyars never again invaded Germany, even at the request of Pope John XII who would later try to usurp Otto. This same pope, however, was currently in need of an ally and it was he who was soon to crown Otto Holy Roman Emperor.

In the meantime Otto had succeeded in fortifying and strengthening Germany's borders and establishing peace in Germany by 960. His successes furthered his own fame and when he was again called to Italy, there was no one who would oppose his coronation.

Otto Becomes the Holy Roman Emperor

Shortly before his death Alberic II had his own son named pope. This young Octavian was only eighteen years old when he was selected, in 955, and changed his name to Pope John XII. When Alberic II passed away Octavian also took the secular arm of the government in hand. He continued to call himself Octavian as civil leader but John XII as pope. He was often seen wearing full military garb and regalia, and dressed himself in armor as well as in pontifical robes. He is notorious as one of the most vile and despicable of pontiffs in Roman Catholic history. He considered his role as pope more of a joke than a sacred responsibility and once consecrated a priest in a stable. He irreverently invoked the pagan gods and was even accused of Satanism, although it is likely these were more sardonic jokes to Octavian than sincere invocations. Still worse were crimes which few could prove, but which most all had heard of. Octavian/John XII was known to rape young women who went to the Holy City on pilgrimages as well as crimes of murder, castration of a priest, sleeping with his own mother and sisters, and arson. Some may doubt these accusations but the evidence is as solid as any in the distant past. Still, none can contest that this same Pope John XII turned the Papal Palace into a brothel of prostitutes. Most heard of his immaturity and sexual liaisons but word of the more dark side of his destitute lifestyle had not reached the ears of King Otto when the young pope requested Otto return to put down a rebellious Berengar in 962.

Upon assuming the civil authority Octavian was challenged by Berengar II. Octavian/John XII had no loyalty to Otto, but he needed Otto's strong arm to secure his own position. Having been sent a plea for help, Otto the King came and subjected the rebellious Berengar in little time.

Too long had passed since a true Emperor sat on the throne. Otto had proven his capabilities over the whole Empire and it was he to whom the call came when help was needed. By the agreement of all, Otto was to be named Holy Roman Emperor. Otto's strong leadership was what the Empire desperately needed and, in 962, Pope John XII obliged the people and crowned Otto Emperor of Holy Rome.

Following the coronation Otto put into writing a pact which consolidated the relationship between emperor and pope that had been unspoken, but accepted, throughout the middle ages. It was agreed that only the Pope could crown the Emperor but that the emperor must be represented at all papal elections. Thus the two were, in theory, equal but separate entities. A sort of balance of power was decreed between the civil and spiritual leaders of the empire.

Nevertheless, John XII still sought civil power for himself. No sooner had Otto, the newly crowned Emperor of Rome, left for East Frankonia (Germany), than Octavian/John XII began to conspire against him. In fact, John XII's conspiracy even involved the very man whom he had sought to crush with Otto's help; Berengar II. John XII had hoped to eliminate opposing civil authority in Italy but seeing that Otto was now the supreme authority, by John's own hand, he turned to his former enemy Berengar and even dispatched a letter to the Magyar tribes east of Germany requesting that they invade Eastern Frankonia so as to keep Otto preoccupied. The Magyars, however, had no taste for battle with Otto. They had yielded to his supremacy and when Otto heard of John's plot he returned to Italy only to find the gates of Rome closed.

Despite the the Roman populous' apparent support for the pope, the people knew they could not withstand Otto's army if he wished to invade so the gates were finally opened and Otto held a Synod to review charges against the pope. When Otto heard the charges he found them hard to believe and often took the side of the young boy by saying, "he is just a boy." As more evidence was presented, however, it became obvious that the pope was no mere child, but a beast. Strangely enough the accusations at the Synod concentrated not on the charges of rape and murder but on improper behavior such as hunting. This was partly because the Synod wanted only hard evidence, but it was ironic for like the Clinton impeachment trial, the serious crimes were neglected for lack of proper proof, while more insignificant charges were hurled venomously. One is almost amused to read that hunting was among the more serious charges leveled against John XII.

When Otto heard all the charges he showed amazing mercy and offered the pope a chance to respond to the accusations and/or repent and reform. Otto included the charges of murder, incest, perjury, and sacrilege in his letter, but the pope responded by sending back a terse response, written in poor Latin, threatening to excommunicate him. Otto then sent a messenger asking the pope one final time to "reform your morals and your Latin." The messenger, however, was unable to find the pope, for he had fled Rome along with many valuable vessels and relics from the Lateran.

With the pope fleeing Rome it was up to Otto to chose a new pope. He carefully examined the situation and wisely decided that the job would best be left to a devout layman. The Papacy had become so debased over the years that selecting one of John XII's bishops would doubtless only feed the fire. A young layman was then chosen who became Leo VII. Although this move was best for Rome and the office of the Holy See, it did not sit well with the people of Rome.

Rome had once been masters of the world, and masters tend to become proud. So proud had the Romans become that they themselves allowed the government and church around them to become base. Such corruption does not occur without the apathy of the people and the very citizens of Rome had lost their dignity for arrogant pride. When they saw that the Emperor had selected a mere layman, without the people's consent they grew restless. Although the people never offered an objection to the sham elections of Marozia's son, nor to Alberic's son, nor countless other puppets of consuls and kings, they became irate at having a foreigner choose their pope. John XII soon returned with Berengar's help and started yet another uprising. John XII wreaked revenge on those who had testified against him, mutilating some and executing many others. This short lived reign of terror was soon squelched by troops loyal to Otto.

This was the fourth time that Otto had suppressed tyranny in Rome. He now had Berengar II brought to Germany where he could keep a close watchful eye on him. Still, Otto did not need to punish John XII, for he had fallen victim to his own sins when he was murdered by an irate husband who caught him with his wife. Unfortunately, Otto would be needed a fifth time, for the people of Rome would again prove that corruption in government is a symptom of a debased populous.

When Leo VII died another pope was elected by Otto's will. This John XIII committed no rapes or murders but brought on the wrath of the people because he had been chosen by a foreigner. The people again rebelled and were again vanquished. This time Otto had lost patience. He had shown great mercy numerous times; mercy to his younger brother, mercy to his rebellious son Liudolf, mercy to Berengar thrice, and even mercy to John XII whom Otto had given numerous chances to repent. Now Otto executed several Senators and banished the Consuls. He and his pope blinded many persons as punishment and executed thousands. Italy would have to learn submission. He decided to take up residence in Italy to insure the loyalty of the populace where he would remain for almost a decade, leaving for home only shortly before his death.

Otto's Final Years

In these final years Otto expanded the boundaries of the empire. In Denmark, the home of the dreaded Vikings, Otto succeeded in bringing about the submission of the barbarous people who had plagued Europe for so many years. He forced the famed Eric Bluetooth to acquiesce to the empire and to allow the free preaching of the gospel within his lands. This free preaching of the gospel is one of Otto's most lasting legacies. Pagan empires forbade the gospel and persecuted Christianity with fierceness little known even in ancient Rome where a certain measure of law and order often entitled even Christians to a trial. In pagan countries, Christians needed no trial and suspicion of empathy toward Christians garnered no less severity of punishment than believing the gospel. To these cultures Charlemagne and Otto brought the greatest measure of freedom of religion. While modern historians scoff of the idea of religious freedom in the middle ages it must be remembered that the middle ages was an age of *progression* from pagan civilizations where freedom was either absent all together or severely restricted. In the middle ages only Catholics held true freedom but during the *early* middle ages a measure of freedom was given to all, which could not be found in most other countries. Charlemagne had created duchies where Jews could create their own community and live as they saw fit whereas Otto permitted freedom of missionaries where formerly none had existed.

In addition, Otto repaid the Slavic invasions in kind and took Poland, Hungary, and all of Bohemia. These countries were added to the Holy Roman Empire and all declared fealty to Otto. With the alliance of England and the nominal acceptance of France in the Empire it could be argued that Otto's empire exceeded even Charlemagne's in terms of territory. Of course, critics will note that Charlemagne's empire was fully loyal to him and all accepted him as Emperor. Otto could never claim such. England was probably more allies than subjects of the Emperor and France ignored the Emperor, neither declaring independence nor fealty. Many historians even argue that France was no longer a part of the Empire, but this would be an overstatement. France wanted the protection of the Empire *when necessary* but it wanted its independence at all other times. Her policy was to ignore the Emperor whenever possible; an attitude more than occasionally used upon the Pope as well.

During these last years Otto also carefully strengthened Italy much the way he had Germany. This meant he had to protect the Italian borders which had fallen prey to Saracen invaders many times before. This was a touchy problem, though. The Byzantine Empire had kept the land of southern Italy in their Empire, dating back to the time of Charlemagne himself. In order to secure the Italian borders Otto was forced to move into Byzantine territory. Since the Byzantine Empire was an ally of Rome, Otto had to negotiate in order to keep the peace. After many years an agreement was made to marry the Byzantine Princess Theophano to Otto's son, Otto II. The part of Italy in question could then be considered a sort of dowry which the Holy Roman Empire could legitimately occupy. This occurred in 972, shortly before Otto returned to Germany and died.

Otto In History

Otto cannot be said to be as great as Charlemagne for he created nothing new that Charlemagne had not established before him. Nevertheless, Otto may be considered Charlemagne's true successor. What the feeble Carolingian Dynasty could not do Otto did. He reunited the crumbling Empire, restored integrity to the papacy (albeit briefly), saved Italy from themselves, solidified the borders from foreign invaders, and resurrected the decaying Empire. Like Charlemagne, however, he failed to ensure that it would survive without him. Otto's empire was a continuation of Charlemagne's. It offered nothing new, nothing to ensure it could survive without capable leaders. Thus it would be that the history of the middle ages would be a repeating pattern of decay followed by a brief resuscitation led by a strong leader. When this leader died, so also the renaissance would die with him, until seven hundred years later when Martin Luther breached the empire itself.

It is, therefore, fair to say that the Ottonian Renaissance was but a shadow of Charlemagne's renaissance. While the Ottonian Dynasty may not be considered as weak as the Carolingian Dynasty it did not last as long. It was only fifty years after Otto's death that Ottonians fell to a new Dynasty whereas Charlemagne's descendants dragged along mercilessly for well over a hundred years. Otto saved Rome but he could not, and did not, reform its heart. The Holy Roman Empire was still the dying remains of Constantine's Empire; divided and weak. Still, it is this empire from which the modern world emerged and it is this empire to which we owe our own civilizations. No part of the world, whether it be in Asia or Africa, South America or Australia, can deny that it is the bastard offspring of the Holy Roman Empire. An empire which still cries out that it has been buried alive in Europe today.

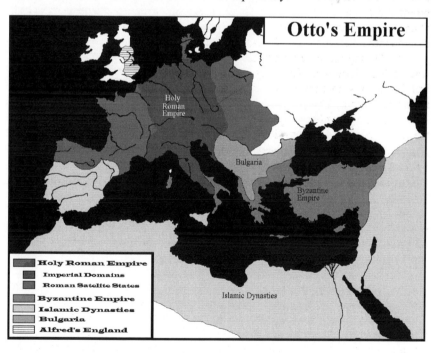

Vaclav Brozik – Otto II's Farewell – 1875

6
—

The Ottonian Dynasty

Great leaders defy the odds and make themselves great but poor leader do not always make themselves poor. Sometimes poor leaders are but victims of circumstances. Too often in history the makings of a great leader are thwarted by events and people over which they have no control. One reason that truly great leaders are so rare is that the cards are stacked against them. So it was with Otto's descendants. Every Ottonian who ever sat on the throne might have been called "the Great" but conspirators, circumstances, and political power plays prevented it. Although the Ottonians were far superior to the Carolingian descendants they did not last even half as long. It is the base and wicked of the world that too often have the upper hand and the righteous only occasionally succeed. So it was with the Ottonian Dynasty.

Otto II Ascends the Throne

Otto II's ascension to power occurred almost without incident, but "almost" was as close as one could get in this day and age. In 974 Otto's cousin, Henry the Quarrelsome, rebelled. Henry the Quarrelsome was himself in the line of Henry the Fowler and resented the fact that Otto the Great had been named heir instead of his line. He had aspired himself to rise to the crown but his methods merely garnered him the unflattering nickname he bears.

In Italy Marozia remained in prison, rotting in a dreary dungeon. Her family, however, continued to rule Rome. Her sister, Theodora the Younger, had a son named Crescentius. He had soon risen to the consulship in Italy and, together with the Crescentii family, ruled Italy in the emperor's absence. Although Otto II had left Count Sicco as his representative in Rome, Crescentius was quick to take advantage of Otto's occupation with Henry and in 974 he rebelled and imprisoned Pope Benedict VI in the Castle St. Angelo. A deacon named Franco, under orders by Crescentius, consecrated Boniface VII as the new pope but when Count Sicco demanded Benedict's restoration Boniface immediately disgraced the tiara by ordering the murder of his predecessor. Benedict could not replace him if he was dead, or so Boniface reasoned. What Boniface did not reason was that the people would despise him for this act.

Count Sicco and troops loyal to Otto stormed Castle St. Angelo where Boniface was held up but Boniface had managed to slip out and escape. More than this, he was able to escape with a great deal of the church treasury. He then fled south to Byzantine Italy where he was supported by the Byzantine Emperor John Tzimisces. The Byzantines were still reeling from the loss of so much of

Italy to the west. Although the eastern and western empires remained allies, Tzimisces secretly plotted a way to regain portions of Italy. As a result, any enemy of Rome was an ally of Tzimisces. For ten years Boniface would remain in Byzantine Italy under their protection until the day he returned to Rome to usurp the throne once again.

In the meantime, Crescentius and Count Sicco came to a compromise in choosing a new pope. Benedict VII was acceptable because he was pro-imperial but he was also an old colleague and friend of Alberic II, who was related to the Crescentii family. Benedict's first act was to excommunicate Boniface VII.

It was in 978 that all Bavaria, Henry's domain, was forced to accept Otto but there was hardly time for peace before news arrived that the French King Lothair had invaded Lorraine, claiming it as the rightful property of France. This dispute dated back to Louis the Pius whose divisions of lands among his sons created the divided nations that exists to this very day. Lorraine had been taken from one son and given to another, and now France claimed it again as their own. This latter conflict, however, must not be seen as rebellion against the empire but as an internal conflict. The French never seceded from the empire but rather claimed that the Carolingian Dynasty continued through their kings. Lothair, therefore, claimed Lorraine as the rightful property of Charlemagne's descendants. Otto again took to the field and with the help of Hugh Capet, future king of France, Lothair was forced to renounce all claims to Lorraine in 980.

With these wars complete, and with no contenders to the throne, it appeared as if Otto II was ready to lead the empire as he saw fit. Nevertheless, circumstances and events would dictate otherwise. In less than seven short years Otto had secured the empire in his name and peace seemed possible. Still only his twenties and with his first child having been born to his wife, the Byzantine Princess Theophano, it seemed as though Otto's entire life lay before him, but he did not know how long that life was to be. Within three years Otto would be dead while still in his twenties. His reign was considered a failure by modern historians but this was through no fault of his own. Indeed, Otto's future might have showed promise but for the betrayal of the Byzantine Empire, whose princess was Otto's empress!

No sooner had Otto secured the empire and brought peace than Boniface made the first of his two comebacks. In mid 980 he had established himself again in the Lateran while Benedict VII was away from the city. Otto II marched on Rome in March of the following year and Boniface again fled, this time to Constantinople. Otto II took up residence in Italy, as had his father before him. History would prove that an emperor was only an effective ruler if he ruled from Rome. For the last three years of his life Otto II resided in Rome and the Crescentii family could but wait and abide their time.

Otto II and Benedict VII became close and worked together closely. Together they outlawed simony, the practice of selling bishoprics to the highest bidder, which had become popular under such notorious popes as John XII. It looked as if the Papacy might be regaining some respectability after the fiasco of the Papal Pornocracy, but the evils of that era would soon rise again. Another task that Otto desired was to further secure southern Italy. Despite the political marriage between Theophano, the Byzantine princess, and himself the relations between the two empires was strained. This was obvious by the Byzantine Emperor Basil Bulgaroctonus' support of Boniface VII. Southern Italy created a larger problem. Much of the land had been given to Otto as a dowry but with Muslim Saracens creeping closer and closer to Otto's Italy he felt obliged to create a stronger presence in southern Italy which only made Byzantium feel more threatened.

In 982 Otto II set out to crush the Muslim Saracens in Southern Italy. Byzantine Emperor Basil II, however, was more than eager to lend some quiet assistance to the Saracens. Otto's army was brutally beaten and Otto himself retreated to Rome. He contracted malaria but would linger on until December 983. In the meantime Benedict VII died and Otto appointed, without proper election, John XIV in whose arms he died just days after his consecration. Otto II was buried alongside the popes; a distinction unique among all the emperors of Holy Rome for none, save he, may be found in this resting place.

Otto III's Regents

The death of Otto II at so young an age was a blow to empire, not so much that it grieved his death for he was too young to have accomplished anything but it left only a three year old child to claim the throne. This same child of three was kidnapped by Henry the Quarrelsome who had hoped to ransom the baby in exchange for the Imperial title. The Empress Theophano immediately left for Germany where an Imperial Diet demanded that Henry return the child. Certainly Henry could not slaughter a child. If he had it would get him no closer to the throne and would make him a tyrant in the eyes of the people. Henry was forced to obey and released the young boy to his mother.

Immediately after the Empress left Italy for Germany Pope John XIV's position was threatened. The people of Italy did not favor him because he had not been duly elected and national pride made them suspicious of a pope so close to the imperial family. In April the antipope Boniface VII made his move. With Byzantine funds to back his return to power, and the assistance of the Crescentius family, Boniface returned to Rome and had John XIV imprisoned as an impostor. John was beaten, starved, and possibly poisoned. He died in the St. Angelo dungeon four months later.

Since Otto III was still a mere child the Empress Theophano ruled in his name. Nevertheless, she exercised little control in Italy. For the next ten years Theophano, and later Otto's grandmother, Adelaide, would rule as Empress in his stead. They were wise enough not to assert their authority too much but to stay in the background. As a Byzantine Princess, as well as western Empress, Theophano enjoyed the support of both the east and west. She therefore devoted herself to raise Otto III as best she could. The best education was provided for him and three of his tutors would later raise up to become popes, one of whom would betray him. Gregory V, John Philagathus or John XVII (XVIII), and Sylvester II all knew the young Otto. Gregory was the grandson of Otto the great and Otto's cousin. He also served as Chaplain to Otto. John Philagathus was Otto's godfather. Sylvester, better known at this time as Gerbert of Aurillac, was a learned and exceptionally well educated man who not only tutored Otto but was also a musician for Otto's church. Gregory would become the first German pope, Sylvester the first French pope, and John would become a severe example of what happens to those who betrayed Otto and Rome.

With the Empress spending most of her time in Germany, the country of Italy, and Rome in particular, again fell prey to the Crescentii family. Crescentius I had died the very year Boniface VII returned to Rome, and in his place John Crescentius now sat as consul and patrician. Boniface, however, was hated and despised by the people. He had stolen Vatican treasures and committed treason by conspiring with Byzantium. He murdered two previous popes and now called himself the Vicar of Christ. The not so affectionate name that the public had given him was "Bonifatius." In 985 a revolt erupted and Boniface was murdered. His body was dragged into the street naked where people kicked, beat, and stabbed the dead body. His deceased remains were brutalized for some time before it was safe to take the body for burial.

With a new election ready to take place John Crescentius wanted to insure that a pope would be elected that would not take away from his authority. The Empress resided in Germany and the pope was the only real threat to the Crescentii rule. Crescentius knew, however, that Boniface, who had been raised by Crescentius I, had created a reaction against puppet popes who abused their authority. He decided the wisest thing was to compromise. He backed John XV, who agreed to take a minimal role in temporal affairs and to devote himself to the spiritual duties of the office. John XV was then elected and consecrated.

The Pope, the French, & the Empire

In 987 the King of France Louis V (surnamed Louis the Do Nothing and Louis the Lazy) died in a hunting accident. He was to be the last of the Carolingian kings. Ever since the fall of Louis the Fat, the French had continued to argue that only Charlemagne's descendants alone could rule as legitimate emperors. While Germany set up its own emperors, the French politely ignored them and set up for themselves Carolingian kings. Nominally, they continued to be a part of the empire, and their allegiance to the Church was never questioned. However, the relations between the French clergy and the Roman clergy would continue to decline. The fact that the papacy supported the Germanic line of emperors doubtless did not sit well with the French who would have preferred French emperors. Again, they politely ignored this and continued to serve in the empire as independent minded vassals of the pope, if not the emperor. Nevertheless, as time passed the relations between the French clergy and Roman clergy continued to become strained. The first controversy had occurred as far back as Pope Leo IV and his public disputes with Hincmar and Lothair. Hincmar and Lothair were eventually forced to acquiesce to the pope but occasion conflicts continued, with Rome ending up on top each time. From this time forward the battles would become more and more heated. In each case, however, the fact remains that France never departed from the empire, nor as vassals of the pope.

The death of Louis the Do–Nothing left France in a dilemma. The long line of Carolginians was beginning to dwindle. The French had opposed the Germanic emperors largely based on the fact that they were not the descendants of Charlemagne. They had argued that the emperor's must be of Carolingian descent and rejected all other. In France, however, the Carolingian Kings had become as incompetent and weak as any emperor ever had. They were faced with a choice. Elect yet another weak Carolingian king or Hugh Capet, an important Duke who had alliances with both Otto II and III. The French magnates agreed that it was time to abandon the Carolingians and chose a real king.

In 987 Hugh Capet became the first in a long line of Capetian rulers. It is ironic that many modern scholars list his ascension as the break with the Holy Roman Empire. There can be no doubt that there was now a clear division between the eastern and western portions of the Holy Roman Empire but Capet hoped to further forge his alliance with the eastern segment of the Holy Roman Empire, not breach from it. Already a colleague of the still young Otto III, he arranged for a synod to meet in 991. The archbishop of Rheims, Arnulf, was an illegitimate son of one of the Carolingian kings and was accused of treason against Hugh Capet. He was deposed and Otto III's mentor and tutor, Gerbert of Aurillac, later Pope Sylvester II, was named the new bishop.

This move might have improved France's relations with the emperor, but it angered the pope. Pope John XV demanded that Arnulf be reinstated and that Gerbert step down. The French clergy declared that the papacy had violated the sacred trust by its corruptions and no longer had the authority to enforce its will. Gerbert himself, a future pope, derided the decadence to which the papacy had fallen and defied the pope. Several synods were held over a course of three years. In the end Pope John XV was victorious. The French were forced to succumb. Gerbert stepped down, but the demotion was good for him. Otto III was now officially of age and invited his old friend and mentor to accompany him to Rome.

At this same time Pope John XV also was successful in negotiating peace between Normandy and England. The two northern nations had been on the verge of war when the pope averted hostilities and negotiated a peaceful settlement between the two parties. Still greater for the empire was when the Duke of Poland offered his whole realm to the protection of the Holy See. Although Poland had already become a part of the empire, as vassals, the Duke had hoped that the pope could provide more protection for his realm, as well as a higher level of respect and dignity for the realm. He had hoped to become a true nation of the empire, and not just a vassal state.

Despite these successes abroad, John XV had more trouble in his home. John Crescentius had died in 988 leaving Crescentius Nomentanus as the supreme power of Rome. This Crescentius was far worse that the others. He called himself emperor and ruled as a corrupt tyrant. Bribes were the common mode of business and the pope was treated with remarkable contempt. Once Crescentius even refused French dignitaries admittance to the papal palace unless they paid bribe money. John XV was a virtual prisoner to the new Crescentius, and in 995 John XV fled to Sutri where he was able to send a dispatch to Otto III, asking for him to come and rescue Italy. Otto III immediately embarked with Gerbert of Aurillac but before he could arrive John XV had died of a fever.

Otto III Comes of Age

Although still a teenager, Otto III had officially come of age in 994. He had barely ascended to his true rule when he received word that Italy, yet again, needed to be liberated from tyranny. With his old friend Gerbert in tow he descended on Italy only to find Pope John XV dead. The people, fearing both Otto and the corruption that had plagues the papacy for so long, declared that any man he should nominate would be elected pope. At this time he would pass up Gerbert, later having him appointed Bishop of Ravenna instead, and chose his former chaplain and cousin, who chose the name Gregory V. Gregory immediately returned the favor by formally crowning Otto III.

The next day Otto passed judgment on Crescentius Nomentanus. As a just Christian emperor he showed leniency and had planned banishment alone, but upon the foolish advice of Gregory V he even commuted that sentence and Crescentius was forgiven. Perhaps Otto forgot, or never knew, how much pride the Italians had. He himself had the greatest respect for Rome and was, although its people did not fully realize it, their greatest ally. In the years to come Otto would plan to make Rome again the seat of power for the whole empire and meticulously drafted plans on how to make Charlemagne's dream of a Christian Rome a reality. Otto III dreamed of the greatness of Rome as a truly

Christian Rome; something it had never truly been. Nevertheless, its proud and arrogant people resented the presence of a Germanic pope even more than they resented having a Germanic emperor. When Otto returned to Germany a month later rebellion would crop up, led by Crescentius Nomentanus; but in the month before Otto departed, he still had much to do.

Soon after Otto's mercy to Crescentius he had learned of another upon whom he should have mercy. Having been contacted by Gregory V it seemed that after fifty four years Marozia, now in her nineties had not yet mercifully died. Her body was withered and malnourished so that she was barely able to stand. Otto III and Gregory V decided to show mercy. She was readmitted into the Church, absolved of her sins, and mercifully executed. Despite being one of the most vile women in history she cannot help but inspire pity; betrayed by her own son she lingered on for over half a century in the worst of dungeons with no companions, nor love, nor hope. Perhaps these protracted years led her to repentance or perhaps justice was served, but hopefully both.

Now Otto began to lay out his designs for a new Rome. Although his plans for a Christian Rome were just beginning he knew that a revived Roman Empire could never be without the Byzantine Empire. He therefore desired to strengthen the always tenuous alliance with the eastern Roman Empire by arranging for a marriage alliance with Constantinople, even as his father had. He selected his godfather John Philagathos as envoy to the capital of Byzantium and returned to Germany to await his reply.

Gregory V was more aware of the Romans distaste for Germanic blood than Otto had been. He had hoped that by showing mercy to Crescentius Crescentius they would return the favor. He also hoped to win over the Italians by showing his support for their cause in the Rheims affair that Gerbert had taken part in a few years earlier. He again asserted that Gerbert had usurped the bishopry of Rheims and that Arnulf was its rightful bishop. He further requested that part of the papal states, which had been taken back by the emperor during of the revolts be returned to the Papal See. This was refused by Otto III. Despite all these measures, which showed the pope was not afraid to stand up to his colleague the emperor, the people of Rome still viewed him as a foreigner.

Not more than a month had passed after Otto's departure before Gregory was asking for his return to protect him. Whether Otto thought Gregory paranoid, whether he was angry for Gregory's stances, or whether Otto was truly too ill to make the journey as he claimed, the fact is that Otto did not offer any assistance. By October Crescentius Nomentanus felt secure enough to stage his new revolt. Gregory V was deposed and took refuge in the duchy Spoleto. With the assistance of the Duke of Spoleto, ally of Otto, he attempted to retake the Vatican but twice they were repelled from Rome, unable to secure victory. Having failed to achieve a military victory he went to Lombardy where he secured the support of many bishops and excommunicated Crescentius.

Crescentius' response was to install a new pope and declare Gregory V an impostor and pretender to the tiara.

John Philagathos had returned recently from Constantinople with an Imperial envoy from the east. He found himself returning to a Rome in revolt. Crescentius needed a new pope and John seemed a good choice. Crescentius reasoned that John was Otto's godfather and, therefore, might not incur the emperor's wrath if he were named pontiff. Moreover, John's envoy from Byzantium was well aware of the political situation and relished the idea of causing a split between Rome and the "Frankish Emperor." John was named Pope John XVI in place of Gregory V, but John was to be nothing more than Crescentius' puppet, and confined to purely spiritual duties.

By this time Otto had intervened. He still resided in Germany for the time being but sent his demands to Rome. John had agreed to acquiesce to all of the emperor's demands but Crescentius intercepted the Imperial messengers and had them imprisoned. In December of 997 Otto III began to march into Italy. John fled but it was not until February 998 that Otto again took possession of Rome, storming Castle St. Angelo and seizing Crescentius. He had shown mercy before but what followed this time was to be an example to all.

Crescentius Nomentanus was executed but Pope John XVI was not so fortunate. He had his eyes gouged out and his nose, tongue, and lips were mutilated. He was ridden backwards on a donkey through Rome, as was the ancient Roman custom, and sentenced to live out the rest of his days in a monastery. Otto III finally realized, as all the great emperors did, that no emperor could rule effectively unless he ruled from Rome. Otto decided to make his palace in Rome and there he would stay.

Otto & Sylvester

The following year Pope Gregory V died at age thirty. Some suspected foul play by poison but others say he died of malaria; a distinction hard to make in those days. In the year since his restoration he had excommunicated the new French King Robert II for his incestuous marriage but despite this, and also because of it, he strengthened the position of France in the empire. He again asserted the authority of the papacy over France, and France was again forced to comply. This was, however, the highlight of his last year and his relation with Otto III was amiable but doubtless not as good as Otto had hoped. Gregory had tried to satiate his enemies with compromise but refused to relinquish authority in France. The loss of power under the Crescentius rule had only made the pope more determined to assert his authority elsewhere in the empire. With the loss of the pope at so young a age Otto was now left to find another pope. He promptly replaced the first German pope with the first French pope, his old friend Gerbert who took the name Sylvester II.

Sylvester II immediately tried to secure France's position in the empire. He, who had been called the usurper of Arnulf, archbishop of Rheims, now affirmed that Arnulf was rightful archbishop. His friendship with both Hugh Capet and Otto III also helped to ferment friendship between the rival regions of the empire. It was his relationship with Otto, however, that helped the most. Otto III needed a pope that he could work with if he was to ever create his vision of a *true* Holy Roman Empire. Sylvester was more than willing. Together they ruled virtually side by side as partners.

In 1001 Otto III returned to the Lateran the "Pentapolis" region which had once been a part of the Papal States. He did this after previously denying the request to Gregory, and despite his recognition of the "Donation of Constantine" as a fraud. This requires some comment. The "Donation of Constantine" was a document that alleged to have donated large portions of Italy to the Church by order of Constantine the Great. The document first appeared, however, four hundred years after Constantine and had been used by the pope to earn Pepin's respect. This document had been accepted as authentic ever since, up until after the Reformation. Even most of the Reformers believed the document to be real. The fact that Otto III claimed the document to be a forgery, which is now known to be true, but gave Sylvester the land anyway, shows two things. First, Otto was far more keen and intelligent than other emperors. Second, Otto donated the land out of respect to his friend Sylvester and not out of obligation. This latter remark is crucial in understanding the last few years of Otto and Sylvester's reign. Together they formed a unified government that worked as one.

Later that same year Sylvester worked feverishly to promote the Church in foreign countries. Thanks to him the Holy Roman Empire expanded without even the lifting of a sword. Poland and Hungary were now Christian nations and Sylvester earnestly worked to develop the Church in these regions. Poland had annexed into the empire under John XV and now Sylvester sent King Stephen I of Hungary a royal crown, making him a vassal king of Otto. Further, Sylvester opened formal relations with Prince Vladmir of Kiev who had become the first Christian ruler of what would become Russia. Still more, he opened relations with King Olaf I of Norway who made Christianity the official state religion. While these later two kingdoms remained separate from the empire the alliances served to strengthen both the papacy and the empire.

Among Sylvester's domestic duties he worked to reform the Church from the corruptions of the previous decades. One way in which he had hoped to do this was the ill advised notion of Priestly celibacy. So prominent was Sylvester that he would easily have eclipsed most other emperors. Had he and Otto lived much longer there little telling how great the empire might have become. Their vision of a truly Christian Roman Empire would never be realized, however.

As the Italians had done many times before they grew tired of foreign rule. Despite all that Otto had done, and could have done, for Rome they saw him as a foreigner who had appointed foreign popes. Nationalism rose its ugly head again. In early 1001 the Italian city of Tibur had revolted. The city was immediately retaken and peace established but Otto showed great mercy toward its inhabitants and forgave the populous. This enraged the Romans who demanded the entire city be razed to the ground and all its people be executed. In February mobs of rioting Romans marched the streets and finally stormed the palace of Otto. As the palace lay under siege Otto managed to escape and flee to a monastery where he sought the aid of his cousin Henry of Bavaria.

Aid would not arrive in time. Otto III died a young man. His dreams of a Christian Rome would also die with him. Ironically, the emissaries that had been sent to Constantinople seeking a marriage alliance returned with Princess in hand only to find her groom deceased. The marriage might not only have created an alliance but, as was Otto's dream, reunited the two empires again into a single Roman Empire but it was not to be.

Otto had been an effective ruler for only a little over five years. In those brief years he had been a just and fair emperor. He had reduced taxation and relaxed requirements for tributes from foreign vassals. He had aspired to restore the glory of Rome as a truly Christian State and sought to follow Augustine's formula of a Heavenly Kingdom on earth. He was exceptionally well educated and devout in faith. He humbly called himself "Servant of the Apostles" and "Servant of Jesus Christ." He was of German blood but lived with a mixture of Romanism and Christianity. He seemed out of place in his time. In Germany he was relatively unpopular for neglecting his home country and for reducing tributes required to Germany while in Italy he was viewed as a foreigner.

Some believe that Otto had been poisoned by the vindictive widow of Crescentius Nomentanus while others argue he died of malaria. One thing is sure. He, Gregory V, and Sylvester II, a year later, would all die young men under uncertain circumstances. In all likelihood poison was the perpetrator of all three and the Crescentius family the conspirator of the same.

Like Otto, his friend, Sylvester was also a controversial figure. He was exceptionally well educated and had been a pioneer in the abacus and in celestial globes (all educated people knew the world was round). His talent for math and the sciences led many to create fanciful legends about his being in league with the devil. This was partially because the medieval sciences were amalgamated with occult notions and astrology, but Sylvester was mainly interested in mathematics. Despite this it had been said that Sylvester had sold his soul to the devil to become pope. Others argued that he secretly practiced sorcery and magic. One legend even says that he had a mystical occult stone head which spoke secret mysteries to him and that he repented on his deathbed for selling his soul to the devil. Together with Otto, they make a fascinating study in medieval history.

Otto III might have been the greatest emperor that the empire ever knew but the irony is that the very people, Romans, whom he had hoped to elevate were his demise. Their own arrogance and pride blinded them to Otto's beneficial attitude. They could only see a foreigner. Otto III's dream of a restored Roman Empire fell with him, but had he studied the prophetic theologians of the day, and today, he would have realized that the true revival of the Roman Empire was not for a Christian but for the anti–Christ. According to age old interpretation, continued down to today among many evangelicals, it the anti–Christ who will revive the Roman Empire and reunite the whole of Europe but this empire would be the last. So Otto's dream was really a curse. It led to his own death despite a promising future and the Holy Roman Empire would continue to decay, awaiting the one who truly is said will revive it, only to share its fate.

The Rise of Saint Henry II of Bavaria

Henry of Bavaria was descended from Henry the Fowler and was the son of Henry the Quarrelsome. When Henry the Quarrelsome had been exiled to Bavaria following his kidnapping of Otto III, the young Henry of Bavaria spent much time in a monastery learning from the abbots and monks. He had patched up the sour relationship with his cousin and became a trusted colleague of Otto. He was a devout Christian who donated lands generously to the Church, would work fervently to reform the Church, and install men of integrity into the ever increasingly corrupt Church. He would eventually be canonized by the Church and made Saint Henry.

When he received news from Otto that he needed assistance, Henry set out to Italy in defense of his friend but when he heard news of Otto's death he ceased his march and returned to Germany. The loss of Otto, who left no heir, not only left the empire without an emperor but Germany without a king. Henry was the most likely choice for king of Germany but he did not wish to leave the decision up to the dukes without his presence. Germany then took precedence over the empire.

This decision may have been bad for both the empire and Germany. Although Henry would become Holy Roman Emperor and follow in the footsteps of the Ottos, his decision showed how fragmented the empire had become. For Henry it was more important to secure his position in Germany first, despite the obvious fact that the emperor was supreme over the whole empire. In fact, the emperor was only supreme over those who accepted his authority. Ever since Louis the Pious the emperors had little recognized authority outside of Germany and even in Italy the emperor often had to use force. France had ignored the emperor for well over a hundred years and the new additions to the empire, Poland and Hungary, presented themselves as vassals to the pope, not the emperor. This was particularly true in Poland where Henry's authority was rejected for the Polish King. The pope could hurl anathemas and threaten excommunication but the emperor had to result to brute force and conquest. Although allegedly coequals it was the pope wielded authority across the whole empire from Poland to France and from Burgundy to Hungary. By contrast Otto III had no control over France or Poland. The emperor's main control over these countries was through the pope whom he had appointed and whom many emperors would seek to control.

It was now up to Henry to start from scratch and gain what control he could in Germany. Once he had been accepted he almost immediately turned to Poland and went to war. The new Polish king Boleslaw the Brave, he argued, would have to accept him, not just the papacy. This same Boleslaw rose to prominence by martyring the Bohemian king Wencelas. "Good King Wencelas," or Saint Wencelas, had promoted missionary activity in Bohemia (modern day Czechoslovakia) which was still partly pagan. At Boleslaw's behest, he was slain on the steps of a church, becoming a martyr and patron saint. Now Henry argued that Boleslaw would have to be his vassal, and not just the pope's. The war would continue to rage for sixteen years with Henry occasionally leaving the war up to others so he could deal with Italy.

Historians have pointed out that, despite Henry devotion to Christ and the Church, he allied himself with the pagan Liutitian tribes against the Christian Poland state, even promising to reduce the number of missionaries allowed into the region. The apparent hypocrisy seemed a necessary evil to Henry who believed that Poland would have to accept his rule or else fall out of the empire's grip. However, Henry would have to take a brief interlude in the war, for the situation in Italy demanded his attention.

Italy in Henry's Absence

With Otto's death the Italians were again vying for power. Arduin was named the king of Italy by dukes and nobles while the bishops and clergy ardently opposed his nomination. In Rome, however, John Crescentius II now came to power and ruled dictatorially as Patrician. He forced Pope Sylvester II to deal strictly with religious ceremony and not to interfere in politics. A year later Sylvester would die, allegedly poisoned by Crescentius Nomentanus' widow (she was also John Crescentius II's mother), the same woman that supposedly poisoned Otto III. John Crescentius II then had John XVII elected pope.

In 1003 Henry marched into Italy. The clergy of Italy had asked for his help in removing Arduin from the throne and Henry came to claim the title for himself. His armies were able to take control but Arduin himself escaped unharmed. Scandal hit as Henry's armies looted and pillage many cities. Saint

Henry's men apparently did not share his Christian convictions and the scene was that of atrocities. Despite this, Henry was a far better and more just ruler than any Italy had. That very year Pope John XVII tried to negotiate for Henry to come to Rome and claim the Imperial throne, but John Crescentius II, upon hearing this, became violently angry. He took immediate steps to see that John XVII made no further attempts to communicate with Henry, and John XVII would not, for the pope would die in December under unknown circumstances.

With the papal office vacant again, John Crescentius II now had yet another pope elected. This one, he hoped, would be more submissive to his will. The new Pope John XVIII did not attempt to crown Henry Emperor but in Pavia, in early 1004, he did crown Henry the King of Italy. It is alleged that he also sought to bring Henry to Rome but Crescentius resisted the idea. What the exact situation was is unknown. John XVIII would surely have born Crescentius' wrath if his request had been public but with the death of two popes in the previous year (each probably connected with the Crescentius family) Crescentius may have felt that three would place his own position in doubt. Regardless of how the situation played out Henry returned to his war with Poland and John XVIII returned to Rome and fell under the tight grip of Crescentius. He continued as pope until 1009 when Crescentius probably forced him to abdicate. During these years John XVIII had little control. He was able to establish a See in Bavaria and at one point played his hand in another battle of "Gallicism" with France. This occurred when the French clergy tried to force some abbots to burn papal bulls. John ordered the men to appear before him for judgment and even threatened the French King Robert II with excommunication if they did not appear. Again, the French were forced to submit.

When John XVIII abdicated, by Crescentius' orders, Sergius IV rose to the papal office. His nickname was "Pig's snout" and he was yet another pope held under the thumb of Crescentius. He would also be the third pope to try to negotiate Henry's return to Italy to claim the Imperial diadem. By this time, however, a political rivalry had developed between the Crescentius family and a Tusculan family, also descended from Theophylactus. In May 1012 both Sergius IV and John Crescentius II died, only six days apart. The counts of Tusculum now secured power in Rome, but the surviving Crescentii did not give up easily. Benedict VIII was elected pope with the backing of the Tuscalans but a certain Gregory was elected antipope by the surviving Crescentii.

The Interregnum Ends

Benedict VIII had bought his election with bribery but he was also aided by the fact that he was the son of Count Gregory of Tusculum. His brother Romanus then assumed the civil authority of Rome. The Crescentii were forced out of Rome and held up in some mountain strongholds but

Benedict led armed forces which were able to penetrate and crush the Crescentii. This forced the antipope Gregory to flee to Germany to beg the help of Henry.

When Gregory arrived, Henry told him to cease all papal activity until he had decided the issue. When he arrived in Rome, however, he decided in favor of Benedict. The Crescentii family had been corrupt dictators whose relationship with the Germans was notoriously poor. Although Benedict was scarcely a devout pope he was a keen politician and skilled military leader. He immediately sought to make Henry Holy Roman Emperor and establish good relations. In February 1014 he crowned Henry II but an armed revolt by supporters of the long officially ousted king Arduin threatened the new emperor. A small scale war occurred but Arduin's men were soon subdued and he was sentenced to live out his days in a monastery. Henry II was now the unquestioned Emperor of Rome.

Immediately after his coronation and the deposition of Arduin, Henry and Benedict proceeded to enact clerical reforms, that Henry had long sought, in a synod. Among the reforms that Henry strove for was clerical celibacy. He doubtless believed that the sexually debased conduct of previous popes could be curbed by the enforcement of celibacy but by denying men lawful wives, it would inevitably lead to more sexual misconduct, not less. Nevertheless, in 1022 they agreed to outlaw concubines, which had been permitted by old Roman law, and forbade marriage for certain priestly offices. It would not, however, be until over a century later that the celibacy of the priesthood was strictly required and enforced. Among the reforms passed in 1014 were laws against simony and age requirements. The later was as a result of the papal see having been given to young children or aged feeble men who had been puppets. Ironically, some claim that the very next pope would be only ten or twelve years old upon ascension, although this is disputed.

Upon the conclusion of the synod Henry again left for Germany leaving behind a viceroy to enforce his will in Italy. He allowed Benedict the authority to act militarily against any threats. This Benedict did with fervor. Over the next few years while Henry was waging war with Poland Benedict was forcing defiant Italian cities to again accept Rome as the center of Italy's power. Then in 1016 he led an army again the Saracen threat in Sardinia. Meanwhile Henry had finally come to terms in Poland. Poland would retain its king and have semiautonomous authority but would acknowledge Henry as emperor of the empire, and Poland with it.

Henry & Southern Italy

The Byzantine Empire had long held on to part of Southern Italy, even after Otto II claimed much of the land as dowry. Over the years Constantinople had not given up hope of regaining Rome but invasions from the Arabs and, more recently, the Bulgars had prevented them from seriously governing their own western realms, let alone annexing Rome. As a result of the prolonged Bulgar war the southern Italians, themselves tiring of Saracen raids as well as lack of interest and help from the east, were now growing restless of their eastern rulers. Not long after Benedict had shown strength in defeating the Muslims, Melus of Bari revolted against the Byzantines.

The political situation had changed. The old Crescentii family despised the Germans and longed to return to the Byzantine (eastern Roman) Empire. The new Tusculan family, however, were smart politicians, if not good people. They knew that the strength of the empire lay in the west and in Henry II. They sought to strengthen the west rather than the east. Benedict had further invigorated the Church's alliance with the Normans and increased their power and authority in the empire. The Normans in return lent troops to him and he in return slyly rendered aid and assistance to the rebellion, including the lending of Norman troops to Melus.

This rise of Norman power certainly was not Benedict's doing, however. In recent years France had lost any real control over the region and the new Norman dukes were themselves to become powerful rulers. The most famous of whom, William the Conqueror, would rise to dominance less than a half a century later. For now, however, the Normans were still a relatively small country and their troops were unable to defeat the Byzantine army that had arrived in 1019. Even though Benedict had not openly participated in the rebellion it was obvious what role he had played in it and the Byzantines promptly moved north.

Benedict VIII now went to visit Germany, and seek Henry's help. He arrived as if he were simply there to show his respect for Henry and the German people, but after his welcome and customary exchanges, he asked for Henry's help in Italy. Henry agreed. In 1021 Henry advanced against Southern Italy and scored a few victories against the Byzantines but he was unable to secure many lands. A truce was enacted that would draw the boundary lines similar to where they had been previously. It was a draw. Neither side made any significant advances nor had they lost much. The Holy Roman Empire and the Byzantine Empire continued in their always uneasy alliance.

The Fourteen Martyrs of Orleans

It was late in the reign of Henry that a seemingly obscure travesty in France occurred. This tragic event often goes unnoticed in history books because it had no connection with the empire as a whole, but it did plant a seed which, when it went unpunished, would later grow into the Inquisition. This tragedy was the public execution and martyrdom of fourteen "heretics" in Orleans France in 1022. This was the first such trial in the middle ages and set the stage for many more in future generations.

Over the past thousand years Christians had suffered persecution and martyrdom. Almost without exception, however, these Christians died at the hands of pagans. The Vikings, Saxons, Magyars, Bulgars, Huns, Parthians, and more recently Muslims had slaughtered Christians with sometimes utter cruelties, but never before had Christians been tried and executed under the charge of heresy. To be sure Popes had excommunicated and banished alleged heretics and occasional riots and confrontations between the early Arians and Trinitarians had resulted in death but since the rise of Charlemagne heresy was not a state crime punishable by death.

It is ironic that the French who had so greatly blasted the tyranny of the papacy were the clergymen responsible for this forerunner of the Inquisition. Stranger still is the fact that these Christians did not seem to preach any "heresy" not preached by some dissent Catholic clergy members. Specifically, the issues concerned the legitimacy of infant baptism and the doctrine of transubstantiation. This later doctrine refers to the belief that the bread and wine of Eucharist are literally transformed into the physical body and blood of Jesus. The Eucharist then became viewed as a second sacrifice for which believers could gain the remission of sins. That these men were condemned for their opposition to transubstantiation is even more astonishing since the doctrine of transubstantiation had *not yet been formally adopted by the Catholic Church itself!* Indeed, it would be another two hundred years before the Church would officially adopt the position.

Nevertheless, in 1022 King Robert II had been warned of the "dangerous" teachings of many laymen, including several nobles. The fact that these were laymen rather than clergy members may have contributed to their persecution for although the French clergy opposed interference by the papacy, the French clergy too had been corrupted by power. The notion that mere laymen were qualified to attack the doctrines and teachings of their bishops threatened their very power. Hence, when King Robert II convened a council the "heretics" were condemned to death by fire if they refused to recant. This was done and the fourteen were burned alive at stakes before King Robert II.

A final note upon these martyrs is prudent. Because accounts of their martyrdom come only from their enemies it is hard to determine exactly who the fourteen were. They have been identified by the Catholics as Albigenses but this term was far too vague, particularly in this day. The term lumped together various sects which range from the later Waldenses to various Cathari sects. Some Protestant historians have erroneously identified these groups as forerunners of the Reformation but this is only partially true. The later Waldenses may indeed be considered true "proto–Protestants" but the Albigenses and similar Cathari sects taught a breed of dualism that wreaked of cultic doctrine, which bare no resemblance to Protestantism or Catholicism. Like the Paulican sect of the east, some of these sects taught that there were two sons of God; the one Christ but the other Satan, His brother. They rejected the

Old Testament as having been written by the evil brother and also preached celibacy for all. Finally, they believed that a Christian who sinned after gaining redemption was instantly lost and could never be brought back to repentance. The problem is compounded by the Catholic's failure to distinguish between these various sects. If these martyrs were early Waldenses then they were doubtless true believers burned for threatening the power of the clergy. If, however, they are to be associated with the later Albigenses then they were probably an obscure cultic sect. This is possible was the martyrs were also accused of preaching against marriage and declaring that absolution was not possible for new sins, although some suggest this is merely an allusion to the "sacrifice of mass." In either case, their death would establish a terrible precedent that gave the state the right to determine orthodoxy under pain of death.

The End of the Saxon Dynasty

In 1024 both Benedict VIII and Saint Henry II of Bavaria died. As Henry left no true heir, the throne would fall to the Burgandians and with it the Ottonian, or more accurately the Saxon, Dynasty would end. Henry himself was a good emperor but he had made many mistakes. He did not share the Otto's love for Rome and so the Romans, despite the new alliance with the Tusculan family, had no love for him. Upon his death the citizens of Pavia actually demolished the Imperial Palace, yet again acting as if their emperor had been a foreign conqueror. His preoccupation with Poland did little to expand the empire, as it was already a part of it, but wasted time and effort that could have been used elsewhere.

The great Saxon Dynasty was really an Ottonian Dynasty. Although Henry was not directly related to the Ottos he was a cousin of theirs and was the most sincere since an Otto. He had strove to enforce and promote the Ottonian system of government appointing many bishops of high moral standards and making grand donations to the Church. He sought to reform the Church of its ills and was in most respects a devout Christian Emperor. This was so of all the Ottonians. They were idealists who had hoped to make Augustine and Charlemagne's vision of a Christian world empire a reality but they each failed. The Italians were too proud and arrogant to allow a German to be their emperor and the Church had become corrupted by the power they had assumed. The Ottonians thought they could restore the integrity of the Church by appointing good men but when they died new men would simply appoint more wicked popes. The system itself was flawed. It was not based on the Bible but on the ancient structure of ancient empires. They believed that good Christian men would make righteous autocrats but the power of autocracy only makes good Christian men corrupt. A thousand years had passed since Christ walked the streets of Jerusalem and two hundred since Charlemagne had unified Europe, but there was not yet a true Christian empire. Over the next few centuries men would realize that the Kingdom of God was not for men to make but for God. The ancient empires were dead and the two halves of the Roman Empire were all that remained, yet prophecy had told men that Rome was to be the last great empire before Christ's. This led to one of two inevitable conclusions. Either Rome would truly become Christ's Kingdom or Rome would fall. For the next five hundred years scholars would dispute which of these was to be but the fall of the Ottonians signaled to many that the former was untrue. Rome *would* fall.

Holy Roman Emperor	Pope	AntiPope (if any)

——————— 924 ———————

——————— 928 ———————

Leo VI

——————— 928 ———————
——————— 929 ———————

Stephen VII (VIII)

——————— 931 ———————

John XI

Fourth Interregnum
(Otto began reigning in 936 but was not
  anointed Holy Roman Emperor until 962)

——————— 935 ———————
——————— 936 ———————

Leo VII

——————— 939 ———————

Stephen VIII (IX)

——————— 942 ———————

Marinus II

——————— 946 ———————

Agapetus II

——————— 955 ———————

——————— 962 ———————

John XII

——————— 964 ———————

Leo VIII   *Benedict V*

Otto the Great (Otto or Otho I)

——————— 865 ———————

John XIII   — 866 —

——————— 972 ———————

——————— 973 ———————

——————— 973 ———————

Benedict VI

——————— 974 ———————

Otto II

                            Boniface VII

Benedict VII   — 974 —

——————— 983 ———————

——————— 983 ———————

John XIV

——————— 984 ———————

                     Boniface VII (2nd time)

——————— 985 ———————

Otto III

John XV

——————— 996 ———————

                            — 997 —

Gregory V   *John XVI (XVII)*

                            — 998 —

——————— 999 ———————

——————— 1002 ———————

King of England	King of France	King of Burgundy	King of Sicily
——— 955 ———	——— 954 ———	——— 937 ———	
Eadwig 959	Lothair	Conrad the Peaceful	
Edgar 975			
Edward the Martyr 979	——— 986 ———		
	Louis V 987		
Aethelred the Unready	Hugh Capet 996	——— 993 ———	
——— 1016 ———	Robert II 1031	Rudolf III	
Cnut (or Canute) 1035		——— 1032 ———	
Interregnum 1037		Kingdom ceded to the Emperor	
Harold 1040	Henry I		
Harthacnut 1042			
Edward the Confessor 1066	——— 1060 ———		——— 1059 ———
			Kingdom of Sicily founded in 1080
William the Conqueror 1087	Philip I		Robert Guiscard I
			——— 1085 ———
William Rufus			Roger II (Adelaide regent)

7

The First Salic Emperors

When Henry II died the people of Italy, and specifically Pavia, again erupted in anti–Germanic fever. They rejoiced at the death of a "foreign" ruler and destroyed the Imperial Palace in a riot but this riot did not result in the overthrow of Germanic rule. Instead it incited the archbishop to immediately call upon Conrad II, surnamed the Salic, to come and liberate Italy from anarchy and to protect the domains of the Church which were threatened by the mobs. Henceforth, the Franconian Dynasty or, as it is more frequently called, the Salian Dynasty (so named after Conrad the Salic) would rule over the empire for a hundred years.

Conrad II

Conrad II was the Duke of Franconia when he received news of Henry II's death. He was a distant relative of the Ottonians and had married a descendant of Charlemagne. He was the most obvious choice to become king of Germany in the absence of any true heirs by Henry. In 1024 Conrad received the crown but a few electors set up William of Aquitaine as a rival king. This forced the various kings of the empire to take sides but when Robert II of France sided with Conrad, William was forced to give in without a fight. The crown of Germany was therefore resolved with little or no bloodshed.

No sooner had his ascendancy to the German throne been completed than he received word from the archbishop of Milan, Heribert (also called Ariberto). The bishop needed help to quell the riots and anarchy which had ensued following Henry II's death. In 1026 Conrad II arrived in Italy but his mere presence was all that needed. The people did not like German leadership but they were acutely aware that Italy lacked leadership of its own. The rioting and anarchy ceased shortly after Conrad's arrival and the people were ready to accept him as their emperor. He was crowned the king of Italy that very year and the following year he received the Imperial Crown from the recently elected Pope John XIX.

In 1022 Romanus, the former consul and brother of Pope Benedict VIII, was consecrated as the new pope. He, however, had created a scandal by bribing his way into the papal see and since he was a layman upon his election, he was passed through all the priestly orders in a single day. Despite this scandal he had been able to patch up the political situation in Rome, including semi–reconciliation with the recently displaced Crescentii family. The people were ready to accept a pope, whatever his credentials, and they were also eager to have an emperor.

The coronation of Conrad was itself significant for several reasons. First, Conrad II had not forced himself upon Rome, nor had he been called to Rome because of a great political crisis there. He was crowned because the people realized that the empire needed an emperor. Second, the ceremony was done with great pomp and featured such notables as the Burgundian King Rudolf III and, more significantly, King Canute (or Cnut) of England.

The latter king is significant for while England may not yet have become a part of the Holy Roman Empire it forged a powerful alliance that would soon take the country into the Empire of Nations. The unique structure of the empire makes it hard to clarify Britain's position in the empire at this time but three facts prevail. First, after attending the ceremony Canute struck a deal with Pope John XIX which would grant England exemption from certain tributes. The facts that tributes had been required indicates that England was not wholly independent of the empire. Second, the marriage of Canute's daughter in 1036 to Conrad's son, the future emperor Henry III, struck a major marriage alliance that would eventually lead to England's inclusion in the empire if it was not already. Finally, the very appearance of Canute at the coronation indicates his prominent position in the empire. It would be rare indeed for a foreign dignitary to be invited to such an event. While this is a possibility it signifies at the very least the importance to which England was slowly rising.

Conrad had little time to celebrate his coronation for after receiving the crown he received news of a rebellion in Germany. He instantly returned to Germany where the rebellion was easily put down and the perpetrators punished. This included members of his own family but Conrad did not spare them, for they too were executed for treason.

The following year yet another revolt occurred. This one was in Poland where Mieszko, the son of Boleslaw the Brave, sought independence from German rule. Like the previous revolt Conrad was able to halt Polish aggression and a truce was arranged which would leave Mieszko with semi–autonomous rule so long as he agreed to remain a vassal of the empire and pay tribute.

The next few years would remain relatively peaceful until the death of Burgundian king Rudolf III in 1032. His death is significant because he had formerly planned to bequeath his entire kingdom to Henry II, but upon the emperor's untimely death Conrad II was to inherit the kingdom, from which he had come. However, Hugh (or Eudes), the Count of Champagne, now claimed the Burgundian throne for himself. He rejected Conrad's claim and revolted. Conrad was again forced to take the field and defeat the pretender to Burgundy's throne. By 1033 Conrad would secure Burgundy (also called Arles at this time) and accept the crown thereof.

Conrad & the Constitution of Fiefs

Accompanying Conrad on the Burgundian excursion was Heribert, the archbishop of Milan, with whom he had become close friends. It is ironic that upon their return to Italy they would soon become enemies for when they arrived yet another revolt had occurred. This one, however, was not an attempt to oust Conrad, but to claim land rights. In Italy the Church and the feudal system had developed in such a way that land left behind by certain vassals was not bequeathed to their heirs but to the Church. A class of citizens known as "vavasours" had increasingly seen the lands of their fathers taken away from them and found themselves being reduced to little more than slaves who worked the land for the Church. While Conrad and Heribert had been away in Burgundy the vassavours had created an upheaval demanding certain property rights.

When Cornad arrived he surveyed the situation and proved to be a just emperor. He sided with the vavasours and lent his support to their cause. This sense of justice displays Conrad's character but it would also alienate his old colleague Heribert. Conrad ordered the restoration of the disputed lands and Heribert was forced, for the time being, to accept his decision. The lands in question were returned to vavasours but it would not be long before Heribert himself was in rebellion.

Having convinced himself that all was well in Italy Conrad set out to subdue the pagan Liutitians east of Germany. This is the same tribe which Henry II had unwisely made a treaty with many years before. Since that time Christian missionaries were barred from their lands and the pagans continued to be a threat to both Christian citizens and missionaries. Conrad resolved to make the land free for Christians and by 1035 the Liutitians were defeated allowing missionaries to enter the territories freely again. In just over a decade Conrad had successfully become king of Italy, Germany, Burgundy, and the emperor thereof. He further had forced Poland to declare fealty to the empire and had crushed one of the last remaining pagan threats to Europe. What he could not do was crush the proud and arrogant spirit of the medieval clergy. News arrived that Heribert had now rebelled in Milan and was refusing to enforce Conrad's will in regard to the vavasours. Heribert declared that he was the equal of the emperor and did not, therefore, need to obey his wishes.

When Conrad II returned to Italy Heribert was arrested and the lands again restored. Nonetheless, friends of Heribert helped him to escape where he set out to gain support for a revolt against Conrad. This time Conrad used wise diplomacy and skill to drive Heribert into hiding where he lost communication with his supporters. Soon he was able to separate Heribert entirely from his base support. After Heribert was no longer a threat Conrad had Heribert deposed and in 1037 called upon the most recent pope, Benedict IX (about whom much will be said later) to ratify the deposition. Initially Benedict had hoped to reach a compromise but Conrad was unwielding. Unable to safely get in contact with his supporters Heribert was effectively left in exile and his supporters quietly died out. The rebellion had come to nought without a fight. The following year Conrad created a Constitution of Fiefs which guaranteed that land could not be taken away from vavasours without a trial by peers and thus secured land rights for commoners. The next year Benedict IX gave in agreeing to ratify the deposition of Heribert. The pendulum had swung and the emperor, for now, was greater than the pope.

Conrad's final years were relatively peaceful. Like many people in that day Conrad died before his time. While on an expedition to Southern Italy he had contracted a fever from an epidemic there. He returned to Germany where he lingered on for a short while before dying in 1039, leaving behind his son and heir Henry III. Like the Ottonians before him Conrad II showed great promise but little is said of him in most history books for his greatest achievement, the Constitution of Fiefs, would soon be ignored and all but forgotten. Not until the *Magna Charta* nearly a hundred years later would the concept reappear. Nonetheless, Conrad II deserves respect as one of the last truly good emperors before the decline of the Imperial dignity.

The Empire Upon Henry III's Ascension

Henry III was only twenty two years old when he took the German crown. Although his right as Holy Emperor was never questioned by rivals or the pope it would be almost seven years later before Henry's formal coronation occurred. Interestingly enough, little of historical value seems to have occurred in these first seven years. He was a devout man who sought peace rather than war. He sought stringently to stop feudal warfare between Christian princes but, ironically, went to war himself to subjugate Bohemia and Moravia. These small eastern countries soon fell into his hands and his control of the east was uncontested. In regard to the western half of the empire he helped to secure his position there by political marriages. Canute's daughter had already died leaving Henry III free to marry to Agnes, the daughter of William V of Aquitaine and Poitou. Strong ties were therefore forged between both France and England.

All these years Henry III had strangely put off his coronation. The reason was doubtless his concern over the papal corruption that had begun anew under Benedict IX. As a devout man he did not want to be coronated by a corrupt pope. Perhaps he waited to see if the situation would correct itself, but when it did not Henry would assert himself to make the correction.

Benedict IX had ascended to the papacy in 1032. He was alleged by contemporary observers to have been only eleven years old upon his ascension but modern scholars have doubted this assertion on the grounds that no one so young could have engaged in as many sexual hijinx and debauchery as he had been accused, if indeed he had not even reached puberty. Benedict IX, like Octavian before him, was accused not only of adultery but of raping young pilgrims. His crimes were alleged to include murder and robbery of pilgrims "upon the graves of martyrs." Simony, or the selling of Church offices, was so common under him that one had said he followed "in the footsteps of Simon Magus rather than Simon Peter." So vile was he that back in 1033 several nobles had tried to assassinate him during mass. Benedict, however, had many friends in high places. His brother, Gregory, was the Roman Patrician and he himself was the son of Alberic III, tracing his ancestry back to the Marozia lineage. It was with that lineage that he had secured the papacy and it was with that support that he kept it.

Finally, in late 1044 the people of Rome revolted. The Crescentii family had sufficiently managed enough support to raise a rebellion against the Tusculans, who supported Benedict. Certainly the Tusculan popes had been no better than those of the Crescentii. By January of 1045 bloodshed had forced Benedict IX to flee to his Tusculum protectors and the Crescentii placed Sylvester III on the papal throne. Benedict argued that he had never formally been deposed and therefore the election of Sylvester III was invalid. He excommunicated Sylvester and, with help from the Tusculans, reclaimed the Lateran in March. He soon realized, however, that the people despised him and were not likely to tolerate him from long. Moreover, Benedict had fallen in love with a cousin and sought her hand in marriage. Although the pope was allowed a wife in this day, her father refused to give him his daughter's hand in marriage unless he resigned the papacy. This would be a grand compromise for all.

In May, only two months after resuming the papal throne, Benedict abdicated in favor of John Gratian, a popular man who was a part of the reform movement which sought, among other things, to outlaw marriage among priests. He was politically a wise choice but he did not gain the office legitimately, for an enormous amount of money (some say two thousand pounds of silver) was secretly paid to Benedict in return for his abdication. The office of the papacy had been sold to the highest bidder. John Gratian took the name Gregory VI. Rome now had two popes, Sylvester III and Gregory VI. Worst still Benedict IX was scorned by his future wife and reneged on his abdication, again claiming to be the true pope.

It was 1046 and Henry III decided he had waited long enough for his coronation. He would receive the crown and he would receive it from the pope of his choice. He entered into Italy and immediately convened a synod to deal with the issue. Gregory VI, Sylvester III, and Benedict IX were all charged by the synod of Sutri with simony. Only Gregory VI appeared before the synod and accounts differ on exactly what happened but what is undisputed is that Gregory VI willing abdicated after formally deposing his rivals. Some scholars argue that Henry III was careful not to circumvent the belief that the pope could be judged by no man. He therefore is said to have forced Gregory VI to execute his judgment upon Sylvester and Benedict and then abdicate. Other accounts give a more respectful accounting to Gregory who is said to have gracefully repented of the sin of simony and stepped down remorsefully. He allegedly asked forgiveness for "usurping the dignity of Christ."

This account is worthy of notice for among Gregory's followers was a monk named Hildebrand, whom he had taught. He would one day rise to become one of the most famous popes under the name of Gregory VII. That the name Gregory was chosen is no accident. Hildebrand saw Gregory as a sort of martyr. Gregory had desired reform but could see no other way to rid the papacy of the tyrant Benedict than to pay the bribe money. When Gregory went into exile, Hildebrand went with him, only to reappear in the pages of history years later.

With Gregory having abdicated the papacy was now vacant. The synod presumably searched all of Rome and could find not a single clergyman worthy. Henry III then nominated a German who became Pope Clement II. This Clement II would crown Henry III as Holy Roman Emperor one day after ascending to the office on Christmas day, 1046. In the following months Clement and Henry would strengthen the role of the emperor. Henry became the Roman Patrician as well as emperor and the Romans were obliged to guarantee that no pope could be elected without the approval of both the patrician and emperor. Inasmuch as Henry was now both, it made him the supreme authority of the papacy. Further, Henry, as the great emperors before him, again made Rome an Imperial City. He knew that the legacy of the empire was in its decent from the Roman Empire. Much of the rebellion and discontent in Italy over the years had stemmed from their pride and belief that the Germans were usurping the once great dignity of Rome. They felt that the Germans were robbing them of their heritage. Henry III again made the Holy Roman Empire a truly *Roman* empire but this honeymoon would not last long for Clement II died of lead poisoning nine months after he had crowned Henry.

With Henry out of Rome, Benedict returned to claim the vacant throne. Many accused him of poisoning Clement and the people were not long in driving him out. Benedict remained entrenched only nine months himself before he looted the Church treasury and fled Rome for his life. He was excommunicated and most likely confined to a monastery where he died eight years later. Some say he died repentant of his sins but others paint the figure of a haunting unrepentant ghost.

Again the papacy was vacant and again Henry III chose a German who took the name Damasus II. Yet again, this pope met his death under mysterious circumstances, for less than a month after assuming the office he died, most likely of poison. Henry III would live to elect two more popes, the first of whom was Leo IX.

The Hildebrandian Popes and the Rise of Normandy

Henry III had a cousin named Bruno. He had served under Conrad II before assuming the bishopry of Toul. Among his close colleagues was the "reformer" Hildebrand who had followed Gregory VI into exile. When Damasus II was declared dead Henry nominated Bruno but agreed that his election would have to be ratified by the clergy and people of Rome. With Hildebrand at his side he came to Rome dressed as a pilgrim in bare feet. He was welcomed with open arms by the people and became the first of the "Hildebrandian popes," so called because of Hildebrand's influence. He chose the consecrated name of Leo IX.

He began to promote reform by encouraging synods in various cities throughout the empire. A true reform would have to have the support of the local clergy so synods were created in Pavia, Rheims, Rome, and other important cities. Simony was to be forbidden and clergy who had violated this law were punished either by deposition or sometimes by penance. Other reforms pushed for clerical celibacy while most could only agree on outlawing concubinage. The clergy were also forbidden from taking up arms as some had done before.

Ironically, along with these reforms came an ominous foreshadowing of the Inquisition to come. The first had actually occurred under the emperor, but was soon followed by the Church. In 1052 while Henry was celebrating Christmas he had heard of Manichean heretics that were gaining a large following. He ordered them to be hung, and so *for the first time* in medieval history the emperor had declared heresy a crime punishable by death. These martyrs had set the stage for the emperor who lent credibility to the action and the Church was now given an ominous choice. A certain Berengar of Tours had become a subject of controversy when he spoke out publicly about the increasingly popular doctrine of transubstantiation. This doctrine held that the bread of communion was literally transformed into Christ's body while the wine was literally transformed into His blood. Despite the fact that this doctrine had not yet been formalized as doctrine within the church it was held to be sacrilegious by many people to attack the idea. Since the teaching of transubstantiation viewed Christ as literally being sacrificed again at Mass (hence the title "Sacrifice of Mass"), to attack it was to attack Christ Himself, or so they argued. Lanfranc of France had become one of Benergar's most livid critics but each side had strong political support. Young William, Duke of Normandy, supported Lanfranc but the Empress Agnes supported Berengar. Since Henry III, Agnes' husband, had himself set precedence by hanging heretics a few years earlier, she could not directly intervene. In 1050 Leo IX decided to officially condemn Berengar's position but he did not yet go beyond this. In the years to come, however, Berengar would continue to preach the gospel as he believed it, and he would not back down. He would later come into conflict with two other popes and his followers would become the first "proto–Protestant" martyrs of the Catholic Church.

Nevertheless, while Leo's promotion of the Hildebrandian "reforms" first began to blossom during his reign they were slowed by the political situation in Southern Italy and the Norman occupation thereof. Back in the early tenth century land had been parceled out by France to the Viking Rollo in exchange for peace. Over the past century and a half the Vikings had become members of the Church and became moderately civilized but they were still mercenaries. The Viking blood in them had not satiated and in the later half of the eleventh century they had undertaken mercenary raids against the Muslims in Southern Italy. As mercenaries, however, they did not stop with Muslims. They were soon marauding in Byzantine territory and threatening the security of the Church's land nearby.

By this time the Normans had attacked and seized land in Southern Italy. Although the acquisitions were in Byzantine territory, not Roman, Leo IX was terrified of the threat of invasion and equally alarmed by raids and incursions against Church property. Leo IX had requested Henry's assistance but Henry took no action and was seemingly unconcerned. In May of 1053 he then decided to take action himself. Despite the Church's new stand against clergymen taking up arms, the pope led a small ill–equipped army against the Normans in southern Italy. Politics, however, is a strange thing for although the Normans had only seized Byzantine lands, the Byzantine Empire seemed more angry at the pope than the Normans. They angrily declared that the pope had no right in their lands. The Patriarch Michael Cerularius virulently began to squash Latin rituals and practices that were not in accordance with eastern Churches and when the pope asked for assistance against the Normans, none was forthcoming from either Henry III or the Byzantines.

In June, only a month after his incursion, Leo lost a battle to the Normans and was taken prisoner at Civitate by Robert Guiscard, the leader of the Normans in Italy. The western Church called Leo a hypocrite for taking up arms, the eastern Church treated him as arrogant, and the emperor did nothing to help him. To heap more ironies upon this was the fact that this Norman conquest would only help the west in the long term. The fall of former Byzantine territories in Apula and Calabria to Norman marauders prevented the Byzantine Empire from viewing this as an act of aggression by the Holy Roman Empire, yet when the Normans became vassals of the empire the lands would fall into Holy Roman territory, thus allowing all of Italy to enter the realm without Byzantine war.

After nine months of hospitable captivity the pope was released and returned to Rome where he would die in 1054. Henry III would then elect Victor II as the new pontiff. Henry would later appoint him the Duke of Spoleto and the Count of Fermo as well. Victor II had followed in Leo's footsteps in many ways. He was not as strong a reformer but he had, like Leo, become preoccupied with Norman aggression and feared that they might invade Roman territory. His position as duke and count also forced him to devote much of his time to politics and was one of the reasons for his concern over Norman occupied Italy. In 1056 Victor received more distracting news.

Henry III was ill and knew he would not live. For years poor health had caused the emperor, who was once considered a man of the people, to stay aloof, rarely showing his face in public. His son was but five years old. The western arm of the Holy Roman Empire was becoming increasingly distant as the Norman aggression had proven and eastern vassals would have loved to have taken advantage of the young child for their own reasons. Henry wanted his son, Henry IV, to inherit the empire so he called Victor and made an arrangement. Victor was to support and secure the throne for Henry IV and to make Agnes the regent until he was of age, but Victor was to act as the real ruler until that time. Moreover, should something happen to little Henry IV Victor would decide who the next emperor would be. This profound trust in Victor left the pope as emperor in everything but name. Upon Henry's death Victor did as asked and showed himself to be worthy of Henry's trust. Henry IV was accepted and named Henry's successor in 1056.

The reign of Henry III signaled a drastic change in the empire. Nevertheless, the changes that would occur could not have been seen by any man and certainly much of the change was not his intention. Henry had showed signs of greatness but also many signs of weakness. He was generally a just and fair emperor whose leniency sometimes backfired as it had with Louis the Pious. Particularly late in his reign, possibly when he was weakened by illness, many parts of the empire neglected his authority and some even openly rebelled. Lorraine, Normandy, Hungary, Tuscany, and even parts of Germany were increasingly independent of the emperor's rule. So also his reform and piety produced bad fruit as well as good. The moral reformation that would continue in the Church had begun largely with him but so did its degradation in terms of political corruption. Henry had been the first emperor to execute men for heresy and thus set a precedent that would lead to the horrors of the Inquisition.

The empire that Henry left to a five year old child would surely have fallen were it not for the increasing political power of the papacy. In the decades to come the emperor would be eclipsed by the pope and by his vassals; most notably, William the Conqueror. The world was about to change.

Eduard Schwoiser – Henry IV at Canossa – 1862

8

The Age of Hildebrand

The end of the eleventh century marked a change in the empire. The early medieval empire was still part barbarian but it was, in many ways, far more Christian than that of the High Middle Ages. The ancient barbaric empires of old were slowly changing due to the influence of Christianity. Despite the corruption of the papacy and the hierarchical status of the pope and emperor, borrowed from ancient civilizations, the empire showed great promise. It had become as great as any empire in history but the corruption of the Church demanded reform. Ironically, the "reform" that Hildebrand brought also brought with it a new brand of corruption. The sexual debauchery and petty ambition of popes was replaced with power such as even emperors never had. Great armies lay at their disposal, doctrinal truth was shifted from the Bible and placed solely in the interpretation of the pontiff, the kings and emperors had to seek the pope's approval, and the authority of the pope was enforced with Crusades and Inquisitions.

Yet this was also an age when Universities blossomed and when the *Magna Charta* was written. It was an age when true reformers risked martyrdom to make the world better and paved the way for both the Renaissance and the true Reformation. This was truly the generation that would change the world, but Hildebrand was not the only important figure from this generation for it was in this same generation that saw William the Conqueror create the foundations of the England of the modern world; the England from which freedom would one day bloom.

The Hildebrandians Struggle for Power

When Victor II died the Hildebrandians were afraid of losing control of the papacy. Their extreme views upon enforcing clerical celibacy, as well as their strict control, made many enemies within the Church. A group of Hildebrandian supporters then elected one of their own without notifying the Imperial Regent Agnes as required. Their choice, Stephen IX, was supported by Godfrey, the Duke of Lorraine, and the Count of Tuscany, and when the Imperial family was finally notified of the new pope, they cordially accepted the pontiff.

The short rule of Stephen IX was relatively unimportant except for two events. The first was the alliance created between the Hildebrandians and a radical reformation group known as the "Patarians." These men, who soon were ardently supported by Hildebrand, favored drastic measures to enforce clerical celibacy and Church discipline. The second was Stephen IX's plan to attack Normans in southern Italy. He needed the assistance of Duke Godfrey and had considered negotiations to make Godfrey emperor in lieu of the child Henry IV. Godfrey had even gone so far as to promise to conquer the Byzantine empire and reunite what was once the Roman Empire. However, upon his journey to meet and negotiate this pact with Godfrey, Stephen fell violently ill. Realizing that he might die, he had the clergy promise not to elect a new pope until Hildebrand, who was on a mission to Germany, returned. This showed the enormous control Hildebrand wielded over his followers and the desire of his followers to keep the papacy in the hands of the reform movement. Nevertheless, upon Stephen's death the enemies of Hildebrand had no desire to wait for his return. The nobles of Tusculum hoped to regain their control of the papacy, and in April 1058, they helped to establish Benedict X as pope.

Upon Benedict X's ascension the Hildebrandian party fled Rome. Without these bishops the consecration of Benedict was performed irregularly by an ally and not the lawful bishop. When Hildebrand's colleagues reached him they turned to Duke Godfrey of Lorraine for support. Nicholas II was elected by them, but this now made two popes, so in January 1059 a synod was held at Sutri with the support of Agnes, the regent empress, and Benedict was excommunicated. Later that month the synod was backed up by Godfrey's troops who escorted Nicholas II to Rome. Bendict retreated to a castle in Galeria where he was besieged. Within a few months the castle's owner surrendered and Benedict was handed over to the soldiers. He formally renounced all claims to the throne but when Hildebrand was promoted to archdeacon he had Benedict imprisoned, formally charged, and deposed. Nicholas II was now pope but only in name. It has been said that Nicholas was like a mule in Hildebrand's stable. He was fed everything. Hildebrand became the archdeacon and chancellor of the Church. So powerful was Hildebrand that his own ally and colleague, Peter Damiani, called Hildebrand his "Holy Satan."

One of Nicholas' first acts was to convene another synod at the Lateran. This synod again affirmed rules and regulations forbidding simony and equating clerical marriage with concubinage. Two other significant rulings were also made. The first relegated the election of popes solely to the clergy. Lay people were no longer permitted to participate in elections and the emperor was only given the right of ratification upon good behavior, thus negating his control. The papacy was no longer to be bound by the people or the emperor, thus the Church had granted itself sole authority to name the most powerful figure in medieval Europe. The fact that Henry IV was but a child doubtless allowed the synod to make such a drastic alteration, in violation of agreements cemented by previous popes themselves.

The second ruling of the council was also spurred by Hildebrand. Berengar, whose criticism of the doctrine of transubstantiation had been condemned by Leo IX, was now called before the synod to answer charges of heresy. He was apparently given a choice of death or renunciation. While he continued to hold fervently to his belief, he did not believe that it was important enough to die for. He officially repented and signed a document drafted by the synod itself, but when he left he again preached against the sacrifice of Mass. Later Berengar would stand trial a second and third time for the same offense.

The next major act of Nicholas' reign was to mark a vital change in Church policy and effect the political structure of the empire. At Hildebrand's urging Nicholas reversed the position of the previous popes and forged a powerful alliance with the Normans. Rather than making the Normans their enemies they would become vassals. The whole of Italy would fall into the empire for the first time and the Normans pledged protection against the Muslim invaders. In the years to come the Normans would prove to be great allies indeed. They took Sicily back from Islamic hands and overshadowed the Germanic rule. This naturally angered the young emperor Henry IV. For a time many German bishops even refused to acknowledge Nicholas. Meanwhile the Norman Robert Guiscard (also known as Wiscard) was named the Duke of Apulia and Calabria. He who had once imprisoned a pope (Leo IX) now solemnly swore fealty to Pope Nicholas. A final benefit of this alliance was the bond that it instantly formed with Sir William, Duke of Normandy; the future king of England.

William : Duke of Normandy

Throughout the history of the Holy Roman Empire the emperor and pope swung back and forth between supremacy and fealty to the other. Sometimes the emperor was the supreme law of the land while other generations saw the emperor as a mere vassal to the power of the pope, yet on rare occasions the power of both was usurped by a "vassal" king. So it was with one of the greatest of "vassals," William the Conqueror. But how, asked some historians, can a vassal be superior to his lord lieges? The whole idea that William the Conqueror was a subject of the Holy Roman Empire seems laughable. Indeed, it would be so if it were not for several undeniable facts; facts that contribute to the unique nature of this empire.

William the Conqueror did not seek to overthrow the empire, nor secede from it. All to the contrary, he greatly expanded it. He never came into conflict with the lands directly under the control of the emperor, and he rode into battle under the banner of the pope. Germany, Burgundy, northern Italy, and the other regions of Henry IV were never touched by William. The fact is that William the Conqueror merely sought to increase his own kingdom in regions over which the emperor had no direct control. Indeed, before he was king of England, he wasn't even a king, but a great Duke. His relations with the emperor and most of the popes were cordial and sometimes even friendly.

The truth is that just as ancient Rome became too large for one man to control, so also the Holy Roman Empire had lost effective control over the west. The emperor ruled in the east but the west, while maintaining nominal fealty, had succumbed to its local kings and lost any unity. William the Conqueror subjugated much of the western Holy Roman Empire in the same way that Charlemagne had subjugated the western Roman Empire. But did not Charlemagne create a final breach between east and west? True, but that breach was caused when Irene was usurped. William had no such problem. The pope would support William in his conquest of England and whatever bitterness the Germans might have been harbored did nothing to effect the government. Decades later when the popes called upon the kings of the west and east alike for the Crusades, they enthusiastically laid their armies, both German and Norman, at the disposal of the pope. Could there ever be more loyal vassals?

The reality is that William the Conqueror effectively divided the Holy Roman Empire into two separate sections without breaking from it. He brought England into the Empire of Many Nations and strengthened the political power of the west. From his reign onward the western Holy Empire would compete with the eastern empire for supremacy of power, although the emperor would continue to be acknowledged by both east and west. From William's day forward England and France would play an ever more increasing role in the history of the empire, and the world. German sovereignty would not relinquish easily, however.

Back in 1035 an eight years old child named William inherited the title, Duke of Normandy. He became a feudal Lord of King Henry I of France. Although born a bastard and raised surrounded by court intrigue, death, and mayhem, he would grow to be one of the most famous kings in medieval history. With so young a duke, armed body guards were placed to protect him from assassins but several of them died in front of his young eyes. Anarchy had ruled Normandy during the years and only his mother was able to protect him from conspiracies and plots to seize his duchy. In 1042 he became knighted, at fifteen years of age, but by 1046 many barons were in revolt. King Henry I of France came to young William's aid. For many years the young William would learn to fight from Henry and his soldiers. In 1049 William had been able to gain control of many of the dukes but he still needed a stronger alliance. He had successfully negotiated a marriage alliance with Baldwin of Flanders which would have given him a great ally against the dukes, but Baldwin was himself in rebellion against the emperor Henry III. Moreover, because the woman chosen for William was a distant cousin, Leo IX condemned the marriage proposal by calling it incest. William was unable to complete the marriage alliance until four years later when Baldwin was no longer a threat to the Emperor. In 1059 William funded and built two monasteries and the Norman alliance with the papacy was strengthened further.

During these years William was in constant contact with his friend and ally King Edward the Confessor of England. Edward had no children and it seemed that he would not have any children. William claimed to have gained Edward's solemn promise to make him heir to the throne following his death. Since Edward was an ally of Emperor Henry III, William's position in no way threatened his position with the empire. Whether or not William ever really obtained Edward's promise is disputed but over the next few years William would remain a close confidant of Edward.

In 1060 William conquered Maine, just outside France. His duchy, which had been in anarchy years earlier, was now easily the strongest in French territory. The Norman alliance only made his duchy stronger when news arrived of Pope Nicholas II's death in 1061.

Pope Alexander II

The death of Nicholas II set the stage for one final battle between the Hildebrandians and his enemies. The Empress Agnes was no doubt angry that the Hildebrandians had attempted to take away the rights of the emperor in selecting a pope. She nominated Peter Cadalus with the support of the Roman nobility and he was elected Pope Honorius (II). The Hildebrandians, of course, were not willing to stand by and see the see stripped from them. Using their new laws of election the Hildebrandians elected Alexander II without laity vote or Imperial approval. The Emperor's pope was backed by the Germanic armies but Hildebrand's pope was backed by the more powerful Normans. In late 1061 Norman troops forcibly installed Alexander as pope. This action only angered the general populous of Rome who were outraged at the violence of the Normans, who were still Vikings at heart. In April of 1062 Honorius' troops then met and vanquished the Norman troops that had been left behind to guard Alexander. The very next month, Godfrey arrived at Rome with a vast army. He did not, however, storm the city but nobly suggested that both popes withdraw until a German court decided the matter.

The fact that the court would be German, rather than Norman, might have been thought to favor Honorius but Godfrey was aware that Agnes' regency had been usurped by the archbishop Anno. Earlier that same year the archbishop had kidnapped Henry IV, the child emperor, and demanded that Agnes turn the regency over to him. She agreed, for love of her child, and Anno was now regent for the emperor he had kidnapped. He was also favorable to the extreme "Pataria" reform party. Naturally, Alexander won the support of Anno, but in May 1063 Honorius laid siege to Rome and was able to bar himself in the Castle St. Angelo. He was able to hold out here for several months while Alexander held yet another synod reaffirming the new stance against clerical marriage and now going so far as to forbid anyone from attending Mass where a clergyman was married. Under the new rules priests and bishops were barred from Church duties so long as they had wives, and pressure was placed on them to give up their wives.

The "reform" which had began as an attempt to purge the Church from decadence was now a political and theological war over marriage. The Hildebrandians called clerical marriage the sin of "Nicolaitism," yet the irony of this is that nothing is said of the Nicolaitans in the Bible except that they were a cultic sect of some sort. They appear only as asides in Revelation 2:6 & 15, each time being mentioned only as a heresy. Some of the Church fathers believed that the Nicolaitans were a licentious sect which is why the Hildebrandian party attached the label to clerical marriage, which they considered licentious. The irony is that 1 Timothy 4:3 condemns those who "forbid marriage." Nevertheless, the Hildebrandians were determined to root out clerical marriage despite strong opposition by married bishops and clergymen throughout Europe. Eliminating clerical marriage would not be easy.

In the meantime, the threat of Honorius still loomed large. Another synod was convened which would try both popes on charges of simony and of using force of arms to seize the tiara. The obvious bias of this synod can be seen in that Alexander was allowed to preside over the very synod which was to try him! He swore an oath to Anno, and then Honorius, who had refused to attend, was formally anathematized. Alexander II was now the undisputed pope and true Lord of the Realm.

William the Bastard Becomes William the Conqueror

In 1066 Edward the Confessor of England died without an heir. Three people now claimed the throne. Harold Hardraade III of Norway wanted to take the kingdom for himself while both William of Normandy, irreverently called William the Bastard by his enemies, and Harold of Wessex claimed to have been named the true heir by Edward, but the documents, if they ever existed, are long since gone. The fact that Harold of Wessex would have had access to any such formal declarations indicates that there either were none, for he did not produce them, or that the document had truly named William of Normandy and was hence destroyed. Regardless of whom Edward really named as his successor, if anyone, it was William of Normandy that had the support of Hildebrand and his pope, Alexander II. Hildebrand had called William his "best beloved" and Alexander sent the papal banner to William for him to carry into battle in his conquest of England.

Three armies were now ready to converge on the tiny island. Had all three armies met at once there is no telling what might have happened to English history but they did not. Harold Hardraade arrived first and fought the forces of Harold of Wessex. Harold of Wessex prevailed but his forces were diminished as a result of the battle. Three days later William arrived on the coast of England and met Harold at the Battle of Hastings. Despite the losses sustained against the Norwegian king it looked as if Harold might control the day when William's troops began to retreat. Alas, this was but a trick for once Harold's troops emerged from their entrenchments William turned and met the enemy in the open field. The outnumbered troops of Harold were now easy prey and William carried the day.

On Christmas day, 1066 William the Conqueror was crowned the king of England by three papal delegates at Westminister Abbey. The Normans now controlled England, and England had become a part of the Empire of Many Nations. Two years later, King Sancho of Aragon in Spain also delivered his kingdom up to the pope. The Holy Roman Empire now covered almost all of Europe from Hungary to Normandy. Still, had William merely conquered Britain and done nothing else, history might not have taken the path it did. The old England was still a land ripe for invasion with only small concentrations of urban life. It had several grand cities to be sure but it also had a vast rural landscape which needed to be protected and brought under control.

William set out to make Britain a modern country. Grand castle fortifications were build throughout the country. William promoted the Church and expanded its control in Britain, but he was a rebellious vassal. While he respected and honored the Church he wanted the Church free from corruption and the Church had not proven capable. He resided over synods himself and paid tribute to Rome but he did not allow the pope to interfere with his direct control of Britain. He also began to establish the feudal system in England, which had not formerly been enacted in that country. Unfortunately, while this provided better protection it also meant that the right of the people to the land was stripped of them. Land was parceled out to knights and the people became serfs. To better understand this, the feudal system itself should be examined.

Because the ancient empires had no police their only form of protection came from the emperor's, or king's, armies. Obviously injust kings or emperors left the people with no real protection at all. Tax money went to the kings and emperors, not to civil service. Consequently, the early middle ages developed a system that was, for that day, the best possible way of insuring protection on a local level. Knights were given the right to live off of the land in exchange for the protection of the people. The old land owners worked the land and gave the knight whatever he needed in exchange for his service to the people. In a way, the old knights may have been a forerunner to the modern police who live off local taxes. However, unlike the police, the right of the knights to the land eventually came to supersede the land owners. When a land owner died, it was not his son who inherited but the knight. The original land owner's son was then given permission by the knight to work the land, but the land belonged to the knight. This would soon equate the "serf," or land worker, to little more than a well treated slave. The lands were no longer his own, but the knights who protected him.

Another aspect of the feudal system was its structure which could either give the king greater control or greater enemies. Like our system of government, it was recognized that a king could not effectively control every province without regional governor, as they were called in the old Roman Empire. In the feudal system the emperor ruled over the empire, kings over their respective kingdom or country, dukes ruled over duchies, counts over counties, and below these were the barons and the knights that served under them. This allowed for tighter control of respective regions but it also created powerful dukes and counts who often rebelled against their kings. This was the situation which William's conquest of England created for his duchy in France. Normandy was officially a part of France. In regard to Normandy William continued to swear fealty to the French king Philip but he also kept a tight control on Normandy that kept it effectively under his control. Philip I of France had many problems of his own. Over the years the weak and ineffectual control of France allowed various dukes and counts to wrest effective control of their duchies or counties from the king. William was the least of Philip's concerns.

This was the great irony of France. The French kings, who had long since wrenched effective control of France away from the emperor, were now seeing their own duchies and counties stripped away from them. With the appearance of French duchies under the control on an English king conflict was sure to arise someday. Indeed, it eventually would. This situation would lead to conflicts between France and England which would continue for hundreds of years. The sons of William the Conqueror inherited not only the throne of England, but also the duchy of Normandy. As years progressed the question of whether or not Normandy was a French province or an English one would lead to the Hundred Year War and Joan of Arc.

A final piece of importance during William's reign was his attempt, began in 1086, to create The Domesday Book. This book was a detailed account of every city and town and county and shire through England. The people were not overly happy about the census. Many people resisted and there was some violence. The people viewed this as a clear attempt to decide how to increase taxation and steal land. It would take many years to complete but the Domesday Book remains the quintessential document that historians use to evaluation the society and economy of that day.

The next year the problems of an English king ruling a French Dutchy were realized when a neighboring band of Frenchmen raided Normandy. William took the field and defeated the invaders but he received a mortal wound and died on September 9, 1087.

The Last Days of Alexander II

When William the Conqueror had secured England for himself he had the support and blessing of Alexander II and the powerful monk Hildebrand. William would outlive both of them but in the twelve short years in which Hildebrand ruled as pope he was able to change the course of history more so than William. His reign was decades in the makings. He had been the true guiding force behind several previous popes including Alexander II.

Alexander's last few years were largely unproductive but they did help to set the stage for Hildebrand's ascent after him. This was particularly true because the conflict that had arisen between him and the now of age emperor Henry IV. Many of these problems could be traced back to Henry's youth. When he was a child the Empress Agnes had acted as regent but she was not a politician. She is often described as a devout unworldly woman who turned the authority of the realm over to her dukes and counts. Unfortunately, her choices were often ill–conceived. The men to whom she gave authority would later show little loyalty to her son. One of these was Rudolf, Duke of Swabia, who had married Agnes' daughter. By means of the marriage she hoped to create an ally but she also created an eventual rival to the throne. Moreover, she lost her regency when Anno kidnapped young Henry IV in 1062 and demanded that she turn the reigns of government over to him.

In 1065 Henry IV officially became of age and the following year he was married, by previous political arrangement, to a noble named Bertha. Naturally, political marriages are hard. In a polygamous society political marriages do not interfere with the king's real love life but for a monogamous society such marriages leave both hearts longing. Less than devout kings would simply hide a lover or have flings but the devout were left little choice. Henry IV decided that he wanted a divorce in 1069 but Alexander II strongly objected to it. After some minor backbiting Henry IV agreed to keep his wife and forgot about the divorce.

The second and final conflict between Henry and Alexander is the one that would have repercussions in the later rule of Hildebrand. In 1071 the archbishop of Milan had died. Henry IV, as emperors had for many generations, nominated an archbishop of his choice named Godfrey and he was consecrated by bishops who supported Godfrey. The Hildebrandian party, however, was furious. The Milanese bishops had long resisted the arguments of the Hildebrandians that forbade clerical marriage. Alexander II and Anno then selected their own Patarian bishop who would forbid marriage. When Henry and Godfrey refused to back down Alexander II took drastic steps, which would be exceeded by Hildebrand years later. Alexander II, afraid to excommunicate the emperor, instead excommunicated five of Henry's royal counselors. The antagonism between the so–called "reform" party of the Church and those who supported clerical marriage would only grow wider. The Milanese had two archbishops and the Church had created a schism. Less than two years later, in 1073, Alexander II died.

Hildebrand Becomes Pope Gregory VII

Upon Alexander II's death, in 1073, it became clear that there was only one real choice for pope. Hildebrand was a mere monk, usually considered at the low end of the totem pole as far as being nominated to the papacy, but his power was undisputed by this time. The people overwhelmingly supported his election and he is alleged to have been swept up and carried by the people of Rome. As pope he chose the name Gregory VII, after his old friend and colleague Gregory VI whom he saw as a sort of martyr for reform. This irony, since Gregory VI had been guilty of simony, has been treated and interpreted in many different ways. Indeed, there are few people in medieval history, or any other time, that have been as controversial as Gregory VII (Hildebrand). He has been revered as a Saint, which he did attain by canonization in the early seventeen century, but he was also condemned as an antichrist. His own friends spoke adulently of him yet one of his closest of friends also called him "Lord Satan."

Gregory VII, more than any other man, made the High Middle Ages. Everything in it, good and evil, might never have existed were it not for him. He clearly and indisputably elevated the papacy far above the emperor and ruled as a dictator. He hoped to subjugate all Catholics kings to himself and had a desire to reunite the east with the west. Although the crusades would not begin until after his death the crusades were originally planned by Gregory. He was the supreme power of the age. Still, his Church "reforms" brought with them not only reform but also decadence; a new kind of decadence. Theological dissension could not be tolerated in Gregory's mind. "Heresy," meaning anyone who disagreed with him, was the vilest of crimes. His militant means of enforcing his decrees set the standard for the later Inquisition and literally created "the Church Militant." Hereafter, the Church would be referred to with two separate operations. There was the "Church Triumphant" and the "Church Militant." Both terms were used by the Church themselves to refer to the spiritual Church and the earthly Church, yet this irony has not escaped many of its detractors, for the medieval Church only rarely saw the two as separate. In medieval theory, borrowed from St. Augustine, the heavenly Church reigned on earth. The line became increasingly blurred over time.

Even though Gregory VII (Hildebrand) had been one of the guiding minds behind restricting papal elections, so that lay people could not vote, he was truly made pope by the people. There is a dispute among scholars as to whether or not Gregory VII had actually asked for Imperial recognition but it seems that he did not. Gregory VII believed his commission came directly from God, and he would struggle zealously to reduce the Imperial authority.

Nevertheless, Gregory did not immediately concern himself with the emperor. The emperor was busy himself. Since Henry IV had reached age he began to try to retake control of lands effectively lost, though still nominally under his authority, when Agnes was regent. This brought Henry primarily into conflict with Rudolf, Duke of Swabia, whose marriage to Agnes' daughter made him a rival to the throne. The two did reach a treaty in 1074 but when the tomb of Henry IV's young son, who had died in childhood, was desecrated by Rudolf's supporters war again broke out. With the support of the people, outraged by the desecration, Henry was able to secure victory in 1075, and he crowned his son Conrad as heir with the support of the German princes.

As for Gregory, his early days divided between devising plans for a crusade, which he felt might be a step toward reuniting the two halves of the Roman Empire, and his "reforms." In regard to reform, the promotion of clerical celibacy was a major issue which would come to the forefront in a few years. In the meantime, Gregory hoped to establish control of all bishopries by requiring the nomination of *all* bishops to be made by him, not a king, duke, or even emperor. This was called the right of investiture, which Gregory now claimed as his own. As for the crusades, Gregory saw himself as leading the crusade personally, despite recent canon law forbidding a pope for bearing arms. Of course, Gregory often ignored laws he disliked, while creating new ones to support his own views. For example, as a monk he was very attached to the idea of clerical celibacy but the majority of bishops throughout the empire opposed such a doctrine. Bishops were married in virtually every city and county in the empire. The "worst" offenders, however, were the Milanese bishops for they were second only to Rome in authority and they resisted the Patarian edicts more than any. Only the Patarian archbishop of Milan, Anno, was a true friend to Gregory.

Despite the great number of married bishops the tide was turning in favor of Gregory and the Patarians. Ever since the previous popes had begun to promote clerical celibacy a number of bishops took wives (after lawful but private ceremonies) to live with them in secret. They feared the long arm of the pope but this did not give married priests an air of legitimacy. To the common man it looked as if the priest had something to hide. Why, if marriage is justified, do these priest hide their wives and live secretly? Why is a wife hidden like a concubine? Although some areas, like Britain, continued to hold clerical marriage ceremonies in full view of the public, the secrecy of many priestly marriages played into the hands of the pope.

Unlike the previous popes Gregory realized that forming synods and condemning clerical marriage was insufficient if the synod were unable to enforce its rules. Ever since Henry III the idea of clerical celibacy had gained significant ground and won the support of Gregorian (or Hildebrandian) synods but the majority of bishops throughout the realm, and particularly in Milan, ignored the synod. They asked, justly so, why, if this be true, did the idea of clerical celibacy not arise until the recent decades? Had not previous popes been married? Did not the priests of the Old Testament marry?

Gregory's response was to forge documents in an attempt to prove that clerical celibacy had always been canonical law. These documents were presented at a synod and by 1079 (at yet another synod) clerical celibacy, for the first time, became canonical law (even though Gregory would convince many that it had always been so). This tactic showed Gregory's mentality. He believed his goals were noble but for him, the end justified the means. If lying, forging, and even brute force were necessary for the final righteous goal, so be it! This attitude would soon turn on him, however. Even many of his closest friends would tire of his despotic rule, for forgery was but the first step. The synod would still carry no weight without enforcement. Gregory then pulled out another tool for its enforcement. First, he commissioned all counts, dukes, princesses, and kings to use force if necessary to enforce the decrees of the synod, to which Gregorian opponents had not been invited. He forbade married priests and bishops from officiating or performing their duties. Worst of all, he stirred up the uneducated peasants by warning them of the dangers of receiving mass from heretics, and threatening the masses with excommunication as well.

The result was atrocities. Some priests were castrated by mobs. Wives were dragged from their homes and charged with prostitution or put in convents. Many bishops were driven from their lands and their homes and the vilest of sins was committed; children were separated from their fathers by force. Contemporary sources mention many suicides by grieving wives and mobs ruled the day.

Even this was not sufficient or Gregory. He still needed direct control of the churches and bishops, which popes had never really had. By stripping the right of investiture away from kings and emperors he achieved part of his goal but he also had to make the clergy loyal to him, and him alone. In the name of "simony" Gregory also made it a crime for any bishop to earn a living or make money from any source other than the Church. They were also to swear an oath of loyalty to him. This too was to be enforced by kings and mobs. In only two short years Gregory had done much for his "reforms" but he had also made many enemies. His strong arm tactics and win–by–any–means mentality turned many of his own colleagues into secret enemies.

The Schism of Emperor and Pope

In 1075 a stage was set for the confrontation between Gregory and Henry. Henry had finally achieved peace in Germany and now resolved to rid himself of the corrupt archbishop. To the joy of the Milanese, he used the centuries old right of investiture to nominate a new archbishop in place of Anno, who had kidnapped Henry when he was child. Gregory was enraged. In December Gregory wrote to Henry and sternly warned him not to interfere. He compared Henry to King Saul of the Old Testament and compared himself to the Prophet Samuel. Such arrogance, however, did not suit Gregory at the time. Gregory had too many enemies already because of his militant means of rule. On Christmas day, while conducting Mass, a Roman nobleman named Cencius attacked and kidnapped the pope from the Church, but this was too much for the people. Gregory was still a pope and the Romans could not tolerate such actions so they stormed Cencius' residence and rescued the pope. By late that afternoon Pope Gregory VII was finishing mass.

In Worms Henry gathered many bishops for a synod to deal with the pope while in Pavia a group of Italian bishops gathered to condemn the pope. At this Diet of Worms in January of 1076 Henry deposed Pope Gregory with the support of twenty–six bishops who refused allegiance to the pontiff. Later that year in Pavia, the other group of bishops excommunicated the pope for illegally separating families. Gregory's response was eventually to lead Germany into civil war, for he not only excommunicated Henry but he dared to declare Henry deposed and further asserted "I forbid Henry to govern the kingdoms of Italy and Germany. I absolve all his subjects from every oath they have taken or may take; and I excommunicate every person who shall serve him as king." Gregory also excommunicated all the bishops that had dared to excommunicate him.

The result of this might have come to nought were it not for the thirst that many German princes had for power. Nobles and knights took sides. Unfortunately for Henry the countess of Tuscany, Matilda, was among his enemies. She was also his aunt. Agnes too supported the pope and was present when the deposition was made. She urged her nephew to reconcile with Gregory. In October the princes of German were ready to vote for a new king unless Henry could resolve the situation with Gregory by the first of the year. What followed would change history forever.

The winter of 1076–1077 was so cold that history says the Rhine river itself froze over. It was at that time that Henry undertook the long journey to Italy. No one seems to have known what to expect. When Henry arrived in Italy he was greeted by a large army of Lombards who offered their services to overthrow the corrupt pope, but Henry refused. He had not come to conquer but to reconcile. However, when Gregory heard that Henry had met up with these troops he assumed the worst and fled to Matilda's castle in Canossa. Upon Henry's arrival he did not lay siege to the castle but sued for peace. The pope believed he had Henry where he wanted him. He ordered Henry to strip himself of his crown and all imperial vestments, to bring them to the pope directly, to declare himself unworthy, and do penance as directed by the pope. So Henry approached the castle where he stripped down to nothing. He was given a rough scratchy tunic, which monks used to punish themselves, and told to fast and pray for forgiveness. In the cold snow of the mountains, Henry stood there barefoot for three days until he was near death. The pope still refused to forgive the emperor but Matilda, the matron of the castle herself, begged the pope. Henry would die if he stayed there any longer. It is said that even the soldiers and knights of Canossa wept for Henry and his devotion. So callous was the pope that his best friends called him a tyrant. It was not until the fourth day that Henry was brought into the castle and he was then made to swear to submit to the pope's judgment. He further was told not to exercise his authority until the pope should return his crown at a time and place to be decided by Gregory.

The humiliation did not save Henry's crown but further jeopardized it. The excommunication was lifted but the emperor had not regained his crown. In March 1077 Rudolf was elected anti–king in Henry's place with the approval of two papal delegates. Although Gregory was wise enough not to be officially involved, he refused to respond to Henry's request that he condemn the usurpation. Henry had been betrayed and civil war erupted. The Saxons supported Rudolf but the common people favored Henry. For three years war would rage and death would fill the coffers because of Gregory's pride.

The Civil War Years

When Henry went to war with Rudolf in 1077 Gregory turned his mind back to "reform" and further establishing papal control over kings and nations. He asserted his authority over many kings and used forged documents to prove that popes had always had this authority and had used it before. That very year the Countess Matilda ceded her entire county to the pope.

Gregory was, however, wise enough to know who he could push and who he could not push. In regard to the Normans Gregory was moderate. He befriended William the Conqueror and never tried to interfere too much with his realm, despite the fact that William was the one king who never seriously enforced Gregory's rules on clerical celibacy. In fact, a council in England at Westminister Abbey refused to annul the marriages of priests although it did forbid future marriage. Still, the Normans were Gregory's best allies and he could not afford to alienate them. Nevertheless, all his quest for power actually dampened the Holy Roman Empire, for he deposed the Polish king Boleslaw, and forbade them ever to even call themselves a kingdom again. From that time forward Poland would only nominally be a part of the empire. Gregory would further intervene in Byzantine politics and declared an emperor of Constantinople "deposed" (though he was not a part of the Holy Roman Empire) because he had made an alliance with Henry IV. It is only natural that the pope's interference in political sovereignty would lead to civil wars and strife in various kingdoms just as it had in Germany.

In 1079 Gregory now turned himself to the issue of "heresy." He had, by brutal means, forced clerical celibacy on bishops and now, with the help of more forged documents, introduced it into canonical law, as if it had always been there. Later that year he called forth Berengar of Tours for a third trial on the issue of transubstantiation. As had happened twice before Berengar defended his view and declared that since Christ had been crucified once for all, and because he could not be crucified all over again (cf. Romans 6 & Hebrews 6), the sacrifice of Mass could not be valid. Berengar denied that Christ was sacrificed again at Mass. With the help of still more forged documents Gregory "proved" Berengar wrong again found him guilty. Berengar was faced with death again and yet another letter of renunciation was written for Berengar. Yet again he signed it only to go forth and preach what he had renounced. This entire situation was unique. Since the Church had not yet developed the Inquisition it did not know how to deal with Berengar. The pope had condemned his view and with the precedence set by Henry a heretic could be burned but what could they do with a man who would so easily renounce his views only to go back out in the streets and preach again. The Church was attempting to reform itself, not plunge itself in tyranny. This is the irony, for the reforms of Gregory VII would bring tyranny, not true reform. Berengar was able to live out his life to a ripe old age of nearly ninety but his followers would not. Within a few decades heresy hunters would root out the Berengarians and persecution of fellow Christians would become a part of history.

In January 1080 Rudolf's soldiers dealt Henry a critical blow. Henry was defeated and Gregory now believed it was safe to officially endorse Rudolf for the crown. In March 1080 he again excommunicated Henry and backed Rudolf as the rightful heir to the throne. Gregory further had the audacity to utter a "prophecy" that within months Henry would die or surrender. The prophecy was false for it was Rudolf who died, not Henry. The army of Henry had lost another decisive battle at the Battle of Elster but Rudolf had his hand cut off in battle and died later that day from blood loss. The rebels had no king. They would eventually elect Hermann to succeed Rudolf as their claimant to the throne but Hermann was weak and Henry was again the effective ruler. He was now able to turn his attentions to the despotic vicar.

In June 1080 Henry held his own council composed of many deposed and excommunicated bishops who opposed the ruthless rule of Gregory. They officially deposed Gregory VII and elected Guibert as pontiff in his stead, under the name Clement (III). Even Clement's enemies admit that he was a man above reproach. He commanded the respect of many men but it was his staunch opposition to the tactics of Gregory that had earned him excommunication from that pope. For the next sixteen years Clement would reign as pope, but the Gregorian Popes also remained. It is a testament to the weakness of Henry IV and the strength of the Normans that the Gregorians won out, and the middle ages would plunge into tyranny.

For now Henry had to make his pope legitimate and reclaim his crown from Gregory, who still held the diadem he had taken at Canossa. In the spring Henry marched into Italy and defeated the Countess Matilda's troops. He was then able to continue on directly to Rome unopposed. When he arrived, however, he was surprised to find that the Romans were unwilling to open the gates for him. Gregory had many enemies but he still had many supporters and the Romans were among his most loyal. Henry was forced to retreat until he could return with a larger siege army. That army returned in 1081 and 1082 but withdrew both times. Sieges were long tedious tasks and often involved starving the besieged out. In this case, however, Henry did not want to alienate his own subjects so there was restraint used in the siege. This is probably one reason that the siege was never completely finished until March of 1084 when his troops entered the city. Gregory retreated to the castle St. Angelo where he prepared for another siege but Henry was content with the crown, knowing that Gregory could not escape. It was arranged for Gregory to lower Henry's crown down on a long rope from the castle top. After retrieving his diadem Clement was officially installed and consecrated as the new pope. A week later Clement officially crowned Henry the Holy Roman Emperor.

Their victory was, nevertheless, short–lived for, in May, Henry learned that Gregory's Lord Protector, Robert Guiscard, was approaching from the south with an army of over thirty–five thousand men and both he and Pope Clement bid a hasty retreat. Ironically, but poetically, what followed would only cement Henry's claim to the throne and lead to Gregory's exile and disgrace.

Robert Guiscard : Guardian of the Pope

Robert Guiscard was a Norman mercenary when he first set foot in Italy decades before. His military tactics amounted to raids on villages and pillaging while he took the citizens hostage and ransomed them for money. He was a harsh leader whose Viking heritage still showed through, even though his nominal Christian faith restrained some of the more savage aspects of the Viking heritage. Still, the fear which the Normans inspired is obvious by the fact that Pope Gregory VII himself had originally considered Guiscard a dreaded enemy and had excommunicated him for pillaging too near the Papal domain.

Despite his barbaric nature, Guiscard was a wise politician and knew how to seize power without the sword, as well as with it. In 1080 he vastly solidified his position by marrying his daughter to the Byzantine Prince Constantine, son of Emperor Michael VII, and he also reconciled himself with Pope Gregory VII by taking his side against Henry IV on investiture. It was worth it for Guiscard to surrender his right to appoint bishops in exchange for a chance at becoming the Papal protector. However, his plans for Byzantium were thwarted when a usurpation occurred and Michael VII was overthrown and deposed. The new emperor did not trust Guiscard and imprisoned his daughter Helen, the princess, in hopes of keeping Guiscard in line. Instead, Guiscard invaded the Byzantine Empire with hopes of making himself emperor.

Robert Guiscard had managed to put the empire on the defensive and landed on the shores of Epirus when his invasion was called off. The Pope needed help against Henry IV. This was 1083 and Guiscard was forced to obey.

120

If he neglected his duty to the pope he would surely lose Italy. Guiscard decided that the Byzantines would have to wait.

If the old Holy Roman Empire was a Germanic empire, as many claim, then surely the western segment of the Holy Roman Empire was a new Norman empire. The Normans were quickly rising to become masters of the empire. The Germans would continue to dominate the eastern Holy Roman Empire, but the Normans could now be said to be the master of the western Holy Roman Empire, including southern Italy. They were still but one empire, but the dangers of splitting into two separate empires was real at this time. The struggle between the German emperors and the popes would determine the outcome and this was to be but the first battle. The result of the battle could be anticipated by none for there was no literal battle and the Norman victory turned into a German one by virtue of the atrocities the Normans committed upon the innocent Romans.

At the end of May 1084 Gregory's protector finally arrived with a massive army of over thirty–five thousand men. The army itself was a mixture of mercenaries including Lombards, Normans, Apulians, and even Saracen Muslims. With Henry's retreat, however, the army was starving for "action" and action they got. If the enemy was gone then they had won a victory and Rome was the spoils. After reinstalling Gregory VII in the Lateran Guiscard's men engaged in an age old pagan tradition. "To the victor goes the spoils." As had happened since ancient times, and was preserved among the Muslims, though softened in the Christian age by Charlemagne and his successors, the victor had the right to take anything from the conquered city. In Islamic tradition rape was a rite of conquest just as the old pagan civilization had done. Now the Norman Guiscard, still a Viking at heart, unleashed his men.

Women, including nuns, were raped. Buildings, homes, and even churches were pillaged and destroyed. Thousands of citizens were sold into slavery. Death and mayhem raged yet the greatest proof of the evils wrought on Rome in those days is the destruction, waste, and ruins of the great city itself. So severe was the destruction that literally half of the city was said to lay in ruins. For decades after the rampage history recounts pilgrims despairing at the ruins of Rome left behind by the Norman raiders. The people who were fortunate enough to survive saw this as a judgment from God. The great city which once boasted over a million residents now dwindled to under twenty thousand. After the brigands had left, Gregory and Guiscard were forced out of Rome by the people themselves.

The Fall of Gregory/Hildebrand

Not long after the atrocities of Rome Gregory would die alone in exile. His last words are alleged to have been "I have loved righteousness and hated iniquity; therefore I die in exile." Yet one of this allies noted the hypocrisy of such a self–righteous remark, noting, "how in exile if the whole world is thine?"

Such was Gregory. Like many other controversial figures in history Gregory has drawn a mixture of admiration and hatred from scholars. Ironically, Gregory VII is revered by some evangelical Protestant historians while he is equally vilified by some Catholic historians. He was canonized by Rome in 1606 to the protest of many. The last emperor of the Holy Roman Empire, Napoleon Bonaparte, is quoted as having said that if he could not have been himself he would have liked to have been Gregory VII.

In these last days the pope showed his usual mixture of mercy and arrogance. He officially absolved all his enemies with the exception of Henry and Clement whom he damned, and there seems little doubt that he truly believed he could do this. In a letter to William the Conqueror, Gregory implies that he is able to answer for William's sins and serve as intermediary between him and God. Gregory most literally set himself up in the place of Christ. In previous generations the pope was only known as the "Vicar of Peter," but beginning with Gregory VII the papacy would be called the "Vicar of Christ," paving the way for many theologians and scholars from the twelfth century up to the Reformation that would call the pope "antichrist." This is not to say that these men, discussed in the coming chapters, believed that the pope was *the* antichrist, as is sometimes erroneously supposed, but that he was *an* antichrist. According to 1 John 2:2, an antichrist was anyone who set himself up in the place of Christ. This Gregory had done by claiming to be the sole spokesman for Christ.

It is of the strongest irony that this man, who had hoped to make the whole world part of a Holy Christian Empire, actually dealt the Holy Roman Empire its severest wounds at a time when it was reaching its heights. His arrogant treatment of the king of Poland resulted in Poland's effectual loss to the Holy Roman Empire from Gregory's reign onward. Although the German Emperors would continue to hold a grip on Poland, and they would remain nominally a part of the empire, they had been alienated by the papacy and would increasingly distance themselves from the empire's authority. Moreover, Gregory, by his arrogance and alienation of Henry IV, lost a prime chance to see Kiev Rus, later to become Russia, brought into the empire. After Henry's wife, Bertha, died he took a Kiev princess as his bride but the antagonism that Henry and the Gregorian popes had instigated would carry on. Eventually Kiev would become Greek Orthodox, and break into its own Russian Orthodox Church. Russia would never become a Catholic country. Had Gregory, and his successors, worked with the kings and the emperor, the Holy Roman Empire might have stretched clear into Asia, without a sword ever having been lifted.

The truth is that Gregory may have known himself that the power of the papacy was too great for him. He is alleged to have desired never to have become pope, because he knew he would use that power to its fullest extent.

Gregory VII had been a monk and much of his theology came from that fact. Monks flogged themselves and abstained from all worldly things. As a monk he was celibate and in his mind, if celibacy was good enough for him it was good enough for everyone. Gregory believed that all priests should behave as monks. His stern discipline came from the abuses which he cast upon himself. Monastacism had itself evolved from eastern monasticism, which had borrowed from Gnosticism and the belief that the body was evil; a hindrance to the spiritual. The fervor with which Hildebrand the monk punished himself was now the same fervor with which he now pushed upon the clergy at large.

There is no doubt that Gregory sincerely believed he was doing what was right but he also believed that the end justified the means, and it was in this way that he paved the path for the Crusades and the Inquisition. He used force, threats, excommunications, and forgery as a means to an end. Among his forgeries were documents produced that claimed both Pope Gregory I and Pope Innocent I had deposed previous emperors, which they had not, and the infamous Pseudo–Isidorian Decretals which were heavily circulated at that time. In this *Decretum*, or Code of Canon Law, which fell into use from his time onward scholars have now proven that of three hundred and twenty five quotations from popes of the first four centuries, only eleven are legitimate. All the rest are fabrications or alterations. These documents and others were the means by which Gregory, and later popes, could claim that the Catholic Church had not changed since the time of Christ! They simply changed the facts to fit what they wanted.

This belief, that the ends justified the means, stemmed from Gregory's self–righteousness. He truly believed that he was a Saint and even declared as much. While he did not directly claim inerrancy for himself he did declare that the Church could not, and *never has*, erred. Since Gregory had to forge records to prove that this Church agreed with him, his hypocrisy seems obvious. Nevertheless, his view of the papacy set them above every man on earth. The pope, so he believed, could not be judged by any man and his judgment was final in all matters. So great was his esteem for himself that he even declared that he had the right of intercession for man's sins. As briefly aforementioned, in a letter addressed to William the Conqueror, Gregory wrote "if I am to answer for you on the dreadful day of judgment before the just Judge ... do you not think that I must very diligently provide for your salvation."

So then did Gregory really believe that he had the power to save men's souls or damn them? It would seem that he did. So Gregory single–handedly changed the course of history and brought about the most abrasive hierarchy of the High Middle Ages. This first "reformation" of the Church ended the sexual hijinx of immature and insecure popes and replaced them with a self righteous breed of tyrants. The Inquisition, the Crusades, and the corrupt power of the Church were to be his legacy, though he did not live to see them. The end *does not* justify the means.

Holy Roman Emperor	Pope	AntiPope (if any)
──────── 1002 ────────	──────── 999 ──────── Sylvester II	
	──────── 1003 ──────── John XVII	
	──────── 1003 ──────── John XVIII	
Saint Henry II of Bavaria	──────── 1009 ──────── Sergius IV	
	──────── 1012 ──────── Benedict VIII	*Gregory (VI)* *─1012─*
──────── 1024 ────────	──────── 1024 ──────── John XIX	
Conrad II	──────── 1032 ──────── Benedict IX	
──────── 1039 ────────		
	──────── 1045 ──────── Sylvester III	*Benedict IX*
	──────── 1045 ──────── Gregory VI	
	──────── 1046 ──────── Clement II	
Henry III	──────── 1047 ──────── Benedict IX	
	──────── 1048 ──────── Damasus II	
	──────── 1048 ──────── Leo IX	
	──────── 1054 ──────── ──────── 1055 ────────	
──────── 1056 ────────	Victor II	
	──────── 1057 ──────── Stephen IX (X)	
	──────── 1058 ──────── *Benedict X*	
Henry IV (Early regents were Agnes & Anno)	──────── 1059 ──────── Nicholas II	
	──────── 1061 ──────── Alexander II	*Honorius (II)* *─1072─*
	──────── 1073 ────────	

9
—

The Age of the Crusades Begins

The death of Gregory VII seemed at first to bring some peace and stability to the realm. Even Robert Guiscard, the pope's Lord Protector, died a few months later during a siege against the Byzantine Empire. Pope Clement (III) was invited back to Rome where the people eagerly accepted him, but the Normans were not content to let this be the end of the story. Gregory VII had been the best of Norman allies and the Normans saw Clement as nothing more than a German puppet. Had the Normans been willing to accept Clement, Gregory might have been just another sour footnote in history but they were not. The Normans soon elected their own popes and upon the ascension of Urban II the Gregorian popes would overshadow the Clementine popes. It was with Urban II that the Crusades began and the history of Europe changed forever.

Before the Crusades

The passing of Gregory and Clement's installation in Rome gave Henry IV the legitimacy of rule that he had hoped for all these many years. Only the weak rival Hermann caused Henry IV trouble but Hermann was unable to gain the military victories or support that his predecessor Rudolf had. In Southern Italy the death of Robert Guiscard threw Norman Italy into a power struggle between two brothers; Roger and Bohemund. In the meantime, the Norman prince Jordan of Capua was able to gain enough stability to try to reinstall a Gregorian pope.

After a full year Jordan pressured Gregory's supporters into nominating a new pope, ignoring Clement (III)'s legitimacy. They chose Victor III, who had been a close friend of Gregory's despite some public disputes. The people of Rome, however, were not about to allow any such usurpation. They remembered the last time the Normans had come to install a pope against Clement and they had not forgotten. The ruins and crumbled buildings still remained as a testament to the barbarity of the Normans. Clement was the true pope and the Romans would accept no other. Rioting and violence cropped up in the city and Victor fled for his life before being consecrated. For a time Victor was content to accept the failure and live quietly as a monk but the Normans were not. A year later in March Jordan of Capua put pressure on Victor to convene a synod in Capua, his own abode. The synod, of course, recognized Victor as the true pope and declared Clement an impostor. It was now up to Jordan and other Gregorian allies to enforce the synod's ruling.

The political situation was difficult. Jordan did not want a repeat of Robert Guiscard's affair in Rome but there was no doubt that a pope could not be recognized as legitimate unless he was consecrated and was ruling from Rome. A siege would take years and would surely send Henry IV to Clement's rescue, but Jordan had to gain access to the city in order to make Victor's ascension official. His troops decided that St. Peter's Cathedral was sufficient for his cause because St. Peter's was not enclosed in the main city. It had at one time lain beyond the walls of Rome but was later enclosed by a new wall to protect it from invaders. This new section of Rome was called the "Leonine City." Jordan resolved to lay siege to this section of Rome and then use St. Peter's as Victor's palace. The plan worked. By May Jordan's forces were able to penetrate the Leonine section of the city without breaching the main walls of Rome. Victor was consecrated but Clement's own troops lay within Rome and fighting immediately broke out over control of Leonine. Victor fled but was urged to return by the Countess Matilda, one of Gregory's greatest allies. With her assistance Victor's place in St. Peter's seemed assured but in July Victor heard rumors that Henry IV was returning to Rome to assist Clement. Once again Victor fled, but this time he would never return. Stricken by a serious illness he died in September.

It had seemed that the position of Henry IV and Clement was secure but they underestimated the will power of the Normans. It would be almost another year before another Gregorian pope would be elected but this one, Urban II, would eventually prevail. Though he would die while Clement still lived, it was he whose rule established the Gregorian line of popes, and it was he who called forth the first Crusade.

The Rise of Pope Urban II & the Call to Crusade

All seemed well for Henry IV in 1087. He crowned his son, Conrad, king and had seen Victor III's bid for the papal tiara fail but in 1088 the Gregorians, with Norman backing, again elected another pope, Urban II. In terms of history there seems little doubt that Clement was recognized by all but the Gregorian party and the Normans of Italy as the true pope. Victor III and Urban II by all rights appear to have been antipopes, but history shapes reality. Modern Catholic canons and historians all call Clement (III) antipope and list both Victor III and Urban II as true popes. Those who lived at the time, however, knew that who was the antipope and who was legitimate would depend upon the events of the next decade.

It was to be many months before the Normans and Gregorians again felt strong enough to elect another pope and even then they were forced to elect him south of Rome. This new pope, Urban II, realized that his papacy depended on his ability not only to establish himself in Rome but also to win over the kings, dukes, and counts of the Holy Roman Empire. This would not be an easy task, but by winning over kings it would be an easier task to win the support of that king's dukes and counts. In Italy Urban already had the support of the Norman dukes as well as the Countess Matilda. In Germany the followers of Hermann lent their support as well. Urban resolved to strengthen the bond between his allies in Italy and those in Germany. One of Henry's most hated enemies in Germany was Guelph of Bavaria. Urban arranged for a marriage between him and Matilda, creating a powerful political force. This marriage was strictly political and when it ended in divorce in 1095 Urban offered no criticism.

The importance of the marriage alliance went far beyond the reign of Urban II and Henry IV, for the Guelphite party became strong advocates of papal theocracy for centuries. Their enemies, the Ghibellines, favored a mild form of separation of church and state. The two parties would war with one another, often literally, for many centuries. For the time being it merged two armies and two powerful political figures. Urban's next step was to expand this support by establishing himself in Rome. Unlike the situation during the reign of Victor III, the Normans were able to penetrate the city of Rome and establish Urban. This, combined with Urban's affirmation of Gregory VII's decree against investiture, led Henry IV to plan to rid himself of the "antipope."

In 1090 Henry entered Italy and began his march to Rome. Matilda and the Normans provided Urban with ample defense but Urban still felt safer outside Rome. The war continued until Henry suffered a severe defeat in 1092. This occasion further created the belief that Henry was a weak emperor, and in 1093 after Hermann died his followers were looking for a new rival. Urban made his move. He prompted Conrad, Henry IV's son, to set himself up as king. Conrad agreed and was crowned the king of Italy, under the Countess Matilda's protection. Henry IV now was forced to deal with a rebellious son, leaving Urban II relative freedom to act in Rome. The tide was now shifting. In 1094 Urban II gained possession of the Lateran with lavish bribes. Clement (III) was betrayed for profit and forced to retreat to the Castle St. Angelo.

With Urban II now in possession of the Lateran his position in Rome seemed relatively secure. Fighting would continue between Clement's troops and Urban's, like the Chicago mobs of the twenties, but Urban now resided at the proper papal palace. The Norman dukes of Italy, Matilda and Guelph, and now Conrad of Germany supported Urban II. Only the French and British provinces needed to be won over (the Spanish were too concerned with the Moors in Spain to play a sizable role in the politics of the pope and only Aragon was recognized as a part of the Empire). England was Urban's next challenge. Upon William the Conqueror's death the lands of Britain and Normandy were split between his two sons. Robert took over the lands across from the English channel while William II became king of England. The Normans were already close allies of Urban but William II had been neutral toward Urban. Urban began serious negotiations with William II to secure his support. After much discussion Urban willingly surrendered many concessions to William including the requirement of royal permission for papal legates to enter England. This concession gave England much freedom from the tyranny of later popes for a time, although the archbishops of Canterbury soon took the effectual place of papal legates in the enforcement of papal rulings.

With Britain falling into line, only France remained but France would be more difficult. King Philip I had divorced his wife, to live in sin with Bertrada, the wife of Count Fulco. The scandal had rocked the king of France since it first occurred in 1092. In October of 1094 a synod had excommunicated Philip as another one did in 1095. As an excommunicated king Philip needed the support of at least one pope to keep his already weak throne stable. Urban was willing to override the synods' decision and lift his excommunication if he would return to his old wife, or at least this was the *official* condition. The real bargain was doubtless a lifting of excommunication in exchange for Philip's support of Urban against Clement. This occurred not long after Urban's call for the Crusades which occurred in Clermont, France.

Thus, by 1095 Urban had succeeded in wresting support from Clement in Italy, parts of Germany, France, Normandy, and even Britain. He promised Conrad, Henry's rebellious son, the imperial crown in exchange for an oath of fealty which he gave that year.

Urban was now strong enough to convene a synod in Piacenza, Lombary. This synod was held in the open field because it was attended by over four thousand clergy and allegedly over thirty thousand laymen. First, Urban brought forth the second wife of Henry IV, a Kiev (Russian) Princess, whom Henry had married after the death of his first wife. There she recounted Henry's deviant sexual acts upon her person and defamed his character. Henry was made to look like a vile despot whose own wife shuddered at the thought of him. After hearing the charges (no rebuttal was permitted) Henry and pope Clement were damned. The "sins" of simony and Nicolaitism were reaffirmed and Berengar, who still preached against the doctrine of transubstantiation, was again condemned as a heretic. However, unlike previous popes, Urban II now declared that heretics could be tortured and burned. Soon the followers of Berengar would find themselves the victims of this edict. Berengarians were first persecuted in mass about 1099 or 1100. Those who were not executed were exiled. These persecutions, the first of many which would follow, should be the first true examples of Protestant forerunners.

The success of the synod in Piacenza led to another synod in November 1095 at Clermont. At this synod Urban first raised the call to the Crusades. For many centuries the once great Eastern Roman Empire, or Byzantine Empire, had been slowly beaten back by Muslims. The Saracens and Seljuk Turks ravaged the lands that had once belonged to the Romans and, despite all the political turmoil and dissension between Constantinople and Rome, the two were still allies. There was a brotherhood felt between the Holy Roman Empire and the

Byzantine Empire. This bond was in part because they were Christians, even as the Holy Roman Empire was nominally Christian, but this bond was also because they both secretly dreamed of reuniting the empires into one Roman Empire again, as it had been hundreds of years earlier. Indeed, even when skirmishes and battles raged between the two there were almost always negotiations ongoing which discussed the reunification of the empires. From Charlemagne, who had sought to unify the two empires, that he had himself divided, by a marriage proposal to Empress Irene, to Urban's nemesis Clement (III) the empires always discussed reunification, though it remained a distant dream.

Now Urban called forth all Christians to defend their brethren against the Muslim heretics who had desecrated the Holy Land and murdered their Christian brothers. Although some have criticized the very idea of a Crusade, the Crusade, like many wars, was a mixture of justice and politics; good and evil. The Seljuk Turks had come into possession of the land by conquest and these Muslims were unlike any who had preceded them. Their savagery and cruelties made even Muslim citizens despise them. They turned on their own Islamic brothers and, when they took the land from the Saracen Muslims (who had taken the land from the Byzantines), they wreaked evils that the Byzantine Emperor and Pope were only too eager to recount in order that the spirits of the west might be stirred up against them. Stories were told, probably true, not only of desecration, rape, and murder, but of the most heinous of tortures and blasphemy. Christians were forced to urinate in baptismal pools while others had their veins cut open and were forced to be baptized in their own blood. Not only were women raped but homosexual rape of boys and priests was reported by the east as well. Turks were said to place bets on how many strikes it would take to cut off a Christian's head. Among the worst of horrors, which was no doubt true, was a torture where a Christians stomach was cut open and their intestines pulled out like a rope while they still lived. The intestines were tied to a pole and the Christians were forced to walk around the pole until they died or until their entire intestines fell out.

Such atrocities cannot be doubted. While Christians had once been able to visit the Holy Land during Muslim occupation, the invasion of the Turks made this impossible. The Turks were not considered heretics but pagans. The west forwent their wars with one another for a war against the pagans. It was a spirit that seemed noble and just. The idea of the Crusade stirred up images of King Arthur legends and medieval chivalry but there were, even at this time, several things that hinted at the terror to come. Urban, like Gregory before him, seemed to believe he had the power to absolve sins. Consequently, he promised that any and all who went on the Crusades would be absolved of their sins, whatever those sins might be. This made the Christian Crusaders little different from the Muslims who were promised instant translation to Paradise if they died in a *Jihad*. Implicitly, however, it also meant, if they were assured of salvation, that they could commit any sins they wished in the meantime. As Church Historian Philip Schaff put it, the Crusades called forth the most noble and great warriors of Europe, but it also called forth the worst elements; murderers, rapists, vagabonds, thieves, and lowlifes. So it would be. The Crusades began as a noble call to defend Christian brothers evolved into a despicable political power play with men whose souls were now free from conscience and whose deeds rivaled those of the ancient barbarians. The Knights exchanged their shining armor for armor rusted with blood stains and their chivalry for a barbarian spirit.

The Peasant's Crusade

The Crusades had been in the making for centuries. The Muslims had first taken Jerusalem from the Byzantine empire back in the seventh century but the Saracens knew the advantages of politics. When the Islamic Dynasty was in its golden age pilgrims were permitted to visit the city and both Christians and Jews, with limited freedom, were allowed to live within its walls. Nevertheless, as with all great empires, the Muslims soon began to war among themselves. The Shi'ite sect created a faction which was pitted against the Orthodox Sunnis. Although the Shi'ites are often erroneously referred to as "fundamentalists" they were, in fact, a new sect or cult of Islam different from the fundamentals of traditional or orthodox Islam.

In Persia the Seljuk Turks conquered Bagdad and turned on their own Muslim allies. They savagely conquered Syria and the Holy Land, taking it from the Saracens. Christians were persecuted in heinous ways and pilgrims were no longer safe. It was the eleventh century when Christians and Muslims alike cried out against the brutal oppression of the Turks. As long as Christians had been allowed to live in the Holy Land and pilgrims were permitted to visit unmolested the Byzantine Empire was on good terms with their Muslim neighbors but with the Turks all that changed. The boundaries of the Byzantine Empire were driven back to within fifty miles of Constantinople itself and cries of all the people of Syria and Palestine went out to Europe, for the Byzantines were no longer strong enough to defend them.

So fervent was the call to the Crusades that many of Henry IV's most loyal knights left to be a part of it. Henry himself was silent and said nothing to discourage his knights from the undertaking. Indeed, the Crusades seemed to grow far beyond the dispute of who was the true pope. In fact, when Robert, Duke of Normandy, led his army through Rome he ignored the pleas of Urban's troops, who requested assistance in overthrowing Clement. The Crusade was for the cause of Christianity, not the papacy. The call stirred up in people visions and prophecies, but not all were fooled. Many came to believe the Crusades to be a curse but the majority wholeheartedly embraced it. There can be no doubt that the people knew and believed in their hearts that history was about to change. The whole course of human history would be altered; they just didn't realize how it would change.

The First Crusade was primarily made up of two separate segments. The first segment was the real military Crusaders made up of Knights, Counts, and Dukes. These were the real soldiers. The second element, however, has become known as the "Peasant's Crusade." This was the more notorious segment that was doomed to failure.

The so–called Peasant's Crusade had been created largely at the instigation of Peter the Hermit, a mad sort of monk who paraded around Europe looking like an Old Testament Prophet. He was a short unkempt man who rode barefoot on a donkey. To the modern mind he was but a bum. To the medieval mind he was like John the Baptist who wore camel skin clothes and was "a voice crying in the wilderness." Peter gained a large following, but his "soldiers" were neither warriors, nor organized. This segment was composed of the most uneducated, illiterate, and superstitious people. It was also comprised of murders, rapists, thugs, and cut throats who went along in search of bootie and fun. They had no discipline and took few provisions. Estimates of the size of the army have varied but the lowest suggest that Peter the Hermit personally led at least twenty thousand men while four other peasant armies followed. It should be obvious that with such large numbers and few provisions the peasants would survive only by pillaging and plundering.

Because the peasant armies were poor and uneducated they could see no need to wait or organize. They were the first to leave on the Crusade while dukes and knights spent time putting their affairs in order and making preparations for the long journey. These peasants, however, did not even realize how long the journey would take. They set out in April of 1096.

Now these peasant armies were comprised of five separate divisions each of whom went their own separate ways. The first division to leave was that of Walter the Penniless. They chose to take the path through Hungary and its king, Coloman, was more than willing to allow passage through his country. The army made it all the way to the border of the Byzantine Empire before any trouble started but when they arrived there the Byzantine commander at Belgrade asked them to await orders. The peasants found themselves unwilling to wait and began to pillage the nearby Hungarian cities. They were met by Hungarian soldiers and death was the inevitable result. Soon order was restored and Walter's army was sent on to Constantinople but not far behind him was Peter the Hermit himself.

When Peter arrived at the Hungarian border Coloman had agreed to allow him passage but warned him that pillaging would be met with the severest of punishment. Again they crossed the country with little difficulty until they reached the border near Belgrade. The Hungarians remembered the pillaging of Walter's men and relations were therefore poor to begin with. When the Byzantines again asked Peter to await orders the peasants became restless. It is alleged the actual rioting and violence began over an argument concerning the price of shoes. Whatever the cause violence erupted soon enough. Over four thousand Hungarians were killed and the store houses were plundered. Houses were stripped of their wood so the peasants could make rafts to cross the river into the Byzantine Empire and when they arrived they proceeded to pillage and destroy Belgrade itself. The people of Belgrade had abandoned the city and fled to the mountains while the entire city was soon set aflame by Peter's army.

Despite the destruction that was caused, the Byzantine Empire showed generosity. Once Peter regained some control of his men, the Byzantine commander had sent word that provisions and a "military escort" would be forthcoming. However, hostages were taken from Peter's army to ensure no further pillaging would take place.

Back in Germany three other peasant armies remained. These armies were led by Volkmar, Gottschalk, and the notorious Emich. These armies may have had a small admixture of knights and nobles but they were largely peasant armies, none of whom would even manage to survive to make it to the Byzantine Empire. The first, and most notorious, of these armies was that of Count Emich. An anti–Semite, Emich had come to hate Jews.

Ever since Charlemagne Jews had come to Germany to find freedom. Although Jews did not have full rights and privileges they were favored by Charlemagne and were granted their own duchies. Because of their high education they had become the bankers and money lenders of the middle ages, hence the stereotype of the money grubbing Jew. It has often been said that this was the true reason for anti–Semitism for as the average peasant found himself more and more poor, he also found himself more and more in financial debt to Jewish bankers. Taxation was not nearly as bad as it is in this day and age (although it was bad enough) so the peasants blamed the Jews for their poverty the way that later generations would blame taxes. To the uneducated it seemed as if the Jews controlled all the money in Europe and the high interest rates they charged only angered the commoner more. Consequently, accusations of the "Christ killers" came as an attempt to justify hatred for Jews but the real reasons were quite different.

The Jews were well aware of increasing dislike toward them and they were also well aware of Emich's opinions. They wisely sought an audience with Henry IV who made all the Crusaders promise to protect the Jews and cause them no harm. Unfortunately, Emich made no such pledge and his peasant army was not made up of nobles. While Peter the Hermit's army was nearing the border to the Byzantine Empire Emich decided to attack a Jewish village near Spier. The Bishop of Spier, however, took the Jews under his protection and forbade any aggression. Twelve Jews had died before the Bishop was able to safeguard them and the murderers' hands were cut off in punishment.

This did little to deter Emich who doubtless bore a grudge. As his army approached the city of Worms the Jews of that city were not spared.

Although the Bishop of Worms also tried to provide protection Emich's men showed respect neither for Jews nor the right of sanctuary. Many Jews had taken refuge in the Church itself under the Bishop's protection but the men broke into Church and slaughtered the Jews in the very sanctuary of God. Over five hundred Jews died in Worms.

Word of the onslaught and the deeds of Emich soon reached the ears of the Archbishop of Mainz, Rothard, and when Emich arrived at Mainz he found the gates of the city closed. Still, Emich had friends inside Mainz who managed to open the gates a day later. Emich stormed the city and laid siege to the Archbishop's palace itself. Rothard was forced to flee and the Jews of Mainz were slaughtered by the thousands. By now Jews throughout Germany were fleeing to their Christian friend's homes in hopes that they would hide them. Other Jews fled to the palaces of the Archbishops or other bishops. Many Jews lives were spared by the protection provided by these Christian men and women, as well as by the Church itself, but Emich continued to wreck havoc across Germany. His army slowly made its way to Hungary, pillaging the countryside and murdering Jews wherever they encountered them.

Volkmar's army had not been as fractious as Emich's but they heard of, and took inspiration from, Emich's actions. When they arrived in Prague, now a part of Czeckoslavokia, they began to murder Jews and fight with the civil authorities who tried to prevent the attacks. Volkmar then moved on to Hungary where Coloman, already upset with the previous Crusader's ventures, did not wait long. As soon as Volkmar's men began pillaging they were set upon by the Hungarian soldiers and routed.

The final peasant army was led by a monk named Gottschalk. His army too had persecuted Jews in defiance of both the Emperor and the Church. Like Volkmar, his army was given permission to pass through Hungary so long as they behaved themselves. They did not and they were massacred by the Hungarian army. Only Emich's peasant army remained of the three and it had been slowed in progress by its unauthorized excursions against the Jews. When Emich finally arrived at the Hungarian border Coloman was unwilling to allow Emich passage under any circumstances. Emich then attacked the Hungarians and, being a Count, had enough knowledge and skill to prepare a siege against a relatively unguarded castle near the border. Despite his military prowess, his army was still made up of peasants, vagabonds, and cutthroats. The army of Emich soon fell to the Hungarians.

Many Christians saw the failure of Emich, Volkmar, and Gottschalk as proof of divine judgment for the treatment they had shown the Jews, and those who protected them. Others believed that the judgment was cast upon the whole Crusades. Of the first, there is no doubt. The persecution of Jews was neither sanctioned by the Church nor the emperor and angered most all who heard of it. The failure of these last three armies to even reach Byzantium illustrates the folly of the entire peasant's crusade. Surely even Peter's army was destined for failure.

Peter could no longer expect any more peasant armies to arrive but he was having enough trouble with his own. As they crossed the Empire toward Constantinople Imperial guards watched to make sure that the army stayed in line. Despite this the undisciplined armies of Peter still engaged in pillaging and mayhem which led to conflicts with the Byzantine soldiers. At one point a full scale battle erupted and Peter was forced to flee, along with five hundred men, up a mountainside. After the battle was over Peter met up with the survivors. Over a quarter of the army had died in the battle.

Again, the Byzantine Emperor was willing to forgive the army. He needed their help and was in no position to start a war with so many foreign troops in the very midst of the empire. When the army finally reached Constantinople Peter was called before the eastern Emperor Alexius Comnenus. It was obvious to the emperor that neither the army nor its leader were prepared to fight a real war against the Turks but it was equally obvious that the troops could not remain in Constantinople or its suburbs. Rioting, theft, murder, and vandalism was already being reported. The emperor suggested that Peter move his troops further east and await the arrival of the real western armies. Peter was wise enough to agree but the peasants were not and would not wait long for help to arrive.

Walter the Penniless had died shortly after arriving at Constantinople so Peter absorbed his army and together with his own moved east toward Nicaea, which was in Muslim hands. As Peter's army moved east they became more and more savage. Although Christians still lived in many of the lands the peasant army treated the inhabitants equally; with utter cruelty. Without regard for Christian or Muslim the peasant army not only pillaged the countryside but, starving for food, were said to have roasted babies on spits. Personal disputes and animosity increased among the army and Peter's authority was in question. As hostilities increased the army was fragmented. One group chose to follow Rainald who was one of the few nobles that had come with army.

In the summer, before all of the real armies of the Crusade had even left Europe, Rainald's men besieged and captured a relatively undefended castle at Xerigordon. The Turks immediately responded. The water wells which provided the castle were cut off and Rainald's men were dying of thirst. Some cut open their horses and drank their blood while others drank urine to survive. Rainald was forced to surrender but the Turks promised only to spare those who renounced Christianity and convert to Islam. Rainald obliged and the Turks took the castle. Some renounced their faith while others were executed. The vast numbers of the army that Peter once held were now dwindling hopelessly. Peter the Hermit left those who had been loyal to him and went back to Constantinople to seek help. He would never return to these men for they would be slaughtered before he ever could. Only attractive young women and men were spared, being sold as slaves. All the others were butchered. The Muslim Turks piled the bones of the victims up into a pyramid and thus ended the peasant crusade.

The Crusaders Ally with the Byzantine Emperor

The real armies of the Crusades were made up of five different groups. They were led by Hugh of Vermandois, Godfrey of Bouillon, Bohemund of Taranto, Raymond of Toulouse, and Robert of Normandy. Each of these men were renowned and respected in their realms. Hugh was the brother of King Philip of France, Godfrey had been a hero of Henry IV's army, Bohemund was the son of Robert Guiscard, and Robert was the son of William the Conqueror.

Hugh's troops were the first to leave. The Crusades had been first proclaimed in France where the Council of Clermont occurred and King Philip's brother was among the first to pledge himself to the cause. He set sail for Constantinople by ship in October 1096, the same time that Peter's the Hermit's peasant army was falling to the Turks. The ships encountered a storm and were wrecked but most survived. The soldiers of Hugh were well disciplined and there were no reports of serious raiding or pillaging. Hugh was well received and showered with gifts by eastern emperor Alexius Comnenus who had his own motives. Alexius was well aware that the presence of so many foreign soldiers in his country could easily backfire. He had himself been invaded by Robert Guiscard just years earlier. He, therefore, asked Hugh to pledge his loyalty to himself and to promise that all land which had been captured by the Turks would be returned to the sovereignty of the Byzantine Empire. He did not require that the Holy Romans could not establish lands beyond the old Empire for this would create a buffer between the Byzantines and the Turks to which Comnenus would have no objection. Hugh gladly pledged his fealty and waited for the arrival of the other armies.

Godfrey of Bouillon's troops would be the second army to arrive. Godfrey had been one of the great heroes of Henry IV, in his war with Rudolf, and it was he who had cut off Rudolf's hand and had thus given the blow that would kill Rudolf. He was acclaimed by friends and foes alike as a man of great honor and chivalry. While some modern scholars have questioned some of his motives and actions it seems that his motives were never questioned even by his contemporary enemies. He was devoted to the Church, but not to the pope. His allegiance to Henry IV, therefore, did not put him at odds against Urban II, though he may have believed Clement to be the true pope. This must be understood for the Crusades extended far beyond the question of Urban's legitimacy and was, in fact, a major cause of it.

In character Godfrey, except for Raymond of Toulouse, was the most chivalrous and noble. His knights sometimes complained that he spent so long in giving thanks to God for dinner that the dinner was cold by the time he was finished. Like Charlemagne before him, he was devout and sincere but he was still a warrior at heart. He was a man of his word but his word was not easily given. He was a rigid soldier whose virtues were offset by his German blood and temperment.

Godfrey sold all that he had and took his wife and children with him. He did not expect to return but hoped to establish his home in Jerusalem. Following him on the Crusade was his brother, Baldwin, whose character was less noble. Since Godfrey came from Germany the shortest route was through Hungary but Hungary had already had five armies enter through its borders and none had left without pillaging and destruction. King Coloman was reluctant to grant the right of way but upon meeting Godfrey he came to trust him. He agreed to let the army pass but only if Baldwin's family was surrendered as prisoners. Baldwin and his family were to be released only after Godfrey's men had passed through to the Byzantine Empire. Godfrey agreed and sternly warned his soldiers that death would be the punishment for raids.

All went well and Godfrey's troops entered into Byzantine territory peaceably. It was December, a year after the call to Crusade, when Godfrey's troops heard rumors that Hugh was kept a prisoner. If he was a prisoner, he was a prisoner in a guilded cage but the men assumed the worst. For over a week the army ransacked and wrecked havoc upon the countryside. Messengers from Constantinople arrived and convinced Godfrey that all was well. He restored order to the troops and continued on to Constantinople where he met up with Hugh.

When there Comnenus tried to make Godfrey pledge loyalty, as Hugh had done, but Godfrey refused saying that he had given his pledge to Henry IV. Discussions continued for some time but Baldwin had been left in charge of the army in Godfrey's absence. Again trouble erupted in April of Holy Week and a battle broke out between Baldwin's men and the Byzantine troops. Soon order was restored and Godfrey agreed to give his pledge to Comnenus so long as it did not conflict with his pledge to Henry IV.

Bohemund arrived almost immediately thereafter. Bohemund was the son of Robert Guiscard and had warred with his brother over the possession of Guiscard's domain. He now pledged himself to the cause of the Crusade and set sail with his nephew, Tancred, for Byzantium in October. Like his father, Bohemund's Viking blood still boiled. He was a pretentious knight who set his own personal ambition above the Church but he had the prestige and respect that few other knights could command. He did not have the good of the Church or Christianity at heart and many of the knights wished that he had never come. Like his father he could be exceedingly cruel and barbaric, as well as treacherous. He was quick to take the oath of loyalty to Alexius but only because the oath meant nothing to him. The other Crusaders were by no means quick to take an oath of loyalty but once they gave it they kept it. Such scruples and ethics did not interfere with Bohemund who once ordered spies roasted on a spit and cooked for dinner.

Nevertheless, Bohemund was a politician and knew when to behave civilized as well as when to be barbaric. After their arrival in Byzantine lands Bohemund ordered that no pillaging should occur. There was, however, one notable exception. When the army passed by a town of Paulican heretics Bohemund doubtless remembered Urban II's words when he declared heresy punishable by death. The Paulicans were a dualistic sect that, among other things, believed that Satan was Jesus' brother. This was more than enough to incur Bohemund's wrath. The Paulicans were burned in their houses and then the troops moved on.

Two other armies remained before the forces were assembled. Raymond IV had traveled with his ally the Bishop of Le Puy. Robert, the Duke of Normandy, was the commander of the final army. He was the son of William the Conqueror and had inherited the Norman duchy but his brother, William II of England, had attacked his lands many times claiming it as a part of the English inheritance. When the Crusades began Robert made amends with his brother and sold the duchy to William II in order to finance his expedition. Of these last two armies Raymond's troops seemed the most undisciplined and several skirmishes occurred in Byzantium. As the actions of his army displayed, Raymond was not a great general but he was the most noble and chivalrous of the Knights of the Crusade. When civility and humanity abandoned the Crusaders for greed and revenge Raymond was the usual voice of reason along with the Bishop of Le Puy.

Once all the leaders were assembled in Constantinople the emperor again had to insure their loyalty. The greatest problem, however, was that Bohemund and Raymond both desired to become the commander of the united army. Naturally the two held each other in enmity. Raymond had also been reluctant to swear allegiance to Alexius Comnenus but he was convinced by his comrades that it was for the best. In the spring of 1097 the forces moved on from Constantinople ready to battle the Turks, but they moved on as separate divisions. No unified leader had been elected.

The Capture of Nicaea and Antioch

The first target of the Crusade was the city of Nicaea roughly fifty miles from Constantinople. The armies surrounded the city walls and prevented any one from entering and leaving. The citizen's only hope was the return of the Sultan who had left on business believing that the peasant armies he had defeated so easily months earlier was the best that the Holy Roman Empire had to offer. When he heard of a new army of soldiers mounted with glistening silver clothes and shields, he hastily returned to protect Nicaea and when he arrived he found that these soldiers were no peasant army. The barrage of arrows that he sent down upon them were usually deflected by armor and shields such as the east had never seen. On even footing the Turks were no match for the Knights of Europe and the Sultan retreated.

Not long afterward the city of Nicaea surrendered, but they surrendered at night to the Byzantines. When the Crusaders awakened in the morning the Byzantines had already taken the city. The incident was political strategy by the emperor, and proved somewhat embarrassing to the Crusaders, but Alexius Comnenus was generous to both the Crusaders and the captured Turks. The Europeans were showered with gold from the Sultan's coffers and the Turks were treated generously. Still, some resentment and bitterness began to well up and dissension among the Crusading armies first appeared. They agreed to proceed on to Antioch.

The Sultan at first tried to lay a trap for the Crusaders and again rained arrows down upon the unsuspecting soldiers but Bohemund and Robert took up defensive positions and used shields to deflect most of the damage while Raymond, Godfrey, and Hugh circled around and attacked the Sultan's men. Once again the Sultan was forced to retreat and this time he realized that he was no match for the European armies on the battlefield. He decided to try to the age old tactic of leaving destruction in the wake of his retreat. The Sultan's men pulled all the way back to Antioch but they pillaged, burned, and destroyed their own cities on route. Villages and towns were abandoned and left useless to the enemies. This tactic worked well. For months the Crusaders marched through what had become, it seemed, desert wastelands. There was no food to be found and a drought left them thirsty as well. The horses died first and the Crusaders found themselves forced to eat them. When the rains finally came they came in buckets. The desert was replaced with swamps and the Crusaders progress was substantially slowed as their heavy armor made them sink further into the deep mud.

Eventually the Crusaders separated and took different routes to Antioch. Tancred and Baldwin followed the route through the Armenian area of Cilicia where Tancred found many Christians who still lived in the lands. These people willingly opened their gates to him and welcomed them as deliverers. Baldwin, however, followed close behind and when he arrived at Taurus he demanded, in as much as he outranked Tancred, that Tancred hand the city over to his authority. Tancred reluctantly agreed and when reinforcements arrived Baldwin refused them admittance into the city, fearing they might challenge his authority. That night the reinforcement army camped outside the gates when it was discovered that not all the Turks had fled. Some remained behind and staged a surprise attack on the army at night. The massacre was severe and even Baldwin's own men despised him for his selfishness. Later Tancred, at the instigation of other knights, reluctantly agreed to attack Baldwin's army in retaliation for Taurus. When the battle was over the two made amends but it had become clear that Baldwin had lost the respect of the Crusaders and many of his own men.

Before the armies reached Antioch Baldwin had an offer from the Armenian city of Edessa. The city lay east of what the Crusaders had planned on taking but the people of the city were desperate to be liberated from Turkish rule. The Christian Prince of the city therefore promised to adopt Baldwin as his son and name him heir if he would come and liberate Edessa. Baldwin agreed and abandoned the Crusade. With a few loyal troops he headed for Edessa where he established his rule. Not long after taking the city, however, Baldwin was cited in a conspiracy to overthrow his new father. Prince Thoros was butchered by the people and Baldwin became their prince. He now had what he had wanted, a small kingdom of his own. This tiny state was but a fraction of what he had once hoped for but it was the best he could do for the Crusaders were now well aware of his selfish motives. Motives that even led to a failed rebellion by the people of Edessa not long afterwards.

The rest of the Crusaders mobilized on Antioch. The city itself was one of the best fortified in the country. A huge wall with four hundred towers surrounded the city. Raymond recommended an immediate attack but the others suggested that they wait for reinforcements and request siege engines from Alexius Comnenus. Scholars have disputed which was the more sage advice but what resulted is fact. The armies of the Crusaders waited long months and soon ran out of food and provisions. Raids on neighboring lands and the purchase of food from local Christian towns also ran dry. Desertions began to arise, including Peter the Hermit, who had joined the regular army after the failure of his peasant army. Tancred heard of the desertion and caught up to Peter, dragging him back before the leaders. Peter was chastised but forgiven.

After five months reinforcements finally arrived and news that the eastern emperor Alexius was marching to assist the Crusaders lifted spirits for a short while. The Turks, however, were also waiting for reinforcements. The first set of Turkish reinforcements came just after the Crusaders'. The Crusaders managed to beat off the Turkish troops with the loss of many lives but many months had passed and as of yet there had been no real attempt to take the city. Worse yet, Bohemund, whose character seemed borrowed from his ambitious father (Robert Guiscard), was already stirring up dissension by trying to secure the rule of Antioch for himself. Raymond firmly held that the oath to the eastern emperor should be upheld and the city returned to him. It was June 1098 before Antioch would finally be taken.

News had reached the Crusaders' camp that Kerbogha was leading a large Muslim army to support Antioch. More deserters fled the Crusaders' encampment when the battle appeared imminent. Bohemund, however, had secretly negotiated a pact with a traitor inside Antioch. A groups of knights slipped into Antioch and opened the gates. The armies rushed in and took Antioch only days before Kerbogha's army arrived. The victory was, nevertheless, short lived for now the siege army had become the besieged and Kerbogha set up in the very camp abandoned by the victorious Crusaders.

The events that followed would change the long term impact of the Crusades; not in terms of their success which was all but assured by this time, but in terms of the future of the Latin states of Palestine and Syria. The Bishop of Le Puy had accompanied Raymond and is often considered to have been the spiritual leader of the Crusades. While war had always been savage, and particularly in the middle ages, the Crusaders did restrain themselves to some extent under his guidance. Chivalry and the Cross tempered the brutality of the Normans, but only moderately. With Kerbogha standing outside the gates a new "spiritual" leader emerged.

Peter Bartholomew was a rascally man of disrepute. He had come to Antioch with claims of repeated visions by St. Andrew. He told the leaders of the Crusade that St. Andrew's visions had tormented him for many months and had revealed that the location of a sacred relic. He declared that the Holy Lance, that pierced Christ's side, was buried beneath St. Peter's in Antioch. The Bishop of Le Puy doubted the story, especially since the supposed Holy Lance was already said to be residing in Constantinople. Despite this the leaders decided to search anyway. St. Peter's had been turned into a stable by the Muslims and it was not uncommon to hide relics under sacred ground if danger was coming. After much digging a lance was discovered and a sign in the sky, supposedly a meteor, heartened the spirits of the people and the army. Raymond led the armies out of Antioch with the Holy Lance before him and this surprise attack, from people Kerbogha thought would be on the defensive, prevailed. The Muslim army was routed and the Crusaders had secured Antioch.

This victory lifted the spirits of all but was followed by the death of the Bishop of Le Puy a month later. Disease often accompanies war and the bishop was among the first stricken. Peter Bartholomew, however, despised the bishop who viewed him as a charlatan and declared another vision in which it was revealed that the bishop had descended to Hell for a number of days as punishment for his disbelief, before ascending to Heaven. Immediately, many people took a disliking to the "prophet." Moreover, Bohemund resolved to keep Antioch for himself and when it was found that the eastern emperor's army had turned back and did not come to rescue the Crusaders as promised, Bohemund had justification for the renunciation of his oath of loyalty. The other leaders argued with Bohemund and in the end, to ensure his claim was not taken from him, Bohemund withdrew from the Crusades and called Antioch his home.

Europe During the 1st Crusade

The Crusades did not alleviate many of the problems of Europe. Henry IV was still faced with a rebellious son and Urban II was increasingly gaining the respect of the people. In this latter sense, the Crusades were a success.

Urban II was now the true pope in the eyes of most all Europe but as long as Clement remained holed up in the Castle St. Angelo he was a threat and mob violence continued throughout much of the years. Finally, through bribery the Pierleoni family succeeded in ejecting Clement from St. Angelo and the entire city of Rome fell into Urban II's hands in August 1098. Clement fled to safety and awaited an opportunity to return.

For Henry IV the situation also improved somewhat. His rebel son did not endear himself to many of the German princes and in 1098 many of them agreed to accept Henry V as heir to the Imperial throne. Conrad continued as an anti–king but his weakness made him no severe threat to Henry IV. As Clement's position weakened Henry attempted to make amends with the papacy and would at one point suggested leaving on a Crusade himself in exchange for the lifting of his excommunication. Even though Henry never did go on a Crusade, the request would further weaken the position of the Clementine popes and assure the eventual victory of the Gregorian popes. Henry was, in essence, admitting the legitimacy of the Gregorian pope's excommunication.

The Siege of Jerusalem

It was not until January of 1099 that the Crusaders embarked for Jerusalem. Bohemund and Baldwin were not with them, for they had abandoned the cause for profit. One might have hoped that the remaining nobles, who were indeed more chivalrous than the aforementioned, would then have left a noble mark upon history but in the absence of true spiritual leadership and the bitterness of the past few years, the hope of seeing their dreams fulfilled before the walls of Jerusalem filled them with thoughts of Joshua's conquest. In the days of Joshua, because human sacrifice was practiced by the old inhabitants as well as other reasons, not even women and children were spared. To the Crusaders, with a few exceptions, this was a new conquest commissioned by God against the heathen. To be sure, there were still noble chivalrous warriors who put their own life on the line to protect the innocent, but the majority were filled with Viking fervor. The conquest of Jerusalem ensured not only the establishment of a Latin state in Palestine but also its fall. The Christians who had once viewed the Crusaders as liberators would soon distrust them. The siege was to be a testament to the change that had occurred in history. The innocence of the old Holy Roman Empire, and it was innocent compared to the barbarian culture they had emerged from, was now over. The barbarians had once become Christians. Now these "Christians" became barbarians all over again.

The journey from Antioch to Jerusalem lasted almost five months, during which time more bitterness and infighting occurred. The "prophecies" and dreams of Peter Bartholomew were now declared to be frauds by his critics and Bartholomew agreed to undertake a "trial by fire" to prove his innocence.

141

In this old pagan tradition, incorporated into Christian European theology, one could only survive if his heart was true and pure. So Bartholomew ran through the blazing fire with the Holy Lance in hand. He survived the initial test but the fire had done its damage. He lingered on until finally dying days later.

When the Crusaders reached Bethlehem they were greeted with cheers as the crowd even kissed the feet of many Crusaders. Such was the condition of the Holy Land under Turk rule. So severe had it been that even Muslims despised the Turks. This fact, however, did not necessarily play into the Crusader's hands for the Egyptian Fatamids also hated the Turks and likewise had designs on Jerusalem. While the Crusaders had been delayed at Antioch the Fatamids had gained possession of Jerusalem and instituted a moderate government. The Egyptians had even negotiated with both the Byzantines and the Crusaders in hopes of reaching an agreement on the parceling of Turkish lands but both sides demanded Jerusalem for their own. When the Crusaders finally arrived at the gates of Jerusalem in June 1099 it was the moderate Fatamids that they were besieging, not the Turks.

The Fatimids were not as cruel as the Turks but when they had taken possession of Jerusalem they exiled every Christian in the city. This only inspired the Crusaders and reinforced the idea that the siege was a war against heathenism. They immediately began the siege, but soon found that they would be unable to penetrate the mighty defensives of Jerusalem without siege equipment. Despite attempts by the Egyptians to blockade English and Byzantine fleets several ships slipped by the blockade and landed at Joppa. There the siege materials were delivered only about a week after their arrival. A huge "castle" tower was built, with a huge cross upon it, and placed on wheels. It was armed with catapults, and was so tall that the men could jump over the enemy walls.

In July, a priest named Peter Desiderius declared that the Bishop of Le Puy, whom the whole army had revered, appeared to him in a dream and promised victory in nine days; if they would march around the walls of Jerusalem in bare feet while fasting with repentant hearts. The army agreed to undertake this and did so to the mocking of Muslim soldiers' jeers and laughter. Nine days later the "prophecy" would be fulfilled. At night on July 13 the Crusaders, now numbering only thirteen thousand men, began to shovel dirt into the trenches that surrounded the walls so that the towers and scaling ladders could be used. Boulders and boiling oil were poured over the walls but the Crusaders protected themselves the best they could. On the morning of the 14th, nine days after marching around the walls, the Crusaders began to pour into Jerusalem.

Much space had been devoted to the savagery of the Crusaders which followed, but the chivalry of some soldiers and knights should not be scorned. The onslaught which occurred was not orchestrated by the leaders of the Crusade, but by a wanton mob made up of mercenaries over which most of the princes had lost control. Memories of the unthinkable savagery of the Turks beat the Crusading mobs into a frenzy. Muslims and Jews alike were slaughtered in the streets regardless of their age or sex. Of the butchers the Tafur were the most notable. They may have been the survivors of Peter the Hermit's peasant Crusade or some other group but they had no armor and were penniless. They fought like wild animals and were so savage that the Knights secretly despised the lot of them. They had been guilty of cannibalism during the Crusades and were the predominant butchers of Jerusalem. Of their leader, Godfrey and the other knights once commented, "all of us together cannot tame the King Tafur."

Despite this terrible testament to the Crusade there is no evidence that the leaders of the Crusade played a direct part in the atrocities. Godfrey cannot be shown to have been involved at all and Raymond, for a price of gold, ensured the safety of several of the leaders of the Muslims; escorting them out of Jerusalem to safety. So also Tancred showed chivalry, free of charge, for he had trapped many Muslims in a mosque and when they surrendered to him to he took them under his protection and promised over two hundred that they would not be harmed, but such nobility was not to be found in the hearts of those Crusaders who had survived the long journey. Bitterness at their plight, anger at the persecution of their brethren, feelings that this was a war against heathenism, and the darkness of the human heart inspired many of the Crusaders to spare neither women nor children. These men forced their way past Tancred and his men, willing to fight even their Christian brothers for the right to strike down the heathen. The Muslims in the mosque were murdered and Tancred's cries were of no avail. Even the Jews were not spared, for when the Muslims expelled all the Christians from Jerusalem the Jews remained. They were viewed as traitors who cooperated with the Muslims in their persecution of believers. Many Jews had taken refuge in a synagogue and were placed under the protection of Tancred, but the mobs (probably Tafur mercenaries) ignored Tancred's banner (the symbol of his authority, showing that those under it were not to be harmed) and the Jews were burned alive in the synagogue.

Exaggerations of the slaughter that occurred claim that the blood and bodies on the dead piled up to a horses bridle (a phrase borrowed from Revelation's prophecy of Armageddon) and suggest, with some legitimacy, that their armor was covered in blood from head to foot. The savagery is said to have prevented the west from ever gaining the trust of the Muslim peasants, whose support was essential in establishing a lasting state. For the time being Jerusalem and the Holy Land belonged the Holy Roman Empire but the events of July 14 would ensure that it would not remain a part of the empire. Even the best of the Latin Kings of Jerusalem found it impossible to erase the memory of the butchery and it was this carnage that inspired the Muslims to drive the Crusaders from the land with even greater zeal than the Crusaders had shown in taking the land.

It seems almost prophetic that within weeks of the capture of Jerusalem Pope Urban II would die. He did not even live to hear the news. Even more, the majority of those who had been so crucial in the Crusades would die within a few years. Urban died fifteen days after the fall of Jerusalem. Godfrey would become the first Latin King of Jerusalem but died five days after the first anniversary of the city's fall. The Bishop Le Puy died before Jerusalem had even fallen, and many of the others faded from the pages of history shortly thereafter. The Crusaders typified the High Middle Ages which they may sometimes be considered to have inaugurated. It was a mixture of the greatest of nobility and the vilest of barbarity. It was a time of honor and savagery; of gallantry and of atrocity. It was the beginning of the late middle ages.

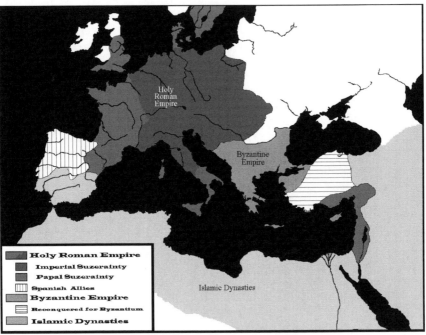

The Holy Roman Empire circa 1100

Holy Roman Emperor	Pope	AntiPope (if any)
──────── 1056 ────────		
	──────── 1073 ────────	
	Gregory VII	
		−1080−
	──────── 1085 ────────	
	──────── 1085 ────────	
Henry IV	Victor III	
	──────── 1087 ────────	Clement (III)
	Urban II	
	──────── 1099 ────────	
		−1100−
		Theodoric
		−1102−
	Paschal II	Albert
		−1102−
		−1105−
──────── 1106 ────────		Sylvester (IV)
		−1111−
	──────── 1118 ────────	
Henry V	Gelasius II	Gregory (VIII)
	──────── 1119 ────────	
	Calistus II	−1121−
	──────── 1124 ────────	
──────── 1125 ────────		Celestine (II)
	Honorius II	−1124−
Lothair II	──────── 1130 ────────	
		Anacletus (II)
──────── 1137 ────────		−1138−
──────── 1138 ────────	Innocent II	Victor (IV)
		−1138−
	──────── 1143 ────────	
	Celestine II	
Conrad III	──────── 1144 ────────	
	Lucius II	
	──────── 1145 ────────	
	Eugenius III	
──────── 1152 ────────		
	──────── 1153 ────────	

King of England

William Rufus
—1100—
Henry I
—1135—
Stephen
—1154—
Henry II
—1189—
Richard the Lionhearted
—1199—

King of France

Philip I
—1108—
Louis VI
—1137—
Louis (The Younger) VII
—1180—
Philip II Augustus

King of Jerusalem

1099
Godfrey (Lord Protector)
—1100—
Baldwin
—1108—
Baldwin II
—1131—
Fulke
—1143—
Baldwin III
—1162—
Amalric (Amaury)
—1173—
Baldwin IV
—1184—
Baldwin V
—1186—
Guy
—1187—
The Fall of Jerusalem

King of Sicily

Roger II (Adelaide's Regency)
—1127—
Roger II
—1154—
William (the Bad) I
—1166—
William (the Good) II
—1189—
Tancred
—1194—
William III
—1194—
Henry IV conquers Sicily

10
—

The Fall of the Franconians

The Crusades had done more to ensure the survival of the Gregorian popes than any military excursion against Henry IV ever could. The success of the Crusades further strengthened the power of the papacy and weakened Henry's claims. Even Henry would soon be seeking reconciliation but he was to be replaced by a spoiled son whose character was lacking in Christian virtue. The Franconian (or Salian) Dynasty was about to fall.

With the rise of a new Kingdom of Jerusalem and the expanse of the Holy Roman Empire into England, Normandy, and Spain, the role of the emperor, whose authority was only felt in Germany and Italy, diminished until it would be revived a half a century later by Frederick Barbarosa. The popes were now the true masters of the Holy Roman Empire stretching from the middle east to the coast of the Atlantic Ocean, but their struggle was not yet over. Indeed, their struggle would never truly end for emperors are not eager to surrender their authority easily.

The Rise of Pope Paschal II

Upon the death of Urban II, Paschal II became pope. Immediately he sought to ensure that his throne would not be threatened by Clement (III), who was held up in Albano, and Norman troops were dispatched to drive Clement further away into hiding. Clement died the next year but his supporters still clung to the hope that the Gregorian popes would fail. Despite Clement's failure he was a better man, and a better pope, than Urban. Few questioned his character and integrity but many could question the motives and character of the Gregorian popes. While Paschal was away on business Clement's supporters met secretly at night in Rome. They elected and consecrated Theodroic as pope but his reign was to last but a few months. When Paschal returned with Norman troops Paschal attempted to flee to Germany, hoping that Henry IV would support him. Instead he was captured and imprisoned in a monastery by the Normans.

That same year another feeble attempt was made to raise a Clementine pope. Albert (sometimes called Adalbert) was elected by the Clementines but rioting in Rome ensured that he would never sit on the papal throne. He fled to the safety, so he thought, of Marcello, but through bribery he was handed over to the Normans who imprisoned him in another monastery. Paschal's ascension was assured and even Henry IV was wise enough to recognize the fact. It would be another four years before Paschal's enemies would appoint another rival pope, named Sylvester (IV), but after warfare between Paschal's supporters and Sylvester's the latter was eventually forced to Ancona where he remained until Henry V's coronation.

By the time of Clement's death Henry IV was desperately trying to make amends with the pope. He had outlived two enemy popes but he had not outlived his excommunication. It seemed that Henry was willing to do anything; anything except forfeit his right of investiture. This was the issue that neither Henry nor Paschal would waver on. By this time the emperor was clearly the second fiddle to the papacy and if the emperor had not the right to appoint his own bishops then he feared he would become little more than a puppet of the pope. Owing to the vast power of the bishops this was not entirely paranoid but England's Henry I, who had become king in 1100, had agreed to forfeit investiture on the condition that the appointed bishop give homage to the king. France, likewise, required an oath of allegiance to king. Henry, however, would not compromise and his relation with Paschal deteriorated quickly.

The Kingdom of Jerusalem

Jerusalem was now under the sovereignty of the Holy Roman Empire but it had no king. Raymond was first offered the crown but refused saying that no king should sit where Christ was crucified. Godfrey was then offered the crown. He accepted but only on the condition that his title be "Lord Protector of the Holy Sepulcre" for he too felt that no man should wear a crown of gold where Christ had worn a crown of thorns.

There was little time for Godfrey to celebrate. He was forced to move south where he planned to ambush the Egyptian reinforcements before they could reach Jerusalem. With the victory that followed the Kingdom of Jerusalem was assured. Unfortunately, for all Godfrey's virtues he was insecure. He felt threatened by the knights who could have made his kingdom stronger. In one instance a city agreed to surrender to Raymond but Godfrey halted the surrender because he saw it as a slap in face that they would not surrender to the Lord Protector. His insecurity and anger over such trivial matters soon led to the defection of Raymond and Robert of Normady who, tired of the quarrels, departed home for Europe. This severely weakened Godfrey's kingdom but it made him realize how frivolous he was being. Godfrey learned to be chivalrous in victory as well as defeat and to deal more fairly with his colleagues. He then made Tancred the Prince of Galilee and his loyal vassal.

In the meantime, Daimbert, the papal legate, was on his way from Rome. Daimbert (sometimes called Dagobert) was the corrupt archbishop of Pisa who was loyal to the Gregorians popes. He had set sail with a Pisan fleet which had pillaged and sacked numerous Byzantine cities on route. The Emperor Alexius of Constantinople even gave orders to prevent sacking and several sea battles were fought. Daimbert finally found port near Bohemund's

Antioch where the two began to plot against the eastern emperor, but when Raymond and Robert arrived they chastised both men. Bohemund was already considered a traitor to both Alexius and the Crusaders, and Daimbert endangered the papal claims to Jerusalem by plotting against Byzantium. Daimbert relented and set out for Jerusalem while Raymond took possession of Lattakieh in the name of the eastern emperor.

Daimbert arrived in Jerusalem in time to celebrate Christmas. A Patriarch of Jerusalem had already been named but that man, Arnulf, was corrupt and despised by the people. He had even tortured Christians in an attempt to find where they had hidden sacred relics. Arnulf was now deposed and Daimbert become Patriach of Jerusalem.

With the new King and Patriarch the feudal system was brought to the middle east. Godfrey also strengthened the position of the Hospitallers (later to be developed into the military order of the Knights of St. John or rather the Knights of the Order of the Hospital of St. John) who were a religious order established, before the first Crusade, to protect hospitals throughout the land so that pilgrims would be safe from harm and have places where they could rest and heal on the long journey. With the establishment of a Latin Kingdom Godfrey now bestowed generous gifts upon the order and its leader, a monk named Gerard.

The position of the Crusaders had been solidified by Godfrey in the year following Jerusalem's capture, but it is hard to tell what kind of king Godfrey would truly have been for he died just after the first anniversary of Jerusalem's capture. He was by all accounts devout and sometimes chivalrous but he also suffered from pride and distrust. He could be brash and brazen, which could have cost lives on at least one occasion. His conscience, however, seemed to tempter most of these character flaws. The first part of his administration showed both of these characteristics but as time passed he seemed to learn how to be a good king, as well as a good leader. Nevertheless, his death after just one year makes it impossible to tell exactly how the kingdom would have grown, and in what direction it would have taken.

Upon his death word was sent to Daimbert, to whom Godfrey had bequeathed Jerusalem. Daimbert, along with Tancred, decided that Bohemund should be the next king of Jerusalem but another embassy, led by Arnulf, the expelled Patriarch of Jerusalem, sent a message to Godfrey's brother Baldwin declaring the people would accept him as Godfrey's heir. The supporters of Baldwin feared that the papacy might seize control of Jerusalem through Daimbert and many knights even took possession of defensive towers lest Daimbert's supporters gain control of the city. This seems ironic indeed for Bohemund was loyal to no one but himself. The choice of Bohemund by Daimbert and Tancred would be odd unless they believed that he was willing to grant them almost anything for the title itself. Nevertheless, when Bohemund was captured by Muslims and carried into captivity the issue was decided. Baldwin became king of Jerusalem.

Baldwin, for all his character flaws, knew how to conquer and fortify his conquest. The once massive Crusade army which had entered Palestine, sometimes exaggerated to have been over a quarter of a million, was down to a few thousand. Jerusalem had been won but the land was still filled with treachery and bandits. Many cities still belonged to Muslim lords. A pilgrim traveling to Jerusalem could expect starvation, thirst, robbery, rape, and even worse. The Knights of St. John gave protection to pilgrims but they were too few in numbers to make an adequate police force for the entire Holy Land and they had not yet truly established themselves as a military order. If Palestine was to be secured then reinforcements were needed.

Paschal commissioned new recruits to come and relieve the Crusaders but the new batch of Crusaders were not destined for success. The first group from Lombardy was led by the Archbishop of Milan, Anselm. When they arrived at Constantinople Raymond met up with them and became their commanding officer. Against the advice of Raymond the army decided to rescue Bohemund from his Muslim captors but the army was ambushed. The knights and soldiers fled in terror and Raymond himself was forced to retreat with no knights left to protect him. The wives and children, who had accompanied their families on the Crusades as pilgrims, were left to the Turk devices. Young attractive women were raped and shipped off to harems, healthy children were sold to slave markets, and all others were slaughtered.

Raymond, the most noble of the Crusaders, was made the scapegoat and was arrested for treason. Allegations circulated that he fled as a coward and had even arranged the ambush. Tancred was given charge of the prisoner but after many protests Raymond was eventually released on the condition he abandon Lattekiah which Tancred promptly took over.

In the meantime, two more Crusading armies met the same fate. The later was commanded by Hugh, who had left the first Crusade after Bohemund's treachery. In the ambush which claimed this army Hugh received wounds from which he would die and the Archbishop of Thiemo was captured and martyred for refusing to convert to Islam.

These Crusades of 1101 were a disaster. Baldwin had no choice but to consolidate the conquest with what little men were left. He granted the Hospitallers booty from Joppa and greatly increased their prestige. They were now the most important source of health and well–being for pilgrims but they were not yet a military order and could not provide much protection beyond the walls of their hospitals. Baldwin was forced to consolidate the conquest with what he had left. One of his best warriors, however, was Bohemund who lay in captivity but the Turks were as greedy as they were brutal. Bohemund's freedom was purchased and upon his return he set out for Europe to solicit more Crusaders. When he arrived in Italy Bohemund turned Paschal against the eastern emperor and declared that the Crusade should concentrate on the Byzantine Empire. His father had tried to conquer Byzantium and now, with the support of a weak and gullible pope, Bohemund brought new Crusaders to attack Alexius, but these Crusader were also doomed to failure, for Bohemund was captured in battle once again and forced to swear fealty to Alexius. He did so, but then returned to Europe, disgraced and defeated.

Tancred took over the northern Syrian states for Bohemund, Raymond now moved to the region south of Syria, and Baldwin controlled Jerusalem and the southern area. Until his death Baldwin would work to secure the lands and seize the cities in Palestine still controlled by Muslims.

Britain and Normandy Before Emperor Henry V

William II had bought Normandy from Robert before his brother had left on the Crusades. He had been corrupt, rude, blasphemous, and unjust. When William II died in a hunting accident Robert was already on his return trip from the Crusades. Because William II left no heir, Henry I, both William's and Robert's brother, became king. Realizing that Robert would soon return Henry acted fast. His coronation and ascension were completed only weeks before Robert's return to Normandy. Immediately the stage was set for war, but the war was short lived. In 1101 a treaty was signed which gave Henry I England and Normandy was returned to Robert along with a promise of £2000 a year.

All seemed well until the year of Emperor Henry IV's death. In 1106 war erupted between Robert and Henry, but this war ended with Robert's capture. He was placed in Henry's dungeon and remained there for twenty-eight years before his death. The victory did not help Henry to solidify his power. Normandy was hard for Henry to control from across the English channel and the French still claimed it as a Dutchy of their own. King Louis VI of France and Count Fulk of Anjou were at constant war with Henry over Normandy.

This disputed area would lead to conflict between England and France which would last for hundreds of years. Normandy had once been a Dutchy awarded to the Vikings in a peace pact but as the Norman power grew so also did Normandy's independence. When William the Conqueror became King of England it was only natural that Normandy and England were one country, but on his death the lands were split between William II and Robert. Despite the temporary reunification after Robert left for the Crusades, Normandy became a controversial land issue such as was rarely rivaled in history. If Normandy was a part of France then the French could be said to have conquered England (through William the Conqueror). If so then does England belong to France? If England does not belong to France then surely Normandy belongs to England but if a French subject, William the Conqueror, becomes King of England then how can he remain a French subject? The dispute would continue to rage creating such legendary figures as Joan of Arc and its final resolution would not occur until the end of the Hundred Year War in the fifteenth century.

The Ascent of Henry V

The Imperial authority of the Holy Roman Emperors had steadily diminished since the fall of the Ottonians, and Henry IV knew that what little authority he had left needed to be salvaged. Following Pope (or antipope) Clement's death Henry began to try to reconcile with Paschal. When Paschal asked for new recruits in the Crusade Henry even offered his own services but for a price. The price included allowing Henry to maintain his right of investiture but this was too much to ask from the Gregorian popes. Paschal refused and when Henry's son, Henry V, revolted in 1104 he found a powerful ally in Paschal.

Those who were discontent with Henry's rule were numerous. Much of the dissatisfaction had to do with Henry's lack of standing in the Church but a large portion of the resistance came from the nobles who felt that Henry was diminishing their rights in favor of *ministerials* who were sort of civil servants. Henry V's rebellion was backed by Bavarian nobles and assisted by the Church who desired to rid themselves of the pope's enemy. In December of 1105 Henry V captured his father and imprisoned him. He was forced to "voluntarily" abdicate his throne in favor of Henry V, with the full support of Paschal, but the Lotharingians resented a son who would commit such crimes against his own father. When Henry IV was released they helped him to regain his throne but he was not to live long. Despite all that his son had done, Henry V was still his son and his heir. Henry IV forgave his offspring and died in March 1106.

With Henry V's ascent assured the controversy of Henry IV did not die. The pope remembered how Henry had challenged his authority and had the emperor's body exhumed from its grave by the local bishop. It was declared that he could not be buried on consecrated grounds and after the body was removed the arrogant bishop refused to hold Church services until the stench of Henry's spiritual pollution could be properly fumigated.

The Church now believed that it had a loyal puppet on the throne but they learned otherwise very quickly. After trying, with only moderate success, to reunify Germany and ensure fealty from Poland and Hungary, Henry V set out for Italy to officially receive the Imperial crown, for it had long been acknowledged that only the pope could confer that title. The year was 1110 and Henry did not come asking, but telling. He refused, like his father, to surrender the right of investiture and when the pope refused to coronate him without the promise Henry promptly imprisoned the pope in his dungeon. After many long months in prison Paschal still seemed reluctant to budge until Henry pulled his trump card. The antipope Sylvester (IV) was seen near Rome. There was no official relationship to Henry V yet, but that was intentional. Paschal could acceded to Henry's demands or Sylvester (IV) would be recognized as legitimate pope. Paschal relented. In April 1111 he conceded the issue of investiture. He also agreed to allow Henry IV to be buried on consecrated grounds but only if Henry V would promise to circulate the rumor that his father had sincerely repented on his deathbed. It was further promised that Paschal would never excommunicate Henry but he would have to make Sylvester (IV) renounce all claims to the papacy. With these promises made Henry V was officially bestowed the Imperial diadem and made the last Franconian Emperor of Holy Roman.

Promises Reneged

The Church was angry not only at Henry V for his treatment of the pope, but also at the pope for so easily giving in to Henry's demands. The following year a large gathering of Bishops formed a Church council and nullified Paschal's decisions on the grounds that they had been forced from him. The right of investiture was again stripped of the emperor and, despite Paschal's promise, Henry was excommunicated. It seemed that the only change between Henry IV and Henry V was the roman numeral at the end of his name. Paschal actively opposed Henry V and in 1113 he had even opened negotiations with the Byzantine Emperor Alexius Comnenus, at his instigation, on his becoming the Holy Roman Emperor as well. Such a move would have reunited the two empires but it came to naught.

Despite the excommunication Henry had no desire to immediately return to Italy. Germany was still fragmented with disloyal Counts and Dukes who refused to give Henry much more than nominal authority. The excommunication did not help matters but Henry believed he had struck a coup when a marriage alliance was made between him and Henry I of England. Henry I's daughter, Matilda, was given to Henry V as his bride. Since Henry I had no legitimate children, though he had many illegitimate ones, Matilda was the heir to the throne. Henry V dreamed of taking England into his sovereign domain and actively tried to support Henry I against France but troubles at home prevented any real success. With the urging of the Archbishop Adalbert a new rebellion broke out and civil war erupted again. The fermentation of unrest by the Church was effective and in 1115 Henry lost Saxony to Lothair of Supplinburg, who became the Duke of Saxony, and eventually the next emperor.

The apparent loss of Saxony was appeased by news of the Countess Matilda's death in Italy. Countess Matilda had been one of the most staunch supporters of Pope Gregory VII and an enemy to the Emperor. She had bequeathed all her lands to the pope on her death but Henry saw the opportunity to seize her powerful lands for himself. Pope Paschal called upon the Normans to defend the Papal states but Urban and Paschal had been too successful in the

Crusades and most of the ablest Normans were in Palestine. By 1117 Henry V had secured most of the disputed lands and arrived in Rome where he made Paschal crown his English wife, Matilda, Holy Roman Empress.

The next year Pope Paschal II died and the stage was set for a new struggle. The Clementine popes had failed but there was still much antagonism against the Gregorian popes. Their arrogance and tyranny created many enemies. But for their alliance with the Normans it is unlikely that the Gregorians could ever have survived. However, the Normans were now largely in Palestine and their weakness was evident. When Gelasius II was elected and consecrated only three days after Paschal's death a Roman nobleman immediately kidnapped Gelasius and imprisoned him but the people still respected the spiritual office. Such behavior could only be tolerated by the emperor, and only him because he had the military might. The city prefect demanded the release of Gelasius and mobs of citizens were ready to back up the prefect if necessary. Gelasius was released peaceably and yet no sooner was he released than news of Henry V's coming to Rome sent Gelasius into hiding.

When Henry arrived in Rome he dispatched a letter to Gelasius' colleagues demanding his return and saying that he wished only to negotiate a settlement in regards to investiture. Gelasius showed no backbone and refused to budge. He further declared that he would hold his own council to which Henry was apparently not invited. Henry then appointed an archbishop named Maurice as a new pope, who took the name Gregory (VIII). Gelasius himself tried unsuccessfully to seize Rome and drive out Gregory (VIII) but his troops were no match for those of Gregory. Gelasius again retreated and died, a feeble old man, the next year.

Papal Struggles and a Concordat

When Pope Gelasius died his supporters elected the son of the Count of Burgundy under the name Callistus II. Gregory (VIII) himself had never been able to achieve the backing and support of the people, which in itself displayed the lack of respect which Henry V garnered. In 1118 the German nobles had even ordered Henry to return from Italy or else they would overthrow his rule. Henry had no choice but leave. Gregory had clearly been elected as a ploy of Henry. Had Henry commanded more respect Gregory might have succeeded but he did not. The Romans themselves were inclined to accept Callistus even though Gregory held the city. Finally, Gregory was forced to leave for Sutri when he learned that Henry V had betrayed him. Henry, always a politician, realized that Gregory did not have the support of the people and he was willing to compromise with Callistus if necessary. This news sent Gregory fleeing but the army of Callistus besieged the city of Sutri and the populous, faced with starvation or worse, knew that Henry V was not interested in rescuing them.

They turned Gregory (VIII) over to Callistus who brought him back to Rome for a mock trial.

Gregory was paraded around backwards on a camel where the people threw rocks and food at him. After having humiliated Gregory, Callistus had him imprisoned for the rest of his life in a monastery, the prison of popes. Now only Callistus remained. The year was 1120 and not long afterwards the German princes, tiring of the conflict that had gone on for over fifty years, urged Henry to resolve the situation by compromise. At the instigation of the princes and nobles a concordat was arranged at Worms in 1122. This concordat agreed that the symbols of spiritual authority, a ring and crozier, were to be conferred by the pope but that the emperor would bestow the sceptre as a sign of temporal authority. Furthermore, the ceremony was to take place in the presence of the emperor. This concordat was ratified at the First Lateran Council in early 1123.

In matter of fact the concordat was little more than a political treaty. It did not explain or clarify exactly what would happen if the emperor and pope disagreed on the appointment of a particular bishop although the emperor could object to the election of bishop on certain grounds. Nowhere is the situation fully resolved. For Henry and Callistus, however, it was a symbol that they could work together as they were suppose to. Whether it is a testament to their strength or weakness is a matter of opinion for neither would live long beyond this, and the reign of both hinges upon the concordat. Callistus died in 1124 and Henry V died the following year, the last of the Franconians.

Jerusalem During the Henry V's Reign

The first Crusades had been a success despite some atrocities, such as occur in most every war, but now petty ambition and selfish backbiting threatened the kingdom of Jerusalem. It was only because the knights knew that unity was essential to their own survival that they came to each other's aid when necessary. Only Godfrey and Raymond showed true chivalrous honor but Godfrey died in 1100 and in 1105, after having been betrayed by Tancred, Raymond died.

Raymond had been the most noble and virtuous of the knights of the Crusade. Of the major knights only he and Godfrey honored their word to the eastern emperor. He spared those Muslims who surrendered in battle and showed chivalry when those around him were butchering the innocent. Out of his own pockets he paid money to ransom many of those who had been taken captive. Despite the wealth that he had at home he never abandoned the Holy Land, even when Tancred had kicked him out of Syria and, most noble of all, he declined the offer to become King of Jerusalem out of respect for Christ. He was devout and pious. Had Raymond had more leadership ability the Crusades might have had a different ending but the two best knights of the Crusades, Godfrey and Raymond, died too soon.

Of the great knights of the first Crusade only Baldwin and Tancred remained. Tancred had some of Raymond's chivalry but he had more of his uncle Bohemund's petty ambitions. He could be as ruthless and treacherous as he could be honorable. Baldwin, likewise, displayed similar traits. When a city surrendered to him he treated them with the highest respect and honor but to those that refused to surrender he was merciless and cruel. It was intentional. He wanted his enemies to fear him and his allies to respect him.

With what few men Baldwin had to aid him he slowly took over important cities which still rested in Muslim hands. In 1103 the important sea port of Acre was taken. In 1105 the Egyptians failed in an attack on Palestine but Baldwin also failed when he boldly attempted to invade Egyptian lands. In 1110 Tripoli and Sidon fell into Latin hands but Baldwin was never able to take Ascalon or Tyre, both of which were vitally important cities.

During these years guerrilla warfare was common. As the Muslim Turks of Palestine were cut off from their allies they could only hope to hold out in fortified cities and hit the Crusaders whenever possible. For their part the Crusaders tried to make Palestine content with Latin rule. Religious tolerance was permitted for Muslim and Jew and racial intermarriage became commonplace. Despite the fact that the Christians were hopelessly outnumbered by their Muslim enemies surrounding Palestine the Crusader's cause was helped by their seeming unity. Although their personal squabbles and fights showed that their unity was only out of necessity, the Muslims warred openly amongst themselves. In the years before Baldwin's death no fewer than a half dozen Islamic rulers had fallen by exiles, assassinations, treachery, conspiracy, or other means. The Assassins, from the word *hashishayun* for the Hashish drug they used, had become a prominent political tool of some powerful Islamic Emirs.

Among the Christians there was certainly much fighting and backbiting but they cooperated because they knew they had to. An example, however, of the type of infighting that did occur was the deposition of the Patriarch Daimbert whom Baldwin despised for plotting a usurpation with Bohemund years earlier. Daimbert was replaced by Arnulf, while Tancred had fought with Baldwin of Edessa, the King's cousin, who succeeded him in that region.

In 1112 Tancred died of typhoid fever, though some speculate poison, leaving a powerful Syrian state. He was only thirty six years old. He would be replaced as the Prince of Antioch by a knight named Roger, while a certain Joscelin, who had been exiled by Baldwin of Edessa, became the Prince of Galilee. Only Baldwin, king of Jerusalem, remained but in 1117 two lunar eclipses occurred followed by the sighting of the *aurora borealis*. To the medieval world this signaled disaster and within a year seven of the world leaders died including the great Byzantine Emperor Alexius, Pope Pashcal, and King Baldwin.

Baldwin II was King Baldwin's nephew. He had become the Prince of Edessa and was rising to prominence as a just ruler. He would be the last King to have fought in the first Crusade. In terms of character Baldwin II was more devout and chivalrous than his namesake but he was still a rigorous politician. He had accused Joscelin of treason and exiled him from Edessa, yet it was Joscelin who recommended him to succeed Baldwin. This irony can only be explained by Joscelin's conscience for he had once secretly desired to inherit Baldwin's estates. When Baldwin had learned of this he tested Joscelin by feigning serious illness. Joscelin betrayed his intentions when he grew excited at the prospect of Baldwin's death. He ask the Prince, "how do you fare?" to which Baldwin replied, "better than you think." He then leapt from his bed and imprisoned Joscelin for a short time. Joscelin apparently learned his lesson and became one of Baldwin's best allies. Baldwin II in return made amends with Joscelin and awarded him his old fief of Edessa.

With the royal throne of Jerusalem Baldwin II inherited his nephew's problems. Palestine was still plagued by rogue Muslim Turks who held out in a number of cities. The Crusaders held most of the major cities of Palestine but Tyre and Ascalon still eluded them. That same year Gerard, head monk of the Hospitaller order, died. He was replaced by Raymond of Le Puy who was distressed that the road to Jerusalem was so treacherous and dangerous. He helped turn the Hospitallers into a military order of Knights, later called the Knights of St. John, whose job was not only to provide places of rest and entertainment, but was also to safely escort pilgrims to Jerusalem. They were a sort of police force who was accountable solely to the pope, and not to any king, duke, or count. At this same time the Knights Templar became the second military order founded by Hugh of Payens, who spent much of his time in Europe recruiting members for the order.

These military orders differed from regular knights, not only in that they were solely accountable to the pope, but also in that they took a vow of poverty. They were truly armed monks, not mercenaries. Part of the tragedy of the first Crusades was the fact that so many of the soldiers had been mercenaries with no code of honor. They came to pillage and plunder. The military orders did none of this. They were seen as the friends of the common man, while regular armies were often distrusted. Together these military orders served as a police force which helped and assisted the King of Jerusalem in many ways, though they were not directly under his sovereignty. Baldwin II was more than pleased to have that help. Indeed, the Templar Knights would soon rise to become the most famous and mysterious knights of history. As a religious order they were armed monks who vowed no human warmth. They were not even allowed to hug their own mothers. Privacy was not permitted. Each member belonged to the other members. They founded their headquarters on the spot where they believed Solomon's Temple had rested, hence the name, and they later developed rituals which put them in conflict with the papacy. For the time being, they were the pope's warriors. They had no allegiance to Baldwin directly, other than that they served the same cause. They became the elite warriors of Palestine and developed an intricate spy system. The Templar's power would one day rise to such heights that even the popes would fear them.

In 1119 a massive Islamic army of Turcomans moved toward Antioch. Its leader was a vile Emir name Ilghazi who would promise safe passage to those who surrendered only to slaughter them. His army was also made up of rouges and mercenaries that made the atrocities of the first Crusade, for which they have been so harshly judged, look like harmless fun. When Roger heard of the army he sent word to Baldwin II but he preferred not to allow Ilghazi to besiege Antioch before Baldwin II could arrive, so he rode out to meet Ilghazi at what came to be called the "field of Blood." Ilghazi's army routed Roger's army. Roger was lucky, for he fell in battle, but those prisoners who survived were paraded back to Ilghazi's home city only to be tortured to death for the people's enjoyment.

While Ilghazi was reveling in his victory over Roger, Baldwin II had time to arrive and secure Antioch, which had been left undefended. The arrogant revelry of Ilghazi had cost him his prize. Baldwin II and Ilghazi met in another battle in which both sides claimed the victory. Ilghazi had secured more prisoners which he brought before his people for the usual entertainment of torture and death, but Baldwin II had ensured that Antioch was not taken and Ilghazi was never again to make another attack on the fortress. Now, with Roger dead, Bohemund II was the rightful heir to Antioch but he was only ten years old so the Patriarch of Antioch served as regent in his stead.

In 1122, and again a few months later in 1123, disaster struck. In two separate incidents the Muslims had captured Joscelin and King Baldwin II himself. An ambush had taken the two most prominent knights of the realm and they were imprisoned in the Emir's castle, but Joscelin had many friends in that countryside and when the Emir's army was out attacking a city about fifty men entered the castle in disguise as merchants and monks. They then seized the castle with relative ease, inasmuch as the garrisons were away on a raid. There were too few of them to expect to make their escape all the way to Christian lands so Joscelin agreed to slip behind the lines and go get help but Baldwin II chose to stay with his friends in the castle. Joscelin arrived to late. The Emir had returned and executed all but Baldwin II, who was too important to slay. Joscelin's army was itself defeated and the latest Patriarch of Jerusalem, Gormund, acted as regent of the kingdom until Baldwin could return.

Not long after this the Emir had died and his son desired to ransom Baldwin II for profit. A huge sum was paid and Baldwin II was released. He returned to Jerusalem where the people cheerfully accepted him back. In his absence Gormund had managed to capture the important city of Tyre, with Venetian assistance, in 1124. The kingdom of Jerusalem was slowly reaching its height of power by the time of Henry V's death.

Summary of the Franconian Dynasty

The Franconian Dynasty had, as with many others, begun with promise but it rapidly deteriorated. Although Conrad II did not make a great name for himself, he was by all rights a good and capable emperor. He was also a political leader, not a spiritual one. Throughout Conrad's reign theology and the Church played a small role. Upon the ascension of Henry III, this changed. A devout Catholic, Henry III served as a loyal minion of the Church throughout his reign. What he did he did for the good of the Church, or so he believed. Henry had bought entirely into the medieval theory of the Church and it was through his active support that the Gregorian popes rose to power.

Despite Henry IV's pitiable reign, he was not really an enemy of the Church, nor a bad emperor per se. He was the victim of circumstances that his father had created. The Church was now declaring, for itself, temporal powers that it had never sought nor claimed in centuries past. Henry's main failing was his arrogance and his inability to accept failure. His actions, both good and bad, made him appear weak and his groveling before Gregory VII symbolized the change that history was to make. The pope was now sovereign over the emperor and nothing Henry could ever do would change the image that he created on that day.

The long tenure of Henry IV was largely a weak and unstable one. Had Henry been stronger, or wiser, history might not have taken the course that it did, but history is inevitable. Henry V did little more than continue in his father's footsteps; the same father he had himself usurped with the aid of the popes, whom he later opposed.

Ironically, the main thing for which the Franconian Dynasty may be remembered was that which it had no part in: the Crusades. The Crusades were neither as noble as the Europeans dreamt, nor were they as barbaric and atrocious as is believed today. It was a war as grand and as grave as World War I was for the modern era. The Turkish invaders were scarcely innocent victims, though the innocent often died along with the guilty. It symbolized the rise of the west, and the decline of the eastern Roman Empire. It saved the Byzantine Empire, yet it also betrayed them for wealth and power.

With the Franconians the Imperial authority of Germany was diminished and the papal authority rose to new heights. For the first time heresy was made punishable by death and the true gospel began to slowly be suppressed in favor of political bishops. It is ironic that the removal of bishop's investiture by the kings created a far more political bishopry than had ever existed before. In the centuries past, kings preferred bishops that would not interfere in their politics. This meant that most, but certainly not all, nominated bishops who would be concerned with religion, and not politics. Nevertheless, the evils of simony became apparent as bishops literally bought the offices for money. The Church now stripped the kings and emperor of this right and bishops were now to be nominated by the pope himself. The result was that bishops throughout Europe were made to be loyal to the Gregorian popes.

For all that had happened over the centuries, local communities had once had bishops who were independent of the corruption of the early medieval Papacy. Milan in particular was renowned for its devotion to the older, more pure, faith; and that region would soon see the rise of Protestant forerunners; most notably, the Waldenses. With the rise of the Gregorian popes, and the decline of the Franconian Emperors, all that was to change. Independence could not be tolerated if the pope was truly to be sovereign.

The Franconian Dynasty can be defined in a single sentence. It was the age when the pope became the true sovereign of the Holy Roman Empire and the emperors, with few exceptions, became figureheads.

11

—

Two Houses at War

The Franconian or Salian dynasty had weakened the authority of the Holy Roman Emperors and with it, the position of Germany in the empire. The once great Germans were now second fiddle to the Normans, whose barbaric nature was still obvious at times. Just as the proud Italians had constantly been in revolt against Germanic leaders, the Germans were too proud to be content with figurehead emperors. They wanted an emperor who could restore the glory of Charlemagne and restore the empire to its supposed Germanic roots. The Franconians had not proven themselves to be strong leaders and the Germans decided to reject the hereditary right of the throne. Two houses then began to vie for the position. The House of Supplinburg would rise first by election, but the famous House of Hohenstaufen claimed the right of hereditary rule. Elective monarchy was pitted against hereditary monarchy.

The struggles for the imperial throne were not the only struggles of this era. The pontiffs too had succumbed to petty rivalries and bickering. Rival emperors would set themselves up against one another and two rival popes would anathamize one another for almost a decade. The imperial throne would be resolved before the papal throne was resolved, and from the House of Hohenstaufen would arise emperors who would indelibly carve their niche into the pages of history. The rise of the House of Hohenstaufen might be considered the last ditch efforts by the emperors to preserve the old empire as it was known under Charlemagne but before they could do battle with the popes, they would have to do battle with the House of Supplinburg.

Honorius II Usurps the Papacy

Shortly before the death of Henry V, Pope Callistus had died. A debate broke out among the clergy as to who should succeed him. The now old school Gregorians wanted one of their own ranks installed but many protested that the investiture issue had been resolved and that the papacy should move on to other things. A compromise was reached and Celestine (II) was unanimously elected pope, but before the consecration could even be completed armed soldiers broke into the assembly, brutalized Celestine, and demanded that he resign.

Celestine could do nothing more than offer his resignation and die from his wounds not long afterwards. In his place Honorius II was installed without ever having been elected. Bribes were paid to the prominent politicians and families of Rome, along with threats, to ensure that Honorius' ascension was not challenged. A short time later Henry V died. Had not the struggle ensued between the House of Supplinburg and the House of Hohenstaufen there is no way to tell what would have happened to Honorius, but with bitter rivals vying for the imperial throne papal recognition was vital and there was currently only one pope. Honorius II was never challenged.

The House of Supplinburg

Lothair II (sometimes reckoned as Lothair III by those who accepted Emperor Lothair's son as a legitimate successor) had rebelled against Henry IV and helped in Henry V's rebellion against his father. However, after Henry V's accession, and his appointment as duke of Saxony, Lothair turned against Henry and rebelled. Saxony had become independent under his rule but with the royal throne empty Lothair seemed the most logical choice for king, and emperor. He was from the House of Supplinburg and was certainly one of the most powerful dukes of Germany as his successful rebellion against Henry V had shown, plus he was an ally of the popes, unlike the previous emperors. In 1125 Lothair was elected king of Germany.

The election was immediately contested by the remaining heirs. The House of Hohenstaufen, so named after its great castle, claimed the right to the throne. Conrad was the grandson of Henry IV as was his brother Frederick, the duke of Swabia. They revolted and civil war was imminent. Lothair then took the unprecedented step of asking the pope, controversial Honorius II, to confirm his election. Conrad, however, also had powerful allies. The Archbishops of Milan were historically unfavorable to the papacy. They had never loved the Gregorian popes and did like the usurper Honorius. Milan, from whence the great Archbishop Ambrose had risen centuries earlier, had always been independent minded and was the region from which many Protestant forerunners emerged, including Claudius the "Protestant of the Ninth Century." The Milanese Archbishop Anselm was in sympathy with Conrad and with his support Conrad was crowned king of the Lombards in northern Italy. The position bolstered Conrad's claim to Germany.

Honorius excommunicated Conrad and Anselm. Civil war was the result. For two years Germany was at war with itself until Lothair successfully seized Nurnberg and Speyer, two of Conrad's strongest fortresses. By 1129 Lothair had largely secured Germany. Conrad maintained his title as the king of Lombardy where he stayed with Anselm's backing until he could bide his time.

Papal Schism

No sooner had the civil war in Germany died down than a new schism would erupt. Honorius II had seized the diadem with violence so it is perhaps a testament in his favor that he was an insignificant pope whose reign came to nothing. Aside from his support of Lothair his most memorable testament was the official recognition of the Knights Templar, which had the strong backing of Bernard of Clairvaux, a prominent theologian who was quickly rising in prestige among the empire. When Honorius died in 1130 he had only a few loyal colleagues and it was only logical that a schism would erupt between his followers and the rest of the clergy.

Among Honorius' best ally was Aimeric, his chancellor. When Aimeric realized that Honorius was dying he took he pope away to a quiet monastery so that no one would know exactly when he died. Upon his death Aimeric then secretly buried the body and spirited away to Rome where he and Honroius' supporters secretly elected Innocent II. As the sun rose on February 14, news spread throughout Rome that a new pope had been elected in the seclusion of the night and the majority of cardinals were incensed. The cardinals held a new election in public and allowed the entire populous of Rome to witness the election. A Messianic Jew (Jewish convert) named Anacletus II was duly elected pope and both Innocent and Anacletus were consecrated on the same day, February 23, 1130.

Each pope knew that his legitimacy would not depend upon whose election was canonical but upon who could secure the support of the kings and people of the empire. Anacletus began with the strongest support, owing to his manner of ascension. The people of Rome thoroughly backed him. By the end of the year Innocent had fled to France to muster support there, while Anacletus gained his most powerful ally in the Norman Roger II of southern Italy. Ever since Robert Guiscard had conquered the former Byzantine lands of southern Italy the land had been divided into several duchies, but it had never been united under a single king. The Normans had become allies of the popes but they had never truly submitted themselves to the emperor's authority. After Robert died the dukes fought with one another for supremacy, but this fighting was itself interrupted by the Crusades. Now Roger II had come into possession of the duchies of Apulia, Calabria, and Sicily making him the most powerful duke in southern Italy. He wanted one more thing; a king's crown. Anacletus agreed to make Roger II the first recognized King of Sicily in exchange for his support against Innocent II, and he was coronated on Christmas day, 1130, thereby uniting all southern Italy into a single Norman country.

Innocent never had a military ally as strong as Roger, but he made himself a powerful spiritual ally in France, and with that ally Innocent would eventually prevail. Bernard of Clairvaux had become a prominent and well respected theologian and abbot. So popular was he that Martin Luther, four hundred years later, is said to have preferred Bernard to St. Augustine. In some respects Bernard's theology was compatible with Protestant theology, for Bernard emphasized Christ above all, but Bernard was still a medieval Catholic and that meant that the Church, and its pope, were Christ's representatives on earth. Once Bernard came to trust Innocent he became his greatest spokesman. Within a year Bernard had convinced both the French King, Louis VI, and the

English King, Henry I, to support Innocent. Of the main countries of the empire only that of Lothair II remained undecided. In March of 1131 Innocent met with Lothair to begin long negotiations on his recognition. Innocent agreed to bestow the Imperial crown on Lothair, whose struggles with Conrad had prevented this recognition, but Lothair also wanted the right of investiture restored to the crown.

Anacletus had nobly agreed to submit the dispute to arbitration and to abide by the decision, but Innocent refused. He had apparently already finalized his agreement with Lothair. It was decided that, in exchange for his support and military aid, Lothair would be crowned emperor of the Holy Roman Empire and Innocent would also surrender the vast estates that the Countess Matilda had bequeathed to the papacy. In August of 1132 Anacletus and Roger II were anathematized by Innocent II. Of the major kingdoms of the empire three now supported Innocent, but military aid could not be expected from France or England and the Kingdom of Sicily was far stronger than Germany's. Nevertheless, Lothair wanted the imperial crown and, in 1133, he set out for Rome with his army to overthrow the supposed antipope Anacletus.

In Rome Norman soldiers and Anacletus supporters held out in the Leonine City and St. Peter's but Lothair was able to capture the heart of Rome including the Lateran. There, on June 3, Innocent kept his promise and crowned Lothair Holy Roman Emperor amid the backdrop of a besieged city. An interesting side–note is the fact that Lothair held the stirrup of the pope. This symbolic gesture showed humility on Lothair's part but was more significant, for it was the task of menial peasants. It showed that the pope was the emperor's sovereign, a fact not lost on later emperor Frederick Barbarossa. Not long after his coronation Lothair was forced to retreat from Rome. From the Leonine City the supporters of Anacletus were able to stage raids and harass his army. He was doubtless aware as well that Roger II would not sit idly by without sending reinforcements. Lothair made his retreat with Innocent to Pisa while Bernard continued to try to win peaceable support for their cause.

Lothair's short lived victory was interrupted by news that Conrad had risen in rebellion again. In 1132 Conrad had first reentered Germany and defeated Lothair's troops. His desire to be coronated emperor allowed him to ignore the usurper temporarily but he now returned to restore his lands. Conrad was not one to surrender easily. With Roger II in southern Italy and Conrad invading German lands Lothair did not want a war on two fronts. By 1135, when it was obvious that Conrad would not easily disappear, he came to an agreement. Conrad would cease the revolt and in exchange Lothair would pardon him and restore all the lands that had once been his. The extent to which Conrad bartered for the right of accession cannot be determined but when Lothair did die the electors chose Conrad over Lothair's son–in–law with little debate.

This peace settlement freed Lothair for duty in other parts of the realm. In 1135 Denmark became a vassal state of the emperor and Polish kings again submitted to German rule after years of dispute. Now Lothair was free for another campaign against Italy. In the meantime Bernard of Clairvaux had been tirelessly at work and in 1136 he was able to convince Milan to switch their support from Anacletus to Innocent. This was a critical loss for Anacletus. His staunchest supporters had been the Italians. With Milan now favoring Innocent only Roger II and the Normans remained by his side. This same year Lothair launched another expedition into Italy with the purpose of driving Roger off the continent. He was initially successful. Roger II was forced to retreat to Sicily and rival dukes were appointed in southern Italy by Innocent and Lothair. By 1137 virtually all of Italy had been secured by Lothair but on his return trip to Germany, Lothair died. At this same time Bernard, hoping to avoid more war, agreed to a meeting with Roger at Salerno where a debate was held between Anacletus' supporters and Innocents. Bernard was said to have been the most eloquent. He made the analogy that the pope was like Noah's ark. If Anacletus was the ark then all the empire would drown except for the Kingdom of Sicily. If, however, Innocent was the true ark then the empire would be saved. The analogy is, of course, false and really boiled down to "we have more supporters than you." That Anacletus was properly elected seemed irrelevant at this time for many years had passed. The present was deemed to be of supreme importance and Bernard won the debate.

The result of the debate was the effective loss of Roger but Roger was still not willing to accept Innocent unless concessions were made. Negotiations continued while Anacletus held out in Rome. His death, however, came a month later in January of 1138. His supporters elected a Victor IV to replace him but it was obvious that all support was lost. In May Bernard negotiated a peaceful solution. Victor IV promised to surrender the papacy to Innocent and Bernard promised that no further action would be taken. Innocent, however, lied. As soon as Innocent took possession of Rome a council was held at the Lateran and he reneged on his promise. Victor and his allies were banished against the angry protestations of Bernard, who had made Innocent pope.

From Conrad's Ascension to the Roman Rebellion

When Lothair died the electors of Germany chose Conrad over Lothair's heirs. Ironically, even though Lothair had risen to the crown by denying the right of hereditary rule his heirs now claimed it for themselves. Henry the Proud was the duke of Bavaria and Saxony, and was Lothair's son-in-law. War broke out but within a little over a year Henry had died. Despite this, Henry's brother, Wulf, now claimed the throne on hereditary grounds and the war continued.

In Italy, the death of Lothair gave Roger II opportunity to restore his lands in southern Italy. It was 1139 when Roger II marched all the way into Rome, after reclaiming his old lands, and seized Pope Innocent II. Innocent was forced to acknowledge Roger as the King of Sicily and its kingdom. Roger then released Innocent and set about solidifying his kingdom. He refused, however, to acknowledge Conrad III as emperor. This fact proved to be of little consequence since Conrad was too busy at war with Wulf.

Germany had seen little real peace since the time of Henry III and the civil wars of the last decade began to take a toll on the public spirit. It was fortunate when Conrad was able to reach a temporary peace accord with Wulf. Wulf had lost a critical battle back in 1140 and two years later his defeat seemed imminent. A treaty seemed the only way for Wulf to save himself and inasmuch as Conrad had done the same with his enemy Lothair II, Wulf decided it was best. The terms did not favor Wulf but it did bring some peace. Nevertheless, disorder continued from Poland to Bavaria to Bohemia and beyond. Conrad would remain occupied in his native lands until the call for the second Crusade went out in 1146. Indeed, Conrad would be so busy that he was never able to have the Imperial crown formally bestowed on him by the pope.

During this difficult time the French continued to spar among themselves. King Louis VI spent most of his reign forcing robber barons to submit to the king's justice. In Spain the Catholic kings bickered amongst themselves while they continued their long war against the Muslims. Normandy proved no more peaceful. The struggle between the English crown and France intensified over the years. Henry I of England had arranged a marriage alliance between Matilda (the widowed Empress of Henry V) and Geoffrey (Count Fulk of Anjou's son) back in 1128. Fulk had been one of the claimants to the onetime duchy of Normandy and he had hoped that the alliance would allow Normandy to peaceably be accepted as a part of England but Fulk left for Palestine in 1129 to become heir to the throne of Jerusalem and by 1135 Henry and Geoffrey were openly at war with one another.

Henry died in 1135 and, because of Geoffrey's war with Henry, his claim to the throne was weakened. The majority of the English supported Stephen of Blois, Henry's nephew, as heir to the throne. Naturally war erupted between Geoffrey and Stephen. Both gained prominent supporters. The foremost of Geoffrey's allies was Robert of Glouchester. During the course of the war Stephen was captured by Geoffrey's men but Robert of Glouchester fell into the hands of Stephen's army. The two were traded for one another and the war continued.

Back in Rome Innocent's prestige was quickly diminishing. His rise had largely been due to the influence of Bernard, whom he had alienated somewhat after his refusal to pardon Victor IV. In 1141 King Louis VII, the new king of France, had refused to accept an appointment made by the pope so Innocent placed an interdiction on anyone who offered the King shelter. Then, in 1143, the pope gained the enmity of the people of Rome and Arnold of Brescia forced his way into the pages of history.

From the Founding of New Republic of Rome to the Second Crusade

The depravity and corruption of the Roman Church had first brought the reformer Otto the Great to power over a hundred years earlier. The previous attempt to reform the Church from within had risen to its peak with Gregory VII but it only further polluted the Church with power, as it had Gregory himself. Now a lesser person in history, but no less in stature, arose by the name of Arnold of Brescia. Arnold was a monk who critically and vocally spoke out against the luxurious living of the Church. He called on the Church clergy to take a vow of poverty and even went so far as to proclaim that a priest could not be saved unless he was poor. In 1139 he was exiled from Italy for "inciting" the people against the clergy. He moved to France, but at Bernard of Clairvaux's instigation, he was also exiled from there. He then moved to Zurich near the ever independent minded Milanese. There he remained until resurfacing in Rome about 1143.

Arnold of Brescia had been a disciple of Peter Abelard who had recently been declared a heretic. Abelard was philosopher who treated Christian doctrine mystically. He was a proud, arrogant, sarcastic, but eloquent speaker whose personal life, as well as doctrines, made Bernard of Clairvaux into a powerful enemy. He had secretly married a woman and fathered a child whom he refused to support or care for. He later abandoned his secret wife who went to a convent after her father had him castrated. He died about the same time that Arnold began his revolution in Rome.

With the corruption of the Church and the schism of the papacy, Arnold found the always proud Roman people ready to reject the temporal claims of the papacy. Gregory VII had powerfully asserted the temporal control of the pope but in less than fifty years it was clear that the popes were no better than the emperor's of old. Arnold beseeched the people to reject the pope and reestablish the old Roman Republic. He asserted clearly the inalienable rights of men and of Christian laymen. The people followed his lead and set up an independent senate which refused to recognize the pope's sovereignty over Rome in any temporal sense. Rioting once again enveloped the city.

Once the city had been secured, and the military support of Innocent thwarted, Arnold wrote to Conrad III. He begged the emperor to come and receive his crown from the senate, not the pope, and tried to win his support for the democratic movement. He slyly reminded Conrad that "the pope and the Sicilian are united in an impious league to oppose our liberty and your coronation." He also requested that Conrad take up residence in Rome as the old emperors had, and as the great Holy Roman Emperors had, calling it the Capital of the World.

167

Had Conrad agreed to the request the course of human history would almost certainly have changed. Whether that change would have been for better or worse can only be speculated upon for the people of the world were not yet ready. This was no where more obvious than with the Romans themselves. Though Arnold of Brescia is considered an ancient forerunner of the American forefathers he, and his followers, were proud Romans. Their Republic would last only ten years and was truly a revival of the old Roman Republic, not a new Christian one as Arnold preached. One could not tell a great difference between the Rome of the papacy a decade earlier and the Rome of this New Republic.

Of Arnold himself, controversy had surrounded his character. Some claim him as a Protestant forerunner while others see him merely as a politician. The truth is that he was both and neither. In theology he held, with Protestants, that the Eucharist was but a memorial and rejected infant baptism but with the Catholics he held to most other doctrines save the primacy of the pope. He was obvious inconsistent in regard to salvation by faith, since he held poverty as a requirement for the salvation of the clergy. Politically he did not wish to distance Christianity from government, only the Church from the State. This important distinction seems lost on many of this age, for they do differ significantly. Although unrealized, Arnold's democratic republic was to be based on Christian principles of human rights and on the supremacy of God and Christ over man. Man was not to be his own master but was entrusted with government of the people, and it was their responsibility to protect those God given rights.

The Republican experiment was to intrude upon the papacy of six popes but the first to witness its rise died the year it appeared. Innocent was the making of one man; Bernard of Clairvaux. When he lost that man's respect he also lost the favor of the people, although Bernard never tried to be vindictive or turn the people away from Innocent. Innocent had arrogantly asserted his authority over many people but in the end was defeated by them. Roger II forced Innocent to accept his claim to the Kingdom of Sicily, Louis VII outlived Innocent and returned to the French throne intact, and even the people of Rome were in insurrection against his rule. In September Celestine II became the next pope but, like many popes of that day, he was already aged and frail. His reign lasted only a little over five months. During that time he lifted the interdiction against Louis VII and, after initially revoking Roger II's claims, came to terms with the Kingdom of Sicily and Roger. At Bernard's instigation, Celestine was forced to distance himself from his teacher (and Arnold's), Peter Abelard, and vowed to orthodoxy.

When Celestine II died another pope was destined to rise and fall within a year's time. This time it was Lucius II but his death was his own fault. He refused to accept the New Republic of Rome. Giordano Pierleoni, a Jewish Christian, and the brother of former antipope Anacletus, became the Patrician of Rome and the New Republic. Lucius therefore resolved to head up his own military troops against the senate. Lucius attempted to besiege the Capitol where Pierleoni and the insurgents held out, but large stones were hurled down in place of boiling oil. Lucius fell prey to a heavy stone and died on February 15, 1145. Even as he lay dying word that Edessa had fallen to the Turks in Palestine was already being sent back to Rome. The Second Crusade was about to begin.

Palestine Before the Second Crusade

Baldwin II was king of Jerusalem when the Latin Kingdom was at its height. He was a balanced king who mixed his devotion to the Church with a military prowess against the Islamic invaders. He was also wise enough to realize that he was growing old and had no male heirs. If the Christian Kingdom of Jerusalem was to survive his death then it needed a strong successor and there could be no time for disputes among claimants. He decided to adopt the aged Fulk of Anjou as his successor in 1129.

That same year the old Emir of Damascus had died. Damascus had been the main stronghold for the Islamic threat, just east of the Kingdom of Jerusalem, and without an Emir Baldwin II believed this was the best possible time to strike at the heart of the Muslim enemies. He had attempted to besiege Damascus when news arrived that Joscelin was at war with Bohemund II, the heir to Antioch who had recently come of age. Without their help Baldwin was unable to take Damascus so he withdrew and set out to make peace among the northern Princes. By the time this was done Damascus had a new ruler and the Christians had lost the opportunity to take the city. It was at this time a new Emir in Syria named Zengi rose to power in opposition to both the Franks and Damascus and it was he, surnamed the "Pillar of Faith," who ultimately threatened the very existence of the Christian Kingdom.

Bickering among the northern Princes had thwarted Baldwin's chance to strike a blow to the Islamic resistance and further selfishness by those same Princes would further enhance the cause of the Muslims. Bohemund II died in battle while still in his early twenties. This left Antioch with a small child as heir. His mother, Alice, was Baldwin II's daughter. When Baldwin II heard the news of Bohemund's death he set out to Antioch to examine the situation and appoint a regent. Alice, however, was a corrupt power–seeking woman who did not have the good of the kingdom at heart, but her own ambitions. She immediately declared herself regent of Antioch and sent a messenger to the Muslim Emir Zengi promising to betray Antioch into his hands in exchange for the right to rule.

Fortunately Baldwin II intercepted the messenger. When he arrived at Antioch Alice had the gates locked in his face. Joscelin arrived to help in the siege of Antioch when loyalist inside the city were able to rush the gate and open it for Baldwin. He forgave his daughter and took her to Lattakieh where she could be watched. She would, however, return again to try to usurp the Kingdom at the expense of the people.

In 1131 Baldwin II lay dying. He knew that his death was near and had himself made a monk in his final days. He was buried in the Holy Sepulchre following his death on August 21, 1131. That same year Joscelin died from wounds he received in battle. The last of the old guard of Crusaders had died and with them died the zenith of the Kingdom of Jerusalem.

Fulk's ascension to the throne was interrupted by news that Alice was again trying to usurp the rule of Antioch, this time with the support of the northern Princes. Fulk defeated her forces in 1132 and generously exiled her again to Lattakieh, where she would again bide her time. Fulk was now the acknowledge king of the Kingdom of Jerusalem, and the Princes of the north acknowledged his sovereignty, but the pettiness of Queen Melisende jeopardized the peace of the kingdom.

Fulk's wife, Melisende, had been having an affair with another noble. When the affair was made public, Melisende's lover, Hugh of Le Puiset, fled to Egypt where he formed an alliance and returned with an Egyptian invasion army. The invading army was crushed and Hugh was captured, but Fulk showed great leniency to Hugh by giving him only three years in exile while he punished an assassination attempt on Hugh by having the culprit's arms and legs torn off. Fulk was more and more becoming a puppet to his domineering, and unfaithful, wife.

These circumstances further harmed the Kingdom of Jerusalem because it prevented Fulk from siezing the opportunity to crush Muslim opposition in Damascus and Egypt. Zengi had been engaged in war with Bagdad and had left his region under the control of his son, who was hated by the Muslim populous for his cruelty. He had once even walled up his brother for suspicion of treason. The Egyptians were also embroiled in their own wars. The Caliph of Egypt had even executed forty Emirs and murdered his own son. The opportunities to exploit these travesties came and passed as Zengi returned and regained control. Zengi now turned his attention to the Franks where he would wage war for the next decade.

Zengi slowly began to chip away at the Kingdom of Jerusalem. He was a better warrior than the previous Islamic leaders and showed more honor that his predecessors. At one point he even allowed Fulk to escape with his life in exchange for the surrender of the city he was trapped within. It is almost certain that the city would have fallen or else Fulk would never have trusted Zengi, but Zengi was true to his word.

Matters were worsened when news arrived that Alice had again installed herself as regent of Antioch. This time she had the wide support of the local populous, as well as that of Queen Melisende. Fulk secretly sent a message to Raymond of Poitiers, a knight in the English King Henry's court, and arranged for him to marry Alice's nine year old daughter. The marriage legally annulled Alice's regency and made Raymond the new regent. In 1137, however, Raymond found Antioch besieged by the Byzantine Emperor John Comnenus who was demanding that the previous pacts be honored and that Antioch be delivered to himself. With Fulk's knowledge and permission Raymond agreed to make Antioch a vassal of the Byzantine Emperor and swore allegiance to him.

This alliance helped to forestall the inevitable. With the Byzantines and Franks finally cooperating the Muslim threat was slowed but not halted. The pact between the Byzantines and Franks was, nonetheless, a fragile one marked by a riot and even threats of war. When John Comnenus died in 1143 the alliance folded. The last great hope of the Crusaders against Zengi came when Fulk forged an alliance with the Damascus Emir who feared Zengi and felt no threat from the Christians. Unfortunately, Fulk died (the same year as Comnenus) in a hunting accident after falling off his horse. He left the kingdom to his thirteen year old son, Baldwin III, but Melisende was the regent in his youth.

Although Melisende had a change of heart in her later years and devoted herself to the Church and charity, she was still a weak Queen who knew nothing of ruling. Alice would finally gain her regency of Antioch under Melisenda's reign, but the women would see the Kingdom of Jerusalem begin to crumble within a year. In late 1144 Joscelin had left Edessa on an expedition when Zengi seized the opportunity to attack. Joscelin sent for help but Raymond refused to help and the Queen's troops were slow in coming. Joscelin never returned to protect Edessa and without military support the walls finally gave. Zengi conquered Edessa in December of 1144. While the western Christians were slaughtered, the eastern Christians were treated with leniency in hopes of gaining their supports against the westerners.

The fall of Edessa signaled the beginning of the end of the Kingdom of Jerusalem. Although the kingdom would persevere for another forty years, its decline and fall began with Edessa. The kingdom had lost its unity and would see itself ruled by child kings. The only hope of preserving Christian Palestine was in a Second Crusade.

The Second Crusade

Pope Eugene (or Eugenius) III was elected on the very day that Celestine II died. He was forced to flee to Viterbo because of strong opposition from the Republican senate in Rome. From there Eugene ruled for most of his reign. Though he was a disciple of Bernard of Clairvaux, Bernard was surprised at his election, believing Eugene to inexperienced. His first real act of consequence was to call a new Crusade. He commissioned Bernard of Clairvaux to preach the Crusade and at one point Bernard was even slated to lead the armies, although Bernard decided against it.

Ironically, the Emperor Conrad was to be the first emperor to lead a Crusade and yet Eugene did not want the Emperor to go. Instead he went to France to enlist the help of Louis VII. The reason for Eugene's attitude was a selfish one. He had hoped that Conrad would lend military support to overthrow the Republican Senate and to crush Roger II, King of Sicily, whom Eugene despised. His mistake was in commissioning Bernard to preach for Conrad soon fell under Bernard's spell and vowed to leave on the Crusade himself. Hence the Second Crusade was to be led by a king and an emperor. The armies themselves were said to be larger than those of the First Crusade.

From France came King Louis the Younger (VII). Despite his fallout with Pope Innocent years earlier he was a devout Catholic. From among the previous French Kings few had been of any worth. Hugh Capet broke with the weak Carolingian line of kings but the Capetian kings were little better. France was ruled by local barons whose interest were purely selfish. They were called "power barons" since they sought merely their own power and riches. The Kings of France had spent much of the past century trying to subjugate the Dukes, Counts, and Barons of France but most of these were too busy fighting amongst themselves. The dispute over Normandy further typified the troubles of France at this time. Now Louis VII was eager to leave his kingdom for the glory and promise of the Crusades. The arrogant Eugene had even promised what Christ alone could give to those who embarked on the Crusade; the remission of sins.

Along with the emperor Conrad, several other kings accompanied the Second Crusades. The Polish King Boleslaw IV and Vadislav of Bohemia followed the emperor. One other man of importance embarked with the emperor; his nephew and heir to the throne, Frederick, the Duke of Swabia, known later to history as Frederick Barbarosa. So great were the Crusading armies that Bernard of Clairvaux declared "villages and towns are now deserted" and "everywhere you see widows whose husbands are still alive."

As with the First Crusade the large number of mercenaries and lowly men, who formed the armies, all but guaranteed lack of discipline. Pillaging and violence were common. Like the Peasant's Crusade there were attacks on Jews throughout Germany which were neither sanctioned by the Church or the emperor. Only Bernard was able to order the miscreants to return to their homes and leave the Jews in peace. In Conrad's army pillaging and even murder occurred on a somewhat regular basis once they reached Byzantine territory. Conrad himself could only send his apologies to the Byzantine Emperor and allow the Byzantine army to deal with undisciplined soldiers as they saw fit. In one case, however, after an entire village was burned down, Byzantine bandits wreaked revenge and killed a German magnate. Frederick Barbarosa believed that a monastery nearby must have housed the bandits so he slaughtered its inhabitants and burned the monastery to the ground.

The French army proceeded along a different route and showed much greater discipline than Conrad's. Louis VII was respected for his piety if not his leadership. In England, though no king accompanied them, many soldiers also left for the Crusades, but many stopped to help the Spanish reclaim their lands from the Muslim populous there. Spain was quickly rising to become a Catholic country and the Muslims were on the defensive. Portugal received much help from Flemish mercenaries while the rest of the English Crusaders continued to travel toward the Holy Land by sea.

In October 1147 Conrad's army left Constantinople and Nicaea, and was heading towards Antioch when they were ambushed by Muslims. The Byzantines had made a treaty with Muslims in this part of the country and word was passed that the emperor of Constantinople would take no action against those who attacked the Crusaders in honor of the treaty. It has been estimated that only a tenth of Conrad's army survived. He and Frederick, along with the survivors, retreated where they met up with Louis VII. The armies of the Second Crusade had not even reached the Holy Land before its troops were radically diminished. Louis blamed the apathy, and "treachery," of the Byzantines but Conrad apparently held no grudge.

When the armies arrived in Jerusalem battle plans were drawn. During the call to the Second Crusades Zengi was assassinated by his own eunuch. His two sons divided the kingdom amongst themselves but Nuradin had become the strongest of the two sons. He had hoped to conquer Damascus, which both he and the Christians desired for its strategic importance. The Queen had previously broken the alliance that the Christians once had with Damascus, but Damascus had still taken no action against the Christians. The princes bitterly argued for days. Many wished to attack Nuradin's stronghold in Aleppo while others argued that Damascus was critical. It was finally agreed that Damascus should be the Crusaders' first objective.

Regardless of whether or not the plan was sound, the siege was not. The Crusading army fought among themselves and many of the Knights who had opposed the Damascus expedition were said to be deliberately lax in their duties. It was even said that the Damascan Emir had paid large sums of bribe money to some of the Crusaders to sabotage the siege attempt. After only four short days Conrad lifted the siege and retreated, furious at the lack of cooperation he had received and at the poor military advice which he had been given. In July 1148 the Second Crusade ended, only days after its first expedition. Conrad left for home.

The Aftermath of the Second Crusade

The Second Crusade had been a disgrace. Conrad's willingness to give up so easily was a reflection not of his cowardice but of the selfish bickering that embroiled the Kingdom of Jerusalem and its princes. Conrad could not hope to win a war if the princes were not united. Indeed, many of the princes of Syria and Palestine refused to even attend the Jerusalem conference where the siege of Damascus was planned. One incident illustrates the rapacious squabbling of the princes. Raymond of Tripoli was the heir to Raymond of Toulouse, the great chivalrous Knight of the First Crusade. When the Second Crusade came he had heard that Alfonso–Jordan of Toulouse was accompanying them. This Alfonso was another heir of Raymond of Toulouse and Raymond of Tripoli feared that he might claim Tripoli as his inheritance. Alfonso died under mysterious circumstances soon afterwards and Raymond was suspected of having him poisoned. Alfonso's son, Bertrand, then set out to overthrow Raymond but seeing that his own people would not support him, Raymond made a pact with Nuradin and Damascus. The two Muslim Princes came and crushed Bertrand, restoring Tripoli to Raymond.

The incident shows the real reason for the Second Crusade's failure, but for the Crusaders themselves a scapegoat was needed. Louis VII immediately accused the Byzantine Emperor Maurice of complacency and conspiracy. He entered an alliance with Roger II of Sicily but Conrad would not cooperate. A Third Crusade was preached, but this Crusade was supposed to be against Byzantium, not the Muslims. Even Bernard of Clairvaux was caught up in the fever, but without Conrad's support (who had made an alliance with the Emperor Maurice) the Third Crusade could not occur. An attack on Maurice would be an attack on Conrad III so long as their alliance was firm. The Third Crusade would have to wait.

The situation in Europe now seemed more important than that of Palestine. Conrad was disturbed to see an alliance between Roger II of Sicily and Louis VII of France. The Holy Roman Empire was truly an "empire of many nations" and those nations did not always accept the authority of the emperor. The pope had usually been the peace maker but Eugene's loyalties were divided. He was a friend to Louis VII and Conrad but was neutral towards Roger II. Moreover, Eugene still wished for Conrad to dispose of the Republican Senate in Rome. In 1148 the pope had taken the step of excommunicating Arnold of Brescia but since the people of Rome had never even allowed Eugene to take up residence in the city, the excommunication meant nothing. In 1149 Eugene had bartered with Roger II in exchange for his support against the senate. Roger II besieged Rome and forcibly installed Eugene in the Capitol city, but once Roger II left the people were again in revolt. Arnold called the pope a "man of blood" for his violence and Eugene was once more forced to flee Rome.

It was clear that Conrad needed to reclaim his authority and bring some unity to the empire. He had never officially received the Imperial Crown from the pope because of the circumstances of his reign and the Second Crusade so it was agreed that he should come to Rome, remove the Republican Senate, and receive the Imperial diadem. The decision was probably not easy, for the senate had offered to bestow the crown on his head as well. Doubtless, the reverence that most of the empire still felt for the papacy, despite its scandals, caused Conrad to want to receive the crown from Eugene rather than the senate. Nevertheless, his decision was delayed until 1152. Conrad would assemble an army and meet the pope at Rome in the Fall, or so he planned. Conrad III died on February 15, leaving Frederick Barbarosa as the new emperor.

Philipp Foltz – Frederick Barbarossa and Henry the Lion – 19th Century

12

The Reign of Frederick Barbarossa

Charlemagne was the greatest emperor in European history. Otto the Great followed in Charlemagne's footsteps but was far inferior to him. Frederick Barbarossa hoped to follow in their footsteps and restore the glory of the empire, which had diminished since the fall of the Carolingian and Ottonian dynasties, but he was far inferior to both Charlemagne and Otto in moral aptitude as well as achievement. Charlemagne and Otto strove to do what they believed was right. Frederick's motive was political. Although he was sometimes in the right, it was not religious devotion which drove him, but political ambition and a firm belief that the emperor must be the temporal authority of the empire, not the pope.

In many ways Frederick Barbarossa was his own worst enemy. He had the opportunity to change history but it is ironic that he often did the opposite of what he professed to believe. When political opportunity struck he took it, regardless of its long term effects. It was he who crushed the dreams of a republican government and allowed a pope whom he despised to crown him. His ego drove him to make enemies over frivolous gestures and his more noble aspirations fell to his selfish ambitions. It is ironic that the emperor, who first clearly placed himself against the Gregorian popes, was in reality a secular Hildebrand. Barbarossa and Hildebrand were much alike save that one was an emperor who represented the State while the other was a pope who represented the Church.

It should not go unnoticed that Frederick Barbarossa was the first emperor to actually coin the term "Holy Roman Empire." Previously the empire was simply the "Roman Empire" distinguished from the "Eastern Roman Empire," or, preferably, the more mundane "Eastern Empire." On occasion, the empire had been called simply the "Christian Empire" or even "*the* Empire," with the meaning "the" being self evident. The omission, however, has been construed to be a sort of backlash against Italy and the Romans who were often viewed outside Italy as arrogant and proud people. The Germans and French revered Charlemagne, the English Alfred the Great, and the Byzantines looked to Constantine while the Italians still looked back to Augustus. The term "Holy Roman Empire," first employed by Barbarossa, was used in official letters to address the subjects of the kingdom. It acknowledged the Roman legacy, as well as providing a connection to the "Holy Roman Church." The term would soon fall into fairly common usage among the successors of Barbarossa, and is the title which has survived throughout history, yet neither Barbarossa nor his empire were truly holy. Greatly revered among the German people Barbarossa was hated by the Italians. In reality, he was somewhere in between.

Frederick Barbarossa cannot be declared "great" by any means, but the grandeur and spectacle of his battles with the popes are considered one of the great dramas of history. He would later be eclipsed by another Emperor Frederick as the House of Hohenstaufen began to emerge as the great enemy of the medieval popes in a time when the political power of the papacy was beginning to reach its zenith. Despite this, the emperors of Hohenstaufen failed because of their own sins and ambitions, the very things for which they rightly condemned the papacy.

The Ascendancy of Frederick

Pope Eugene had succeeded in securing Conrad's support against the Republican Senate in Rome when he died. When Frederick Barbarossa was elected to succeed Conrad on March 4, 1152 he sent notice to Eugene. That notice was worded in such a way that Eugene could have no doubt he would have to begin negotiations anew. Frederick I refused to accept himself as a vassal to the pope and violated the Concordat of Worms by appointing several bishops. Moreover, Frederick announced that the treaty between Conrad and Byzantium was Conrad's, not his own. This left Frederick free to ally himself with Roger II, if necessary. The decision was tactful and forced the pope's hand. Eugene III had an uneasy alliance with Roger II but he did not trust the Normans. The Republican Senate of Rome was still a threat to the pope's power and he desperately needed Frederick's support. Aware that the Roman Senate had themselves vied for the recognition of the emperor, and had offered the crown to Conrad as well, Eugene was quickly forced to come to an agreement with Frederick Barbarossa.

On March 23, 1153 Eugene III and Frederick I reached an agreement which was called the Treaty of Constance. Frederick agreed not to recognize the Roman Senate or ally himself with Roger II without the pope's permission. In exchange Eugene would crown Frederick emperor. Providence, however, refused to let Eugene carry out the treaty, for he died in July. Anastasius IV was elected on the very day of Eugene's death. The coronation of Frederick was naturally delayed while the new pope established his rule.

Anastasius showed promise in his brief reign but is considered a weak pope, for he had sympathies with the Republican Senate and also granted concessions to Frederick. He, alone among the popes of Arnold's Republic, was permitted to reside in Rome. There Anastasius did not interfere with the Senate and even began construction on a new palace. In regard to Barbarossa, he ratified the appointment of bishops which the emperor had made in defiance of the Concordat of Worms. Whether Anastasius did what was right, or whether he was weak as his critics suggest, his brief reign was a peaceful interlude. Like many popes he was an aged man before ever assuming the pontifical chair. He died in December 1154.

Upon Anastasius' death Hadrian IV was able to secure his election. Hadrian, the only Englishman to ever sit on the papal throne, was known to be a harsh, strict, and even arrogant man. He had once been transferred from an abbotry because of a large number of outcries from the people, but he later assumed the bishopry elsewhere. Unlike Anastasius, he was completely unwilling to grant concessions to either the Roman Senate or Frederick Barbarossa. He held the crown that Frederick wanted, and with that crown he would crush the New Republic once and for all.

While negotiations were ongoing with Barbarossa the Senate was itself eager to gain recognition from Frederick. Sporadic violence was nothing new in Rome, particularly between the Arnoldists and the pope's supporters, but when a cardinal was attacked and injured by one of Arnold's supporters, the pope, for the first time in history, placed an interdict upon the whole city of Rome. The interdict forbade the entire populous of Rome from participating in the sacraments or blessings of the Church. In some ways an interdiction was worse than excommunication, for officially excommunication only forbade participation in communion whereas interdiction forbade participation in any and all sacraments of the Church. Although the idea of excommunication had, by this time, taken on the idea of complete separation from the Church and Christ, thus implying the very soul of the man was lost, interdiction was little different.

Despite Rome's opposition to the temporal, or political, control they still deeply respected the spiritual authority of the pope. The attack on a cardinal was obviously a sin and the people of Rome were desirous to make amends and restore communion. This was only done by promising to abolish the Republican Senate and by exiling Arnold of Brescia. Although Arnold was banished the Senate, which had always existed in some form, did not entirely live up to their promise and quietly ignored the pope. At one point their bickering reached such a point that Frederick had even refused to listen to them. The pride of the Romans was countered by the pride of the Germans.

When Frederick Barbarossa arrived in Rome he was asked to hold the pope's stirrup as the Emperor Lothair had done. This act of subservience was refused by Barbarossa and immediately angered the pope. He threatened to withhold the crown if Barbarossa did not comply, while friends of the emperor argued that this was merely a courteous tradition. The next day Barbarossa reluctantly complied but deliberately held the wrong stirrup. After this frivolous and childish display Hadrian placed a new demand on Frederick before he would bestow the crown; the execution of Arnold of Brescia. Arnold was then brought back to Rome where he was executed.

At the execution Arnold bravely stood before his executioners and refused to recant. He maintained that the materialism and worldliness of the

179

Church had destroyed its innocence. He faced death so bravely, as a martyr, that Frederick himself is said to have been moved and repented of obeying the wicked pope's orders. Arnold's body was burned and the ashes were thrown into the Tiber river so that no one would worship the remains or provide him a Christian burial.

Although the New Republic would linger on for several more years, it had died with Arnold. Part of the blame lies in the Romans themselves. The great advantage of a democratic republic is also its greatest drawback. The people get exactly what they deserve. There would be no less than three failed attempts to revive a republican government before the American forefathers succeeded. Not long after their success, however, a French republic ended in anarchy. Republics must rely on the justice and the sacrifice of its populous to survive. When it becomes hedonistic, selfish, and debased, it inevitably falls. So Arnold of Brescia's republican experiment failed after only a little more than a decade, though its remnants lingered on for a few decades.

Now was time for Frederick's coronation. Significance should be attached to the fact that Hadrian IV altered the ceremony in a manner which illustrated the pope's superiority to the emperor. Following the ceremony the Roman people did not give Frederick the glory that other emperor's had received. Furious at Arnold's martyrdom and that Frederick had scorned the Senate's offer to bestow the crown, the city erupted in mob violence. Barbarossa mounted his horse and personally participated in the army's attack upon the Roman mobs. The revolt was quelled with blood but the situation again became untenable for both the emperor and the pope. Frederick left for Germany, having won the crown, but having lost the respect that the people might have given him. He had betrayed the senate and people of Rome for the papacy he despised. This fact was not lost on Hadrian who would soon become Frederick's bitter enemy.

Hadrian Allies with the Normans

King Roger II of Sicily had died in 1154. His son William, nicknamed William the Bad, ascended to the throne of Sicily, or the Kingdom of Naples as it is sometimes called. Immediately, a power struggle erupted as various Norman barons refused to accept William and sought to enhance their own power. The situation placed the Papal States in harms way, as William was at war with barons throughout southern Italy.

For the pope the rebellious barons were a good thing. Although the Normans had previously allied themselves with the popes, it was always a precarious alliance. The Normans had not always shown themselves to be true lovers of the Church, or the pope, and Hadrian had hoped to rid himself of William. Consequently he entered into an alliance with the Byzantine empire, and the rebel Normans, against William. Frederick Barbarossa did not enter the fray. The German princes were not interested in the squabbles of southern Italy, though the emperor would have seriously loved to extend his rule into those regions.

Without the emperor's help William quickly put down most of the rebellious barons and laid siege to Benevento where the pope had held up since he fled Rome. As the siege progressed starvation and famine caused many people to desert Hadrian and flee the city. It was only a matter of time before the city fell. Hadrian agreed to the Concordat of Benevento which recognized William as the rightful ruler of the Kingdom of Sicily. The territorial boundaries which the pope recognized, however, included Naples, Apulia, and Capua, which were viewed by Frederick as fiefs of his dominion. This was a violation of Hadrian's agreement with Frederick.

Messengers were dispatched to explain the situation to the emperor. The letter attempted to sway the emperor by declaring that the Church had given Frederick much *beneficia* and was capable of bestowing more. This word, "*beneficia*," could be translated in the emperor's tongue as either "benefit" or as "fief." The later would imply that the land belonged to the Church and was given to the emperor as a gift. This enraged Frederick, who would never accept his empire being considered a "fief" of the pope. The cardinals were sent packing and returned to Hadrian in defeat. Again the two men engaged in childish banter over trivial matters. Each wished to appear the dominant force of the empire and neither was willing to yield even the most insignificant of matters.

Hadrian's Native Land

In England and Normandy the war between King Stephen and Geoffrey of France, once Henry I's heir, had continued. Geoffrey died in the early fifties and by 1153 Stephen reached an agreement with Geoffrey's widow to adopt Geoffrey's son, Henry, as heir to the throne. This brought temporary peace to England but Stephen died a year later in 1154.

When Henry succeeded Stephen it was to be the first peaceful transition in over a hundred years. His kingdom was at the time the greatest in all of Europe and he was richer than Frederick Barbarossa. The war over Normandy was seemingly halted since Henry was the natural son of the Duke of Anjou in France, and along with Normandy many duchies throughout western France fell under his dominion. The kingdom of England stretched all the way down to Spain covering the easternmost part of France and most all of the British island. Only northernmost Scotland and the tiny island of Ireland evaded his kingdom.

It was at this time that Hadrian IV wrote to Henry II and made a startling request. Ireland, although always Catholic, had never yielded to the political sovereignty of the pope. Ireland had never fallen into the Holy Roman Empire, and never desired to. Hadrian argued that all Christians lands, even

Ireland, were given to the Church under the alleged Donation of Constantine. He then told Henry that he was giving sovereignty over Ireland to him and, in a disputed bull, he gave Henry the authority, in the name of the Church, to conquer Ireland and force its submission. Henry, whose reign coincides almost exactly with that of Frederick Barbarossa, did not immediately undertake this task, for matters with Thomas Becket a few years later would occupy much of his time.

Frederick Invades Italy

Frederick desired to expand his empire and his finances. The papal states held much tax revenues and territory which the emperor wanted. A few decades earlier the Countess Matilda had bequeathed her land to the pope, but in the reign of Lothair, Pope Innocent had agreed to restore the land to the emperor. In the conflict which arose between Conrad and Lothair this territory again fell into the papal states and Barbarossa now wanted it back.

The banter between Hadrian and the emperor had grown increasingly worse, and even took on a racial tone. The Emperor declared that the papal states were the gift of Constantine, not the empire the gift of the popes. To this Hadrian replied rhetorically, "What were the Franks until Pope Zacharias welcomed Peppin? What is the Teutonic king now until consecrated at Rome by holy hands?" The war of words had now become a war of Germanic supremacy verses Roman supremacy. Racial overtones overshadowed the conflict. In 1158 Frederick marched his army into Lombardy and captured Milan. He then formed the Diet of Roncaglia, in which he asserted the imperial authority over northern Italy and levied *fodrum* taxes against the residents. Imperial castles were to be built from which imperial officials could enforce the emperor's decrees. The cities themselves would be allowed "self–government" so long as it did not conflict with those Imperial decrees.

Hadrian was furious at the actions and threatened excommunication. He had planned a military alliance against Barbarossa and so he gave the emperor forty days to withdraw the diet or be excommunicated. Hadrian, however, would die before the time elapsed. On September 1, 1159 the pope was dead and the empire's fate would rest upon the decisions of the next pope.

The Second Major Schism

The Clementine popes had seemingly met their failure with Victor IV and the Gregorian popes appeared to prevail, but with the death of Hadrian another schism was to erupt as another pope, Victor IV, challenged Alexander III for the papal title.

After Hadrian's death the electors were split over his successor. The Gregorian party elected Hadrian's closest advisor, Cardinal Orlando (Roland)

Bandinelli, under the name Alexander III, while the pro–Imperial party elected Cardinal Ottaviano under the name Victor IV (for the previous Victor IV was not recognized as a true pope). It is ironic that the first challenge to the Gregorian popes since Victor IV now chose that same name, but it is not at all surprising that fighting, bickering, and even fisticuffs erupted when Alexander III attempt to place the pontifical robes upon his person. Eventually, the fighting forced Alexander to take refuge in the Vatican, near St. Peters in the Leonine City, while Victor held Rome proper. Each was consecrated by their supporters a few weeks apart and a new schism was born.

As had occurred numerous times before, the emperor was appealed to as the arbitrator. Barbarossa had actually been at siege against the Lombard city of Cremona when he heard what happened. He lifted his siege and then convened a council in Pavia in 1160 to decide the matter. Both parties were invited to attend and defend themselves but Alexander politely refused. He may have suspected that Barbarossa knew he had been the one who advised Hadrian to excommunicate Frederick but whatever his real reasons he tactfully declined to come, knowing that he would not accept the verdict if was unfavorable. The council itself was made up of bishops from both Germany and Italy. It could scarcely have been considered a kangaroo court but the conflict that Hadrian had with the emperor made the decision seem unduly influenced by him, despite the unanimous verdict. They declared Victor the true pope and excommunicated Alexander III.

Alexander III was prepared. He had already excommunicated Victor, even before the council, and he now anathematized Barbarossa. He then sought the support of the kings of Europe and the countries of the empire. As had been the case with Urban II, the task was political. Sicily obviously sided with Alexander. Spain was loyal to the papacy but not to the emperor. It is somewhat debatable at this time whether or not Spain was truly even a part of the empire. Its kings certainly paid no taxes to Barbarossa and some had even used the title "emperor" for themselves, before being rebuked by former popes. They were subject to what may be called the "papal empire" at that time but they had no desire to be put under the thumb of a German prince. Spain, then, easily declared themselves for Alexander, the enemy of Barbarossa. France too had secret animosity against the German emperors. They had long declared that the heirs of Charlemagne were French and not German. They had given up seeking the Imperial throne but were more than eager to throw off what little authority the emperors still wielded over France. Louis the Younger (VII) then declared himself for Alexander at a meeting in Toulouse alongside his dreaded enemy Henry II of England. This latter king proved a particular victory for Alexander.

Henry II had been in a long war against France and Louis the Younger. The two had no great love for each other but each desired to keep his kingdom under their own sovereignty. Frederick Barbarossa's attempts to install Imperial rule in Italy were seen as a possible forerunner to more direct control elsewhere in the empire. Henry II declared for Alexander III, alongside his enemy Louis. Despite this, Alexander would have to play his cards carefully for two years later Thomas Becket would become the Hildebrand of England and Alexander needed to keep the king's support without undermining Becket.

In the meantime Germany, Bohemia, Norway, and Sweden declared for Victor IV. Italy, however, was split. Rome and Tuscany supported Victor who was even able to take up residence in Rome. The northern Italian cities, or Lombards, saw Barbarossa as a despot. They had long despised German rule and sought Italian kings. These cities would eventually form a coalition known as "the Lombard League," which Alexander III would one day lead. It was with these cities that Barbarossa's challenge remained. By 1162 Frederick's army was marching through Lombardy. He took Tortona and besieged the great city of Milan. Alexander III was forced to flee to France where he would remain for three years.

In Italy Barbarossa was prepared to make a terrible example of the defiant Milan. The once proud city, perhaps the greatest in Italy behind Rome, was razed to the ground. The city reduced to ashes and rubble. The plan backfired. Rather than scaring the people of northern Italy into submission it rallied them against his tyranny. The travesty had the emotional impact of the World Trade Centers in New York city. Rather than installing fear, it provoked anger. Frederick, believing himself victorious, left Italy but the citizens of Cremona immediately undertook the task of rebuilding Milan. It was at this time that the Lombard League was formed to protect themselves against Barbarossa. It was with this deed, as well as his execution of Arnold of Brescia, that Barbarossa's failure was insured.

Thomas Becket & England

It was this same year that Thomas Becket became the archbishop of Canterbury. England had begun to rise to prominence among the empire a few years earlier. While the power of the emperors continued to diminish over the next few centuries, England would wage its own spiritual warfare, paving the way for both the Reformation and democracy. Geographically, financially, and perhaps even politically England was the greatest of all the Holy Roman nations during the reign of Emperor Frederick Barbarossa and King Henry II. It is, therefore, ironic that Henry II is primarily known for his defeated battles against Thomas Becket.

The history of the Holy Roman Empire cannot be adequately told without the history of its most important kingdoms, even if they were only nominally a part of the empire. The kings of France, England, and the Spanish kingdoms acknowledged Barbarossa in name only. What he did in Italy had little effect on them, but what they did had significant effect upon him. Their support of Alexander III is a case in point. Henry II's support was essential to the pope's battle against the emperor and it had to be played with caution. Henry II was not an apostate but he was certainly not a devout man either. He had expanded his kingdom by marrying Eleanor, the ex–wife of his rival King Louis VII. By making her his bride much of the French inheritance she owned became his domain. This marriage, however, did not stop his licentious shenanigans, in which he was often accompanied by his chancellor, Thomas Becket.

This Becket was a strong and able leader who even served as regent when Henry was off the isle of Britain. He was a very public figure who was extremely loyal to his monarch even leading soldiers in battle in disputed French lands. He was also ambitious. One might say charitably that he desired to do the best job he could in whatever he did. This was the problem. When Henry II helped to appoint Becket the Archbishop of Canterbury, Becket had himself warned the king that he would loose a dear friend. Whether in jest or a serious warning, Henry found it was the truth. Becket immediately took up the cause of the Church against the State, and even demanded concessions that Alexander III dared not ask. Indeed, it was Alexander who once ordered Becket to back down to the king's request. Debates about Becket's character and motives will rage until Judgment Day but herein I will present only the undisputed facts.

In 1161 the Archbishop of Canterbury, Theobald, died. Becket had been tutored under the Archbishop but refused to visit him in his dying days. It was nearly a year before the vacant office was filled and it was Becket, at the behest of King Henry II, who filled that vacancy. Soon afterwards, the feud between former friends erupted. Not only did Becket oppose Henry's tax laws and excommunicate a baron but he also refused to turn over a clerk to stand trial for murder. According to ancient law clerks were members of the ecclesiastical orders and could only be tried in an ecclesiastical court, not a civil court. Because the ecclesiastical courts tended to be lax on those it convicted, if convicted at all, the corruption of the clergy grew more rapidly. Clerks were of the lowest order and had recently become the most scandalous. When a certain Philip of Broi was accused of murder the ecclesiastical court acquitted him. Henry II now demanded that the culprit be handed over to stand trial. Becket heard the case himself and sentenced Philip to a light sentence. Henry was furious and within a year a council was convened to deal with the issue of clerical exemption from prosecution.

Becket opposed any concessions to the king but even Alexander III's legates urged Becket to accede. It seemed as if Becket alone, against all the other bishops, dissented but he finally consented himself, though he would later repent of it. The *Constitution of Clarendon* was then formed only to become the same type of divisive issue that investiture was for Hildebrand.

The constitution itself was composed of sixteen articles. According to the it clergy accused of crimes shall be liable to the king's law, but to insure that the power was not abused the local bishops may be present and twelve peers would hear the case to the decide the matter. This is obviously a forerunner to the trial by jury system used in America. It was designed to protect the clergy from possible abuses of the law by the king. Becket was still not pleased, for in addition to allowing clergy to stand civil trial for their crimes, the constitution forbade that any of the King's nobles could be excommunicated without first consulting the king. Other restrictions were also placed on how and when excommunication could occur.

Excommunication, from the days of Gregory VII (Hildebrand) to the days of Becket, was the most powerful weapon that the Church had at its disposal. Long ago when the great emperor Theodosius was excommunicated by the Bishop Ambrose it meant little except that Theodosius was excluded from Church services until his repentance. No one, not even the bishop himself, doubted the salvation or faith of Theodosius. However, from the time of Gregory VII, who dared declare that Henry IV's very salvation depended upon his submission, excommunication became an instrument of damnation. The bishops themselves were now held, at least officially, to have the power to damn one's very soul to hell. Not only could they forgive sins in confessionals but they could pass eternal judgments as God's spokesmen on earth. Henry II hoped to deter this abusive power, for Becket had already excommunicated a baron.

One other obscure passage in the constitution was a section that forbade bishops from leaving the country without the king's permission. This section was important, for almost immediately after relenting, Becket changed his mind, repented, condemned the entire constitution, and attempted to leave England to seek out Alexander III. However, he was forced to return due to bad weather and was arrested. Becket was charged additionally with misconduct while in the office of the Chancellory but he refused to answer saying that no man could judge him save the pope. He threatened excommunication of any and all who passed judgment on him and then escaped in the night disguised as a monk. From there he fled to France, the land of Henry's enemy, Louis the Younger.

Alexander still needed Henry's support at this time but he also wanted to protect Becket. He urged both sides to compromise but this did not hinder Becket from excommunicating any and all who had written, approved, and/or defended the *Constitution of Clarendon*. This included a great number of English bishops. Henry responded by seizing all of Becket's property and impounding all the tools used for the ritual of excommunication.

For the next six years Becket would remain in exile in France. During these years the debate did not die. Most bishops supported the king but the pope was far more secure by 1169. Two rival popes had already come and gone leaving only a weak rival that even Barbarossa was reluctant to endorse (see below). With Alexander's security, he began to support Becket more strongly. Henry, however, refused to back down and even went so far as to add six new articles to the constitution. When, in 1170, he had his son crowned king (co–

186

regent) by the Archbishop of York, he was held to have gone too far. By tradition only the Archbishop of Canterbury could perform such a coronation. Both Becket and Alexander III excommunicated all involved including the Archbishop of York.

Fearing an interdict, Henry II met with Becket and a truce was arranged. Becket would be allowed to return to England with his property restored. Becket, nevertheless, did not lift the excommunications, not even of the Archbishop. When he returned to England in December, 1170, his days were numbered. In a fit of rage Henry II was heard to have said, "is there none of my thankless and cowardly courtiers who will deliver me from the insults of this low–born and turbulent priest?" Four nobles heard the remark. On December 29 they entered the Church of Canterbury and ordered Becket to lift the excommunications. When he refused they attempted to drag him from the Church but he resisted. At that time he was then struck down and murdered near the altar.

Although some bishops themselves had actually declared that Becket had suffered the wrath of God, the people were outraged. A priest had been butchered in Church by agents of the king and the sacrilege was more than enough to anger the people, but Henry, like most kings, was not popular with the commoner to begin with. Becket became a martyr against despotism. The pope even sainted Becket less than three years after his death. It is the quickest elevation to sainthood in history and one cannot help but think that Alexander's motives in so doing were suspect, for the death or martyrdom of Becket did more than anything to insure Alexander III's success. Henry II could not now alienate himself from the pope. Henry would eventually do penance, even being flogged by the bishops, abbots, and 240 times by monks. It was the deepest humiliation of a king by the clergy since Emperor Henry IV lay in the snow for days before Hildebrand. In this case Henry II was at the mercy of the bishops and the pope. In 1171 he finally undertook the conquest of Ireland under the authority of the pope, bringing that Catholic country for the first time into the Papal Roman Empire.

The Persecution of "Heretics"

Alexander III, following in the footsteps of the Gregorian popes, undertook not only to enhance his power and authority, but to abuse it. Believing it was his sacred duty to compel people to believe the truth as he saw it, Alexander began to instigate the persecution of several "heretical" sects in France and England. Interestingly enough, the source of some of these "heretics" was Germany, with whom Alexander was in a pitched spiritual battle. During the time that he spent in exile in France he used his authority to persecute both Cathari and Waldenses, although the latter was not yet known by this name.

187

The two sects were different and yet the Catholic Church has often failed to distinguish between them. The same mistake has been made by many Protestant historians, who are eager to list them as forerunners to the Reformation. In fact, it is fair to consider the Waldenses as forerunners of Martin Luther, but not the Cathari, despite some similarities. Another dispute is whether or not some of the persecuted really were Waldenses, or were merely followers of an "unnamed author," as the Catholic bishop's themselves charged.

The Cathari had been recognized as an established sect for some time but the Waldenses were not yet distinguished from them. Exactly from whom the Waldenses came is hotly debated. In less than a decade a man named Waldo would found a group who took vows of poverty and were nick–named the "Poor Men of Lyons" because they originated from Lyons. Some believe the term "Waldenses" derives from Waldo's name. If this is so then the sects persecuted by Alexander III could not truly have been Waldenses since they had not yet appeared on the scene. Others have argued that "Waldenses," or "Valdenses," comes from the Latin word for valley, for many of them lived in the valleys of Piedmont in northern Italy. Regardless, it is clear that Waldo did not invent a new religion but clung to an older apostolic view which many believed had been abandoned by the Catholic Church and its warring popes.

If this first sect was not Waldenses then what were they? Catholic bishops have suggested they may have been Petrobrusians or Berengarians. The Berengarians have been mentioned previously. It is possible that these men were Berengarians but it is also likely that they were Petrobrusians. These men took their name from Peter of Bruys, who lived a half a century earlier. This Peter echoed Berengarius in many ways, condemning infant baptism and the sacrifice of Mass, but he met with the rage and hatred of the people when he burned many crosses, believing them to be idols. The people then threw him on the fire and made a martyr of him.

These men differed from the Cathari in that they rejected the Cathari's notions of dualism, disdain for the Old Testament, sexual abstinence for life, and the belief that one who sins after conversion could not again regain salvation. In these teachings the Cathari are indeed considered heretics by Protestants as well as Catholics. It was toward these groups, that Alexander aimed his wrath.

A Cathari sect, made up of eight men and two women, were burned at the stake in Cologne, France in 1163, but in England two years earlier a group of about thirty men and women had fled Germany on account of religious persecution and landed on the shores of England. This sect, whether they be Waldenses, Petrobusians, or Berengarians, did not escape the eye of Alexander and the Church. They were ordered punished for their heresies but Henry II refused to pass judgment without a hearing. On his orders a council was convened at Oxford and the prisoners were interrogated.

After interrogation, which apparently did not include torture, the prisoners professed to be Christians but called the Roman Church the "Whore of

Babylon," an apostate Church prophesied in the Book of Revelation, and condemned both infant baptism and the sacrifice of Mass or transubstantiation. The council, presumably with Henry's backing, was reluctant to execute the "heretics." Instead they were branded on the forehead after being scourged, even as Christ was. They were then exiled with the brands as a mark, warning that anyone who harbored them or gave them shelter would risk arrest. Nevertheless, whether Henry and the council intended death as their punishment, that was the inevitable result for the cold winter caused the death of all with no one to offer them shelter. The Gregorian popes were staining their robes with the blood of martyrs.

Stirrings in Palestine

It is necessary to again pause in the history of Barbarossa, for in the Kingdom of Jerusalem events were forming which would lead to another Crusade; one which Frederick himself would one day embark. Since the fall of Edessa the fortunes of the Crusaders continued to decline. Baldwin III died in 1162. He had originally become king in 1143 when he was but thirteen years old. His mother, as regent, tried to maintain effective control and it was because of her advice that the failure of the Second Crusade is often attributed. Damascus had an alliance with the Kingdom of Jerusalem while Nuradin was ravaging the northeast and threatening to cut Jerusalem off from the Christian east and west. By attacking Damascus Jerusalem had made an enemy of its only Muslim allies and allowed Nuradin to emerge victorious in the northeast.

Baldwin III himself might have been a great king under different circumstances. Indeed, even under the circumstances he is usually credited with being the greatest king of Jerusalem. He was a devout, intelligent, and a seemingly innocent young man. In battle he refused to retreat while his soldiers still fought and he likewise refused to leave the dead or wounded behind. He was the first king to have been born in the Holy Land and is said to have been a capable leader who garnered the respect and love of his people and even that of his enemies. However, it was not until after the Second Crusade that he had gained control of the Kingdom of Jerusalem. His mother was a domineering and power–mad woman who had brought the kingdom to the verge of collapse. Baldwin III had tried to claim the throne from her many times after coming of age but she obstinately continued to hold it for herself and the spoiled princess Constance, who resided in Antioch. Together they might have brought the kingdom down had not Baldwin III seized power in 1152.

With the assistance of his knights and the people Baldwin was secretly crowned king in the Holy Sepulchre and his army then blockaded both his mother's aides and her messengers, who were shut up with her in the citadel. Eventually even her allies abandoned her and she was retired outside Jerusalem, being forbidden from ever returning. It was at this time that Melisende, perhaps remorseful for her sins, devoted herself to the Church and charity. In the meantime her son set about prolonging the fall of the kingdom of Jerusalem. Unfortunately, Constance had married a vile noble, if that be an appropriate term, named Reynald. He had used his soldiers to loot and pillage Byzantine territory, even raping nuns and murdering children. He had also tortured a Patriarch which enraged the young Baldwin. In time Baldwin would deal with Reynald, but for the time being such atrocities committed against Christian brothers alienated the eastern empire and furthered weakened the north, thus isolating Jerusalem between Muslim threats from the south and east with only a weak and decadent northern ally to assist. Baldwin III decided that the strategic conquest of Ascalon off the coast of the Mediterranean would be the best strategy.

The walls of Ascalon were said to be impregnable and the fortress had food enough to withstand a long siege but after a few months the army was able to set the walls afire causing part of the wall to collapse. The Muslims withstood the initial attack but were routed when they emerged from the city to attack. The people of Ascalon sued for peace and Baldwin permitted everyone within the city to leave with their possessions in peace. Ironically, the people, spared by the just Baldwin, were later ravaged by Arabs when they were found wondering in the Egyptian desert.

The fall of Ascalon was to the Muslims what the fall of Edessa had been to the Christian west. It was a rallying cry for Muslims which Nuradin was quick to take advantage of. He made an alliance with Damascus and entered the city as the new Emir. Damascus had fallen into Nuradin's hands without a fight. However, Nuradin fell ill after this and his days as a warrior were numbered.

After taking Ascalon Baldwin decided it was time to fortify the north. He did not despise the Byzantines, as did the Franks and Normans, and so he sought a marriage alliance with the emperor. Having married a young princess named Theodora he set out toward Antioch. Reynald knew his days were numbered if he did not act fast. He had ravaged the emperor's lands and his sins disgusted Baldwin. These two men were too strong for Reynald and he knew it so he decided to feign repentance. He rode out to meet Emperor Manuel Comnenus dressed in traditional repentant garb sackcloth, walking barefoot, and with a sword pointed at himself. He offered the hilt to the emperor symbolizing his willingness to die for his sins. Crawling on hands and knees he convinced the emperor of his sincerity and Manuel Comnenus believed that mercy was a virtue of the eastern emperors. Reynald turned Antioch over to Comnenus and festivities took place for over a week. Baldwin and Manuel Comnenus had at least seen a true alliance between the Franks and Byzantines that might have saved the Kingdom of Jerusalem, but it was not to be. Soon after Comnenus left, Reynald decided to attack the Turks on his own. He was then captured and remained in their dungeons for sixteen years. Baldwin became regent of Antioch but his days were also numbered.

Queen Melisende died in September 1161 and Baldwin was grief stricken. As he rode back from Antioch, where had been when he heard the news, he stopped by Tripoli. There he became violently ill and died a short while later, a young man still in his early thirties. There has been much speculation that he was poisoned and indeed, in those days it was hard to distinguish between poison and several diseases such as malaria. The circumstances, however, were suspect particularly with his death so close to that of his mothers. The kingdom had lost its greatest king and the only man that might have saved the kingdom. Even Nuradin is alleged to have said of his enemy's people, "we should pity them, they have lost such a prince as the world no longer possesses." Indeed, with his death the tides of war would shift to the Muslims and to Nuradin's successor, Saladin.

The Tide Turns in the West

The second Pope Victor IV died in April, 1164. Immediately, with the backing of the prefect of Rome and Frederick's own chancellor, a new pope was elected as Pascal III. Although Frederick allegedly had nothing to do with the sham election, he was naturally quite eager to ratify the new pope's election. Nonetheless, the unorthodox manner of Pascal's election made many sympathizers switch allegiance to Alexander III. Even a number of German prelates now supported Alexander III over Pascal. Barbarossa assured Pascal, at the diet of Wurzburg, that he would not accept Alexander but the people of Rome soon invited Alexander to return to the Holy City.

In 1165 Alexander left France and returned to Rome, but Frederick Barbarossa was not long in following. Alexander's ally in Sicily, William the Bad, had died and William II, later to be surnamed "the Good," was but a child. Alexander could not count on help from the Normans. Barbarossa then returned to Rome with an army and managed to seize control of the Leonine City where Pascal III performed a second coronation of Frederick I. Alexander was forced to flee Rome which soon fell into Barbarossa's hands. Alexander fled to Lombardy where Barbarossa had few friends following the savagery at Milan while Frederick was forced to return to Germany after his army came down with the plague, which killed over two thousand soldiers including the emperor's chancellor.

It was during the next few years that Alexander's fortunes changed. He established himself as the head of the Lombard League and found the political climate increasingly in his favor. The Byzantine emperor Comnenus I had longed dreamed of reuniting the two empires and again made overtones to Alexander. This alliance would have threatened both Norman Sicily and the Lombards, who in turn catered to Alexander in hopes of securing his support. With this unspoken threat in back of him Alexander further allied himself with

William II's regent in Sicily and gained the full support of the Lombards against Frederick.

Back in Rome what little support still existed for Pascal was fading quickly. Even Frederick had suggested that both Alexander and Pascal should step down for a new election. With a new Senatorial election to be held in 1168, Pascal was disturbed at hearing the Senate candidates suggest that the recognition of Alexander III was in their best interest. Soon Pascal became fearful and sealed himself in St. Peters where he died of unknown causes.

Again, another pope was set up by the pro–imperial party in Rome. He took the name Callistus (III). Nevertheless, Frederick did not immediately recognize him. Instead he surreptitiously supplied the new pope with money to fight for his recognition. This was done in hopes of placing more pressure on Alexander III but he was not willing to cast his lot with Callistus. The tide had turned toward Alexander and Barbarossa waited to see what effect the new pope would have. Alas, the support that had once existed for Victor IV was all but gone. Alexander's supporters were gaining and the "pro–imperial" popes were quickly loosing reputation. Frederick then sent letters to Alexander suggesting that the emperor might be willing to recognize him but Alexander was wise enough to know why. He would not concede to Frederick and no compromise was reached. In 1174 Frederick Barbarossa began his fifth military expedition into Italy in hopes of ridding himself of the Lombard League and Alexander III.

Barbarossa destroyed the city of Susa and marched into the valley of Piedmont. He laid siege to Alessandria, which itself had been named after Alexander. In 1176, after nearly two years of war, Frederick had made little headway. An armistice had been signed at one point but, when Frederick's ally (Duke Henry the Lion) refused to send reinforcements, Barbarossa was forced into a crucial battle which he fought at Legnano. The battle ended with Frederick's defeat. Now Frederick had no choice but to reconcile with Alexander. No help was coming from Henry the Lion and the Lombard League was too formidable a force. His only chance of surviving was to make peace with the Alexander.

At the Peace of Venice in 1177 Alexander III was recognized as the legitimate pope and Callistus (III) was degraded to his former post with no further punishment. On Barbarossa's behalf the treaty acknowledged Frederick's second wife as legitimate in the eyes of the Church and for the first time Spoleto, and several other regions of Italy, were officially recognized as a part of the Holy Roman Empire. The ceremony was a momentous event which is often portrayed as a second Canossa where the emperor was degraded before the pope. In fact, while the ceremony was certainly a triumph for Alexander there was nothing in the ceremony that could be seen as similar to Canossa. It was Alexander's triumph but it was also the emperor's triumph, such as it was, for he was now acknowledged by the pope, his wife declared legitimate, and most of Italy was officially a part of Barbarossa's domain. Neither side had won a complete victory, but Alexander III scored the most points.

The Last Days of Alexander III

From 1177 to 1189 were years of peace and prosperity for Frederick Barbarossa. In Germany he solidified his power and restored the country to the prestige it once held so long ago under Otto the Great. He banished Henry the Lion to England for his failure to come to his aid earlier and took Burgundy under his wing through marriage. He also made a marriage alliance between his son and the Princess Constance of the Sicilian Kingdom. His son was then given the title of Caesar, in the tradition of the ancient Romans. From outward appearances Barbarossa looked to have restored the Holy Roman Empire. Germany, Burgundy, Sicily, and Italy were under his sovereignty and even the ancient Roman titles were re–ignited under him. For the first time the empire was officially called the Holy *Roman* Empire and his son was Caesar, second only to the emperor, as had been the case before the sack of Rome.

These years helped to make Barbarossa a legend in Germany, but outside Germany Europe was anything but peaceful and prosperous. Alexander III's victory had been short–lived. In 1179 he held the Third Lateran Council, but the effect was the further alienation of the people of Rome. The council itself sought to enforce more Gregorian reforms. It was, at the time, the largest council in history. Following Gregory VII's prohibition against clerical marriage many clergy had merely taken up concubines. The council now promised punishment for those who held concubines (which had formerly been outlawed anyway) and placed an age limit of thirty years for being elected to the bishopry. It also began to create sympathy for a Crusade against the Cathari and Albigenses sects of Southern France and paved the way for the Inquisition which would become formally adopted in five years time. Most importantly, however, was its attempt to prevent any more schismatic papal elections. It was this which angered the Roman people for the new rules provided that only cardinals could elect a pope and that the election must be by a vote of no fewer than two thirds. This law would strip the Roman people of the right to vote in papal elections as had been guaranteed by Louis the Pious back in 824.

The lingering followers of Arnold, and the Roman Republic, already distrustful of Alexander, then expelled him from Rome, sending the pope again into exile. The people elected Pope Innocent (III) and installed him in Rome. Alexander, however, bribed one of Innocent's protectors, a knight, who betrayed Innocent and handed him over to allies of Alexander. He was imprisoned in an abbey for the rest of his life. Alexander, nevertheless, was still unable to return to Rome. He would die less than two years later in 1181. Upon the return of his body to Rome the people threw objects at the casket and covered it with insults.

Alexander had won Barbarossa's consent, but never the affection of the people of Rome.

The Rise of Saladin

Although Baldwin III's death may have spelled death for the kingdom of Jerusalem, the next few kings fought valiantly for the survival of the kingdom. They overcame great odds to sustain the kingdom against the Muslim hoards that outnumbered them. Amalric (or Amaury) was crowned the new king of Jerusalem in 1162. He had inherited a kingdom which was strong in itself but was surrounded by enemies. Nuradin held Syria which bordered the Kingdom of Jerusalem to the east and to the south lay Egypt. The Byzantine alliance in the north left most Franks with little comfort. The sole thing that prevented Nuradin from conquering Jerusalem was the enmity between him and Egypt. So long as Egypt and Syria were at odds with one another, and the Muslims were fighting among themselves, the Kingdom of Jerusalem would survive, but Amalric's great mistake was his desire to expand the kingdom into the riches of Egypt.

In 1168 Amalric decided to invade Egypt and annex the southern kingdom. Speculation about whether he was seduced by Egypt's great riches or whether it was merely an ill–advised campaign is irrelevant. All that is relevant is that Shawar, the Sultan of Egypt, who had once been Amalric's ally, now turned to Nuradin and Shirkuh (an ally of Nuradin) for help. Thus Shawar, Nuradin, and Shirkuh created a formidable alliance. Shirkuh's nephew was a young Saladin who would one day become the greatest of Muslim warriors. This same Saladin rose to power in Egypt by betraying Shawar and assassinating him while on a pilgrimage. When Shirkuh died in 1169, Saladin became the Sultan of Egypt and Nuradin's newest ally.

Amalric's invasion had failed. Although he had taken a few critical cities he was unable to secure Cairo or to hold on to his Egyptian possessions for long. By 1170 Saladin had control of Egypt and even succeeded in expeditions into Palestine where he slaughtered every man, woman, and child in Gaza save those knights who had held out in the fortress. These Saladin could not force out, but the incident proved that Saladin was now a greater threat to Palestine than Nuradin. In 1174 both Amalric and Nuradin died. The stage was set for a new power.

Baldwin IV would be the last king of consequence in the Kingdom of Jerusalem. A young man who suffered from Leprosy, and has thus been called the "Leper King," he overcame great odds but ultimately met with failure. Under Saladin most of Islam had become united against the Crusaders. Only a few Muslim enemies hampered Saladin, including the "Assassins" whose name comes from the drug "hashish" upon which they would become high before engaging in a suicide mission. Like modern terrorists, they were suicidal assassins intent upon spreading fear and dread, but they were not a major military power. Nevertheless, these Assassins ironically were allied with Baldwin IV for a short time when Saladin attacked Aleppo. Aleppo was one of the few Muslim cities which still held a treaty with the Crusaders and the Assassins were also allies with its Muslim inhabitants.

Saladin was soon forced to retreat but did not let up his assaults on Palestine. When he heard news that a huge Crusader army was attacking northern cities held by Saladin's allies, he decided the time was right to attack from the south rather than sending a rescue army. The south could not be heavily defended with such a large army to the north so he marched toward Ascalon with an army made up of Egyptians, Turks, Nubians, and Ethiopians, as well as Kurds and Sudanese. The army is said to have been made of close to thirty–five thousand men while Ascalon was defended by Baldwin IV, whose army was less than four hundred. Because of the great protection of the walls, it was more than possible for Baldwin to hold out until help arrived but Saladin knew this. He also knew that Jerusalem was the prize so he abandoned the siege and proceeded north, burning farms, slaughtering villagers, and leaving desolation.

Baldwin IV decided to act. With his small army, and soldiers from Gaza, they followed the army of Saladin and waited for an opportune time to ambush them. In 1177 when Saladin's army was crossing over a wadi following a great rainstorm, slowed up by the waters and mud, Baldwin attacked. It must be remembered that even soldiers fear for their lives. When they feel abandoned or open to attack, like all men, they panic and flee. Many dropped their weapons to lighten their load so they could get out of the deep mud, thus leaving them unarmed to face the enemy. Baldwin is said to have fallen before the "true cross," or at least the icon so–called, and prayed for victory with tears. Having done so his army routed the massive force of Saladin. Saladin's only recourse was to retreat, but even in retreat he sought to leave desolation behind him. Wherever he could villages were burned and razed while the people were butchered. Nevertheless, the victory for the Crusaders, with but a few hundred men, was a major setback to Saladin who asked for a two year truce to heal his wounds. Since the Crusaders were equally wounded, the truce was agreed to.

Ironically, it was at this time that the Kingdom of Jerusalem began to unfurl. Baldwin IV was dying of leprosy and while the great kings of history have often been those who did not look the part, men prefer that their kings *look* and *talk* like a king. As Baldwin IV grew closer to death, his flesh falling off, his men paid less attention to him. Barons and Lords began to ignore his authority including, and especially, Raynald of Chatillon. Raynald defied the truce and began to loot caravans on their way to Damascus. Saladin was angry and demanded that Baldwin honor the truce but Baldwin had lost all control over Raynald. More importantly, Baldwin knew that his time was nearing an end and he desired that the kingdom not be left to Guy of Lusignan, the heir to the throne. Baldwin believed Guy to be a selfish Lord with no real concern for the kingdom or its people. When Guy refused to come to Baldwin's court and discuss succession Baldwin disinherited Sibylla, through whom Guy had become heir, and named her young son heir. This boy was but five or six and was not under the care of Sibylla, but lived with Raymond of Tripoli whom Baldwin desired to be regent.

In the spring of 1184 Baldwin IV died. The last of the good kings of Jerusalem died at twenty–four years of age. Unfortunately, there had been few good kings of Jerusalem. This was, in fact, the main reason for the kingdom's fall. Upon Baldwin's death the kingdom was left to feuding and selfish Lords who were cut off from the Holy Roman Empire, to which they nominally belonged, and at enmity with their Byzantine allies for whom the Crusades had allegedly been undertaken. After him two more kings would sit on the throne for no more than three years, for the kingdom was about to fall, and with it a new Crusade was to come.

Barbarossa Before the Crusade

The next decade would be the glory years for Barbarossa. His rule in Germany and most of northern Italy was again secure and to the German people he had restored much of the ancient pride from the days of Otto the Great. In fact, he was far inferior to Otto, even in respect to Germany and Italy, but to the Germanic race, he was a mythical figure. Nevertheless, before he could ever attain his mythical status he would first have to deal with the papacy, for while the death of Alexander III vanquished one of his greatest enemies, the papacy itself still had no great love of him. Four more popes would rise to power during Frederick's last years and at least one would stir remembrance of Alexander's struggles but fate decreed that Frederick would outlive all his enemies.

The first successor of Alexander was Lucius III. He was one of Alexander's closest advisors but he also had won the confidence of the emperor by acting as a mediator and recommending compromises. In 1184 he and Barbarossa met to finalize and resolve disputes which had not been completed before Alexander's death. They met at Verona (for the popes were still not welcome in Rome by the republic) and there discussed various issues.

Several issues were agreed upon. The first, and most important, is *the charter of the Inquisition*. This charter, properly called the *Ad abolendum*, was the first official charter which provided for the persecution of heretics. Previously the persecution of heretics could only be ordered by the highest Church officials or by the kings themselves. Now, any church court could try alleged heretics, and if found guilty the accused would be given a chance to repent. If no repentance was made then the heretics would be turned over to civil courts of punishment. On the charter of the Inquisition he even threw his glove to the floor as a symbolic gesture that he would do the same with heretics. While this decree did not yet specify the death penalty or torture it paved the way for later enhancements of the law. It declared for the first time that any who opposed the teachings of the Holy Catholic Church and its pope risked their freedoms, if not their lives.

Along with this decretal came preparations for a new Crusade. Although Jerusalem had not yet fallen, the marks were clear. The Muslims hoards were retaking much of what the first Crusaders had reclaimed for the Christian empires of Rome and Byzantium. Now they were marching ever closer to their ultimate prize of Jerusalem. On these issues Frederick showed his full support. He would himself embark on the Crusade in less than five years time.

Among the issues on which they could not agree were the issues of the Countess Matilda's land and the coronation of Frederick's son. The "Matildine estates" issue had gone back to the days when the Countess Matilda had bequeathed her land to the pope. Since then the land had been retaken by the emperor but the popes still claimed this as their rightful possession. The more important issue, however, was that of the coronation of Henry VI. Frederick had recently arranged for the marriage of his son to the aunt of William the Good of Sicily. This political marriage would create an alliance between the Kingdom of Sicily, or Naples, and the emperor. Such was not in the interest of the popes. Since Hildebrand the kings of Sicily had been used to keeping the emperors at bay. With such a political marriage envisioned the Kingdom of Sicily would doubtless become an official part of the Holy Roman Empire. The papal states would be surrounded by the emperor's subjects. Lucius then shrewdly argued that the empire could not have more than one emperor at a time and thus refused to coronate Henry VI while Barbarossa still lived. This was enough for the emperor. He angrily left the meeting and relations between the two grew increasingly worse. Nonetheless, within a year the pope had died.

The cardinals now believed it was time to elect another Alexander. One they believed would stand against the emperor with more vigor. They elected Urban III whose family had perished under Frederick in Milan. It did not take long before Urban was angering the emperor. He again refused to coronate Henry VI and even went so far as to suspend the patriarch who had crowned Henry the King of Italy. When Urban later reneged on a promise to appoint the emperor's candidate to the archbishop of Trier, Frederick decided it was time to take matters in hand. He did not want Urban to escape to France as had Alexander so his troops entered the papal states and surrounded Urban at Verona. Although Urban had been able to get messengers out to Cremona, urging them to revolt, he was soon trapped without even a way to send messages to his allies. Frederick made his demands. He asked only for a new election for the archbishop of Trier. Urban agreed, but no sooner did he agree in words than he was preparing to betray the emperor.

Waiting for Frederick's troops to back off after the new election, Urban planned to excommunicate Barbarossa, but he found that the local cities were unwilling to even harbor him. He found himself having to ride as far as the city of Ferarra to find allies, but he fell ill during the trip and died in October 1187, preventing yet another schism.

With the fall of Jerusalem and the strength of Barbarossa evident, the cardinals were now willing to elect a pope of more temperate character. Their choice fell on Gregory VIII, a former chancellor of the Roman church. He was a good choice for he advocated evangelism over conquest, humility over extravagance, and declared that the Fall of Jerusalem was a punishment by God for the many sins of the Christian west. He urged a new Crusade and sent out legates to proclaim it. Finally, he was able to return to Rome for the people were willing to accept him. If nothing more than a symbolic gesture, this return to Rome would have made a significant impact upon repairing the rift that had occurred since Arnold's martyrdom, but alas, it was not to be. Gregory VIII was already in his late seventies, a long life for the Middle Ages, and after only fifty–seven promising days as pope, he was dead.

Barbarossa had outlived seven popes and four anti–popes. He had restored much of what had been lost since Henry V and he was already becoming a legend in Germany. Nevertheless, he had not exactly been victorious. Alexander III had attained a technical triumph over Frederick and the Lombard League had never submitted to the emperor. He alienated Italy while endearing himself to Germany. France and Britain proved that if they were nominally subjects of the emperor they were equally subjects of the papacy and they were more than eager to ally themselves with the pope against their emperor. Nevertheless, it was Barbarossa who still lived while his enemies lay in their tombs. It was Barbarossa who ruled Italy as well as Germany while Alexander and Urban ruled no more.

Barbarossa had but one final task to perform. Like his colleagues, the kings of France and England, not to mention many others, Barbarossa was about to embark on the Third Crusade in hopes of liberating Jerusalem from Saladin's hands. Although he had vanquished popes, Barbarossa would not succeed in vanquishing the Muslims. It was a Crusade from which he would never return.

Richard Glass – Richard the Lionhearted on the march to the Crusades – 1854

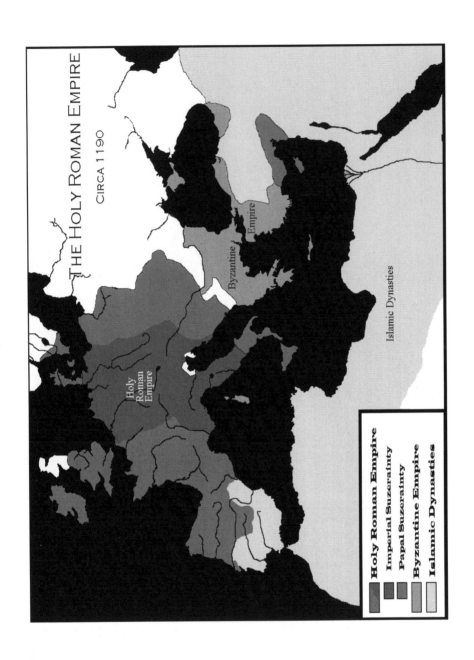

THE HOLY ROMAN EMPIRE

CIRCA 1190

Byzantine Empire

Holy Roman Empire

Islamic Dynasties

Holy Roman Empire
Imperial Suzerainty
Papal Suzerainty
Byzantine Empire
Islamic Dynasties

13

The Third Crusade

The western Kingdom of Jerusalem was on many levels completely distinct from the Holy Roman Empire. Neither the emperor nor the pope had any real authority over the kingdom, which was separated from the west by the Byzantine Empire. Nevertheless, they were tied spiritually to the Holy Roman Empire and that tie was never severed. Even before Jerusalem fell Barbarossa wrote to Saladin warning him of a future Crusade if he did not withdraw. Saladin calmly replied saying, "if this is indeed the letter of a king" then he would find Islam a far more formidable foe than he might anticipate. Indeed, the third Crusade would secure the Kingdom of Acre but would never succeed in retaking Jerusalem.

The Fall of Jerusalem

In 1187 Jerusalem fell to Saladin. A new Crusade was called and Frederick Barbarossa would take up the cross. He was nearly seventy years old when he embarked on the third Crusade. It was to be a Crusade from which he would never return.

The fall of Jerusalem had been in the making for many years. The Kingdom of Jerusalem had been weakening for some time. Baldwin III and IV had prolonged the kingdom's demise but bickering, rivalries, and greed had divided the kingdom from within. The old proverb "divide and conquer" is true, but it was not Saladin who divided the kingdom but the Princes themselves. When Baldwin IV died he had made Baldwin V his heir. The real ruler, however, was to be Raymond of Tripoli, for Baldwin V was but five or six years of age. Raymond, as regent, resumed the truce with Saladin but his regency was short lived for in 1186 the young boy Baldwin died. He had been ill for some time but allegations that he was poisoned by supporters of Guy of Lusignan may be well founded, for Guy heard news of Baldwin's death soon enough that he and his supporters were able to enter Jerusalem and claim the throne even before Raymond could.

Immediately, the kingdom of Jerusalem seemed on the verge of civil war as the rivals set the stage for conflict. Raymond called a parliament while Guy crowned *himself* king of Jerusalem (an act ironically to be repeated by Napoleon in the fall of the Holy Roman Empire). Guy's allies, which consisted of strong military leaders including Gerard, the Master of the Templar knights, held Jerusalem. Gerard was a powerful ally indeed and Gerard hated Raymond with a vengeance, for once, when he was young and in love, he had sought the hand of a woman whom Raymond sold into slavery for her weight in gold. Gerard, now Master of the Templars, never forgot or forgave the arrogant sin. Had he know that Guy's ascension would spell doom for Jerusalem he might still not have cared.

Raymond's supporters, eager to save the kingdom, suggested a compromise. They sought to name Humphrey of Toron king in place of both Raymond and Guy, but Humphrey refused and took the side of Guy. Guy of Lusignan then became the last western king of Jerusalem. He fared no better than his predecessors in harnessing the acts of Raynald of Chatillon who continually provoked Saladin and forced the Crusaders to play their hand before they were ready. Finally, Raymond of Tripoli and King Guy made a last united front to try to stop Saladin. It was the largest army ever assembled by the Kingdom of Jerusalem and had they been truly united they might have succeeded.

Raymond warned Guy that they should wait to attack Saladin because the area where Saladin remained was barren of food and water. In the heat of the summer the armored soldiers of the Crusaders would have been near death before even reaching Saladin's army. Guy was at first inclined to accept this advice but Gerard, again remembering the woman he lost, told Guy that Raymond was plotting against him and urged him to attack immediately. Guy acquiesced and the large army marched in the midday sun with little food or water. By nightfall they stopped to rest in a mountain pass called the Horns of Hattin. From there Muslim archers could rain down arrows and the armored cavalry of the Crusaders had poor ground upon which to charge. The grass fields were set afire, and the Crusaders were trapped.

There, at the Horns of Hattin, the outnumbered troops of Saladin slaughtered the last Christian army of the western Crusaders. The supposed "True Cross" was captured, never to be heard of again, and the survivors were either sold into slavery or butchered by the Muslim Mullahs (Muslim clerics or priests). Only the king and a few of the top knights were spared. Saladin was now free to march to Jerusalem unopposed. He took over the majority of cities in Palestine but Jerusalem held out. Its population promised to fight to the last man and even threatened to burn down the Dome of the Rock and the other Muslim shrines. They promised that Islam would conquer a hollowed burned–out shell of a city. Fearing this, Saladin promised to let the inhabitants of the city leave alive for the price of gold. The inhabitants agreed and the population was spared. Jerusalem was now in Muslim hands.

In the fall of 1187 the Kingdom of Jerusalem had fallen, not yet a hundred years old. A third Crusade was coming and with it would ride the Emperor Frederick Barbarossa and two of the greatest kings of medieval Europe, Philip Augustus and Richard the Lion–Hearted.

Philip Augustus and Richard the Lion–Hearted

The French King Louis the Younger had died in 1180. His successor was Philip II "Augustus." Among the medieval French Kings there was none as strong. France has often been mocked as the country that has never won a war nor been ruled by a true leader. Its kings are usually stereotyped as decadent spoiled brats with time only for sexual shenanigans and daily decadence. Anarchy was jestingly said to be the rule of the land long before the French Revolution brought literal anarchy to the land. Philip II Augustus, however, was the strongest king of France, or perhaps French conqueror would be a better choice of terms, until the very day of Napoleon.

When Louis the Younger died Britain possessed almost half of what is today France, splitting the country nearly down the middle. Philip Augustus would reign for almost half a century. When he finally died, having opposed at one time or another kings, popes, and even the emperor, he had regained much of the lost territories and restored France to a semblance of its former glory.

He was first crowned king in 1179 but the House of Champagne hoped to make him a puppet king. For centuries the dukes and counts of France ruled their lands without much interference from the king. Even as the emperor sought to restore his authority in more than name, the French King Philip II sought to restore the crown to its true authority. He first arranged for a marriage alliance with the count of Flanders in hopes of alienating the House of Champagne. The House of Champagne sought the help of Henry II of England. The exact nature of Henry's assistance is unknown but its motive was to force Philip to turn to the House of Champagne for help against Henry's "threat." Instead Philip negotiated with Henry II and renewed a peace treaty with him. The House of Champagne was then unable to exercise any authority over Philip until years later when they succeeded in turning the Count of Flanders against Philip. A revolt ensued but by 1185 the Count of Flanders was suing for peace. By 1186 Philip Augustus was the true king of France, in fact as well as in name.

In the meantime, coups were in the making in Britain, the enemy of King Philip. Henry had several sons, a number of whom were illegitimate. None of the children were particularly loyal to their father and all sought power for themselves. In 1173 the young Henry, Geoffrey, and Richard had revolted together and invaded their father's land in Aquitaine, but the rebellion was eventually suppressed and the sons were pardoned. Later, in 1183, Richard faced a rebellion of his own as the people of one of his duchies rose against him. They were angry with Richard's brutality in suppressing disobedient barons and called upon the young heirs Henry and Geoffrey to take the lands from Richard. Henry II, however, feared that these brothers might become too powerful and rallied to Richard's aide. In 1183 the young heir Henry had died, leaving Richard as heir to the throne.

Henry II also desired an inheritance for his son John, Richard's younger brother. He demanded that Richard give Aquitaine to John, but Richard refused. Allying with his mother against Henry II, Richard finally turned to Philip Augustus in 1188. Together Richard and Philip rode in battle against Henry II. Henry was forced to acknowledge Richard as heir. He died soon afterwards in July 6, 1189, broken by the betrayal of his sons.

By this time news of the fall of Jerusalem had reached all Europe and both Richard and Philip were eager to embark on the Crusade. Richard and Philip had already broken with one another by this time, their usefulness to one another exhausted, but the Crusades called on all the loyal kings of Europe to come to the aid of the Holy Land. This latest Crusade seemed to have had the most impact upon the young ruthless Richard. He raised money for the Crusade through extortion, robbery, and the plunder of his own people but from then on his character is said to have transformed. He became acutely interested in religion and even sought out the famed theologian Joachim of Floris (also called Joachim of Fiore).

Joachim was himself a unique character. He was a teacher of prophecy and the founder of the prophetic school of thought known as historicism. This view held that the prophecies of Revelation were not merely about the end of the world, but about the entire history of man. The events of Revelation were believed to occur in the past, the present, and the future. The significance of this is of the *present tense* which Joachim invoked. Richard was very interested in Joachim's beliefs about the anti–Christ, but the two did not agree. Richard had apparently been schooled by the Chiliasts of old, who held that the reign of the anti–Christ would be followed by a literal thousand year reign of Christ on earth. It seems that Richard believed the anti–Christ would be a Muslim and that Saladin had come to prepare the way for the anti–Christ. Richard was then to play a critical role in the final war against evil.

The Death of Barbarossa

Germany was far closer to Palestine than France or England so Barbarossa was already in the east by the time Richard and Philip had reached their rendezvous in the Kingdom of Sicily. His army was the largest that the Crusaders had ever assembled, said to number over a hundred and fifty thousand. This time, however, the Crusaders were not welcomed by the Byzantine emperor. Isaac Angelus was hated and despised by many of his own people. The Bulgars and Serbs even promised allegiance to Frederick if he would overthrow Isaac and reunite the eastern and western empires. Nevertheless, there was something profound in the Third Crusade that made the Crusaders forsake their selfish motives, as had not been the case in the first. Frederick declined to overthrow Angelus, although it would have been easy enough. Despite the fact that Isaac had imprisoned Frederick's envoys, he promised not to take the Byzantine kingdom if Isaac would grant safe passage. In fear of Barbarossa, Isaac relented.

It is ironic that one of the greatest emperors of Germany, at the head of the greatest Crusading army ever assembled, died, not in battle, but in an accident. While marching toward Antioch Frederick drowned in a river. The details are unknown. Some say he was bathing, others say he stopped for a drink, still others that he fell off his horse in armor and was swept away. In any case, the great emperor of the Holy Roman Empire died in a freak accident ill–befitting his legacy. In Germany he would become almost a mythical figure. In the centuries to come legends about Barbarossa arose. One legend, reminiscent of the Athurian legend of Avalon, tells of a red–bearded man who lay in an enchanted sleep within the mouth of a great cave awaiting the day that he will awaken and restore Germany to it rightful place among the nations.

Barbarossa's legacy is a mixed one. The German people idolize him to mythological status. The Italians, however, despise him with a hatred beyond measure. They remember him as the butcher of many innocent men and as a conqueror who defied the Holy Church. For them, Barbarossa was a pagan spirit while Germans remember him as a devout king. The truth lay between the two extremes.

In terms of his religion, Barbarossa expressed surprising knowledge. His accusation that the pope was anti–Christ should be evaluated in light of the emerging Joachimites who believed that the prophecies of Revelation encompassed the whole of history and, therefore, saw in current events many of the prophecies of the Bible. Nevertheless, Barbarossa could not be said to have been a truly devout man for, even in the Middle Ages, Barbarossa was barbaric. He certainly believed in God and Christianity, but only intellectually. Spiritually he believed only in himself and in Germany. Religion did not guide his practices, but his practices guided his religion.

In terms of political rule, he was also a paradox. He sought to restore the Holy Roman Empire but did so with an arrogance and self righteousness that made him a secular Hildebrand, with all the same faults. What good he did was negated by his sins. He had executed the visionary Arnold of Brescia and shown little mercy to his enemies, yet he appeared to restore the Holy Roman Empire to its former state. In reality Barbarossa restored only the image of the Holy Roman Empire but in practice it was still as divided as ever. Moreover, the war between the emperors and the popes was just beginning. This war would be for the control of the empire and for its survival.

The Siege of Acre

The death of Barbarossa caused a far greater effect on the army than might be anticipated. One of Frederick's sons, Frederick the Duke of Swabia, assumed command but was incapable of leading the soldiers. Many ambushes left the army in pieces by the time they reached Antioch. Eventually, the remaining soldiers disbanded, died, or retreated to Germany. Richard and Philip had not even reached Palestine when news of the great army's demise reached them.

Richard and Philip soon set out to Acre in hopes of retaking the seaport city. It was critical to any conquest of Palestine because it could receive supplies from the Mediterranean. Any land route would be plagued with perils and occupy far too much time. From Italy to Palestine, by sea, goods could be brought to the Crusaders with relative ease, but Acre had to taken first. Philip and Richard both set off together, but Richard was delayed when some of the ships in his fleet were caught in a storm. The shipwreck survivors found themselves held hostage by Isaac Comnenus, the Byzantine dictator of Cyprus. Richard, therefore, paused from his journey to conquer Cyprus and make it a base for the Crusaders. In less than a month Cyprus was wrenched from the Byzantine empire and made a part of the Kingdom of Acre (as it would soon be called).

By the time Richard finally arrived at the siege of Acre, the city had already been under siege for two years. Guy of Lusignan, former king of Jerusalem, had led the siege in defiance of his promise to leave Palestine forever. He had been released by Saladin (who had to say, "a king does not kill a king") on the sole condition that he leave Palestine. Such chivalry, however, Saladin reserved only for those of noble blood. The common soldiers were butchered by Saladin and Guy reneged on his promise. The arrival of Richard and Philip was most welcome. The army of Frederick of Swabia, what remained of Barbarossa's massive army, was too small to provide any real support. With the addition of the armies of France and England it was believed that Acre could finally fall.

Nevertheless, the siege would continue for over a month. Saladin set up his army on the hills of Acre to harass the Crusaders but feared a direct assault. As a result Acre was eventually at the mercy of the Crusaders. Its inhabitants offered to surrender the city in exchange for the right to leave the city unharmed, but Richard refused. He was eager to gain every concession possible. Under his guidance a truce was agreed upon where the Crusaders would take the city and the inhabitants would be held as prisoner in exchange for Christian prisoners taken by Saladin, as well as the "True Cross." On July 12 Acre was officially taken and the Crusader's base was established.

Despite the apparent success of the Crusade, many of the knights grew tired. The zeal of the Crusade had already worn off. The fighting and death in Palestine was far worse than any they had known in Europe. Disease, searing heat, starvation, and perhaps old fashioned home sickness led many to desire to abandon the Crusade. Frederick of Swabia left with his small army as did Leopold, the Duke of Austria. More importantly Philip Augustus left for France. His motives are considered suspect by many historians for it is well known that he wanted the English land that had once belonged to France, and with Richard in the Middle East, Philip would have little competition in re-conquering those lands from England. Less than a month after the siege of Acre all the great kings and nobles of the Third Crusade were either dead or in retreat except for Richard the Lion–Hearted.

Saladin might have wished they had all remained save Richard. He would find Richard to be not only a brilliant tactician but also as ruthless as any Muslim leader. By mid–August Saladin had still not released his prisoners or returned the "True Cross." Richard decided to make an example. All the prisoners taken at Acre, including women and children, were taken out on the hill of Ayyadieh, where the whole Muslim army of Saladin could see, and were butchered. The act is one reason that many doubt Richard ever had a sincere religious conversion. Some barbarity might be excused for the day in which he lived, but the slaughter of women and children was never justified, or excused, by the devout Christian. Not even in the Middle Ages. Chivalry may not have been as noble as it is often depicted but it was, nevertheless, a code that told soldiers what was and was not acceptable in war and duty. Like the modern Geneva Convention, Chivalry was a code by which all Christian soldiers were suppose to bound. Richard's act, although it would never be repeated, remains the single most despicable act by a Crusader during the Third Crusade. In an act of revenge Saladin executed all his own prisoners and ravaged the neighboring towns. Nevertheless, the act showed Saladin that Richard was there to stay.

The Lion's War

Richard the Lion–hearted was known for his bravery in battle. He was one of those few men, whom Hollywood so often portrays, who rush headlong into battle ahead of his troops. He was never a general who sat behind the lines. It was a boldness, or foolhardiness, which would eventually end his life prematurely, but it was a bravado that earned him respect from both foes and allies alike. He had believed that he could capture Jerusalem by Christmas but he needed more money to partake of the siege. He raised the money by selling the newly captured Cyprus to the Templar knights but it was more than money that he needed.

The Arabs were a desert nomadic people. They knew how to fight in deserts and it was their greatest strength against heavily armored Europeans. The problem was that Palestine was the land of "milk and honey," or so it was before the Arabs arrived. Saladin ordered all the forest and trees stripped from the land surrounding Jerusalem for miles. Saladin wanted to make a desert of Palestine, so that it would be like their land. Saladin wanted every advantage he could get to defeat the Crusaders and so the land of "milk and honey" became as barren as the Dead Sea. That is not to say that all the land was stripped, but even what was left was never cared or nurtured by the nomadic people of the desert. The lands of the Arabs were the Arabian deserts and the sands of Egypt. With Palestine in their hands, the forest became barren and the land their home.

Gustave Dore – Richard and Saladin in Battle – 19th Century

Richard had contemplated a marriage alliance with a Muslim Prince but no Christian Princess truly wanted the marriage. Whether such an alliance ever would have worked is doubtful, but the plan was quickly put on the back–burner when no suitable bride was to be found. He planned to besiege Jerusalem but upon seeing the land surrounding the city made barren, and being aware of the massive stockpile of food and supplies that the Muslims had brought to the city, Richard wisely decided the city could not be taken or held. He and his men retreated to Ascalon only to find rubble where the walls of the great fortress city once stood. Islam was making a desert of the land and of its cities. Nevertheless, Richard was now determined to rebuild the city and its walls and make it a fortress once again.

In the meantime, King Guy and his heir apparent, by agreement, continued to fight. Conrad had secretly met with Saladin for some unknown purpose, but it was a council which met to determine once and for all who would be king of Jerusalem. Guy had been the rightful king, but it was his incompetence that had led to the kingdom's fall. Richard tried to act as arbitrator and the council eventually decided to name Conrad future king of Jerusalem in Guy's stead. Shortly afterwards, however, Conrad was stabbed to death by the Muslim assassins. These Assassins, or *Hashishiyum*, were a sort of terrorist organization led by "the Old Man of the Mountain." They took their name from the fact that they would become high on hashish, in order to make them fearless, before undertaking and assassination. Indeed, the word "assassin" comes from "hashish."

A great controversy exists as to who was the true mind behind the assassination and why. Saladin, Guy, and even Richard were all blamed at one time or another, but most believe it was indeed the "Old Man of the Mountain" who hoped to spread terror and defeatism among the Crusaders. A new king was eventually decided upon. Henry of Champagne was officially named the new king and Richard gave him the Castle of Daron which he had recently captured. In the meantime, Richard, unable to take Jerusalem, laid siege to Beirut, Jaffa, and other crucial cities along the coast. In a relatively short time Richard the Lion–hearted cut out a niche along the cost of the Mediterranean which would form the Kingdom of Acre. Nevertheless, he would never take Jerusalem.

In 1192 Richard had heard that his brother John was attempting to usurp the throne and that Philip Augustus was conquering his lands in the Aquitaine. He decided to return to England, restore his crown and lands, and then return to the Holy Land with a new massive army large enough to take Jerusalem. Saladin had also desired a truce, so they agreed on a treaty that would allow Christians pilgrimages to Jerusalem. The Crusaders would keep the coastal cities they had conquered, while the Muslims retained the rest of Palestine. Richard then left for England, but would never return.

Richard's Betrayal

Had Richard decided to stay in the Holy Land just six more months, the history of the world might have been different for in March of 1193 Saladin died. The Muslims had no real leader to replace him and many of the Muslim factions fought among themselves thereafter. Unfortunately, the Crusaders likewise lacked leadership after the departure of Richard in October of the previous year.

Richard, technically a subject of the Holy Roman Empire, had papal permission to cross by land through Germany toward England. This was the quickest possible route but the emperor, Henry VI, had plans of his own. Leopold of Austria captured Richard and held him for ransom, ransom that Prince John was not eager to pay. For the next couple of years he would sit in a dungeon in Austria. Neither Prince John, nor Philip Augustus, nor the emperor ever interceded in his behalf. He would only be released after Henry VI extracted from Richard a promise to deed his entire country to the emperor. The emperor then promised to return the land as a fief in exchange for a massive payment which Richard himself would have to secure. Richard would die five years later, from injuries received in battle, as one of the most legendary kings of England.

With Richard the Third Crusade had carved out the Kingdom of Acre, but it had also died with his departure. Richard himself was both good and bad. His nobility is exaggerated by legend, as he could be quite the butcher, but his accomplishments on the battlefield can never be disputed. The Third Crusade was Richard's Crusade.

14

Europe Before Innocent

Frederick Barbarosa had been the Hildbrand of the emperors, but if the pendulum had swung back in favor of the emperors with Barbarosa, it would swing back toward the popes with a hammer's force under Pope Innocent III. Nevertheless, while the Third Crusade raged in Palestine, Europe faced a small interlude. Emperor Henry VI ruled opposite the reign of Pope Celestine III. Henry VI had inherited from his father the desire to be absolute ruler of the Holy Roman Empire but had inherited none of his father's diplomacy. He was despised by his own people and called a tyrant. Indeed, his tyranny may well have been one of the leading factors that would lead to the rise of a strong willed pope able to defy the emperors.

Two Henrys at War

Almost immediately after his ascension to power Henry VI had to suppress yet another revolt from Henry the Lion, but it was the news that William II, King of Sicily, had died which was of greater concern for the new emperor. He had long desired to make Sicily a part of his kingdom, even as his father had. He made peace with Henry the Lion as soon as possible and set out for Italy and Sicily.

In April 1191, Henry VI arrived in Rome to find the newly elected pope, Celestine III. Celestine was an 85 year old man who had never even been consecrated a priest. He was a friend and student of the controversial Peter Abelard and it was believed that he would be a peacemaker. He had acted in moderation between King Henry of England and Becket, and had advised leniency against Henry VI's father, Barbarosa. On the 13th he was consecrated as priest, he became pope on the 14th, and on the 15th he crowned Henry VI Holy Roman Emperor.

Henry VI did not stop to celebrate his new title, but immediately set out to secure it. He continued through Italy and made his way to Sicily where William II had died two years earlier. Since no rightful heir remained, Henry VI, by virtue of his marriage to William's aunt, was the rightful heir, but the Sicilians had no desire to see the emperor as their king. They sought out Tancred, the illegitimate son of Roger, and named him the King of Sicily. Henry was determined that Sicily would become a part of the empire once and for all under his direct administration. He besieged Naples, but in August 1191 all news arrived that Henry the Lion had again breached his peace agreement and was in revolt. Henry was forced to retreat and protect his homeland. The war with Henry the Lion would continue to rage for several more years but the turning point was actually because of Henry VI's treachery against King Richard of England. Henry VI needed money and he never stopped desiring to reinstate the absolute power of the emperor across the whole of the empire.

In violation of papal protection and the rules of chivalry, Richard the Lion–Hearted was captured and imprisoned by Duke Leopold V of Austria in December 1192. A few months later he was turned over to Henry VI. The pope raised no loud voice against this breach and when Prince John heard the news he immediately allied himself with Philip Augustus in an attempt to seize the throne for himself. Richard's loyal agents, however, made the task difficult as has been immortalized in the legends of Robin Hood. In the meantime, Richard was at the mercy of Henry VI who wanted nothing less than England itself. Although England had nominally been a part of the greater Holy Roman Empire it had never been under the administrative control of the emperor. Henry VI wanted to change that. Eventually, in February 1194, Richard had reached an agreement in exchange for his release. England would be deeded over to Henry but in exchange for 100,000 Marks plus an additional 50,000 to be received later, Henry would deed England back to Richard as a fief. In this way Henry VI received enough money to continue to finance his war against Henry the Lion while at the same time gaining the prize of England under his official banner.

With help from the money that Henry VI received Henry the Lion was again forced to acquiesce. In March that same year Henry the Lion formally recognized Henry VI. He then arranged a marriage alliance with the Danes. The Guelphs, enemies of Henry VI, then became a strong political force and ally of the family of Henry the Lion. Nevertheless, Henry VI was more interested in Sicily than in future power plays. He ignored the affair, over which he could not object too loudly, and turned his attention to Sicily where Tancred had died, leaving Sicily again without a king.

Henry VI Seeks Absolute Power

In February 1194, only a month before Henry VI made peace with Henry the Lion, Tancred, king of Sicily died. His heir was a mere child, William III. In May, Henry VI reached Italy and began his conquest of Sicily. With a large fleet from Genoa and Pisa the sea was controlled easily by Henry and the land soon fell in place. By November, Henry VI had entered Palermo and he was crowned the King of Sicily on Christmas day.

Henry seized the treasure of the Normans and distributed the Sicilian lands to German *ministeriales*. The Normans were thus stripped of both their lands and their treasure and were made vassals of the emperor. The Kingdom of Sicily had lasted just over a hundred years and with its fall the Norman power was brought to an end. Norman blood continued to reign, particularly in

England but that blood was intermarried with the blood of Saxons, Italians, and French. Sicily was now a part of both the papal empire and the imperial dignity as well.

Henry's task was now to subjugate France. England and Sicily had been forced to recognize Henry's rule and France was to be next. He immediately used his political clout to stir up the French provinces against each other. Soon the King of Aragon found the Genoese conspiring against him. Philip Augustus had his own hands full defending his recently conquered lands against Richard the Lion–Hearted, who had by now returned to power in England and was busy reclaiming his French possession. Thus Henry VI was content to see chaos in France. He did not need to invade France, at least not yet. He would let the kings and dukes batter each other down and make his play later. For Henry the more immediate task was securing the hereditary crown for the emperor.

Since the most ancient of times the crown of Germany had been a hereditary title. When Charlemagne claimed the Imperial dignity, the pact was made that the title must be conferred by the pope. Moreover, Germany had long been Romanized with Roman laws. As a result, there was no longer a guarantee that the king's son would also be king. On several occasions the crown had passed from one family to another and Henry VI wanted to ensure that this did not happen again.

The Guelphs had allied themselves with Henry the Lion's family and thus threatened the House of Hohenstaufen. As a result Henry called for a diet at Wurzburg where he sought to establish the crown as hereditary. This was accomplished by promising the same liberties and rights to the princes of Germany. Thus the princes would also see their own holdings and estates passed on to their own descendants. The plan obviously appealed to those who had the power and at the Diet at Wurzburg the vote was carried. Nevertheless, the issue had not been put to rest, for a minority of those present refused. Henry needed the approval of Celestine III, but Celestine had cut off official relations with Henry. He did not venture so far as to excommunicate the emperor or to take any other action that might incur his wrath but he bided his time. The dispute had gone back to Henry's conquest of Sicily. Sicily had allied itself with the popes many years earlier and was officially under the protection of the pope. Henry had not only invaded Sicily to claim its crown but also refused to recognize that the pope had any feudal claims to Sicily, and even imprisoned bishops in Sicily.

Henry refused to give the lands back to the Church even though he would have remained its king. The issue was part financial, such as who would receive the taxes, but it was also autocratic. Henry wanted supreme power. In October 1196 another diet was convened but this time the emperor was not in the majority. Henry even suggested that the Church would be paid a large annual income but insisted that they renounce their claims to Sicily. In the end, at the Diet of Erfurt, Henry was forced to settle for the promise that his own son would crowned king of Germany later that year.

Henry now began to turn his attention toward the east. He, like many emperors before him, dreamed of again reuniting the eastern and western Roman Empires. Like those before him, he believed he was to be the sole emperor of east and west. By this time the Byzantine Empire, or eastern Roman Empire, was weak and tattered. The Muslims had beaten back the Greeks, and the very survival of the eastern empire had been due in part to the western Crusades. However, more westerners began to see an opportunity to conquer the east, including Byzantium. Whether the eastern emperor recognized this or not cannot be said with certainty, but he had agreed to pay tribute to Henry VI and agreed to a marriage alliance between his daughter and Henry's brother, Philip of Swabia. In the meantime, Henry was planning a new Crusade. Jerusalem's capture was still fresh in the minds of the west and Richard had only just returned to Britain a few years earlier. The treaty he had prepared was already broken and the west had not yet given up hope of recapturing Jerusalem. Nevertheless, Henry VI's plans for a Crusade were put on hold when a rebellion erupted in Sicily, some say at the instigation of Pope Celestine III.

Henry ventured south and brutally quelled the revolt. With savagery Henry crushed the rebels and retained his Sicilian crown, but the price was malaria. On September 1197, at an age of only thirty–two years, Henry VI died of malaria. Celestine III died a few months later on Janurary 8, 1198.

The Fallout and the Double Election

Henry was the epitome of the Middle Ages. A pendulum was swinging back and forth between the emperor and popes; between the autocracy and the Church theocracy. On many levels Henry had come closer than any to restoring the Holy Roman Empire. In terms of autocratic rule he had forced England to recognize the emperor's authority, subjugated Sicily and Italy, and begun work to reclaim France and the Byzantine empire. Yet his brutality and cruelty made him a despot. The Sicilians immediately rose up again, upon news of his death, and the German rule virtually crumbled. Moreover, the Germans themselves would attempt to break the House of Hohenstaufen. Henry had succeeded in defeating his enemies but he had also created many new ones.

Frederick II, Henry's heir, was but three years old at the time of his father's death. The German people were not willing to accept a child as king, knowing that one of Henry's aides would be regent. Immediately the Germans fell into two separate camps. Those who had supported Henry the Lion favored his son, Otto of Brunswick. Otto was related to the English court and was raised under the court of Richard the Lion–Hearted. He had been the earl of York, the count of Poitou, and the duke of Aquitaine, thus Otto was in a great position among the Germans, English, and French. Strictly in terms of his family credentials he seemed a perfect fit. However, in terms of character and temperament he was closer to Henry VI than was Philip of Brunswick, who was chosen by the Hohenstaufen party.

Philip had entered the clergy when he was young, becoming a bishop at Wurzburg, but in 1195 Henry had made him the duke of Tuscany and a year later the duke of Swabia. He was married to the Byzantine emperor's daughter, Irene, and was the brother of Henry VI. Thus his credentials were equally impressive. He was also man of calm demeanor and diplomacy. He was a drastic change from his predecessor, but he was still a Hohenstaufen. The Welf family had long struggled with the Hohenstaufens and among these families power was the bottom line, not who would make a better king.

So it was that following the death of Henry VI all that he had accomplished faded away almost instantly. In Sicily, Henry's estranged wife, the empress Constance, ordered all Germans to leave Sicily and the land was again proclaimed a fief of the papacy. In Germany civil war was inevitable. This laid the door open for another Hildebrand. The pendulum had swung from Hildebrand to Barbarosa and Henry VI. Now it swing back with a vengeance. The old pope Celestine III had shown no backbone against the cruel Henry, so the new election focused on a young, brash and arrogant deacon to be named Innocent III.

Henry's Failure and the Empire's Decline

Barbarosa and Henry had come the closest to regaining Charlemagne's empire, but only in terms of land. In terms of justice and regime they were victims of their own arrogance. The Ottonians had not conquered as many lands but they brought justice to the lands they did conquer. They came the closest to Charlemagne's legacy while Barbarosa and Henry had become consumed with land and titles.

Under the Ottonians Germany, Denmark, Burgundy, Poland, Hungary, and most of Italy had been under the direct rule of the Ottonian Dynasty. England and France were nominally subjects of the empire but beyond their direct control. Under the early Hohenstaufens the emperors could claim little more. England had been forced to formally recognize the emperor's dominion and Sicily was brought under the emperor's thumb but neither would remain obedient for long. Indeed, Denmark, Poland, and Hungary were all ruled by their own kings who acknowledged the emperor as their lord liege but neither Barbarosa nor Henry had the power over these countries that the Ottonians had.

It thus seems that every time the restoration of the Roman Empire seems at hand, an invisible hand sweeps away those who would have accomplished the act. Several of the Ottonians died as youths, Barbarosa was swept away by the raging river, and Henry died of Malaria; all before their grand schemes of reuniting east and west could be realized. It seems then that something was at work over which man had no control. It is little wonder that theologians throughout the ages have written about the Bible prophecies of the fall of Rome. Prophecies that no man could orchestrate, but that inevitably come to pass. Rome was split in two separate halves and no man has yet been able to put the pieces together again. This is from whence the fairy tale of Humpty Dumpty came. "Humpty Dumpty sat a wall, Humpty Dumpty had a great fall. All the king's horses and all the king's men couldn't put Humpty together again." Such is the lesson of history.

14
—

The Age of Innocent

The vacuum created by the double election of Philip and Otto IV was exactly what the papacy needed to reassert its authority. The secular powers had reacted against the Hildebrandian papacy and restored some of its powers but with the tyranny of Henry VI the papacy was now primed to reestablish its supremacy. Whoever would claim the title of emperor must receive the crown from the pope. With two rivals seeking that crown gaining the allegiance of the papacy was essential. War was inevitable, but the support of the Church could accomplish as much as a dozen battles and hundreds of dead soldiers. This was the time when Innocent III asserted papal supremacy over both Church and State. He would declare himself above all men, and just below God Himself. Innocent would become the emperor of all the empire in everything but name. He would wield more power over the empire than any emperor since Charlemagne.

Innocent Becomes "Ruler of the World"

The reign of Henry VI had left a sour taste in the mouth of the papacy. Celestine III had been 85 years old when he was elected and was unable or unwilling to stand up against the youthful and arrogant Henry. He had proved to be ineffective in restraining Henry's conquests or even in retaining the estates that the papacy had once held. In addition to the more noble reasons for opposing Henry, the failure had also meant there was now less money flowing into the papal treasury. With the double election of Philip and Otto, it was clear that the secular state would be in turmoil for a time. This was time enough for the Church authorities to decide upon a young pope who was not afraid to stand up to kings and emperors.

Pope Innocent III was only thirty–seven years old at the time of his election. This was the youngest age at which any known pope (or bishop of Rome) had ever served. In contrast to his predecessor, Innocent was neither meek nor weak. He declared that the pope was not only to rule over the universal Church but the whole world itself. Like most of the wicked popes, he was a lawyer. He immediately set about securing his own power in Italy. After obtaining the oath of allegiance from the Senate he began to systematically replace officials and commune members with those he knew were loyal to him. In so doing he would soon regain control over the duchy of Spoleto and, with the assistance of Henry's widow, Sicily was again made a fief of the papacy, and not of the emperor. The Empress Constance even went so far as to make

Innocent the guardian of her son, and future heir, Frederick II, to take effect upon her death which came in November that same year, 1198. Nevertheless, Markward, the former deputy of Henry VI, refused to release the hold he had on Sicily. In 1199 Innocent declared that any and all who resisted Markward would receive indulgences, and hence the remission of sins, even as the Crusaders did. Among the early "crusaders" against Markward was a young Francis of Assisi who had not yet renounced his life of sin, but whose conscience would be awoken by the evils of the war he even now participated in. The war would continue for some time but the war itself stifled Markward's control and kept Sicily a papal fief.

With Italy and Sicily under Innocent's control he turned his attention to France where Philip Augustus had divorced his Danish wife only months after their political marriage and married another woman named Agnes of Meran. The divorce had been sanctioned by the majority of French bishops but Innocent refused to accept the verdict. He ordered Philip to take back his Danish wife and divorce Agnes. When Philip refused Innocent placed the whole of France under an interdict. This meant that no religious ceremony, act, or function would be permitted to occur within the realm of France, save baptism and confession. Since even courts of justice had clergy present as part of their function, this left France in chaos. After two years Philip was forced to renounce his new wife and return to his political marriage.

This was the first, but by no means the last, time that Innocent had used interdiction upon a kingdom. When Alfonso IX of Leon was found to have married a blood relative, Innocent leveled the sentence of interdiction against the whole kingdom for five long years until Alfonso agreed to abandon his wife. In the meantime, Peter II (or Pedro), the king of Aragon, and Sancho, king of Portugal, had agreed to make their kingdoms a fief of the papacy. Even Poland, which had been officially recognized as a fief of Germany, now declared itself a fief of the Church. Innocent's power now stretched farther than any emperor in history, including Charlemagne. Even Scotland, Ireland, Iceland, and Bulgaria bowed to the will of the pope.

Next on the agenda was the schism in Germany. When Philip had been first elected, the electors had dared to elect him not only the King of Germany, but Emperor of the Holy Roman Empire without the consent of the papacy. It was their hope to nullify the pope's role in the choosing of an emperor, but it instead alienated the papacy who would ultimately play arbitrator between the two rival emperors.

Philip had the support of the German House of Hohenstaufen and the French crown but Otto was supported by the rivals houses of Germany, by the English crown to whom he was related, and the Archbishop Arnulf. After several years Philip's cause was prospering on the battlefield, but in 1201 Innocent had been asked to be arbiter of the affair. His decision was not to based on who would be the better ruler, for Philip would have won that contest, but who would promise the most to the papacy. Otto, not above false promises, pledged to hold nothing back. Otto promised to deed to the pope all the lands of Italy and Sicily. Innocent then officially decided in favor of Otto IV and excommunicated Philip.

The Fourth Crusade and the Sack of Constantinople

The west had not abandoned hope after the collapse of the Third Crusade. The fall of Jerusalem to Muslims still wretched in the hearts of the west. As early as 1199 Innocent had begun preparations for a fourth Crusade and commissioned its preaching. By this time, however, the great nobles of the earth seemed to have disappeared. Richard the Lion–Hearted had died that same year and his depraved brother John became king. Without a devout or righteous bone in his body John was too interested in the war with France to care about Crusades. Philip Augustus had already abandoned one Crusade and had no desire to leave his conflict with England. In Germany the great princes were taking sides in the civil war between Philip and Otto. The lack of education and Biblical literacy in Europe had also diminished the number of princes who really even knew what nobility or chivalry meant. The Christian Empire was again slipping into its pagan roots and the only ones found who would lead the new Crusade were more ambitious men who had little to loose in Europe, but much to gain in the Crusades.

Boniface, the Marquis of Montferrat, was chosen its leader. He is often considered to be both ignorant and arrogant. He considered himself a leader but was easily manipulated by those equally as ambitious as himself; most notably, by the Doge of Venice, Henry Dandolo. The Venetians had promised to furnish a fleet of ships for the transportation of the Crusaders to Egypt, where they believed their base of attack should be directed. The plan seemed sound except that Dandolo required an incredible 85,000 marks in payment. This would be very roughly around $50,000,000 in modern currency. Since the Crusaders could only come up with 50,000 marks Dandolo immediately contrived a "compromise."

The Venetians considered themselves masters of the sea and Dandolo desired to expand and control all the major coastal cities. Zara, the capital of Dalmatia, was under the sovereignty of the King of Hungary, but it was once a Venetian city and Dandolo craved it again. He told Boniface that if he would assist in the capture of the city then the debt still owed would be paid. Boniface agreed, but when the pope heard news of this plot he immediately sent word that no Christian should attack another Christian city except where the city was inhibiting the Crusade. He promised to excommunicate any who attacked the city, but his pleas did nothing.

The people of Zara hung crosses out across the walls of the city so that the Crusaders would know that they were Christians, for they were aware that many Crusaders were ignorant of what was transpiring and many, being uneducated, might even believe they were in Egypt. When they saw the mighty army that had assembled around them they offered to capitulate in exchange for their lives. Dandolo refused. He meant to punish Zara for defecting to Hungary. Some Crusaders refused to participate but others did. The Venetians besieged the city for five days before they surrendered unconditionally in November, 1202. The city was sacked and many of its people reduced to slavery. The pope excommunicated all involved but in the next few months even stranger events would take place.

In April 1203, a letter arrived from the claimant, emperor Philip of Swabia, rival of Otto, along with his brother–in–law, Alexius, son of the deposed Byzantine Emperor Isaac II Angelus. Isaac II had been betrayed by his own brother, also named Alexius, who had blinded Isaac and usurped the throne. In the turmoil which followed the young Alexius fled to the west with his sister, who became the wife of Philip, the rival emperor. Alexius eventually made his pleas to the pope, asking that an army help him to capture Constantinople and restore the throne to its rightful heir. Although Innocent was naturally skeptical of interfering in such a manner, Alexius had made grand promises which appealed to Innocent's own lust for power. He promised 200,000 marks to the Crusaders, an army of 10,000 to be lent to the Crusaders, 500 knights would be kept at all times in the Holy Land for its defense, but most importantly for Innocent was the promise to recognize the supremacy of the papacy and to require the submission of all Eastern Orthodox Churches. To this the pope was open, thus, while continuing to oppose Christian war against a Christian city, he left a small crack in the door saying that it would only be acceptable in "exceptional circumstances." Alexius would provide those circumstances.

In addition to this news also came blessed news for the plunderers of Zara. The pope had rescinded his excommunication and granted absolution to the pillagers of the Christian city of Zara. It is not know exactly to what degree Innocent favored what was to come next, for a month after Alexius' arrival at Zara an uprising occurred in Rome and Innocent was forced to flee. He had not yet obtained the absolute control of Italy he desired, and would not for several more years. In the meantime, he fell ill and received little news of the events which would transpire in the Fourth Crusade. It was only after the deeds were done that Innocent characteristically condemned the actions while taking full political advantage of their occurrences.

Back in Zara the Crusaders were well aware that Alexius, Boniface, and Dandolo were planning another detour. They had been deceived once and had no intention of being detoured again. An organized rebellion broke out among the Crusaders who planned to find another means of reaching Egypt. Fighting had gone on for weeks when Boniface and Dandolo went to the Crusader's camp and made their plea. The crowds began to chant "Go to Acre! Go to Acre!" Upon hearing this, the pleas of Dandolo and Boniface went out and begged them to save the Christian Prince's kingdom. They promised that the city, when seeing their emperor return, would surrender with little or no fighting and that once the city had been secured they would have all the money and soldiers to go anywhere in the Middle East and reconquer Jerusalem. The rebelling Crusaders only relented when Alexius, Boniface, and Dandolo drew up and signed a document promising everything that they had said and agreeing to take them to Syria after a given amount of time. Some Crusaders still deserted, to their credit, but the rest reluctantly agreed.

They set sail for the famed city of the east which had been built by Constantine himself. When they arrived they soon found that the people were not so eager to have Alexius IV as emperor. They had become used to usurpers over the years, for Byzantium had become in many respects as depraved as the west. Corruption and brutality had become the norm for the Byzantine emperors and it was the people who often paid the price. Consequently, the people had no desire to risk their lives by overthrowing Alexius III Angelus. A siege was then the only recourse.

Constantinople was the most fortified and defensible city in the world. Built on the sea, it was surrounded by huge walls and gates from both land and sea. The Venetians attacked from the sea while the Crusaders attempted to level the walls. In the end a few Venetians managed to climb over the walls and spill into the city, but they were hopelessly outnumbered. Their strategy was, therefore, to set fires and burn the city from within. The strategy worked well. Nearly a quarter of the city burned to the ground before the fires were put under control, but the invaders were still held outside the gates. Nevertheless, Alexius III Angelus had proven to be a coward. During the night, when the fire was raging, Alexius III had fled. The next morning the people reinstalled the blinded Isaac II, who had been imprisoned in a dungeon since Alexius III's ascension. The Crusaders were still outside the walls, but Alexius IV's father was back on the throne and he invited his son back. It looked as if everything would end favorably, save the destruction caused by the fire, but Alexius IV was not content to be prince. He wanted to be emperor. In the days that followed Alexius IV had convinced Isaac II to abdicate. Isaac tearfully handed the throne over to his son whom he prayed would some day repent. On August 1, 1203, Alexius IV became emperor, but the young teenage prince was as ignorant as he was arrogant. He released from prison a certain Alexius V Ducas, nicknamed Murzuphlus after his thick eyebrows, who himself had designs on the throne, and made him a trusted advisor.

It seemed once again that the east and west were destined to be reunited for the fortunes of the west were rapidly swinging in favor of Philip of Swabia, the brother–in–law of the new emperor of Constantinople, but as happened so often before, it was not to be. Murzuphlus had Alexius IV assassinated and declared himself emperor. He then sent word to the Crusaders that they must leave his land or suffer the consequences. The Crusaders responded with outrage. They had come all this way on a detour to enthrone the young Alexius who was now murdered by yet another usurper. The siege began anew, but this time Constantinople would not be so fortunate.

After four months of fighting the Crusaders still had not breached the walls, nor had the Venetians been able to enter the city by sea. Murzuphlus arrogantly declared to his troops, "am I not a good emperor? Did you ever have so good an emperor?" Like most arrogant men, however, Murzuphlus was a coward, even as Alexius III had been. When it looked like the Crusaders were gaining the advantage, Murzuphlus fled. On April 12, 1204 the gates of the city were opened and what followed has been called the greatest crime in history. The Crusaders had vowed upon Holy Relics not to despoil any women or to defile any Churches. Those who violated the vow were to be executed. Nevertheless, the ancient pagan rite had not been forgotten; only their vow. For the customary period of three days rape, murder, and pillage ensued. A prostitute was placed upon the Patriarch's chair while the nuns and virgins were raped. Murders were common and plundering of the most sacred places was prevalent.

The crime is justly considered among the worst in medieval history. Nominally Christian soldiers had defiled the most sacred of places, committed the most abominable crimes, and sacred relics were stolen by the dozens. Among the sacred relics claimed as prizes by the conquerors were the "original" crown of thorns, the loincloth supposed to be worn by Christ on the Cross, the arm of St. Mark, the girdle of the Virgin Mary, the rod which Moses turned to a serpent, the sponge which fed Christ on the Cross, a vial of Christ's blood, a vial of Christ's tears, and even John the Baptist's head. The Venetians had conquered the unconquerable city. They henceforth declared themselves rulers of "a half and a quarter of the Roman empire."

Pope Innocent III's reaction is interesting, to say the least. He issued forth a scathing diatribe against the atrocities of the Crusaders but did not excommunicate the participants. Instead, he quickly sent a papal Legate to crown Baldwin of Flanders to become the first Latin Emperor of Constantinople. He further appointed a Venetian as Patriarch of Constantinople. Immediately, the Greek Orthodox Church was besieged by the papal attempt to force his supremacy over them. Latin priests were instituted throughout the new kingdom and the Latin emperors of Constantinople made a small part of the empire a fief of the papacy and the Holy Roman Empire.

Most of the Byzantine Empire resisted. Greek emperors continued to rule in exile for the next fifty years, while the west controlled most of what is modern Greece, the city of Constantinople, and the western tip of modern Turkey. The Byzantine Empire itself was effectively broken up into four principalities. Two separate halves of the empire declared themselves the true successors of Byzantium, while the Greek empire of Nicaea also declared itself a separate kingdom. The east was crumbling and the west, far from preserving their Christian brothers as they had promised in the first Crusade, sped the destruction along. The Latin Empire of Constantinople itself would only last just over fifty years. Far from reuniting the eastern and western Roman empires, the Fourth Crusade resulted in their mutual hatred of each other. The Greeks would never forget the sack of Constantinople nor the papacy's attempt to force their submission.

The Fourth Crusade was the first of three Crusades that would be attempted under Innocent's reign. This Crusade, however, was but a foreshadowing of what was to come. The next two Crusades would show the depths to which the west had fallen in moral aptitude. The Children's Crusade would fail miserably only to be followed by the Albigenses Crusade against "heretics." It seemed as if the west had become pagan again.

The Imperial War

Innocent III had placed his faith in Otto, in opposition to the House of Hohenstaufen. However, Philip was not only winning the civil war, but in 1204 many defections from Otto further enhanced Philip's prestige. These defections included the influential Archbishop Adolf who had crowned Otto earlier. Innocent himself was still in exile from Rome where he would remain for another year. Being preoccupied with solidifying his power in Italy, let alone Rome, Innocent was unable to say much about the Imperial war but it was clear that the tides were shifting away from his candidate, Otto IV.

By 1208 Innocent had been restored to Rome and had finished consolidating his power in Italy as well as many other realms. Otto, however, was virtually abandoned. He continued to fight but the war was being won by Philip with the support of much of the German clergy. Innocent was forced to relent and agreed to crown Philip Holy Roman Emperor, but before the coronation could occur Philip was assassinated. The assassin was an old friend of Philip who had been offended when Philip refused to give his daughter in marriage to his family. Otto was now the only claimant to the throne.

Otto knew that, even with his opponent dead, he would have to appease his dissenters. He immediately set to punish Philip's assassin, to acknowledge Philip as the previous emperor, to request an election for a new emperor, and to marry Philip's eleven year old daughter, thus securing the peace between the Hohenstaufen and Guelphs. The marriage, however, was not without controversy for Otto was a cousin of Philip's daughters within the prohibited degree. Innocent III, who had previously forced Alfonso IX of Leon to divorce his wife for the same reason, now granted papal dispensation to marry the two despite their blood relation. Nonetheless, when she died only weeks later, Otto's enemies remained, perhaps suspicious of her premature death. Otto needed the support of Pope Innocent III so he set out to negotiate with Innocent for the imperial diadem. By this time Innocent was already quite powerful. He had just instigated the interdict against England (of which much more will be said later) and was arranging for the Crusade against the Albigenses "heretics." Innocent was prepared to accept nothing short of complete submission to the pope and acknowledgment of the papal claims to Italy and Sicily. Otto, for the time being, gave the pope everything he asked for and on October 4, 1209 Otto IV was officially crowned Holy Roman Emperor by Innocent III. It would not be long, however, before Innocent regretted his decision.

Religious Dissidents and Sects Before the Albigenses Crusade

It has been shown previously that many of the doctrines of the papacy stemmed neither from the Bible, nor the Church Fathers. For centuries bishops, clergymen, and educated laymen ignored those teachings that they failed to find support for in the Scriptures. Only in recent decades, however, had the papacy and emperor begun to take measures against these men. They first clamped down on disobedient clergymen by reassigning them, demoting them, or even defrocking them. When it became clear that this did not stop the papal critics, other measures became necessary. As much as a hundred years before a few Christians had been executed for daring to dispute the doctrine of transubstantiation, which had still not become official dogma, but most continued to worship and preach on their own. Innocent saw where the problem resided; "lay preachers." Although the "Great Commission" of the Bible declares that all Christians shall preach the gospel, the pope knew that he could never control all people. His hierarchical system made all clergy accountable to him alone, and all laymen were accountable to the clergy. The clergy were then to suppress heresy. This was one of Innocent's most "urgent" desires; to stamp out "heresy," and with it "lay preaching."

Before discussing the pope's war against heresy it is prudent and necessary to clarify how many sects there were in Europe at the time, and how they differed from Rome and from each other. Many of these groups are claimed by Protestants as their forerunners and for some groups this is a fair statement, but other sects bear little true resemblance to the Reformation. In some cases Catholicism lay far closer to Protestantism than the sects of the Cathari and the Amaurians. They were similar to the Reformation only in that they opposed some of the same doctrines of the medieval Church. In regard to what they actually taught, however, they were drastically different.

The origins of these dissident groups, not surprisingly, corresponded with the height of papal power and corruption. They first began to appear at the time of Gregory VII (Hildebrand) when he sought to impose his will upon the whole clergy. By the time of Innocent III the dissident sects were everywhere. They came from both within and without. Indeed, St. Francis of Assisi and even the more prominent Joachim of Fiore were devout Catholics who themselves were dissidents of a sort. St. Francis followed the Waldenses in both their love

224

of poverty and their desire for evangelism and is even believed to have emulated his Franciscan order after some of the tenets of the Humiliati. He sought permission from Innocent for the founding of his order and was reluctantly granted it. It is said that Innocent, upon smelling Francis, had him thrown out before one of his aides informed him that Francis was the one seeking the new order. While Innocent was no fan of either Francis or Joachim, whose teachings in prophecy drew the attention of Richard the Lion–Hearted years earlier, he had his hands full with far greater "heretics." Indeed, the number of religious sects in Europe, beyond the Catholic Church, has varied but was estimated by those at the time as being between seventy and a hundred and thirty. Their followers quite literally counted in the hundreds of thousands. The great Waldenses alone are estimated to have numbered over a hundred thousand solely in Germany.

The most prominent of these sects were the Cathari or Albigenses, the Waldenses, the Humiliati, Berengarians, Petrabusians, Henricians, Arnoldolists, Paulicans, Bogomili, Amaurians, and Beguines. Others have been named the Patarini, Speronistas, Leonites, Circumcisi, Monarchians, Passagins, Josephini, Garatenses, Beghaids, Franziscos, Bagnarolos, Commixtos, Roncarolos, Apostolicals, Luciferans, Warini, Albanenses, Bagnoliesi, Runcarri, Concorrezzi, and the Communellos. The ensuing chart breaks down the most important ones and shows how they differed from both Catholics and the later Protestants.

Before addressing the Cathari, with whom Innocent was most concerned, the Waldenses and their peripheral sects should be examined for they, not the Cathari, would have the most impact upon later history and reformation movements. Unlike the Cathari, the Waldenses were true Christians, in the Biblical sense of the word. Although they took their name from Peter Waldo (also called Peter Valdez), they are know to have predated his leadership. Often being known by the name, "Poor Men of Lyon," they were a group which took vows of poverty. This lifestyle was certainly not unknown before them and did not alarm the Catholic hierarchy, but some of their other teachings began to create concern for the papacy.

Located in the Piedmont Valleys of northern Italy the Waldenses came from the same region whose bishops had long criticized and condemned the papacy for its sins. The great bishop Ambrose had resided in that area and the bishops of Turin, where the famed shroud was kept for centuries, also resisted papal authority. The Waldenses maintained this and opposed the "new" Catholic teachings on prayers for the dead, veneration of the saints, purgatory, and the hierarchy of the priesthood. They also translated the Bible into the vernacular of the people, a fact which angered the papacy, but it was not yet illegal. Nonetheless, what was of the greatest concern to the papacy was their belief in "lay preaching." The doctrine of lay preaching, believed to be founded in Christ's Great Commission (c.f. Matthew 28:16–20 and Mark 16:14–18), lay at the cornerstone of the Reformation and its predecessors. The Catholic hierarchy, however, outlawed *any* preaching by anyone who had not been given a specific dispensation to do so. *Only* the Catholic hierarchy could commission someone to preach and the papacy believed that no one should preach without it. Part of the argument was that it prevented the spread of heresy from uneducated or outright heretical men. The greater reason was the more obvious. It kept all Churches tightly within the grip of the pope.

Under Peter Waldo's leadership the Waldenses began preaching throughout southern France and northern Italy. In 1179 Peter had attended the Third Lateran Council where he had sought papal support. Although Alexander III refused to give him a commission, he was confirmed in his vows of poverty and given leave. Waldo and his followers, however, continued to preach and by 1184 Pope Lucius III issued a bull forbidding the Waldenses from further preaching and condemning Waldo.

By the time of Innocent III Waldo had passed away. His followers continued preaching the gospel but a breach was beginning to develop among the Waldenses. Perhaps spawned by fear of the coming Crusade, or perhaps based on a more sincere dispute, the Humiliati broke from the Waldenses. The break was based on a dispute between their views on the Eucharist as well as Peter Waldo's leadership. The Humiliati accepted Catholic Eucharist, while the Waldenses rejected much of it. The question of Peter Waldo's leadership also seemed to be called into question, doubtless stemming from this debate, but another reason may have been the pope's readying of a Crusade. The Humiliati, although still Waldenses at heart, sought approval from the papacy and it was granted, for a time, by Innocent III. This new Catholic order, however, would be short lived for they too would soon be rejected and scorned, but along with St. Francis, the Humiliati and the Franciscans became the two newest religious orders. Meanwhile, most other sects became the subject of the pope's wrath.

Along with the Waldenses and the Humiliati were four other small Protestant forerunners. These were the Berengarians, the Petrobusians, the Henricians, and the Arnoldolists. Each of these groups would eventually be absorbed in one way or another into the great Waldenses sect, but each began independently. The Berengarians were the followers of Berengar of Tours. Mentioned in previous chapters, Berengar opposed the Catholic teachings on transubstantiation. He was tried several times and released on numerous occasions, often recanting his views only to take up the cause again after release. His followers were sporadically persecuted in France but those who survived the coming Crusade would eventually be assimilated into the Waldenses.

The Petrobusians took their name after Peter of Bruys. This man, like later Protestants, preached against infant baptism, the doctrine of transubstantiation, the sacrifice of mass, prayers for the dead, and the celibacy of the priesthood, but most of all he spoke out against the worship of relics. He condemned relics as a form of idolatry and took his preaching to extremes by burning crosses in bonfires. It was this act which would lead to his martyrdom for an angry mob, outraged that he would burn crosses, threw him upon one of his own pyres. His followers continued to exist until they too became absorbed into the Waldenses, but many were slaughtered in the Crusade along with the Cathari.

Connected to the Petrobusians were the Henricians. They were named after Henry of Lausanne, a one time associate of Peter of Bruys. Nevertheless, unlike Peter, Henry was less inclined to controversial actions. He did speak out against indulgences and the use of relics but did not burn crosses. His preaching was, nonetheless, sufficient to draw the ire of several priests. He was tried in 1135 but released to the custody of Bernard of Clairvaux. Bernard taught Henry and released him, whereupon Henry continued to preach against the heresies of his mother Church. The Henricians obviously drew less attention to themselves than the Waldenses or Petrobusians, but their distaste for relics and icons would draw enough attention to warrant sporadic persecution before the Albigenses Crusade.

The final sect which would eventually be amalgamated into the Waldenses sect were the Arnoldolists. Taking their name from Arnold of Brescia, who had been executed by Frederick Barbarossa not too many years earlier, this sect has sometimes been considered political rather than religious, but this would be a mistake. The concept of a Republican Democracy had taken on a religious nature from the time of Arnold to the Cromwell Republic and even to our own forefathers. The justification was that man is a sinner and is corrupted by power. Only by distributing power amongst the people can the corruption of power be diminished, and only by staying free of political power can the Church remain pure. Like Arnold of Brescia, the Arnoldolists spoke out loudly against the corruption of the Church and its abuse of power. In doctrine they were somewhere between the Catholics and Protestants.

Together, these groups, the Waldenses, Humiliati, Berenegarians, Petrobusians, Henricians, and Arnoldolists created the earliest reformation attempts. They called the Church back to a more pure apostolic beginning and spoke out against some of the emerging doctrines that had been unknown in the earliest days of the apostles. The later Benguines and Beghards were also reform minded groups which began as a religious order like the Franciscans. It was, nevertheless, not these groups that the pope concerned himself with the most, but the more extreme heretical sects. Although actually a compilation of many sects, the Cathari sects were all related to one another. It was with them that Inquisition would first begin.

The history of oppression always begins with fringe elements and then moves toward the center. The Cathari sects were, by both Catholic and Protestant definitions, cults. They had developed from the eastern sects known as the Paulicans and Bogomili. Many of the Paulicans had been slaughtered during the earlier Crusades as the soldiers passed through toward Palestine. The Bogomili continued to prosper for a time in Bulgaria and the eastern empire. As their followers moved west they found many thousands of people who tired of the corruption of the Catholic Church and desired something better. With the instigation of Innocent's interdict Churches were virtually shut down and their doors closed until as such time as Philip Augustus and John of England had "repented" and agreed to submit to the pope's will. It is, therefore, little surprise that people turned to the various religious sects for comfort. In this respect, the proliferation of the Cathari sect was Innocent's own fault. People were turning to those sects who opposed the corruption of the Church; a Church which shut its own doors to the people for political gain.

Although there were many different classes of Cathari, some more orthodox then others, their central doctrines were usually dualistic and gnostic. According to gnosticism all flesh was evil. This meant that Christ could not have literally dwelt in the flesh. For most Cathari there is no resurrection of the dead, baptism of any kind was condemned on the basis that John the Baptist questioned whether Christ was really the one, Satan was believed to be the brother of Christ, and not only was sex forbidden but marriage as well. They rejected the doctrines of purgatory, the seven sacraments, indulgences, and the established Church itself. In addition, they refused to eat meat, rejected the Old Testament as the work of the Devil, and some engaged in a rite known as the *endura* in which followers starved themselves (and sometimes their own children) to death. This act was supposed to be a reflection of asceticism and is reminiscent of some eastern religions. It was also the most heinous of the Cathari's crimes.

As aforementioned, the Cathari themselves are believed to have derived from the eastern religious sects, or cults, known as the Paulicans and Bogomili whose followers made their way westward during the third and fourth Crusades. The Paulicans dated back several centuries and were a dualistic sect who rejected the Old Testament and held, like the Cathari, that matter was evil. The Bogomili were also related to the Paulicans and rejected the Biblical (and Catholic) view of the Trinity. The Amaurians were yet another sect related to the Cathari who took their name from Amaury of Bena who had died in 1204. He taught that love was the only commandment but his other doctrines were clearly deviant. He believed in neither heaven nor hell, denied the resurrection, use of relics, the Eucharist, and openly called the Catholic Church the prophesied "Whore of Babylon."

Religious Sect	Name derived from	Doctrinal beliefs in relation to Catholics and later Protestants	Found in
Cathari (also associated with the Albigenses, Albaneases, Bagnoliesi, and Patarini)	Taken from the Greek word *catharos* meaning to "cleanse." Albigenses, the Catholic name given, is derived from the city of Albi where they originated.	They differed from both Catholics and Protestants in that they were a dualistic sect that rejected the physical incarnation of Christ, the resurrection of the dead, and baptism of any kind. They believed Jesus and Satan were brothers, that Satan created the earth, rejected the Old Testament completely, refused to eat meat, believed sex to be evil, even condemning marriage, and taught the belief in the migration of the soul. They agree with Protestants only in that they also rejected indulgences, purgatory, and the seven sacraments.	South of France
Waldenses (also associated with the Humiliati, the Leonites, the Runcarri, and possibly the Apostolicals)	Believed to be taken from Peter Waldo although the sect predates his leadership.	Considered true forerunners of the Reformation with whom they differed in no noticeable way. They believed in the priesthood of all believers, the sole authority of the Scriptures which they translated into native tongues, they elected their leaders, and taught free salvation by faith through grace. They rejected the Catholic hierarchy, purgatory, prayers for the dead, prayer to saints including Mary, indulgences, the use of relics, and the validity of excommunication.	Piedmont valley in Northern Italy, but it also spread throughout France, England, Germany, central Europe, and even to eastern Europe and Belgium.
Berengarians	The followers of Berengar of Tours.	They rejected the Catholic doctrine of transubstantiation and questioned the authority of the papacy. In most other ways they were Catholics although the later Berengarians, leaning on the Bible, moved toward the Waldenses movement with which they eventually became absorbed.	France, England, and some followers in Italy.
Petrobusians	The followers of Peter of Bruys.	Like the Protestants of later ages they rejected transubstantiation, the sacrifice of mass, use of relics, prayer for the dead, and infant baptism. They also encouraged priest to marry. Like the Berengarians, Henricians, and Arnoldists they eventually became absorbed into the Waldenses movement.	France and central Europe.
Henricians	The followers of Henry of Lausanne.	Virtually identical to the Petrobusians but with an added emphasis on the condemnation of indulgences. They also became absorbed into the Waldenses movement.	France and central Europe.
Arnoldolists	The followers of Arnold of Brescia.	Roughly half way between Catholics and later Protestants, the Arnoldolists were not really a political movement but a religious one. They rejected the Catholic hierarchy, thus spawning their firm belief in Republican Democracy. They also rejected the Eucharist, transubstantiation, and infant baptism. They eventually became absorbed into the Waldenses movement.	Mainly in Italy, but some spread throughout central Europe.

Religious Sect	Name derived from	Doctrinal beliefs in relation to Catholics and later Protestants	Found in
Beguines	Named for the convents.	Began as a convent for lay women. They were largely Catholic in belief save that they were very influenced by the Joachimite Spirituals. They were evangelical, thus violating Catholic dogma forbidding lay preachers, and they also rejected the hierarchy as well as infant baptism. Later they either became absorbed with the Franciscan Spirituals or the Waldenses.	The Rhineland.
Beghards	The Latin name for their order.	Virtually identical with the Benguines save that the Beghards were made up of men. They also became absorbed with either the Franciscan Spirituals or the Waldenses.	The Rhineland.
Paulicans	Named after the apostle Paul since they accepted only the Pauline epistles as valid.	A dualistic sect in opposition to both Catholic and later Protestant teachings. They are believed to have influenced the Cathari. They rejected the entire Old Testament and most of the New, accepting only the Pauline epistles. They probably denied the resurrection as well. In addition, they rejected the use of icons, relics, and the veneration of Mary.	Asia Minor.
Bogomili (also associated with the Patarini)	The followers of Bogomil.	Similar to the dualistic Paulican but they also taught that Satan created the earth and they downplayed the Trinity. They also rejected the Eucharist, the use of icons and relcis, baptism of any kind, and rejected both sex and marriage as sins. Like the Cathari they refused to eat meat. Along with the Paulicans they are believed to have had a significant impact on the Cathari sects.	Bulgaria, the Balkans, and eastern Europe.
Concorrezzi (a distinctive sect of the Cathari)	Named after the city of Concorreggio where they originated.	A Cathari sect listed separately here because this sect rejected the heavy dualistic elements of tranditional Cathari including a rejection of the role of Lucifer in creation. They considered themselves enemies of the Albancases sect of the Cathari.	France.
Amaurians (also associated with the Ortlibenses and the " Brethren of the Free Spirit")	The followers of Amaury of Bena.	Compatible with neither Catholicism nor Protestantism. They were a pantheistic sect that believed God became incarnate in believers. They denied the resurrection of the dead and the reality of both heaven and hell. They also rejected the Catholic doctrines of transubstantiation and the use of relics. They did, however, teach salvation by faith.	France and Strassburg, Germany.
Passagins (also called the Circumcisi)	Named for the Passover since they accepted the Mosaic law. (Circumcisi is from the word "circumcision")	A legalistic sect who held that the Mosaic law was still valid. They worshipped on Saturday and required circucision from all of their followers. Again, they were neither Catholic nor Protestant in disposition. The papacy disliked their love of " Jewish dispensations."	France and central Europe.

It is important to note that the term "Albigenses" was a term used by the Catholics and is applied somewhat generally to *all* the "heretics" of southern France. Consequently, whenever one speaks of Albigenses it should be assumed that the term speaks of many religious sects, not just the Cathari, with whom the term is most often associated. Indeed, any number of other sects, and cults, could be mentioned, for France, as well as parts of northern Italy, Austria, and Germany, had become a haven for dissenters. The corruption of the Church and its departure from the apostolic age fed dissents but perhaps nothing spawned the dissents so much as Innocent himself. The priests of the Church were openly known to be corrupt and to hold concubines, often without even keeping them a secret. Although there is no proof of it, the interdicts which Innocent placed on France and England doubtless only spawned the religious sects to more growth, for where else would the common people go if the doors of the Church were shut to them. Of the estimated ten to fifteen million people who lived in France at the time, no less than a hundred thousand, and possibly as many as half a million, were members of some dissident sect. The numbers vary so greatly because of the exaggerations and misinformation given by both the Inquisitors and later historians. It is likely, however, that the appropriate number rests closer to the high number than the low number for the number of those slaughtered in the coming Crusade itself indicates how great the dissidents were in numbers; so great that Innocent was resolved to obliterate them from the face of the earth.

The Albigensian Crusades Begin

It had been nearly two hundred years since the emperor and papacy began officially executing "heretics," but the persecutions throughout these times were still relatively few and had no major impact on the spread of dissident sects. Innocent aimed to change all that. He made the extermination of "heresy" one of his primary goals. For Innocent a heretic was worse than a Muslim since Muslims did not profess to be Christian.

Southern France, and particularly the county of Toulouse in the region known as Languedoc, had come to be inundated with dissident sects. Since Innocent had first taken office he had written repeatedly to the Count of Toulouse, Raymond VI, asking him to take measures to stamp out the "heretics." His very first year, in 1198, he had sent a papal legate to persuade Raymond to crush the heretics, but Raymond repeatedly refused to slay his own people. In 1203 Innocent decided to try a new legate. Peter of Castelnau was chosen to convince the stubborn count of his duties and Peter was not unwilling, as papal legate, to use all the powers at his disposal. In 1205 Innocent had even began sending legates and letters to Philip Augustus urging him to take action against the heretics and against Raymond, if he would not obey. Philip, however, was still at war with King John of England over the Aquitaine possessions. He had no desire to waste his time, resources, and troops performing tasks for the pope whom he had no great affection for. Raymond had heard of this and realized that he was fast becoming a target of the pope so he quickly promised to eradicate the heretics; a promise he had no intention of keeping.

After two years Raymond had done nothing to execute the dissidents and allegations began to creep up that Raymond was actually a heretic himself. Owing to what is known of Raymond this is unlikely. More than likely Raymond merely saw the folly of brutalizing one's own peasants over religious disputes. He was not prone to fighting in the first place and it is said that what few battles he had previous taken part in, he had failed to even draw his sword. Raymond was merely buying time. Peter appeared to Raymond and leveled many of the charges against him including one charge that he had appointed Jews to public office.

Of this last charge a brief aside is needed. The Jews had once been welcomed by Charlemagne but times had changed radically. As the education of the masses dwindled and the nobility and clergy came to seize all lands in their own names there were few commoners with the education to perform the tasks of banking and other essential functions. The Jews, however, had never lost their desire to educate their children. Most were home–schooled or taught in the synagogues. As a result, by the twelfth century most all lenders and bankers were Jews, since they were the only ones educated enough to perform those duties. Christian commoners were simply not educated enough to perform the tasks anymore. With interest rates ranging from 20% to as much as 80% in some places the people of Europe began to mistrust and blame the the Jews for their problems, calling them money grubbing deceivers. Anathemas and cries of "Christ–killers" became common (showing ignorance of the Bible as well as anti–semitism). Moreover, like the Cathari, many Jews had taken up mystic views as expressed in Kabalistic magic which also flourished in this same area. Indeed, the very legend of the Golum may have come from this land. Jews were, therefore, considered little better than the "heretics" whom the papacy was determined to extinguish.

Raymond was threatened with interdiction and excommunication if he did not make good on his promise to exterminate the "heretics." Moreover, Innocent was already making preparations for a Crusade; one that could be leveled against the heretics or against Raymond himself. Peter met with Raymond for one last time and words were exchanged. Raymond is alleged to have flown into a rage and threatened the legate, who had a bodyguard with him. Peter left Raymond on January 14th 1208 never to see the count again, for a lance was driven into his back while he was on the road by an assailant identified as one of Raymond's servants.

The assassination would give Innocent exactly what he needed to foster the Crusade. Previously, most dukes and nobles seemed less than enthused with the idea of a Crusade against their own countrymen, but the murder of a papal legate fed fire to the flame. Innocent promised that the land taken by the Crusaders would be theirs. He offered indulgences to all who would take "up the Cross." Salvation, it seemed, was the pope's to offer. The Crusade was now taking shape, but it was stalled by Philip Augustus' refusal to participate. He pointed out that Raymond had neither been convicted of heresy nor of the murder of Peter of Castelnau. Philip was still at war with John and he feared that the emperor Otto IV, John's nephew, was entering to an alliance against him. He would not participate in the Crusade nor spare any men.

Raymond, realizing his precarious predicament, tried to rally forces for himself but could find little support. Even the viscount of Beziers, his nephew Raymond–Roger, had refused to co–operate. Raymond had even appealed to Philip Augustus but Philip was as cold to him as he was to the pope. Finally Raymond tried to plead with the new papal legate, Arnald–Amaury, but the legate wanted blood, not repentance. The last ditch effort of Raymond was to appeal directly to the pope himself. He promised virtually anything that the pope would ask and requested a new papal legate. Innocent had already excommunicated Raymond and placed an interdict upon his people. He finally had Raymond where he wanted him but he was not about to abandon the Crusade at this point. He sent a new legate with specific orders to be Arnald–Amaury's mouthpiece. He was told, "the count suspects him, but not you." Moreover, the pope told them to "use cunning and deception as weapons."

Raymond was forced to cede seven castles and a county to the papacy, to be flogged half naked in the Church, to renounce his love for "heretics" and Jews, but he was also forced to fight at the head of the armies in the Crusade he had refused to mount. He even surrendered his own son as a hostage to ensure them of his loyalty. He joined the Crusading army soon afterwards. Arnald–Amaury, the papal legate, was himself the leader of the army which is alleged to have boasted between 40,000 and by some accounts as many as 220,000 men. When his soldiers asked him how they would recognize the Catholics versus the heretics, he replied the now infamous line, "kill them all, God will recognize his own."

Upon hearing of Raymond's humiliation and of the approaching armies, Raymond–Roger, who had earlier refused to help Raymond VI, now realized, perhaps for the first time, that the army was coming after him. He too had many dissidents and Jews in his cities and many of his men were known to be converts to the dissidents. He, therefore, in a terrible fright rode out to meet Arnald–Amaury and offered to make the same concessions as Raymond VI had but the legate wanted blood. It was too late to send the armies home with no spoils. Raymond–Roger was refused the right to "repent." The papacy, which had taken the power to forgive sins from God, now refused to forgive one its princes. He was sent back to await his fate.

Jean–Paul Laurens – The Agitators of Languedoc – 1887

"Kill them all, let God sort them out!"

Raymond–Roger retreated to Carcassonne while the citizens of Beziers prepared to defend themselves against the Crusaders. They believed that if they could hold out long enough Raymond–Roger would return with help. The people of Beizers, however, were not soldiers and soon began to panic. Men abandoned their posts and the soldiers began to pour into the city. Many of the people, particularly women and children, crowded into the Churches for safety but the laws of sanctuary, and human decency, were forgotten. The papal legate had himself given permission to spare no one and no one was spared. Arnald–Amaury wrote gleefully back to Innocent III "neither age, nor sex, nor status had been spared." All the people in the Churches, women and children included, were butchered and the city put to flames. Within a day the entire city was burned to the ground and no one survived. No prisoners were taken. No mercy was shown. Even the Catholics within the city were looked upon as traitors for harboring the heretics. Arnald–Amaury was pleased.

News of the destruction spread quickly. Between Beziers and Carcassonne villages and towns became ghost towns as the people either fled to the forest or retreated to Carcassonne where they believed Raymond–Roger could protect them. The army reached Carcassonne on July 28, 1209. While the terror had caused the small city peasants to flee, it had reinforced the will of the people of Carcossonne to fight. They saw what had happened to Beziers and they knew the fate that awaited them if they failed. For over a week they boldly defended their city and kept the Crusaders at bay when Peter II (also called Pedro), king of Aragon, arrived at the Crusaders camp.

Peter II was the brother–in–law of Raymond VI and his land lay at the border of Carcassonne. Peter's motives have been hotly debated for many years. He was a devout man but did not seem to abide the Crusaders. He had befriended Raymond VI and doubtless knew that Raymond was not entirely a willing participant in the Crusade. He may have feared that an enemy of Aragon might seize control of Carcassonne or it may have been a more devout purpose, but for whatever reason Peter II was prepared to help negotiate a surrender. Again, Arnald–Amaury refused. He still wanted blood. He was still unprepared to forgive. He was, however, talked into allowing Raymond–Roger to leave with a few friends before the city was taken. To his credit Raymond–Roger refused. He would stay with his people to the end.

After another week of fighting the Crusaders had still made little headway, and they were concerned that the people were indeed prepared to fight to the last man. They had remembered the promise of booty, but they also remembered that they had received no booty from Beziers as it had burned to the ground. Arnald–Amaury was forced to make a legitimate effort to compel their surrender so that the city could be taken with booty intact. The people and Raymond–Roger were promised their lives if they would leave the city carrying nothing but the clothes on their backs. The people agreed, but Raymond–Roger was arrested anyway and taken to a dungeon where he died a few months later of dysentery. The Crusaders then plundered Carcassonne. Simon de Montfort was named the new viscount but his task was far from easy. Many of the Crusaders had already claimed to have received their indulgences and thus saved their soul. They, therefore, did not desire to stay on but to return home. Raymond VI went back to Toulouse under probation, Simon was the new viscount, and Peter II was officially the suzerain thereof. Nonetheless, the Crusade was far from over. In fact, it would continue for thirty years with some of the most ironic twists known to history.

Pierre–Roger, who had defended Carcassonne, established a new base at Minerve. Many other dissidents and sympathizing nobles took up castles and estates throughout the land. From Minerve Pierre–Roger conducted raids on

Simon's lands and officials. Major cities, including Toulouse, took in the fleeing dissidents who had escaped the first wave of the Crusade. Moreover, Arnald–Amaury had not ceased looking for blood. Simon obliged him by executing alleged heretics, usually without a trial, but he had asked what to do with those heretics who wanted to repent and rejoin the church. Arnald–Amaury answered that they too should be burned. Simon was brutal and savage, which did not endear him to his new subjects. In one case he had the eyes put out of an entire garrison which had helped Pierre–Roger. Even more division was caused by Peter II's failure to approve of his new vassal Lord.

Raymond VI had quite different problems. No sooner had he returned home than he found Arnald–Amaury making new demands. Not weeks later, he again accused Raymond of supporting heretics and ordered him to dismiss all accused heretics and Jews from his service. Further he ordered the citizens of Toulouse to surrender everyone he had on a list. The citizens replied that those accused had openly professed to accept the Catholic Church so they refused to turn over the prisoners. Arnald–Amaury then excommunicated Raymond VI again and placed an interdict upon Toulouse without consulting the pope. He professed to speak for Innocent even as Innocent professed to speak for God; without bothering to ask first.

In June 1210, Simon attacked the stronghold of the resistance at Minerve. Using the new siege engine called a Trebuchet, a huge catapult like machine that could throw giant boulders as far as 600 feet or more, Simon was eventually able to beat down the walls and the morale of the defenders. After six weeks of bombardment, the people of Minerve agreed to surrender on the condition that all who repented and professed the Catholic Church as the only true Church would be spared. Uncharacteristically Arnald–Amaury agreed but when questioned by his aides, he assured them that few of the heretics would meet those conditions. He was correct. The Cathari leaders were prepared to accept martyrdom with the same spirit that the early Christians had against Nero. Over a hundred and forty were burned at the stake after refusing to accept the pope as their sovereign. They declared the Church of Rome was in apostasy and they would never deny their faith. The seeds of the Reformation were already being planted.

In the meantime Raymond VI had appealed over Arnald–Amaury's head directly to the pope. Innocent again lifted the excommunication saying that Arnald–Amaury had not given Raymond sufficient time to fulfill his promises, but the pope refused to remove Arnald–Amaury as legate. Instead he sent another legate to work with Arnald–Amaury. This merely angered Arnald–Amaury and made him hate Raymond even more. Now Arnald–Amaury decided to set the stakes even higher. After diplomatically promising that Raymond would be fully restored to the church, Peter II agreed to accept Simon as his vassal, but no sooner had Peter made this concession than Arnald–Amaury demanded that Raymond destroy all his castles, remove all Jews and heretics from his service, and numerous frivolous orders were laid down as well. There were to be but two portions of meat to be served on any given day and even the count's clothes were subject to approval by Arnald–Amaury, but the greatest demand of all was that Raymond retire to Palestine and offer his services to the Templar Knights. The demands were probably calculated to drive Raymond against the church, and they succeeded.

The result was civil war. The Church maintained that it was continuing to stamp out "heresy" but in reality the region of Languedoc surrounding Toulouse was fighting for its life and its freedom. Even many loyal Catholics turned to support Raymond, having been angered over the extreme demands placed on him by the papal legate and having seen the atrocities of Simon of Montfort. The new hostilities began in February 1211 when Raymond was again excommunicated, for the third time, and Toulouse was again, for the third time, placed under interdict. Civil war erupted and loyalties changed rapidly. Even Raymond's brother betrayed the cause, but many more defections came from Simon's camp. In June, Simon attempted to lay siege to Toulouse itself where the majority, including Raymond's army resided, but the siege was a dismal failure. Simon retreated, resorting to burning small towns and villages as well as burning alleged heretics alive "with joy in our hearts," but Raymond's army harassed Simon's to no end. In 1212, two things occurred which further damaged Simon's fortunes. First, the Muslim Moors had invaded Spain and a Crusade was proclaimed there. Soldiers were more eager to fight in Spain than against Christians in France. Second, the Children's Crusade (of which more will be said later) had met with humiliating disaster further hampering new recruits to Simon's cause.

By the end of the year, however, Simon's fortunes had changed. Using brutality and fear he was able to get the upper hand on Raymond's supporters. He instigated rigorous new rules which insured that all property and castles would be owned or managed by northerners with no loyalty to the south or to Raymond. Laws were even made that required certain noble women to marry men approved of by Simon. By December 1212 all but two regions of Languedoc had been subjected. It was at this time that history brought a strange twist of fate. After Christmas of that year Peter II of Aragon again appeared in an attempt to forge yet another truce. He had earlier tried to negotiate for the surrender of Carcassonne but met with failure as the petty ambitions of the papal legates intervened. This time it was the petty ambitions of both the legates and Simon of Montfort. He was clearly invading lands for territory. The war against "heretics" was an excuse. Peter II wanted to put an end to the war that threatened his own territory and have his brother–in–law reinstated to the Church but he found the same unreasonable demands that Raymond had encountered. Peter II, therefore, defected to Raymond's cause. He had sent ambassadors to appeal to the pope, but by September Innocent had called Peter

II a liar, a traitor, and a protector of heretics. In September 1213, Peter II and Raymond VI besieged Murat where Simon was held up.

Peter's army drastically outnumbered Simon's. So much so that Peter's pride led to his downfall. He valiantly dressed in regular army's clothes and fought on the front lines, but, because he had outnumbered Simon's troops, he did not bother to wait for reinforcements or even to make use of his massive infantry. The result was a rout; for Simon of Montfort. Peter himself fell in battle and, dressed in regular armor, received no mercy. So it was that Peter II, who had deeded Aragon to the pope as a fief in 1204, now died a martyr to the cause against the oppression of the papacy. The Crusade was far from over but the tides had turned in favor of Simon, and Raymond again retreated to Toulouse. The blood of tens of thousands of Christians had been spilled in the attempt to suppress dissidents who themselves had been created by the oppression and apostasy of the Catholic Church, but much more blood was yet to be spilt.

England, the *Magna Charta*, and Innocent

Innocent could not preoccupy himself with the Albigensian Crusade for he had other countries to conquer and other people to subject. He left the Christians in southern France to their terrible fate and spent much of his time concentrating on England. While the Albigensian Crusade raged, Innocent raged against King John. The initial conflict had nothing to do with King John's oppression or blasphemies but was the result of the choice of a bishop.

King John himself is easily the most despised of all English rulers even above Bloody Mary. He was a cruel tyrant who even raped the wives of his owns dukes and barons. He taxed people severely, stole from Churches, tried to usurp his brother Richard's throne years before, and is believed to have murdered his other brother, Geoffrey. He inflicted terrible punishment on people including encasing one man in lead up to his neck. The people hated him with a vengeance and his own barons and knights despised him as much. These things, however, did not bother Innocent. Instead a dispute arose concerning who would be the new bishop of Canterbury. King John wanted John de Grey while the monks of Canterbury elected a Reginald. Innocent dissolved both and had the monks elect another in an attempt to compromise. The great Stephen Langton was chosen, but John would accept none other than his own man.

The choice of Langton and the ensuing dispute between Innocent and John would become one more great irony of history, for Innocent would fight long and hard on Langton's behalf, but years later when Langton stood up for the rights of the people of England Innocent turned on him and supported John against Langton. For now, John raged against Innocent. He confiscated the property of the Canterbury monks and expelled them. Innocent threatened interdict. John promised to mutilate every Italian in England and expel the clergy if he did so. On March 22, 1208 the interdict took place and many of the clergy fled for fear of their lives.

For six long years the dead were buried without consecration, churches were locked, and, as Catholic historian Peter de Rosa put it, it was as if "England became a pagan land" again. John, however, wreaked his revenge. He confiscated the property of the clergy, drove them out, and kidnapped their concubines (for wives were no longer permitted for clergymen). On one occasion he freed a man who had murdered a priest, saying "he has killed my enemy." In 1212 it became apparent that the apostate John was unconcerned with interdiction or excommunication so Innocent declared John deposed and absolved the subjects of the English crown from their oaths of obedience. Philip Augustus immediately prepared a massive fleet for invasion.

John soon realized that he would loose all England to Philip, even as he had already lost the French territory to him, if he did not make restitution with Innocent. On May 15, 1213 he agreed to deed the whole of England and Ireland to Innocent. He would receive it back as a fief in exchange for 1000 marks every year and complete submission to the pope. Although England was technically already a fief of the emperor Otto IV, Innocent was by this time at war with Otto (discussed below) and the legal merits were of no interest to Innocent. He was interested only in receiving England and its money.

In 1214 the interdict was formerly revoked. Philip Augustus was furious. His invasion plans had to cease for he could not invade papal territory. The people of England were equally furious for he had betrayed them for petty gain. Even Stephen Langton, who had now taken his proper place in Canterbury, took the side of the people in an attempt to oust the tyrant. Civil war erupted and within a year John found himself in dire jeopardy of loosing his kingdom again. His enemies, made up of his former Lords and Langton's supporters, suggested a compromise. At Runnymede on June 15, 1215 John agreed to sign the most outstanding document in medieval history; *the Magna Charta*.

This document was the forerunner of the U.S. Constitution. Indeed, when our forefathers declared their independence they were claiming the rights of the *Magna Charta*. Technically, of course, the *Magna Charta* was but a shadow of the Constitution, but it did check the powers of the king. The charter declared that the king could not confiscate property without trial, taxes could not be levied without a vote from a council, all freemen must be given a trial before their peers, hearings would be held within a reasonable time period, unreasonable punishments could not be levied for petty crimes, and the law could not be kept secret. A total of sixty–two different clauses are listed, each prescribing protection from a particular abuse of the king. Although the charter did not apply to serfs, it was the first document of its kind to guarantee the rights of all freemen against the tyranny of the nobility and, specifically, against the king.

No sooner had John signed the document and restored his fortunes than he appealed to his old enemy the pope, declaring that he had been forced to sign the document and asking that it be dissolved. Innocent immediately took the side of King John against Stephen Langton and the people of England. He declared that Satan had inspired the document and its authors, condemning them all. He declared the *Magna Charta* "null and void for all time" and excommunicated all who continued to accept the document's validity. When Stephen Langton refused to bow to the pope's will declaring that natural law, God's law, "is beyond the reach of the pope himself" he was suspended from his post and London was placed under interdiction again.

The result was yet another civil war. The barons and nobility had even summoned the French Daulphin Louis to come and claim the crown, but Innocent had placed him under a papal ban and refused to let him do so. King John died in 1216, the same year as Innocent, but the issue would not die with them. It would continue on for centuries. One thing that Innocent's actions had done, however, was to alienate both the people of England and much of the clergy. England would never forget the *Magna Charta* nor would they forget the papacy's actions. Wycliff would sow the first seeds for the Reformation a century later, and the seeds for Cromwell's Republic and the U.S. Constitution had already been planted back in 1215.

The Children's Crusade

While England was still under an interdict and while southern France burned under the Albigensian Crusade, yet another tragic story of cruelty was unfolding. Innocent had not ceased to promote the cause of a crusade to reclaim Jerusalem and his agents had long been promoting such a crusade. Nonetheless, with the spectacle of the Fourth Crusade and with crusades in southern France and Spain there were few motivated to undertake such a task, until the strange occurrence known as the Children's Crusade.

In 1212, a twelve year old boy named Stephen undertook to lead a crusade, but it was not a crusade of conquest, but of missionary work. From the minds of young innocents the children who undertook to follow Stephen believed that they would convert the whole of Muslim Jerusalem by appearing outside the walls of the great city and preaching the gospel. In Germany another boy attempted to lead a similar crusade. The details of these events are questioned by historians for they were but children who left no real record of their deeds. Nevertheless, many eyewitness accounts exist, including Innocent's pleas to later Crusaders, showing that the movements did indeed occur and that they both met with tragedy.

What happened to the German Crusaders is unknown. It is believed that there were as many as seven thousand who went on this venture but none ever reached Jerusalem. What happened to the French Crusaders is more clear.

At one point there were as many as thirty thousand children in the Crusading "army" but the French King had ordered them to return home. Some did and some did not. All that is know for sure is that the number to reach Italy was under ten thousand. Some sources claim that Innocent had been appealed to by adults who wanted the children to return home, but Innocent refused to let them break their vow, sending them on. From Italy the remaining children, those who had not returned home or died on the long treacherous journey to Italy, boarded ships bound for Palestine, but instead of going to Palestine they headed toward Africa where the Muslim slave trade was brisk. One of the ships is said to have become shipwrecked killing the children onboard, but the other reached Muslim soil and all the children were sold into slavery. None of the children crusaders were ever heard from again.

The Rise of Frederick II

Innocent was never idle. There is one thing for which he cannot be criticized. While the Crusades raged, while England lay under interdict, Innocent was still busy. This time his fight was with the emperor. Innocent had allied himself with Otto IV against Philip, mainly on the promise that Otto would not claim sovereignty over Sicily, but when Otto officially received the crown from Innocent on October 4, 1209 he immediately set about breaking his promises. Not only did Otto claim Sicily but he also claimed the old Matildine Estates in northern Italy, that had been fought over since Hildebrand/Gregory VII and Henry IV.

Many of the Italian cities welcomed Otto as a protector for they had tired of the oppression of Innocent and had forgotten the oppression of Henry. Towns were given grants exempting them from papal interference and promising a certain degree of autonomy. Whether Otto intended to keep these promises or not may not be known, but it is clear that much of Italy was itself as tired of papal rule as it was of imperial rule. Their choice was Innocent or Otto, and Otto was still unknown to many of them. He might be another tyrant, but he *might* be like the Otto's of old. Some cities resisted but many willingly backed Otto including Milan. Italy seemed to be slipping from Innocent's grasp.

By November 1210 Otto invaded Sicily and succeeded in conquering southern Italy. Innocent, not even months after crowing Otto emperor of the empire, excommunicated him. He immediately set about setting up a rival and gaining support in Germany for the new rival. That rival would be the son of Henry VI, Frederick II of Sicily. Frederick II had also promised to renounce his claims to Sicily in exchange for the pope's support and at Nurnberg an assembly of German princes formally deposed Otto IV and pledged their support to Frederick II, son of Henry IV and grandson of Frederick Barbarossa. Revolt enused in Germany.

Otto returned to Germany in March 1212 and attempted to patch up things the best he could. In September 1212 Frederick II arrived in Germany, setting foot upon German soil for the first time. With the support of the southern princes of Germany and Philip Augustus of France a civil war followed. Otto IV had the support of his uncle King John of England and many northern princes of Germany. The battle lines were drawn across Europe with France and southern Germany against England and northern Germany. Otto and John attempted to invade France but Augustus was a seasoned warrior and the war came to an abrupt end shortly after the Battle of Bouvines on July 27, 1214. The battle was a humiliating defeat for Otto and his coalition soon broke up. Otto himself escaped, blaming his generals, his advisors, and even God Himself, but his power was at an end. Less than a year later, in 1215, Otto was formally deposed and Frederick II was crowned King of Germany at Aachen. He had risen to power by riding the support of the papacy, but he would, in fact, turn out to be a far greater enemy of the papacy than any who had preceded him. His rise is yet one more piece of irony in the papacy of Innocent III.

The Fourth Lateran Council

The last "great" action of Innocent was the gathering of the Fourth Lateran Council. This was the Twelfth Ecumenical Council and was comprised of over four hundred bishops, eight hundred abbots, and delegates representing the emperor and the kings of Constantinople, England, France, Aragon, Hungary, Acre, and many others. It represented most all the kings of Europe and the representative clergy thereof. The grand council then set out to drastically alter history in the Year of Our Lord 1215.

Among the notable events at the Fourth Lateran Council was the first formal declaration of the doctrine of Transubstantiation. For over a thousand years this teaching (that Christ was physical manifest in the Eucharist) was never formally adopted by the Church. For the first time it was a matter of doctrine along with the Sacrifice of Mass (the teaching that Christ was being re–sacrificed at every Eucharist). The council also made confession to a priest mandatory at least once a year. If anyone failed to confess once a year he would be automatically considered a heretic. In essence, it made failure to confess a crime punishable by death.

Among the lesser decisions made by the council was a ban on further monastic orders (although Innocent himself had permitted several in his day) and a provision which required papal approval for the worship of any new relics. Moreover, the council formally condemned the teachings of Joachim of Floris. The main point of condemnation was in drawing too heavy a distinction between the three persons of the Trinity but another matter lay deeper at the heart of Joachim's critics. Specifically, his prophetic teachings.

The ancient Church Fathers had taken the prophecies of Revelation at face value. They believed that the end would occur in exactly, or very close to, the same manner as described in Revelation. By the time of Augustine this type of literalism was scorned as materialistic and worldly. While hypocritically declaring that Christ was ruling on earth now, thus bringing the Kingdom of God to present day earth, they decried that literal interpretations were worldly because they sought an earthly kingdom in the future. By Joachim's time literalism was considered all but heresy. Joachim himself was by no means a literalist, for he leaned heavily on allegory, but he did resurrect the belief that the prophecies of Revelation were literal events. Among his teachings was the belief that the anti–Christ would be a future pope. Indeed, Frederick II would openly accuse later popes of being the anti–Christ, thus Innocent and his papal supporters were more likely attempting to silence the theological teaching that could jeopardize papal power in the future. Innocent himself taught that the anti–Christ and/or the Whore of Babylon were not papal figures of the future but were Muslims.

Still another declaration passed at the Fourth Lateran Council forbade Jews from holding public office and required Jews to wear a distinctive dress. This was done, among other reasons, so that no Catholic would accidentally have sex with a Jewish woman (mistaking her for a Catholic). Innocent favorably compared the new law to the mark of Cain. Anecdotally, one of the colors chosen for the Jews in Italy was red but when a nearsighted man mistook him for a cardinal and bowed to the Jew, the color was immediately changed to prevent any further embarrassing mistakes. Although Charlemagne had a great respect for the Jews times had changed. Jews were looked down upon and stereotyped as rich greedy bankers. They had risen in European society to the extent that they did indeed control much of the banking and lending of the medieval society but for this they paid dearly. Innocent called them "perfidious" and stated that "we condemn the principles of Judaism." Henceforth, the Fourth Lateran Council made the Jews second class citizens and paved the way for their eventual persecution. In this respect, however, the Jews were more fortunate that the dissenting Christians of Europe, for the most important decree of the Council was in response to the objections of Raymond VI and the southern princes of Languedoc.

The most important decree of the council was the formal formation and structuring of the Inquisition. Having been first established in the late twelfth century the Inquisition had no real organization or structure. It had created the legality of persecuting "heretics" by civil courts but offered no real instructions on how they were to be carried out. This had become very evident by the Albigensian Crusade where even Catholics were butchered without trial on the charge of "supporting heretics." The new council outlined many rules. Monks were to try all alleged heretics but torture was not yet sanctioned. If found guilty they were to be handed over to the civil authorities to be burned.

243

Nevertheless, the worst part of the new rules were those that made harboring "heretics," even accidentally without knowledge, to a punishable offense. Thus a prince could not claim to be ignorant. The result, obviously, was that the princes of Europe had a perfect right to inquire into the beliefs of his subjects, even against their wills. Friends of "heretics" were also subject to punishment if they did not report them to the civil authorities. The era of "witch hunting" had officially begun with Innocent's blessings and joy.

Innocent's Reign and Europe's Loss of Innocence

The last year of Innocent's life was spent preparing for yet another Crusade. He had overseen no less than four Crusades in his time, three of which are among the greatest blights in the history of Europe. The Fourth Crusade sacked and pillaged the Christians of Constantinople and resulted in the establishment of the Latin Empire of Constantinople, which Innocent was quick to exploit for his own gains, while at the same time condemning the events which created it. The Albigensian Crusade resulted in the slaughter of ten of thousands (perhaps hundreds of thousands) of Christians, both dissenters and loyal Catholics, who were butchered at the whims of self seeking Crusader Lords. The Children's Crusades had also been a debacle resulting in the death or slavery of tens of thousands of children. Only the Crusade to Spain, against the Muslim invaders, could be considered of any merit but amid all this Jerusalem still remained in Islamic hands.

The next Crusade would remain to be taken up by another pope, for after eighteen and a half terrible years Innocent's reign mercifully ended. Although he had been the youngest of popes he had suffered from frequent fever and died in his fifties, probably of malaria. With Innocent the papacy had reached its height of power, but it had also created with it a renewed since of determination for those who opposed the papacy's power. Innocent had drawn the battle lines and, with the formation of the Inquisition, it became clear that dissent and debate were no longer to be tolerated within the Church. Three hundred years later it was not Luther who left the Church but the ghostly arm of Innocent reaching out of the grave and pushing him away. The Reformers sought to reform the Church, not to leave it. The papal hierarchy had determined that this would not happen. With Innocent, Europe had lost its innocence.

It may be considered frivolous by some to say that Europe had ever been innocent but when one objectively compares the days of Charlemagne and the Ottonian Dynasty to the ancient Romans there was no doubt that Europe was changing. It was, ever so slowly, abandoning its pagan and barbaric ways and moving toward a Christian society. They were still pagan at heart, but the makings of the modern world were slowly beginning to blossom forth. With the rise of Gregory VII, much of this was stifled. While made in the name of God and Christianity, what Gregory VII sought (though he did not know it) was a return to ancient pagan society. What Gregory/Hildebrand impeded Innocent all but shattered.

As aforementioned, his reign saw no less than three Crusades, each of which ranks among the most barbaric and cruel in the history of Christendom. During the fourth Crusade Christians in Constantinople were butchered and raped, while the Albigensian Crusade did the same to the French dissidents. While Innocent had been quick to decry the evils of Christians killing Christians in the fourth Crusade, he joyfully promulgated it against the Frenchmen. Still another Crusade, the Children's Crusade, ended with thousands of Europe's children either dead or enslaved. Yet these sins were not enough for Innocent. He completed his legacy of evil by being the first to formally institutionalize the Inquisition. On Innocent's head lay the blood an estimated thirty million Christians and countless Jews throughout the ages.

One is reminded of the Christian prophesy of the Harlot Church who was "drunk on the blood of the saints and martyrs" (a charge leveled against Innocent by some of the detractors of the Albigensian Crusade). Innocent had reached the peak of power for the papacy. Never again would the papacy hold such complete and autonomous control over the whole of Europe, but they would try. Nevertheless, from history's most evil events often comes some of its brightest events. Following the Holocaust the Jews returned to their homeland of Israel for the first time in 2000 years. Following the ravages of chemical warfare in World War I the entire world, including Stalin and Hitler's Germany, agreed to outlaw the weapons. Following Innocent III, Europe's people began to slowly seek independence from papal power. It would be a Reformation three hundred years in the making, but from that day forward, the battle line was drawn. Innocent had scorned the *Magna Charta*, but to England's people it was still the law. Innocent had slaughtered the Albigenses, but to the millions of dissidents scattered throughout Europe over the years, they were martyrs against the Whore of Babylon and the anti–Christ.

Innocent's reign marked one of the darkest points in medieval history. He is respected and honored by modern historians for his achievements, but in terms of character he remains among the most wicked rulers. He openly declared that "every cleric must obey the Pope, even if what he commands is evil." It is, therefore, the height of irony that this pope, whose power reached beyond that of most any emperor, raised Frederick II as his Imperial protégé, for that same Frederick would spend the rest of his life fighting the papacy and trying to crush the power that Innocent had created.

Kings List (1199–1272 A.D.)

King of England	King of France	Latin Emperors of Constantinople
——— 1199 ———		
		——— 1204 ———
		Baldwin of Flanders
John		——— 1205 ———
		——— 1206 ———
		Henry of Hainault
		——— 1216 ———
——— 1216 ———	Philip II Augustus	——— 1217 ———
		Peter of Courtenay
		——— 1217 ———
		Yolanda (regent)
		——— 1219 ———
		——— 1221 ———
Henry III	——— 1223 ———	**Robert Courtenay**
	Louis VIII	
	——— 1226 ———	——— 1228 ———
		Baldwin II
	Saint Louis IX	(John of Brienne was regent Emperor from 1231-1237)
		——— 1261 ———
	——— 1270 ———	The Latin Kingdom fell in 1261
——— 1272 ———		

Holy Roman Emperor	Pope	AntiPope (if any)
——————— 1152 ———————		
	——————— 1153 ———————	
	Anastasius IV	
	——————— 1154 ———————	
	Hadrian IV	
	——————— 1159 ———————	
		Victor (IV)
		—1164—
		Pascal (III)
		—1168—
Frederick Barbarosa	Alexander III	*Callistus (III)*
		—1178—
		—1179—
		Innocent (III)
		—1180—
	——————— 1181 ———————	
	Lucius III	
	——————— 1185 ———————	
	Urban III	
	——————— 1187 ———————	
	Gregory VIII	
——————— 1190 ———————	——————— 1187 ———————	
	Clement III	
Henry VI	——————— 1191 ———————	
	Celestine III	
——————— 1197 ———————		
——————— 1198 ———————	——————— 1198 ———————	

Dispute over legitimate emperor was not settled
Until 1208 by Innocent III

——————— 1208 ———————		
Philip		
——————— 1208 ———————	Innocent III	
Otto IV		
——————— 1214 ———————		
——————— 1215 ———————		
	——————— 1216 ———————	
	Honorius III	
Frederick II	——————— 1227 ———————	

Holy Roman Emperor	Rival (if any)	Pope	AntiPope (if any)

* – Italicized means claimant was never coronated

——————— 1215 ———————

——————— 1216 ———————

Honorius III

Frederick II

——————— 1227 ———————

Gregory IX

——————— 1241 ———————

Celestine IV

——————— 1241 ———————

——————— 1243 ———————

——————— *1245* ———————

Frederick II deposed

——————— *1246* ———————

Henry Raspe   Innocent IV

——————— *1247* ———————

——————— 1250 —

Conrad IV   *William of Holland*

——————— 1254 —

——————— 1254 ———————

——————— *1256* ———————   Alexander IV

——————— 1257 ———————

——————— 1261 ———————

Urban IV

The double election of   ——————— 1264 ———————

Richard of Cornwall &   ——————— 1265 ———————

Alfonso X of Castile   Clement IV

——————— 1268 ———————

——————— 1271 ———————

——————— 1272 —

Gregory X

——————— 1276 ———————

Innocent V

——————— 1276 ———————

Hadrian V

——————— 1276 ———————

Rudolf   John XXII

——————— 1277 ———————

Nicholas III

——————— 1280 ———————

15

—

Frederick II

Frederick II is sometimes considered the last of the *true* emperors. His struggle with the papacy was the climax of the imperial/papal struggle. His ultimate failure resulted in the papacy's distrust of emperors in general and in their secret desire to ally themselves with the French and Spanish against the German emperors. Thereafter, the title of "emperor" was little more than that. So feeble were the emperors in authority that one pope would even dare to declare himself emperor. The countries of Europe would remain unified under the banner of the Holy Roman Empire, but it was the papacy who ruled that empire, not the emperors.

Before this fateful day, however, Frederick II would fight a long and protracted war against the papacy. He would openly declare the popes to be anti–Christ and used prophetic utterances while at the same time silencing the dissident Christians who alone could have purged the Church of its corruption and power. Like Barbarossa, his grandfather, he assured his own failure by his proud arrogance and unwillingness to see beyond the Imperial crown. He fought solely for his crown, not for the freedom of Europe. He sought only his own ambitions, even as his enemies did. Frederick II's reign is one of the great sagas of the Middle Ages, but it is also a reminder of why the emperors died out so many years later. They proved little different or better than the papacy. The people's choice was between a tyrant pope or a tyrant emperor. They were forced to choose between two different types of monarchies. Arnold of Brescia's dream of a Republican Democracy would have to wait. The English dream of the *Magna Charta* would not find its dawn until Cromwell. Frederick's dream was less noble.

The Eastern World Before the Crusade

The events of the eastern world were crying out to the west. When Frederick II received his crown at Aachen in 1215 he had spontaneously promised to go on a Crusade to reclaim the Holy Land, but he did not. He declared that he would go when he had put his affairs in order, but it would soon become clear that those affairs would take years, and they would take clear precedent over the Crusade he had promised. Although Frederick II had promised to turn Sicily over to his son Henry, he instead made him king of Germany and set out to make a monarchy of Sicily. He began to insure that all officials, soldiers, and administrators were accountable to the King alone. The new pope was not happy.

When Innocent III died he had been replaced by Frederick II's former tutor, Honorius III. Honorius reminded Frederick that he had promised to keep Sicily separate from the Imperial crown, and that he had promised to lead a Crusade. After much stalling and delays from Frederick, Honorius set a mandate for Frederick to keep his vow by 1217, the date that he declared the Fifth Crusade must be prepared to depart. He believed the disturbances in the east far outweighed any in the west. Even the newly established Latin Empire of Constantinople was on the verge of crumbling.

Baldwin of Flanders had become the first Latin Emperor of Constantinople soon after the conquest of the Fourth Crusade, but the people of Constantinople had not forgotten the atrocities that had been committed by the Crusaders, nor did they forgive the arrogant papacy who now outlawed Greek worship and required all citizens to practice the Catholic form of worship. Baldwin had also seized lands from Greek nobles and distributed those lands to his knights. Soon the Greek people of the Latin Empire were plotting revolt with the aid of King of Bulgaria, Calo–John (also called Kaloyan). The emperor was caught unaware. When the revolt occurred many Latins were slaughtered and word came of the advance of a large army led by Calo–John with fourteen thousand mercenary Comans. The Comans were among the last pagan barbarians in the region near Moldavia. They were said to be so savage that they drank the blood of their victims and sacrificed Christians on the altars of their gods. Baldwin called his brother, Count Henry, for reinforcements, but did not wait for them to arrive. He was captured in battle and later died in prison, his arms and legs having been hacked off.

Count Henry was able to secure Constantinople from the invaders and to maintain several key cities. He defeated the Bulgars and eventually forced the Emperor of Nicaea to sign a peace treaty, but more importantly he was able to gain the trust of many of the Byzantine people. He treated them with mercy and even spared some of the revolting cities on the condition that they not assemble any large numbers of armed men. The Byzantines themselves were growing fearful of the barbarity of the Bulgarians and the new moderate Emperor Henry suddenly seemed like a better alternative. Henry also entered a marriage alliance with a Bulgarian Princess and even allowed the Greeks to occupy certain positions of authority in court and in the clergy, all of which had Pope Honorius III disturbed. Ambassadors were sent to and from Rome in hopes of convincing the pope that the good will of the people was essential to the survival of the Latin Empire of Constantinople. Honorius did not agree. His legate, Pelagius, forbade Greek worship practices, created forced "tithing" to the Roman Church, and further oppressed the Greek Orthodox Church. Henry tried to mediate but constantly refused to cede Greek Church lands to the pope which further antagonized the papacy. His death is suspected to have been from poison although the medievals were never able to tell poison from one of the many diseases that plagued the lands. This itself made poison the primary choice of assassination. If he was poisoned the most likely suspects were Latins rather than Greeks. In either case, the kingdom was again left without an emperor.

Henry left no heir, but his sister Yolande was married to a Count Peter of Courtenay. Peter began the long trek across Europe to claim the crown, stopping in Rome along the way. There Peter became the only emperor of Constantinople to be crowned by the pontiff. However, this new emperor would never even make it back to the famed city of old. He was captured, along with the Roman legate, and held by Theodore, the despot of Epirus, in 1217. Honorius condemned Theodore but eventually negotiated only for the release of his legate in exchange for which Theodore was pardoned for his sins. It would be two more years before official word would come of Peter's death, having had his arms and legs hacked off. In the meantime Yolanda served as regent in his absence. The Latin Empire of Constantinople was crumbling after less than fifteen years.

In Palestine the Kingdom of Acre faired little better. The promised Fourth Crusade never made it to Palestine and the armies of the "King of Jerusalem" (as they continued to call themselves) were too meager to do much of anything other than maintain their already tenuous position along the Mediterranean shores.

The West had many problems of its own as well. In England the French Daulphin Louis, had invaded England to claim the throne, while a minority council governed in the name of John's son, Henry III, who was but nine years old. It would not be until September 1217 that Louis admitted failure and agreed to withdraw at the command of Honorius.

In Languedoc the Albigensian Crusade started up again as the Raymond family seized several of Simon's cities and castles with the eager support of the citizens. The wicked Simon retaliated by taking Toulouse by force, imprisoning most of its people, taxing the rest, and stripping them of their freedoms and often their property as well. When Honorius III ordered Simon to release Raymond–Roger, Simon blatantly defied the pope and continued the brutal oppression of the people including a coup by which he claimed sovereignty over part of Aragon of Spain. Despite the defiance of the pope's edict, Honorius did nothing. For Honorius, these domestic issues were unimportant. It was to the east that he looked.

The Crusade Begins Without Frederick

The date that Honorius had set for the Crusade was September 1217. When it embarked, one crucial man was missing. Frederick II was not aboard the ships that set sail for the Middle East. He again promised to come as soon as he could, but in his place mysterious letters were sent out. These letters, presumed to have been sent by members of Frederick's court, promised prophetic events to unfold in Palestine. They spoke of victory for the Christians and of a great leader who would come and deliver Jerusalem into their hands. Some of the letters even professed to be from King David himself, promising to return to his home.

Concerning these "prophetic" letters one must consider several facts. First, it was not the year 1000 that apocalyptic messengers predicted the end (save a few of the uneducated), but the year 1260. Based on the prophecy of 1260 days in Revelation, the medievals reinterpreted the days to equal years. Thus the reign of the anti–Christ was to last not 1260 days but 1260 *years*. For many of them the anti–Christ was not an individual, but system or group of individuals. Under the tutelage of Innocent III the teaching that a future pope would be the personal anti–Christ was replaced with the theologically innocuous view that the anti–Christ represented Islam as a whole. Despite the fact that Islam had existed for less than six hundred years, the idea was circulating that Christianity would envelop the globe (and the educated knew the world was round) by the year 1260. Consequently, the Crusades had taken on a prophetic zeal. The passages of Revelation, interpreted allegorically, came to be seen as prophecies of the Crusades. These new letters were designed to assure the hope of the Crusaders and perhaps, as is often speculated, to make Frederick II into a prophetic figure himself. The Crusaders took heart in these prophecies.

In 1219 the siege of the Egyptian city of Damietta had already begun. At the mouth of the Nile, Damietta was strategically important. As often occurred in the Middle Ages the siege went on for many months and the besieged were being starved out. Egypt had called for reinforcements from Syria but the prince of Damietta knew they would not arrived in time. In the meantime, St. Francis of Assisi had arrived in Egypt to attempt a peaceful surrender. The prince Al–Kamil treated Francis with respect, but he left Egypt with no accord, although a brief truce was observed for both sides to lick their wounds. In October Al–Kamil made a shocking offer. He declared that if the Crusaders would leave Egypt Islam would surrender Jerusalem, Galilee, Bethlehem, and return the "True Cross." Whether Al–Kamil could deliver his promises or not the offer was staggering and most of the Crusaders were more than willing to accept the generous terms but the Cardinal Pelagius and Patriarch of Jerusalem would not. They declared that no treaty could be made with the heathen. Moreover, some questioned the strategic reasons for the surrender. They believed that Jerusalem could not be held for long without also seizing certain strategic positions which the Muslims refused to surrender. Hence, they suspected that even if the Muslims surrendered Jerusalem they could retake it easily enough. The treaty was refused.

In November 1219 the city gates were opened to the Crusaders who looked with shock upon the dead bodies strewn in the streets from disease and plague. It is said that only three thousand of the original eighty thousand residents survived. Egypt had called for reinforcements from Syria but they had not arrived in time. Indeed, they might not have arrived in time to save Egypt at all but for Frederick's delay. The Crusaders did not advance upon all Egypt as they planned for they decided to wait for Frederick's army. They were convinced that with his help all Egypt and Palestine would fall, but when Frederick delayed, so did the Crusaders. As Damietta had become a prison to the Egyptian prince, so too would it become a prison for the Crusaders; in time.

Frederick is Crowned Emperor of Rome

The promises made by Frederick II at his coronation in Germany had not been fulfilled, but Frederick had argued that his position in Germany was not yet firm for Otto, although deposed, had not yet died and his family had stubbornly refused to surrender the Crown of Otto the Great. By 1219, however, this was no longer the case. Otto was in the grave and the Crown was returned to the true king of Germany. Frederick then promised that he would leave on the Crusade by June 1219. The date came and went while the siege at Damietta continued without him. This time Frederick had another excuse. He had not yet been crowned "Emperor of Rome." Technically, the argument was sound for the papacy themselves asserted that no emperor could reign without being coronated by the pope, so Frederick set out in 1220 to receive his crown.

Even before Frederick left Germany he had issued a decree entitled the *Confederatio cum principibus ecclesiasticis* which declared that the lands of the bishops could be taxed and affirmed the rights of the king to determine the succession of fiefs even if the bishops objected. It further permitted the king to build towns and fortresses on ecclesiastical estates. In short, it asserted firmly, even excessively, the rights of the imperial power over and beyond those of the church. Honorius could not have been pleased but Frederick made many promises to appease the pope. He promised to exempt the clergy from taxes, although his decree declared that he *could*. He further promised to suppress and persecute "heretics." With the same fervor that his grandfather had established, he would crush "heretics," yet it was to the general dissident sentiments of the people, and particularly those of the "heretics," that he later appealed in his condemnation of the papacy.

On November 22, 1220 Frederick's coronation took place. He spoke boldly as a protector of the Church and gave every impression of being the pope's instrument, even as his detractors had said. When Honorius had been forced to flee Rome after another uprising in Rome it was Frederick who came to his aid. The Romans had often tired of papal rule and many a pope had been forced to flee Rome. This time Honorius left as a precaution and Frederick insured his safe return with stern warnings and threats against Roman detractors. Despite this, Frederick did not endear himself to the pope. The pope once again reminded him of his pledge to take up the Cross and Frederick again set another deadline upon which he would embark upon his Crusade. This time it was

August 1221, but no sooner had the words left his lips than he headed south towards Sicily. The Muslim community of Sicily was in revolt.

The revolt was in the same form that it had taken since the Muslims lost control of Sicily and the form that it has taken ever since. It was terrorism or guerilla warfare. Such warfare was hard to quell for the Muslim army was indistinguishable from the common populous. Frederick's solution was to round up all Muslims and place them in an isolated community in Apulia where they could be watched. The rest of the Muslim guerillas were slowly hunted down in the mountains and their leader executed.

After the quelling of the revolt, and the segregation that followed, a strange and ironic change began to occur. While it is possible that Frederick (having been raised in Sicily, where the Muslim population was still relatively large from their occupation centuries ago) had already developed an interest in Islam, it was at this time that he began to study Arabic and the Koran. Muslim prisoners remained at the colony in Apulia where they worked as slaves, but many became bodyguards for him and some served in his army. They not only gained his trust but Frederick clearly showed a liking for some Islamic traditions including the Harem, which Frederick was quick to create for himself. Soon the pope himself objected that Frederick was creating an Islamic community within Sicily.

Although the revolt had been quickly put down, Frederick had not been quick to resume his pledge. He was busy establishing his power base in Sicily. Some of the laws enacted under Frederick seemed trivial at best. There were laws against gambling and even jesting. The result could be one's tongue being cut out. Jews, prostitutes, and Muslims were required to wear separate attire in accordance with the Fourth Lateran Council. Everything was to be under the direct control of the king, who was also the emperor. Moreover, even the marriages of the barons had to be approved by Frederick.

In March 1223, Honorius III called forth all the leaders of the Crusade, along with Frederick II. At the conference it was agreed that money for new Crusades was diminishing with each failure. Honorius was eager to find a way to compel the emperor to embark upon the Crusade, which he had promised, and the titular King of Jerusalem (they were really the Kings of Acre) had given Honorius a promising method of achieving this. A marriage was proposed between the daughter of John of Brienne, the King of Jerusalem, and the Emperor Frederick II. The marriage would make Frederick the King of Jerusalem, make John's daughter empress, bind Frederick to the Holy Land, and John of Brienne would continue to rule Palestine in Frederick's absence.

Frederick readily agreed. He set a date in 1225 for the Crusade and was initially married by proxy to the fourteen year old daughter of John of Brienne, Isabelle. A bishop stood in for Frederick, who was still in Europe, and the new bride was shipped off to meet her thirty year old husband, who held a second official wedding ceremony on November 9, 1225. He then spent his wedding night with another woman while Isabelle slept alone. Matters got worse, for Frederick immediately declared himself the King of Jerusalem and indignantly made it clear that John of Brienne was merely his subject. Even worse, the pope received news that Frederick, whose Islamic sympathies were obvious (owing to his Saracen Harem and Eunichs), was in secret correspondence with the Sultan of Egypt. The year 1225 had come and gone and Frederick had still not embarked on his Crusade. Moreover, the law required that a King appear in his kingdom within a year of receiving his title, but as the year 1226 passed it was clear that Frederick was again shirking his promise of Crusade while still claiming the title, King of Jerusalem. At a conference in San Germano Frederick set yet another date for the Crusade. This time it was to be no later than August 15, 1227. The pope, his former tutor, warned Frederick that if he failed to keep his promise this time he would be excommunicated.

The Albigensian Crusade Continues

The failure of Honorius to compel Frederick to take the Cross and conquer Jerusalem forced him to take a more serious look at European affairs. He had neglected much of Europe in favor of the east, but even the Latin Kingdom of Constantiniple was crumbling. After news of the Latin Emperor Peters' death became official, Robert of Courtenay was named the next emperor of the Latin Kingdom of Constantinople. His reign was, however, both tragic and disturbing. A marriage alliance with the rival Emperor of Nicaea had been arranged in hopes that the Byzantine Empire could again become united with the Latin Emperors. Nevertheless, Robert had neglected his new bride for the love of a French maid whose mother scorned one of Robert's barons. The baron then took the most henous of revenges. He stormed the castle, murdered the maid's mother who had scorned him, and then mutilated the emperor's lover. Her nose and lips were cut off in the fashion of the ancient barbarians. Worse yet, the rest of the barons honored the cruel deed and Robert was forced to flee to Rome in hopes of seeking the pope's protection, but he died on route. The successor, Baldwin II, was but a child and so the kingdom would be left to unscrupulous regents until John of Brienne appeared years later.

Before that tragic day, however, Honorius looked to the French province of Languedoc which was still at war over the Albigenses Crusade against so–called "heretics." The Fourth Lateran Council had done nothing to bring an end to the conflict in Languedoc. Raymond's son, Raymond VII, was now of age and assisted his father in attempting to drive Simon of Montfort from the land. In 1217 Raymond returned to Toulouse as a hero and deliver. During the siege that followed Simon was killed. The people of Toulouse rang out Church bells and rejoiced while the Church made Simon into a saint. Said one bystander, "I have no doubt that if Christ is served ... by ... butchering women and children, then Simon is even now in Paradise." Honorius could not now neglect the civil war, for it was clear that the Crusaders were losing.

Honorius again begged Philip Augustus to have his son lead a new Crusade to Languedoc, but Philip again refused. His son, Louis VIII, had recently been told by Honorius to leave England where he had been attempting to gain backing for the throne there in lieu of King John's child. Neither Philip nor Louis were particularly interested in the pope's Crusade, but when the pope suggested that one of Philip's rivals lead the Crusade and claim the land as his own, Philip relented and Louis VIII, future king of France, embarked to Languedoc. Upon his arrival in 1219 they began by burning Centule d'Astarac to the ground and killing every man, woman, and child therein. When they arrived at Toulouse the siege began earnestly enough, but after forty–five days Louis VIII tired of the Crusade, burned his siege engines so they could not be left for the enemy, and then withdrew all but two hundred knights. His Crusade was over. Louis VIII returned to France.

In the years that followed Raymond died, leaving his son Raymond VII to take up the fight. Amaury, the son of Simon, also took up his fathers claims and the war between Raymond VI and Simon of Montfort became a war between Raymond VII and Amaury of Montfort. Although a truce had been arranged, the truce expired in 1224 and war erupted the very next day. By that year almost all who had been involved in the "false Crusade," as many began to call it, had died. Even Philip Augustus had passed on leaving Louis VIII as the new king of France. The Crusade was a humiliating failure for the papacy, even more so than the more important Crusades to the east. Honorius had no intention of leaving Languedoc in the hands of Raymond's heirs. In 1226 he sent word to Louis VIII that if he would take the Cross again he could claim Languedoc as his own (for the land was disputed since it had once belonged to England and parts of the land were once claimed by Aragon), his soldiers could receive indulgences, and the Church would allow the king to tax the French clergy ten percent of their revenues. Louis VIII quickly agreed and again took up "the Cross."

Raymond had appealed to Henry III of England who was inclined to help until his astrologer told him that Louis VIII would die on the Crusade and leave his kingdom open to invasion. Henry then decided against assisting Raymond, believing that the astrologer's predictions would benefit England. In fact, the astrologer was only half correct. Louis would die, but France would not falter. Upon hearing that England would not help, the people of Languedoc quickly began to recognize Louis as their king, but this was out of fear, not respect. On the march to Languedoc Louis's army needed to pass through Provence and the bridge located at the great city of Avignon. The citizens had once supported Raymond and had been under interdict for many years but they both feared and distrusted Louis. They agreed to let Louis' army pass and submit, but they would not let his army enter the city, so they built a small bridge outside the city where his army could cross, but during their crossing many of the citizens of Avignon attacked the soldiers and killed many of them. Louis smelled betrayal and besieged the city. For three months the siege commenced until they capitulated on favorable terms, for Louis' army had fallen ill and were themselves starving. Louis had also become ill during the siege and died a few months later, before conquering all of Languedoc.

Frederick Embarks on the Crusade

Prior to the deadline set for embarkation troubles with northern Italy threatened to again delay the Crusade. Honorius was determined that this not happen. The problem arose, or at least became prominent, when Frederick called for a Diet at Cremona in Lombardy. The Lombards themselves had long since claimed semi–autonomous rule. Even more importantly, it was a haven for dissident Christians who opposed papal rule and dogma. It was the home of the Waldenses and had become the abode of many thousands of dissidents from Southern France, who had fled the Albigensian Crusade. They, therefore, had little love for the pope, less for the emperor, and none for the newly created Inquisition. It is then no surprise that when Frederick declared, at the diet, his intention to stamp out heresy and assert this authority over northern Italy, the newly reformed Lombard League cried fowl. They protested that previous treaties gave Lombardy semi–autonomous rule and that Frederick was violating the pacts. Milan, the center of the Lombard resistance, became the focal point of Frederick's ire. He demanded their submission and was prepared, if necessary, to go to war. Such a war would obviously have delayed the Crusade even further so Honorius sent legates to attempt a negotiated settlement. In the meantime, the Lombards had even gone so far as to communicate with John of Brienne requesting that he become their protector against his new son–in–law. Frederick himself pleaded with Honorius saying that "the honour of the Roman Church, as well as our own honour and that of our empire" was at stake. In the end a sort of truce was established to insure that Frederick's departure was not delayed. In fact, it was merely the dispute that was delayed.

Five months before the August deadline, when Frederick had last promised to set sail for the east, Honorius died. Despite their differences, Honorius, who had been Frederick's childhood tutor, never took any harsh measures against Frederick. The new pope, Gregory IX, had no such loyalty. He was Innocent III's nephew and had inherited the same arrogance and pride. Indeed, it seemed that Gregory IX was merely looking for an excuse, any excuse, to chastise the emperor and assert papal supremacy over him. That excuse was not long in coming.

The Crusaders assembled in the summer of 1227 at Brindisi in Sicily, but the plague had come with them. Although many thousands died of disease, Frederick did not renege on his promise this time. He set sail as promised, but when his friend and second in command, Louis of Thuringia, died of the fever, Frederick ordered his ship to make port. He immediately left for Pozzuoli where his physicians told him the doctors could cure his fever. Since the dirt and grime of the Middle Ages was one of the major reasons for illness in Europe at the time, it was only natural that the emperor was to bathe constantly in the baths of Pozzuoli. It was also only natural that the new pope, Gregory IX, leaped at the chance to picture Frederick as again shirking his duty by taking luxurious baths while the Holy Land was being lost to infidels.

Having refused admittance of Frederick's ambassadors Gregory IX excommunicated Frederick, accusing him of numerous crimes and sins and even going to such extremes as to suggest that Frederick knew that the staging grounds at Brindisi would cause the plague. He even further hinted that Frederick poisoned Louis of Thuringia to make it look like he died of the plague. The pope's long harangue against Frederick also proved that Gregory meant to humble the emperor, even as Gregory VII once humbled Henry IV. Although Frederick promised to do whatever Gregory asked in exchange for the lifting of the excommunication, Gregory refused to even give an answer. Frederick's response was to attack the evils of the medieval papacy. They, he declared, had forsaken the purity of the early Church for the riches of the Vatican. They had ceased to be the rulers of the spiritual, and had made themselves the rulers of the temporal world as well. He pointed out that the war with King John of England and the atrocities of the Albigensian Crusade were directly attributable to the papacy. He first began to sound the trumpet of the dissident Christian groups that he himself had promised to persecute. He also promised to continue his Crusade with or without the pope's blessing.

This only fueled the pope's anger more greatly. If Frederick were successful on his Crusade in defiance of the papacy it would hurt Gregory's prestige and power. He, therefore, forbade Frederick to go and warned that any Crusaders who followed an excommunicate to Jerusalem would themselves fall under ban. All Catholics were forbidden from associating with Frederick, but they followed him anyway. Gregory then echoed his excommunication and anathamized Frederick a second time, this time for leaving on the Crusade for which he had previously been excommunicated for not leaving for.

It is clear that the people were not sympathetic to the pope's cause and in Rome, where the people had always accepted the papacy's power with reservation, a riot erupted when Gregory turned the Easter Mass into a diatribe against Frederick. The pope was chased from the Church and out of the city where he took refuge at Viterbo. A little over a month later Frederick departed for the east probably unaware that Gregory was recruiting a mercenary army to conquer Sicily and strip the emperor of his power. Frederick was too busy trying to expand his own power to notice, for on route to Acre Frederick took a detour at Cyprus. The kingdom was ruled by the regent John of Ibelin in lieu of the child king, Henry of Lusignan. John was also the king of Beirut. Frederick already considered himself, as Roman emperor, to be sovereign over the kingdom, but he sought to make that sovereignty clear to everyone in every manner possible. He cordially invited John to a grand banquet and then, when everyone was dining, armed soldiers burst into the dining room and held the guests hostage. Frederick then made his demands. He wanted the lordship of Beirut and taxes from Cyprus for ten years. John, bravely, refused to grant the "request" declaring that the court of Jerusalem should decide the issue. When it became clear that he would not relent easily Frederick allowed him to leave after taking many hostages including John's son Balian, but John nobly refused to let his vassals assassinate Frederick when they had the chance. Instead he held out in his castle realizing that Frederick could not delay long. Indeed, Frederick soon found out that Gregory IX was ready to invade Sicily with the assistance of John of Brienne.

Frederick's bride Isabelle, the daughter of John of Brienne, had died shortly after giving birth to Conrad. John of Brienne, therefore, had no more reason to be loyal to the emperor, who had openly tried to strip him of his title, who had neglected Isabelle for a harem, and who was accused of abusing and even murdering Isabelle. He reminded the people of Palestine that the law had required the king of Jerusalem to appear in his kingdom within a year of receiving his title. Since Frederick had not done this, his title was relinquished, especially since Isabelle had died. This situation made it urgent for Frederick to complete his task in Jerusalem, return in triumph, and reclaim his lands. Frederick had no time to delay in Cyprus.

After one and a half months Frederick relented, returned the hostages, and departed for Acre. Finally, in late 1228 Frederick arrived in Acre. He found mixed support. Gregory IX had sent word that anyone who assisted Frederick in any way could be liable to excommunication and his treatment of John of Ibelin had not endeared him to the princes of Acre. Only the Teutonic Knights stood strongly by their emperor. In fact, it seemed as if the only friends that Frederick had were the Muslims. Ironic indeed, for Frederick had become well known among the Muslims through his correspondence with Al–Kamil, the Sultan of Egypt. Al–Kamil had been in a war with Damascus and had promised Frederick that he would deliver Jerusalem up to him if he would help attack Damascus. However, Al–Kamil no longer believed he needed Frederick's help. Nonetheless, he had no desire to enter into a war with Frederick while Damascus still eluded him. After long negotiations Frederick and Al–Kamil agreed to a pact which has, to this day, amazed and confounded both Muslim and Catholic.

According to the treaty Islam would surrender Jerusalem, Bethlehem, and Nazareth as well as the stretch of roads that connected those cities to those already controlled by the Franks. In exchange Al–Kamil asked only that the Dome of the Rock and the mount remain under Muslim control, that Muslim pilgrimages not be hindered or harmed, and they not build up any new defensive structures. Since the three key cities were surrounded by Muslim controlled areas it seems that Al–Kamil was merely buying time for his conquest of Damascus and the consolidation of his kingdom. He doubtlessly believed that Jerusalem could be easily retaken, but he needed to buy time and could not become embroiled in a war with the Franks. The treaty, in accordance with Muslim law, was to last ten years and five months.

The treaty shocked Gregory's supporters. Frederick was seen as having collaborated with the infidels, not to mention that he scored a political coup which he was eager to exploit in the west. The Patriach sent the Archbishop of Caesarea to Jerusalem to declare a papal interdict which would forbid any religious ceremonies from occurring within the city. The arrogant act placed the Holy City itself under ban, but the interdict did not arrive in time. Frederick had already arrived and was eager to be crowned King of Jerusalem. The bishops, however, were well aware of Gregory's threats and told Frederick that they could not crown him. As a result, Frederick, in the Church of the Holy Sepulchre, bestowed the crown *on himself.*

This act, later echoed by Napoleon, was symbolically important. It was both a defiance of the papacy, as well as of Church authority in general. The symbolism since the days of Charlemagne was that God alone makes a man a king. Since the Church represents God it was important for the Church to bestow the crown as a symbol that the king's authority came from God. By crowning himself Frederick, and later Napoleon more blatantly, was declaring that he was king by his own might. The papal interdict had arrived a day too late. Frederick was crowned. He had liberated the city which he had promised to liberate and was ready to return to deal with Gregory's armies that were already ravaging Sicily. He had only a few scores to settle in Palestine first.

First, Frederick attempted to besiege the Templar Knights castle and oust the Patriarch, who had refused to accept his authority for fear of excommunication, but it became obvious that the siege would take many months. Sicily was slipping from his grasp every day. He settled for declaring that the lands of the Templars and Hospitallers now belonged to the Teutonic Knights. He then, finally, decided to return to Sicily, but before he boarded his ship he saw John of Ibelin who came to show his respects and bid the emperor a fond farewell. The chivalrous act was seen by Frederick as an attempt to make him look bad and less than chivalrous by comparison. He responded by cursing John and sold the regency of Cyprus to the highest bidders. Five barons were given control of the land. The result was a civil war. It would take John of Ibelin and his supporters many years to free the island from the oppression of the barons.

Thus Frederick had come to fight Muslims but fought only Christians. He had retaken Jerusalem without a drop of blood, but he left Christian Palestine in civil war. The Teutonic Knights fought with the Templars while the Ibelins warred with the barons for control of Cyprus. Wherever he went the good the emperor had done was undone by the evil he spawned. When he left Palestine he left only a legacy but nothing of any permanence. Nothing he did there would stand the test of time.

Frederick's Restoration

With the assistance of Frederick's father–in–law, John of Brienne, who still claimed the title King of Jerusalem, Gregory had begun the invasion of Sicily. Rumors were spread that the emperor was dead and promises of freedom and independance were made to towns who rebelled against the emperor's authority. Nevertheless, Frederick's soldiers, under the command of Rainald of Spoleto, were able to slow the invading armies long enough for Frederick to return. While Rainald was driven back, the sudden return of Frederick to Italian soil turned the tides. Many of Gregory's cities, upon learning that the emperor was not dead quickly reverted back to loyalty for Frederick out of fear if not love. Frederick crushed the opposition and made an example of at least one city, Sora, which he razed to the ground after executing its inhabitants.

By October 1229, about five months since his return Frederick had succeeded in restoring Sicily to his crown. Gregory IX, who had again excommunicated Frederick for returning from the Crusade, was all but defeated, save the fact that he was pope. He knew that Frederick would not dare to kill a pope if he could avoid it. With this in mind he was receptive to Frederick's negotiations. Gregory was allowed to return to Rome, the Sicilian Church would be exempted from secular jurisdiction, and the Templar and Hospitaller Knights would have their properties returned in exchange for which the pope agreed to lift the excommunication of Frederick and renounce his acts against him. The pact was agreed upon and enacted in 1230. Gregory even, disingenuously, called Frederick the "beloved son of the church."

With Gregory having officially lifted the excommunication from Frederick the issue of John of Brienne had to be resolved. He was Frederick's father–in–law and a friend of the pope. Frederick had claimed the title "King of Jerusalem" and would not surrender it. It was then decided that John of Brienne would be named the regent emperor of the Latin Kingdom of Byzantium for the still child emperor Baldwin. The decision proved to be a good one. John ceased to be King of Jerusalem but became an emperor instead. Moreover, he helped prolong the decaying Latin Kingdom. Invaders from the Greeks came from both north and south hoping to reclaim what they believed was their empire, stripped of them by the Fourth Crusade. John's abilities served to push back the Greeks and keep the kingdom alive for decades to come.

Frederick now had the task of setting his affairs back in order again. Although he had reclaimed power, the situation in Sicily, Italy, and even Germany was far from perfect. In Sicily Frederick enacted the *Constitutions of Melfi* which clearly established the medieval monarchy. It declared that God had established kings to master over men and downplayed the role of Church. It declares Frederick the "emperor of the Romans," Caesar Augustus," and heir to the "divine predecessors" of ancient Rome. The laws themselves were numerous and aimed at increasing the countries finances as well as establishing new laws. Heresy was punishable by death and declared treason, Jews were limited to ten percent interest rates on money loaned, and cities would pay large fines if a murderer escaped justice.

In Lombardy the situation was worse for both Frederick and the pope. The Italians of northern Italy had always resisted papal authority and had become a haven for dissident Christian sects. The distaste for the papacy among the Lombard League had also spread to Rome, where the popes had always maintained an uneasy relationship with the people. This relationship with the Lombards and Romans was further agitated when Gregory IX began to expand the Inquisition and its powers. In 1229, the Council of Toulouse forbade the use of the Bible to laymen and mere suspicion or even rumors were sufficient grounds to bring someone to the Inquisitors. Frederick's *Constitutions of Melfi* allowed the Inquisitors to act upon "even the slightest suspicion of guilt. The trials themselves were usually conducted in secret and the property of the guilty could be seized by the state. Even repentant heretics could be sentenced to life in prison. So great in number were these repentant heretics that some in France complained that they could not quarry enough stones to build all the dungeons necessary. The Lombard League vigorously opposed these measures and defied both pope and emperor.

In Germany there were likewise problems. The German princes had grown to love the fact that their emperor had been absent for many long years, for it gave the princes the authority to act in their own respective regions without interference. However, Frederick's young son Henry was no longer a child. He had slowly demanded that his regent give him more power until he finally marched an army into Bavaria to demand that the regent give him the authority to act. Henry then began to assume control of the state, to which the princes objected. They argued that it was Frederick, not Henry, to whom the authority belonged. Frederick agreed. In 1232 at a council in Ravenna Frederick chastised his son, whom he had not seen since he was but a small child, declaring that his actions detracted from those of the emperor. While Frederick was asserting his autocratic powers in Italy he warned Henry not to intervene in the affairs of the princes who, officially, acted in the name of the emperor. Frederick even threatened to depose Henry if he got out of hand again.

The action did nothing to endear Frederick to his son who probably had to be reminded which prince was his father since he had not seen him since childhood. Henry was also aware that his step–brother, Conrad, was favored by Frederick. Henry's visit had been short, but he had seen the troubles in Lombardy and the frivolity of his despotic father. Upon his return to Germany he immediately began to seek out those loyal to him. Within a year Henry was plotting a coup. Concerning this coup Henry's motives have been debated.

Some see him as a visionary who supported dissident Christian sects (forerunners of the Protestants) and democratic communes. Others see him merely as a fortune hunter. Since little personal information on him remains it is hard to ascertain which is correct. He certainly maintained many allies from the so–called heretics, and the communes, but it is also possible he was merely using them. On the other hand, he was the next in line to inherit his father's kingdom. Was he really so impatient as to risk it all on a coup if, in fact, he did not adhere to the tenants of the dissident Christians and republican sympathies? In any case, his coup would be doomed to failure.

This same year saw Gregory driven from Rome again before being restored by Frederick. It seemed as if he and Gregory were friends and colleagues. They struggled together to subjugate the rebellious Lombards, but Frederick had far less success against Lombardy than he had had against Sicily. Soon Lombardy would find an ally in Henry.

Henry's Rebellion

In 1233 Dominican Inquisitor, Konrad of Marburg, had angered even the local bishops of Germany by his excesses. He had participated in the Albigensian Crusade and massacred both "heretics" and those he held to be sympathetic to them. He later became the confessor to a Hungarian Queen, whom he was accused of savagely beating for her sins. So severely, in fact, that she died, still young, of the wounds inflicted. The people loved this charitable woman so much that she was declared a saint years later and, ironically, Konrad would one day be buried next to her, but before that day, in 1231, Gregory named him the first papal inquisitor of Germany. The Inquisition was being expanded throughout the realms. In 1234 Aragon became the first country to officially outlaw the translation of the Bible under the Inquisition. Germany now had its first Inquisitor in the sadistic person of Konrad. He attempted to root out those bishops who had secretly married (for the unbiblical prohibition against marriage did not deter many) and brutally pursued alleged heretics. The persecutions of dissident Christians was so severe many princes, apparently including King Henry, criticized and resisted Konrad's efforts. When Konrad accused a German Count of heresy the princes and bishops alike became disturbed, perhaps fearing another Albigensian Crusade. An assembly of bishops declared the count innocent at Mainz, but Konrad demanded that they reverse their decision. He angrily left Mainz with the intent of using whatever power he could muster to compel the bishops to heed his will. On July 30, 1233 he was murdered.

Gregory blamed Henry's court and vehemently denounced the princes of Germany and Henry himself. The incident may have actually generated more sympathy for Henry for no one was, at the time, too fond of the Inquisitors. The Inquisition was rightly seen by many at the time as an attempt to enforce papal rule and to control even the private lives of individuals. To be sure, few liked heretics, but what was and what was not heresy varied greatly from person to person, as in any society. The Albigensian Crusade had already become known as "the False Crusade" and the Inquisitors, although not yet embued with the right to torture, were feared for their cruelty.

In 1234 Gregory was once again driven from Rome by the angry people. In Germany an assembly affirmed the right of the "elected king of the Romans," Henry (VII). Frederick again came to the pope's aid in Rome while Gregory came to Frederick's aid and excommunicated his rebellious son Henry. In 1235 Henry responded by forming an alliance with the Lombard League against Frederick and Gregory. The act was to spell doom for Henry. Frederick marched into southern Germany and demanded to know to whom the princes owed their loyalty. It is clear that Henry's support was far less than he had estimated. Through another political marriage (to the sister of King Henry III of England) Frederick had even made allies with the Britains. Frederick's support included many of the German princes, Louis IX (the new king of France), Pope Gregory IX, and Henry III. Henry had no choice but to come to his father and beg for mercy. He lay prostrated on the ground before Frederick for hours before Frederick would even acknowledge his son. He demanded that Henry accept deposition, but Henry refused. He was then sent in chains to a dungeon where he would reside for many years.

The Oppression of Lombardy and the Second Break with Rome

Following the strategic defeat of his son, Frederick immediately set out to recruit a large army to crush Lombardy. The papacy, however, opposed this. Gregory certainly had no love of the Lombards but he feared Frederick gaining too much control in northern Italy. He had already subjugated Sicily, and Gregory felt surrounded. He believed that disobedient Lombards were better than imperial powers to the immediate north and south of him. He, therefore, promised to negotiate a peaceful settlement. Moreover, he suggested that the Crusade in the east needed to be revived. The Franks of Palestine considered the treaty of Frederick's to be invalid, claiming that the Muslim still attacked many of their strongholds. The position of Jerusalem was hardly secure. It was surrounded by Islamic controlled cities and would doubtless fall the day the treaty ended. Gregory, therefore, demanded that Frederick return to Jerusalem and create a true Latin state.

The political strategy altered Frederick's stratagem, but not his goals. He argued that the war against Lombardy was a prelude to the Crusade and he would take east afterwards. He, using Gregory's own hatred of heretics, argued that the Lombards were far worse than Muslims, for they claimed to be Christians. The Lombards were not only the home of the great Waldenses, but also the refuge where the Albigensians had fled, and was even the home of many communes. Indeed, Lombardy, like the Arnoldolists of Rome before them, had retained certain tenants of a Democratic Republic. They were not so naïve as to believe that Italy would become a Republic again but their local cities elected representatives, largely merchants, and worked together with other communes. This angered Frederick more than anything. Like his grand–father, Frederick I, he believed democracy to be both heresy and treason. Had not the Arnoldolists been declared heretics? Frederick saw himself as God's annointed leader on earth and everyone under his dominion had to submit to him completely and unalterably.

In 1235, Frederick began his campaign in Lombardy, seizing the city of Vicenza and burning it. The Lombards appealed to the pope, claiming that prisoners had been mutilated, women raped, and Churches desecrated, but Gregory IX still felt powerless at this time. The Lombards would have to fend for themselves. They did see a brief respite as Frederick returned to Germany in 1236 to see his son Conrad crowned King of the Romans and named heir to the Imperial throne. This act irked Gregory since, in theory, only the pope could name an emperor. Frederick soon returned and resumed his war. By the end of 1237 Milan, the capitol of the Lombard League, promised to recognize Frederick in exchange for recognition of the communal and territorial rights. This would be nothing more than a nominal acceptance of the imperial authority and Frederick refused outright declaring that Milan would have to submit to his "mercy." Naturally, mercy was not a quality that the Milanese recognized in Frederick so the war continued, but in the summer of 1238 Frederick was dealt a blow. His siege of Brescia, the birthplace of Arnold, ended in failure as one of his top men defected for love a woman and promises of wealth. The failure seemed to signal Frederick's mortality and triggered several key breaks with former allies.

The Genoans made a treaty with the Venicians which would secure control of the Mediterranean. Gregory IX was quick to side with Genoa and challenge Frederick's power in the sea, and particularly in Sardina where Frederick had succeeded in placing his illegitimate son on the throne, thereby claiming sovereignty over the island that was once a papal fief. Gregory gave authority to Genoa over Sardina in exchange for recognition of the papal rights to the island. It is clear that Gregory was awaiting an opportunity to again challenge Frederick's authority and that a new rift was in the making.

On Palm Sunday 1239 Gregory IX again excommunicated Frederick, but the reasons for the excommunication were even more trivial than they had been the first time. Frederick was not excommunicated for his brutality or savagery or even for his oppression of the Lombard freedoms (although these incidents were mentioned and may have been in Gregory's mind), but rather the official causes listed were his blockade of certain papal legates who were delayed at times, his refusal to give substantive aid to Jerusalem, and the treatment of the Church in general. Gregory consulted with no Church council nor with the Cardinals on these matters. He alone took it upon himself to challenge the emperor and to place a ban upon all those who supported Frederick. Letters were sent out across Europe urging the Kings of Europe to abandon the emperor and support the Church. Frederick was portrayed as an apostate, a Muslim sympathizer, a sexual pervert, a sodomite, a blasphemer, and the "forerunner of the anti–Christ." He called upon all good Christians to form a new Crusade against Frederick.

The letter's reception was mixed. The devout Louis IX of France, who would later become Saint Louis, noted that no council or Cardinals had been consulted and that Frederick had never been heard on any of the charges. Henry III of England was Frederick's brother–in–law but he was also King John's son and England was a papal fief. He feared arousing the anger of Gregory and officially took the side of Gregory although he supplied no troops for Gregory's "Crusade."

Frederick's response was to forbid any priest from carrying out Gregory's interdict thus ordering Churches to be left open in cities favorable to him under pain of Frederick's wrath. He attempted to intercept papal legates and stop the spread of Gregory's letters, but having failed in this he sent out his own propaganda campaign. He declared that he had no trial and had committed no sin. Moreover, Frederick's propaganda pretentiously compared himself to Jesus Christ while Gregory was portrayed as a Pharisee and compared to Pontius Pilate. What is more interesting was Frederick's response to the claim that he was the "forerunner of the anti–Christ." Frederick, who brutally persecuted "heretics," was now appealing to the dissident theology of the Waldenses, Joachimites, and others who believed that a future pope would be anti–Christ. Frederick proclaimed that Gregory himself was the anti–Christ. These claims were particularly influential inasmuch as the popular Joachimite views on prophecy declared that the anti–Christ would reveal himself in the year 1260, only twenty–one years from the present.

The War with Rome

Gregory made grand plans. He had already formed an alliance with the Genoese and Venetians, but he was now planning to have them invade Sicily. Frederick had made no real advancements in Lombardy and soon realized that it was Rome, not Lombardy, that he needed to force into submission. As long as the pope remained free to propagate conspiracy and dissension, Frederick's throne was not safe. Frederick's armies took cities faithful to Gregory in and around Rome, while the soldiers themselves cut off supply routes and intercepted messengers. By February 1240 Rome was effectively surrounded by Frederick's armies.

Rome itself had never been particularly friendly to Gregory, or to the popes in general. Many wished to admit Frederick into the city, and Frederick's own propaganda machine promised to restore the Roman Empire to its former glory with Rome as its capital. The promise doubtless excited many Romans, and on February 22 Gregory was forced to make his plea to the Roman people. He created a procession and carried before him the alleged skulls of Peter and Paul. He declared that it was not for the papacy that they were struggling, but for the Church itself. He claimed that Frederick the apostate would destroy the Church if they did not defend it, and the skulls of Peter and Paul were there to defend the Church if the Romans would not. The people of Rome agreed to defend the city.

It was not Frederick's desire to sack the great capital or to alienate his allies by storming the Churches of Rome so he was content to blockade Rome and wait Gregory out. Already Gregory was facing opposition from within the Church itself. Even the Cardinals were upset that they had never been consulted in Frederick's excommunication. Louis IX of France, whose devotion to God was never doubted, even suggested that Frederick receive a hearing. Finally, Gregory agreed to hold a council on Easter 1241. The representatives, of course, were to made up entirely of those favorable to Gregory. Frederick, therefore, refused to promise the safe conduct of anyone traveling to Rome. In fact, in early May 1241 Frederick's troops attacked and plundered a fleet of Pisan–Genoese ships which were carrying, among other things, two cardinals headed for the council. They were arrested by Frederick and held prisoner for many years. What the results of this war might have been are unknown for, in August, Gregory IX died.

The Papal Elections

Because of the schism between Frederick and Gregory the new papal election became all the more important. Frederick wanted a pope who would lift the excommunication and acknowledge his rights in Sicily and Lombardy while the supporters of Gregory wanted a pope who would continue the war against Frederick. Moreover, each side had plenty of leverage. Frederick himself held two cardinals hostage as well as many bishops. In Rome the Senator Matteo Orsini was virtual dictator and was equally disposed to using unethical methods to achieve his ends.

Since two of the cardinal electors were held by Frederick the remaining ten resided in Rome where Orsini kept them virtually imprisoned in deplorable living conditions prone to disease. He promised to release them when they elected a pope favorable to him. Technically, of course, Orsini was not "imprisoning" them, for it was the usual habit of cardinals to be shut up in private and not to emerge until a new pope was elected. Orsini, however, made sure that the cardinals were shut up in horrid conditions with agents of his stationed where they could hear all the discussions. The plan appears at first to have backfired. The cardinals were doubtless unsympathetic to the emperor who held two of their colleagues prisoner but the treatment of Orsini caused them to be equally ill disposed toward him. In turn they elected one of their own rank, naming him Celestine IV.

Celestine IV's career was all too short. He excommunicated Orsini for his treatment of the cardinals, but on account of the living conditions in which he was placed, he fell violently ill and died just over two weeks after being elected. Once again, Rome was without a pope and the cardinals were pressed from both sides. This time it was Frederick who seems to have exerted the most pressure. He is said to have warned the cardinals that if they wanted their colleagues released they would have to elect someone favorable to him. He continued to surround Rome and blockade the city so that the cardinals were afraid to leave. They opted to remain in Rome with a slightly more reserved Orsini than risk being captured by Frederick. In the meantime they could not come to a decision on who to name pope. It would be nearly two years before that decision came.

In the long interim between the election of popes, Frederick decided to call forth his imprisoned and rebellious son, Henry. For seven years Henry had sat in a dungeon where his father had placed him. With increasing criticism of his treatment of the cardinals and the effective siege of Rome, Frederick may have wanted to appease critics by reconciling with his son, who had the sympathy of many of his detractors. Whatever reasons for Frederick's decision he claimed he wanted to reconcile with his son. When news arrived, however, Henry thought the worse. He had rarely seen his father and certainly did not know him except by his reputation for cruelty. On the journey to meet Frederick Henry escaped his captors and rode his horse off a cliff, preferring a quick death to whatever his father had in store for him. Frederick is said to have been heart-broken but whatever remorse he had did not alter his heart. Frederick continued to destroy everything good thing he had done by his own pride, arrogance, and thirst for power.

The news that Frederick's own son feared him so greatly doubtless did little to enhance his prestige and esteem among Europe. Indeed, Frederick was finding the princes and Kings of Europe increasingly angry at his attempts to halt, or slow, the election of a new pope. Public opinion grew that Frederick wanted to prevent a new pope from being elected at all. In early 1243 Frederick finally agreed to release the two cardinals he held prisoner and await the results of the election. Those results came in June. The new pope was a Genoan aristocrat and lawyer who despised Frederick. He named himself after the pope who had so fiercely fought against Imperial power before. He was called Innocent IV.

New Papal Strife

On June 1243 Innocent IV took up the sword of Gregory IX. Although Frederick bestowed his congratulations to Innocent and tried to open negotiations for a lifting of the ban, Innocent paid money to mercenaries to attack Frederick's soldiers even while he was pretending to negotiate with Frederick. He may also have sensed that Frederick could not long continue the war, for events in the east were demanding his attention.

In the Kingdom of Jerusalem the treaty had been broken after the death of Al–Kamil. In 1240 Jerusalem had been reconquered by Muslims with relative ease. Although the Franks had once again reclaimed the city by this time it was clear that the entire Kingdom was in jeopardy. Recently the Muslims themselves were involved in civil wars but the eastern Muslims had employed the assistance of the Chorasmian mercenaries. These mercenaries were particularly brutal and cruel. Their women fought along side them in battle with the same savagery as the men. Already they were advancing toward the Holy City and the Kingdom of Jerusalem.

The Latin Kingdom of Constantinople faired no better. Baldwin II had come of age and replaced the able regent John of Brienne. Baldwin, however, displayed little competence or leadership against the invading armies of Nicaea. In fact, he would even enter into an alliance with the Turks and pagan Comans in hopes of defeating the Greeks. He even entered into a blood pact with the Comans, which included the drinking of blood, and participated in the sacrifice of a dog to the pagan gods. These pagan rituals did nothing to enhance his leadership skills.

Even closer to home was the flood of the Mongols. Hungary, a part of the empire, had been ravaged by the invaders who were already threatening Germany itself. Decades earlier Genghis Khan had united the tribes of Mongolia, both Mongols and Tatars, and conquered China itself. By the time of his death his empire stretched across to the Adriadic. The Mongols mainly sought tribute in the form of gold and slaves. They formed a vast empire across Asia and the hoards were now pressing hard against eastern Europe. In response to the threat Frederick issued edicts against the Tatars and urged the princes of Germany to defend the homeland, but Frederick himself remained in Italy.

It is little wonder that by March 1244 Frederick had drafted a treaty which would agree to the withdrawal of all Imperial forces from the papal states and grant many other concessions to the pope in exchange for a lifting of the excommunication. The treaty would have agreed to most everything Innocent had asked for, save acknowledgement of papal suzerainty in Lombardy. Nevertheless, the new pope had delayed an agreement until he was able to secretly slip out of Rome in disguise with the assistance of Genoan family members. He headed to Genoa in the summer of 1244 and reached Lyons in December. The move not only humiliated Frederick but was a tactically wise political move, for Lyons was under the dominion of one of Frederick's closet allies, Louis IX, who now supported Innocent's call for a Church Council. Louis had, in fact, been asking for a council to decide the issue and decried Gregory for making the decision without a trial. Frederick could not now move his armies to Lyons without alienating his ally Louis and appearing to be in an all out war with the Church itself.

During this brief time period the situation in the east deteriorated even worse. Jerusalem, for the fourth time, fell to Muslims. This time it occurred with the assistance of the Chorasmian mercenaries who savagely slaughtered the Christian population, desecrated the tomb of the Holy Sepulcre, and burned the bones of the Christian Kings who were buried there. They even massacred those whom they had solemnly promised to let leave the city in peace if they would lay down their arms.

The council, known respectively as the First Council of Lyons or the Thirteenth Ecumenical Council, met in the summer of 1245 and officially addressed the problems in Jerusalem, Constantinople, the Mongol invasions in eastern Europe, and, of course, Frederick II. On the issue of Jerusalem the pious king, Louis IX, promised to lead another Crusade to preserve the Holy Sepulcre. On the second issue Baldwin II had traveled all the way from Constantinople to plead for assistance but received little of what he wanted. Frederick's counselor had suggested that he assist Baldwin in securing Constantinople but that was not to be. Instead, Baldwin II began to sell off the relics of Constantinople to raise money. The alleged skull of John the Baptists, the baby linen of Christ, the sponge that allegedly was used on Christ on the Cross, the Holy Lance, and the supposed rod of Moses were all sold off for profit and disappeared into history. All these treasures and the money they raised could not save Constantinople which would fall back into Greek hands in 1261.

Another interesting item on the agenda was a complaint by the clergy of England that the foreign clergymen appointed since Innocent III humbled King John, were abusing their offices, and extracting too high a tribute for the papacy. They pleaded on behalf of the common law of England, avoiding mention of the *Magna Charta*, but Innocent IV merely demanded that the bishops of England affix their seals to King John's charter, thus confirming their agreement with the tribute demanded. The event is obviously eclipsed by the war with Frederick, the invasion of Mongols, the crumbling of Constantinople, and the fall of Jerusalem, but it was a sign that dissatisfaction with Rome was growing in England, even among the bishops. England was becoming the isle of refuge for distant, perhaps fleeting, thoughts of freedom and justice. It would be the land from which the Reformation was first preached, more than a century before Luther, and from which Republic Democracy would first rear its head again.

The issue of Frederick II was perhaps the most important item on the agenda. Frederick had been invited to the Council but instead sent Thaddeus as his counselor to plead his case, although he was said to be coming to Lyons personally. Thaddeus denied Frederick had a harem, claiming they were merely "dancing girls," and promised virtually everything the papacy had been asking for, but Innocent IV challenged whether or not he would keep his word. He suggested that Frederick would merely renege on his promises as soon as the excommunication was lifted. To this Thaddeus said that Louis IX and Henry III would act as sureties to ensure that faithfulness of Frederick. To this Innocent curtly responded that he would merely antagonize two more princes of the empire. It was becoming clear that Innocent did not want to merely humble Frederick but to topple him altogether.

On July 17, 1245 Innocent ordered Frederick, the excommunicate, deposed. His right to rule was stripped from him as an unrepentant sinner. The charges of blasphemy, sacrilege, and immorality were repeated along with a call to a new Crusade; one against Frederick. Saint Louis IX urged the pope to show restraint, but Louis is said to have found "very little of that humility which he had hoped for in that servant of the servants of God." Louis IX was leaving on a Crusade to the Holy Land, while Innocent was preparing for a Holy War against Frederick on European soil. There was nothing Saint Louis could do to stop it.

An Unholy Crusade

Frederick II was more than willing to oblige the pope if he sought war but he first appealed to the kings of Europe. He warned them that his fate might one day befall them and he appealed to the dissident Christian sects that he once persecuted. His letters spoke of how the Church had strayed from its early days of poverty and humility and become corrupt and decadent and rich. In this he is sometimes, erroneously, seen as a voice of Reformation centuries before the Reformation but, in fact, he was merely saying the words that all common men knew. The words did not come from his heart, for he had himself burned many of the "heretics" who had dared preach the very words he now used. He was backed into a corner. His lack of sincerity and the people's hatred of his tyranny were the real cause of Frederick's downfall, for the pope's armies and plots were not sufficient. Even the pope's assassination attempt had failed.

In early 1246 the plot to assassinate him was revealed by his closest confidants. What was disturbing is that it was many of his closest confidants who were conspiring. They had become too arrogant and brazen and too many people knew about the plot. Nevertheless, the assassins were close enough to realize when they were betrayed. They escaped Frederick's grasp before he could capture them. Two of them fled to Rome where they were protected by Innocent's cardinals. Others took refuge in Sala and Capaccio, both of which were besieged by Frederick. When the cities fell the bodies of the conspirators were mutilated, burned, and cut up into pieces which were sent out to various cities in Italy as a warning. The brutality again backfired.

Oppressive taxation and the corrupt and all–powerful central govenment made many cities side with the papacy. Lombardy, Sicily, and the

Papal estates were all in various stages of revolt. Frederick was forced to go to war again to reclaim his rights.

In Germany civil war was erupting. Innocent had not been content to depose Frederick, but Conrad IV as well. Conrad was now King of Germany and Innocent may have feared that having Frederick's son as lord in Germany would hinder his plans. In any case, Innocent was resolved to bring down the entire House of Hohenstaufen, not just Frederick. Conrad was now excommunicated and deposed, apparently for having the wrong father, and Henry Raspe was elected king by sympathizers of the pope in May 1246. In August of that year Conrad was defeated at Frankfurt and retreated into Swabia. There Henry followed him, but in early 1247 Henry fell ill during a prolonged siege at Ulm. He died on February 16, leaving the papal party without a king.

It was not until October that the papal party had found and elected Henry Raspe's successor. William of Holland was a popular choice and soon gained general recognition. He was crowned king of Germany at Aachen, the traditional place, on November 1, 1248, but did not secure Germany all at once. Conrad maintained strong support himself and was able to regain control of the Rhineland. The war would continue until Frederick's death at which time Conrad abandoned Germany for the struggle over the Sicilian crown.

In Italy, Frederick II faired no better. His allies were the tyrant Enzio, who had helped against Lombardy years earlier, and Thaddeus of Suessa, his counselor. War in Italy raged but Frederick, prompted by Saint Louis who was also urging the pope to make peace, still sought compromise. He promised to spend the rest of his life in the Holy Land fighting the Muslims if only Innocent would agree to coronate his son Conrad as emperor and revoke their excommunications. When the pope refused Louis was said to be irate. He was soon to leave on the Crusade but Innocent was taking too many of the soldiers and money and diverting it to his Crusade against Frederick. Louis was forced to leave for Egypt with far fewer troops and supplies, but also with Europe in chaos. He had tried to negotiate between the stubborn pope and the emperor, but to no avail.

By this time Frederick was at Parma in northern Italy. He sought to make a statement by building a new capital city within sight of the besieged Parma. He called the city Victoria and the plans for it were extraordinary and exotic. It was to be modeled after Rome and featured a menagerie of exotic animals and, of course, a large harem. The city was, however, an arrogant presumption by Frederick for one day the Parmesans formed a large sortie and stormed out of the gates late at night. They flooded into Victoria, still in the early process of being built, and slaughtered many soldiers. They torched the city and stole many valuables that Frederick had left there including the famed imperial crown which was once worn by Otto the Great. The greatest blow, however, was the loss of Thaddeus who was captured and, in mock imitation of

Frederick's cruel punishments, his hands were cut off before his ultimate fate that year.

The loss of Thaddeus in 1248 was devastating. Moreover, Frederick seemed to become increasingly paranoid of his own advisors. Thaddeus had been faithful but Frederick trusted none of the others. One advisor, Piero della Vigna, was respected by Frederick's enemies as well as by Frederick because of his justice and moderacy. In 1249 Frederick had him arrested. He was accused of stealing money and rumors of an assassination attempt were also circulated, although most discount this. In any case Piero was blinded and chained to a pillar in a dungeon. Piero found no recourse except to bash his head against the pillar until he died. The betrayal of Piero, the phoney charges (so most believe), the cruel punishment, and the suicide of Frederick's most honest advisor left Frederick looking all the more a tyrant; especially since his few remaining allies were men such as the savage tyrants Enzzilino and Ubertu.

The Crusade of St. Louis

Saint Louis was one of the best kings of France and one of the few true Christian kings of the Middle Ages. He was a devout man who worked as a volunteer at hospitals where he washed bedpans, washed the feet of beggars, and as king he abolished the age old pagan ritual of trial by combat, which had for so long been incorporated into Christian language and law. He was faithful to his wife and spent many hours in prayer. He was also a very calm and determined man who only became angry when he caught men in sin. A product of the Middle Ages he has sometimes been criticized for cruelty but his "cruelties" were as a dove compared to a lion for while Frederick II mutilated people for alleged crimes Louis once punished some men by placing them in a small boat and dragging them behind the fleet on its long trip to the Crusades.

Saint Louis was forced to abandon his efforts at negotiating a peace settlement in favor of the Crusade for which he had fought so hard. Jerusalem had fallen to the savage Chorasmian mercenaries and the Kingdom of Acre (or Jerusalem as it was still called) was in danger of collapse. Frederick II had left the kingdom in a state of conflict. Although he had reclaimed Jerusalem, he had set the Military Orders against one another and divided the princes against themselves. When Louis arrived at Cyprus he arranged for the warring princes to make a two year truce with each other and began to plan his siege of Damietta in Egypt. During this time an emissary arrived from Mongolia. After the death of Genghis Khan the empire was divided among his relatives. Guyuk Khan, Genghis' nephew, ruled over northern Asia from Peking to modern Russia. Recently he and his army had been converted to Christianity. His emissary arrived and offered a treaty with Louis that would result in the collapse of Islamic power in the east and a unified Christian Palestine ruled jointly by Latin and Mongolian Christians.

Alexandre Cabanel – St. Louis : A Prisoner in Palestine – 1878

After a careful examination of their sincerity Louis sent many gifts back with a message that he would accept the alliance with much rejoicing. Unfortunately, when the emissary arrived Guyuk had died and his wife, who was still a pagan, was ruling in his stead. She sent an answer saying that the alliance would not happen but she would expect many more gifts, unless Louis wanted to meet her Mongolian armies. This was perhaps the first omen that the days of a Christian Palestine were ending.

Louis set out for Egypt in May 1249. Many scholars, looking back in retrospect, have questioned the Crusader's obsession with Egypt. It was believed that the key to securing Palestine lay in the conquest of Egypt. Certainly Egypt had become the most powerful of the Muslim states, or at least of the Muslim states who were actively involved in Palestinian affairs. Nevertheless, it was removed from Palestine and its conquest would be virtually impossible. The Egyptian held all the advantages and the Crusaders had none. In retrospect, it would have been far better to secure Palestine and build up heavy fortresses at key points in the Middle East where invading armies would have to pass, but retrospect makes tactical decisions much easier. Right or wrong, Louis set out to conquer Egypt and his campaign began promisingly.

The Sultan of Egypt had kept his own generals in so much fear that they were unwilling to make any decision without him lest the plan fail and they bear his terrible wrath. As a result the fleet of Louis sailed into Egypt and landed with no real resistance. Indeed, the Egyptians abandoned Damietta to await orders from their brutal Sultan. Saint Louis had captured Damietta with barely a fight. It was hailed as a miracle and contributed to Louis' religious aura. Unfortunately, there were to be no more miracles in Egypt. The Sultan had died and a power struggle was in the making in Egypt. Louis believed that it was time to strike at Cairo itself.

The attempt to siege Cairo proved to be disastrous. Louis was always cautious, hoping avoid unnecessary loss of life or failure, but again historians have looked back in retrospect and shown that his delays and caution actual led to his defeat. The Egyptians were also patient and waited until disease and pestilence hit the Christian camp. Finally, in the spring of 1250 the Christians were all slaughtered except for the princes who could bring a hefty ransom. King Louis himself was captured in April while the Egyptians hung the heads of Christians on the walls of Cairo.

It was at this time that Baibars, the famed Muslim warrior, betrayed the new Sultan and seized power in Egypt. He had the Sultan's heart cut out and then came to Louis. Faced with threats of torture and death Louis stood firm and refused to renounce his faith. He offered money for the release of his princes and negotiations soon took place. Eventually, standing fast against his tormentors, Louis agreed to pay over 400,000 livre, the yearly revenue of France, in exchange for his men's release and his own release was granted in exchange for the surrender of Damietta. Saint Louis would sail to Acre where he remained "the uncrowned king of Jerusalem" for several years but he was never able to reclaim the Holy City and never set foot in it.

The Death of Frederick II and the Aftermath

The capture of Saint Louis by the Muslims did nothing to help Innocent. The French were convinced that the diverting of money and troops to the pope's "Crusade" against Frederick was to blame for the capture of their beloved king. The pious and devout King of France stood in high contrast to the arrogant and unforgiving pope. Innocent's Crusade was already shaking the faith that the average person had once held for the papacy and pressure was now increasing for Innocent to make peace.

Innocent had another problem. Frederick, although on the verge of defeat, was close to threatening his safety at Lyons. He wrote to Henry III seeking refuge in England when his fortunes suddenly and dramatically changed. On account of illness Frederick retired to southern Italy where he died on December 13, 1250.

The pope exclaimed "let heaven and earth rejoice." The enemy of the papacy had died, but Innocent IV was quick to declare that the Crusade was not at an end. Conrad IV remained to be dealt with. He solemnly declared that those loyal to the Church must support William of Holland and overthrow Conrad. For many years Europe would be thrown into turmoil as the papacy sought to unseat Frederick's children. Conrad IV came to Sicily to claim his hereditary right there but died in 1254. Only Frederick's illegitimate son Manfred remained, who also claimed the regnal title of Sicily, but Innocent would die himself in 1254 before Manfred fell. It would not be until 1257 that another election for emperor took place and that election resulted in a controversial double election where two separate emperors claimed the title. Innocent's war was fought for the supremacy of the papacy, but in reality he dealt the initial blow that would lead to the fall of the Holy Roman Empire. He broke the power of the emperors once and for all.

The Legacy of Frederick II

Frederick II is one of the most controversial figures in the Middle Ages. He is viewed by one historian as a visionary and a as tyrant by another. He is always viewed as the "Stupor of the world." His struggle was one of the great spectacles of the Middle Ages. He looked like the ancient emperors of old, talked like a Renaissance man, but lived like a pagan barbarian. He might have been great but was instead corrupt and despotic. It was fear of his tyranny that gave support to Innocent's war, not love of the papacy. He was his own worst enemy.

With the fall of Frederick II the Imperial dignity of Germany would never again be the same. The papacy had succeeded in crushing the Imperial authority of Germany with a vengeance, but in so doing spelled its own destruction. The emperors had always promised to protect the Holy See but without any authority the emperors could no longer do so. The papacy did not have any real military strength of its own; only the powers of the spiritual sword. While these powers could be potent indeed, they were insufficient to keep the empire together for long.

With the virtual collapse of imperial power in Germany the papacy tried to find allies elsewhere. They would eventually try the French and the Spanish but neither could restore the fortunes of the empire. Indeed, in the final days of the Holy Roman Empire it was again the papacy who threw their lot with Napoleon and in so doing destroyed the last remnant of the empire that they once ruled with an iron fist.

To be sure the emperors of Germany continued to exist for another five hundred and fifty years but the death knell had been sounded. Anarchy would reign in Germany for many years before the emperors could restore order, but by then it was clear that if they could not keep order in Germany, how could they keep order in Europe? Certainly the emperors deserve as much blame for their collapse as does the papacy, for both Barbarossa and Frederick II might have restored the fortunes of Rome had they not allowed their own petty pride and thirst for power to destroy them. Truly the Catholic teaching, "pride comes before a fall," is accurate. The first of the deadly sins destroyed the Roman Empire. Nevertheless, the failure of the emperors proved once and for all that the age of empires could not long endure.

Kings and empires survived in a world of anarchy because they brought order amid savagery and chaos, but amid civilization kings and emperors only suppress freedom. The Reformation was already in the making. It would not blossom until two hundred and fifty years later but the seeds were already sown. The Crusades, the Inquisition, the papacy, and the failure of the emperors to maintain order all planted the seeds that they would themselves try desperately to uproot. The *Magna Charta* could not be obliterated with a simple decree, nor could the Bible be hidden by outlawing its translation nor by placing it on the Index of Forbidden Books (as would happen years later). They lived in the hearts of minds of men who saw the need for freedom amid the rising oppression.

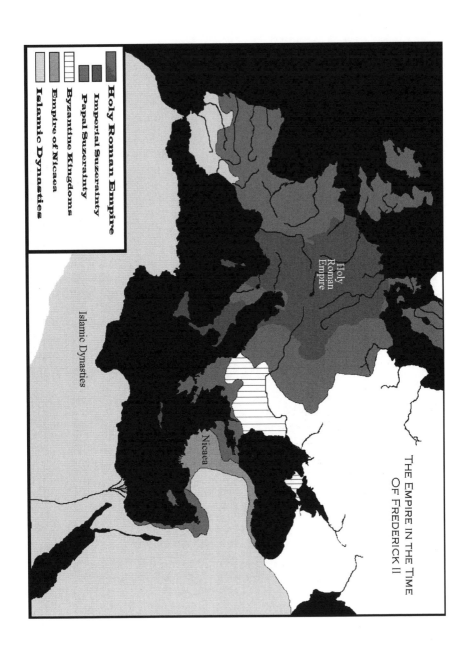

Holy Roman Empire
Imperial Suzerainty
Papal Suzerainty
Byzantine Kingdoms
Empire of Nicaea
Islamic Dynasties

Holy
Roman
Empire

Islamic Dynasties

Nicaea

THE EMPIRE IN THE TIME
OF FREDERICK II

16

The Great Interregnum

It may have seemed that the desire of Innocent IV was not only to crush the Hohenstaufen dynasty but the imperial dignity altogether. In the two decades following Frederick II's death no less than three different individuals claimed the title of emperor but none were recognized by all and none were crowned by the pope as tradition required. Sometimes referred to as "the Great Interregnum," this period saw the controversial "double election" for emperor and the murder of the entire male lineage of the Hohenstaufen. It saw the papal alliance with France, the fall of the Kingdom of Acre, the fall of the Latin Kingdom of Constantinople, the invasion of Mongols, and the death of one of Europe's greatest kings, Saint Louis IX of France. They were by no means unimportant decades.

The War Against the Hohenstaufen

The death of Frederick II was not enough for Innocent IV. He was resolved to extinguish the entire house of Hohenstaufen. He declared that the Crusade should now be diverted to Germany to support William of Holland against Conrad IV. He also sought to install his own king in Sicily. At first he sought out Richard of Cornwall who was a rich earl in England and had led several expeditions in Palestine after the Fifth Crusade. Richard, however, thought better of entering into a situation which would require conquest at great expense and controversy. He refused. Innocent then turned to the King of England himself. Henry III considered the offer on behalf of his young son Edmund, but no agreement was reached. Innocent again looked elsewhere for his puppet king. Charles of Anjou, the brother of Saint Louis was offered Sicily and was at first inclined to agree but for the angry denouncements of his brother, the king. Louis did not want Charles to embark upon the Crusade believing that they should remain neutral in the conflict, in which Louis clearly sympathized with the Hohenstaufen.

While Innocent was trying to place the kings of Europe (particularly Sicily and Germany) under his wing he was also trying to check the rising number of dissident Christian sects which seemed to be cropping up daily. In 1252 Innocent IV ratified the use of torture in the Inquisition and established it as a permanent institution. The Dominicans and Franciscans were named the officiators of the institution. This was indeed an irony, and proof of the depravity to which the papacy had brought low most all the orders. The Franciscans had begun as a pacifist order but as their popularity grew the papacy

279

began to seek more and more control over the order. Originally many of the order, including Francis while he yet lived, resisted papal control. Some of these monks eventually formed an effective new order known as the Franciscan Spirituals. These Franciscan Spirituals came to adopt many of the teachings of the Joachimites and would ultimately come under the Inquisition of their brothers. Some other religious orders who opposed the new teachings and doctrines of the Church, as well as the political abuses of it, also came to fell under the sporadic, and sometimes, incessant, persecution of the Inquisition. The most notable of these orders after the Franciscan Spirituals were the Benguines and Beghards from the Rhineland.

These events forced Conrad IV, who felt relatively secure in Germany, to come to Italy to claim his Sicilian heritage. It was clear that the pope planned an invasion of Sicily and Conrad wanted to make the prospect unpleasant for anyone attempting to do so. His premature death in 1254 brought a brief respite to Sicily and it seemed as if the war might come to end. Innocent IV was willing to negotiate with Manfred, the illegitimate son of Frederick II, for regency of Sicily in exchange for Manfred's acknowledgement of the pope as overlord of Sicily. Nevertheless, Manfred was soon in open rebellion.

Manfred was not the only one in open rebellion. The English bishops had been reluctant to accept papal interference in English and resented the appointment of Italians to local bishoprics, knowing full well that these men were appointed for their loyalty to the pope and not for their qualifications. The Bishop of Lincoln, Richard Grosseteste (also called Grosthead), was among the most rebellious. He refused to collect ten percent taxes for Innocent's "Crusade" and refused to install the Italian bishops demanded by Innocent. When Innocent responded with threats of excommunication Grosseteste responded with words, "I disobey, resist, and rebel." In a time when the Bible was slowly being supplanted, and even suppressed, Grosseteste preached the Word of God and has often been considered a forerunner of Wycliff. He showed clemency to the Jews and even went so far as to declare that the pope should be tried for heresy himself. He argued that it was the papacy which was guilty of heresy, and not those persecuted by the Inquisition. He further compared the pope to the anti–Christ and eloquently debated the apostacy of the papal office. He stood out as one of the first voices of the Reformation, two hundred and fifty years before it occurred. When he died, in 1253, Innocent believed he had recorded a triumph, but Innocent soon followed him to the grave. When Innocent IV died, in December 1254, it is said that the ghost of the bishop Grosseteste appeared to him beckoning the pope to come to his doom. To be sure the story is probably apocryphal, but there is no doubt that Innocent's death was prophetic of the dramatic shift which was about to take place in the war against the Hohenstaufen.

Manfred, Italy, and the Papacy

Innocent IV had died in Naples with his Cardinals by his side. When the Cardinals began to leave for Rome the mayor of Naples bolted the gates and demanded that they elect a new pope then and there. This type of coercion was nothing new to papal elections over the past few centuries and was certainly one reason for the increasing corruption of the papacy. The Cardinals did not, however, protest too loudly and settled upon Alexander IV only a few days after Innocent's death.

Alexander IV is usually glossed over quickly in history as a pope of little importance who merely followed his predecessor's policies. This is in large part because his entire pontificate was largely embroiled and tied to the war with Manfred. He excommunicated Manfred in 1255, and like Innocent IV before him, he began to freely attempt to distribute lands to whomever he pleased. He unsuccessfully enfeoffed Sicily to Edmund, King Henry III's son, who had been offered the land years early. However, when Henry failed to come up with the money needed for a conquest of Sicily, Alexander axed the deal. In Germany he disputed the rights of Conrad IV's son, Conradin (meaning "little Conrad" who was but a child) and attempted to negotiate for the rights of Alfonso X of Castile (known also as Alfonso the Wise) to the duchy of Saxony in his stead, for he was related to the Imperial families of Germany through both his grand–parents. Thus Alexander was equally disposed to destroy the entire house of Hohenstaufen although he met with little success.

In 1258 Manfred had successfully gained control of all Sicily and been crowned king at Palermo. He then turned his attention north seeking to bring the whole of Italy under his control. Matters worsened for the pope when the people of Rome offered to make Manfred a senator in 1261. That same year Manfred had secured the support of even some Lombard cities. Worse still for Alexander was the fall of Constantinople to the Greeks who reclaimed their capitol after nearly sixty years. Additionally, the Mongol threat was continuing to plague eastern Europe and Germany was now faced with a controversial double election which Alexander did little to resolve.

The Double Election

Conrad's death in 1254 left William of Holland as the sole claimant to the title "king of the Romans." Despite this, the papacy was in no hurry to crown him, or anyone else, "emperor of Rome." Germany was itself a divided country ruled by powerful magnates who wanted no interference from a powerful king, let alone emperor, and who were desirous to maintain their own authority. Frederick II had rarely set foot in Germany and let the various princes of Germany do whatever they wanted, for good or evil. When Frederick's son, Henry, had attempted to check the power of the barons and princes he was deemed a rebel and imprisoned by his father. By this time Germany was ruled largely by seven magnates who had gained the sole voting power for king. When William of Holland died in 1256 the magnates delayed on a new election until called upon. The archbishop of Cologne told the electors that they should elect someone rich enough to support the title, but weak enough that the electors would not fear him. The result was large scale bribery and a double election.

Alexander IV had forbade the electors from electing Conradin under threat of excommunication. Only two other real candidates remained; Richard of Cornwall and Alfonso the Wise. Richard of Cornwall was the son–in–law of Frederick II, an earl, and had become one of the richest men in England. He had fought in the aftermath of the Fifth Crusade and been considered a candidate for the King of Sicily by Innocent IV. He was also the second son of King John and had acted as regent for Henry III one year when he was out of the country. Alfonso the Wise had become king of Leon and Castile. He was the grandson of the emperor Philip and his mother was the grand–daughter of Frederick Barbarossa. He was a scholar who modeled the laws of Castile after Roman law and had done much to unite Spain against the Muslim states. Along with the king of Aragon, he was the most important king of Spain and also aspired to German inheritance.

Both Richard and Alfonso heavily bribed the electors. Initially, Alfonso gained four of the seven votes but one, upon further payment, changed his vote to Richard of Cornwall. He ventured to Germany and was crowned king of the Romans on May 17, 1257 but when three of the electors who had voted for Richard found that they received less money than the other electors they protested by belatedly changing their vote to Alfonso who was unable to come to Germany on account of concern for Spain. Richard, therefore, stayed in Germany and tried to garner support for his crown. Through lavish bribery he won the support of the Rhineland, but was unable to gain further support when he was forced to return to England, in 1259, to aid Henry III against some barons. He returned to Germany in 1260, but stayed barely a year.

Alexander IV did little to resolve the double election and when he died in 1261 his pontificate had amounted to little. Manfred had succeeded in taking most of Italy, Constantinople had fallen, the Crusade of Saint Louis had been abandoned, Mongols were invading the east, and a double election made the imperial dignity seem a joke. On August 29, 1261 the former Patriarch of Jerusalem was made pope under the name Urban IV. A Frenchman, Urban was never able to live in Rome as the Roman people were now in open defiance of the popes. They favored Manfred and rejected the papal dictators. This may have been one reason that a Frenchman was elected pope. The papacy had increasingly fell in ill with the Roman people and not too many years later the papacy would even move to France, making Avignon its capital. Regardless of the intent, it is clear by now that the papacy was at odds with the very people who lived in the papal estates. The war in Italy was becoming a personal one.

Urban had no time for the double election and put it on the backburner. Throughout his short tenure Urban completely ignored the double election and left it unresolved by the time of his death.

Saint Louis Returns

After four years in Palestine Saint Louis IX returned to France following news of his mother's death. One of the few truly good kings of history Louis had managed to establish diplomatic ties with Muslims in Palestine but failed to retake Jerusalem. Upon his return to France England was again trying to reclaim the lands that had been disputed and fought over for so many years. Louis was able to bring this conflict to a temporary, but noble, end. At the Treaty of Paris in 1258 Henry III acknowledged the sovereignty of France over all the lands on mainland Europe save the Aquitaine which Louis allowed Henry to possess as a vassal. So great a reputation had Saint Louis that he would even negotiate for peace between Henry III and some barons who had rebelled against Henry.

In France, Louis cracked down on the abuses of officials, outlawed prostitution, trial by combat, and even punished corrupt clergymen who claimed the protection of the papacy. Such protection, however, did not dare to oppose the king whose virtue made the pope's look like demons. Europe's best king returned in a turmultuous time.

The Scholars of the Age

Despite the dark and oppressive time which was arising the High Middle Ages were also a time when the Universities were again returning to prominence after the death of the Carolingian Renaissance. Perhaps the oppression of truth made the minds of the weary more curious to know what was forbidden to them, or perhaps it was inevitable that the dark times would call forth men who wanted a way out. Of course many scholars are not men of enlightenment. Such a paradox is the lesson of history. Men such as Roger Bacon and, to a lesser extent, Albertus Magnus, were paving the way for the age of science even while dabbling in the occult and mystic superstition. On the other hand men like Thomas Aquinas were providing the intellectually weak papacy with fuel for fire. From this generation three men stand out. Their contributions are both negative and positive, good and evil.

The first of them was Albertus Magnus. Born in Bavaria, Albertus (or Albert) became a Dominican and moved to Cologne where he is best known. He begun to dabble in the mysteries of science, as the medievals knew it. His science blended the occult with science, and mysticism with logic. He was one of the first to deduce that the poles of the earth were too cold to be inhabited, but his real notoriety was in his pursuit of alchemy. Alchemy, of course, was based on a misconception about chemistry. Albert knew that some substances could be changed from one to another but, without any knowledge of modern chemistry, he assumed falsely that any substance could be changed to any other. He maintained that there were only a few selected elements in the world, such as wind, earth, water, and fire. This was borrowed from the ancient world which naturally limited his abilities. He integrated his studies with ancient occult magic with which he was most identified in his age. People, by and large, saw him as a mystic and a magician who dabbled in the dark arts, but he was also a Catholic Theologian and among his best students was the young Thomas Aquinas.

Thomas Aquinas, like many before him, had desired to integrate the philosophy of the ancient classics with the Catholic dogma. Many had tried before him and many had failed. In the days of the apostles, Paul had openly declared that the "wisdom of this world is foolishness in God's sight" (1 Corinthians 3:16). The apostles rejected Plato and Aristotle which were, in fact, one of the reasons that the ancient Romans called the Christians ignorant and unlearned. After all, who would reject the "great thinkers?" Certainly this argument, false as it was, had an impact upon the early church, for as early as Origen, the Church Fathers sought a way to make Christianity acceptable to the philosophers. Origen integrated certain aspects of Platonic thought into the Church but it was not until Aquinas a thousand years later that Aristotle was made compatible with Catholic doctrine.

Aquinas used "reason" as a logical means to prove the message of the Church. In some respects his work is monumental as history has declared. Certainly his arguments for the existence of God are echoed to this very day among Creation Scientists (those scientists who oppose evolution), but in most other ways he ventured into the very areas that the apostles had forewarned about. He attempted to prove Catholic dogma based on logical presumptions, but those presumptions are not always true. In short, Aquinas was the first to give the medieval popes a systematic doctrine of their teachings. In the years previous dissident Christians, or "heretics," had attempted to prove that many of the teachings of the Church were neither in the Bible, nor logical. Catholicism (and we should by this time distinguish it from other forms of Christianity whether Eastern Orthodox or "heretical" dissident Christianity) did not yet have a systematic theology. It was faith by decree without justification. Aquinas provided the Catholic hierarchy with a systematic theology which would eventually be declared by Leo XIII the standard for Catholic orthodoxy.

Thomas Aquinas taught, as did the medieval Catholic Church (which has remained virtually unaltered to this day), that the papacy had supplanted the imperial authority and the pope was above all men. He declared that submission to the pope was necessary for salvation itself. So also baptism was held to be essential to salvation. So much so that if a child dies without baptism he cannot attain salvation, but is eternally lost. He also taught that purgatory was essential to purge men of their sins. In short, he legitimized every foreign doctrine of the Church which had failed to be taught by the apostles. He further promoted the use of the death penalty against "heretics" as well as the use of force, and torture. Indeed, he may well have had a hand in Innocent IV's decision to make torture a legal means of extracting confessions from "heretics."

Among Aquinas' foremost critics was the Scottsman known as Duns Scotus. He was a loyal Catholic, but differed from Aquinas in the use of Aristitole to prove the faith. He argued certain teachings, such as transubstantiation, cannot be proved with logic but must be accepted on faith through the Church. However, the reverence and esteem in which Aquinas was held would eventually lead to equation of Duns with "dunce." Men who rejected Aquinas' logic were thus called "dunces," a term which is comparable to "dumb" or unlearned.

The last great scholar of his age was in fact little known in his own age. Roger Bacon, and Englishman, is now considered a pioneer in the field of science. Like Albertus Magnus, Bacon did intermingle his science and superstition, but he was actually far closer to modern science than his more popular predecessor, for Bacon made much use of experimentation. He observed that even the smallest stars were larger than the earth and was one of very few who openly promoted the teaching of Hebrew and Greek, the languages of the Bible. On the mystic side he believed that the stars could effect personality, even as the moon's gravity effected the tides. Such arguments continue to be used to this very day by modern astrologers. These beliefs, popular as they may have been to the medieval mind, earned him a reputation as a necromancer and magician. It was not until the Renaissance that Roger Bacon's writings became known to the scholarly world again.

Urban IV and Charles of Anjou

Urban IV was not one to shy from bloodshed. He issued an edict in 1262 condemning the great Waldenses of Lombardy as well as the other dissident sects, and cults, of northern Italy. The Inquisition was given full authority to root out the dissenters. Urban also took up the cause of the two previous popes in his war against the Hohenstaufen and Manfred. He delicately resolved Edmund's claim to Sicily since the English king's son could not raise the money for conquest and again offered the kingdom to Charles of Anjou, the brother of Louis IX. Although Louis had earlier forbidden Charles from venturing to Sicily, he was now convinced that the war would not end peaceably and reluctantly gave permission for Charles to claim Sicily for himself.

Having heard that Charles, and his army, were now prepared to march into Italy Manfred was resolved to make peace with the pope. He agreed to recognize the papal suzerainty in Sicily, to pay tribute, and would also lead a Crusade against Constantinople with Baldwin II (the former Latin emperor of

Constantinople who had fled to Italy to seek his help). Urban rejected the terms. Instead Charles agreed to pay 50,000 marks, promise an annual payment of 10,000 gold ounces, and agreed not to accept any offer for the emperor's crown or other royal or dignitary position. Despite these promises Charles renegotiated the agreement after Manfred had forced the pope to take refuge at Orvieto.

With Ubran holed up against Manfred, Charles was now in a position where the pope could not refuse his help. He demanded that he be permitted to accept the Roman offer to make him a senator. Manfred responded by petitioning the Roman Senate to make him emperor. This was a flattering display, for the Senate had long ago lost the right to elect the emperors. Nevertheless the Senate acted with caution and did not act on Manfred's request. In the meantime, Manfred continued to press forward against Urban, who fled further, this time to Perugia, where he died on October 2, 1264.

The Fall of the Hohenstaufen

The election of a new pope was delayed for many months. Pressures from within and without forced the election at Perugia. Clement IV, another Frenchman, was elected. He came to Perugia in disguise as a monk for fear of Manfred's men and, in February, the war was resumed. Clement preached a Crusade against Manfred and urged Charles to make haste in coming to Italy. Within a year Charles' army was crossing into Italy. He was crowned King of Sicily by the pope and on the 26th of February 1266 he entered into battle with Manfred's army. On that very day Manfred fell in battle and died. Charles was king of Sicily and only one Hohenstaufen remained; the young Conradin.

The rule of Charles did little to comfort the Sicilians or Italians. In defiance of his original promise to the pope he attempted to gain control of northern Italy. His rule proved not only no better than Manfred's, but worse. Several Spaniards and their princes, who had ties to Manfred, were now in rebellion against Charles. Tunis was even considered a vassal state of Sicily and refused allegiance. Moreover, the excesses of Charles government caused even some of his own supporters to turn on him. Most notably, the city of Rome. Even several of the Roman families that had supported the pope, now turned to Conradin and asked him to come and claim his inheritance.

Conradin was only fourteen years old when he made the pledge to come to Italy and claim his inheritance. By his side were young princes including Frederick of Baden whose age was comparable to Conradin's. They had little expertise in war but Charles' hands were full. The Berbers were in revolt, the King of Tunis had invaded Sicily, the Muslims of Sicily resisted Charles, and the Roman families of Orsini and Annibaldi (his former supporters) were now ready to acknowledge Conradin. Clement excommunicated Conradin and all his supporters, but in July 1268 he was nevertheless received with rejoicing at Rome. With most of the rest of his opposition in retreat or crumbling Charles looked to Conradin and, at a battle fought on August 23, 1268, Conradin was captured and his army fell in battle.

The capture of Conradin was not sufficient for Charles, nor for Clement. Innocent IV had hinted many years later at the extermination of the male lineage of Frederick II. On October 29, Charles obliged. A trial was held and Conradin was prosecuted as a land robber and thief. Clement did nothing to interfere, and, in fact, is believed to have been the master mind behind the act. Conradin was executed along with his colleagues as a common criminal. The boy prince Frederick, and his friend Conradin, himself a sixteen year old boy, were executed at Naples to the disgust of all Italy. The devotion and justice of Louis IX did not extend to his brother.

The papacy had thus succeeded in finally exterminating the male lineage of Frederick II, but in so doing created animosity between themselves and Rome; even all of Italy. They had proven themselves no better than the tyrant kings and made a mockery of the Church.

Gregory X and the Resolution of the Imperial Schism

Clement IV made no attempt to truly resolve the double election. When he died shortly after Conradin's execution Europe had neither a pope nor an emperor for a period of nearly three years. Richard of Cornwall returned to Germany in 1268 and stayed a year, again trying to stir up support for his imperial bid. He married again to a German princess in hopes of appeasing them but there was little desire for a true emperor. The princes of Germany did as they pleased and sought no order. Robber barons and knights plagued Germany and the corrupt ruled without a true king to stop them.

In Italy Charles ruled without justice. In France the great Louis IX decided to leave for another Crusade, but soon after his stay in Carthage his army caught the plague and Louis was not immune. The great king of Europe died in 1270 and was brought back to France where he was honored by the people who did not wait for the Church to declare him a saint. He was the most beloved of all French kings and one of the few truly good kings of history. His death left Europe without the land without a leader. No undisputed emperor sat upon the throne, no pope ruled the land with his a spiritual sceptre, and now there was not even a strong king. Pressure was mounting for the election of a new pope but the French and Italian supporters fought amongst each other. The papacy had been ruled by French candidates for many years and the Romans had not even permitted the last two popes to set foot in the "Holy City." The Cardinals had been imprisoned, threatened, and lock up until they finally elected Gregory X in September 1271.

Gregory X almost immediately called to convene another general council. In honesty, it was time for a council. The empire was in disarray and a council was the best means to bring together the kings and bishops of Europe.

Of course, many councils only served to further divide Europe. Exactly what Gregory had in mind for the Fourteenth Ecumenical Council, or the Second Council of Lyons, would have to wait for the council was three years in the making as messengers went out even to Constantinople inviting the Greek Emperor Michel VIII Pelaeologos to send representatives in hopes of ending the strife between east and west.

In 1272, Richard of Cornwall died leaving only the rival claimant of Alfonso the Wise. Gregory became the first pope to attempt to solve the great schism of the emperors, but he did so by declaring a new election. He told the electors that if they did not elect an emperor, he would. Alfonso's appeal for the crown was then referred to the electors anew. As had been the case earlier, the princes of Germany secretly desired neither a king nor an emperor. The pope's insistence forced them to an election but it was an election in which Gregory kept a careful watch. Charles of Anjou put forward his nephew, Philip III, the new king of France. Such a candidate did not sit well with the German electors. Neither did Alfonso' bid for the crown. King Ottokar II (or Otakar II) of Bohemia was also a candidate but he was far too powerful and the princes of Germany feared him greatly. Instead they settled upon the meek and peaceful Count Rudolf of Hapsburg. He was a godson of Frederick II, thus satisfying Hohenstaufen sympathizers, but he was clearly a vassal of the pope; loyal and obedient to his authority. Most importantly, he provided a German alternative to Ottokar. He was elected and on October 24, 1273 Rudolf was crowned king of the Romans at Aachen while preparations for his coronation as emperor of the Romans were delayed on account of the coming council. Gregory, nevertheless, did recognize him in exchange for the renunciation of all claims to Sicily, Rome, and the papal estates, as well as a pledge to lead a new Crusade which Gregory was planning.

In the meantime, the crowning acheivement of Gregory's short reign was the convening of the Second Council of Lyons, or Fourteenth Ecumenical Council. The council convened in the spring of 1274. Chief on the agenda were a new Crusade planned by Gregory, the reunion of the eastern and western empires, and new measures on how to elect a pope. The later had clearly become a problem with the previous elections, including Gregory's own election. Abuses and corruption as well as threats and bribery were known to occur. The absense of a pope for nearly three years also decreased the faith that the general public had in the elections. The Fourteenth Ecumenical Council decreed that a new election must be held not more than ten days from the death of the previous pope and that no contact with the outside world must be made until the election is over. Several other decrees were also made in hopes of correcting the abuses.

Perhaps the most interesting of items on the agenda was the reunification of eastern and western empires. Ever since the Roman Empire had divided there had been talk of reuniting, but the reunion never occurred. When the Fourth Crusade was diverted to Constantinople it seemed as if the schism would only widen, but the Byzantine Empire was now on the verge of collapse. After the destruction caused by the west, the invasions from Muslims and Mongols, the Byzantine Empire was now clearly willing to negotiate, especially since it was well known that Charles of Anjou, now King of Naples, was planning a Crusade against the Greeks in an attempt to reclaim Constantinople for the Latins. The Greek representatives' appearance at the council was a clear message which Charles vigorously attacked. He insisted that the Greeks could not be trusted and should not be listened to. He pleaded for the right to invade Byzantium, but Gregory silenced Charles and even forced him to renounce his title of Senator of Rome which he had held in defiance of the pope. Gregory appeared to score a coup when the Greeks pledged their willingness to accept papal authority and even religious mode of worship. The grand plan, however, fell through when the Greek clergy rejected the already ratified plan. Gregory's death two yeas later insured that the long dreamt reunion of the Roman Empire would not occur.

Another intriguing event was the appearance of Mongol representatives. Ever since Mongols had appeared to Saint Louis in the east it was clear that the Mongols wanted to form a coalition against the Muslims. Many of the Mongol representatives even received baptism. Such an event further spawned and enhanced Gregory's plan for a new Crusade to reclaim Jerusalem once and for all, but this plan too died with him two years later. There would, to be sure, be a few other feeble Crusades, but the days of a grand Crusade led by the Christian Kings of Europe against the Muslims were dying. Already the general public at large believed the Crusades to be false and many clergymen even cried out that the sins of the west were the reasons for fall of Jerusalem. Indeed, the eastern Latin Kingdom was collapsing. Antioch had fallen in 1268 and the warrior Baibars was now threatening Acre. People were more concerned with the situation in Europe than in the east.

Of the final items on the agenda included a reaffirmation of a previous edict forbidding new religious orders. This edict had been slowly forgotten but ironically, the Dominicans and Franciscans were exempt from it. The orders of the newly formed Inquisition were given clear exemptions from many laws and regulations placed upon all other orders.

The Council seemed in many respects a dramatic success but with Gregory's death the dreams of the Council faded. The Byzantine Empire remained apart from the west and at enmity with it, the Crusade dreamt of was never truly realized, and the corruption of the Chruch was only deepening. Gregory would die of fever in January 1276 having reinstalled the Imperial office but having done nothing else of lasting influence. Whether his dreams were truly for good or evil only God can tell for his reign was too short to see the fruits of his plans.

Summary

Some recon the Great Interregnum to be merely the three years between the death of Conrad IV and the election of Richard and Alfonso. Others count the interregnum as extending to the rise of Rudolf. Of course, in theory every emperor had to be anointed by the pope. Since no emperor since Frederick II had been anointed it could well be argued that the Great Interregnum extended from Frederick II's death until Rudolf's ascension. Nonetheless, the rights of the papacy in approving the emperor was one of the very issues that was in dispute, thus the legitimacy of Conrad IV, Richard of Cornwall, and Alfonso the Wise will perhaps never be resolved in the minds of historians.

The age itself was an age anarchy and chaos in Germany, and civil war in Italy. It was a continuation of the war against the Hohenstaufen and saw the brutal extermination of the male lineage of Frederick II. The papacy had permanently supplanted the emperors in power and authority. It also destroyed the confidence which the common man had in the papacy but more importantly the papacy had destroyed its own protector. Without a strong emperor the popes would find themselves unable, incompetent, and incapable of ruling. They would eventually be driven out of Rome by the people and establish themselves in alliance with the French. They had once been protected by the German Kings but turned to the Normans of Sicily. When the Sicilians came under the control of the Hohenstaufen, and eventually Charles, they then turned to the French for support. The love affair would itself be short lived.

17

The Calm Before the Storm

From the reign of Innocent IV to the death of Conradin under Clement IV the papacy was corrupt and power seeking. The height of arrogance, however, occurred under Pope Boniface VIII. Before his ascension to the papal crown eight popes would reign over a period of less than twenty years, but only Rudolf of Hapsburg sat on the Imperial throne until 1291. It was a period of peace between the papacy and emperor. It was a calm before the storm.

Rudolf Against Ottokar

In the years since Frederick II rose to power Germany had become a country of robber barons. The term itself, as well as "highway robbery," took their names from this time. Barons and princes would levy taxes and tolls as they willed. Many roads and particularly bridges were set up for tolls to be collected so that anyone traversing the road or passing the bridge would have to pay a tax. The duchies and counties of Germany became as if they were separate states and, indeed, Hungary, Poland, and Bohemia were just that. Now Austria, Saxony, and the other territories also threatened to become effectively separate states ruled by a powerful prince. Among the most powerful of all these princes was Ottokar II of Bohemia.

Rudolf proved to be an effective king by tearing down the castles of robber–knights and barons and stopping highway robbery. He brought order back to Germany and during his reign laws concerning the *ministeriales*, a sort of civil servant, were codified. In the south the codified laws were called the Swabian Mirror and in the north, the Saxon Mirror. With the suppression of robber barons the greatest threat to Germany was believed to be Ottokar. He was the grandson of the emperor Philip of Swabia and the strongest princes since Henry the Lion. He had inherited Bohemia and Morovia, been elected duke of Austria and acquired through marriage or conquest Babenburg, Carinthia, Carniola, Styria, and Istria. In addition he was actively seeking control over Poland, Lithuania, and even Hungary.

To reduce the threat from Ottokar, and weaken his position, Rudolf, with the support of the other German princes, convened a Diet at Regensburg in 1274 which ordered Ottokar to surrender Styria, Carinthia, and the dukedom of Austria. Ottokar consented but the princes did not consider the issue resolved. When Ottokar reasserted his authority in Austria he was placed under ban by the empire and Rudolf invaded his lands that same year, 1276. In a few months Ottokar was forced to yield to the Treaty of Vienna which ordered him to renounce his claims to all lands save Bohemia and Moravia which he had inherited from his father, King Wenceslas.

During these turbulent times Alfonso X of Castile continued to assert his claims to the imperial crown. He insisted that his crown had been awarded legitimately years earlier, arguing that Richard of Cornwall was a usurper and that he was being denied his rights. Having appealed to Gregory, the pope was eventually successful in talking Alfonso into renouncing his claims in 1275. Rudolf became the sole claimant to the title, but had not yet received the Imperial diadem. Although Gregory had agreed to coronate Rudolf, troubles, and lack of funds, prevented Rudolf from venturing to Italy. The trouble was again Ottokar. In 1278 Ottokar had again reasserted his claims over Austria and was marching on Vienna. The war was, nonetheless, short–lived for Ottokar fell in battle at Durnkrut on August 26.

Years later the question of who was the rightful heir to the former provinces of Ottokar were called into question. Rudolf justly acknowledged the rights of Ottokar's heir, but only in regard to Bohemia and Moravia. He awarded Austria and Styria to his two sons whom he was anxious to insure as heirs. Much of his later years were spent trying to secure the right for his oldest son to inherit the throne but the German princes were leery of a hereditary crown. They continued to resist any promise of making the House of Hapsburg hereditary heirs to the throne.

Four Popes – One Year

Following the death of Pope Gregory X, Innocent V was elected. Another Frenchman, he was also a friend of the famed Catholic theologian Bonaventura and the first Dominican to become pope. He requested that Rudolf postpone his coronation as emperor while he settled on differences between the papacy and King Charles of Naples who was now as great a threat to the papal control in Italy as had the Hohenstaufen. In fact, there is no doubt that Charles had wanted to control the pope. The extent to which he exercised control over Innocent is unknown but the pope did confirm Charles right as a Senator of Rome and eventually employed strong arm tactics against the Greek Emperor Michael Pelaeologus sending envoys to tell him that Charles intended to conquer Constantinople if he did not submit to the decree of the Fourteen Ecumenical Council.

He died only six months after ascending to the papal tiara. This time Charles made sure that he would have a pope of his choosing. He manipulated Gregory X's rules for a new election to force the election of his partisan Cardinal Fieschi. Among the rules were that the electors should forced to fast if they did not elect a new pope within a certain amount of time. Charles then virtually starved the electors until they chose who he desired. The Cardinal chose the name Hadrian V and his first act as pope was to declare null and void the new rules for electing a pope. It was also his only act for he fell and died only a month after being pontiff.

In Viterbo, where the electors were currently residing, the mayor attempted to compel the latest election according to the rule of Gregory X, but when they informed him that Hadrian V had nullified to rules there was rioting and violence. The rioters are generally believed to have been people who wanted to secure the election of a pope favorable to their own political allies or they may have been mere hooligans who sought any excuse to riot, but by the time the violence was quelled it was clear that the Orsini, not Charles, would control the papacy.

The Orsini family was now the most powerful political family in Rome. One of the Orsini was a Cardinal who aspired to the tiara himself. He soon realized, however, that he would not be able to garner enough support to win so had a meek man chosen who was more than willing to let Orsini, as his advisor, run the papacy. Pope John XXI was a Portuguese scholar who liked nothing better than sitting in his private cell and studying. He had no real political ambitions and virtually agreed to let Orsini rule in his name.

That his name was chosen as John XXI requires a brief comment for there was no John XX. In fact, the level of education had sunk to an all time low a century before and even the scholars of the age made notorious mistakes. Many historians of the day place a Pope John XX in the tenth century but modern historians are unsure why. The truth is that a popular fairy tale had actually become accepted as history by many medieval scholars. It is the legend of "Pope Joan." According to the story a woman disguised herself as a man in order to become pope. She was discovered only after giving birth to a baby while mounting a horse. After the discovery she was supposed to have been stoned to death by irate citizens. Of course, the story is completely mythological, but it was accepted by historians until it was discredited in the 17th Century. It is likely that Joan's "papal name" would have been John, hence the absence of a Pope John XX is actually because of the general acceptance of the legend of Pope "Joan," known officially as John XX. Regardless, John XXI turned the reigns of government effectively over to Orsini.

Among Orsini's first actions was the punishment of the rebel rousers at the election of Pope John XXI. Orsini was made to look like a champion of free elections. He also resumed negotiations with Rudolf for his coronation and sought again the submission of Constantinople to Rome's authority. Once again it looked as if Constantinople was willing to do so when John XXI died. The ceiling of his study had fallen in and killed the pope, only eight months after his election. There is no evidence to suggest that the accident was not an accident but it is clear that Orsini benefited from his death. Orsini was recognized as the real power behind John's papacy and he was the natural choice to succeed him. Charles' partisans, however, were determined to prevent his election for it was clear that Orsini was a rival of Charles, as was his family. Nevertheless, after six long months Orsini gained enough votes to win election and named himself Pope Nicholas III.

England, France, and Spain

Rudolf had no real authority outside of Germany. The countries of the empire acknowledge fealty to him but only nominally. Philip III of France had sought the imperial crown from himself and certainly was not anxious to obey Rudolf. Likewise, Alfonso of Castile and Leon had lost his bid for the imperial diadem. England had ceased to be a fief of Germany when it was made a fief of the papacy. In either case England was a part of the empire, but in reality they desired to be neither a fief of the emperor nor the pope. It should not be overlooked at Charles of Naples, the brother of Philip III, had also had aspirations to the imperial throne although his aspirations were but fleeting dreams. Thus the kingdoms of the empire were once again effectively divided against one another.

In England, King Edward I Longshanks came to power. He came on the heels of the dissident sentiment of the English people. Still reeling from papal interference in their country and the attempt to suppress the *Magna Charta* the English people, and even some of the clergy, sought autonomy from outside influence and guarantees of the rights established in the *Magna Charta*. Edward had risen to power with a reputation for cruelty even before he departed on the Crusade with King Louis IX. Indeed, the Crusade might have been an attempt to restore his reputation which was diminishing among the people. When King Henry III died, Edward was forced to pay homage to his cousin King Philip III of France for the French regions of his territory as had been arranged by Saint Louis. Historians are divided on Edward's motives toward Parliament but he did give recognition to Parliament, saying "what touches all must be approved by all," and even expanded its role, forging the way for the House of Commons. Some consider him a good and noble king while others despise him for his military intrusions into Wales and Scotland. Both countries were fiefs of England but were ruled by their own kings. Edward wanted direct control over each country. The former was eventually subjected to direct English rule after years of war, while Scotland continued to resist and rebel. Many of these rebels were led by William Wallace until he was betrayed by Robert the Bruce and executed. Years later, in Edward's final years, Robert the Bruce himself revolted and reconquered most of Scotland.

In France, Philip III, surnamed "the Bold," had come into conflict with the King of Aragon, Peter (III) the Great, over the rights of his nephews to rule in Aragon. The French and Aragonese had long been in conflict over territories between the two, including Toulouse which had become so prominent in the Albigensian Crusades. Philip's nephews laid claims to Peter's throne. Peter had married Constance of the Hohenstaufen and was the son of King James I of

Aragon. In 1276, Philip declared war and supported the rebels against Peter. The war would, however, ultimately end in failure as Peter retained his throne and quashed the rebel army.

Charles In Italy

At the time of Nicholas's election Rudolf was still embroiled in his conflict with Ottokar. In eyes of Nicholas, Charles was the predominant threat to Italy. Nicholas was not to be a puppet to Charles. Nicholas, whose family were powerful politicians in Rome, opposed Charles' authority there and in northern Italy. He even compelled Charles to resign his office as Senator of Rome and made a provision that prohibited any prince from holding that office without papal dispensation. He, moreover, made himself senator for life in Charles' place.

Despite his clear opposition to Charles he was a tactician in his policies. He resumed negotiations with Rudolf for a coronation and arranged for a marriage between Rudolf's daughter, Clementia, and Charles' grandson. The marriage alliance would give Burgundy to Clementia and diminish Charles' authority in northern Italy. It also made the emperor a relative of Charles, thus insuring family ties that Nicholas hoped would further keep Charles in line. This diplomacy continued throughout his reign. While he vigorously opposed Charles' desire to launch a Crusade against Constantinople he placed more rigorous demands on the east in the negotiations for reunification.

Nicholas also tried, futility, to negotiate peace between Philip III and Alfonso the Wise who were in a war over the rights to Navarre. The other notable of his reign was his moving the papal palace to the now famous Vatican. He is remembered largely, however, for nepotism. A member of a powerful political family in Rome, Nicholas granted many high Church offices and awarded other benefits to his family members. Dante so despised the pope that he placed Nicholas in the bonds of hell itself. He died in the summer of 1280.

Charles himself was ambitious. His brother was King Philip the Bold of France but he had little of true significance. He had once been a Senator of Rome and in 1277 had purchased the title "King of Jerusalem" from Maria of Antioch, even though the titular name of a kingdom now all but dead meant nothing except prestige. The only true authority that Charles held was as King of Sicily. However, he sought to expand his power eastward. He had lobbied hard for the papacy to let him reconquer Constantinople and was actively asserting his authority in northern Italy. With the death of Nicholas, Charles was determined once and for all to install a puppet pope who would bow to his whims.

Disorder followed Nicholas' death. For six months no decision could be reached until Charles finally arrested members of Orsini's family, including two cardinals, and forced the election of Martin IV (so called because

295

Marinus I and II were sometimes called Martin II and III). Martin was another Frenchman of mild temperment who was a close partisan and friend of Charles. He was also easy to control. Under Martin IV King Charles had gained effective control of the papacy.

Almost immediately, he proved a loyal ally of Charles. After having been made Senator for life, Martin IV gave papal dispensation transferring the office to Charles, thus making Charles a senator for life and granting him control over the rectors of the papal states. In 1281 he excommunicated the Greek Emperor Michael VIII Palaeologos and gave full backing to Charles' plan for a Crusade against Constantinople.

The Division of Sicily

With his long unrealized dream near reality Charles was confident that he could reconquer Constantinople and add it to his domain. The Crusader fleet was being assembled in the spring of 1282 on the main island of Sicily, but Charles' ambitions made him blind to the sufferings of his subjects who were furious at heavy taxation and oppression. On March 30 the Church bells rung out at the hour of vesper (announcing the evening). Those bells, however, were also a signal. Although the exact details are disputed, the Sicilian Vespers Revolt, as it came to be called, erupted at the ringing of the bells. Sicilian mobs rampaged declaring, "death to the French!" The French were then driven off the island of Sicily.

Soon after the revolt the Sicilians sent representatives to Pope Martin IV asking that they be made a papal fief in exchange for Communal rule. Martin, ever the puppet of Charles, refused outright, thereby causing the Sicilians to turn to Peter the Great of Aragon. Since Peter was married to a Hohenstaufen, the Sicilians argued that he was the rightful heir to Sicily. Peter heartily accepted and only a few weeks after the Vespers Revolt he was sailing for Sicily. Peter took the crown of Sicily and formed an alliance with the Byzantine Empire who was fully aware of Charles' plans to launch a Crusade against them. Peter then advanced northward on the Italian mainland.

Martin excommunicated Peter, but the act did little to harm his authority. Martin was seen by all as a puppet of Charles. So much so that even the papal city of Perugia renounced Martin. Charles was loosing the war. Martin's only hope of taking the Sicilian island back for his master Charles was to declare a Crusade against Aragon. In 1285 the Crusade was preached to the French, who would naturally have sympathies with their king's brother, but that very year Philip III of France, Peter the Great of Aragon, Charles of Anjou and Naples, and Martin IV all died natural deaths. It must have been God Himself who had decreed to put an end to a Crusade which should never have been preached. The end result of the escapades were merely the failure to reunite the eastern and western Roman Empires and the separation of the kingdom of Sicily into two separate kingdoms known as the Kingdom of Sicily on the main island and the Kingdom of Naples in southern Italy. Although the two kingdoms would sometimes share the same king there would never again be officially reunited until the 19th Century. Far from uniting Europe, the papacy's policies were dividing Europe and crumbling the once great Roman Empire.

From Honorius to Rudolf's Death

It was beginning to seem as the fall of the Carolingian dynasty was happening all over again. Even as had happened in those dark days, Europe was united in name only. Each country was ruled by different kings, often in conflict with one another. The universal emperor Rudolf had not yet even been coronated and the universal pope could not even control Italy. These days, however, were not long in remaining, although the people of Europe might well have wished that these days would have remained. Before the rise of Pope Boniface VIII three more popes would sit in the Vatican and another emperor would rise to power following Rudolf's death. Nevertheless, these days are important in understanding how, and perhaps why, the power structure of Europe was changing. The old Republican ways had died with Caesar, the Imperial ways had died with Gregory VII, and the Papal way would not hold sway forever.

Honorius IV succeeded Martin IV and was well received in Rome amid the hope that he might loose the binds that had held the papacy prisoner to hated French Angevins. He was, as several previous popes had been, elected Senator for life and was one of only a handful of popes at that time to reside in Rome. In his policy towards Sicily and Naples he again attempted to reunite the kingdoms under Charles' heir, Charles II.

The situation was delicate, although Honorius did not treat it as such. Peter the Great's oldest son, Alfonso III, had become the new King of Aragon while his younger son, James, was crowned the King of Sicily. However, Charles' son, Charles II, had been captured in battle and was being held prisoner. Charles had agreed to renunciate his rights to Sicily in exchange for the Kingdom of Naples and his freedom, but Honorius was furious at Charles for attempting to make the concession. He refused to lift Alfonso's excommunication and would not ratify the treaty that Charles had signed.

Among Honorius' other acts was his condemnation of the dissident sect known as the "Apostolicals," encouraging their persecution. He also resumed negotiations for the coronation of Rudolf but the pope died only a month after negotiations resumed. Yet again, Rudolf was disappointed. He would again have to wait and wait he did, for there would not even be another pope for nearly a year. The electors argued and when illness fell upon the cardinals a suspension was ordered. It was not until February 1288 that Nicholas IV was elected.

The first Franciscan to be elected pope Nicholas was a partisan of the important political family of Colonna who were descended from the old Counts of Tusculum. He was elected Senator for life and repaid the Colonnas, appointing them to important positions in the papal states and in Rome. He attempted to ally Castille with France against Aragon, but Philip the Fair had no real desire to embark on a Crusade in Spain. Nevertheless, Nicholas had Charles II crowned king of Sicily after he agreed to pay homage to the pope and not to take any office in Rome or the papal states. Since James held Sicily the coronation was merely a declaration of the pope's support but he would have to fight for Sicily if he wanted it.

In 1289, Edward Longshanks had negotiated a peaceful settlement between Charles II, Philip the Fair, and Alfonso III of Aragon. The treaty promised that Alfonso would be released from the sentence of excommunication if he accepted Charles as King of Sicily. Since his brother James was the actual king the treaty merely separated Alfonso from his brother, cutting off any military support that Alfonso might have afforded him. James then was left to fend for himself against the kingdom of Naples. However, fortunes changed when Alfonso died in 1291 without an heir. James became the king of Aragon as well as Sicily, thus placing the army of Aragon at his disposal.

The year 1291 was not a good year for Nicholas. Not only did James inherit Aragon but the Kingdom of Acre in Palestine was dealt if final blow. The fall of Acre in May 1291 signaled the end of Christian dominance in the Holy Land. Like the fall of Jerusalem, the Catholics were largely to blame themselves. One out of every nine people in Acre was said to be a prostitute, about half of whom were Muslim women used to such treatment. The decadence and petty infighting among the Catholics made them oblivious to spies within the city and the Islamic armies are believed to have known everything that happened within the walls. When the Crusaders sent word back to Nicholas of the desperate need for new soldiers the people had already grown tired of the Crusades and were well aware of the corrupt motives behind the papacy's request. As a result only a few hundred soldiers sailed for Acre. Ironically, most of the help came from James II of Sicily with whom the pope was at war. However, when the mercenaries arrived they found the money promised them was not sufficient. They went on a rampage and killed every Muslim they could find, identifying them by their beards and dress. Many Christians (those who wore beards) were also slain.

Egypt, which had tolerated the presence of Acre in exchange for peace in Egypt, was outraged and demanded the perpetrators be handed over for execution. Acre tried to appease Egypt but after much bickering they did nothing. A few months later an army of 200,000 Muslims from Egypt arrived outside the gates of Acre. Within a little more than a month Acre fell. Some of the Muslims raped both women and children, but all the Muslims slaughtered the inhabitants of Acre. The Catholics knew they could do nothing but fight to death for the Muslims were not taking prisoners. Acre fell on May 18, 1291.

Nicholas could little to stir up the passions of the people when news arrived of Acre's fall. The Crusades were for all intensive purposes over. Nicholas had to be content with ruling Europe. He sent out missionaries to Kubla Khan of the Mongol China who was even then consorting with a young Marco Polo. Nicholas also began to resume the discussions for Rudolf's coronation. The long delayed coronation had often been because of the death of a pope but this time it was the death of Rudolf which was to insure the coronation never occurred. He died on July 15, 1291. Less than a year later Nicholas IV followed him to grave.

The Ascension of Adolf of Nassau

Rudolf had a been a good emperor but not a strong one. The Princes of Germany preferred it this way. They still did not desire a strong emperor and they feared what might happen if the office became hereditary so they opposed the election of Rudolf's heir, Albert. They agreed that they should not elect one of their own rank for fear of creating more strife. The result was similar to the events that led to the double election of Richard and Alfonso.

Adolf, the Count of Nassau, was a vassal of the King of Bohemia. Considering that Rudolf had gone to war to oust Otokar of Bohemia one might have assumed that the electors would have thought better of nominating one of Bohemia's vassals but Adolf offered the electors many possessions and rights that they could not refuse. He was elected "king of the Romans" and emperor designate in May 1292. Within a few years the electors would regret their decision.

The "Angel Pope" and the Devil

After the death of Nicholas IV there was a vacancy in the papacy of over two years. The Orsini family wanted to regain control of the papacy but the Colonna family did not wish to loose the control they had under Nicholas. A stalemate was reached which dragged on years. A third party which entered into the fray was certain Benedict Gaetani (also known as Caetani). He was a corrupt man who not only slept with a mistress but with her daughter as well. He desired the tiara but was much disliked for his arrogance. For all his arrogance and for all the enemies he had made, he did have one decided advantage. He was shrewd and cunning. Realizing that he could not be elected, he moved to the shadows. Historians debate on what role Gaetani, later known as Boniface VIII, really had in the events to come but he was certainly the beneficiary.

After two years of bickering a hermit, named Peter (or Pierre) of Morone, is said to have sent a letter to the Cardinals. The hermit had a reputation as an ascetic, a miraculous healer, and a prophet. Like many hermits, in his day, and generations before him, he had the aura of a John the Baptist. Like the popular vision of John he was scraggly little man whose devotion to God was doubted by none. He resided in a cell he had made in a cave atop a mountain. He was the anti–thesis of the papacy of years past; humble and poor. He had no possessions, was uneducated, naïve in the ways of the world, and had not bathed in years. The letter is said to have read that the Church was without its leader and that if the Cardinals did not elect one soon God's wrath would fall upon them. The letter was received by Benedict Gaetani.

The Cardinals now changed their plans. For years the corruption of the papacy had been so apparent that the common man had long dreamed that an "angel pope" would one day arise and restore the papacy to the apostolic days. Here was as a "prophet" and hermit who beckoned the Church back to those days. They unanimously elected Peter, although he did not ask for it.

Peter was a unique figure. He was member of the Franciscan "Spirituals," who were later persecuted as heretics for their rejection of the Inquisition and their allegiance to Joachim of Fiore. They were not really forerunners of the Reformation but they were strongly ascetic and harkened back to the days of the Church in poverty. They resisted many of the changes that occurred in the Church and broke away from the main stream Franciscans, who were by now the leaders of the Inquisition along with the Dominicans. In some ways Peter looked like an "angel pope." He refused to ride into Rome adorned like a prince but instead rode around on a donkey like Jesus. Unfortunately, for all his virtues he was uneducated, naïve, and gullible. He was already over eighty years old and may well have suffered from Alzheimers. He often made several appointments to the same office, having forgotten that the office had been filled by him days earlier. He was also easy to manipulate.

He took the name Celestine V in July 1294, but the control his advisors exercised over him was evident immediately. He moved to Naples where Charles II resided and his decisions were manipulated in most every way by that king. A treaty had been reached with James II of Aragon and Sicily who agreed to relinquish Sicily, but his brother, Frederick, had been acting as regent and refused to leave. Instead, he was proclaimed king and hailed by the Sicilians as the "new Frederick."

He had, at Charles' request, agreed to reinstate the age old edict which allowed kings to reside over, or "protect," the election process of a new pope. In fact, the new pope did little himself. He had Gaetani and others to run the daily offices of the pope while he retired to his cell to practice his ascetic lifestyle. The only acts he did of his own accord involved giving away the riches of the Church to poor, which angered the Cardinals to no end. It was at this time that he began to regret ever having taken the office at all. He is said to have proclaimed, "O God, while I rule over other men's souls, I am losing the salvation of my own." Indeed, he came to believe that demons had a role in his election and feared for his very soul. Voices were said to call out to him beseeching him to resign his office. It was Gaetani who advised Celestine that it was proper to step down and voluntarily abdicate his throne.

On December 13, 1294 Celestine became the first pope to voluntarily abdicate the throne. His reasons were outlined as follows; "of his humbleness, the quest of a better life and an easy conscience, on account of his frailty of body and want of knowledge, the badness of men, and a desire to return to the quietness of his former state." Within two weeks time Gaetani was the new pope under the name Boniface VIII, but as for Celestine, he never attained his dream of returning to his former estate. Boniface could not allow Celestine to roam around freely so Celestine was confined to cell and kept under guard.

Some historians maintain that he was not treated poorly but that he tried to escape once only to be captured cannot be denied. Moreover, he died two years later, most say by starvation. To his successor Boniface, Celestine is said to have utter this prophecy; "you leaped on the throne like a fox, you will reign like a lion, and you will die like a dog."

Summary

With Innocent III the papacy had reached its height of power and the imperial office was forever damaged. The decline of the imperial dignity took nearly half a century. The decline of the papal office would not take nearly as long. On the heels of Innocent's victory Boniface VIII arose, at one time claiming to be both emperor and pope. The fact is that the people, however, apathetic they might be, were never led around on a leash as often depicted by film makers and others. The people came to despise the papacy more and more. The rise of Boniface signaled the beginning of the decline of the papacy.

Rudolf's reign brought a semblance of sanity back to Germany but there was not even a glimmer of restoring the emperor's office to the ancient "universal sovereign." He remained a sovereign in name, and the other king's of Europe paid him homage but they did as they pleased. The "emperors of Rome" were hereafter largely German kings with vassals among the weaker states. The kings of Bohemia, Hungary, Poland, and other states continued to bow to him while the kings of France and England sometimes sought to usurp the dignity for themselves. Throughout these coming times the office of the emperor was never forgotten, but it was but a fading shadow of its former glory. The real power resided in the papacy which even now was beginning to crumble.

Perhaps Celestine was a prophetic image of the Church itself. He was proof that the Church was not ready to return to apostolic poverty or surrender its power. The corrupt now ruled in place of the righteous and there was no one who could reform it. That would one day be the lesson of the Reformation; if the Church could not be reformed, it must be abandoned.

Although Bonfice still lived in when Dante wrote, he reserved a place in Hell in Canto 19

Gustave Dore – Dante's Inferno Canto 19 (Boniface's place in Hell Reserved) – 19th Century

18

The Reign of Pope Boniface

Boniface VIII was the most arrogant of all the popes. It said of Boniface, "he was admired my many, feared by all, and loved by none." Even in his daily life he was demeaning to all around him, once denying an office to man because he thought he was too ugly. Boniface made no attempt to make men like him for he believed he was above that. He did not attempt to hide his love affairs and reveled in making snide remarks.

So hated was he that centuries later a certain Fancois du Jon would reinterpreted Joachim's belief that the anti–Christ would rise in the 1260. He argued that Christ was crucified in 34 A.D. and, therefore, the anti–Christ had risen to power 1260 years after that. This would be the year 1294; the year that Boniface took office.

Boniface was like Gregory VII and Innocent III in his presumptions of power, but he was unlike in them in that it would be he who would, symbolically speaking, bow before the King of France, even as Henry IV once bowed before Gregory VII. Gregory had humbled an emperor. Philip the Fair would humble a pope. With Boniface came disgrace upon the papacy. It was a disgrace that would never die. As Dante, who lived in his day, said, he turned the Vatican into a sewer.

Boniface VIII Receives His Crown

Celestine V had ridden into Rome on a donkey. Boniface rode into Rome one a white horse in full dress and regalia escorted by the kings of Naples and Hungary. At the ceremonies a terrible storm erupted and the wind put out all the candles in the Church. This was believed by some to be a terrible omen of what was to come. The people of Rome already knew the real Boniface and when false rumors spread that he died a few days later sporatic celebrations erupted. When it was learned he had not died, the papal physician was then called "the second most hated man in Rome."

No sooner was Boniface been crowned then he annulled all the privileges that Celestine had granted. He awarded many church offices to relatives and deprived the Colonna family of many of their offices and titles. He also received news that Celestine V had escaped his place of retirement. Soldiers were sent out to quickly retrieve the former pope and a careful guard was placed over him to insure that he did not again leave the tower of Fumone where he was held until his death.

Philip and Boniface Collide

While Edward Longshanks was attempting to gain autonomous control over the English fiefs of Wales and Scotland, Philip the Fair decided he wanted autonomous control over the French fief of Glascony, which happened to be ruled by Edward. The fight, of course, went back centuries. Having been conquered by a French vassal, William the Conqueror, the English kings had claimed William's inheritance in both England and France. At one time England had ruled more than half of modern day France, but Philip Augustus reclaimed much of the land and Saint Louis IX arranged a truce which would deliver all of former France to the French King save Glascony which would belong to the English king on the sole grounds that it remain a French fief and that the King of England pay due homage to the French king for this fief. As the treaty declared, Edward Longshanks had fulfilled this obligation when he ascended the throne and paid homage to Philip the Fair. Now Philip wanted Glascony back in his sole possession. War was the obvious result.

Edward turned to the emperor Adolf for help. In exchange for 10,000 pounds of sterling Adolf agreed to ally himself with Edward against Philip. Having heard of Adolf's alliance with Edward Philip might have feared that the emperor would actually keep his word and invade France. He needed money to pay his troops and build arms and he needed them fast. In a feudal society, however, private entrepreneurs were few and far between. The commoner had little to tax and even stiff taxes furnished little to the king in times of war. Much of Philip's career, and particularly his conflict with the papacy, involved dubious ways of raising money. The first of these methods was simply to tax the institution which had much money; the Church. The clergy bitterly complained to the pope of this new taxation.

Boniface was quick to respond. In February 1296, he issued the papal bull *Clericas Laicos* which reaffirmed that taxation of the clergy was forbidden without papal consent. The bull, however, was done with the typical Boniface flare. It was held by the king to be presumptuous and arrogant in its assertations. It opened with the statement that the laity has always been hostile to the clergy and asserted clearly that the state was subject to the pope in everything. Moreover, it declared an automatic excommunication to any king who did levy such taxes. Philip the Fair responded by prohibiting the export of all goods and outlawing the presence of foreigners in France. This meant that trade with Rome was abolished, cutting away at the pope's finances, and that the clergy, who were mostly foreigners, were to be expelled. The measure was not technically an attack on the papacy and Philip did not openly refuse to obey the pope's bull but the actual message was clear. If the pope does not let Philip tax the clergy then the pope will loose much of his revenues and much of the clergy would be expelled from France.

Had Boniface been faced only with reduced revenues and the bitter conflict with Philip he might not have backed down, but when the Colonnas family of Rome began to stir up dissension Boniface had little choice but to back down. The Colonnas had suffered at the hands of Boniface who was rapidly replacing Colonna family members with his own family members and degrading the family publicly. Moreover, the death of Celestine V was considered suspicious by many people. The Colonnas family implied that Boniface had Celestine killed by driving a nail through his head while others suggest that Celestine starved to death. In either case, Boniface had too many troubles at home to become embroiled in a protracted conflict with France. He was obliged to write reconciliatory letters to Philip. Philip, however, was but a teenager at the time and was almost as arrogant as Boniface. It is natural that the two came into conflict, even when Boniface was forced to back down. He tried to appease Philip by stating that the clergy might voluntarily donate money to held Philip's cause, but could not be taxed. In almost every case Boniface offended Philip with his attitude and flair for supremacy, even while trying to appease the king. The conflict was eventually resolved when Boniface canonized Saint Louis IX, Philip's grandfather, and permitted the taxes, but the fumes were to burn for some time.

The Colonnas Revolt

The Colonna family's dispute with Boniface erupted into a full scale revolt when they raided a papal convoy carrying treasure in May 1297. The revolt forced Boniface to settle matters with France and concentrate on eliminating his political enemies in Rome. He excommunicated all the Colonna, deposing two Cardinals who were members of the Colonna family, and calling for a Crusade against the family.

The family responded by asking for a council to investigate the death of Celestine. They then made a quick retreat to their fortresses and castles, well aware that the papal army was ready to march. The army was led by Charles of Valois, Philip the Fair's brother. Nevertheless, Philip refused to loan 100,000 pounds to his brother for the venture, since Boniface had been so reluctant to give money for his war against Edward. Regardless, the money was not needed. Their strongholds fell one by one over a year's time. At Palestrina the two Colonna Cardinals were besieged. When they realized that they could not hold out against the papal army they threw themselves on Boniface's mercy. They emerged from the city walls and prostrated themselves before the pope. Boniface stripped them of their titles and their estates which were given to the Orsini family. The two cardinals, however, escaped to France where they were protected in Philip's court.

Of more importance to Boniface was his complete humiliation of the Colonnas by the complete destruction of their last place of refuge. Nevertheless, the two cardinals escaped the fate of their city and its remaining populous. The city was leveled save the cathedral. Six thousand were reported slain in the walls of the city and the great monuments of history were destroyed. The city once held the house of Julius Caesar and a palace with a grand mosaic dedicated to the Virgin Mary. Neither were spared. The Colonnas family had been humbled by Boniface at a terrible price.

An Imperial Schism

No sooner had the German electors elected Adolf king of the Romans than they found that Adolf was more interested in money and power than anything else. Although he had allied himself with Edward Longshanks against Philip the Fair he did not keep his promises. No sooner did he receive the money than he spent it at war against the heirs of the former emperor Rudolf. Moreover, he entered into negotiations with Philip the Fair promising to ally himself against England if Philip would pay large sums of money. Soon even the king of Bohemia had abandoned him and was ready to accept Albert, the heir of Rudolf.

In 1298, the electors called a council which Adolf was ordered to appear before. He was to give an account of his actions since becoming emperor. When he failed to appear at the council, Duke Albert of Austria, member of the Hapburgs family and son of the emperor Rudolf, was proclaimed king and Adolf was deposed on June 23, 1298. The decision did not sit well with Boniface who declared that only a pope could depose an emperor. He backed Adolf who finally appeared, but with an army at his side. Albert has also had enough foresight to bring his own army and, on July 2, a battle raged at Gollheim in which Adolf was slain. Albert was crowned king of the Romans in August that year.

Despite the victory for Albert his recognition for emperor would not come for years. Boniface refused to recognize Albert's legitimacy, calling him a usurper. Philip, who had earlier been refused the Imperial throne, would have liked for Boniface to make him emperor but the pope's animosity had not subsided. He refused to set up Philip as a rival, preferring another candidate; *himself*. Boniface did not immediately pronounce this, for he had too many enemies at present, but there seems little doubt that Boniface was already planning his own self–coronation.

The Year of Jubilee

With the destruction of Palestrina, the subjugation of the Colonnas, and temporary peace with Philip, Boniface believed he was at last at the peak of his power. Indeed, he was. He declared a grand celebration called the year of Jubilee. His bull declared that any and all, save the Colonnas and a few enemies, would be given plenary indulgences for their pilgrimage to Rome. Thus all who came to Rome for the celebration of Jubilee would receive the remission of sins without so much as needing to embark on a Crusade and slay "heretics."

The celebration was a protracted event which brought great wealth to the city. It is said that there were over 200,000 pilgrims in Rome with 30,000 new ones daily replacing the departing ones. According to contemporary historians, clerics had to stand by the altar of St. Peter's day and night gathering up offerings with a rake. The grand celebration was also a chance for Boniface to make his most arrogant of presumptions.

Among the pilgrims to Rome during the year of Jubilee were envoys from the emperor designate Albert, king of the Romans. The envoys were greeted by the pope dressed in full imperial regalia. He told the envoys simply, "I am pontiff, I am emperor." The message was clear and repeated, "*I*, I am the emperor." Later he held a procession through the streets of Rome dressed in imperial garb with heralds declaring, "I am Caesar! I am the emperor!" Albert made no response to this claim and the kings of Europe seemed to largely ignore it. Boniface had no respect among royalty and most looked upon his wild pretensions as the ramblings of a madman. Boniface would hold this pretension until 1303 when he was forced to recognize Albert in a futile attempt to save his own papacy against the wrath of Philip the Fair. It would, in fact, be too little, too late.

Marco Polo

It is necessary to pause from the story of Boniface and his royal enemies to make mention of another event which occurred at this time. Marco Polo, having recently returned from his journey's in China and the east, was imprisoned by the Genoese, who were rivals of the Polo family. There, in prison, he dictated his story which soon draw the attention of the world at large.

It might perhaps seem out of place to discuss a mere traveller in the history of the Holy Roman Empire, but there can be no doubt that the meeting of the far east and the west had a profound impact upon the course of history. Not only did it bring gunpowder and other technical achievements, but more importantly it stirred the imaginations of the people to a world far beyond their own. One might say that the unexplored world of the east was the science fiction of the Middle Ages. The "final frontier" of *Star Trek* was merely an attempt to displace the mysteries that men once imagined might have existed on the earth in some unexplored region. It was one reason for the famous journey of Columbus, but it was Marco Polo who first stirred that imagination.

More than a half century earlier Genghis Khan and his hoards swept out of Mongolia conquering China and sweeping westward to the Adriadic. Upon Genghis Khan's death the vast empire was divided among his heirs, at least one of whom had become a convert to Christianity. Other Mongol leaders were interested in Christianity, more because the Christians were the enemies of the Muslims than for love of Christ. The Mongols had often sent emmisaries to the Latin and Greeks seeking alliances. It was for this reason that contact with the east first became important to the Holy Roman Empire. Dreams of reconquering the Holy Land were fading as the Latin States were crumbling, but the appearance of Asians in the courts of European kings and princes stirred the imagination of at least a few.

Marco Polo's father had been an ambassador and traveled to the east. There he had met with the new Mongol Emperor of China, Kublai Khan. In 1271 he departed for a second time, this time taking his young son, Marco. There he spent nearly twenty–five years in China serving in various capacities in the court of Kublai Khan. When his story was penned in 1295–1296 it was seen as a grand epic romance. It has been compared to the Arthurian legends, and indeed, this is how it was received by many who doubted its accuracy. It sparked the imagination of what lay beyond the bounds of the then known world. When Marco Polo was asked on his deathbed to retract what he said, Marco replied that he had told only half of what he saw.

The War Erupts Afresh

At the height of his power Boniface again attempted to reassert his power over the kings of the earth. In England he challenged Edward's right to rule over Scotland, with which he was at war, declaring that Scotland was a papal fief and had been since ancient antiquity; a questionable statement. The English parliament responded by informing the pope that the king had no obligation to heed the papal see in matters of temporal authority. The statement was a clear reaction against the days of Gregory VII and Innocent III wherein such authority was held to exist at the mere pleasure of the pope. Of course, Gregory VII and Innocent III were wiser than Boniface, and Boniface did not press the issue. Indeed, he could not, for Philip was about to lay his hands upon the ancient frontiers once claimed by the emperor alone.

In 1301 Philip become embroiled in a dispute with a French Bishop named Bernard Saisset. He had the bishop brought up on charges, which many believed were false. He was tried and imprisoned. He then asked, or ordered, the pope to degrade the bishop. Boniface was outraged. For many years the clergy was not to be tried by secular courts, let alone to be defrocked by an ambitious king. Boniface is said not to have bothered examining the case when he condemned the trial and those responsible. The response of the king was staggering. A document was circulated declaring that the king should expand his frontiers to Rome and denied the papacy any and all secular power. If the Church had gone too far in declaring secular power, Philip now went too far in interfering in Church affairs. He seized Church property, yet still sent legates to

Rome to ask for money toward a Crusade. When the legate arrived with a negative answer, Philip had the legate arrested and tried as a traitor.

In reaction to these extreme measures by Philip, Boniface issued a bull in December calling for a council to be held in Rome in which the king and his advisors were called to present an account of their actions. The bull brazenly asserted the authority of the Church over the kings and princes of the earth. When the bull arrived in France, a forgery was made which exaggerated the claims of Boniface, thus making it sound far more audacious. The bull then evoked the sympathy for the king and was thrown into a fire by the king's chief advisor, whom many believe forged the document. Philip then called French parliament and other representatives to convene a council of their own which asserted that the French crown had no allegiance to the Church. In a letter to the pope, Philip begins by addressing the pope as "your infatuated Majesty."

It was to be tit for tat and Boniface was not willing to let Philip be more arrogant than himself so he called a council of his own, which convened on Halloween day, 1302. The result of the council was a bull entitled *Unam Sanctum*. This bull is one of the most infamous bulls of history despite the fact that it presented nothing new. Everything that was presented in the bull had been proclaimed before, but never so blatantly. In years past, the blasphemous assumptions were disguised in a barrage of theological streams of thoughts. E.g. "the vicar of Christ represents Christ, the Church is the spiritual authority, therefore submission to the pope and the Church is essential since submission to Christ is required for salvation." Boniface did not attempt to water down the underlying doctrine. He states flat out in the last lines of the bull, "every human creature is subject to the Roman pontiff – this we declare, say, define, and pronounce to be altogether necessary to salvation." Thus, for the first time the Church *clearly*, formally, and brazenly declared that *no one* can be saved without blind submission to the pope.

Again, it must be asserted that this was not a new teaching. It had been taught by Innocent III who declared that every cleric must obey the pope "even if what he commands is evil," but his statements were directed at the clergy and never formalized in a bull. Now, in formal writing, was a document that could be held before an uneducated general public. It quickly became the most widely known and derided bull in medieval history. The legates who carried the bull were arrested by Philip and imprisoned. Furthermore, at his own council he ordered that Boniface be called into account by a general council. Among the charges leveled against Boniface were sexual immorality, simony, heresy, sorcery, incest, and the murder of his predecessor. The battle lines were clearly drawn.

Boniface was now faced with a difficult decision. His words would clearly not alone prevail against Philip. Philip would not back down easily. Boniface was faced with admitting that he could not be both emperor and pope. He needed an ally who could command an army, and that ally would have to be the emperor designate, Albert. To this end Boniface was now willing to recognize Albert as emperor and coronate him if he would come to his aid. On April 30, 1303 Albert made an oath of allegiance to the pope and promised that none of his sons would be elected king without papal consent. In essence he acknowledged that the papacy was supreme over the emperor and that the office of the emperor existed at the will of the pope. He had earned his crown, but at the expense of the imperial office.

Despite the emperor's humbling, it was a hollow victory. Albert was to be emperor but Boniface was to loose his throne. The emperor was of no help to Boniface when one of the most notorious acts of medieval history unfolded in September of that same year.

The Assault of Anagni

Boniface was prepared to formally announce the excommunication of Philip and his colleagues. He personally, as vicar of Christ, would damn Philip's eternal soul. Far from the simple punishment that shunned an unrepentant sinner (as was once leveled against the great Theodosius) excommunication now meant nothing less than eternal damnation. Ambrose and the ancients would never have envisioned such a thing, but neither would they have envisioned why the excommunication would never occur.

Boniface was at his retreat in Anagni when terror besieged the city. Philip's advisor, William of Nogaret, had devised a plot, with Philip's approval, to capture the pope and forcibly bring him before a Church council to be deposed. On September 7, 1303 mercenaries appeared before the walls of the city led by William of Nogaret. The estimated number of troops varies from five hundred to as many as two thousand; mostly horsemen and calvary. The gates of the city were treacherously opened by the pope's own captain of the guard and the onslaught began.

The soldiers poured through the streets and sacked the palaces. They were joined by the Colonnas family who had suffered so much at the pope's hands and Sciarra Colonna himself struck down the archbishop of the city. The blood of many, civilian and clergy, were spilled when Sciarra appeared before Boniface's palace with the demands of Philip. Surrender, restore the dignity of the Colonna family, and resign his office. Boniface looked down upon his enemies and refused. The storming of the papal palace began almost immediately. Soldiers broke in and offered the lives of any who would tell them where the pope was hiding. Resistance was relatively meek for the soldiers far outnumbered Boniface's guards. Nevertheless, blood stained the floors of the palace when Sciarra broke into the audience chamber. There he was greeted by the pope, dressed in full regalia sitting arrogantly upon his throne. Boniface may have gambled that they would not dare to kill a pope, or he may have been truly willing to die as he professed. In either case, he defied them even as they stood before with swords drawn.

Sciarra demanded his resignation but Boniface refused. Sciarra was ready to strike the head of the pontiff when Nogaret entered the court and intervened. He told Sciarra that Boniface must be brought back alive to Philip to stand trial before the council. Sciarra was forced to back down. Instead, he sacked the papal palace and the goods and treasures it housed were either destroyed or carried away as booty. Symbolic of the event was the image of an overturned and broken urn which allegedly contained the milk of the Virgin Mary. Blood stained the floors of the papal sanctuary along with the "milk" of the Virgin.

The Death of Boniface VIII

The image of a pope being taken by force of arms stirred even the apathetic members of Anagni. The Orisini family had no great love for Boniface but they had no desire to see what might befall the city that allowed such a tragedy to occur. Many of the mercenaries in Nogaret's service had already left with their booty and the denizens of Anagni had suffered much at their hands. Now it was their turn to rise up. Three days after the sack of their city they attacked the remaining soldiers. The soldiers were driven from the city and pontiff was physically rescued, but it was too late to rescue his spirit. Boniface was a broken man.

Whatever happened to him over the few days that he spent imprisoned, it had broken his will. The once arrogant pope who stood before armed soldiers willing to die was now said to beat his head against the wall and chew on his arm like a dog. He died a month later from injuries the he had received. As the prophecy of Celestine said, he leaped on the throne like a fox, he reigned like a lion, and he died like a dog.

Summary of Boniface's Reign

Even as a storm had raged at the coronation of Boniface, a storm raged at his funeral. The storms were prophetic for his reign was like a storm which and left destruction in its wake. In many ways Boniface was an unimportant pope. He brought nothing new to the papacy and was really more corrupt and power hungry than many before him but his reign marked, both symbolically and literally, a Rubicon in the history of the Middle Ages.

Even as the popes had humbled the emperors, the popes had now been humbled by a king. They were soon to come under the dominion and control of the French. The emperors had taken five hundred years to fall from prominence; the papacy but a hundred. It was now the kings of Europe themselves who held the supreme power, but it was a power they could not wield without destroying the unity of the Holy Roman Empire, and the continent it embraced. To be sure, they tried to maintain this unity, but their rejection of both emperor and pope would further cause the empire to crumble. It could not long endure as a divided kingdom, nominally held together by two powers that the kings cared nothing for at all.

Philip had sought to become emperor. He could not claim the title so he claimed the power thereof. With him the papacy was to be subjected but it was with him that the fall of the Holy Roman Empire began to come to fruition. The seeds had been planted with the division of the empire, with the humbling of Henry by the papacy, and many other factors too numerous to be listed, but in his own arrogance Philip had begun the disintegration of the only force that could hold Europe together. For better or worse, the corrupted Church was all that kept Europe united. With its further degradation over the years to come, the call for Reformation would signal the end of the empire as a unifying force and the rise of the modern age.

Holy Roman Emperor	*Rival (if any)*	Pope	*AntiPope (if any)*

– Means the pope ruled from Avignon

——————— 1272 ———————

——————— 1280 ———————

Martin IV

Rudolf

——————— 1285 ———————

Honorius IV

——————— 1287 ———————

Nicholas IV

——————— 1291 ———————
——————— 1292 ———————

——————— 1292 ———————
——————— 1294 ———————

Adolf

Celestine V

——————— 1294 ———————

——————— 1298 ———————

Boniface VIII

Albert

——————— 1303 ———————

Benedict XI

——————— 1304 ———————

——————— 1308 ———————

Henry VII

Clement V*

——————— 1313 ———————

——————— 1314 ———————
——————— 1316 ———————

John XXII*   *−1328 −*

Louis the Bavarian   *Nicholas (V)*
    −1330 −

——————— 1334 ———————

Benedict XII*

——————— 1342 ———————

——————— 1347 ———————   Clement VI*

——————— 1352 ———————

Charles IV   Innocent VI*

——————— 1362 ———————

Jaques de Molay, Master of the Templar Knights, is burned at the stake (pp. 317–321)

Unknown artist – A Depiction of the Execution of Jacques du Molay – 19th Century

19

—

Philip, the Would–be Emperor

Philip had long dreamt of becoming the emperor, but his emnity with Boniface ensured that he would not be nominated, and the electorate was now controlled by German princes who did not desire a strong king; and Philip was a strong king, if not a good one.

Philip had to be content with being the most powerful king of Europe, but he still wanted more. He wanted money to finance his campaigns, and if he could not be emperor, then he would be the next best thing. He would control the most powerful office in the whole of the empire; the papacy itself. Philip is greatly respected by many historians, and by the French, but his legacy is not a good one. Nothing he did would ultimately benefit the empire or the church. He would drive the Jews from France, destroy the once great Knights Templar, and make the papacy his personal puppet. He only real legacy was to make France a power player in Europe, but it is the end to which that power was used that marks Philip. Some believe he was a devout Catholic, but if he was, then he was of the same "devotion" as Gregory VII. He was arrogant, self–righteous, and believed that the end justified the means.

Pope Benedict XI

Even the death of Boniface did not satiate Philip. He continued to demand that Boniface be put on trial, echoing back to the Cadaver Synod. He was supported by the Franciscan Spirituals, as well as a number of Cardinals. The new pope, Benedict XI, was not about to let the memory of Anagni be forgotten. Benedict did not, however, want to antagonize Philip too much. Much of his wrath was spent on the Franciscan Spirituals, who hearkened the Church back to a more pure and noble day. He even had Arnold of Villanova, a leading Franciscan Spiritual and physician to Boniface, imprisoned without trial.

In regard to Philip, Benedict was more political. He delayed as much as possible, but in March, 1304, Philip's envoys arrived offering to "accept" any absolution that the pope might infer upon Philip and his men. The statement is intriguing and shows Philip's arrogance, even at this time. Nevertheless, Benedict complied and absolved Philip of misdoing. A month later, he agreed to pardon all who were involved in Anagni, save Nogaret himself. Despite this, Benedict later called Nogaret and all his accomplices (whom he had just pardoned) to appear before him on pain of excommunication to answer charges for the atrocities of Anagni. This edict was sent out on June 7, and the trial was set for June 29, but the pope fell violently ill and was unable to carry out his threat. He lingered on for a month, and died on July 7, 1304.

The official cause of death was acute dysentery. Certainly this was not uncommon in the unclean Middle Ages, but the pope lived like a king and was not confined to a dungeon, nor trapped in a beseiged city with the dead. Rumor spread that poison was placed in his figs, which he snacked upon daily. Given the nature of dysentery (a form of severe diarrhea), this is almost certainly the case. The main suspect was obviously one of King Philip's sympathizers. The next pope would not be elected for nearly a year, so no cardinal was in a position to believe himself the immediate beneficiary of Benedict's death. Philip, however, would gain nothing more than the papacy itself.

The Church in Exile

It would be eleven months before a new pope was selected. Their eventual choice is ironic, to say the least. The French party desired another French pope, while the Bonificians desired a pope who would avenge the atrocities at Anagni. Eventually, the Bonificians were split, with a number willing to comprimise on a French candidate whom they believed would be sympathetic to Boniface. What they got was the first of many papal puppets who never set foot in Rome.

The term "Babylonian Exile" is used to refer to the time when the papacy dwelt in Avignon. The Biblical allusion is to the time when the Jews were exiled in Babylon, away from their beloved Jerusalem. Clement V never crossed the Alps. The beloved city of Rome was abandoned by the papacy for the next seventy years (ironically the same amount of the time the Jews spent in exile). Clement eventually settled on Avignon, at the southern end of France, as the new papal seat of power. When the people challenged Clement, he responded, "where the pope is, there is Rome."

The reasons for his move to France are given out of his own mouth. He said that he feared "to cause pain to our dear son, the King of France." Even the coronation of Clement was said to have sent a terrible omen to the years to come, for a wall fell, killing twelve men including a brother of the king, and a brother of the pope.

No sooner had Clement took office than he wrote bulls absolving the King of France from crusade vows, any obligation to return moneys stolen from the church, and sanctioning the Flemish who were now in rebellion against Philip. Philip finally had his puppet.

Edward Longshanks and Philip

The Flemish uprising had reopened the wounds that Philip had thought he had closed years before in the Angevin possessions of France. Edward

Longshanks of England and Philip had been at war for many years over the disputed Angevin territories. In 1303, however, Philip gave his daughter Isabella to be betrothed to Edward II, heir to the throne of England. This was a welcome truce for Edward and Philip both. Philip wanted to concentrate on the Boniface affair, while Edward wished to divert his troops northward to the disobedient Scots. Neither side had made much headway in the Angevin lands, so the betrothal was agreed upon and Edward turned his attentions to William Wallace.

After the death of the last of the loyal Scottish rulers, Edward had decided to rule Scotland directly. The Scots, however, were unwilling to accept a puppet king, especially given Edward's reputation for cruelty. William Wallace had led the revolt, but in 1304, he was betrayed by Robert the Bruce, and defeated. He went into hiding but was found in near Glasgow in August 1305. From there he was taken to trial where he was disemboweled, quartered, and beheaded. The barbaric act did little to gain the sympathy of the Scots, and in in 1306 Robert the Bruce himself rebelled, seeking the Scottish crown for himself.

Most of the fighting was, at this time, within Scotland, and against Scottish rivals. The family of John Comyn was pitted against Robert's. By 1307, however, John Comyn's family was defeated. That same year Edward Longshanks was en route to Scotland, to crush Robert, when he died. Edward II was unable to carry his father's mantle. In fact, his barons so despised him that much of Edward's reign was spent trying to regain control of England, let along Scotland. Edward had given the earldom of Cornwall to Piers Gaveston, whom the barons believed was Edward's homosexual lover. They demanded he be removed, and murdered him years later. Edward II was to rule for twenty years, but it was not to be an effective reign, and the husband of Philip's daughter is said to have shunned her for the company of men. Nonetheless, Philip had greater concerns.

The Destruction of the Templars

It is said that even before Clement's coronation, Philip demanded that Clement give in to the plans he had developed against the Templar Knights. These events are among the notorious and mysterious of history. Legends have arisen to explain the king's obssession, but most scholars believe that the true motive behind these events was nothing more than the thirst of money.

Philip was financially in great debt. He had spent money for dowries, for his war efforts, and for his own luxuries, and he was said to owe many hundreds of thousands of pounds to French banks. Philip needed money and was not above deceit, or even murder, to get his wishes. Most of the bankers he was indebted to were either Jewish or Templars. In 1306 Philip expelled all Jews from France and seized their assets, and money, for himself. Jews were driven out of the country, even had been done by Edward Longshanks a few years earlier.

In 1305, Queen Joan, Philip's devout wife, had died. Philip is said to have been so heartbroken that he once considered abdicating his throne and spending the rest of his life trying to reclaim the Holy Land, but whatever repentance he briefly had from the remorse over his wife was not to last. It was this same year that he first began to press against the Templars.

The Templars were the richest of the Crusader Knights. They took their name from the Temple of Solomon. Their rites and rituals are still seen to some extent in Masonic lodges (even their symbol is of the instruments that Solomon used to build the Temple). Such rituals included what is called "mystery" rites. In these rites, initiates learn new "secrets" as they gain rank in the order. Low order initiates know only the basic tenets of the order, but the higher ranks allegedly learn new rites and secrets. According to Philip's preposterous accusations, these rites included such acts as worshipping the idol Bafomet (which was connected to the Muslim religion), Satan worship, sex with demons, sodomy, and kissing other knights on the navel. A total of a hundred and twenty–seven charges were made.

Despite these accusations (and perhaps because of them, for they seem extreme in any age), Clement resisted Philip's push to eradicate the Templars. Instead, he placated Philip by revoking Boniface's infamous bulls, *Clericas Laicos* and *Unan Sanctum*. Nevertheless, in 1307 Philip's confessor, and a papal inquisitor, began to arrest Templar Knights and extract confessions through the use of torture. The terror began on October 13. The victims were all Templars, even down to the master of the order itself, Jacques de Molay. After "confessing" due to torture, the charges and confessions were again presented to Clement. Among the less absurd charges was the accusation that the order granted absolution for sins; something which the popes now claimed for themselves, and denied to all others. In 1308 Clement then gave in to Philip and ordered the prosecution of all Templar knights wherever they might be found. Clement ordered their prosecution throughout the empire. Some countries were more obliging than others. Spain, Portugal, Italy, and even Germany were lackluster in their zeal to eradicate the knights. Trials were held, but many were found innocent and released. In England, Edward II reminded Clement that torture had never been legally enacted in Britain. Clement then demanded it be enacted and Edward II quickly caved in. The pope's papal inquisitors appeared in England to teach the art of torture and the Templar families and houses were eliminated from the island.

Many knights died under torture, fifty four were burned at the stake in a single day in Paris, and hundreds more died in prison. In 1312, a council was called at Vienna to settle the Templar issue. The majority on the council wanted to grant new trials to the Templars, citing the fact that torture had extracted false confessions. Clement, however, was now Philip's puppet. Using his "apostolic" power, he overruled the council and ordered the abolishment of the Templar order on March 22. The property of the Templars was officially bequeathed by the pope to the Knights of St. John, but Philip nevertheless seized 260,000 pounds as "reimbursement" for the cost of the trials.

Imperial Hopes

Before the destruction of the Templars was complete, Philip again set his eyes on the Imperial diadem. He knew that he could not get enough support to win the crown himself, but he hoped to make the emperor his puppet, even as he had made of the pope. In 1308, Philip denounced Emperor Albert, saying that he had taken a "vassal's vow" to Boniface (thus defacing the Imperial throne), despite the fact that Albert had entered into an alliance with Philip against Boniface in 1299. That alliance, however, was broken when Albert accepted the diadem from Boniface in exchange for an oath of obedience. The two soon became bitter enemies, and shortly after Philip's denunciations, Albert was assassinated by his nephew, John of Swabia, who is now known to history as the "Parricide."

Philip immediately put forth his brother, Charles of Valois, as the emperor nominee. However, the German princes were by no means eager to have a member of Philip's family on the throne. As a compromise the Archbishop of Trier, Baldwin, nominated Henry of Luxemburg, a vassal of Philip.

The election of Henry VII was acceptable to Philip. Although he did not gain the control he had desired, a Frenchman, and his vassal, was now on the throne of Charlemagne. Henry VII immediately set out to solidify his crown by subjugating the disobedient Bohemians and driving the rival Hapsburgs out. He then set forth for Italy, to reclaim what was once the country of the emperor.

Henry VII in Italy

Italy had long been the domain of the emperor in name, but it had also long been rebellious. The Lombards in particular had rebelled against the authority of the emperors, preferring to govern themselves through communes. Henry was aware of the feelings and sentiments of the Lombards and other Italian peoples. Unlike Frederick II, Henry was willing to accept compromise for their allegiance.

In 1308, shortly before Henry VII's election, Clemeny V had given papal sanction to persecute Waldenses sects in Lombardy. Since the Inquisition had already been founded, there was no reason to specifically ask for the popes permission, but they kept him informed of their pursuits, and he gave them his blessings. According to the surviving documents, a certain Dulcinus of Novaria, his wife, and a hundred and forty other Christians witnessed the gospel and

319

practiced their faith in a manner not sanctioned by the papacy. By order of the inquisitors, Dulcinus was torn limb from limb, as was his wife, and the other members were burned at the stake. It was not long after their martyrdom that Henry VII marched into Lombardy with 30,000 soldiers.

The people were tired of the brutality and savagery of the papal Inquisitors. The Archbishop of Milan, Ottone Viscounti, openly opposed the papal party. His prominent family also consisted of Mateo Viscounti, the Captain General of Milan. Mateo had been driven out of Milan by his rival, and papal sympathizer, Della Torrie. When Henry VII entered Lombardy, he returned with Mateo by his side, in 1310. The Lombard insisted that a community had an inborn and natural right to govern themselves, even as the Arnoldolists had believed, but they were willing to accept Imperial authority in theory. Henry agreed to allow them semi–autonomous rule in exchange for their loyalty and the Iron Crown of the Lombards. Henry thus won Lombardy without a fight, but antagonized the pope.

Henry soon began to march south, but his success in Lombard was not to follow him southward. In 1309, Robert of Anjou succeeded Charles as the king of Naples. He was a member of the Guelf party, enemies to the Ghibelline (pro–Imperial party) and the Viscounts of Milan. Henry would, therefore, be unable to sway Robert without a fight. Florence and Naples were in rebellion, and when Henry approached Rome, to claim his Imperial crown, he found it occupied by Robert's troops. They occupied St. Peters, but the Lateran was taken by Henry. On June 29, 1312, Henry was crowned Holy Roman Emperor by three cardinals in absentia for the pope.

Henry finally demanded that Robert surrender the city, and when Robert defied the emperor, Henry declared Robert, and his followers, guilty of treason and subject to execution. Philip the Fair soon found that his vassal was no longer content to be a vassal, and he ordered Clement to intervene on Robert's behalf. Clement threatened excommunication if Henry acted against Robert. He even preached a crusade against all cities who failed to submit to Robert. Things might soon have come to a head, had Henry not died in 1313.

The Fall of Philip

With the death of another emperor, Philip had still one more chance to try to control the Imperial throne. He put forth his second son, also called Philip, and ordered Clement to push hard for his election. Once again, Philip was to be denied. The German electors were split and a double election pitted Louis (or Lewis) the Bavarian against Frederick the Fair. Civil was to engulf Germany until 1322, when Frederick was defeated at the Battle of Muhldorf, confirming Louis as the rightful emperor.

The Imperial troubles could not concern Philip, for his last days were his worst. He had achieved many victories through his papal puppet, but he would win little in his last years. A few years earlier, Philip seemed unbeatable. Even before Clement agreed to extinguish the Templars, the pope had formally absolved Nogaret of all guilt in the incident at Anagni. Nogaret had insisted that the atrocities were done without his consent (although he had done nothing to stop them), and that the assault was a religious act of faith against the wicked pope. Clement absolved Nogaret, praised Philip for his zeal against Boniface, nullified Boniface's bulls, and passed his own bull (in 1311) declaring that France was the New Israel. All of this despite the fact that the Ecumenical Council of Vienna declared Boniface innocent and a true pope.

All these victories seemed to fade in the final years of Philip's reign. The Flemish were now uprising against French rule in the Aquitaine, scandals would rock the royal family, and the Templars would defy the king one last time, before their ultimate martyrdom.

1314 was a particularly bad year for Philip. First, a scandal erupted over two squires who were tried and executed for having an affair with Philip's daughter–in–law. The Flemish proved a nuisance as well, but most significant was the fact that the Templars reared their heads one final time. Jacques de Molay had confessed under torture to the crimes of the Templars, but now, years later, he stood before the Cathedral of Notre Dame with Geofrrey de Charney, the grand–preceptor of Normandy, and declared that he had only confessed to stop the torture and by the command of King Philip his Lord. He declared that the Templars were innocent. The wounds were opened anew, and suspicion of Philip's motives was again brought to public attention. The very next day, March 11, Philip ordered both men committed to the flames. According to legend, Molay shouted out from amid the flames, beckoning both Clement and Philip to appear before the judgment seat of Christ with him in less than a year's time.

One month later Clement V died. He had betrayed Rome, the Templars, and the papacy itself for Philip. His papacy marked the official beginning of the "Babylonian Captivity" and furthered the persecution of those who would dare to reform the church. Under his pontificate the Benguines and Beghards (two more Franciscan religious orders) were condemned and outlawed. One of the Franciscan Spiritual's leaders, Peter de Olivi, was also condemned posthumously. Thus, the new Franciscan order had little resemblance to the order that St. Francis had founded so many years ago. The Franciscan Spirituals continued to exist, but would come under increasing persecution. Many of them began to merge with the Waldenses movement, which had also suffered persecution under Clement, but some would continue to fight for recognition.

Still one more scandal rocked Clement's papacy, although it was unknown until his death. Clement had sent for much wealth from Rome, and upon his death, his will dispensed the riches among his relatives. He had believed that the money belonged to him, and not the Church of Rome or the papal office. John XXII was to spend many years trying to reclaim much of the treasures lost by Clement.

Not long after Clement's death, Napoleon Orsini sent messengers to Philip and begged the king to allow the new pope, whomever he might be, to return to Rome. He warned that the "Eternal City was on the verge of destruction" and that only the return of the papacy might save it. Anarchy reigned in Rome, but Philip would have none of it. The papacy was his and he needed the pope near his realm in order to insure its obedience, but death was to put an end to Philip's tyranny. Philip died that same year.

Summary

The reign of Philip proved that kings could be more poweful than emperor or popes. While once the emperors had been supreme, the popes usurped that power. Now the kings attempted to usurp the power of the popes. Europe was still a single empire in name, but it was increasingly divided amongst warring kings. Philip's rule marked the beginning of the French domination of European politics, but it was also the height of French power. The successors of Philip could not maintain the power that Philip had corrupted. The period of "Babylonian Captivity" created a vacuum in the Europe that left anarchy in Italy and provided no leadership to the rest of Europe. The Holy Roman Empire was decaying with every day that passed, and there would be none who could ultimately save it from its eventual, but far away, demise.

20

—

The Bavarian Hope

The grand scope of the wars between the papacy and the emperors had passed. Frederick II was the last to wage that war on such a grand scale, but he was not the last to wage that war. Louis the Bavarian is often forgotten history, but not because he was not important, but rather because Europe had grown weary of the battles. The emperors and popes were no longer looked upon with awe and respect by the kings of Europe, so the war that would rage between Louis and the Avignon popes remains more of a footnote to the great battles of history. The truth is that the people of Europe no longer cared who won. The Avignon popes were not taken seriously by the average peasant or king, although they still wielded great political power and caused many a martyr to die. Likewise, the emperors were a figurehead, remembered and respected, but they were no longer looked to as saviors of the empire.

Much of Louis' reign shows an emperor fighting a loosing battle, yet it was a battle he could easily have won, if the people of Europe had been behind him. With every victory, he found the people's rejoicing turn to apathy. With every defeat, he found the apathy of the people only encouraged the papacy. The Middle Ages were as much the fault of the people's apathy, as of the corruption of the papacy and royalty. The lessons of history often repeat themselves, and the lesson most often repeated is that the common man is short sighted and thinks only of tomorrow, but never the day after. Apathy is ally of dictators and fools.

Pope John XXII

After the death of Clement V, the poet Dante wrote to the cardinals, begging them to elect an Italian pope, but the French were not about to surrender their grip upon the papacy. Violence and rioting delayed the election for nearly two years when the cardinals finally elected a seventy–two year old cardinal–bishop. Nevertheless, John XXII was not to die until he was nintey.

He wasted no time asserting his authority; only slightly less arrogantly than Boniface VIII. He did not solve the double election of the emperor, which resulted in a civil war which was still raging in Germany, but instead seized the opportunity to declare that the pope was the lawful vicar of the empire in the absence of the emperor. He ordered Louis and Frederick to appear before him so that he could determine who the emperor would be, but Louis refused, realizing that the meeting would be little more than a bribe fest. John was furious at Louis and quickly became his bitter enemy. He even pressed for King

Charles IV of France to suplant Louis although it came to nothing. Thus, instead of ending the double election peaceably, he declared himself ruler of the empire, and became antagonistic toward Louis.

John then set about expanding the work of the Inquisition. John pressed against the Franciscan Spirituals. On December 30, 1317, he abolished all convents under the control of the Spirituals, listed many "heresies" of which they were guilty, and ordered sixty–four of the most prominent Spirituals to Avignon to answer the charges. Michael of Cesena, the general of the Franciscans, appeared to defend the Spirituals.

The main charge was that the Spirituals continued to maintain their vows of poverty. John declared this heresy and insisted that Christ and the apostles all owned property. Regardless of who was correct, the Spirituals continued to insist upon their vows of poverty and refused to submit. They were turned over to the Inquisition and four of them were burned at the stake on May 7, 1318. The Franciscan Spirituals soon realized that they were targeted for persecution, even as had the Albigenses, Waldenses, Templars, and others. Many fled to the safety of Sicily, but some, including Michael of Cesena and the Spiritual leader William of Ockam, would eventually find an ally in Louis the Bavarian. In the meantime, they rotted in prison under the supervision of the Inquisition.

Persecutions were also ordered against the Waldenses movement. Christian dissidents, both Franciscan Spirituals and Waldenses, spread from France to Bohemia, Poland, England, and Italy. Lombardy, often a haven for dissident Christians, was no longer safe when Robert of Naples defeated the Viscounti at Sesto in 1319. Robert's position in Italy seemed secure enough that he moved to Avignon to show the pope his support, but the Lombards, along with the Spirituals, would soon be looking to Louis to throw off the papal boot.

Louis' *Defensor Pacis*

In the election Louis had gained five of the seven votes. Frederick had only two, but it was on the battlefield that the true emperor was to be determined. In 1322, at the battle of Muhldorf, on September 28, Louis captured Frederick the Fair. However, Luxemburg, home of the previous emperor, allied itself with France and John XXII against Louis. John declared that the pope even had the right to nullify an emperor's election.

The hostilities arose, in part, from Louis' support of Milan. The Viscount had returned to Milan after a victory over the Guelfs at Vaprio. John XXII had then ordered Robert of Naples to besiege the city of Milan for harboring heretics. Louis sent an imperial governor to Milan to support the Viscounti family and reassert imperial rule in Italy. He also ordered Robert to lift the siege of Milan. John XXII was furious. Louis had already allied himself with the Franciscan Spirituals and was now defending the Waldenses abodes in

Lombardy. John declared that Louis was himself a heretic and excommunicated him in March, 1324. Louis response was quick. In the *Sachsenhausen Appellation* on May 22, Louis pronounced that John XXII was himself guilty of heresy, and called for a general council to reform the Church. In the *Defensor Pacis* (or *Defender of the Peace*) Louis' Franciscan Spiritual advisor, Marsiglius, wrote one of the most overlooked and important articles in medieval history. The treatise was a call to the Reformation two hundred years before Luther's successful call. It also called for an Arnoldolist form of elective monarchy hundreds of years before democracy would effectively return to Europe.

Specifically, the *Defensor Pacis* pronounced in matters of religion that the papacy was to live in apostolic poverty (as the Franciscan Spirituals taught), that the church had no authority in temporal affairs, that the church was properly the community of believers (as opposed to the institution of the church government), that the church has no right to judge, let alone execute, heretics since men are accountable to God alone, that no man had the right to excommunicate or place interdiction upon another, that the Scriptures alone are the true basis for faith, and also that the pope was not the successor of Peter and thus could be deposed. It was the Reformation doctrines two hundred years before. The influence of the Waldenses and Franciscan Spirituals was obvious, but it was not only religion upon which the *Defensor Pacis* dwelled. In matters of government, it presented the belief that the people were the true sovereigns of the empire. The people had the right to elect representatives to make the laws. The document went even further. It said that the people ought elect the emperor himself and that the emperor could also be deposed on bad behavior. So the emperor himself now declared that he was subject to the people and could even be deposed! Such profound wisdom was not to be ultimately rewarded, however. Louis would find support, but ironically, many of his very supporters used the very works he promulgated to deny him the authority with which he might have made his dream a reality.

The battle lines were clearly drawn, but the kings of Europe made their choices based on political power, not choices of right and wrong. Austria sided with John XXII against Louis. Such an alliance would have meant another prolonged war had not Louis shown the statesmanship which was often mistaken for weakness. The Austrians were supporters of Frederick the Fair, Louis' one time rival. Frederick had been imprisoned since his capture in 1322 and the Austrians were still sympathetic to him. Louis, therefore, made a pact with Frederick. He would make Frederick a king in Germany, under Louis' authority, if he would bring the peace. Frederick heartily agreed and Louis, emperor of the Holy Roman Empire, formally made Frederick king. The pact showed the unique character of Louis. The king of Germany was also one and the same as that of emperor, but Louis made Frederic king and co–ruler in order to bring peace. Louis was still emperor, so what need had he of a title? It was a humility that was too often mistaken for weakness, and Louis' enemies would remember that "weakness."

In the meantime, Louis had averted another civil war, but the powerful Duke Leopold now threatened his power again. He noted how easily Louis had surrendered the crown of Germany to Frederick, so Leopold used his own pressure to try to force Louis to surrender the imperial diadem itself. It seemed as of Louis was willing to comply and abdicate his throne when Leopold died in February 1326. Louis retained the imperial crown and had a strong ally in Frederick. With Germany again secure, Louis returned once again to Italy, and Milan in particular. On May 31, 1327, the Milanese awarded Louis the Iron Crown of Lombardy. He then marched to Rome in defiance of John XXII.

The Imperial Crown

The pope did not reside in Rome, but in Avignon. He was not well liked in the "eternal city," which had never forgiven the popes for defecting to France. When Louis arrived in Rome, the spirit of Arnold of Brescia was alive and well. The *Defensor Pacis* was received with open arms and on January 11, 1328, Louis the Bavarian became the first Holy Roman Emperor to be crowned by representatives of the people. Louis was made Senator and Sciarra Colonna, official of Rome, placed the crown on his head. It harkened back to ancient Rome itself and stirred the memories of the glory long past. Unction was performed by three excommunicated church officials, sympathetic to Louis, but the coronation was to be the first medeival coronation by the people themselves. Louis' wife was also crowned empress.

The celebrations continued as the people and Louis both declared "Jacques of Cahors" (John XXII) to be deposed for heresy on April 18. Indeed, John XII, who condemned so many on the grounds of heresy, taught a doctrinal form of "soul sleep" which is universally considered heresy by both Catholics and most Protestants. Even John's supporters eventually convinced him to back down from his support for "soul sleep" (the teaching that the dead do not see Christ until Judgment Day).

In May 1328, Michael of Cesena escaped with William of Occam and another prominent Franciscan Spiritual. They fled to the protection of Emperor Louis, whose court harbored Christian dissidents. That same month, Louis had pressed for the election of a new pope, on the grounds that he people had deposed John XXII a month earlier. The selection was a Franciscan Spiritual who took the name Nicholas V. Louis himself placed the papal tiara upon his head and his legitimacy was hailed and promoted by Michael of Cesena and William of Occam.

John XXII now called for a Crusade against Louis and offered Lombardy to the French crown if he would conquer it. However, the French crown was not competent to do so. Since the death of Philip the Fair, four kings sat on the throne. Louis X the Stubborn ruled briefly for two years but his reign was marked by a scandal involving his wife and the charge of adultery. She was later found strangled to death in prison. Louis spent most of his time trying to accumulate money to pay off Philip's debts. His son, John the Postumous was but a child who died days after he was born (he is sometimes called Joan based on the uncertainty surrounding the child's death). Philip V the Tall was suspected in the death, and became king immediately after the child's demise. Charles IV then succeeded him and reigned six years. Much of his reign was spend at war with Edward II of England, his brother–in–law. He died this very year, and Philip VI of Valois had only just assumed the throne. John XXII could not seriously expect his help, but he pressed for a Crusade anyway. Not surprisingly, he was met with apathy.

Louis appeared strong and had won the support of both Italy and Sicily. Even Robert of Naples remained neutral. The love affair, however, was short. The common man is concerned with his own daily life, and not the annals of history. Louis' best ally, Sciarra Colonna, had died and when Louis demanded a tribute of 10,000 florins from Rome, the people turned on him. They defiantly refused tribute, reminding him that the people were sovereign by his own decree. In August, Louis left Rome to the jeers of the people. With him rode his "idol" Nicholas V. The fickle people of Rome drove out their own emperor and pope, proving that apathy is the real villain of history.

Unknown Artist – Coronation of Ludwig (Louis) IV – 19th Century

327

The Tide Turns Again

Despite the rejection of the Romans, Louis' position was still strong in Italy. He went to Pisa where Michael of Cesena and William of Occam placed John XXII on trial in absentia. A straw figure was placed in pontifical robes and the trial commenced. Nicholas V excommunicated John XXII and called for a general church council in Milan. The straw figure was condemned, degraded, and paraded around Pisa, where the people finally burned the straw figure in effigy. This was to be the last triumph of the Franciscan Spirituals, for things soon took a dramatic turn. Apathy was the rule of the land in those days. Nicholas' call for a church council was ignored, and Louis' *Defensor Pacis* was taken as an excuse to reject imperial authority altogether. The Swiss now formed the Swiss Confederation, seeking independence from Germany rule and in January 1330, Frederick the Fair died leaving parts of Germany in rebellion once again. John XXII rejected Robert of Naples, who had been neutral in the affair with Louis, and turned to John of Bohemia. He promised John all of Robert's lands if he would invade Italy. Robert now found himself allied with the Lombards and Viscounts.

Louis was forced to leave Pisa and return to Germany where he struggled to regain control of the princes. Nicholas stayed behind and found himself the target of invading armies. In May, John XXII sent word to Nicholas that his life would be spared and that he would be well treated if he would surrender and renounce his title. Nicholas gave in. On July 25, 1330, he renounced his office and title and was led to Avignon with a rope around his neck. He declared himself a "schismatic pope" before John XXII and was confined to the papal palace as a prisoner under house arrest. He died three years later. John XXII only survived him a year.

The Hundred Year War Begins

The imperial war which had begun anew in 1330 was to continue for many years, but changes occurring in England would eventually be to the benefit of Louis. Edward II's wife, the daughter of Philip the Fair, had invaded England with her lover, Baron Robert Mortimer, and usurped the throne. Edward II was forced to abdicate for incompetence. She and Mortimer ruled in Edward III's stead, since he was but a teenager. However, in a few years Edward staged a coup of his own and had Mortimer executed. His mother, the French princess, was forced out of public life. Edward renewed war with Scotland after Robert the Bruce's death, but it was his relations with France that were of the most importance.

The French were the masters of the papacy, and eagerly sought to gain the imperial throne for themselves as well. French royalty had been pushed forward as imperial candidates on several occasions. Now, with the death of

John XII, the French again pushed for another French papal puppet. Cardinal John of Comminges was denied the office, because he refused to promise to keep the papacy in Avignon. In his place, Benedict XII became the first inquisitor, trained in the art of torture, to become pope. Benedict proved that the French were not willing to relinquish control of the papacy. Benedict immediately began to press for Louis' abdication. It was obvious that the English would make great allies against the French, and it was to be that alliance which would give Louis his greatest victory.

In 1336 Robert of Naples succeeded in driving John of Bohemia out of Italy, giving a severe defeat to Louis' enemy, but more important was when the Flemish revolted in the Aquitaine. Philip VI's soldiers squelched the revolt with a brutality which resulted in the deaths of thousands of Flemish. The atrocities did nothing to strengthen the French position in the Aquitaine, but instead created mass sympathy for English rule in the region. Edward III took up their cause and, in August 1337, he allied himself with Louis. The Hundred Year War bewteen France and England was officially begun that very year.

Louis was now strong enough to call for the Frankfurt Diet, with the support of the Archbishop of Mainz. In May 1338, the Diet met. John of Bohemia made his submission to Louis, Edward III was given the imperial vicarate of the Lower Rhine, and at "the Rhense on the Rhine" the council confirmed that the election of the emperor did not require papal confirmation. It was a reaffirmation of the *Sachsenhausen Appellation* and the *Defensor Pacis*. With Edward III as a loyal vassal of Louis, the French were in a poor position to do anything about it. On September 1, 1339, Edward III, citing the fact that his mother was the daughter of Philip the Fair, even went so far as to declare himself the King of France, and invaded. The battle of Creamy dealt a major blow to French power and in June 1340, the French Navy was defeated, dealing another decisive blow to the French cause. Unfortunately for Edward, his money was becoming depleted. Without money, he could not finance his war. The Hundred Year War was, therefore, a war interrupted by many truces and pauses. This was to be the first of many as both England and France paused to resecure their finances and their military capabilities.

The Fall of Louis

Benedict XII died in 1342 having accomplished little. He was derided by his contemporaries as a drunken man, unfit for public office. He was to be replaced by a pope who had many sexual partners and whose extravagant lifestyle rivaled the most obnoxious of kings. Clement VI was to continue the papal policy against Louis and to turn parts of the papal palace into torture chambers for his inquisitors.

Louis' position seemed strong not but a few years earlier. However, he made a dreadful mistake when he sought to establish for his son, and his descendants, a heritage (for he knew that the imperial diadem was no longer a heriditary title). When Margaret, the Queen of Luxemburg (from whence Henry VII had come), expelled her husband, Louis declared that their marriage had never been consumated, thus insuring that Luxemburg would belong to the Queen. In 1342, he then betrothed his son to Margaret, making him heir and ruler of Luxemburg. The plan backfired. The French despised Louis and took the defense of Charles of Moravia (Henry VII's grandson and the son of John of Bohemia). He claimed Luxemburg as his own, but with the assistance of Clement VI, he would claim even more. Clement VI called for a new imperial election, ignoring Louis' claim the throne. With Philip VI preoccupied by war with England, Charles became the pope's candidate for emperor. Of French descent, grandson of Henry VII, and ruler of Moravia, Charles made a formidable candidate. He made many promises to the pope, pledging to acquiesce to all the pope's wishes.

Louis realized that the Luxemburg affair was viewed as a coup of sorts, and his enemies again raised their heads. Louis was again willing to sacrifice everything for the good of the empire, and his son. In August 1343, Louis was willing to bow to all twenty–eight articles which the pope had laid down, including abandoning his Franciscan Spiritual advisors; among whom were the great men Marsiglius, Michael of Cesena, and William of Occam. Even more, Louis promised to abdicate his throne, in exchange for which, he asked only one thing. Louis asked that his son be made emperor in his stead. Despite this willingness to complete debasement, the arrogant pope refused and instead called upon God to strike the emperor with insanity and to blind him. He invoked nature itself to strike him down with thunder and lightning, and placed a curse upon his family; declaring that Louis should see his own children struck down before his eyes. For three years the debate raged until the German electors convened and elected, by a majority (but not unanimous) vote, Charles of Moravia as emperor. A new civil war might have loomed but for the events of next year.

1347 was a strange year in many ways. In Rome, one of the most unique stories unfolded, although its importance was largely anecdotal to medieval thought and culture. Cola de Rienzo was a fascinating orator who mesmerized audiences with grand dreams of restoring the glory of ancient Rome. He had been sent to Avignon as an emissary of the people and flattered the pope. When he returned to Rome, the pope had given his sanction to Cola. It is not clear if the pope knew what Cola had in mind, and it is certain that Clement did not know *everything* that Cola had in mind, for the pope would later excommunicate him, but it is certain that Cola had the blessings of the pope in his early ventures. He had told the pope that Rome was a "den of theives" led by the nobles. Anarchy and chaos had reigned there for sometime. Cola had garnered support among many of the people of Rome, and on May 20, 1347, Cola de Rienzo orchestrated a "bloodless revolution" in Rome.

"M. S." – Cola de Rienzo – 19th Century

Cola summoned the people to a parliament on Capitoline Hill where he assumed the ancient titles of "Tribune" and "Augustus." He ordered many reforms, bridling the abuses and excesses of the nobility, and ending anarchy. In so doing, he obtained the hatred of the nobles of Rome, whose families had ruled for hundreds of years. The Orsini and Colonna families united, and awaited their opportunity. In the meantime, Cola's power went to his head. He began to make the most bold of claims, and created a brotherhood whose purpose was to spread peace and justice to the four corners of the earth. On August 1 he decreed all Italians were citizens of Rome and sent out to the cities of Italy invitations to a grand assembly in Rome. He declared that he was revoking all the privileges which Rome had granted to both emperor and pope since the time of Constantine and told the Italians to prepare for a new imperial election, conducted by themselves alone. He dared to call Charles of Moravia and Louis the Bavarian to stand before him, and even demanded that the German electors and Cardinals appear before him to defend their right to vote.

These statements were too much for those outside Italy, if not for the Italians themselves. Clement VI declared Cola a heretic, a pagan, and a criminal. He excommunicated Cola and sought his arrest. The Orsini and Colonnas now rebelled. Cola's soldiers beat them off on November 20, 1347, but by December 15, Cola was forced to flee and live among the hermits. His grand revival of ancient Rome lasted only seven months.

The incident with Cola de Rienzo might seem insignificant in the grand scheme of the empire, but his reappearance in Rome years later, and eventual martyrdom, inspired the imaginations of men in Rome. It also diverted attention from the conflict between Charles IV of Moravia and Louis. That conflict, however, never came to fruition, for at the end of 1347, Louis died while boar hunting. Although there is no evidence to suggest an assassination, and no one proclaimed such, the death was conveniently timed. Such accidental deaths were not uncommon, especially among kings whose thrones were coveted. In any case, Louis' passing ended the dream of a Reformation, of a restored Roman Empire, and of a truly elective monarchy of the people.

Summary

The Bavarian Hope of the empire was nothing more than a fleeting dream. In many ways Louis was one of the great emperors of history, but in many other ways, he was one of the weakest. He was a man of great humor and personality, of humilty and modesty, and a lover of both justice and the people. His association with the dissident Christians of Europe shows that the Reformation was already in the hearts and minds of many people, two hundred years before its time, but the majority of the masses were still apathetic. It was not truly Louis' weaknesses which proved his failure, but the people of Europe itself. The kings were happy to see Louis fail, thus enriching their own power. The peasants were too concerned with the routines of daily life to risk life and freedom for their children's future.

Louis had made laws punishing robber barons, was well as forbidding tolls and road taxes. He had bodly proclaimed, at his own expense, that the emperors are subject to the people and called forth a reformation of the Church. He protected the Waldenses and Franciscan Spirituals, showed mercy to his enemies, and defied the Avignon popes. He was even willing to surrender his throne for the peace of Europe. For all these things he can be called great, but for these same things, he was considered weak. His willingness to abdicate to avoid bloodshed made him appear fearful, although he had fought a long war against Frederick the Fair in his early days. His antipope had proven a failure and had been humiliated before John XXII. In the end, he died with no more authority than he had in the beginning. Italy was in rebellion, Germany was divided, and the rest of Europe offerred nothing more than nominal allegiance to the once great emperors.

For all his failures, he left behind a legacy. The legacy of a man calling out for justice amid injustice. The *Defensor Pacis* remains a singularly important document. It is like the voice of Anne Frank from the Holocaust. It seemed to be drowned out by the cries of the dead. The voice could not be heard over the marching of the Nazi soldiers, but when the soldiers were no more, when the Holocaust was a memory, Anne Frank's diary was found and the solitary voice of one of Hitler's victims is remembered today while Hitler's dreams lay in the gutter. So also, Louis' dream would be forgotten until it was taken up again by men like John Wycliff, John Huss, Martin Luther, and Oliver Cromwell. Louis was the Bavarian Hope.

Unknown Artist – The Black Plague – 19th Century

21

—

The Time of Judgment

The middle of the fourteen century was most literally a time of judgment. Not from man, but from God. This was acknowledged in the hearts and minds of the great theologians and even the common man. The Black Death ripped through Europe, killing an estimated third to one half of the population. The Hundred Year War dragged on mercilessly, and the Babylonian Captivity deepened the scar that the Roman Church had already created upon itself. The events of this time planted the seeds for the Renaissance and the Reformation. It is not so ironic that the term "Babylonian Captivity" was used to describe the papacy's plight in these times, for like the Babylonian Captivity of the Bible, it was a time of judgment and chastening which warned the people that God would not be patient forever. If the people would not love God, then they would be chastised. This was Europe's chastisement.

The Coming Storm

Charles IV's transition to power did not come without troubles. Not only were Louis' supporters reluctant to accept Charles, but there was much anger over the electorate in recent years, which had been among the causes for the recent double elections and civil wars. In the earliest of days, each of the major tribes was awarded a vote along with the three prominent archbishops. However, several of the tribes had passed into history, becoming merged with others, and several new German territories emerged as well. Originally, the Franks, Swabians, Saxons, and Bavarians all cast votes, but now the count of Palatinate was allowed to alternate voting with the Bavarian ruler. Also the king of Bohemia, by territorian expansion, effectively possessed two votes, hence Charles' election was seen as tainted. Moreover, it was well known that Charles had promised the pope to renounce all rights to the papal states, Sardinia, Corsica, Sicily, and other states. He further promised to step foot in Rome only on the day of his coronation and to leave that same day. He also recognized all papal claims. In short, he had been seen to have purchased the title from the Avignon pope.

Gunther of Schwarzburg was set up as an antiking, but Charles bought him off, paying a large sum of money to make Gunther renounce the title. In 1348, Edward III of England, Louis ally, was offered the Imperial throne, but Edward thought the better of it. He was already in financial trouble financing his war with France. Two years earlier he had invaded the Aquitaine with his son, the Black Prince, but a truce was declared the following year. Edward knew that to claim the title he would likely have to raise more money to fight a civil war in Germany. Whatever the reasons, Edward III declined the generous offer. Charles is seen to have won the right to the throne through diplomacy rather than war.

In Italy Clement VI worked to remain master of Italy, even while the papacy was absent in Avignon. Back in 1337 Frederick III of Sicily had died. Although Robert of Naples was heir by pact, Clement had turned on Robert because of his apathy against Louis and his resistance of John of Bohemia. Robert was denied his inheritance. He died in 1343 and was replaced by Andrew of Naples. When, in 1348, Queen Joan was accused of murdering Andrew to assume the crown herself, Andrew's brother (Louis the Great of Hungary) invaded Naples and claimed the throne on behalf of his deceased brother. He sought justice against Queen Joan. Since Joan was the countess of Provence, as well as the Queen of Naples, she fled to Clement VI in Avignon, which lay within Provence. After Joan agreed to sell the city of Avignon to the papacy for the bargain price of 80,000 florins, the wicked pope quickly defended her, acquiting her of the crime of murder and supporting her against the great king of Hungary.

It was against this backdrop that the Bubonic plague, or Black Death, settled upon the shores of Europe and spread like widefire throughout the land, leaving desolation in its wake.

The Black Death

The bubonic plague, or Black Death, first hit Europe from the east. In October 1347, a small fleet of Genoese ships arrived at Sicily from the Crimea. They brought with them death. They were marked by large carbuncles or boils under their arms or upon their groins. These sores were sometimes as large as three to four inches and accompanied by fever, vomiting of blood, shortness of breath, a foul odor emanated from their persons, and they possessed a black tongue. The victims were fortunate in that they all died within three days of the first symptoms. This was the pattern. The plague quickly spread to Italy, France, and Spain in 1348, making its way into England, Sweden, Scotland, and Germany in 1349, and from there moving into Hungary and the Baltics. It spared no one, neither man nor beast. Cats, dogs, sheep, chickens, horses, and people were its victims. In England as many as 5000 sheep were said to have died in a single day. People fared no better. Villages and cities were virtually wiped out. Three fifths of the population of Florence died, half of Flanders met their fate, and in Venice an estimated 100,000 people died. In Marseilles, it is said that 57,000 people died in a single day. Even the city of the pope, Avignon, was not spared as half of its population succumbed to the disease. In England, it is believed that half of the country died from the Black Plague, or around two and half million people.

The immediate results of the plague devastating. Mass graves were dug to hold all the dead, but fear of the plague soon led many not to bury the dead at all. Streets were strewn with dead bodies. Fields became barren as there was no one left to tend the fields, resulting in famine and starvation. The price of food and other necessities became excessively high while land and sickly livestock were sold for pennies.

The people hid from one another. Many families abandoned their own wives and children for fear of the disease. Distrust also became to crop up against the Jews, who seemed to be little effected by the plague. Most now believe that it was the clean lifestyle of the Jews. Others believe that it was because Jews kept cats which reduced the number of rats in their land. Regardless of which is true, it was suspected that the Jews had caused the plague by poisoning water wells. 200 Jews were burned in Strasbourg, while similar pograms were created in France, Spain, Austria, Poland, and Germany. To his credit, the pope protected Jews in Avignon. However, the pope was rarely seen in those days as he hid alone in the papal palace, hoping to escape the Black Death. Those who did not blame the Jews, blamed Clement and his sins.

Such a disaster, such as has never been recorded in history before, ulimately led to some beneficial changes in Europe. It forced the empire to change in many ways. First, it spelled the beginning of the end of serfdom. With lands barren, the lords of the castles needed anyone they could get. Competition for the working class was discovered, and the poor could go where they were wanted, and where they would get the best benefits. Second, was the loss of control which the papacy was forced to endure. With so many of the inquisitors dying out, the tight grip with which the church held upon the local cities of Europe began to slip. It would take many years before the papacy was able to again silence the cries of the dissident Christians, but by that time, it was too late. The dissident Christians began to speak out more freely and condemn the corruption and heresy of the Church of Rome. This was perhaps the most important change. Europe became receptive to the calls for reform.

The Jews were not the only group which seemed to have escaped the jaws of the Black Death. Along the region of northern Lombary, near the Swiss alps, from Milan to the Piedmonte valley, the Black Death barely touched. This was the region best known for harboring the "heretical" Waldenses and other dissident Christian sects. It is, perhaps, little wonder that many saw the Black Death as a judgment from God for the sins of Europe. The imagery of Revelation in the Bible came to mind. "The first angel went and poured out his bowl into the earth; and it became a loathsome and malignant sore upon the men who had the mark of the beast and who worshiped his image" (Revelation 6:2).

Of course, not everyone reacted in the same way. Some became flagellants, who beat themselves in hopes that their own self–punishment would abate the judgment of God. Others followed the old pagan tradition, "let us eat and drink, for tomorrow we die." Bars and brothels seemed to thrive while the fields and markets were empty, but for most the apathy which had greeted Louis the Bavarian's call for reform was passing away. Out of the dark plague there would arise a desire for reform and education. The Renaissance would blossom shortly after, and the calls for the Reformation had already begun. Among the most prominent of the early pre–reformers was a John Wycliff of England, who was in his twenties during these days, and about whom we shall read much more later. The "wrath of God," as many called the plague, ended the apathy that had doomed the High Middle Ages and signaled a change that would one day result in the Reformation itself.

Europe During Innocent VI's Pontificate

When the plague had passed, cities tried desperately to put back the pieces. No city seemed more desperate than Rome, the spiritual capitol of the empire. City officials wrote to Clement VI, saying that upon the shortness of life, they request that he reduce the number of years between Jubilee, which had been established by Boniface VIII, from one hunderd years to fifty years. A new Jubilee would bring pilgrims, and money, to the once great city. Clement agreed, and further granted indulgences who those who went on the pilgrimage without the permission of their superiors, monks, abbots, or husbands. The new Jubilee proved successful for Rome, but it left a striking memory in the minds of the pilgrims themselves. Even the poet laureate, Petrarch, visited the city but was despaired to see the once majestic city reduced to its current state. Rome, which once housed over a million people in ancient times, was now a city of but 20,000, having been plagued by war, corruption, pestilence, and the plague.

The year of the Jubilee saw the death of Philip VI who was succeeded by King John II the Good. It also saw the capture of Cola de Rienzo, who had ventured to Prague in hopes of enlisting Charles IV. He uttered "mystic prophecies" but the emperor betrayed him to the Church. Cola was taken to Avignon where Clement imprisoned him in the papal palace. Clement died in December, 1352.

The Cardinal college, which elected the popes, had feared that the previous popes were too free and loose in appointing whomever they wanted to papal college. The emperors had their time of power, the popes had their time of power, the kings had their time of power, and now, the cardinals believed, was their time of power. They elected Innocent VI on the promise that new cardinals should not be elected unless there were fewer than sixteen, that all new cardinal appointments be approved by two thirds of the college, and that half the papal revenues go to the college. Innocent VI agreed to gain the office, but no more than six months later he denounced the agreement as an infringment upon the papal rights and nullified it.

Among the first acts of Innocent VI was to restore the work of the inquisition and renew the persecution of the Franciscan Spirituals. The

Spirituals, and other dissidents, were handed over the inquisition and many burned at the stake. Innocent was undertaking the task of restoring the depleted ranks of the inquisitors and drew the wrath of Saint Bridget of Sweden. Bridget was a woman who had formed the Bridgete order based on similar principles of the Franciscans. She worked with the poor and moved to Rome in 1350 where she worked tirelessly to restore the papacy to Rome, to feed the poor, and return Rome to its former glory, but for all her desire to see the papacy return to Rome, she declared that Innocent was a persecutor of Christ's sheep.

Nevertheless, Innocent's most grand dream was to restore the papacy to Rome, but he feared going back to Rome in the midst of anarchy. Italy had become ruled by tyrant political families and was not deemed safe for the pope. Innocent, therefore, resolved to bring Italy under subjugation in one way or another. He appointed Gil de Albornoz, a Spanish cardinal who had fled Spain after the rise of Peter I of Castile, to subject the rulers of Italy to papal control. He also, wisely, released Cola de Rienzo, and sent him to Rome in hopes of securing the support of the people. However, Cola's return to Rome in August 1354 was not as glorious as either Cola or the pope had desired. A mob riot erupted two months later, and Cola attempted to escape in disguise as a commoner, but he was discovered and murdered on October 8, 1354. Cola de Rienzo became seen as a martyr to many, but in reality he was no Arnold of Brescia. Cola was a man of ego, pride, and self grandeur. His visions for a restored Roman empire stirred the imaginations of men, but was never thought out or planned. It was like the charge call of a trumpet blast, but with no army to hear its call.

The next year Rome had yet another visitor. This time it was the emperor. Charles IV had stopped in Milan to recieve the Crown of Lombardy, and arrived in Rome on Easter, 1355. He stayed only a day, in accordance with the promise he had made to the papacy. He was coronated in absentia by the pope's cardinal and left hastily before the night fell. Petrarch is said to have been disappointed in the emperor. Indeed, the Romans were disappointed in many. Petrarch, Saint Bridget, and Cola de Rienzo all had reason to dispair. At no time in history was Rome's history quite so tragic as it was in those days. Even the sack of Rome in 476 did not leave a real scar on the city. Many of the people, including the Senate and Churches, continued on as they always had, save that the German invaders became the new Consuls under the Emperor Zeno. In the 1350s and 60s Rome seemed almost desolate, but of course so did much of Europe following the Black Death.

The Black Death had put a temporary end to the Hundred Year War between France and England, but it was to be but a temporary end. The truce was broken when King John the Good executed a prominent English prisoner. War with France was renewed the same year that Scotland surrendered to King Edward. Edward III's son, the Black Prince, then invaded southern France in 1355. Charles II of Navarre, John's his son–in–law, had made a secret alliance with Edward, but he was discovered and on April 16, 1356 John the Good had Charles imprisoned. His forces then moved on to meet the Black Prince near Poiters. It is there that the Black Prince struck a decisive blow against the French. It is said that more Frenchmen surrendered than there were Englishmen to receive them. King John the Good was among the prisoners taken.

King John was taken to London where Edward forced him to sign two seperate treaties, but each was, in turn, rejected by the French as illegitimate. It was clear that they were not going to accept any treaty signed by the king while he was imprisoned. The pope begged Charles IV to intervene on behalf of King John, but Charles ignored the plea. Charles was himself busy with the famous Golden Bull.

In 1356 Charles IV presented the Golden Bull, which established the new rules for electing the emperor. In years past, the elections had been hotly disputed as the parties debated the fairness of the older system which had become antiquated to some extent. Charles hoped to settle those disputes, while enhancing the power of the Bohemians. According to the Golden Bull, the new electorate was to composed of three archbishops and four princes, as had been the case previously, but now the archbishops and princes were specifically identified. The Archbishop of Mainz, Trier, and Cologne all possessed a single vote. The princes were henceforth to be the King of Bohemia, the Duke of Saxony, the Count of Palatinate, and the Margrave of Brandenburg. The Golden Bull thus robbed the Austrians and the Bavarians of a vote. More significantly, it omitted the papacy. This omission was a shrewd move. Since the papacy was not specifically mentioned, it was hard for the papacy to condemn the Bull. After all, the Bull did not *deny* the papacy the right to confer the crown, as had always been the case, but neither did it *confer* that right.

Charles Golden Bull is often considered his crowning achievement, but in reality, it was the manner in which he created the power of Bohemia. He made the king of Bohemia hereditary, giving that king one vote in the imperial election, but making the king the supreme member of the electorate. He founded the University of Prague and began to make other significant expansions to the city, which would soon become the new capitol of the empire. Those who claim that the Holy Roman Empire was a German institution had to admit that it was becoming a Czechoslavokian one. Charles took measures to insure that it stayed that way. Under the new law no Bohemian subject could be called before a court outside Bohemia, nor could an appeal be made outside Bohemia. Furthermore, Charles found that he could gain a significant financial advantage by protecting the Jews, or one might cynically say, requiring protection money from the Jews of Bohemia.

Pope Innocent VI might have objected to the Golden Bull, and its omission of the papal rights, had he not been preoccupied with the protection of Avignon. France was no longer the power that it once been, and following the Black Plague, anarchy reigned in many parts of the land. Mercenaries and plunderers regularly attacked Avignon in those days. Innocent was forced to sell off the papal treasury so he could begin construction of walls and military fortifications to protect the city.

In 1360 Innocent was finally able to negotiate the Treaty of Bretigny between England and France. King John the Good was offered his freedom from prison on the condition that he pay 3,000,000 gold ecus and surrender much of the Aquitaine to Britain. Edward would renounce his title, the King of France, and hold a royal hostage in John's stead until the money was paid. On October 9, 1360 John the Good was released and returned to France. Upon returning to France, however, he found that he could not raise the money he had promised. Further, he received news that the royal hostage of England had escaped. There was no longer a political reason to honor the treaty, but John's honor and chivalry would not tolerate it. It was for this reason that he was called John the Good, for he was not a strong king but a good man. He set sail for England and surrendered himself to Edward III for his inability to keep his promise. John would die in 1364, remembered not for his achievements, which were few, but for his honor.

In 1361 the Black Death returned to some parts of Europe. It was a small reminder of the judgment that had appeared to fall upon the empire, and the Babylonian Captivity was seen as a part of the reason for that judgment. It is not insignifant then that after Innocent's death in 1362, Urban V would make a significant effort to restore the papacy to Rome.

Urban's Dream

Urban V replaced Innocent as pope on September 28, 1362. He had grand dreams which including a restoration of the unity between the Eastern and Western Roman Empire, a new Crusade, and the return of the papacy to Rome. The poet Petrarch had written Urban, as he had the previous popes, asking him to return. Urban's answer was more favorable this time. The French kings were no longer as powerful as they once were, and the papacy had lost, rather than gained, power while in Avignon. Urban also found his dreams of a Crusade and the reunification of east and west were hopeless unless Italy was reunited and Rome was again the spiritual capitol of the empire.

Under Innocent, Gil de Albornoz had besieged rebellious cities in Italy and was even now at war with the Viscount of Milan. Urban demanded that Albornoz lift the siege and make peace. He then ordered the restoration of the Vatican which had fallen into disrepair. Likewise, the Lateran had burned a second time in 1360. Neither papal palace was habitable, but the Vatican could be repaired more quickly.

The same year that Urban made peace with the Viscount, King John the Good of France died. Charles V the Wise succeeded him and immediately came into conflict with Navarre over Burgundy. The British, however, were lending careful support to the King of Navarre in hopes of harming Charles' position. Meanwhile, in May 1366, emperor Charles IV visited Urban in Avignon and promised to provide an escort to Rome if he so desired to return there. Charles eagerly sought a return to Rome, and an end to French domination of the papacy. A year later, Urban finally agreed. He departed for Rome and arrived on October 16, 1367. His stay there would not be permanent, but it would be significant. In the three years that he resided there, he received many royal visitors. The Queen of Naples and the King of Cyprus both stopped in Rome to show their respects to the pope, but most significant were the appearances of the eastern and western emperors. Charles IV visited Urban in October 1368, but Byzantine Emperor John V Palaeologus' arrival in 1369 was of the most importance. The eastern empire had been pressed hard by the Turks and was on the verge of collapse. While the west had once been weak during the glory days of the east, it was now the east which desperately sought a return to the days of glory. So desperate was their need that they forgot the attrocities which led to the Latin Empire of Constantinople and begged the pope to call for a new Crusade.

Urban insisted that if such a reunion or Crusade were to occur, the east would have to accept papal authority and worship. John formally signed a document submitting to Rome and affixing his imperial seal upon it. He then performed an act of obeisance, kissing the feet of the pope before all, and officially became a Catholic. Neither act, however, was sanctioned by the eastern clergy and John was greeted back in Constantinople with apathy. Although John was to reign for another thirty years, he found himself constantly fighting usurpers and Ventians as well as Muslims. The reunification and the Crusade were again but futile dreams.

This same year Charles the Wise of France renewed war with England, renouncing the Treaty of Bretigny and setting out to reclaim the Aquitaine by the hand of his war general, Bertrand du Guesclin. 1369 also saw another outbreak of the Black Death in some areas of the empire. Rome too experienced its problems. As was often the case in history, many Italians opposed papal interference and resisted Urban's return. In 1370 Perugia revolted. Urban placed them under an interdict, but the interdict backfired. The Viscount began to hire mercenaries to harass Urban's men and the Romans themselves rose up. Urban fled to the safety of Viterbo. Although peace was restored to Rome, Urban had decided he needed to return to Avignon. Petrarch pleaded with the pope to stay and Saint Bridget prophesied that if he left he would die an early death. Urban ignored both and arrived at Avignon on September 27, 1370, but he fell violently ill almost immediately after arriving. Within less than three months, on December 19, he died. Urban had sought to restore the papacy to Rome, but his last act was return to Avignon where he was greeted with death.

The Babylonian Captivity Ends

The official end of the Babylonian Captivity was not truly the work of a pope, but of providence, for Gregory XI was not only reluctant to move to Rome, but had decided to return to Avignon, even as Urban V did before him. Providence, however, stepped in and saw that Gregory died before that return. Even then, Avignon did not release the papacy easily, but a Great Schism erupted as both Rome and Avignon elected their own popes. Nevertheless, the papacy of Gregory XI is a fitting prelude to this conflict and illustrates the era in which Europe lived. The pope defied two Saints, persecuted the dissident Christians, began a war with Italy, and condemned the great John Wycliff. Two elements were in motion. The first was the movement to reinstall the medieval Church as it was during its height of power. The second was the call to reformation. One of the two elements would have to be triumphant, and the other would have to be extinguished.

Gregory resolved to continue Urban's plans for reunifying Italy. The papal estates were in danger of seceding and becoming independant states. In many regions anarchy continued to reign and the Viscount Bernabo had become a virtual dictator whose tyrany caused him to besiege Piedmonte, the home of the Waldenses. Gregory, for his part, cared not an ounce for the Waldenses, but Bernado had become a threat to the papal power as well. Gregory therefore formed a league against the Viscount, placed an interdict upon his cities, and began to preach a crusade against him. Nonetheless, the Viscount was only one of the problems in Italy. Florence revolted against the hierarchy itself and unfurled a new red flag upon which was printed the word "liberty." Gregory's responce was to place an interdict upon Florence as well. Moreover, he dared to declare any and all who opposed Florence would have the right to plunder the city and makes slaves of whomever they found there.

Soon the virtual whole of Italy was in rebellion from Viterbo to Perugia. Gregory therefore decided to take more tangible actions. Ten thousand mercenary soldiers were detatched under the control of Cardinal Robert of Geneva, who would later become the first antipope of Avignon. His orders were to force the submission of the Italian cities in whatever manner possible. In this the ruthless Robert was more than obliging.

It soon became clear that even the military conquest of Italy would not suffice to bring peace to Italy. It was the presence of the pope in Rome that alone could save the papal estates. Saint Bridget, who died in 1373, had written Gregory early on and warned him that he must come to Rome. Her words, however, were harsh upon the stubborn pope. She declared that the pope "is worse than Lucifer, more unjust than Pilate, and more cruel than Judas." After her death, another female Saint arose in Rome. As a youth of Catherine of Siena had a vision of Christ whom she said had betrothed Himself to her, placing a wedding band upon her finger. That was 1367. From that time on she became a medieval Mother Teresa. Like Bridget, she too was to become sainted, and like Bridget before her, she too wrote to Gregory, urging him to return to Rome. In fact, in 1376, she appeared before him in Avignon to make her plea in person. She was not the only one to make her plea before the pope, but not all were pleading on behalf of Rome. Charles V of France sent a delegation, headed by the Duke of Anjou, to try to dissuade Gregory from leaving. The deciding factor may have been the fact that the Romans threatened to elect a new pope in Rome, if Gregory did not come in person. Gregory knew that the only way to avoid a great schism was to go to Rome, but the Great Schism was inevitable.

On September 13, 1376, Gregory left for Rome. A large fleet and mercenaries accompanied him. Gregory had been forced to borrow 30,000 gold florins from the king of Navarre in order to finance his return, but the pope still brought with him an estimated 125,000 florins. He arrived in Rome on January 17, 1377. This date marks the *official* end of the Babylonian Captivity, although it is, in fact, an artificial mark used by historians. Gregory would only survive this date by a little more than a year and he had fully planned on returning to Avignon. The great schism that he had hoped to prevent came inevitably after his death, but in the year interim, Gregory would prove that it was more than a Roman pontiff that the empire needed; it was a reformation.

John Wycliff's First Trial

The increasing sentiment of dissident Christian has already been discussed, but the coming years would strengthen their numbers, while inciting greater persecution. Even the secretary of the emperor, John Milicz, was executed for demanding a reformation and condemning the Roman hierarchy. That occurred in Bohemia in the year 1374. Meanwhile, in England John Wycliff became among the first scholarly dissidents. Called the "Morning Star of the Reformation" and a "Reformer before the Reformation," John Wycliff was a professor of divinity at Oxford University. In recent years he had begun to preach not only against the corruptions of the church, as others had dared to do in the past, but, like the Waldenses, he began to preach against the doctrines and teachings which he believed were the inventions of the church, and not found in the Holy Scriptures. He criticized the doctrine of transubstantiation, declared that the papacy should be abolished, defined the church as the body of believers rather than a material institution, and he condemned the acts of excommunication, pilgrimages, clerical celibacy, and articular confession. Like the Franciscan Spirituals he believed that the church had no right to own property and even went so far as to say that the government could repossess church property if necessary. Mostly, however, Wycliff was know for making the first translation of the Bible into English. He declared that the Bible ought to be translated into the tongues of the common man, even as the Waldenses had done before him.

As an Oxford scholar, the church was at first some what reluctant to pursue him but as time passed his language stirred them to action. Moreover, his support for the confiscation of church property by the king angered the clergy to no end. They were also taken aback by Wycliff's blunt manner. In criticizing the doctrine of transubstantiation Wycliff used to mockingly ask if the priests broke Jesus' arms or legs when they broke the bread. His translation of the Bible was perhaps the last straw.

Formerly, Wycliff had been protected by the Duke of Lancaster, John of Gaunt. The Duke was a son of Edward III and a powerful figure which the church feared. It was he who had, with Wycliff's help, seized certain church properties. However, a certain Alice Perris, at the bequest of a dominican friar, seduced the now feeble minded King of England and arranged to have the Duke arrested. Alice was believed to be running the country behind the scenes. In 1376 the "Good Parliament" met to address grievances by the people against the king. Wycliff corresponded with the Parliament by letter and Parliament agreed to banish Alice and free the Duke of Lancaster. Further, they appointed twelve regional governors over England who would act under the authority of the king, who was no longer able to act for himself. The situation only further antagonized the clergy who viewed Wycliff as their dreaded enemy.

On May 22, 1377, Gregory wrote no fewer than five seperate bulls to England officials condemning John Wycliff. He addressed one to Edward III, one to the archbishop of Canterbury, one to the bishop of London, and another to the University of Oxford itself. Wycliff was ordered to appear before the tribunal of William Courtenay, the bishop of London. Wycliff was to be condemned for nineteen seperate heresies. However, bickering soon turned into fighting. When Lord Percy, the marshal of England, suggested that Wycliff should be allowed to sit during the prolonged trial, the bishop bitterly protested, insisting that the defendant should remain standing. The tribunal soon became a ruckus and erupted into a riot. Wycliff was escorted to safety by the Duke of Lancaster and there remained under his protection until the tumult died down.

The archbishop demanded the Duke's imprisonment and the clergy hurled accusations against Wycliff and John of Gaunt, but the commotion was temporarily drowned out by the death of Edward III, and followed soon after by the death of Pope Gregory XI. Wycliff survived his first trial.

A Generation Passes Away

The condemnation of John Wycliff was, in the present context of the pope's administration, but a small thing. Gregory had done far more than condemn with words. In the year that Gregory spent in Rome he actively pursued the persecution of the Waldenses and other "heretics." In France, Provence, Spain, and Germany Gregory pressed for the Inquisition to repress heresy ruthlessly. It is said that in France the prisons themselves were

345

overflowing and could not house all the heretics. Only in England were "heretics" like Wycliff protected.

The repression of Gregory XI backfired. In February of 1377, Robert of Geneva, the pope's legate, ordered a savage attack on the city of Cesena. The people of that city had executed some of Robert's mercenaries after they raped numerous women in the city. Robert besieged the city and ordered them to surrender to his justice. They agreed to surrender in exchange for clemency but Robert then had the eight thousand residence killed, including children. The blood–bath resulted in a popular uprising. Rome also followed the uprising, rebelling against the atrocities. Gregory fled to Anagni where he began preparations to return to Avignon. Soon it seemed as if the entire papal estates would again be lost, when Bernabo Viscounti proposed a peace conference for March, 1378. Gregory, however, would die before the conference was finished.

Gregory was not the only leader to died in 1378. The emperor Charles IV also passed away that same year. His last few years had not been bright. He coronated his son, Wencelas (also called Wenzel), without the pope's consent, and upon hearing of the pope's displeasure, he sent out a formal letter requesting the pope's approval, which he back dated before the coronation. Moreoever, in hopes of avoiding conflict with Charles V of France (who had succeeded in reconquering much of the land lost to England, and who had recently made a new truce with England) the emperor transferred the kingdom of Arles to the French Dauphin, making it a formal part of France. Despite this apparent weakness, Charles is remembered for his Golden Bull which distanced the election of the emperor from papal interference.

1378 thus saw the death of both emperor and pope. Moreover, Edward III had died in 1377 and Charles V the Wise would follow them to the grave soon afterwards in 1380. A generation had passed away. They had lived to see the time of judgment, but what followed would be the Great Schism that furthered crippled the once great power of the church, and spawned the preaching of Wycliff, Huss, and others.

22
—

The Great Schism

The Babylonian Exile of the papacy lasted seventy years, even as had the original Babylonian Exile of the Jews had lasted seventy years. The Great Schism would officially last about forty. For over a hundred years, Europe was without a true spiritual leader. It is for this reason that the voices of dissent grew louder, despite the oppression of the Inquisition. Wycliff, Huss, the Franciscan Spirituals, and Waldenses all gained significant followers, as did other Christian dissidents and martyrs over the next hundred years. The Black Death, the Hundred Year War, the weakening imperial authority, and the complete collapse of the papacy as a true spiritual voice beckoned both the common man and the prince back to a time when the Church was pure and simple. This was to be an age of evangelism and of martyrs.

The Schism Begins

A generation was passing away. Wencelas would succeed his father as emperor, Charles VI was to succeed his father of king of France, and Richard II was to inherit the reign of England. A new pope was now needed. The death of Gregory XI had allowed Italy to regain control of the papacy, but it was not to be as easy a task as they had thought. A mob, alleged of up to ten thousand men (although this is almost assuredly an exaggeration) assembled outside the Vatican and demanded an Italian, preferably Roman, pope. However, in the seventy years that the papacy dwelt in Avignon 112 of the 134 cardinals appointed by the popes were Frenchmen. That left very few Italians to choose from. Outside of the Roman Orisini family, whom they would never elect, there were three Italian candidates, but the cardinals did not want any of them. The closest they could do was to elect a native of Naples in the south.

Roman guards had sealed the Vatican off, but not from the mobs. Rather they sealed the cardinals *in*. They set bonfires and banged their spears against the walls. When rioters broke into the Vatican, the cardinals performed a ruse. They pretended that they had elected an aged Italian cardinal pope, placing him in papal dress and placated the crowd. When the crowd mobs died down, one cardinal is believed to have said, "it is better to elect the devil than to die." They then formally elected a drunkard from Naples. Urban VI was enthroned on April 18, 1378 and within a few months he earned such hatred from the very cardinals who had elected him, that they would turn on him and set up the first antipope of the Great Schism.

Urban VI was renowned for his arrogance and pejorative attitude. Immediately after obtaining the office, his advisors suggested restraint, to which he responded, "I can do anything. Absolutely anything I want!" He was demeaning and insulting to everyone around him, including his allies. He called the prominent Roman cardinal Orsini "*sotus*", meaning retarded or clownish. He was also known to go into constant tirades for no apparent reason. He degraded and humiliated even envoys from kings and princes. It was not long at all before many of the cardinals who had elected him believed him to be instable and/or insane. Within a few months the French cardinals began to slip out of Rome and assembled at Anagni. On August 2, only three and a half months after electing Urban, the same French cardinals issued a decree declaring that the election was null and void on the grounds that the election had been conducted under fear of the Italian mobs. They called for him to abdicate. An act which was not forthcoming. One week later, they declared that the pope was deposed.

Fearing the pope's wrath cardinals moved to Naples under the protection of Queen Joan (or Joanna). She had been supported by the Avignon popes against Louis the Great of Hungary, whose son now laid claim to Naples. She had reclaimed the throne of Naples after Louis' departure and later married Otto of Brunswick. She also recognized the French Duke Louis of Anjou, brother to King Charles V, as heir to Naples. She was, therefore, perfectly loyal to the French. The French cardinals, therefore, found a solid ally in Urban's homeland. On September 20, the cardinals elected one of their own; Robert of Geneva. This was the same Robert of Geneva whose atrocities and brutality had slaughtered so many in Cesena. On October 31, Halloween, he was coronated Clement VII, officially marking the beginning of the Great Schism. War was inevitable.

The Battle of the Popes

The first battle was for Rome itself; literally. Clement's mercenaries held the famed Castle St. Angelo. Urban's troops were determined to drive them out of the castle, which stood in the shadow of the Vatican. In April, 1379, the very walls of the grand castle were beaten to the ground. The famed castle would have to be rebuilt, but for now the victory was all that was important. Urban's troops drove Clement's from Rome and secured the city. Clement retreated to Naples and the protection of Queen Joan.

The sides were soon to be drawn. France, naturally, sided with Clement (VII), along with Burgundy, Savoy, Naples, the Spanish states, and Scotland. Urban managed an impressive display of support from England, Sweden, and most of Germany and Italy, but his coup was perhaps the support of Saint Catherine who mocked the French cardinals for claiming to be pressured into the decision. She reminded the people that the cardinals had

348

already deceived Rome into believing that they had elected a Roman, only to find out that they had lied. How could they now claim that Urban was a pressured choice, when they had already lied to the Romans about their choice? She declared that they had elected not a Vicar of Christ, but an anti–Christ.

Despite the protection of Queen Joan, Clement found that the people of Naples supported their native pope. Fearing reprisals from the people of Naples, Clement left for Avignon only a month later. Urban then excommunicated Joan of Naples and named Charles of Durazzo, the son of the Hungarian King Louis, the king of Naples. He was crowned by Urban in 1381 and in June of that year he had seized both Naples and her Queen who was imprisoned in the castle at Muro. In May 1382 she was said to have been executed for the old charge of having murdered her first husband, but others say that she was suffocated in her cell; hardly a legal execution.

Like the cardinals who had elected Urban, Charles III of Naples (Charles of Durazzo) soon found himself turning on the pope. Urban had made Charles king, but was almost immediately trying to rule the country through him. He demanded territory in Naples be given to his nephew. Charles was quickly growing tired of his benefactor. When Clement sent an army to Italy, Urban left Rome for Naples. Charles saw this as a prime opportunity. He held Urban in confinment, as a "guest." With Clement's army, led by Louis of Anjou, pressing into Naples, Urban acquiesced to Charles' demands, but fortunes were soon to change. Louis of Anjou was a son of the French King John the Good. He was crowned the king of Sicily by Clement and named the true heir to Naples. His campaign had been solid until his untimely death before a critical battle had even begun. Without their leader, the army of Clement was defeated and a major setback was issued. This was the year 1384. Charles now had little to fear, but neither did Urban. Charles was therefore resolved to get rid of Urban once and for all. He is alleged to have conspired with six cardinals to place Urban under a council of regency. In other words, he would be held a virtual prisoner in the Vatican and be made a puppet pope. However, Urban got wind of the plot and his wrath was fierce.

Urban arrested and imprisoned the six cardinals. They were then subjected to ruthless torture. Charles attempted to come to their rescue and capture Urban. He blockaded the pope's fortress at Nocera, near Pompeii, and besieged the castle. The pope is said to have gone to window of his castle each day to pronounce excommunication upon all the besieging soldiers. It seemed, however, that Urban's defeat was inevitable when the Genoese came to his rescue, and slipped Urban out by sea, past the blockade. Urban had not forgotten to bring his victims with him. One cardinal was released at the bequest of Richard II of England, but the five other cardinals were never heard from again. Different stories arose as to their manner of death, but none can be confirmed. There seems, nevertheless, little doubt that Urban had them murdered.

349

The failure of Charles to get Urban seemed unimportant after news of his father's death in Hungary arrived belatedly. He set of for Hungary where he was assassinated by rivals for the throne. Louis II of Anjou now claimed Naples, with the blessing of Clement. He resumed the invasion that had begun with his father and, in July 1386, was hailed by the people of Naples as their king. Urban's fortunes continued to decline as he now found that his rescuers were demanding money not to turn over to Clement. He was forced to pay the mercenaries and spent the next two years sailing about from Lucca to Pisa and elsewhere trying to recruit his own mercenaries to retake Naples. In October 1388, he finally returned to Rome, but the people had grown to hate him, like everyone else. He died one year later; some say of poisoning.

Although one might think that Clement won this war, the true outcome of this war has never been officially decided even by the Catholic Church or its councils. The popes who resided at Rome are considered the true popes, and to be fair, Urban was properly elected despite the claims of the French. Nevertheless, Urban had proven why the popes left Rome to begin with. They had long ago ceased to be spiritual leaders and succumbed to petty political power. Clement was no better, a butcher to be sure, but he had the tact which Urban lacked. He bowed and scraped when needed, and even offered to call a general council to resolve the Great Schism. He outlived his rival, but the Romans were not about to return to the days of the Avignon exile. They were to elect a new pope in Rome and the Schism was to continue for many decades.

Beyond the Papacy

Europe had to go on about its business just as if nothing were transpiring among the popes. In the east, the emperor Wencelas proved lazy, if not useless. He resided not in Aachen, but in Prague and left Germany to its own devices. Anarchy was to be the result for nearly a decade. Wencelas did little to resolve the Great Schism at this point.

In France a child inherited the throne of Charles the Wise. Charles VI, sometimes called the Mad, was a mere boy of eleven years, but upon adulthood he proved to suffer from some malady which made him mad for months at a time, followed by several months of calm. His bynames are "the Well–Liked" and "the Mad" which illustrate how his temper and personality swung from time to time.

England also had a boy king, but the real power was the Duke of Lancaster, John Gaunt. This same Gaunt had once befriended the controversial John Wycliff, but that friendship would one day prove too dangerous for Gaunt. After the condemnation of Pope Gregory XI, Wycliff did not cease his activities. The Great Schism only fed the support which Wycliff had. He began to write and circulate Bible tracts and sent out "pore priests," or lay preachers, for which the Waldenses had suffered persecution. This "pore priests" were usually students or alumni of Oxford. They spread throughout England preaching the gospel wherever they went, and infuriating the bishop Courtenay. Courtenay called for Oxford authorities to try Wycliff. This time Gaunt took the side of the Church. He forbade Wycliff to speak anymore on the issue. It may have been Wycliff's opposition to transubstantiation that angered Gaunt, or it may have been a purely political decision. In either case, Wycliff did not cease.

This same year, 1381, saw the outbreak of the Peasant Revolt. Still reeling from the Black Death, the economy of England (particularly among the lower class) was terrible. Despite this, and in part because of it, England had increased its tax rates as much as three fold in the past five years. In addition, the oppressive actions of the archbishop of Canterbury against alleged "heretics" angered the people who felt victims of what is today called "witchhunting." When a new tax was proclaimed the people began to revolt. Tax collectors were killed and riots ensued. Worse yet, Simon of Sudbury, the archbishop of Canterbury, was siezed and decapitated. Although the revolt had nothing to do with Wycliff's supporters Courtenay blamed the death of the archbishop on Wycliff and other "heretics." When the revolt died down, Courtenay, the new archibshop of Canterbury, called for a synod to deal with Wycliff. The synod came to known as the Earthquake Synod, for shortly after it convened an earthquake shook the synod. Wycliff and others saw it as an omen from God, but Courtenay remain unswayed. The council condemned Wycliff's teachings and ordered Oxford to bar Wycliff from the school. However, it took an act of Parliament to enforce the ruling as Oxford was at first reluctant to obey the order.

Ironically, Richard II, now of age, personally ordered Oxford to supress the teachings of Wycliff but within a year he married Anne of Bohemia, Wencelas' sister, connecting him to the imperial family. Anne, however, was a devout woman and a great admirer of Wycliff. It is, perhaps, for this reason that when Pope Urban VI called Wycliff to appear before him, Richard II apparently delayed in sending him. The reason for the summons was, in part, because Wycliff had condemned the indulgences proclaim by Urban for those who would embark on a Crusade against Clement (VII). The summons was never obeyed, for Wycliff fell ill and died on December 31, 1384. His most famous disciple, Queen Anne of Bohemia, also died that year. As a result, many of Wycliff's followers, known as Lollards, moved to Bohemia while others spread throughout England. Wycliff was to prove one of the most significant voices in medieval history. His was the voice that foreshadowed the Reformation and earned such disciples of John Huss. He escaped martyrdom in his lifetime, but many of his followers would not.

The Schism Continues

1389 saw the Diet of Eger in which peace was established in Germany after nearly ten years. Despite this peace, Wencelas was still seen as

351

unconcerned with German affairs. The princes of Germany began to demand an Imperial Governor to oversee Germany so long as Wencelas lived in Bohemia, but he refused. The Germans were increasingly angry with the emperor whom they saw as incompetent.

In Italy Urban VI had died, but the people of Italy were not content to let Clement (VII) declare a victory. If they had, then the Babylonian Exile would most likely have continued. The cardinals, therefore, elected Boniface IX who promptly excommunicated Clement. He resisted Clement's call for a general council to resolve the schism and began to reassert his power in Naples. Louis II was now the king of Naples, but he had been appointed by Clement. Boniface, therefore, took the mantle of Ladislas, the son of Charles of Durazzo, and king of Sicily. Boniface would spend many years assisting in the financing and support of Ladislas' conquest of Naples, but that war would drag on for over a decade before Ladislas' eventually victory.

Clement now realized that the death of Urban did not seal his victory. He arranged for a marriage alliance between a French Duke and a Viscounti woman, thus securing the support of Lombardy. In 1391, Charles VI, now in his twenties, suggested a plan of having the pope installed in Rome. Charles offered to personally escort him there to insure his protection, and doubtless besiege Boniface's supporters. The move would have been designed to gain the support of the Romans but insure that French popes remained. This plan, nevertheless, was never enacted.

Ultimately, the people of Europe, including France, began to insist that abdication was the only way to end the terrible schism. Clement refused, as did Boniface. Neither would give way to the other. When Clement (VII) died in 1394, Boniface embraced the hope that he had emerged victorious, but like Clement, he too was to be disappointed. Benedict (XIII) was elected to replace Clement on the condition that he abdicate if necessary to end the schism. Of course, had they truly desired to end the schism, they would not have elected another pope at all. Benedict did not keep his promise. Cardinals urged to two popes to meet and even suggested that they both abdicate but Benedict issued a Bull against the cardinals' request. In the meantime, Boniface was quickly becoming the master of Rome. Another Jubilee had brought money to Rome and in 1398 Boniface used knowledge of a plot against him as an excuse to disolve the power of the Republic and insure that all Senators were nominated by himself alone. Thus the Roman Senate was made a puppet to Boniface.

That year a council in Paris was called, without the popes. Eleven French archbishops and sixty French bishops met and agreed to renounce their obedience to Benedict. When Benedict, who had promised to abdicate for the cause of peace if necessary, refused to step down his papal palace was besieged. Benedict was to remain a prisoner of his own palace for years to come, but he would never step down. Finally, in 1403 the French had a change of heart.

Urged by Louis, the duke of Orleans, parliament agreed to profess allegiance to Benedict once again. One year later Boniface died.

Once again, the Romans were determined not to allow the papacy to return to Avignon so they proceded with yet another election. As with Benedict, the new pope was made to vow that he would abdicate if necessary to end the schism. As with Benedict, he lied. Innocent VII was immediately challenged by the new emperor to meet with Benedict and resolve the conflict.

The Temporal Authority

The world did not sleep while the popes fought for authority. The dukes and princes of France divided effective control of France among themselves, as Charles VI was deemed incapable of rule due to his madness. Wencelas too increasingly beginning to be seen as incapable, and earned the nickname "the Indolent." In 1397 he headed to France to attempt, unsuccessfully, to end the schism. He had scarcely set foot in Germany since becoming emperor, ruling from Prague instead. In 1400 the princes of Germany demanded that Wencelas come to hear their complaints, but when he refused, they deposed him and appointed in his stead Rupert of Palatinate. Two years later Wencelas was deposed even as the king of Bohemia by his half brother Sigismund. He was to be imprisoned for years until promising to allow a royal council to rule. He was permitted to return as king of Bohemia, but only as a puppet king. Despite this, Rupert did not immediately gain recognition. He set off toward Rome in hopes of gaining Boniface's support. En route he aided Florence in there dispute with the Viscount of Milan, who was a strong supporter of Wencelas. He besieged the Viscount but lost a major battle outside Brescia. He thus returned to Germany, uncrowned.

Wencelas was not the only king to loose his throne during these years. Louis II of Naples was finally driven out of the country by Ladislas who became its king and in England Richard II had lost his throne to a coup by Bolingbroke, his old enemy. When Richard was out of the country, in Scotland, Bolingbroke invaded England and won the support of the nobility. Richard surrendered to Bolingbroke, who took the name Henry IV. Four months later Richard died in prison, allegedly starved to death. This change would not favor the Lollards (the name given to the followers of Wycliff). Although Richard II had chastised and warned the Lollards, his wife, Queen Anne, had been a Lollard. Richard had sent warning letters to Walter Brute, Wycliff's successor, but took no real action until 1399 when Parliament first proclaimed heresy punishable by burning at the stake. England became the last of the medieval states to accept the death penalty for heresy. Upon Henry's succession, the Lollards came under increasing oppression. In 1401, even the bishop of Lincoln, William Swinderby, was burned at the stake in London. Many Lollards began to flee to Bohemia, where Queen Anne had lived. Others remained in England where they were persecuted for many years to come.

The persecution was not restricted to England, however. In Lombardy the Inquisitors had been at work as if there had been no schism at all. Nevertheless, the Waldenses were generally well protected amid the valleys, surrounded by mountains and passes which were easily defended. Still, the inquisitor Borelli had made an effort to sieze as many Waldenses as dared to venture outside the valleys. He had executed over one hundred and fifty men, women, and even children before he devised a grand plan for eradicating at least one Waldenses abode. It was Christmas eve, when no one expected an attack. Borelli and his troops rode into the valley of Pragelas and the slaughter began. Women and children fled for the mountains, but of those who escaped Borelli's men many died in the freezing mountains where it is said that frostbite made many men's arms and legs break off like a tree twig. The fifteenth century was to begin the age of martyrs, discussed in the next chapter.

Along with the Waldenses, the Hussites faced a crusade as well (pp. 362–364)

Jaroslav Cermák – Hussites – Defending the Passage – 19th Century

354

Three Popes, One Church

The schism had nearly reached it climax. The entire church was disgraced by the spectacle. Benedict and Innocent were still vying for power. Although Rupert had never been coronated by the pope, Boniface did give his backing to Rupert by claiming, erroneously, that Wencelas had been deposed by the authority of the papacy (Boniface's papacy). Now Innocent was the Roman pope. Innocent gained the support of Ladislas, asking him to supress the latest Roman revolt in exchange for recognition of his rule of the kingdom of Naples. The Romans, however, were angry with the papal oppression and did not easily back down. When Innocent's nephew executed eleven prominent Roman citizens, in a failed attempt to force the submission of the rebels, the people reacted with yet another revolt. Innocent fled the Vatican to Viterbo while Ladislas held up in the Castle Saint Angelo.

In order to regain the trust of the people, Innocent insisted that he had nothing to do with the actions of his nephew, although he did not punish him, and he excommunicated Ladislas, ordering him to leave Rome. Innocent VII, who had been elected in 1404, did not long survive his return to Rome. He died in 1406, just two years after becoming pope.

Gregory XII was elected to replace him. Like those before him, he promised to abdicate if necessary to end the schism and made a great show of his willingness to do so. Gregory and Benedict had planned to meet but neither did. Ladislas is said to have had a hand in the decision not to meet. It was, therefore, the church bishops who decided that it was time to take things into their own hands. They, with the urging of Emperor Wencelas, England, France, and Castile, called for general council at Pisa in 1409 and invited both popes to attend. Both refused and called councils of their own, which would be made up, of course, of their own supporters. With the death of the duke of Orleans, Benedict's most ardent supporter, Benedict was forced to flee Avignon to a fortess near the Pyranees and by the sea where he could make an easy escape if besieged. Gregory had Ladislas as a protector and even imprisoned advocates of the Council of Pisa. Obviously neither pope was impressing the members of the council.

When the council convened in March 1409 it was decided that the only way to end the schism was to depose both popes and elect a new one. Alexander V was elected the new pope. Unfortunately, Gregory and Benedict did not go away. Instead of ending the schism, there were now *three* popes.

The Schism Ends

Three popes reigned. Benedict was still supported by most of Spain, Portugal, and Scotland. Gregory was supported by Naples, Sicily, Hungary, and the schismatic emperor Rupert. Alexander enjoyed the support of England, France, Bohemia, Prussia, Lombardy, and the emperor Wencelas. Once again, the schism proved that it would not die so easily. Alexander saw that a reconquest of Italy was needed to eliminate Gregory. Louis II, who had lost Naples to Ladislas, was now commissioned to undertake a new reconquest of Rome and Naples. Alexander never saw the conquest completed. He died in 1410 and yet another pope was elected. The last of the schismatic popes was to be John (XXIII). John's background was a soldier, not a scholar or theologian. It is said that he denied the resurrection and the immortality of the soul. Some said he even denied the existence of God. Nevertheless, it was believed that a warrior pope was necessary to end the schism once and for all.

Despite John's military prowess, his first real coup was in persuading Ladislas to abandon Gregory in exchange for recognition. John went to Rome but soon found that Ladislas' loyalty turned with the wind. Gregory had persuaded Ladislas to betray John and in 1413 he fled Rome. Yet another council was called to address the schism. This was to be the Council of Constance. Only John attended the council, but upon seeing that it was not favorable to him, he fled the council and condemned it. He was, however, captured and returned to the council as a prisoner. He was to remain a prisoner for many years. The Council of Constance deposed Gregory and Benedict and accepted the abdication of John. The popes were tired, and one was a prisoner. Finally, the schism was officially ended and Pope Martin V became the first post–schimatic pope in 1417.

Despite the end of the schism, the church was not unified. The Babylonian Captivity and the Great Schism had proven to many people that the papacy was not truly the Vicar of Christ. Dissident Christians from Wycliff to Huss to the Lollards and Waldenses began to flourish. The papacy believed that its survival depended upon the crushing of these "heretics." Even before the schism had ended, martyrs were being created almost daily as the two and three popes could agree only on condemning their critics. The age of martyrs had already begun.

<u>Holy Roman Emperor</u>   *<u>Rival (if any)</u>*   <u>Pope</u>   *<u>AntiPope (if any)</u>*

* – *Italicized means claimant was never recognized*
* – *Means the pope ruled from Avignon*

———————— 1347 ————————

                       ———————— 1352 ————————

                       Innocent VI*

Charles IV

                       ———————— 1362 ————————
                       Urban V*
                       ———————— 1370 ————————
                       Gregory XI*

———————— 1378 ————————   ———————— 1378 ————————

                       Urban VI   *Clement (VII)**

Wencelas

                       ———————— 1389 ———
                       Boniface IX   *−1394 −*

———— 1400 −

                       ———————— 1404 −
                       Innocent VII

Rupert

                       ———————— 1406 −
                       Gregory XII   *Benedict (XIII)**
                              — 1409 —

———————— 1410 ————————   *Alexander V*
Robst   *— 1410 —*
———————— 1411 ————————   *John XXIII*
                  — 1415 — −1415 −
                       ———————— 1417 —   *−1417 −*
                                       −1423 −

Sigismund   Martin V   *Clement (VIII)*
                              — 1425 —
                       Benedict (XIV)
                                       −1429 −
                       ———————— 1431 ————————

———————— 1437 ————————

Vaclav Brozik – Huss Before the Council of Constance – 1883

Karl Lessing – Huss Before the Stake – 19th Century

23
—

The Age of Martyrs

The fifteenth century proved to be the age of martyrs. Christian dissidents were no longer an insignificant minority and were becoming a political danger. Once upon a time the Waldenses had only ventured from their valleys to preach the gospel, but now Oxford scholars, like John Wycliff, had disseminated tracts and spread to Bohemia. Bibles were being placed in the hands of common men, who could see for themselves that the Bible conflicted with the actions and teachings of many popes. The papacy was resolved to exterminate these "heretics" once and for all.

The Martyrdom of John Huss

The stir created by John Wycliff did not abate. In fact, like the Christians of the early church it seemed, as Tertullian had once said, "the blood of the martyrs was the seed of the church." In this case, it was the seed of the Protestant Church. Although Richard II's wife, Queen Anne, had been a follower of Wycliff, Richard was obedient to the clergy who sought to repress the gospel of Wycliff. In 1399 burning heretics at the stake first became legal in England. Despite this, Wycliff's teachings spread even to the clergy and nobility. In 1407, William Thorpe, a priest, became a Lollard convert and was executed by order of the Archbishop of Canterbury. John Aston, one of Wycliff's most prominent disciples, was imprisoned for life. In 1408 the Council of Oxford outlawed Wycliff's English translation of the Bible and promised excommunication to anyone possessing an English copy of the Scriptures. These actions, and others, drove many of Wycliff's followers to Bohemia, the home of the beloved Lollard Queen Anne, late wife of Richard II.

In Bohemia (the Czech Republic and Slovakia of the modern day) it is said that the Reformation began in 1403. A Bohemian knight named Jerome of Prague had first brought the writings of John Wycliff to Bohemia in 1402. A certain professor at the University of Prague, John Huss, already familiar with the Scriptures, became a strident advocate of Wycliff and his teachings. He preached at the Chapel of the Holy Innocent of Bethlehem as well as at his academic institution, but protests over his teachings erupted quickly and in 1403 the university condemned Wycliff's teachings. Huss, however, continued to preach at the Chapel of Bethlehem and earned a large following. The people of Bohemia were eager to hear the Word.

A few years later, after repeatedly refusing to cease his preachings, Huss was deposed as synodal preacher and denied the right to preach. Huss refused to obey. The clergy, the pope, and the antipopes, all spoke out against Huss, but the Great Schism had not yet ended and the popes were too busy at war with each other to effectively deal with Huss. This was, in part, because Wencelas protected Huss. The spiritually defeated emperor remained the King of Bohemia, but turned to alcohol in his despair after being deposed as emperor. It seemed as if Wencelas was also looking to religion, although his devotion was suspect. In any case, the popularity of Huss, and his support from Wencelas, led to Huss' reinstatement at the University of Prague in 1409. In 1410 the antipope Alexander V issued a bull ordering Huss' writings burned and outlawed any "unauthorized" preaching in any "unauthorized" area.

After the bull, Huss, with Wencelas' support, appealed to the other antipope, John (XXIII), but John was no more favorable. He excommunicated Huss and ordered the Cardinal Colonna (who would later become Pope Martin V) to handle the situation. When Huss continued to his preaching an interdict was proclaimed against the whole city of Prague, forbidding any Churches from opening or performing their sacred duties until Huss was silenced. Wencelas backed down and ceased to openly support Huss. He promised to root out heresy, but still pleaded with the antipopes to let "Master Huss ... be allowed to preach the Word of God in peace." Once again, Huss not only refused to cease preaching the Word of God, but when John (XXIII) called for a crusade against the King of Naples, Ladislas, Huss condemned it, declaring that the pope had no right to call for a religious war. He boldly declared that the remission of sins came only through repentance to the Lord Jesus Christ. Jerome of Prague supported Huss in these matters as well.

Matters came to a head when Huss made a public display against the papal bulls. The two bulls of John (XXIII) were hung on the necks of two students who were dressed as prostitutes. They were then drawn through the city on a cart. The imagery was drawn from the Biblical Book of Revelation in which an apostate church is depicted as a harlot. The display backfired. Three of the students involved in the display were executed and Huss took their bodies to the Chapel of Bethlehem where they were treated as martyrs. The clergy then demanded the arrest of Huss and Prague was again placed under interdict.

Wencelas, once a Huss supporter, urged Huss to go into exile for the benefit of the people of Prague. In 1412, Huss obliged. Nevertheless, Huss did not cease to preach the Word of God or write Bible tracts. He was protected from the clergy by nobles and lords within their castles. From these strongholds Huss continued to proclaim the gospel and condemn the apostasy of the Catholic Church. He declared that "it is better to die well than to live wickedly." Soon, Huss would have a chance to prove those words.

In 1410 Rupert died. Robst, a member of Charles IV's family was elected emperor, but he died after only fifteen weeks. In 1411, Sigismund, the King of Hungary and son of Charles IV, became the new emperor. Sigismund was determined to end the Great Schism and called the Council of Constance, but he was also determined to end heresy. He promised Huss safe conduct and ordered him to appear before the Council of Constance. That safe conduct was violated. Huss was to remain imprisoned until council had made its declarations.

Huss appeared before the Council of Constance and attempted to defend his positions, but the council was more like a circus at times as the clergy merely shouted over Huss. Sigismund testified against Huss and promised that he would deal not only with Huss but his "pupil" Jerome of Prague. He was condemned, defrocked, degraded, and turned over the civil authority for punishment. Technically the Church could not sentence someone to die, but the Church made sure that the civil authorities could, and that those civil authorities would obey the Church. Huss was turned over to Sigismund for punishment.

In July, 1415, Huss was taken to his place of execution. Over one thousand guards were placed to insure that there was no insurrection. The bonfire raged with his own writings and translations of the Bible being used as fuel for the fire. Huss prayed. He refused his confessor, delaring that he had no need of one. As he was set ablaze Huss began to sing hymns to the Lord. His ashes were scattered in the Rhone river so that no one would be able to say where his body lie. He died the most famous martyr of Czechoslavian history, even above that of the "Good King Wencelas" of old. The new King Wencelas had abandoned Huss, but his followers would not. It is truly fair to say, as the saying goes, that the Reformation began in Bohemia in 1403.

Persecutions In England

Two years before the death of Huss, England would make martyrs of their own. Richard II had died in 1413. Henry V became the new king. He had grand schemes. Henry hoped to win the Hundred Year War and establish his authority throughout England, Scotland, and France, but he also dreamed of extinguishing the Lollards. This he would do with a brutality that few other English kings had dared. In this same year that he took the throne Henry ordered his knights to obedience of the papacy, even though the Schism was not to be resolved for several more years. Henry found that several of his best knights were Lollards.

Lord Cobham, or better known as Oldcastle, was a knight of some renown. He was very popular among the people for his chivarly and honor. Oldcastle eloquently informed Henry that he owed his obedience to the king, second only to Christ Himself, but that he could not swear obedience to the pope, whom he called an antichrist. Henry V, upon hearing these words, abandoned Oldcastle. He was excommuncated and condemned to death.

That same year, at Parliament, Henry V pressed for several pieces of legislation, which he received. In order to finance his war with France, which he planned on renewing soon enough, 10% taxation was placed upon the people.

In addition, was legislation made against the Lollards. Henry V declared that anyone found to own a copy of the Scriptures in English would forfeit not only their own possessions, but those of their heirs and family. Even their life was forfeit. Moreoever, the right of sanctuary was denied to heretics, even though murderers and rapists could still exercise that authority. The result was that thousands fled England, died, or were imprisoned. Another of Henry's knights, Roger Acton, was even arrested for arguing with a priest over theology.

Sir Oldcastle, had been sentenced to die, but Henry granted forty days for Oldcastle to repent. Nevertheless, by year's end he had escpaed the Tower of London, allegedly with the help of Sir Roger Acton. Oldcastle fled to Wales, but in January 1314, Acton was seen again. He was apparently at the head of an army of 20,000 people. The army was called a Lollard army, although it is doubtful that all the soldiers were truly Lollards. A rebellion was in the making only a year after Henry's accession. However, the clergy had forewarned Henry and he met the army, defeating them in the fields. Acton was executed and Oldcastle was accused of conspiring with him, because of his association with Acton on the Lollards. In fact, Oldcastle was in Wales. The uprising had been Henry's own fault for his oppressive policies.

In 1315, the Council of Constance, after having Huss martyred, ordered that the bones of John Wycliff were to be exumed and burned. The act was not carried out until 1328 after Martin V threatened England for their failure to comply.

In 1317, Sir Oldcastle was captured. He was returned to London where, on December 15, he became a famed martyr. He was one of the first knights to be persecuted by the church for his faith in Christ. These events proved that the dissidents were no longer mere malcontents or uneducated rabble. The dissident Christians of the Middle Ages were now among the Universities and nobility. The names of the martyrs were to fill up eight volumes (over a thousand pages each) in John Foxe's unabridged "Acts and Monuments," better known as "Foxe's Book of Martyrs."

Jerome of Prague and the Hussite War

The Council of Constance was convened for nearly four years. It ended the Schism but widened the gulf that had seperated those discontent with the church. It condemned Wycliff and had Huss martyred, but did not stop there. These events outraged the people of Prague. Four hundred and fifty two nobles and knights signed a letter addressed to the Council of Constance condemning their actions against Huss. They declared Huss a righteous man and swore to defend the right of the Hussite preachers with their blood. These men formed a league which would act as a police force designated to protect the free preaching of the gospel in the streets of Prague and insure that the preachers were not harassed by the clergy or anyone else.

The council demanded that those who signed the letter appear before the council, but they defied the council. The council was indignant. In 1417 they chose to martyr another Hussite. Jerome of Prague, the friend and confidant of John Huss, had been warned by Huss not to come near Constance. Though Jerome was a knight, Huss must have known that Sigismund's safe conduct was not necessarily an assurance. Nevertheless, Jerome was captured and Sigismund ordered him brought to the council in chains. He was kept in stocks when he was not before the council and finally ordered condemned, even as his friend Huss had been. Before being committed to the flames the honorable knight was stripped naked. Like Huss, he sang Bible hymns while the flames engulfed him. Like Huss, he was hailed a martyr.

That same year the University of Prague, in defiance of the church, began to offer communion in the style of the Hussites. The people of Prague no longer felt that the Catholic Church had any authority over them; only the gospel. Although Wencelas never took steps that would threaten his rule, he supported the people wherever possible. When the council elected a new pope in November, 1417, they chose the Cardinal Colonna of the famed Roman family. He was also the same cardinal who had been given the task of stopping Huss' preaching by John (XXIII). Taking the name Martin V, he would resume the task he had failed to achieve under John, but not before insuring that his rule was unquestioned.

Although it was the Council of Constance that had ended the Schism and declared Martin pope, Martin enacted legislation which would insure that no council could ever question his legitimacy. He declared that no appeal could be made to a council over the pope and eventually disolved an edict which had required church councils to meet regularly. Then, on February 22, 1418, he issued a bull, *Inter cunctos*, which condemned all "heretics" who supported the "pestilential doctrine of the hæresiarch, John Wycliff, John Huss, and Jerome of Prague," regardless of sex. Fearing loss of power, Wencelas acquiesced, but upon so doing, he found his court emptied of supporters. One of his greatest military leaders, John Zizka (who was known for his one–eye, having lost the other in a battle), left and headed a sect of the Hussites, known as the Taborites. These Taborites were so named because they build a city fortress atop a steep mountain named Tabor. The Taborites were to known as the more militant faction which opposed the Catholic Church in virtually every manner was prepared to defend itself from attack. In July, 1419, they marched through the streets of Prague in a procession to display their faith. However, when a magistrate threw a rock at the crowd, a riot ensured. The Taborites broke into convents, monasteries, and churches, leaving monks and priests dead, and destroying the idols of the churches.

Not long after these events, Wencelas died. Since he left no heir, the emperor Sigismund, Wencelas' half–brother, was next in line to become Bohemian king, but the people despised him as the murderer of Huss and

Jerome. When a merchant named John Krasa was executed for defending Huss, the people became more outraged and defied Sigimund. The emperor finally declared a crusade, as did Pope Martin V. It is estimated that 150,000 soldiers came to invade Bohemia. It was to be the most imposing crusade of its kind and harkened back to the Albigenses Crusade. Catholics were sent to kill Christian dissidents.

Zizka and his militant Taborites led the defenses, and Zizka proved to be a worthy adversary. In fact, he is viewed as having revolutionized military tactics. What made his victories so impressive was the fact that his soldiers were mere peasants whose weapons were largely pitchforks and scythes. Nonetheless, Zizka did have some weapons at his disposal, including a handful of recently invented cannons, and he knew how to use those weapons to his advantage. Zizka mounted the cannons on mobile wagons, thus creating the first mobile artillery. Using these mobile artillery units, Zizka was able to force the enemy to attack before they were ready or to force them into disadvantageous territory. He also unified his military units, merging infantry, calvary, and artillery into single tactical units, instead of requiring seperate commanders for each as had been the case previously. In a battle outside Prague in 1420, Zizka routed the first wave of Sigismund's crusader army on a hill which came to be named after him. Pitchforks proved the better of armor and swords and crossbows, but now the weapons of the defeated enemy were in the hands of Zizka's army.

A second campaign by Sigismund also failed, as the knights are said to have fled in cowardace before Zizka's peasant army. Two other campaigns also failed. Once it is said that ten to fifteen thousand of Sigismund's troops fell compared to fifty of Zizka's. Unfortunately, both sides of the army failed to showed chivalry. The Taborites proved barbarous and took few prisoners. The Catholics burned their prisoners, or sold them into slavery.

Although Zizka had lost the sight in both of his eyes by this time, he still proved to be a more capable commander than Sigismund. When Zizka died in 1424, he was replaced by Procopius Rosa, a Hussite priest, who decided to take his army on the offensive. The Taborites invaded Germany and spread acts of terrorism throughout the land. They did not intend to occupy Germany, but to terrorize it until the Germans ceased their invasions of Bohemia. It is claimed that Procopius burned and destroyed as many as five hundred churches and monasteries.

In 1431 it was decided that a cardinal should lead yet another campaign, allegedly of nearly 200,000 soldiers. On August 14 that army was defeated by Procopius. Martin V finally decided to call another council in an attempt to save face and resolve the Hussite problem. The Bohemians were invited to attend that council at Basil, which would first convene in 1431, but would not close until 1449.

Jules Lenepveu – Joan of Arc Burning at the Stake – 1890

Joan of Arc and the Hundred Year War

France created a number of martyrs of her own. In 1417, shortly before the end of the Council of Constance, Catherine of Thou, along with an entire convent of nuns, were burned alive for being anabaptists. The anabaptists were a sect similar to the Lollards and Waldenses except they were predominantly identified for their belief that only adults should be baptised. They were, thus, called ana– (re) baptists since they "rebaptised" those who had been baptised by the church as children. They are also the predecessors of the modern Baptists.

Additionally, in the city of Flanders, in 1421, "a great number" of Waldenses were burned at the stake as heretics. Many others could be cited, but perhaps no other French Martyr is as famous as Joan of Arc. She could not, however, be called a *Christian* martyr, but rather a *French* martyr. She did not die for her faith in Christ, but for her devotion to Charles VII.

To understand the importance of Joan's actions, the events of the Hundred Year War need to be examined. The war had undergone a long truce when Henry V of England decided to reassert the English crown's claim to the whole of France. After capturing Harfleur and Agincourt, in 1415, from France, Emperor Sigismund came to England to show his support for Henry and enter into an alliance with him. Sigismund agreed to break the alliance of France with Genoa by use of force, if necessary. At the Battle of Seine in August 1416 the English navy established supremacy over the English Channel. English troops could freely pass over the channel without harassment, but the financing of the war was more difficult. Henry decided that he would make the conquest pay for themselves. Captured French territories were stationed with permanent English garrisons and taxation was levied to finance the English's king's conquest.

For many years the people of these disputed lands were largely unconcerned with whether their king was French or English, but the heavy taxation and presence of English troops began to distress the people. The French people were particularly distressed as Henry did not stop with the lands long disputed between England and France, but instead made his goal the ultimate conquest of *all* France. In January 1419 the capital of northern France, Rouen, surrendered.

A few months later, the young French Dauphin Charles, heir to the French throne, murdered the Duke of Burgundy, with whom his own mother had allied. The Dauphin had assumed, although still a teenager, the regency on account of Charles VI's madness. His mother had then formed an alliance with Duke John the Fearless, which Charles saw as a threat to his rule. It was at an official meeting before Charles that the duke was murdered. Philip the Good became the new duke and immediately allied himself with Henry V against the murderer of his father. Charles' plans had backfired. With Burgundy pressing France from the south and the English from the north, the French agreed to the

Treaty of Troyes in which the Princess Catherine was married to Henry, making his son heir to the French throne. A truce was declared.

In 1422 Henry V and Charles VI both died. Henry VI of England claimed the French throne as did the Dauphin Charles, now Charles VII. The war resumed. The English again made inroads with the assistance of the Burgundians. Burgundy captured Paris itself and in October, 1428, England besieged the city of Orleans. It is at this time that a young uneducated (she could not even write her own name) peasant girl named Joan of Arc arrived at Charles VII's court.

Medieval France was superstitious. The cult of Mariology often saw visions of Mary and, in an age of sexual immorality, virgins were looked upon as especially spiritual. Legends soon grew that a virgin would one day come and liberate France. The "prophecy," sufficiently vague enough, became the clarion of Joan of Arc's mission. The young girl had seen visions of St. Catherine and St. Margaret who urged her to go the king. The young Joan, but sixteen years old, tried on more than one occasion to visit Charles VII, but his knights thought her a silly maid, until January 1429 when her persistence paid off. She was led into the court, but it is said that Charles hid himself among the courtiers. Joan allegedly walked up to him directly and acknowledged him as the king. The act impressed Charles. She urged the king to be coronated, but since Reims was the designated place of coronation, it was impossible, for the English controlled that region. Joan promised that she would retake the city of Orleans and lead him personally to Reims. Although Charles doubted her visions, and even suspected that she was a witch, his advisors reminded him of the "prophecies," and noted that she could rally support even if she was a failure.

In April 1429, Joan and a few hundred soldiers slipped into Orleans with supplies. The English had the city virtually surrounded but were caught unaware by the small force which entered the city. The next month Joan led sorties out of the city and suceeded in taking several small forts which the English had built to assist in the siege. Within a week the English (who were used to seeing sporatic and futile defense from the French) lifted the siege and made their retreat. Charles was again leary of travelling to Reims, fearing English reprisals, but several of Charles' best soldiers joined Joan of Arc. In June another battle was won by the French at the Battle of Patay. The English had considered Orleans a fluke, lost by overconfident and lazy soldiers, but their defeat at Patay broke the aura of the unbeatable English. Soon Joan led Charles all the way to Reims where he coronated as King of France on July 17, 1429, seven years after claiming the throne.

Joan's popularity was enormous, but Charles had no real hopes of retaking Paris from Burgundy and, to the dispair of both Joan and the French loyalists, he retreated. Charles had been crowned, and that was all he wanted. Joan tried to convince Charles to attack Paris he consistently refused. In

September Joan's army was disbanded and Charles remained in safety at Loire. Eventually Joan was able to lead some small troops against Burgundy, but the king and his best men stayed behind. On May 23, the following year, Joan was captured in a battle against the Burgundian Frenchmen. Charles made no attempt to ransom her, rescue her, or bargain for her release. Two days later the University of Paris demanded that Joan be tried as a heretic. She was examined by the French Inquisition and charged with crimes ranging from believing in the assurance of salvation (a proto–Protestant doctrine), to witchcraft, to wearing men's clothes. She was even tried with attempted suicide after she nearly died during an escape attempt. Upon examination it was proven that Joan was indeed as virgin as she claimed, but her visions were discarded. She was threatened with torture but Joan said that even if she confessed to crimes under torture, she would retract them the next day. The inquisition decided that torture was not needed.

On May 23, 1431, exactly one year after her capture, the University of Paris declared that Joan was a heretic and was prepared to hand her over to the secular authorities, who alone had the legal authority to execute heretics. However, Joan wavered and agreed to recant. She was sentenced to life imprisonment on the condition that she renounce her views and wear women's clothes, but no sooner had she recanted then her conscious began to gnaw at her. She was found wearing men's clothes again and announced that the voices of St. Catherine and St. Margaret had chastised her for her treason against them. She recanted of her recantation. By law there was but one punishment for a relapsed heretic.

On May 30, 1431, Joan of Arc was allowed to make her confession (which was unprecedented for condemned heretics) and receive Communion. She was burned at the stake while a Dominican held high a cross where she could see it all times. Joan of Arc was executed by French authorities, not English. It is likely that no one, French or English, had desired to see her executed, but the laws of the Inquisition made it impossible not to. She had "relapsed." Although the English were not actively involved, the French court was under the influence of the Burgundian allies of England. Joan's death became the battle cry (figuratively) for the French and the tides of the Hundred Year War began to change. The worthless king Charles VII would live to see England driven completely from the European mainland and by 1453 the Hundred Year War was brought to an end, with Charles the victor.

The Empire in the Early Fifteenth Century

The pontificate of Pope Martin V was predominantly concerned with the war against the Hussites, the restoration of Rome, and the promotion of Martin's family, the Colonnas. Once again Rome had fallen into anarchy over the years. Martin began to restore the Lateran and other monuments, as well as brining law and order back to the city, but he also enriched the Colonna family at the expense of the church and people. His main concern, however, was in promoting the war against the Hussites. Nevertheless, he was bothered by two antipopes who remained a lingering reminder of the Great Schism. Benedict's colleagues had refused to admit defeat at the Council of Constance. Upon his death the three of his cardinals elected Clement (VIII). Without any real support, however, the new "pope" and his cardinals spend their pontificate locked in a fortress surrounded by Spanish troops, making proclamations that no one listened to. Only upon the Aragon King Alfonso V's request did Clement finally decide to step down. Yet one other reminder of Schism remained. Of the four colleagues of Benedict one was absent from the "election" of Clement. He, alone, elected Benedict (XIV) in 1425, but almost from that moment on Benedict disappeared into history; literally. Nothing more is known of Benedict from the day of his election onward.

Sigismund had more troubles than his war with the Hussites. The Muslim Turks were threatening the borders of Hungary, Sigismund's home. In 1428 he led a crusade against the Turks but had no more success than he had against the Hussites. The Turks were becoming a dominant force which would shortly crush the Byzantine Empire and conquer Constantinople. Sigismund realized that the war with the Hussites was threatening his war with the Turks, and the war with the Hussites was increasingly unpopular among the people of Europe. Charles VII consistently refused to sent troops to assist in the war, arguing that they were needed for the Hundred Year War, and the common man saw it as another Albigenses Crusade. Pope Martin even found many placards placed throughout Rome making ambigious threats. Although the Council of Constance required church councils to meet regularly, and established their supremacy over the papacy, Martin had consistently refused to convene councils, despite his promise to do so. The pressure became so great that, in 1431, Pope Martin V reluctantly agreed to call a council at Basil (or Basle) which would address the Hussite war and Church reform, but Martin died before it convened.

Eugene IV was elected to replace Martin. It was he who would inherit the Council of Basil, with which he would come into conflict in the years to come. In the meantime, Eugene took measures against the Colonna family that had been enriched during Martin's pontificate. He attempted to repossess the properties given them by Martin in the papal estates. The result was violence which would increase over time.

In Basil, on the day of the council's opening, a single prelate appeared. The official opening of the council was delayed four months. The Hussites had been invited to sent representatives, but few trusted the council, particularly after what had happened to Huss and Jerome at the Council of Constance. Nevertheless, the council eventually grew to five hundred members, although only twenty were said to be cardinals. As a result, votes were given to lower clergy members. Emperor Sigismund, on his way to the council, took a detour and stopped in Milan where he received the traditional Iron Crown, signifying him as King of the Lombards. He did not, however, receive the imperial diadem at this time. Part of the reason may have been the new schism that was developing between Eugene and the council. Angry at the council, which he viewed as a threat papal authority, Eugene issued a papal bull in December, disolving the council. The council refused and, borrowing from the power granted to them by the Council of Constance, they ordered the pope to appear at the council. Eugene was denounced by University of Paris and within a year the council was threatening to depose the pope if he failed to appear before them in person.

Emperor Sigismund wanted to avert another schism, and receive his imperial crown. He, therefore, travelled to Rome where Eugene coronated the emperor in May 1433, but no agreement was reached until December when Eugene reluctantly revoked his bulls.

Owing to the conflict between the council and pope, the Bohemians eventually came to trust the council and as many as three hundred delegates were sent to Basil. A peace was declared which would permit the Hussite community to worship using their own communion and granted other concessions that gave Hussites more freedom of religion. The compromise angered both the pope and the Taborites. By this time the Hussites had broken into several different sects. The militant Taborites opposed any compromise with the Catholics while the Ultraquists favored the council's agreement. So hostile were the Taborites to this that a massacre began in Prague, resulting in the death of an estimated 22,000 people. Now a civil war erupted between the moderate Hussites and the militant Taborites, but this war would effectively be won on May 30, 1434 when Procopius and his army were defeated at Lipon. Procopius fell in battle and the remaining Taborites proved no match for the Ultraquists. Mount Tabor would not fall until 1452, but the moderate Hussites had won their freedom and in 1467, the Bohemian Brethren formed their own church, seperate from the Catholic Church, fifty years before Martin Luther.

The same year that the Hussite war ended, a new one began in Rome, if can be called a war. In fact, it was another revolt, led by the Colonna family. Eugene, like many other popes, was not popular in Rome and his oppression of the Roman family eventually led to another uprising. Disguised as monk Eugene attempted to slip out of the city, but when he was recognized he barely escaped with his life. He fled to Florence where he would reside for almost ten years.

With the Hussite war being resolved, the council's main goal was now the reform of the church, and that meant the reduction of papal power. One of the more prominent members was Nicholas of Cusa, the famed medieval theologian and philosopher, whose tracts included "on learned ignorance." Nicholas strongly advocated the reduction of papal authority and supported church council rule. Numerous measures were taken to restrict papal abuses and even the right of appeal to the pope was curtailed. Eugene became more than indignant and began to circulate letters to the princes of Europe decrying the council rulings. He was feeling out his support, preparing for a major rift, but he was wise enough to wait until the time was right. That time was not far off.

Ironically, it was the Greeks who gave the support that Eugene needed. The Byzantine Empire was on the verge of collapse. The Muslims Turks had pressed the Greeks all the way to the great invulnerable city of Constantinople itself. The writing was on the wall and only the Holy Roman Empire could possibly save the Byzantines from their fate. The Greek churches even offered to make their submission. Delegates soon arrived from Greece seeking a union. One delegate had come to Basil and another to the pope. The Greeks had wanted to meet in Italy, but the council knew that the pope's influence would be too strong there so they suggested Basil or even Avignon. Eugene then suggested that the council was bartering with Greeks for favor. He sent a bull out in September, 1437, condemnng the synod and calling for a council with the Greeks in Italy. The Greeks chose to go to the council in Florence, leaving the Council of Basil without a voice. It was a challenge between the power of the papacy and the power of the church councils.

In October, 1437, the Council of Basil declared the papal bulls null and void and called the pope to appear within sixty days at Basil. When Eugene refused they deposed the pope on the grounds of simony, perjury, being schismatic, and heresy. That heresy was the denial of the authority of the church councils. A new schism was threatened. Charles VII, eager to gain support for his circumspect coronation under a condemned heretic (Joan of Arc), sided with Eugene, but the emperor had died a month earlier. The new emperor, Albert II, would survive his ascension only two years. Europe was divided again.

A Schism Averted

In 1439 the council made two drastic measures. They first adopted a decree on the immaculate conception which declared Mary free from sin. This teachings, unheard of before, appears to contradict Romans 3:23, and was a signal to dissident Christian sects that councils could no more be relied upon for inerrancy than could the popes. The second measure they took was to elect another pope. Felix V had been the duke of Savoy and founded a monastery after the death of this wife. He was both devout and skilled in politics. He was considered a man of integrity and chivalry; traits uncommon in recent popes. He was, therefore, an ideal choice for pope, and even abdicated his dutchy before becoming pope. His recognition, however, still needed to be won.

Frederick III, of Austria, became the new emperor and would rule longer than any other sovereign. Unfortunately, his rule was so weak that the empire, throughout his long reign, would become increasingly divided.

England, France, Sicily, and other countries of the empire had long since fallen out of effective control of the emperors but with Frederick III even Bohemia, Hungary, and the greater parts of Germany ceased to be obedient to their sovereign. The popes power had fallen, and so had the emperors. The kings of Europe were soon to be united only in name. The Holy Roman Empire was to become a mere ghost of times past, whose nominal sovereigns would linger on for another three hundred years to the present. Frederick could have taken the initiative to save Constantinople and to resolve the newest schism, but he was preoccupied with mysticism. He studied astology, magic, and alchemy, to the neglect of the empire. He remained, for the time being, neutral in the latest schism.

The kingdom of Aragon in Spain declared for Felix, as did the universities of Paris, Vienna, Cologne, and a few others. Savoy and several German princes also supported the new pope, but most others backed Eugene IV. Eugene's real strength laid in the support that the Greeks gave him. The Byzantines were desperate for help and the council, representing the eastern church, had agreed to submit to the pope. It was, however, mere paper work. A miserable crusade failed in 1443 and the Byzantine people rejected the agreements. The Armenians deposed their patriarch while the Jacobites, Copts, and others disavowed the council. Only the Nestorians seemed willing to accept Roman Catholic rule. Despite this, Eugene was seen favorably throughout Europe for his efforts to unite Christendom. In 1443 he recognized the king of Aragon's claims to the kingdom of Naples in exchange for his allegiance. Alfonso V abandoned Felix and Frederick III came to the winning side. Felix began to seek a way to abdicate favorably, but he would have to wait. It would not be until two years after Eugene's death, in 1447, that Felix was able to amicably abdicate. That was, in part, due to the intercession of Charles VII, who negotiated a favorable peace with Nicholas V, the new pope of Rome.

Felix was to be the last antipope. No other pope since has been challenge by a rival claimant. Like a number of the antipopes, he was a better man than the "true" claimant, but as is often the case in history, it is the powerful who rule, not the just. Eugene had crushed the attempted reforms of the Councils of Constance and Basil. He had destroyed any form of democratic government within the church and reasserted papal supremacy, albeit nominal. The popes would never again return to the days of Innocent III, but they would try. Thus the age of martyrs coincided with the futile attempt to return to the height of medieval power, but those days were passing, for not only was this the age of martyrs, it was also the age of the Renaissance.

The Renaissance

The Renaissance is a term often connected to the arts and sciences. Indeed, the Renaissance did spur movements in the arts and sciences. However, the Renaissance was far more. It was an intellectual movement spawned by religious reform and the desire for a pure church. The dissident Christians of the Middle Ages wrote far more than Bible tracts and did far more than preach from the street corners. The Renaissance officially began with Roger Bacon and ended with Erasmus in the middle of the sixteenth century. Dante wrote of the ills of the church and produced one of the most famous pieces of medieval literature. Michaelangelo produced art that reflected the real world, a realism that made people look at the world as real, rather than ideal. The Renaissance was an intellectual movement. It was spawned by the creation of universities, which in turn had created Wycliff and Huss.

The Renaissance was, as some believe, the beginning of the Reformation. That is not to say that the Renaissance artists, writers, or thinkers were Protestants, although some were (or would have been). Nevertheless, the Renaissance was a clarion call for change. It meant that the current path of the Catholic Church would have to change. Some wanted to return to a more simple day when the Bible was supreme, but others wanted to move away from the church all together. Some were forerunners of the Reformation. Others, the "humanists," modeled themselves after the Greek philosophers of old. Many worshipped Plato and Aristotle, rather than God and Christ.

In literature the great names were Dante, Petrarca, and Coccaccio. Each was Catholic, but each criticized the direction of the church and called the church back to the purity of the early church. If alive today they would probably prefer neither the Protestant nor Catholic Church, but something in between. To this day, their literature can be found in any bookstore or any library.

In art Leonardi DaVinci and Michaelangelo ruled the day. DaVinci mixed art with science. The artists were so detailed in their study of the human body that medicine benefitted. The bodily organs were examined along with muscles and sinews. Reality, not mysticism, ruled the artist of the Renaissance, and that reality sparked a curiousity that fed the sciences and the universities. Although the sciences were still steeped in medieval magic (sciences like alchemy) men like Leonardi DaVinci caused the sciences to look beyond their magic and to delve deeper into the mysteries of nature.

Finally, there were the thinkers of the age. Some of these men were called "humanists" but the term seems too vague. Some idolized Plato and Aristotle, but others were devout religious reformers. The universities were filled with both kinds, and a mixture of the two. There was what some called a "revival of paganism" which coincided with the movement for Reformation. The two were flip sides of the same coin. They both opposed the medieval religion of the church but disputed how to change. These were the men that the last of the medieval popes, princes, and kings were to fight against. It was safer to secretly hate all religion, than to appeal to the Scriptures. The church officials hated the humanists of the secular bent, but they feared the religious reformers.

These were the intellectual movements of the fifteenth century. These were what began to fill the universities and occupy the minds of the great thinkers of the age. It was inevitable that the Renaissance would lead to the Reformation, and perhaps the popes knew it. Perhaps that is why the persecutions of the fifteenth century were so severe. The papacy was in a war for survival as they saw it. They could not shut down the universities but they could persecute the Lollard and Hussite professors. This is why the persecutions were not only aimed at stopping the spread of "heresy" but also aimed at taking control of the universities (something all dictators try) but it was destined to fail.

The War of the Roses

Before returning to the martryrs of this age, it is necessary to address the changes in England. A martyr dies for his faith. A soldier dies for his king and country. Sometimes a soldier is a martyr, but too often they die for kings who seek only their own power. The War of the Roses produced no martyrs, but it was, nevertheless, an important part of the political events of the fifteenth century.

When England was driven out of France, Henry VI became mad. His insanity lasted for a year and a half, during which time Richard, the duke of York, became lord protector, the regent. He had hoped to become king, but when Edward, prince of Wales, was born to Henry in October, 1453, his right to ascension was challenged. Henry had an heir. Not willing to risk loosing his power, Richard eventually took to the battlefield. The heirs of York wanted to wrest the throne from Henry's heirs. The houses of York and Lancaster would battle for decades in what bacame known as the War of the Roses.

In 1460 King Henry VI was captured at Northampton. Richard at first claimed the throne for himself, but killing the king would not endear the house of York to the people or princes, and Henry would not willingly abdicate, so they agreed to allow him to rule on the condition that the house of York be named heir to the throne in place of his son, Edward. The house of Lancaster, meanwhile, was not content to see their captured king turn the throne over the Yorks, or deprive the young Edward of Wales of his inheritance. In December, 1460, Richard of York was slain in a battle at Wakeland. The victory, however, would not last and Richard's son, also named Edward, took to the battlefield. He won a great victory at St. Albans in February, 1461 and proclaimed himself king. In March his army routed Henry at Towton, Yorkshire, forcing Henry V, Edward of Wales, and Queen Margaret to flee to Scotland where they would remain for several years. Edward of York was now unchallenge at home and was crowned king in London on June 28, 1461. The war, however, would not end. It was just beginning.

The Papacy in the Mid–Fifteenth Century

The reign of Nicholas V brought some measure of peace and stability to the papacy. It was he who peaceably ended the new schism that had threatened the church at the Council of Basil, and it was he who is called the first of the Renaissance popes. He founded the Vatican library and supported the artists of the Renaissance. Nicholas had taken to restoring Rome and declared another Jubilee in the year 1450 that brought money and prestige back to Rome. He coronated Frederick III in 1452, which would prove to be the last time that an emperor would be so coronated in Rome. That fact alone showed that the empire of old was passing into history. The emperors were no longer masters of the empire and the power of the papacy too was fading quickly. The most momentous event in Nicholas' reign was news of the sack of Constantinople. The Byzantine Empire, the eastern Roman Empire, had fallen to the Ottoman Turks.

News of that the Muslims Turks were now at the fringes of Europe sent shock waves throughout Europe, but oddly enough, it was not a big enough shock to stir the people of Europe into putting aside their petty conflicts. Nicholas was able to secure the peace of Italy where Milan, the Lombards, Florence, Venice, and Naples all agreed to make peace and work together, if necessary, to combat the Islamic threat, but the rest of Europe voiced distress with their voices alone. Hungary was now the front line against Islam, but Frederick III was incompetent to do anything. Nicholas died in 1455 before a new crusade against the Muslim threat could be organized.

Callistus III replaced Nicholas and made his ambition the destruction of the Muslim threat, but Callistus fought a loosing battle. He had reversed the sentence in Joan of Arc (at the request of Charles VII who hoped to justify his coronation by the hands of a condemned heretic) but France still offered little in the way of help for a crusade. A small fleet was put together, and Alfonso of Aragon was placed in charge, but Callistus became furious when he learned that Alfonso was diverting the fleet to settle old debts with the Genoese. Callistus died only three years after taking office, failing in his attempt to put together a new crusade.

Pope Pius II was the next to assume the papal tiara. He too desired to put together a grand crusade to take back Constantinople, but, in fact, he was too busy dividing Europe to unite them. He placed the good of Europe second to the good of the papacy. In a papal bull, the *execrabilis* of 1460, Pius proclaimed that church councils could in no way override the will of the pope. He declared that any appeal to a council from the decision of a pope would result in damnation and curses which only the pope himself could lift. He promptly began to tear down all that the Council of Basil had done and chastized the council for ever having made peace with the Hussites. Pius compared himself to

Melchezedek and excommunicated a popular German duke for refusing to enact some of his legislation.

Ultimately, Pius did nothing to unite Europe. Frederick's incompetence had not only decreased the power of the emperors, but the princes even appealed to Pius to depose him. Nevertheless, Pius was no stronger a leader. The emperor and papacy were fading from glory past. The Holy Roman Empire was now little more than a series of nominally united kingdoms whose kings were usually at war with one another. Soon the papacy would find its last hope in the rising power of Spain; a power they hoped would be able to restore the empire under the banner of the papacy.

The final pope of the mid–fifteenth century was Paul II. He was the nephew of Eugene IV and known mostly for his carefree attitude, as well as his neglect of church affairs. He spent most of his time at carnivals, which he brought to Rome frequently. Although he continued to try to put together a crusade against the Turks he was hurt by his own intolerance. The king of Bohemia was the most capable of leaders who might have lead a crusade against the Ottoman threat that was so close to his homeland, but Paul suspected that he was Hussite (a distinct probability) and excommunicated him. More than that, Paul dared to call a crusade against the Hussites! Thus Paul preferred a crusade against Christians over Turks. As a result neither came to fruition.

It was in Paul's day that the first pringing press was brought to Rome. This significant discovery was made a few years earlier with the help of Gutenberg. Gutenberg's Bible is still among the most famous in history. The press allowed copies to produced in large numbers without the need for scribes. At first the printing press was hailed as a miracle of technology, but the Catholic Church soon came to realize that it put books in the hands of the commoner. Most dangerous to the Church was the fact that it was soon available to put Bibles, translated into the tongues of the common man, into their hands. One can honestly say that the Protestant Reformation owed its success in no small part to the printing press, for it made it possible for the peasant, as well as the noble and clergy, to be able to see the Word of God, and eliminated the necessity of relying upon a bishop for truth.

Storm Clouds Gather

If there was a pause in the persecution of dissidents it was a brief one, but it would resume with a vengeance in the late fifteenth century with crusades and the formation of the Spanish Inquisition. The Spanish Inquisition was itself approved by the will of Sixtus IV. This pope ranked among the most corrupt and vile of the fifteenth century. He is best known for his complacency (although not participation in) the murder of rival Medici family members.

Sixtus abused his powers to enrich his nephews, whom many believed were actually his own sons by his sister. Chief among the family rivals were

Julian Medici and Lorenzo Medici of Florence. Sixtus' nephew and the pope's captain of the mercenary guards discussed a plan to eliminate the two in the presense of the pope. There was some arguments over the plot, and it is not known if all agreed, but that all knew has not been denied by historians of that day, or among modern historians. On April 26, 1478 Julian Medici was stabbed to death by two papal priests during a church service. Lorenzo managed to escape with his life, but the revenge that the Medici took was severe. Sixtus' priests were mutilated before being executed and the captain of Sixtus' guards was beheaded. The Medici also arrested some of Sixtus' relatively although they were not believed to have been privy to the plot.

Sixtus reacted to this news by declaring an interdict against the city and preparing for war. He had the king of Naples at his disposal and was ready to strike when news diverted his attention away from the Medici. In 1481 the Muslim threat had succeeded in taking Otranto, a city on the heel of Italy's boot. The Islamic threat was now firmly on European soil. The death of Mohammed II, however, insured the Catholic victory in Italy and the threat was abated.

Sixtus was also the first pope to license brothels, and was even accused of having served as a pimp to the nobility, as well as acts of sodomy. Furthermore, he was the first pope to apply indulgences for the benefit of the dead. That practice, buying salvation of departed sinners, brought much money into Sixtus' coffers. When Sixtus finally lay dying it was said that three children were used to offer a blood transfusion in hopes of keeping the pope alive. Instead, all four died. Sixtus is remembered as one of a number of vile medieval popes, but he is best remembered for his approval of the formation of the Spanish Inquisition.

The Rise of Spain and the Spanish Inquisition

For centuries Spain had been almost insignificant in the history of the Holy Roman Empire. It had been composed of many small Christian states and controlled in the south by the Islamic Moors. For nearly four hundred years war raged in Spain. Castile, Leon, Aragon, and Portugal were the four main Catholic states. However, when Alfonso the Wise rose to power he had attained the royal throne of both Castile and Leon. Ever since that time Castile and Leon, although techincally seperate for many decades, shared a common king and, hence, became a single state.

In 1466 Ferdinand II, the son of John II of Aragon, was made the king of Sicily. He was married to Isabella, a princess of Castile in 1469. The marriage had itself been arranged in hopes of uniting Spain. That would itself come to pass in 1479, when John II passed away. Isabella had become Queen of Castile five years earlier. Castile and Aragon were now effectively one state, and that state was to become the most powerful in all of Europe. Soon Spain succeeded in driving the Moors completely off of the European continent. Only

Portugal remained a seperate state, and for a time it appeared as if it might have become one with Spain as well. Isabella's daughter had been made Queen of Portugal through another arranged marriage, but when she died in 1498, the kingdom returned to the Portugese heirs.

The power of Spain was due in large part to the power of Ferdinand and Isabella. The famous king and queen are considered among the greatest of Spain's history, but they were by no means tollerant rulers. They were devout Catholics who believed that all "heretics" and unbelievers had to be blotted out. Moreover, they had come to suspect "repentant" heretics and doubted the sincerity of Jews who had converted the Christianity over the years. These Jews were called *conversos* or *maranos*. It had been long alleged that many of these Jews were secretly practicing the Jewish faith while pretending to be Catholic for their own safety.

In fact, while some doubtless did, there is good reason to reject this argument, put forth by Ferdinand himself. By the old Spanish law the papal Inquisition could not touch anyone who was not a member of the Catholic Church. Jews could be punished by the state for offenses, but could not be prosecuted for heresy (since they were not Catholic) until after 1492 when Innocent VIII placed traditional Jews under the Inquisition's juristiction. This was because popes themselves had declared openly that a dissident Christian was worse than a Jew precisely because he professed to Christ, whereas the Jew did not. It was deemed blasphemy to oppose the papacy if you professed to Christ. Consequently, Jews were actually safer (before Innocent's proclamation) if they *did not* profess to being Christian. The truth is that many of the *conversos* were what are called today Messianic Jews. They were Jews who accept Christ as Messiah, but reject the Catholic teachings as foreign to both the Jewish and Christian Bibles. To this day Messianic Jews continue to worship on Saturday and practice Jewish rites such as *barmitzvah*. These acts were considered an affront to Ferdinand in 1478 and he wrote to Sixtus IV demanding the formation of a *Spanish* Inquisition, independant of the papal Inquisition.

The Spanish Inquisition differed from the papal Inquisition in several ways. First, it was the only Inquisition *not* under the direct control of the papacy. Even though Ferdinand and Isabella were devout Catholics they did not trust the papacy. Ferdinand therefore pressured the pope to allow the Inquisition to be under the direct control of Spain itself. Since the Spanish king also controlled Sicily and Naples, the pope was not eager to alienate his strongest, and closest, ally. The Spanish Inquisition was, therefore, placed under the control of an inquisitor–general whose power was absolute. Isabella's confessor, Thomas de Torqemada, became the first inquisitor–general and set the "standard" for the brutal inquisitors to follow. So powerful was he that even the sovereign pope could not grant absolution to those under condemnation by the Spanish Inquisition!

The second, and subsequent, differences were in the canon of Inquisition law. Unlike the papal Inquisitions torture was not only used to extract confessions, but also to "purify the soul." In other words, torture was used regardless of whether a suspect confessed. The accused had no recourse, save to the inquisitor–general himself. Suspects were also expected to hand over the names of all their accomplices. Even rumors were deemed reason to be apprehended. Eventually, in 1515, the inquisitor–general was even given the authority to sieze the highest of nobility for the slightest suspicion.

Inquisitors were given the right to bear arms in public, even as soldiers were. Consequently, they did not need to seek the civil authorities help in arresting suspects. Moreover, the inquisitors claimed to be exempt from civil law!

The greatest difference between the papal and Spanish Inquisition was in their method of payment. Papal inquisitors were bishops whose salaries were paid by the church; the inquisition being a part of their duties. In the Spanish Inquisition, the inquisitors were full time "servants." All the property and inheritance of heretics (with a few exceptions such as a wife's dowry) were subject to confiscation, and the properties themselves were used to pay the inquisitors. Thus the inquisitors could steal any suspected heretic's property for their own. They even had the audacity to charge family members for the price of torturing their heretical family member! Some tortures cost more than others.

In terms of guilt, the deck was obviously stacked against the accused. Any person, no matter what his background, religion, credibility, or criminal history, was permitted to testify against the accused, but only a non–relative (as far back as the fourth generation) of good standing in the Catholic Church could testify in his own behalf.

Punishment for heretics varied greatly, but were always humiliating and severe. In addition to loss of property, men and women (and children twelve or older) could be stripped naked and scourged before all to see. Ceremonies were required of the "pentinent" heretic which was also made a public spectacle, often attended by the king and queen themselves. Various tortures were used to purify the souls of the pentinent, and some were imprisoned for life in dungeons that drove men insane. Of course, some heretics were "handed over" to the civil authority. In this respect the Spanish Inquisition remained the same as the papal Inquisition. Technically, the church could not condemn a man to death, but if the civil authority did not burn the condemned heretic, then he would be accused of heresy, excommunicated, and tried himself. The civil authority never reviewed a case or offered leniency. The punishment was always death in the flames.

In Inquisition wasted no time. Less than two years after its establishment by Sixtus IV the prisons of St. Pablo were overflowing and prisoners were transferred to the grand fortress of Triana. The first victims were almost exclusively *conversos* and/or Messianic Jews. Thousands of Christian

Jews were brought before the Inquisition and hundreds were executed. In 1485 an act of desperation led the assassination of the chief inquisitor of Saragossa. Peter Arbues was struck dead, allegedly while in prayer. The retaliation was severe. The suspected perpetrators were quarted, beheaded, and/or burned alive. In 1867, pope Pius IX canonized the savage inquisitor Peter Arbues.

In 1492 the pope finally gave permission to expand the Inquisition to non–Christian Jews. An estimated 170,000 to as many as 400,000 (the numbers are debated) Jews, both traditional and Christian, were driven out of Spain. A hundred thousand entered Portugal, but a few years later they were given the option of baptism or death. By this time it is conservatively estimated that nearly 10,000 victims were burned alive and another hundred thousand subjected to various other tortures and punishments. The Spanish Inquisition was to be one of the darkest pages in history and illustrated the attempt of the Spanish to remain in the dark ages long after much of Europe had entered a new dawn. The Spanish Inquisition would not be formally disbanded until decades after the Holy Roman Empire itself had fallen.

The War of the Roses Ends

The resolution of the War of the Roses once again interrupts the history of the martyrs of the fifteenth century but is essential in relating the rise of the Tudor dynasty in England. Edward IV had become king of England in 1461 when Henry VI, along with his heir Edward of Wales, fled to Scotland. However, Edward's reign would not last due, in part, to his own making. Richard Neville, the earl of Warwick, became Edward's most powerful ally at court. While Edward spent his time revelling with women and wine, Neville was the real source of power. It was Neville who defeated Henry's forces when they returned in 1464. Henry was finally captured and imprisoned in the Tower of London in 1465. Nevertheless, Neville had a falling out with Edward who resented his power and began to deny Neville's wishes. The breaking point was when Neville believed he had made an alliance with France's new king, Louis XI, only to find that Edward had secretly made an alliance with France's enemy, Burgundy, with whom Louis XI would spend his entire reign at war.

Louis XI was forced to negotiate with Charles the Bold of Burgundy, but when Charles learned that Louis' forces were attacking Liege, even as they were in conference, Charles arrested Louis and imprisoned him. Louis was finally released after making concessions and began to plot with the earl of Warwick to restore Henry VI. In 1469 Neville arrested Edward and restored Henry. Edward was imprisoned, but his supporters eventually forced Neville to flee to France, and Henry was returned to the Tower of London. Meanwhile, Neville, with Louis XI's troops, invaded England in the fall of 1470. This time it was Edward who fled, but he too returned with an army, and in May 1471 the

Prince of Wales was killed and the Lancastrian army defeated. Henry VI was then murdered in the Tower of London.

In revenge for Louis' support of Neville, Edward invaded France in a coordinated attack with the Burgundians. Louis made alliances with the Swiss confederation against Burgundy but the daughter of Charles the Bold was now the wife of Maximillian, Frederick III's son and heir. Charles was, therefore, part of the imperial family. When Charles was killed in 1477, Maximillian claimed the right to Burgundy, which Louis was reluctant to give. Both Edward IV and Louis XI died in 1483, but the heirs of Edward were would soon fall and the Lancastrian struggle was renewed.

Edward V ruled for but two months. A boy of twelve years of age, his uncle, Duke Richard of Gloucester was the Lord Protector of the realm. Richard, however, wanted more and he openly called Edward a bastard and ordered deposed. Edward was never seen again, leading many to assume that Richard had him murdered. The apparent murder of a young boy, and other abuses of King Richard III, caused several uprisings. The Lancastrians found a somewhat distant relative of the Lancastrian dynasty through a widow of Henry V. Henry Tudor became the claimant to the throne and an alternative to the hated Richard. With the support of the Lancastrians, Henry defeated Richard at Bosworth Field on August 22, 1485. Richard died in battle and Henry Tudor became the first of the powerful Tudor dynasty, ending the War of the Roses.

The Persecutions of Innocent VIII

The election of Innocent VIII is said to have been one of the two most turbulent elections in history. The second was the election that followed Innocent's death. Mobs ran through the streets committing murder, rape, and pillaging whatever they could find. The nobleman Jerome Riario, who held the Castle St. Angelo was murdered, and his wife was forced to hold the castle against all besiegers. Amid the turmoil Innocent VIII was elected secretly in the middle of the night.

Innocent was known for his gaity of life and did not fail to acknowledge that he had many children out of wedlock. Unlike previous popes who tried to hide their illegitimate children, Innocent openly acknowledged his. Appointments to public office were openly sold to the highest bidder and the cardinals voted themselves a raise; already being paid as much as some royalty, on average several hundred thousand dollars a year in modern currency.

During his pontificate one of the two heirs of Mohammed II had fled to the isle of Rhodes where he was apprehended and eventually sent to Rome. The new sultan of the Ottoman kingdom did not want his brother, Djem, to return lest he usurp the kingdom so he agreed to pay Innocent 40,000 ducats a year to keep him a prisoner and also agreed not to invade Italian soil. Innocent was more than eager to obligue but Djem was not exactly an unwilling prisoner. He was treated like royalty and received a welcome which would have been fitting the emperor. He was surrounded by an escort throughout his life, but walked freely in Rome and lived in a grand mansion. The people of Rome are said to have treated him as the new Marco Polo from the east.

Innocent's reign is best known for his instigation of the Inquisition against witchcraft in Germany and for his crusade against the Waldenses of Piedmonte Valley. The first was issued in a bull in 1484. Witchcraft was the technical designation for certain pagan religious practices which still occurred infrequently in the Middle Ages. However, the medieval state of the Catholic faith was itself steeped in superstition and magic. The sign of the cross was supposed to ward off evil spirits, exorcisms were performed not only on people but even on wheat fields to insure a good harvest. Curses were also used to drive off vermin and to kill weeds. It is only natural that if the faithful engaged in such practices, how much worse should they believe the practices of witches and heretics! As time passed the most absurd myths and legends grew about the practices of secret witches and Satanists.

The papal bull, entitled *Malleus Maleficarum*, was first accepted in Germany and slowly began to influence England, which was slow to impose its orders. Spain, naturally, followed in line as well with the Spanish Inquisition adding witches to its list of victims. Interestingly enough, witchcraft had been wont to have been prosecuted in the past because the people feared the curses which witches might have placed upon them, thus the papal bull urged the people to cast off their fear and extinguish the threat of witchcraft. Not only were those who experimented with mystic or pagan beliefs apprehended but false accusations abounded, although many were burned at the stake just the same. Paranoia, or even vindicative accusations, were common. The history of "witch hunting," as it is called today, was just beginning.

Innocent's most cruel edict was his command for a crusade, not against the Muslim Turks, but against the Waldenses of Piedmonte. Two armies, one French and the other papal, were to enter the valley, one from the north and the other from the south, and act as a vice, crushing the Waldenses "heresy" once and for all. The French army entered in 1488. Many villages fled their cities and retreated to large caves where they had enough supplies to last a year or more. Realizing that it would be a trap to enter into the caves after them, the French army set massive fires in front of the caves. Some Waldenses fled into the swords and arrows of the French while most suffocated to death. The papal commander boasted that there were three thousand victims, including four hundred children.

Meanwhile, the papal army, led by the legate Cataneo, moved up from the south. He was greeted by two men of high stature from the Waldenses valley who pleaded "do not condemn us without hearing us." Cataneo only became more confident that the Waldenses were desperate and unable to put up a fight. This was his mistake. He divided his army, over 35,000 men, into groups of more than twenty divisions, believing that they could take out the villages independently. He sent each division off in seperate directions with instructions to obliterate any villages they encountered and to meet up at Pra de Tor, meaning Meadow of the Tower because of the tall mountain which encircled it.

Many of Cataneo's troops failed to meet their rendezvous. The Waldenses had at their disposal nature and the terrain of the mountains, the cold, and the valleys. The smaller armies were hurt by the elements and overcome by the enemy. Despite the victory of some of these Waldenses, most retreated into the heart of the valley where they would be surrounded by mountains and where the enemy could only enter in a few narrow passes.

The Waldenses had little to defend themselves. They had bows and arrows, used for hunting, but little else. They beat their plowshares into pikes and made barracades to slow down Cataneo's army. Behind the Waldenses' front line ministers prayed aloud, calling out to God for help. When the attack began the papal army was making headway. The captain mockingly ridiculed the praying ministers when he struck dead by an arrow. The papal army panicked and eventually fled from the peasant army.

Cataneo reorganized the remaining soldiers and tried again. This time when he came to site of the old battlefield, it was abandoned. He believed the enemy had not expected him to return. He confidently marched his troops into the ravine that lay before the vast valley. It was a trap. Boulders were cast down upon the army and an avalance of rocks slew many. Waldenses troops then charged in from the north, while many of Cataneo's soldiers trampled over other soldiers in an attempt to escape to the south. Cataneo's expedition failed miserably. So great was the victory of the peasant Waldenses that the young prince of Turin asked for a conference with the Waldenses leaders. They met with him and he was so impressed by them that he declared that he had been mislead by the pope in permitting the assault. He recounted that the papal legates had even told him how the Waldenses were deformed cyclops, cursed by God for their heresies. Thereafter, the prince made peace with the Waldenses and promised no further incursions would be permitted during his lifetime.

Precursors to the Reformation

There are actually many precursors to the Reformation, many of whom have been aforementioned; two of whom follow. However, there were many more that could never be mentioned. For example, John of Goch, also called John Pupper, and John Wessel were men who preached the gospel that was to be echoed by Protestants many years later. Neither of these men, however, preached to large groups or became notorious through the empire. For that very reason they escaped persecution. In fact, it was not until after Martin Luther that their writings and sermons became known to Germany at large, but their small local communities knew and heard the messages. Although they taught the doctrines of Wycliff, Huss, and the Reformers, their quiet lives kept them from the hands of the Inquisition, who had many more of these preachers than they could keep track of. One such preacher was John von Wesel (not John Wessel).

Wesel taught that the Scriptures alone were the basis for authority, he taught that excommunication was invalid, that the priests had no authority over the soul, that indulgences were useless, that transubstatiation was not essential, that the popes should be disobeyed when in error, and that God alone saves through faith. This German preacher was accused of being a Hussite, although he had no direct communications with them. Soon he was taken to trial before the Inquisition, but being an old man, he could not endure the threatened tortures. He renounced his views and was sentenced to life imprisonment. He escaped death, and hence martyrdom. There were many like Wesel. They wanted Biblical reform but had not the heart to endure martyrdom or torture. Had they all had the strength that few bear, the Reformation might have begun many years earlier.

The Martyrdom of Savonarola and the Close of the Fifteenth Century

The fifteen century closed with the martyrdom of one of Italy's most famous. It is also closed with the discovery of the New World. This New World would perhaps symbolize the new world that waiting around the corner in the sixteenth century. The Reformation would literally create a new world in Europe and end the Middle Ages. With it the Holy Roman Empire was dealt its mortal wound. It would linger on three hundred more years, but the wounds could not be sealed and the empire slowly bled to death. Spain was to be the empire's last hope, but this is to be discussed in the next chapter. Here, it is appropirate that the age of martyrs ends with the death of Italy's "prophet" and child, the friar Girolamo Savonarola.

There has been much debate as to whether Savonarola was a precursor to the Reformation or whether he was a loyal Catholic. Both claim him as their own. In truth, he belongs to both. Like modern evangelical Catholics, he claimed to be a loyal Catholic but blinded himself to obvious contradictions between the medieval theology he nominally accepted and the Biblical doctrines he expounded. For example, he believed in the seven sacraments but was clear that these sacraments constituted the *result* of grace, despite the fact that the official position of the Church was that they *dispense* grace. Such contradictions are not uncommon among people, and typified his entire life and ministry. While officially accepting the doctrine of the papacy, Savonarola defied Pope Alexander VI repeatedly. He also created the first, and only, democratic theocracy. An oxymoron? Perhaps, but this is one of the very things that made Savonarola so revered in history. Truly Savonarola belongs to both the Protestant and Catholic, for he sought to reform the Church, and promoted the Scriptures as the sole source of truth. He placed Christ alone as the dispenser of grace and called for judgment on the wicked within the church, but he never denied the Holy Church; only its officials. Martin Luther considered him his precursor. So does history.

Following the death of Innocent VIII, the papal tiara was literally put up for sale. Alexander VI won the crown and earned the distinction among historians of being the most corrupt and debased pope since the papal pornocracy. He openly fathered many children, several of whom occupied prominent positions in his court, including one accused of murdering another of Alexander's sons. He also held a concubine whose husband was paid off with gold. Much of his reign will be discussed in the next chapter, but his decadence is important inasmuch as Savonarola spent much time preaching against his depravity and earned his wrath.

Savonarola first began preaching over a decade earlier. In a time when Hebrew was chastized as the "Jewish" language, he emphasized studying the Bible in the original languages, including Hebrew. His preaching, however, emphasized repentance and judgment. Some compared him to John the Baptist, who preceded Christ's coming. In the Middle Ages, he was to John the Baptist as the Reformation was to the coming of Christ. He said that he took "the Scriptures as my sole guide" and condemned wickedness of the clergy, declaring, "the care of the souls is no longer their concern ... they have not only destroyed the Church of God, they have built up a new Church after their own pattern." He even went so far as to cry out, "Arise and come to deliver thy Church from the hands of the devils, from the hands of tyrants, from the hands of inquisitous prelates." However, it was Savonarola's prophetic visions that most disturbed the Church in his early days. According to Savonarola, he had visions of God's judgment upon the Church symbolized by a sword falling from heaven. Of his "prophecies" there both hits and misses, but it was one of his hits that sparked the most significant actions of his career, and antagonized Rome far more than his declarations that Rome was the new Babylon.

Savonarola prophecied that the French King Charles VIII would invade Italy and experience momentary success. He also predicted Charles' ultimate failure. Perhaps it was an educated guess, for Charles' ambitions may well have been guessed. Related by marriage to the Spanish family, who were the heirs of Naples, Charles began to place claims on Naples himself. In order to understand this, however, it is necessary to briefly catch up on past events that have been bypassed.

Frederick III had reigned longer than any other emperor in history, but his incompetence made the office of the emperor a joke. The princes of Germany and the surrounding countries had tried to convince the popes to depose Frederick, but they would not obligue, so Maximillian, Frederick's son, was named co–regent in 1486. Maximillian was married to the prominent

Burgundian royal family, which antagonized the French, but strengthened Maximillian's position in Europe along with his regency over the Netherlands. The co–emperor, however, was not the true emperor yet and in 1488 the Swabian League was formed to protect itself and southern Germany from mercenaries and invaders who threatened it. One of those threats came from France itself. The Swiss confederation, along with Hungary and Bohemia, had allied against Frederick. Although they planned no invasions, their opposition to the emperor allowed the French Count of Armagnac to send brutal mercenaries into south Germany in an attempt to break German power.

Charles VIII, who had not proven competent himself, paid large sums of money to King Henry VII of England in exchange for Englands promise to renounce claims to French territory and abandon Normandy. With Germany and England at bay, he began to direct his efforts to a campaign to capture Naples. In 1494 he began his march in Naples and soon came upon Florence, the home of Savonarola. The "prophet" had spoken of his coming months earlier and warned the people that the powerful Medici family, who had ruled the city as dictators, must be driven out. He declared that God would make Florence like a new Jerusalem and the center of Christendom, even as Rome once was many centuries ago. He received Charles, who had marched unopposed into Italy and told him that he would capture Rome. That he did, and on May 12, 1495 he was crowned king of Naples, but he did not realize that the pope, Milan, Austria, Venice, and others were behind him, ready to invade. Charles was forced to retreat to France, and quickly lost all his new territory as fast as he had gained it.

With the banishment of the Medici family, who were already in Rome poisoning the pope against Savonarola, a new government had to be formed, for the former was little more than a monarchy run by the head of the Medicis. To that end Savonarola mimicked Arnold of Brescia (another would be Church reformer) but Savonarola's government was both more idealistic, and more democratic (as opposed to republican). The new government of Florence consisted of two councils. The first council consisted of 1500 people who then elected a supreme council made up of eighty elders, and yet the councils did not have a president, for Savonarola delcared that Christ alone was the king. Thus a democratic government, with Christ as the nominal head, was established in Florence. This was the third attempt to resurrect the ancient republic of Rome, but Savonarola did not envision this as a reestablishment of an ancient Republic, but as a true theocracy. Savonarola himself had no official role in the government, although it was obviously of his making.

It was at this point that Alexander began his battle with the prophet of Florence. On September 9, 1495, Alexander sent a letter to Savonarola prohibiting him from preaching and warning him not to intervene in government affairs (which the popes did all the time). Savonarola ignored the letter. Two more were sent. The last, appearing in October, officially forbade him from preaching either in public or in private and was more threatening in tone. For a time Savonarola obeyed, but in February, 1496, he was not only preaching again but he was specifically preaching about the evils of the papacy. He even declared, "of old, priests called their bastards nephews, but now they call them outright sons."

Savonarola soon found himself the target of conspiritors and assassins, whose failure may be attributed to the protection afforded Savonarola by his allies in Florence. Within a year Alexander excommunicated the great friar. All were forbidden from associating with him or even conversing with him. Once again, Savonarola remained silent and did not preach for a time, but a year later, in February, 1498, he again took to the pulpit and denounced the high clergy saying, "they are worse than Turks or Moors. They traffic in the sacrametns and sell benefices to the highest bidder." He spoke of the clergy's concubines and reminded the people that the pope openly enriched his illegitimate children at the expense of the people. He then called for a general council to depose the pope. Alexander threatened an interdict upon Florence if they continued to tolerate the excommunicate.

Allies of the pope called for the ancient rite of trial by fire. Savonarola refused, since many had long abandoned the barbaric practice, but others still believed that only by miraculously escaping the flames could Savonarola prove himself a prophet. Soon a friend of Savonarola, Fra Domenico, offered to take his place. When the trial date came there was much delay and arguments over whether Domenico should go into the flames naked or be allowed to carry items with him. Soon a rain storm came and the trial was cancelled. The people were furious and a mob broke out, accusing Savonarola of cowardice. Mob violence seized the city and Savonarola was abandoned to the pope's allies.

In April, 1498, Alexander VI gave orders that confessions were to be extracted from Savonarola and his close friends. Torture insured those confessions, including the friar who now denied he was a prophet at all. The "confessed heretic" was ordered by the pope to be executed by hanging. At the execution the clergy declared that Savonarola was to be eternally seperated from the "Church militant and the Church triumphant," to which he replied, "not the Church triumphant, for that is not yours to do." He was then hung and his body burned. The ashes, like those of Arnold of Brescia and John Huss, were thrown into the river so that no one might know where his body rests.

Holy Roman Emperor	*Rival (if any)*	Pope	*AntiPope (if any)*
		———— 1431 ————	
———— 1437 ————			
Albert II		Eugene IV	*—1439—*
———— 1440 ————			*Felix V*
		———— 1447 —	
		Nicholas V	*—1449—*
		———— 1455 ————	
		Callistus III	
		———— 1458 ————	
		Pius II	
Frederick III		———— 1464 ————	
		Paul II	
		———— 1471 ————	
		Sixtus IV	
		———— 1484 ————	
		Innocent VIII	
		———— 1492 ————	
———— 1493 ————		Alexander VI	
		———— 1503 ————	
		Pius III	
Maximillian		———— 1503 ————	
		Julius II	
		———— 1513 ————	
		Leo X	
———— 1519 ————			
		———— 1521 ————	
		———— 1522 ————	
		Hadrian VI	
		———— 1523 ————	
		Clement VII	
		———— 1534 ————	
Charles V		Paul III	
		———— 1549 ————	
		———— 1550 ————	
		Julius III	
		———— 1555 ————	
		Marcellus II	
		———— 1555 ————	
———— 1556 ————		Paul IV	

24

Spain and the New World

The discovery of the new world was to have a profound impact upon the old world. It opened new horizons and stirred the imagination as not even Marco Polo had. Dreams of reclaiming the Holy Land and the eastern borders were largely forgotten for the hopes of the new world and its land. Change was everywhere.

The Voyages of Columbus

One of the most popular myths of the twentieth century is that Columbus set out to prove the world was round. In fact, all educated people knew this since ancient Egypt where the scholars of their day tried to measure the size of the earth by measuring, at different locations, the shadows which the sun cast at noon and comparing the differences. Scholars came to believe that the earth was quite large, and, in fact, they were very close to being accurate. Columbus never had to argue for a round earth, he had to argue for small earth. The riches of India and China beckoned Europe, but the journey to the east was not only troublesome, but nearly impossible. By land there was the Muslim threat, as well as mountains and deserts and an impossible stretch of landmass. By sea, one had to sail down below the tip of Africa and up through the Indian sea. Columbus believed there was a shorter way; around the globe.

Columbus' motives were religious, not political. He was a man driven by a belief in the great commission of Jesus. "Go into all the world and preach the gospel to all creation" (Mark 16:15). Colmbus was propelled by his desire to spread the gospel and by the prohetic interpretation of Joachim of Floris.

Born in Genoa, Italy, Columbus was always a sailor at heart. He tried to win support for his venture from king Henry VIII of England and the Portugese, but finally he turned to Ferdinand and Isabella. He placed the size of the oceans between Europe and India at one quarter their actual size. Scholars and priests warned the king and queen against the venture, but Columbus earned the respect of Isabella, who was to prove Columbus' best ally. It could have been that the financial risk was small compared with what might be gained, or it may have been Columbus' quotation of Bible prophecy, including Isaiah. The NIV tranlsation of Isaiah 40:22 even speaks about "the circle of the earth."

Columbus was granted dispensation to undertake the journey, but they took only as much food as he believed was necessary. In short, had the New World not been waiting on the other side of the Atlantic, Columbus' men would have starved. It was for this reason that they had threatened mutiny, not fear of falling off the earth. Three ships and ninty men sailed across the Atlantic and as the supplies began to run short, the men began to panic, fearing that Columbus was indeed wrong, but on October 12, 1492 they saw San Salvador near Cuba. The natives there spoke of cannibals on the mainland to the south, but these natives were not particularly hostile. Columbus gathered together cigars, sugar, tobacco, cotton, and learned how to make hammocks which soon became standard in all ships. He then brought news of the New World back to Spain.

Nicolo Barabino – Columbus at Salamanca – 1887

Settlements followed and Columbus was put in charge. However, the officials that the king and queen sent with Columbus did not like the fact that their master was a commoner and often sought to usurp Columbus' authority. The second expedition was paid for with money stolen, or confiscated, from Jews who were now fleeing Spain under the weight of the Spanish Inquisition. When they arrived at the New World, Columbus tried to establish colonies as best as he knew how in a medieval time (for the Middle Ages had not yet passed, particularly in Spain). Indians were used as laborers and some of their lands were appropriated for the European settlers. Troublemakers among the Indians were shipped back to Spain where they became slaves. Although modern revisionists have made much of this, it was actually Columbus who lobbied for the gentle treatment of the Indians and their conversion, rather than conquest. Nevertheless, there is no doubt that Columbus, master that he was of the sea, had trouble knowing how to govern towns. Sometimes he was too lax with discipline, while at other times he compensated by being far too harsh. When one settlement was devastated by renegade Indians who rebelled, Spain's officials were quick to point the blame at Columbus. His second voyage ended on June 11, 1496.

In Columbus' absence, Alexander VI had partitioned the New World between Portugal and Spain. This was ratified on June 7, 1494. The division would not create any immediate problems, but would eventually lead to conflicts on the New World. In the meantime, Columbus continued to encounter more problems on his third voyage. Another rebellion caused him to request an administrator from Spain to help him, but when Bobadilla arrived, on August 23, 1500, he replaced, rather than assisted, Columbus. When Columbus refused to surrender authority, he was imprisoned. Some skirmishes occurred between Bobadilla's men and those of Columbus. On the trip back to Spain Columbus refused to allow the chains to be removed. His plan worked. Isabella was shocked to hear that the discoverer of the New World had been brough back in chains and ordered his immediate release. She would not, however, give him back his command of the colonies. It had become apparent that for all his greatness, he was unable to govern colonies.

Columbus eventually gave up on the New World and instead tried to sell Isabella on a new conquest of Jerusalem. The calls for a crusade against the Turks had lost their zeal over the years, but Columbus, armed with Bible verses, aimed to gain Isabella's support for a new expedition. She reminded Columbus that such a conquest would be impossible without money. She, therefore, urged Columbus to instead take a new expedition to try to find a way through the New World, for by this time it was clear that the New World was not the Indies, as Columbus had originally thought, but a new continent.

Columbus left on his final voyage on May 9, 1502. He was never able to found a way around, or through, the giant continent. On November 7, 1504 he returned to Spain with the bad news. Less than a month later, on November 26, Columbus lost his most trusted ally. Isabella died. Columbus would never return to the New World and himself died, a forgotten man, on May 21, 1506.

The Empire Before the Conquistadors

When Columbus returned the Spain he found that Pope Alexander VI had died a year before. Pius III, the "nephew" of Pius II, had been elected to replace him, but survived only twenty–six days from his election. It is believed that he would have called a general council to attempt another reform. Of course, there is no way of telling what would have happened. It may have, and probably would have, been yet another feeble attempt at reform resulting in little more than minor administrative changes. In any case, the cardinals had no desire in seeing a reformatory council and the next pope was selected through open bribery. Julius II, the "nephew" of Sixtus IV, was elected pope.

Called the warrior–pope, Julius made his career ambition the reunification of Italy under the authority of the pope. This was not an easy task. For years Italy had been divided amongst itself and wars were constant over the succession to the throne of Naples. Charles VIII of France had claimed Naples his own, but the Spanish kings also laid claim to the inheritance of Naples.

The imperial problem was also Julius' concern. The painfully long reign of Frederick III weakened the empire to the extent that Maximilian, Frederick's son, was named co–emperor and regent even before Frederick died. Maximilian I inherited the Netherlands and Burgundy through marriage alliances and his son, Philip, was given in marriage to Spanish royalty. When the Hungarian king died without an heir in 1490, Maximilian wanted the throne, but the electors instead chose King Vladislav of Bohemia. War was the result but a truce gave Maximilian the inheritance of Hungary *if* Vladislav died without an heir. When Frederick died in 1493, Maximilian had already expanded his authority through marriage alliances and peace pacts, but he was still not a particularly strong emperor. His main task for years would be to drive the Turks from the south–eastern borders of the empire.

In 1499 the borders of the empire were safe enough that Maximilian set out to force the Swiss confederation into submission. The plan failed and in 1500, at the peace of Basil, the Swiss nominally accepted imperial authority but, in fact, became virtually independant, paving the way for Switzerland's defection from the empire decades later in the Reformation.

Another result of this war was the increasing fear among the German princes that Maximilian was trying too hard to reassert his authority. They had not liked Frederick's weakness, but feared a strong emperor. Consquently, the princes of Germany gathered together at Reichstag and created a supreme council of twenty one electors, made up of princes, bishops, and other high officials, who seized some of Maximilian's power to keep him in check. They even toyed with deposing him.

Despite Maximilian's growing power, it was Spain which continued to grow in dominance. The imperial family had married into the Spanish royal family and future emperor, Charles V, would be raised a Spaniard. Ferdinand's daughter, Catherine of Aragon, was given in marriage to the new king of England, Henry VIII as well. Even Portugal married into the family of Ferdinand and Isabella, causing hope that Portugal and Spain would be united, but that hope died along with Isabella's daughter and the Spanish heir who had died in childbirth. The throne of Naples was also claimed by Ferdinand, but the new French king, Louis XII, also laid claims to Naples (the old Neopolitan king had been in marriage alliances with the French and Spanish causing debate over who was the proper heir). That claim was first laid by Charles VIII when he had invaded Italy years earlier. Louis was no less ambitious.

Louis had already laid claim to Milan. Now he wanted Naples. In 1500 Ferdinand and Louis agreed to divide Naples betwixt themselves, but the treaty was not to last. Within a year war erupted and France was driven from Naples. Meanwhile, Julius, the warrior–pope, was busy forcing the submission of Italian cities, personally leading the armies.

It was in 1508 that Europe's princes began a series of conflicts and alliances that would illustrate how precarious the Holy Roman Empire's unity really was at this time. The Venetians, who had never truly submitted to the empire, were now the object of Julius' wrath. In fact, Maximilian was prevented from coming to Rome because of the Venetian threat. Julius, therefore, coronated Maximilian *in absentia*. Unwittingly, Julius himself had thus negated the real necessity of the emperors coronation by the pope; something not lost on later emperors. For the time being, however, Julius' concerns were more with the Venetians. Julius, Louis, Ferdinand, and Maximilian all entered into an alliance against Venice. Part of the alliance was based on the fact that Louis had promised Maximilian and Ferdinand that both Milan and Burgundy should be bequeethed to the future emperor Charles V, their grandson, if Louis failed to produce a male heir. This pact, however, soon fell apart, when Louis backed a general council of Tours (sometimes called the council of Pisa, since that is where it opened) which set out to depose Julius and instigate more reforms. The council itself was an utter failure, but several of its motions were significant in showing the increasing dissatisfaction of the people with the medieval order.

Venice was forgotten and Maximilian, Ferdinand, and Henry VIII of England all turned against Louis. In 1510 Julius backed Spain for the right to Naples and the Spanish power grew to southern Italy where Ferdinand became king of Naples. The "Holy League," including Henry VIII, invaded France several times, although no major conquest were acheived.

The council of Tours, however, defied the pope, printing up coins with the promise, "I will destroy the name of Babylon," a prophetic reference to Rome's decadence. They also tried to win back Maximilian by offering *him* the papal tiara if he would depose Julius. This would have been a return to the days of Constantine who himself was both emperor and pontiff. Maximilian is thought to have seriously considered the offer, but decided it was far too risky.

Julius responded to the council by calling the fifth Lateran Council. This council acheived nothing, other than to negate the force of the French council. The only thing it decreed, other than the typical insignificant administrative changes, was to affirm the bull of Boniface VIII, declaring that the pontiff was the supreme authority.

Julius died in 1513. Nicknamed "the terrible" he was a cruel warlike pope, but the Romans viewed him as a patriot for his reassertion of Roman (or at least papal) authority throughout most of Italy. King Louis XII followed Julius to the grave two years later, being replaced by Francis I. In the meantime the Spanish Inquisition was growing in power and authority. By the time of Louis' death, in 1515, the Spanish Inquisition had even been given authority to arrest the highest noble and the slightest suspicion and the right to defend themselves with blood. The crimes punishable by the Spainish Inquisition now included unauthorized production of non–licensed books, which Ferdinand and Isabella had outlawed years earlier with the Index of Forbidden Books. During these years the Spanish Inquisition executed an estimated 4000 people and subjected 80,000 more to torture.

A year later Ferdinand of Spain died. Ferdinand and Isabella are often considered among the greatest kings of Europe, but they were only so in terms of the success of their political achievements. Ferdinand and Isabella were the driving force behind the Spanish Inquisition and the oppression of Christian dissidents. Given the honorous title of "Catholic Kings" they were the epitome of late medieval rulers. They ruthlessly enforced their will and denied the common man the freedoms that the nobles enjoyed. In the last days of her life Isabella became known as Isabella the Mad on account of mental instability. Nevertheless, there is no doubt that they remain the strongest and most powerful of rulers in Spanish history, and among the most powerful in European history as well.

Charles V, the grandson of both Ferdinand and Emperor Maximilian, became king of Spain in 1516. Three years later he would become emperor upon his grandfather's death. It was Charles who would face some of the most important trials in the history of the Holy Roman Empire. It was also he who gave sanction to the conquest of Hernan Cortes.

The Expedition of Cortes

The New World had seen settlements but no real conquests. Ponce de Leon did conquer Puerto Rico in 1508 to 1509, but he was known more as an explorer than a conqueror. Hearing legends of a fountain of youth, he set out to find the fabled fountain, discovering Florida. Hernan Cortes was to be first of the real conquerors of the New World. Although he has been chastized in an age of political correctness, much of the criticism is ill deserved. It is true that Cortes could be ruthless, and he even accused of having poisoned Ponce de Leon, who had been sent by Charles V to investigate allegations of wrongdoing in Honduras. In fact, it may have been the officials who had confiscated Cortes' land who were the real culprits, since they had far more to loose than Cortes who believed himself a victim of their rebellion. In any case, a man must be judged by the era in which he lived, and for all his cruelty, Cortes was a man who knew when to show mercy. In fact, it was this very quality which made him one of the greatest conquerors in history, for he would set out for Mexico with four hundred soldiers and succeed in conquering an empire estimated to have a populous of over a million people.

Cortes youth hinted at some of his characteristics. He contracted Syphillis as a young boy and was delayed going to the New World because of an injury he sustained while trying to escape the house of a married woman. When he first arrived in the New World he was a clerk to Velasquez, the conqueror of Cuba. There he fell out of favor by a love affair with Velasquez's future sister–in–law. He was imprisoned but agreed to marry her in order to get back in his graces. Cortes soon rose to become the "mayor" of Santiago and a wealthy man, barely thirty years of age.

In 1517, Hernandez Cordoba returned from a voyage to the mainland. He brought back reports of gold, as well as horrifying reports of human sacrifice and cannibalism. In 1519 Cortes was selected to go to the Yucatan. It was to be more of a foraging expedition than an expedition of conquest, but Cortes had other ideas. He left on February 10 with eleven ships, sixteen horses, and five hundred and eight soldiers. After landing ashore, they soon encountered hostile Indians. The first battle Cortes faced enemies numbering around 15,000. With cannons, crossbows, calvary, and strong armor Cortes fought off the force, whose superiors soon sent an embassy. Cortes ordered them to abandon their idols and send their leader to him. They replied that they had already sacrificed their leader for ordering the disasterous attack.

It was here that Cortes first learned of the barbarity of the Aztec religion. Those critics who decry the loss of the Aztec "way of life" under Cortes must ignore that it is the Indians themeselves (not Cortes) who tell of the Aztec society's savagery. It has a distinction in history as being the most barbaric in the history of the world. According to their religion the world was destined to end and be consumed every fifty–two years, unless the gods were appeased. Human blood was the "food of the gods." Worse yet was the manner of the sacrifices. The victim's heart had to be removed while he was still alive. Five men would hold the victim down while the priest cut open his chest and carefully removed the still beating heart. Once the victim had finally, mercifully, died his body was then thrown down the steps of the pyramids where the body was to be eaten in an act of "ritual cannibalism." Still worse than this was the sheer number of sacrifices required. The indians themselves declare that they sacrificed 20,000 victims a year, and boasted that on the dedication of their most sacred temple 80,000 victims were sacrificed during the opening ceremonies. Where did the Aztecs get all these victims? By conquest. Captured enemies were to be the sacrificial victims. Consequently, the Aztecs required two things to keep their system going. First, they forced the empire into submission out of sheer force of terror, but secondly, they had to gain new victims by the thousands every year. The result was the emperor often created conflicts with surrounding tribes to foster war, while at the same time using the wars as a way too keep the people in submission and fear.

From these Indians Cortes also first learned of Montezuma II (also called Moctezuma). The people of Mexico lived in abject fear of him. They told of his cruel tax collectors who raped their wives and children before their very eyes. He learned that sodomy, use of hallucinogenic drugs, polygamy, astrology, and necromancy were among the sins of the Aztecs. Most importantly, he learned that Mexico was yearning for a deliver. Cortes and his troops toured a small city and saw the temples soaked in blood. Many of the soldiers began to doubt Cortes' plans. He had gone far beyond the foraging expedition authorized by Velasquez, and was plotting more.

Cortes began to display some of the wisdom that allowed him to conquer an empire. He ordered no plunder or rape. He also made an example of one man who been caught stealing from the Indians and had him executed. Cortes sought the friendship of the Indians, not their hostility.

Soon they moved far up the coastline and began to build Vera Cruz. There Cortes became governor, and as such he was no longer bound by Velasquez. He had requested, and received, authority from Charles V. Still, some soldiers doubted the whole venture and longed to return home. Following an attempted mutiny, Cortes cut the feet off one man and executed others. To end the future possibility of a mutiny, and to insure that the men were one hundred percent dedicated to his venture, Cortes then ordered all the ships burned. The entire fleet was scuttled. There was now only two choice left to the men; conquer the Aztec empire or be sacrificed to their gods.

Cortes' March to Mexico

Cortes had already established a passive relationship with nearby Indians. They were told to abandon their idols, sodomy, and sacrifices. Their willingness to do so, even if many did so reluctantly, has been variously interpreted. The Aztec legend stated that the god Quetzecoatl would one day return to reclaim his land. Quetzecoatl himself is described as having white skin, which the Spaniards appeared to have by comparison to the dark skin of the Indians. Moreover, the prophesied return of Quetzecoatl was said to come from the east as had the Spaniards, yet the most startling of prophecies was that the arrival of the Spaniards coincided almost exactly with the year in which Quetzecoatl was supposed to return. Thus, many attribute the Indians submission to the belief that the Spaniards were gods. However, while this myth certainly assisted the Spaniards in inducing fear in the enemies eyes, it was not particularly useful to allies. Some of Cortes' soldiers died, and one had even been executed by him. If Cortes had pretended to be a god his lie would have been discovered and angered his allies. More importantly, Cortes did not require the people to worship himself, but Jesus and the Virgin Mary. Cortes did not feed, at least openly, the myth that they were gods. To do so would have been disasterous. So why did they follow him? Two alternatives present themselves. First was their thirst for a peaceful religion. It is said that seeing these great magnificent warriors humbly bow before their idols (of the virgin and child) struck the people of Mexico who were used to barbaric gods who demanded sacrifice. This leads to the second alternative. They followed Cortes because they hated Montezuma. The Aztec religion remains the most barbaric in the history of man, and it is only natural that the people of Mexico were awaiting a deliverer. All three of these factors were involved, and Cortes was careful foster them to his advantage. Wherever Cortes marched, he displayed as much force, or mercy, as was necessary to win them over as allies.

On the march to Montezuma's capital Cortes gained many Indian followers include Malinche, a woman who became Cortes' translator and his most trusted ally. She would help him to understand the motives and actions of the people, and guided him in knowing whether to trust or distrust the Indian people. This was an easy task for many of the same Indians who became Cortes' allies, first tested him by trying to kill him. It was necessary for Cortes, throughout the march, to display his military prowess, but he also had to show mercy and accept the very friendship of those Indians who had laid traps for him. In one particular battle an estimated 140,000 Indians (perhaps exaggerated) took on Cortes and his allies. It is unknown how many of Cortes Indian troops died, but only one Spaniard was said to have been killed. The route earned the respect of the Tlaxcalan Indians who now pledged to help Cortes.

Throughout Cortes' march Montezuma had sent spies and embassies to speak with Cortes. He was watching, and testing him. Montezuma feared the coming of Quetzecoatl and the loss of his throne. The embassies contantly bartered with Cortes, even promising annual payments of gold to the Emperor Charles V if Cortes promised not to enter the Forbidden City. Cortes knew Montezuma was scared. He also knew that Montezuma was using his power to try to stir up the local tribes against him. He, therefore, announced that the local tribes owed no taxes to Montezuma and cut off the hands of all the tax collectors sent by the emperor of Mexico. He then sent the back to Montezuma.

Cortes next stop was the city of the Cholulans, not far from Montezuma's capital. The Tlaxcalans warned Cortes not to trust the Cholulans, but Cortes continued on with as many as forty thousand (some souces claim a hundred thousand) Tlaxcalan troops. As he had done before, Cortes entered the city and eventually made allies of them. As with all the Indians, it was an uneasy alliance. Cortes was always leary of treachery, and as they neared the captial a trap had indeed been laid, but was exposed with the help of Malinche. Cortes arrested the leaders and laid his own trap for the army that awaited him. In the end, all that lay between him and Montezuma's capital was a great lake.

Entry Into Mexico City

The captial of the Aztec empire, called Mexico–Tenochtitlan, was a city built on an island in the middle of a lake. The only way to reach the island was across one of several large drawbridges, which measured several miles in length. The city was impossible to take by force of arms. Once they bgean to cross the bridges, they bridges could be withdrawn leaving them as open targets and no way of escape. Cortes' Indian allies tried to talk Cortes out of entering the city, insisting that it was a lethal trap. Cortes sent the Indians home with many gifts and continued on with the four hundred Spanish soldiers he had left. Several thousand Indians remained with Cortes, but most had returned home.

Inside the city, Montezuma had tried all the magic arts, as well as his political skill, to make Cortes turn back. Curses, hexes, and spells were used contantly to no avail. He finally sent a new embassy to Cortes, granting him entry into the city. The soldiers feared the trap they had been warned about and sight of the massive bridges must have struck them with both awe and fear. They could not win if attacked, but there was no attack. The people of Mexico–Tenochtitlan gathered by the tens of thousands to look at the legendary warriors who had landed on shore with five hundred soldiers, slaughtered hundreds of thousands of Indians, and even now counted four hundred in number. The sight of their magnificent horses also intrigued the people. On November 8, 1519, Cortes' army marched across the five mile long bridge into the forbidden city unopposed.

On the other side of the bridge Cortes was met by Montezuma who declared, "I have seen you at last. I have met you face to face. I was in agony for five days ... this was foretold by the kings who governed your city ... you have come back to us; you have come down from the sky." Despite Montezuma's association of Cortes with Quetzecoatl, he seemed to know that Cortes was mortal, for Cortes himself relates how Montezuma opened his coat and said, "see that I am flesh and blood like you."

For many days Cortes and his soldiers lived in the city as honored guest, but Cortes knew that it could not last. Montezuma was still the emperor of Mexico, and Cortes, honored and fearer or not, could not expect to become a permanent house guest. He had spent much of the time trying to teach Montezuma about the Catholic faith, but Monetzuma refused to allow him to tear down their idols or halt the sacrifices which continued daily. The very sight of the sacrifices doubtless filled Cortes' men with terror, as did the sight of walls laced with the skulls of literally hundreds of thousands of victims.

Things came to a head when news arrived from the coast that an ill–fated rebellion had taken place in one of the towns. Cortes believed that the rebellion had been secretly fostered by Montezuma, who was still looking for a way to drive Cortes out of Mexico without personally confronting him. Cortes, therefore, confronted Montezuma. For hours they argued, but Cortes demand was simple. He wanted Montezuma as a hostage. He promised Montezuma all the respect and courtesy due a king, but he would not allow Montezuma to roam around freely. At the time Montezuma need only have called out to the guards, but Montezuma also feared for his life and may have still be taken by the legends of Quetzecoatl. Finally he agreed and from that day on Montezuma lived in the palace where the Spaniards lived and never was he seen without a

Spanish "escort." Montezuma was now Cortes puppet king, who ordered the rebel leader brought before him.

The rebel leader was burned at the stake and the empire of the Aztecs was declared a part of the Holy Roman Empire. Montezuma himself was made a subject of Charles V, the Spanish king and new emperor of the Holy Roman Empire. More than that, Cortes now felt secure enough to forbid the sacrifices and to throw down the idols. The act led to open revolt. Warriors filled the streets and Cortes' men were forced to hold out in the palace. Cortes offered to leave Mexico if Montezuma would negotiate a temporary truce, and allow them time to build new ships so they could leave the continent. Montezuma agreed and a truce was established, including the surrender of the lead conspirator, Cuitlahuac, but more bad news from the coast further damaged Cortes' hopes. Spanish allies of Velazquez arrived with orders to seize control of Cortes and his towns. A Spanish power play was to disrupt his plans to conquer the Aztec empire.

The Retreat from Mexico

Cortes left a man named Alvarado in charge of the capital while he and a number of the men left to deal with Velazquez's troops. Narvaez was in charge of the Velazquez's force, as he remained behind in Cuba. Using diplomacy Cortes caused many of Narvaez's men to abandon him, but Cortes was still outnumbered. They met on the field of battle where Cortes emerged victorious. He pardoned Narvaez's men if they would join his forced. Thus Cortes gained reinforcements, albeit the hard way. He returned to Mexico City with more men, but he soon learned that Narvaez had already sent ambassadors to urge Montezuma to revolt. Alvarado feared an attack and had many unarmed peasants slaughtered and butchered. When Cortes returned, the city was in a state of panic. Streets were deserted and a forboding fell over the men. Cortes urged Montezuma to calm the peoples' fear, even agreeing to release Cuitlahuac. That was to be his greatest mistake.

Cuitlahuac, upon his release, met with leaders of the Mexicans and deposed Montezuma. He was elected the new emperor. The rebellion began anew. The Spanish, for the first time, suffered heavy losses as the seemingly infinite Mexican troops continued to pour into the streets. The bridges were also controled by the Mexicans. Cortes asked Montezuma once again to negotiate a truce, but Montezuma was no longer their emperor and Cuitlahuac did not want a rival emperor alive at all. Montezuma was struck down by his own men. Cortes was forced to fight his way through the crowded streets and across the bridge to make his escape. The Mexicans still pursued him. They were said to be outnumbered 25,000 to one, but Cortes made good his escape when the Aztecs made the critical mistake of meeting him the open field, after he had escaped the city. There, with armored calvary, the Aztecs were beaten back at the battle of Otumba. As Cortes' men were in retreat, the Aztecs ceased their harassment and returned home. That was their greatest mistake.

Six months after arriving in Mexico City, Cortes had been driven out, June 31, 1520. He arrived at Tlaxcala and found that the Tlaxcalans were still eager to have him as an ally. Centuries of barbarity made their desperate to help Cortes, who had conquered so many with so few. There Cortes set camp, healed wounds, and awaited reinforcements. By April, 1521, Cortes had received reinforcements along with the support of tens of thousands of Tlaxcalan Indians. He now had over a thousand Spanish troops, including a hundred calvary men, as well new muskets and cannons. In addition, he would have over two hundred thousand Indian warriors who had pledged their allegiance to Cortes. Boats were also completed so that they would not be forced to march across the bridges without naval assistance.

The Conquest of Mexico

The battle for Mexico City would last for two months. How many tens of thousands died (the total casualties are believed to be well in the hundreds of thousands) will never be known for sure. Cortes divided his army up into three seperate divisions which would attack the three main bridges with the help of Cortes' navy. The Mexicans fought ruthlessly, working in shifts while other warriors rested. Captured Spanish soldiers were sacrificed, their faces skinned and mounted. They then threw the soldier's arms and legs at the Spaniards, telling them, "eat the flesh of your brothers, for we are gutted with them." Those atrocities only made the Spanish fight all the harder, for they knew that they would be shown no mercy if taken alive.

The Indian allies of Cortes showed no more mercy than the Mexicans, and the Spanish reported, to their horror, that they too ate the flesh of the fallen enemy. Within Mexico City there was soon no food other than the dead, and the Mexicans refused to eat their own dead; only those of the Spanish and their allies. Cortes' men had blockaded the city so that no supplies or help could arrive. It was, in many ways, a medieval siege. The Mexicans were not given time to regroup, to resupply, or to rest. After two long months, the living conditions were deplorable. Cortes pleaded with them to surrender, but they refused, until one day, on August 13, 1521, the emperor was caught trying to escape by canoe. He begged Cortes to let the remaining people evacuate. Cortes obligued.

Cortes had landed in a new world with only five hundred soliders and, two years later, conquered a country larger than Spain whose population numbered in the millions. He had stopped the atrocities of the most debased culture in history and brought them civilization. Although condemned by many historians for his destruction of their way of life, an unknown Indian slave described his own sentiments toward the Spanish conquest, saying, "the great freedom we now enjoy is malicious because we are no longer forced to fear anything." The truth is that Cortes was viewed by the Mexicans as a benevolent leader. After centuries, and hundreds of thousands of human sacrifices, the people of Mexico longed for a freedom they could neither know nor enjoy.

This new country was called "New Spain" and was added to the dominion of the emperor Charles V. The amazing success of Cortes led to the desire of more Conquistadors to conquer the New World, but the new Conquistadors would never acheive the success that Cortes enjoyed. Their atrocities would forever condemn the conquest as a conquest for lust of gold and power, rather than for the hope of bringing the gospel and civilization to barbaric cultures. The paganism of the Indians was to be driven from this new land, but the legacy left by the Conquistadors was one of destruction.

Pizarro's Expedition

Just as the Crusades came to known for their abuses, the Conquistadors were also known for their cruelty and excesses, but like the First Crusade, whose success spurred the future crusades, so also the conquest of Cortes filled many a Spanish soldier with dreams of gold and conquest. The First Crusade was not as bad as those which followed and Godfrey bears too much blame for the atrocities committed in it. So also Cortes bears much of the criticism for the cruel Conquistadors who followed. Whatever one may think of Cortes' harsh discipline, he knew how to show mercy when necessary and he knew when he would be going to far. Viewed strictly as a military leader, Cortes was one of the best. His leadership qualities, however, were lost on those who followed.

Emperor Charles V needed money and the gold sent back by Cortes was promising. The expense of conquest was by no means small, but the promises of wealth beyond imagination filled the heads of the Spaniards. Ponce de Leon had set out in search of a Fountain of Youth, and legends of El Dorado, the city of gold, would inspire Francisco Orellana to set out in search of it, but reality is a harsh mistress. Pizarro's conquest was the only other truly successful conquest, but Pizarro's conquest was indicative of the barbarity of the Spaniards. The Incan empire was subjugated, even as had the Aztecs, but it left a stain on history.

Pizarro had originally left in November 1524 in search of gold and glory but his expeditions seemed doomed to failure. Starvation, disease, and Indian attacks killed many men until Pizarro was finally left with only thirteen followers. Some of his own men called him a butcher and few trusted his leadership. Nevertheless, word came that the Incan Empire was in disarray. Their emperor had died. Pizarro knew the stories of Cortes and how he had conquered the Aztec Empire. He also knew that two rival emperors were claiming to be the successor of the Incan Empire. The time was ripe.

The Incan sacrifices were not as cruel as the Aztecs but they were both incessant and aimed at the most innocent. Children the usual victims. The defeated in battle could often find themselves buried alive. When the Incan emperor had died his servants were sacrificed along with him in order to serve him in the next world. Meanwhile a civil war was brewing between the pretenders to the throne. In May 1532, Pizarro set off for the Incan capital, now with 160 men.

On November 16, at Cajamarca, Pizarro came face to face with Atahuallpa; one of the imperial claimants. With him was a friar and his soldiers, many of whom remained hidden. The friar told Atahuallpa of their faith but the Incan simply showed contempt and ridiculed the strangers. When he threw the Bible to the ground Pizarro's men emerged from hiding and slaughtered many unarmed people in the crowds. The massacre of Cajamarca is often seen as the symbolic turning point in the history of the Conquistadors. They had changed from deliverers to brutal conquerors. So savage were the Spaniards that Pizarro was forced to physically defend his prisoner, Atahualla, from his own men. In fact, Pizarro was the only Spaniard to receive a wound that day; and that was from his own men as they tried to kill Atahualla.

The Incans, divided amongst themselves, mustered an army of 35,000 men but the superior weaponry of the Spaniards prevailed. Thousand of Incans died and several thousand more were taken prisoner. The defeated and seemingly abandoned Atahuallpa attempted to ransom himself. Gold and treasures of unimaginable wealth were given to the invaders. Atahuallpa even ordered his men to root out rivals, perhaps fearing that they planned to usurp him but in fact exploited by Pizarro to further weaken any possible resistance. When the ransom had been collected, Pizarro pointed out that there was not as much as promised (although there was far more than Pizarro probably had ever imagined). Pizarro ordered that Atahuallpa be executed.

The prisoner was taken to be burned at the stake, but upon learning his fate, Atahuallpa begged not to be burned. His pagan religion decreed that if his body were burned, his soul would be lost for eternity, much like the ancient Egyptians who believed that the body was necessary for the afterlife. He was then informed that the only way to avoid burning as a heretic was to become a Catholic. Atahuallpa agreed and was then garrotted (a vice like machine which strangles the victim to death).

The Fall of Pizarro

After the execution of Atahuallpa Pizarro and his men marched toward the Incan capital, Cuzco, which they reached on November 15, 1533; almost a year to the date of the dreadful massacre at Cajamarca. There Pizarro set up a puppet king, Manco, who was a legitimate son of the previous emperor. The Incan empire became a province of the Holy Roman Empire, but its emperor,

Manco, was merely biding for time. As Pizarro stripped the Incans of all the gold and wealth they could find, a rebellion was growing. Rape, murder, and a complete lack of discipline were common among Pizarro's soldiers. Pizarro was incompetent to do anything about it, if indeed he tried. He was corrupt and hated even by his own men. He soon earned the hatred of the Incans, who would have accepted his rule had he been just. Instead they rose in rebellion. After several years Manco escaped Cuzco and became leader of a massive revolt. In February, 1536, Cuzco became besieged by the Incan rebels.

The siege lasted six long months. Cuzco was burned with fire but held out. Finally, when the rebels supplies were exhausted they lifted the siege and retreated. However, Pizarro could not follow up the victory because a certain Almagro staged a coup in which Pizarro and his captains were captured and imprisoned. Pizarro was released upon his promise to leave Peru and return to Spain, but no sooner was Pizarro released than he put together troops loyal to him and advance to reclaim his empire.

On April 26, 1538, Pizarro's men defeated Almagro who was tried and executed as a traitor. Meanwhile, Manco had been waging a guerrilla war. Having defeated Almagro, Pizarro sought to exterminate the remaining rebels under Manco's leadership, but the task was not so easy even with the superior weaponry of the Spaniards. Manco was headquartered in Machu Pichu which was ideal for defense. The guerilla warfare which he employed prevented Pizarro from taking the city and, in fact, Manco would outlive his oppressor who died at the hands of assassins loyal to Almagro's son. In 1541 Pizarro, the conqueror of the Incans, was murdered, not by Indians, but by Spaniards.

The Last of the Conquistadors

Mancu survived Pizarro but he would not survive Pizarro's brother, Gonzalo. Mancu was himself assassinated by Spanish troops in 1544. The Incan Empire had fallen and became absorbed into the grand Holy Roman Empire. Gonzalo Pizarro and Francisco Ornella resumed the conquests and exploration of South America. They set out down the Amazon river where one or the other searched for the fabled El Dorado, crossed the Andes Mountains, discovered the Emerald Forest, and brought back stories of cannibal women and Amazonian women. Their quests were legendary but they were also ultimately failures. The great conquests of Cortes and Pizarro were over. All that seemed to be left for the Spaniards was the quest for gold and glory.

News returned to Charles V of the atrocities and conditions imposed upon the Indian people by the conquistadors. Priests, theologians, and even some of the conquistadors themselves had written to the emperor protesting the treatment and exploitation of the conquerors. He was the emperor of the New World; he should treat them as his subjects. To that end, on April 16, 1550 Charles ordered all conquests to halt until the matter had been debated. The final decision, however, reinstated the conquests of the New World. Had Charles halted the conquests altogether history might have forgiven Pizarro. He did not.

Nevertheless, the glory of the conquistadors was passed. They had already stripped the land of its gold, and the people of their rights. The end of human sacrifice was a noble deed but the new rulers replaced sacrifice with slavery. On his deathbed, Mansio, who had served with Pizarro, wrote to the then ruler of Spain and declared that the Catholics of Spain had destroyed a great civilization. So steeped in a guilty conscience was his last words were, "I beg God to pardon me, ... seeing that I am the last to die of the conquistadors."

Nicholas Maurin – Cortes Halts Human Sacrifice – 19th Century

25
—

The Reformation

The Reformation was nearly four hundred years in the making. Ironically, most of the attempts to reform the church had actually resulted in more corruption, rather than less. Gregory VII had replaced the decadence of the tenth century with the corruption of power in the later centuries. In more recent years, the church councils had tried to make reforms but their changes were superficial and administrative, rather than substantive. Moreover, many of their reforms were later nullified by the popes themsevles. The great irony of the Protestant Reformation is that most of the Reformers did not intend to break away from the church; it was the church that drove them away.

The Ninety–Five Theses

The papacy had long become a political office. Many popes had sat on the throne who had no true interest in religion or the Bible. Leo was one such pope. The former cardinal was a member of the famed Medici family and more interested in power than religion. He is even believed by contemporaries to have doubted the historicity of the Scriptures. It was shortly before Leo's ascension that a monk named Martin Luther visited Rome.

Martin Luther proudly boased that he was the son of a peasant. His religious conversion began one day when lightning struck near him and he realized that he was not ready to meet his maker. He became a monk and began to search earnestly for the Lord. While many monks studied Aristotle and Aquinas, Luther's studies were in Augustine and the Bible. Although a devout Catholic, he began to see contradictions in the Catholic faith. He would not, however, admit to these contradictions until much later in life. As is human nature, he instead tried to reconcile them as best he could. When he visited Rome he was struck by the fact that the Romans openly spoke of the crimes committed by the popes; crimes Luther had once believed were mere fables and slander. He was also shocked by the open sale of indulgences, which was used to pay for the construction of St. Peters at the Vatican.

It was the issue of indulgences which first stirred Luther to action. In his quest for God, he found that the Bible taught that justification was by the merciful grace of God, through faith. Within the church, however, rituals and sacraments were held to be the manner in which grace was dispensed. Luther reconciled these things the best he could, but the sale of indulgences was too much. How could the soul of one lost in Purgatory be bought for money on earth? Had it not been bought with the blood of Christ?

On All–Hallows eve, October 31, 1517, Martin Luther undertook an action which would forever change his life, and the world, although it was an insignificant act in itself, and one which Luther would never have anticipated would stir the world as it did. He did not intend for it to be an act of rebellion or to divide the church. He nailed to the door of the church ninety–five theses protesting the sale of indulgences. The act of nailing a thesis to church doors was not uncommon. As people came to church they would see, and read, about whatever the thesis was about. It was designed to stir debate, but this time it stirred too much debate. Many people agreed wholeheartedly that the sale of indulgences was a corruption of Catholic dogma. Others defended it as Catholic orthodoxy. Ironically, the thesis nowhere challenged any of the orthodox Catholic doctrines; not even the principle of indulgences themselves. It only attacked the trafficing and sale of indulgences. Nevertheless, implicit in the thesis was the fact that the church hierarchy was unnecessary in obtaining salvation. By removing the role of the priesthood in the process of salvation, and implying that repentance and faith alone were essential, the church felt threatened.

It is the height of irony that the Catholic Chuch, not Martin Luther, pressed the issue. Had they ignored the thesis, the Reformation would probably have never taken place at that time, but the church had become arrogant and the brutal persecutions of the fifteenth century had not abated. Any dissention, however meager, had to be dealt with. Leo, at first, thought little of it; thinking it an argument between the Augustinian monks and the Dominicans. He left it to the German bishops, but it became clear that Luther would not back down, and that he was gaining the attention of many people.

Tetzel, who had been commissioned by the pope to sell indulgences, is alleged to have boasted that he saved more souls from purgatory through his indulgences than St. Peter through his evangelism. He published his own theses condemning Luther's but the students at Wittenberg, where Luther resided, burned the theses. Luther was becoming a hero to many in Germany. Leo, realizing the dangers, now ordered Luther to appear in Rome within sixty days and renounce his "heresies." That order was given on August 7, 1518. Later that month, when Luther failed to reply, he sent a letter to the powerful German elector, Frederick the Wise, and ordered him to deliver this "child of the Devil." Nonetheless, Frederick was predisposed to support Luther, not the pope. Instead, he ordered a Diet at Augsburg and offered Luther safe–conduct.

In October the diet met. Cardinal Cajetan acted in behalf of Leo X. It seems apparent that Cajetan knew that he was not there to convert Luther to repentance, but to convert Frederick to the Catholic cause. He disingenuously spoke well of Luther while trying to convince Frederick that he was a heretic, and demanded that Luther recant. Luther responded that he could do nothing against his conscience and that he must obey God rather than men. Cajetan had already had a papal mandate allowing him to excommunicate Luther and threatened to use it, but we must wonder why he was reluctant to do so. Once again, we must assume that Cajetan was well aware of Frederick's sympathies. Nevertheless, as Luther began to realize that Cajetan had only one true purpose, to extract a recantation or to deliver him to Rome, Luther fled the castle and headed to Wittenberg.

While in Wittenberg, and well aware that Pope Leo would soon take to more severe measures, Luther wrote several treatises to the princes of Germany, the clergy of Germany, and the common man. Each treatise was written specifically for each of the classes and designed to support his cause. The first treatise, "Address to the Christian Nobility of the German Nation," emplored the princes of Germany to protect the church and its people. It urged the leaders of Germany to call for a general council and appealed to German pride over Roman arrogance. The second treatise, "Concerning the Babylonian Captivity of the Church," was addressed to the clergy and began to outline the doctrines for which Protestantism is known. It emphasized salvation by faith through grace, the rejection of the sacrifice of mass, the reduction of the seven sacraments, the supremacy of Scripture, and rejected papal authority. His final treatise, "Freedom of a Christian Man," was addressed to the pope but probably intended for the German people. It emphasized faith, rather than the church, as essential to salvation. He also promoted the teaching of the "priesthood of all believers," thus negating the power of the Catholic clergy.

In addition, Luther had begun to write to both Frederick and the Pope Leo. His letters show that he wanted reconciliation but he was unwilling to sacrifice his faith. In desperation he called for another general council, but soon realized that the councils were little hope or comfort. He declared that the Scriptures alone were the basis for his faith and solemnly promised that he was prepared "for all," predicting possible martyrdom. These works were compiled between the years of 1519 and 1521. During that time much was taking place in Germany.

In January, 1519, it was apparent to the pope that Germany revered and honored the monk Martin Luther. Leo, who was not a religious man, played the diplomat. He could not allow Luther to challenge the sale of indulgences, upon which the papal treasury was so dependant, but he was not eager to alienate the elector Frederick, who was one of three possible candidates to replace the aged Maximilian, who would die later that year. Leo, therefore, sent a legate name Karl von Miltitz to negotiate with Luther in person. At the time Luther told Miltitz that he had no desire to divide or seperate from the Catholic Church. He only wished to reform it. Luther promised not to divide the church. No other agreements were reached. Miltitz had seen, in his brief stay in Germany, how Luther was revered. Luther was only saying what the people had longed thought. Revolution seemed in the air and Miltitz did not want to fan the flames. He was content to hear Luther's promise to urge calm and remain loyal to the church.

That same month, on the nineteenth of January, Emperor Maximilian died. Pope Leo had not pressed the issue with Luther because he had not wanted to alienate Frederick the Wise, whose vote as elector would help decide the next emperor. Frederick was a just ruler who himself was to become a candidate for the throne. Leo wanted someone more devoted to the papal cause.

Charles V Buys the Crown

The new candidates for emperor were many, including Henry VIII of England. Nevertheless, only three candidates were viable. These were Francis I of France, the Saxon Elector Frederick the Wise, and King Charles of Spain, the grandson of both Maximilian and the famed Spanish rulers Ferdinand and Isabella. Although Frederick would have been the best ruler, known for his justice and wisdom, he declined the offer, citing his age. The two main candidates were then Francis I and Charles, who were to become the most bitter of rivals. Francis showed great promise in his early days, earning the respect and reverence of the French people. He might have been the best option after Frederick. Charles would have been the worse selection. He was an ambitious man with little regard for justice. His best strength was his mind. Few knew what he was thinking, until he made it known. He was not rash in his decisions, but firm in enforcing those decisions, whether they were good or evil.

Leo X seemed at first to support Francis, but he may have been trying to get concessions from Charles. As the candidates each vied for support, Leo shifted from Francis to Frederick, and finally to Charles. It is unlikely that Leo ever truly wanted Frederick the Wise to be emperor, but he was a diplomat who knew the power of gaining allies. Charles, although still a teenage boy, knew enough about politics to know what would really sway the election. For the equivalent of about $50,000,000 dollars, Charles bought the election, although Frederick refused to take any money for himself. Charles was soon to find that the imperial diadem cost far more than money.

National pride was as much a reason for the fall of the Holy Roman Empire as anything else. The "King of the Romans" was increasingly becoming more a king of Germany than a universal emperor and the Germany people, particularly its princes, were increasingly unhappy with seeing foreigners rule over their land. The emperors of old had come from France, Italy, Sicily, Burgundy, Czechoslovakia (or rather Bohemia), Spain, and even England and Holland. The electors, therefore, now required that the emperor (regardless of where he was from) would not appoint anyone to office in his court that was not a native born German. Germany, not Rome, was to become increasingly the dominant power in the Holy Roman Empire; so much so that that in its waning days it would be considered nothing more than a "German empire," devoid of anything universal that it once had.

For the time being, a Spaniard (albeit half German) sat on the throne, and with him he brought the most vast land possessions that any emperor had held since Frederick II, whose possessions were in many cases largely nominal. Charles V was to become the king of the Romans, king of Spain, king of Naples, king of Sicily, ruler of the Netherlands, Duke of Milan, the heir of Hungary, and the emperor of New Spain (Mexico, Cuba, and the American possessions). He had dreams of restoring the universal sovereignty of the emperor. This was the extent of his understanding. He did not have the vision to see the Reformation for what it was. He did not have the foresight to truly become great. Said one historian;

> "Charles could see the German Reformation only as an insurrection, a religious aberration, a political crime. The conflict of the monk and professor, Martin Luther, was not only personally incomprehensible to the world Emperor, but it filled him with horror and loathing."[2]

Leo thought that Charles would be loyal to the pontiff. He was mistaken, for while Charles was no friend of the Reformation, he was not truly a friend of the papacy. He saw only political allies and political threats. The Reformation was secondary to the Turks, and the papacy was only useful as long as it was useful to himself personally. Charles was to play an important role in the coming decades, and while his hatred for the Reformation was obvious, he eventually came to the wisdom that it was best not to intervene in its ultimate progress, so long as it did not threaten his power. Charles was a man consumed with a thirst for power; not a concern for the spiritual. This was the man to whom Luther would soon come face to face; a young teenage emperor who was secretly in negotiation with Leo.

The Burning of the Bull

On December 10, 1520, Pope Leo X did as he was expected. He sent a papal bull excommunicating the monk Luther. From a secular viewpoint, ignoring the spiritual meaning, this would have meant being ostracized, exiled, or worse, but the people had grown weary of the oppressive Inquisition and the wars leveled agains the Hussites, Waldenses, and Albigenses. The people were sympathetic to Luther, and it was this fact, as much as Luther himself, that led to the Reformation. Had the people not been ready for reform, Luther would have been just another martyr, but the people were ready.

Luther responded to the bull by writing a treatise entitled, "Against the Bull of Antichrist." In it he decried the state of the church and hinted that the pope might even be the prophesied anti–Christ who was to come. At a large bonfire, held by students at Wittenberg, Luther made one last gesture. Along with the books traditionally cast into the fire by students, Luther tossed the papal bull itself. The act was a blatant defiance of the pope's authority and a challenge. He was daring the pope to enforce his will, if he could.

The burning of the bull is significant for numerous reasons. In addition to the spiritual meaning, it showed that the papal Inquisition could not act without the support of the secular state and the people. Not only did the people gather around Luther to support him, but many knights and nobles also offered their allegiance. Luther, a simple peasant monk, became a symbol. The Reformation was inevitable and Luther was simply the man history chose to become its vehicle. The papacy could not ignore him anymore.

Luther at Worms

In 1521 Charles V called for a diet in Worms. One of the purposes of the diet was to deal with the Lutheran "heresy" but Frederick the Wise, as well as other princes, sided with Luther and insisted that he could not be condemned without first being heard. Charles finally agreed to give Luther a hearing, despite protest from Catholic officials, and on March 6 he commanded Luther to appear before the diet with the promise of safe conduct. On March 28, perhaps to influence the diet, the pope issued another bull excommunicating not only Martin Luther, but all his followers as well.

Luther had heard of Charles' secret correspondence with the pope as well as the fact that Charles had allegedly burned all Luther's writings. Charles' first true acts as emperor was to attempt to put a clamp on Luther. By now even Leo realized that this was far more than a simple theological debate; it was a challenge to the Catholic Church itself. Charles had hoped to silence the monk. Friends, colleagues, and even princes reminded Luther of what happened to Huss, who had also been offered safe conduct. To this Luther replied that although Huss was burned, the truth was not, and Christ still lives. He was determined to go.

In April Luther arrived in the city and greeted by a calvalcade of knights and throngs of people. This was a clear indication that, unlike Huss and the martyrs of the Middle Ages, the people were no longer willing to subject themselves to the Inquisition quietly. Charles was to become acutely aware of the public support for Luther. On April 17, Luther stood before the emperor, six electors, papal legates, archbishops, dukes, princes, counts, royalty, and other high officials. He is said to have been in awe at the high powers that had gathered to his trial.

Johann Eck, representing the pope and emperor, showed Luther his writings and asked if he wished to recant of anything found therein. Luther, struck by the magnitude of the proceedings, asked for a day to deliberate. On the following day Luther entered the court a seemingly different man. He had spent the night in prayer, asking for courage, and had prepared a speech, to

410

which he ad–libbed some new material. In that speech he declared that he could not violate his conscience unless shown from the Scriptures that he was in error. Since Luther himself had asked for a general council, the papal legate pointed out that Luther's "heresies" had already been condemned at the Council of Constance, to which Luther's answer angered the emperor, and delivered another crucial blow to Catholic thinking. Luther declared that the councils erred. Even his strongest supporter, Frederick the Wise, later said he had wished that Luther had not challenged the authority of the councils, for to the Catholic mind it was a challenge to every council back as far as the Council of Nicaea (which Protestants also accept as valid).

After the hearing Martin Luther closed with the ad–libbed words, recorded by eyewitnesses, "Here I stand. I can do not otherwise." Luther was prepared for martyrdom if necessary.

Charles had already made up his mind. He said to his aides, "he shall not make a heretic out of me!" However, Charles had not made up his mind how to deal with Luther. The papal legates urged him to arrest Luther, saying that safe conduct to a heretic is null and void. Frederick and others implored the emperor to keep his word. Charles agreed, but began to lay a trap for Luther. He sent letters to Rome in which he makes clear that he believed Luther would flee to Bohemia, the home of the Hussites. Soldiers and inquisitors were stationed along the way in hopes of waylaying Luther and capturing him en route to Bohemia, but Luther did not go that way. Instead Luther went to Wartburg where he was secretly protected inside the castle by Protestant princes.

Charles passed an edict which (not wishing to antagonize those princes with Protestant sympathies) he did not sign until after the departure of Frederick the Wise. The edict put Martin Luther under the ban and commanded that all Luther's writings be burned, forbidding their reproduction, publication, or sale, and further declaring that any and all magistrates should seize the heretic and hand him over for execution. It also placed all Lutheran followers under the ban, but the ban was impossible to enforce in those duchies, counties, and districts which were ruled by princes who favored Luther. Charles would either have to go to war or to ignore the Protestant issue for as long as possible. Owing to French threats against Spanish interest in Milan, as well as a Spanish revolt, Charles was forced to chose the latter while he went to Spain. Luther was safe.

Hadrian VI

Leo X died in December 1521. Charles was fundamental in securing the papal election for Hadrian VI, his former tutor. He believed that Hadrian would be a close ally, but he was to find in Hadrian's short tenure that politics has no life long friends.

In Hungary, the Turks, under Suliman the Magnificent, were besieging Belgrade. Charles was too preoccupied with the Muslim threat to be concerned with the enforcement of his edict of Worms. Moreover, Charles would need the help of the Lutheran princes if he were to succeed against the Turks. To that end, a diet in Nuremberg was called and began in December, 1522.

The papal legate condemend Lutheranism and continued to insist upon Luther being handed over to the Inquisition, but admitted that the curia was itself at fault for many problems. It promised a reform at some future date. The diet failed to produce any real results, but the Lutheran princes made known that they would not persecute their evangelical subjects. The diet ended in 1523 as problems between Hadrian and the emperor began to develop. Against Charles' wishes, Hadrian maintained neutrality in the war between Francis and Charles (over the duchy of Milan and other possessions). When Charles came to believe that Hadrian was being paid off by France, he prepared to invade Lombardy, which forced Hadrian to ally himself with Henry VIII, Francis I, Milan, Austria, and other Italian allies. War seemed to be temporarily averted when Hadrian died.

The Reformation Outside Germany

The years of Luther's exile were not silent, although Luther himself was seldom seen or heard. Luther spent that time mainly writing, including the preparation of a German language Bible. It was, therefore, not Luther who preached the gospel but a vast array of Christian preachers throughout Europe. It was as if they had been waiting for a sign. The failure of Charles V and Leo X to execute their will upon Luther or bring him to "justice" was a clarion call for men of God to preach the gospel as has not been done openly for centuries. Philip Melanchthon, a friend of Luther and a teacher, picked up the cause in Germany. In Switzerland, a chaplain and priest named Huldrych Zwingli preached the gospel before ever having heard Luther. In England too there was a stirring, although Henry VIII tried his best to stamp out the Protestant "heresy."

Philip Melanchthon came to known by many as the voice of Luther. He was a famed preacher whose knowledge of the Bible helped to formulate the Biblical doctrines for which German Protestantism is known. He emphasized the Bible as the source of authority, even as Luther did, and became second only to Luther in the minds of most German Protestants.

In Switzerland Zwingli was by this time preaching against the celebacy of the priesthood, urging the people to cast down their idols and icons, and preaching the supremacy of the Scriptures. This was from the same man who had once earned a papal commission. Unlike Catholic preachers, Zwingli did not preach lectures on theology, but exegesis of the Scriptures. He would read through the Bible and expound upon the meaning, directly from the text. This was new to the people, who had been used to sitting through lectures in which the Bible was rarely quoted, if at all. He became more controvertial when he condemned the sacrifice of mass and infant baptism. Soon he favored baptism of adult believers, which came to known by critics as rebaptism, or anabaptism. Although Zwingli is not considered an anabaptist, the Anabaptist movement was also beginning about this time.

The Anabaptists, forerunners of the modern day Baptists, are generally believed to have grown out of the Swiss Reformation movement, although this is disputed. Many Christian dissidents did differ with the Catholic Church in regard to infant baptism, but the movement as it developed should rightly be traced to the Swiss. Martin Luther maintained the Catholic teaching of infant baptism, but many believers insisted that baptism was a sign of a believer's repentance and spiritual rebirth, and hence it should only be performed on adult believers. Zwingli was somewhat neutral on the issue, but as time passed Conrad Grebel and other Christians seperated from both the Swiss Reformation and the Lutherans, who hated the idea of "rebaptizing" Christians. This particular movement had no ties to any government, prince, or king, as did Lutheranism, and later, Calvinism. The result is that the Anabaptists were to come into conflict with both Catholic and Protestant princes. With no prince to protect them, the Anabaptists became the predominant martyrs of the sixteenth century.

As for England, the history of the Reformation is perhaps as interesting as that of Germany for it did not take a purely religious path, although its source was religious. Henry VIII was a devoted Catholic, but he was also a man used to getting his way. He despised Luther and was devoted to the Catholic cause, but his desire to break with papal domination and become head of the church himself would one day lead him, under Protestant influence, to break with the empire. In the meantime, Henry VIII devoted himself to supression of Protestantism.

In England a group of theological scholars formed what was called "little Germany" because of their devotion to the Reformation cause. The most prominent members of this group were William Tyndale, Thomas Cramner, Nicholas Ridley, Hugh Latimer, and Thomas Bilney. Most of these men would later emerge as important figures in the government and religion of England, but only William Tyndale drew much notice at this time. He had begun work on an English translation of the Bible, but since Wycliff's translation had been outlawed, it was obvious that Tyndale would not be legally permitted to undertake the task. Wycliff's version had been suppressed and few copies still existed, but Tyndale hoped with the aid of the new printing press to distribute copies throughout England. This led him into conflict with King Henry VIII.

King Henry VIII hated the Reformation and had written a diatribe against Luther for which the pope bestowed on Henry the title "Defender of the Faith." Henry would not tolerate William Tyndale who fled to Germany in

1524. There Tyndale completed his copy of the New Testament, even as Martin Luther was finishing his German translation. After many difficulties with the Catholic heirarchy, who attempted to prevent the translation from being published, Tyndale, protected by Protestant princes, sent copies of the Scripture back to England in 1526. His Bible would one day be placed in all the churches of England (before King James' authorized version replaced it), but while Tyndale yet lived, the Bibles were burned wherever found by Henry's men. Tyndale too would be burned when he was finally captured at Antwerp in 1536, a martyr to the Reformation cause.

The Peasant Revolt

Along with the reform movements in Europe was a political movement, closely associated with the Reformation, but apart from it. The Reformation was largely a religious movement which sought to free itself from papal domination, but in rejecting the authority of the established Catholic Church, the authority of the civil authority was also called into question for the Holy Roman Empire and the Holy Roman Church were virtually the same thing. Consequently, it is only natural that some followers of Luther, and also those who were unconcerned with the religious matters, began to take on a political faction, even as the radical Hussite sect (the Taborites) had done.

This movement was not a unified one and had no single leader, but rather it was a movement which emerged from dissaffected people throughout Germany. Hundreds of years of serfdom, taxation, and oppression weighed on the peasant people who had been longing for freedom. Many believed Luther would be their deliverer, although they would be proven to be sorely mistaken, for when he called upon to cast his lot with the peasants Luther betrayed them and sided with the nobility.

The revolt itself was years in the making. In 1521, when Luther had passed through the city of Erfurt on his way to Worms, a large demonstration had taken place supporting Luther. Since the bull of Leo and the ban of Charles condemned the supporters of Luther as well, two priests who had taken part in the demonstration were excommunicated. At news of this, the people erupted into a riot, destroying sixty Catholic priests' homes. The local magistrate had done nothing to stop this. This was but one example of the fervor that was growing in Germany and which would lead to the Peasant Revolt of 1524–1525.

Although the revolt had no single leader, two men emerged as the voice of the people. The first was a one time follower of Luther, named Andreas Karlstadt. Karlstadt had been a strong supporter of Luther but bitterly broke with him of the question of violence and the sole authority of the Scriptures. Karlstadt was a mystic, reminiscent of some charismatic sects. He believed that the "inner light" given by the Holy Spirit should be elevated to the same level as the Scriptures. From this, he believed that God was calling him to free the people from oppression. He took a wife and urged other priests to do the same. He even declared that priest *must* marry based on his view of 1 Timothy 3:2. He angered the Catholic heirarchy by his iconoclasm, wherein he would destroy all the images and icons of local Catholic churches, declaring them idols. Finally, he cast off all scholarly learning and titles, dressing as a peasant and calling himself "Brother Andreas." Hence, Karlstadt became a sort of revolutionary John the Baptist.

A second leader who was to emerge was Thomas Munster, who is sometimes considered the father of communism. Munster and some of his followers made up the "Zwickau prophets" who preached a violent social reform. He was believed to have been associated with the radical Taborites of Bohemia, but he was a mystic like Karlstadt. Soon Munster openly declared that godly peasants have the right to slay the ungodly.

Acts of violence by peasants cropped up increasingly in Germany and many peasants began to refuse to sell food to anyone who did not back their reform movement. Although Luther had no part in the social upheavals, the Catholic Church blamed Luther and called a diet at Nurnberg which sought to repress Protestantism and the preachers of the peasant movement. The edicts it created, however, were virtually impossible to enforce, since even Charles' ban of Luther had not been enforced.

In 1523 the peasants began to organize into the "Eternal Covenant of God" and a single voice was created. They passed their demands on to the nobility in 1524 by means of a program, "Twelve Articles of the Swabian peasants," which asked, moderately enough, for the right to elect their own pastors, the abolition of slavery, freedom to hunt and fish, lower rent, better pay, and the abolition of the right heriot, by which a widow was robbed of her inheritance (the land instead given to nobles). They declared that all these things were supported by the Scriptures and that would withdraw the demand if it were proven not to be in the Bible. Charles and the nobility ignored the request and did not bother to give an answer. In the summer, the revolt began.

The massive number of peasants, poorly armed with pitchforks and the like, caught the princes and knights off guard and outnumbered. Palaces, castles, convents, libraries, and homes were burned to the ground and men (especially priests) were tortured, imprisoned, hung, and even burned at the stake. The cruelty of their actions led not only to sympathy for the nobility, but also led Luther to choose the most harsh language possible in condemning the revolt. Luther made an exhortation to peace in May, 1525, and implied that the demands of the peasants were fair enough, but when the exhortation failed to lead to peace, Luther chose sides, and he chose that of the princes. Not only did Luther condemn the rebellion but he did so in the language for which his enemies have always condemned him.

Luther was given to inflammatory speech on many occasions. Jews remember how many anti–Semitic tracts Luther had written were circulated in

Nazi Germany, but Luther, who inherited his anti–Semitism from his German ancestors, often spoke without regard for the inflammatory consequence. He never persecuted Jews, nor did he probably intend for the consequences of his inflammatory remarks against the peasants, but the consequences were severe.

Luther raved against the "rapacious and murderous peasants" and urged the princes of Germany to "stab, kill, and strangle" them like the dogs they were. He even declared that reasoning with the rebels was useless, and that they could only be stopped by violence suppression. Luther got his wish.

The war was cruel and brutal. On May 25, 1525, at the battle of Frankenhausen, the last of the peasant revolt was put down. Hundreds of prisoners were taken and executed, but the casualties numbered well over a hundred thousand. Andreas Karlstadt escaped the mayhem and moved to Switzerland where he became a professor. Thomas Munster, however, was apprehended and tortured. Two days later he was executed and the peasant's revolt was dead. With it serfdom continued until after the fall of the Holy Roman Empire itself.

The War of Charles V

Charles V was still prevented from taking action against the evangelical reformers in Germany on account of his war with France. A few years ealier Charles helped to secure the election of a pope, as he had done before, that he thought would be his ally. This time it was another prominent member of the Medici family, who took the name Clement VII. Like Hadrian, Clement's loyalty could be bought. When Francis succeeding in conquering Milan, Clement was quick to ally himself with the victor, but his position became untenable when Francis was defeated and captured at the Battle of Pavia in 1525. He then quickly reconciled with Charles.

Francis I, king of France, now found himself a prisoner to his bitter enemy. Charles demanded a third of French territory, the renunciation of all Italian lands, and several other provinces including Provence. Francis steadfastly refused saying that he would rather suffer in prison than to demean the dignity of France so greatly. So Francis would indeed remain a prisoner in a tower in Madrid for many years. The Spaniards knew how to break the spirit, but Francis persisted in his refusal until January, 1526, when he signed the Treaty of Madrid. Charles' triumph, however, was brief, for not only did France refuse to honor the treaty but Clement once again changed sides and in May, 1526, entered into an alliance with Francis, Milan, and Venice.

Charles was furious and prepared an army of Spanish troops and German mercenaries. He kidnapped Francis' children, whom he held hostage, and made ready his army to invade Italy. However, Charles dared not leave Germany in a state of choas. He was at war with the very papacy whom the evangelical reformers were in rebellion against. Charles, therefore, authorized

416

the Diet of Speyer, which established a temporary truce with the Reformers. The diet did not nullify the edict of Worms but instead suspended it until a general council might be called to reform the Church properly. It declared "every State shall so live, rule, and believe as it may hope and trust to answer before God and his imperial Majesty."

The result was a general truce that allowed the Reformation to flourish for many years. The states, duchies, counties, and cities of Germany declared themselves in sympathy with either the Protestant or Catholic causes and became havens for those followers. Although Frederick the Wise had died, his brother John the Steadfast, was just as sympathetic to the Protestant cause as his brother, and became the new Saxon elector. As a result, Saxony, as well as the vast region of Prussia, became Protestant lands.

With Germany's security insured against revolt or civil war, Charles' army invaded Italy. Their goal was nothing less than the city of Rome itself. On May 6, 1527, the troops broke within Rome's walls. Clement fled to Castle St. Angelo while the soldiers sacked the great city of Rome, destroying, raping, pillaging, and plundering. Even St. Peter's tomb was robbed and the corpse of Pope Julius II had been vandalized as well. Clement's castle soon fell and the pope was imprisoned by Charles.

Clement was finally released on December 6, 1527, exactly seven months after the infamous sack of Rome began. Rome had been sacked many times before, but only once before by professing Christian soldiers, and never by the emperor's hand. As part of the agreement for Clement's release Charles lamented the sack of Rome which he blamed entirely on mercenaries and also repented that "his soldiers" has imprisoned the pope. For the pope's part he was apparently forced to promise to coronate Charles, although the coronation would not take place for many years. It seemed that while Charles had reconquered his Italian estates, he had suffered a public relations nightmare by his treatment of the pope, Francis, and the sack of Rome.

Although Clement and Charles were reconciled, Francis and Charles were still at war. Charles held Francis' children and demanded that the treaty of Madrid be enforced. The war would continue on until pressure from Francis' mother and Charles' aunt forced the two to bring the long war to an end. Called the "ladies' peace," Charles agreed to renounce his claims to Burgundy while Francis renounced his claims to Milan and Naples. Charles also released the children of Francis in exchange for 2,000,000 gold crowns. This pact was concluded at Cambrai in August, 1529, and established seven years of peace, before the two rulers went again to war.

In the interim Charles and Francis were free to address other problems. Charles turned first to the Reformers of Germany. The first Diet of Speyer had been a mere truce. The diet had been recessed during Charles' war and never officially concluded, so a second Diet of Speyer took place in 1529. This diet clarified exactly what was, and was not, to be tolerated before the promised reformatory council. Specifically, it did not grant tolerance to the followers of Zwingli or the Anabaptist sect. The diet also gave orders that the Anabaptists were to be put to death. This brought protest from the evangelical princes, which gave the Reformers, for the first time, the title "Protestants."

Now it was finally time for Charles' coronation, but Rome would never accept the emperor on account of the terrible ravages it put through at the hands of this soldiers. The pope, therefore, ventured to Bologna where, on February 24, 1530, Charles V became the last emperor before Napoleon to be crowned by the pope and the first to be crowned outside Rome.

The Honored Martyrs of the Reformation

The martyrs of the Reformation take up five one thousand page volumes (in small print) of John Foxe's "Acts and Monuments," better known as in its abridged form as "Foxe's Book of Martyrs." Thieleman van Braght also compiled a huge volume entitled "Martyr's Mirror" which records many of these martyrs. The volume of this material is a testament to the work of evangelical historians. The numbers, in truth, may not be any greater than those of the Middle Ages, save that their names and records are meticulously recorded by believers and preserved in the records of Foxe and van Braght, as well as others, whereas many of the records from the Middle Ages were either lost, burned, or are merely the records of the Inquisition itself, which present a biased representation of their trials.

I will not venture to give a complete history of the martyrs of this age, for that task would be incompatible with a history that attempts to compile a thousand years into a single volume. A brief memorial to some of the names recorded, however, will suffice to not only honor their memory but remind the reader that even during the Reformation the persecutions did not stop. In fact, to their shame some of the Protestants retained their medieval roots and assisted, to a lesser degree, in the persecutions of the Anabaptists.

The names of some of the martyrs recorded in this time period between the first Diet of Speyer and the peace of Nurnberg, in 1532, a period of less than ten years, are Caspar Tauber, Hans Koch, Leonard Meister, Felix Mantz, George Wagner, Melchior Vet, Michael Sattler, Leonard Keyser, Thomas Hermann and sixty–seven members of his congregation, Weynken of Claes, John Walen, Leonard Schoener and seventy of his congregation, Hans Schlaeffer, Leonard Frick, Leopold Schneider, Wolfgang Ulman, Hans Pretle, "Little Hans," three ministers known only as Thomas, Balthasar, and Dominicus, Hans Feirer and his family, Vilgard of Schoeneck, Caspar of Schoeneck, Hans Langmantel, George Blaurock, Hans van der Reve, Vigil Plaitner, John Hut, Wolfgang Brandhuber, Hans Niedermair and seventy other followers, Carius Prader, Anna of Freiburg, Daniel Kopf, Wolfgang of Mos, Thomas Imwald, George Frick, Mankager of Penon, Barbara of Thiers, Agatha Kampner, Elizabeth Kampner, Anna Maler,

Ursula Maler, three hundred and fifty unnamed victims at Altzey, Philip of Langenlonsheim, George Bauman, George Gruenwald, the Brother Alda, George Steinmetz, Martin "the Painter," Wolfgang Eslinger, Pain Melchior, Walter Mair, George Zaunringerad, Veit Pelgrims, Lambrecht Gruber, Hans Beck, Laurence Schumacher, Peter Plaver, Hans Taller, Hugo Kraen, Mary Kraen, Ludwig Fest, Christina Haring, Sicke Snyder, William Wiggers, Henry Does, John Esch, Henry of Zutphen, John le Clerc, John Costellane, Wolfgang Schuch, John Huglein, George Carpenter, Leonard Kenser, the widow Wendelmuta, Peter Filsteden, Adolphus Clarebach, Nicholas of Antwerp, Johannes Pistorius, Matthias Weibell, George Scherrer, and Henry Fleming.

These men were largely made up of the Waldenses and Anabaptists sects, which were not under the protection of the Lutheran or Catholic princes, and make up but a small number of the martyred dead.

Civil War Averted

During these critical years Charles was caught between his love for the Catholic Church and his desire to wage war against Suleyman the Magnificent. His temporary peace with Francis allowed him to divert his attention to the Islamic threat in Eastern Europe but the treaties of Speyer were mere truces and were not sufficient to unite his princes against the Turks. The Catholics viewed the Protestants as far worse that Muslims because they were heretics. The Protestants also had a profound mistrust of the church of the Inquisition and the church of the Albigenses Crusade. The Protestant princes were living in fear of a new crusade leveled at them by the mother church. Under these circunstances Charles could not fight off the Muslim menace even as it was laying waste to Hungary, of which his brother Ferdinand was now king. Consequently, not long after the "ladies' Peace" was finalized, he called for a new diet at Augsburg.

Charles had been urging Pope Clement to call for a general council to resolve the Protestant schism but Clement saw councils as a threat to his own authority and constantly made excuses. The Diet of Augsburg was therefore the emperor's attempt to resolve the dispute among the princes, if not the church. The diet was not, however, a remission of the edict of Worms, and Charles wished this to be made clear. Luther was represented by Melanchthon and others, while he remained under the protection of the Saxon elector.

Another critical element of the diet was Charles' refusal to give an audience to the Zwingli supporters. Charles had already preodained that Catholic doctrine would emerge triumphant and only Lutheranism was a true political threat to his empire. Consequently, the Lutherans were the only dissident or evangelical Christian sect given a voice at the diet. Nonetheless, even the Lutherans had many restrictions placed on them. For example, the emperor demanded that no Lutherans evangelize or preach the gospel in

Augsburg while they were present; a condition that was not obeyed with regularity.

The Lutherans were asked to present a "confession" of their faith and to have it read before the diet. On June 25, 1530, the Augsburg Confession presented the doctrines and teachings of the Lutheran Protestants. Charles fell asleep but the rest of the diet seemed duly impressed. The duke of Bavaria is said to have even been greatly angered at the papal legate for exaggerating the "heresies" of the Lutherans, and the legates themselves were disappointed that the confession was not more anti–Catholic as they had hoped it would anger the sleeping emperor. Instead, the confession simply presented the Christian faith as they believed it was held from the time of Christ until the corruption of the church.

The confession was signed by numerous princes of Germany including John the Constant (also called John the Steadfast), elector of Saxony, and his son, Duke John Frederick. They did this knowing full well that if could cost them their electorate, for the emperor's sympathies were known from the beginning and when the Catholic legates read their response, it was fully endorsed by Charles, although he had not even heard most of the Augsburg Confession, as he had slept through it.

Once again, the Augsburg diet resolved nothing. As a result, the emperor called a recess in November which sparked fears of a civil war. It was well known that the emperor had promised the pope that he would suppress all heresy. When the recess of the diet was called, the Protestant princes believed that Charles was going to crush them by force. Only a month later, the evangelical princes agreed to form the Smalcaldian League which was a defensive pact, promising to come to each other's aid and prepare for a civil war. In March the League was finanlized at Smalcard where John the Steadfast promised to defend their faith against any and all enemies, including the emperor himself. This pact sent shock waves throughout Germany, but Charles was wise enough to see that a civil war now would only lead to the success of the Muslim invaders. To prevent that end, he convened a new diet one month later and secured the "peace of Nurnberg" which once again established a truce between Protestants and Catholics and pledged to take action against their mutual foes; the Muslims. That treaty was ratified on July 23, 1532.

The Fall of Zwingli

Under the preaching of Zwingli, which some argue predates Luther's theses, the Reformation had spread throughout the Swiss confederation. Caught between France and Germany, the Swiss often found themselves at odds with their Catholic neighbors; the "Five Cantons." These rulers despised the evangelical preaching of the Swiss Reformers and often persecuted those who dared to preach within their territories. When Jacob Kaiser, a Zurich minister, was burned at the stake by the Catholics a war nearly erupted. In fact, led by Zwingli, two armies met near Cappel but did not fight. Zwingli urged the destruction of the Catholic army while it was still possible, but cooler heads prevailed and a peace treaty was enacted in June, 1529. That treaty guaranteed the parity of Protestants and Catholics in the eyes of the law. However, the treaty was destined to fail. The Cantons argued that the tolerance guaranteed in the treaty only applied to Protestant territories, and did not extend to their own. Economic sanctions soon followed. Zwingli again insisted that war was the only way to preserve their freedoms. The Protestant Swiss eventually gave in and the Cappel War was renewed, but it was the Catholics who prevailed.

In October, 1531, the Swiss Protestants were routed and a severe blow to the Swiss Reformation was dealt when Zwingli himself fell while attending a wounded soldier. His last words were alleged to have been, "they can kill the body, but they cannot kill the soul." Zwingli's body was not allowed to rest. The Cantons took the body and tore into four pieces, then burning those pieces and mixing the ashes with the ashes of pigs before being thrown to the wind.

The defeat did great harm to the Protestant cause, but it also strengthened the Swiss resolve. War continued until the second religious peace was signed in November. The status quo was maintained and the Protestants of Zurich were given certain freedoms within their cities, but not in Catholic territory.

With the loss of Zwingli the Swiss Reformation was taken up by three evangelists; William Farel, Peter Viret, and Antoine Froment. Still, there was another who was soon to flee to Switzerland from France. He was to become one of the most influential and famous reformers of history; a man whose influence is, in many respects, felt today more strongly than that of Martin Luther. That man was to be John Calvin, under whom Switzerland would eventually emerge as an independant Protestant country, seperate from the Holy Roman Empire.

England Defects fom the Empire

One of the great ironies of history is that Henry VIII, a man who despised the Reformation cause, would be the first king to make his country a Protestant country. His reasons were, of course, purely political, but his advisors and colleagues had far more in mind than political freedom.

The chief actors in these events, along with Henry VIII, were Thomas Cromwell, Thomas Cramner, and Hugh Latimer, as well as Nicholas Ridley.

Thomas Cramner had been a member of "little Germany" and an associate of William Tyndale. He had, however, escaped persecution and even entered the service of Henry VIII when Henry sought theological scholars to find Scriptural grounds for justifying a divorce he was desperately seeking from his wife, Catherine of Aragon (who was also Emperor Charles V's aunt). Henry blamed her for his inability to produce a male heir and desired to marry his mistress Anne Boleyn. Naturally, the pope was not willing to grant a divorce from the emperor's aunt; especially since his position with the emperor was tenuous at best. Cramner was, therefore, commissioned to write a treatise defending a divorce on the grounds that Levitcus forbade marriage to a brother's widow (Catherine had been married to Henry's brother). This treatise was written in 1527 but came to no avail as the pope was still a prisoner to the emperor, Catherine's nephew.

The marriage problem was to plague Henry for several years when, in 1530 a certain Thomas Cromwell entered Parliament. Cromwell had clear sympathies with the Reformation cause, although he was a politician and knew how to approach the subject tactfully and shrewdly. In defense of the king, or so it was made to appear, he began to attack the papacy and authority of the Catholic hierarchy in England. Cramner, a friend of Cromwell's, was now Henry's chaplain and was dispatched in an embassy to meet with Charles V to help secure the divorce, but he also had a secret mission; to meet with the Protestant princes of Germany. That same year, 1532, Thomas Cromwell pressed legislation that would seperate the Church of England from Rome and establish Henry as the head of the church. The latter portion of this proposition was doubtless to ease Henry's concerns over Protestantism. As the man who had been named Catholic "Defender of the Faith" by the pope, he most likely would not have supported the defection of the English Church had he not been named its head. The fact that he was being named as the future head of the Church of England would later anger evangelicals and lead to the Puritan movement which sought to "purify" the Church of England, but for the time being it was a political neccessity, and in 1533 the Act of Restraint of Appeals to Rome was passed, declaring that no appeal could be made to Rome. Henry was now free to divorce and the Church of England was no longer a part of Rome.

The seperation of the English church from the Roman church, combined with the divorce of the emperor's aunt, completed the defection of England from the Holy Roman Empire. Queen Mary, known as Bloody Mary, would later attempt to restore England to the church and empire, but her death and the subsequent rule of Queen Elizabeth forever established England as a Protestant country, free from the control of both pope or emperor.

On July 11, 1533, Pope Clement VII excommunicated Henry, but no one cared. The people had long grown weary of Roman oppression and threats of interdicts, excommunications, and the like were no longer of any merit. Thomas Cramner became the first Protestant Archbishop of Canterbury while Nicholas Ridley turned Cambridge into a Protestant University. The Reformation seemed to be flourishing in England until it ran afoul of the king. Henry VIII was still a Catholic at heart and soon took measures against both Thomas Cromwell and Hugh Latimer, one of the leading voices of the Reformation in England.

Latimer was to remain imprisoned in the Tower of London for many years for teaching contrary to the decrees of Henry, but Cromwell suffered a worse fate. It became apparent to the king that Cromwell's true agenda was to turn the Church of England into an evangelical Protestant church. On June 10, 1540, Thomas Cromwell was arrested on charges of heresy and treachery. He was condemned without a trial and executed on July 28. His martyrdom signaled to the evangelicals of England that seperation from Rome was not alone sufficient to break with the doctrines and corruption of the medieval past. The struggle between Protestantism and Catholicism was just beginning, but as England was no longer a part of the Holy Roman Empire, its history must be temporarily abandoned here until the reign of Mary Tudor, whose futile attempt to restore the country to Rome and Aachen earned her the name "Blood Mary."

The French and Swiss Reformations

Francis I had been restored to the French throne and freed his children at great expense. His bitterness was not lost, nor did Charles forgive his enemy. Their peace was destined to last but a few more years, during which time Francis vented his antagonism against the Reformation movement. Francis was a great admirrer of the famed humanist scholar Erasmus, who had been a friend of Zwingli and one time supporter of Luther. Erasmus, however, soon came to resent the Lutherans for being little different, if not worse, than the Catholics. Francis too had some sympathies with the Reformers, as both his wife and mistress were Reformation supporters. He was even said to have read the works of Philip Melanchthon, but Francis could not tolerate their Republican ideals. From Arnold of Brescia to Girolamo Savonarola to the later Oliver Cromwell, the evangelical Christians had rejected monarchy for a Democratic Republic of some kind. With the rise of Protestantism rose an increasing desire for republican institutions and representations. This made Francis very uneasy with evangelicals.

The first recorded French Protestant martyr was Jean Valliere who was burned at the stake in Paris back in 1523. Persecutions from this time were sporatic and, relatively speaking, mild. Francis did nothing to either encourage or discourage persecutions so the French Huguenots, as the French Reformers were called, were subject to the toleration, or intolerance, of their local communities. This would, however, change in 1534 after the "Affair of the Placards." A certain servant of the king named Feret was zealous for the Protestant cause but he was neither especially wise nor a man of restraint. He wrote inflamatory tracts on Catholicism's practices that were viewed as nothing more than sheer blasphemy. Rather than promoting the Reformation cause, they merely derided the Catholic doctrines. He placed these diatribes on placards which he placed throughtout the communities, including one upon the king's bedchamber. When the king found the blasphemous placard upon his own chamber doors he became irate and lost any tolerance that he had once had for the Reformers. Already embittered by years in prison and the treatment of his sons at the hands of Emperor Charles, Francis had lost all restrain himself. He was no longer the great king of learning, but a bitter old man who unleashed his wrath upon the Huguenots, Waldenses, and Anabaptists.

The placard incident was the breaking point for Francis, but his sentiments had been changing slowly anyway. He was disturbed by rumors of some strange beliefs and practices among the Reformers. The most famous incident involved the city of Munster. Two years ago the followers of Thomas Munster migrated to the city of the same name. Eventually these men, who were living among the Anabaptists (with whom they were identified), soon gained control of the local government and evicted all people who would not yield to their communistic society. Private property was confiscated and the city government controlled everything. According to the beliefs of these "Anabaptists" (although they were really Munsterites) the world was coming to an end and their communistic theocracy was the model for the coming new world. Monogamy was replaced with polygamy and the "prophet" Jan Bokelson, along with his twelve elders, became dictators of the city. Three years later, in 1536, the Elector of Cologne, along with several neighboring princes, finally overthrew Bokelson and established the Catholic theocracy in Munster again. The incident forever stigmatized the Anabaptists, even though the Munsterites were only loosely affiliated with them. The scars from this incident became propaganda not only against Anabaptists, but against all Protestants.

In France, a year before Munster's overthrow, Francis already began the persecutions that would last, with intermissions, until the rise of Napoleon. Prisoners were filled with those suspected of the Protestant heresy and Francis even declared that he would not spare his own sons if they were supected of the heresies. He also ordered a suspension of the printing presses until he could arrange safeguards to insure that no heresy was printed. Huguenots were burned at the stakes throughout France and some were suspended by rope and slowly lowered into the fires, so as to prolong their deaths.

It was at this time that evangelicals fled France to neighboring countries. The Protestant city of Zurich and other Swiss cities became a haven for many of these refugees including one John Calvin. This same Calvin was destined to become the most influential theologian since Augustine, to whom Calvin was deeply indebted. During his early years in Switzerland he wrote the first volume of his famed *Institutes of the Christian Religion*. The book became instantly popular and earned Calvin the respect and admiration of Protestants throughout Europe, but mostly his influence was to had in Geneva, Switzerland.

Switzerland had for some time been a semi–autonomous state. It remained the nominal subject of Charles but practiced its government as it saw fit. Before the Reformation Geneva had been the Sodom of the empire in many ways. Prostitution was not only legal but sanctioned by the government and every vice from gambling to drunkenness to sexual debauchery was practiced. When William Farel first came to the city he was greeting with hatred and anger but by 1535 Farel had won over the city government. The Great Council of the Two Hundred pronounced an edict on August 27 of that year removing all images from churches, abolishing mass, and establishing Protestantism. Calvin was to find a loyal follower in Farel and the Council who accepted his word almost without question. He was asked to draw up Articles of Faith which were imposed upon the city. Among the articles included excommunication for sins, which Calvin (unlike most Protestants) maintained was a valid practice. Strict enforcement of the religious code was practiced, and on July 29, 1537, the Council went so far as to require all citizens to assent to the Confessions of Faith or be banished.

This plan eventually backfired and those opposed to Calvin soon rose to prominence in the Council. When Farel attempted to ban all holidays save Sunday, the Council forbade him to preach. Determined not to back down or to allow the Council to silence his free speech, Farel continued not only to preach but to speak out against the Council itself. In April, 1538, the Council then took the measure of expelling Farel and Calvin from Geneva. Calvin was to spend the next three years in exile, but he was destined to return, and change Switzerland forever.

Charles, Paul, and Francis

In 1534 Pope Clement VII died. Pope Paul III, a brother of Pope Alexander VI's mistress, was elected unanimously. Although he was already sixty–seven years old he liked to live like a young man. The Vatican became a place of carnivals, masquerade balls, and feasts. He was an opulent pope who commissioned men such as Michelangelo and Leonardi da Vinci.

Paul inherited a church in crisis. The Reformation was flourishing and the emperor, although master of a larger territory than any other, was loosing control of his German princes and unable to drive off the Muslim invasion of Hungary. The Reformation struck at the heart of the Holy Roman Empire in that it struck at the Holy Roman Church. The church and empire were virtually one and the same since the time of Charlemagne. To destroy one would ultimately lead to the destruction of the other. Clement had consistently refused to call a reformatory council, as the Reformers and emperor had asked, because he feared it would mimimize his power. Paul knew he had to call a council, but he also knew that it had to be one sympathetic to his cause. The originally called the council to convene in 1537 but it was to be delayed until 1545 at Trent.

During this period Charles had held back the advancement of Suleyman, although he was never able to break Suleyman's progress as a whole.

Charles finally went back to Spain where he spent much of his time. Germany was left largely to itself although Charles, always eager to check the progress of the Reformation, did pass an edict against the Anabaptists in 1535. The edict declared not only death for those who practice adult baptism but also ordered that anyone who fails to report on persons suspected of being Anabaptists shall likewise be subject to punishment. Even those who repent and "are truly sorry and penitent" were to be executed by the sword, rather than being burned at the stake. Finally, the cruel edict commands that no subject shall be permitted to asked "for mercy, forgiveness, or reconciliation for the aforesaid Anabpstist, or ... presenting any petitions for this purpose, on pain of summary punishment."

A year later Charles resumed his war with Francis after challenging him to personal combat. The two men were determined to kill each other, but their war was to no avail. The only thing accomplished by the war was the delay of the promised reformatory church council, which was twice delayed on account of the waring parties. In 1538 another truce was declared. Once again, Charles turned his eyes toward Suleyman and Hungary, but the Hungarian capital was to fall in 1541. Ferdinand, Charles' brother, pleaded for help but Charles' plans were of no avail. He laid siege to Algiers but was unsuccessful. Finally, he broke off the war with the Turks when he heard that Francis was again besieging Milan. The French king and emperor were once again to wage war for years until 1544 when the peace of Crespy again maintaind the status quo. Only then was there enough peace in Europe for the long promised reformatory council; the Council of Trent.

Protestantism Before the Council of Trent

The progress of Protestantism continued despite the sins of its greatest names. Because Protestantism involved the striving for political freedom as much as for religious purity, it did not always maintain the later. Both Luther and Calvin were men of their times. They could not completely break away from the culture and thought of their times. The Middle Ages were still in the mindset of the people and even the great scholars of the day felt the influence of those centuries past. Lutheranism was dealt a public relations blow in 1540 with the "Hesse affair."

Philip the Generous, the Landgrave of Hesse, was a Protestant prince who, like Henry VIII, desired to marry his mistress. The mother of the mistress promised to go public with the affair if he did not marry her, but since Philip was already married he began to look for a way around the problem. Philip Melanchthon feared that Philip of Hesse might turn to Catholicsm and ask the pope for a dispensation to divorce. That would have censored the freedoms that Protestants were enjoying under this rule, so, with Luther's knowledge, Melanchthon argued that polygamy was better than adultery so long as the marriage was kept a secret. The justification was preposterous, but Philip of Hesse secretly took a second wife.

When the affair was made public Philip of Hesse fell into disfavor with the emperor and the princes, not to mention the public scandal. Although popes had been known to keep mistresses and sexual sin was quite common in that day, polygamy was considered among the worst perversions. Melanchthon and Luther were implicated in the affair and the cause of Protestantism, shortly before the reformatory council was to meet, was given a black eye.

These were also the last years of Luther, who would die one year after the start of the Council of Trent. Much of those years were spent writings salacious tracts against Jews, Anabaptists, and the papacy. He passed away in 1546, but he was to be remembered in history not for his anti–Semitic tracts or for his complacency in the Hesse affair, but for being the founder of the Reformation and signaling the end of the Middle Ages.

Along with Luther, Calvin stands out as the other great mind of the Reformation, but like Luther, Calvin was not without sin. Another setback for the Reformation, at least in the eyes of the world, was the establishment of John Calvin's tyrannical theocratic state. Geneva had very soon come to regret the exile of John Calvin. He was asked to return to Geneva where he was to establish a theocratic state reminiscent of the medieval church. Ironically, Calvin has been called "the pope of the Alps." His own adherants have compared him to Pope Hildebrand and Geneva has been called the Protestant Rome. Calvin became a symbol to some of the fact that the Protestants were no different, or better, than the popes.

It was in 1541 that Geneva asked Calvin to return. After his departure the Catholic bishop Sadolet had reminded the people of Catholic oppression. Sentiment was turning back to Calvin and Protestantism. The four syndics (Council members) who had so strongly opposed Calvin were all found guilty of criminal acts. Three were executed for crimes ranging from murder to fraud, and the fourth died while trying to escape. All that had once stood in Calvin's way was removed. Although Calvin was at first reluctant to return, he finally agreed. When he arrived he was treated with the utmost honor.

Even though Calvin was never officially a member of the government, his thoughts, opinions, and suggestions were treated as law. The syndics fashioned the government after Calvin's suggestions. It became, much like Savonarola's before him, a mixture of Republicanism and Theocratic ideals. In theory the church and state were seperate but equal. In practice, this was much as it had been under Charlemagne. The two entities were techincally seperated but inasmuch as the church claimed authority over all its members, and the government was expected to assist in shaping public morals, the government began to regulate even the most frivolous of practices. In one case, a man was banished from Geneva for three months for jesting that a braying donkey "prays a beautiful psalm." In another case, three men were imprisoned for three days after they laughed during Calvin's sermon. Still another case tells of a man who was imprisoned for four days for naming his son after a Catholic saint.

The death penalty was maintained for such things as blasphemy, idolatry, heresy, and one young girl was beheaded for striking her parents. Torture too was maintained by the courts, although it was less frequently used than by its Catholic counterparts. Calvin's political enemies also found themselves under the knife. The first victim of this new government was tortured and beheaded in July, 1547, for the crimes of sedition and blasphemy. Another political enemy was forced to parade around Geneva with a shaved head, bowing to his knees and asking both God and Calvin for forgiveness.

To understand Calvin's attitude, one must understand Calvin's theology. Although he is still considered one of the great Protestant theologians of history, to this very day, he mixed Biblical theology with Augustinianism and medievalism. His unique view of predestination was borrowed from fatalism and denied the very existence of free will. Consequently, this mimimalized personal responsibility and increased both legalism and Calvin's arrogance. Calvin was not a man to admit wrong. This is most evident in the infamous case of Michael Servetus who was executed in 1553.

Michael Servetus was a famed scientist, doctor, and scholar. He is credited with the discovery of the pulmonary circulation of blood, as well as being repected for his work as a geographer and astrologer. He was also, unfortunately for him, a theologian. His theology is considered heretical from both a Protestant and Catholic point of view. He denied the trinity, predicted the end of the world in 1585, was accused of denying the immortality of the soul (which he denied teaching), and rejected infant baptism, thus making him an Anabaptists in the eyes of the Catholics and Protestants. The worst part was that Servetus had the flair of Luther in regard to inflammatory rhetoric. He did not just state his views, but denounced those who disagreed with him in a most degrading fashion. This included writings which publically denounced John Calvin and his *Institutes*. He was finally put on trial by the Catholic papal Inquisition in France, but made a daring escape. The Inquisition pronounced the death penalty on him in absentia. He then made his way for Naples by way of Switzerland. It is likely that he did not expect anyone would recognize him, since the Swiss would only know him by name, but Calvin had heard that he might be coming this way, so guards were on the lookout for him. On Sunday, Geneva law required all people to attend church so Servetus went to church where he was recognized and arrested by one of Calvin's men. Servetus, having escaped the Inquisition, was now put on trial in Zurich.

According to Geneva law the accuser was supposed to stay in prison along with the accused so that false allegations would be discouraged, but Calvin's secretary took his place, allowing Calvin to roam freely during the trial. Since Servetus had not actually violated any of the laws of Geneva, the first trial did not result a conviction, but Calvin preached from the pulpit a fiery speech condemning Servetus and pressing for a new trial. In accordance with Geneva law, a second trial could be granted in certain instances, and a second trial began days later. Servetus petitioned the Council declaring that there was no case recorded in history of Christians being tried for heresy by the church before Constantine, noting that he had not violated the laws of Geneva, and requesting counsel. The Council denied him counsel, indicating that the guilty do not deserve counsel. Later the French Inquisition had sent a letter requesting that Servetus be turned over to them for execution. The Council decided that Servetus was to be tried in Geneva, which Servetus was favorable to, for he did no believe until the verdict was read that the Protestants would actually execute.

When the sentence of death by burning was pronounced Servetus (who had formerly been arrogant and flippant toward the court) broke down in shock. He cried and begged for mercy, but it was to no avail. Calvin urged the court to decapitate him in the name of mercy, but the stake remained the court's decision. Servetus' last words were "Jesus Christ, Son of the eternal God, have mercy upon me!" Amid the backlash, Calvin ardently defended the verdict.

This act forever stigmatized the Calvinists. While the Waldenses and Anabaptists, like the early Church believers, walked passively to their martydoms, Calvin was making martyrs of those whom many believed were allies against the papacy.

Luther and Calvin were great men in their age, but like all men, they were a product of their age. While their sins are used as justification for the rejection of the Reformation, they were, in fairness, far more just and merciful than most of their Catholic counterparts of the day. In truth the only pure Christians from this day were those Anabaptists and Waldenses martyrs whose lives and deaths fill the pages of Foxe and van Braght.

Martyrs Before the Council

Between the peace of Nurnberg and the beginning of the Council of Trent there was no shortage of martyrs. Many of the thousands of victims will never be known, but the accounts of the matryrdoms of many are recorded in the writings of John Foxe and van Braght. They include Master Perseval, Justus Imsberg, Giles Tilleman, Martin, Hoeurblock, Nicholas van Poule, Andreas Thiessen, Katharine Thiessen, Nicholas Thiessen, Francis Thiessen, Peter Bruley, Peter Miocius, John Diazius, Archbishop Herman of Cologne, Master Nicholas, Peter Koster, Sybrant Jans, Wilmut Jans, Hendrick van Campen, Stephen Benedictus, Femmetgen of Egbert, Andrew Claessen, Peter Gerrits, Peter Joris, Peter Leydecker, Johanna Mels, Jerome Kels, Michael Seifensieder, Hans Oberacker, George Vaser, Leonard Sailer, Sebastian Glasmacher, Hans Gruenfelder, Hans Peiz, Hans Wucherer, Hans Bartel, Philip de Kreus, Leonard Lochmair, Offrus Greizinger, Michael Wideman, John Styaerts, Peter Styaerts Martin of Vilgraten, Caspar Schumacher, Hans Seyel, Hans of Wels, Apollonia

Seyle, Anna of Rotterdam, Tjaert Reynerts, Arent Jacobs, Hans Simeraver, Walter of Stoelwijk, Dirk Krood, Pieer Trijnes, Claus Roders, Pieter Jans, Jan Egtwercken, Claus Meliss, Aecht Meliss, William Meliss, Heyne Walings, Trijn Amkers, Cornelius Luyts, Claus Dirks, Jacob of Wormer, Seli of Wormer, Claus Claess, Jonker ven der Busch, Balthasar Hubmor, Hans Huber, Leonard Bernkop, Damian of Algau, George Libich, Ursula Hellrigling, Maria van Beckum, Ursula van Beckum, John Claus, Lucas Lamberts, Francis of Bolsweert, Oswald of Jamnits, Andrew Kofler, Hans Blietel, Michael Matschilder, Elizabeth Matschilder, Hans Gurtzham, Quitinus Pieters, Hans Staudtach, Antony Keyn, Blasius Beck, Leonard Schneider, Dirk Smuel, and Jacob den Geldersman.

These are but a few of the names listed. Many names will never be known. For example, in Austria, 1539, a great persecution was unleashed by Ferdinand, the emperor's brother, against the evangelicals. Neither pregnant women nor children were spared and the castle of Falkenstein was filled. The numbers were so great that it took until 1540 to execute all the Christian dissidents that they had rounded up.

Thus the work of the Inquisition had been hard at work even before the "reformatory" council. It was also a foreshadowing of the fact that that council's finding had been preordained.

The Council of Trent

In 1545, the Council of Trent finally convened. It had been delayed for nearly thirty years for fear that it might diminish the power of the hierarchy. However, when the council was convened, it was clear that the hierarchy would be upheld for, far from the universal council which the Protestants had requested, the council was made up solely of those loyal to the papacy. Not a single Protestant prince or bishop was invited. Even as the council was convened to determine the issues presented by the Protestants, Pope Paul III was urging Francis I to exterminate the Huguenots from France, and pressing Charles to take military action against the Protestant Smalcaldian League of Germany.

The Council was itself to outlast Paul, who died in 1549, but its resolutions were as he had predetermined. The Council of Trent rejected Luther's thesis of salvation by grace through faith, arguing that grace is only dispensed through the church and its sacraments. They maintained that there is no salvation outside the Church, which excommunicated all who rejected the council and the papacy. The doctrines of purgatory, mass, transubstantiation, prayers for the dead, indulgences, infant baptism, celibacy of the priesthood, and the authority of the papacy were all reaffirmed. They also maintained that baptism and penance were necessary for salvation. In addition, the Council of Trent authorized two new acts. It declared that the Apocrypha (the Apocrypha are historical writings found in the Greek *Septuagint* that were not a part of the Bible but were included in the Latin Vulgate, which was translated entirely from the *Septuagint*) were canonitical and a true part of the Bible. More significantly, the Council decreed that tradition was on equal authority with the Bible. Hence, unable to answer many Biblical questions presented to it, the Council declared that the writings of Augustine, Origen, Jerome, and others were equal to the Bible in authority. This nullified the need for the papacy to specifically defend their positions with the Bible.

In times past, knowledge of the Bible was so poor that the papacy could make Biblical claims that were completely unfounded. Although the Council of Valencia had placed the Bible on the Index of Forbidden books back in 1229, the Bible was techincally forbidden only to laity and did not address the issue of the printing press, which would produce books without specific knowledge of whether they were intended for the laity or clergy. As a result, the Protestants were armed with the Bible and could show where the papacy was in error. The Council, therefore, placed tradition on an even level with the Bible, and in 1546 the Bible was specifically forbidden in Spain from being printed without clerical approval.

The ultimate findings of the Council of Trent was a complete disavowal of everything that the Protestants had taught and a reaffirmation of everything that the Protestants were protesting. With one fell swoop, the Catholic hierarchy expelled all Protestants from the Church and from the promise of salvation. The Protestants did not leave the Catholic Church, they were expelled. Thus the division between Catholic and Protestant was not one of the Protestant's making, as is often claimed, but by decree of the Council of Trent and the will of the papacy. It also spelled war.

The Smalcaldian War

The Smalcaldian War was a natural result of the Council of Trent. Charles was determined to crush the Protestant cause. He had long delayed in this task on account of war with France and the Ottoman Turks, but these obstacles were removed in early 1547 when Francis I died, shortly after daring to ally himself with the Turks against Charles. Francis' death freed Charles and disheartened the Turks. Charles established a five year truce with the Ottomans and turned to the Smalcaldian League, with whom he was finally ready to recon.

Charles promised the Duke of Bavaria that he would be elevated to elector status if he would help crush the Smalcaldian League. He also promised the Protestant Duke Maurice of Saxony the electorate of his cousin John Frederick, if he would betray him and assist the invasion. With papal support Charles began the war which ended as soon as it began. The Protestants were crushed at Muhlberg. John Frederick and Philip, the polygamous Landgrave of Hesse were captured. The traitor Duke Maurice was elevated to elector of

Saxony and Charles began to institute the counter–Reformation throughout Germany. He attempted to restore Catholicism and reassert imperial control over all the duchies, counties, and cities of Germany, but his ambitious plans of restoring the great imperial dignity backfired. His interference and many arrogant Spanish soldiers antagonized Protestant and Catholic princes alike. In 1548, to appease some of the dissention, Protestants were given very limited freedoms but permitted to live.

The concessions did not solve Charles' problems. Germany was now a country of diverse religious views and powerful princes who did not like surrendering their power to a Spaniard. The situtation elevated in 1551 when Charles named his Spanish son, Philip, heir to the imperial throne and made his brother Ferdinand's son the heir to the King of the Romans (the German King). Ferdinand had already inherited that title several years ago when Charles renounced it in his favor. The problem, however, was not with Ferdinand or his son, but with Philip. The anti–Spanish sentiment among the German princes was acute. The hatred which they felt was intensified at this proclamation. That same year the turncoat Maurice of Saxony turned again; this time against Charles. He, along with other princes, allied themselves with the new French king Henry II, promising him nothing less than the imperial regency itself.

Maurice tried to physically capture the person of Charles himself, but Charles fled in terror. He had not the stomach to fight but left the task to Ferdinand, his brother. Ferdinand fought as best he could and made overtone of peace. Those overtones paid off when in 1555 a diet was held at Augsburg to discuss the terms of peace. Charles was not a part of the procedings and neither was the pope or his legates. In fact, the pope was to vehemently denounce the peace treaty, leading a schism between the future emperor, Ferdinand, and the papacy.

Bloody Mary's Attempt to Restore England to the Empire

Protestantism had made great progress in England under the short reign of Edward VI, Henry VIII's successor. Thanks in part to labors of Hugh Latimer, Nicholas Ridley, and Thomas Cramner the Bible even began to be read in English at church services. Unfortunately, the young Edward was not to live long and Cramner, along with others, conspired to insure that the Catholic heir Mary Tudor did not sieze the throne. They attempted to place the Lady Jane Grey on the throne but the people did not know Mary as Cramner did. They saw this as a usurpation and supported Mary who took the throne in 1553. This was to begin a most savage persecution by the only ruler of England more hated than King John. Mary Tudor was determined to restore the country to both emperor and pope.

As a young child Mary had been betrothed to the emperor Charles, but she was rejected. Now she pledged herself to Charles' son, Philip, the current

432

heir to the imperial crown. This engagement frightened the Protestants who knew what she was planning. If the empress of the Holy Roman Empire were to be the Queen of England then the persecution of Protestants would soon follow. They were right. The Queen did permit Protestants to leave the country in exile rather than face almost certain death in England. The famed Scottish Reformer, John Knox, was one of the first who fled England and went to live for a time among the Calvinists of Geneva.

The new pope, Julius III, was ecstatic over Mary's assension and immediately appointed her relative, Reginald Pole, the Archbishop of Canterbury, a spot vacated by the arrest of the Protestant archbishop. This was another warning to Protestants that the Inquisition was to return to England. In 1554 a futile attempt to overthrow Mary was launched by Sir Thoams Wyat. He was soon captured and executed. The act gave Mary the justification she needed. In reprisal over three hundred Protestants were hung on gibbets or burned at the stake. The persecution of Protestants was just beginning.

The history of Mary takes up over two thousand pages of John Foxe's monumental history, of which most is dedicated to these bloody persecutions. Among the victims of this persecutions were the three great Reformers of England. Hugh Latimer and Nicholas Ridley were both tried in Oxford and found guilty of treason and heresy. On October 16, 1555, both men refusing to recant of their faith, were burned at the stake. Latimer's last words are recorded as "we shall this day light such a candle, by God's grace, in England as I trust shall never be put out."

Thomas Cramner did not escape. He was imprisoned and tortured for many long months. He had been forced to watch the martydom of Latimer and Ridley and under the stress of torture, he was finally made to recant. The Inquisition ordered him burned at the stake but first wanted him to make his recantation public. With his death imminent, Cramner mustered his strength of spirit and defied his Catholic oppressors. He died a martyr in the flames on March 21, 1556.

Others were not spared either. Neither rank nor sex nor age was spared. The duke of Suffolk, Henry Gray, was beheaded. A judge magistrate named Hales drowned himself in order to escape death by burning. Many other nobles and priests, as well as common folk, met with death at the hands of Mary's administration and the papal Inquisition. Even the King of Denmark wrote to Mary requesting clemency for some of the Protestant princes.

During these years Mary did not restrict herself to the persecution of Protestants. She, at the urging of her Spanish husband and prince, Philip, dared to invade France on an ill–fated attempt to reclaim the long lost English territory of years past. The ultimate result was humiliation for England as the only English stronghold left on the mainland of Europe, Calais, was recaptured by the French who viewed the victory as a landmark achievement in throwing the English completely off the continental mainland.

433

Mary, a woman of ill health, mercifully died in November 1558. Her death was not mourned. With the ascension of Queen Elizabeth the persecutions of Protestants was ceased. Protestantism again became the religion of the Church of England, the Spanish claims to the England were rejected (which would lead to conflict with Spain for many years), England was to be permanently seperated from the Holy Roman Empire, and the great country was to enter its golden age. The regin of Mary was the last gasp of medieval tyranny in the history of England and its brutality was to insure, as Latimer said, that the candle of Protestantism was never to fade.

Charles Abdicates

After the death of Pope Julius III, Marcellus II ruled for twenty–two days before suffering a fatal stroke. He had promised to reconvene the Council of Trent and institute true reforms, but his death ended the hopes of a true reformatory council. Giampietro Carafa named himself after Paul III, the vehemently anti–Protestant pope. Pope Paul IV was destined to exceed him in his hatred of Protestantism. He became pope in March, 1555. The "Religious Peace of Augsburg" came in September, 1555. Ferdinand granted a truce between Lutherans and Catholics that was to last for nearly sixty years (to be followed by the Thirty Year War). The treaty did not include Anabaptists, Calvinists, Waldenses, or Hussites; only Lutherans and Catholics. Paul IV was furious and would never forget the "betrayal."

In 1556 Charles V was a defeated man. He retired to a monastery after abdicating the imperial throne to his brother Ferdinand and abdicating his Spanish, Neopalitan, Milanese, Sicilian, and Netherland crowns to Philip. Paul IV refused to recognize the abdication and refused to coronate Ferdinand who had made treaty with Protestants. Never again would a pope crown an emperor. Even when the papacy went to crown Napoleon, Napoleon would snatch the crown out of the pope's hands and crown himself. Paul's arrogance created a schism between the emperors and popes that not even wars had managed in ages past. The empire was crumbling. The promise of Charles' reign turned to dismal failure. Northern Netherlands was soon to be lost to the Spanish crown. Switzerland and England had defected. France was now more an enemy to the emperor than ever before. Only its allegiance to the papacy kept it nominally in the empire, but the very term empire was beginning to become meaningless. Even the papacy no longer wielded control over the empire. Germany itself was divided between Protestants and Catholics. The emperors ruled Germany and Lombardy while the papacy ruled over the Spanish princes and southern Italy. France also remained under papal sovereignty. The empire was dying.

Summary of Charles' V Reign

Charles V was the last gasp for the Middle Ages. He was the last emperor before Napoleon to be crowned by a pope and the last to actively fight for the enforcement of papal doctrines and edicts. He dreamt of the glory days of the Middle Ages while the world at large dreamt of a new world. Charles' reign started with more promise than any before him but ended in disgrace. He might have been the greatest emperor of them all, but instead he, more than any other, signalled the end of the medieval empire. The Holy Roman Empire was no longer a medieval empire, but neither was it compatible with the new world. It was to increasingly take a nationalistic and Germanic flavor, while alienating its mother church. The result was an empire more divided than ever and at war with itself. The pope and emperor maintained an uneasy alliance with each other until the papacy's ill fated attempt to restore the old glory under Napoleon.

It is, therefore, here that the history of the medieval emperors ends, and the story of the modern emperors begins. Their history is not as glorious, nor as glamorous, but it is intriguing nevertheless, for no other empire would linger as long as the Holy Roman Empire. Even in its declining years the empire maintained its claims over vast areas of Europe and clung to the legacy of ancient Rome. The papacy struggled vainly to crush the Protestantism and to stay the rise of democracy in hopes that it too might restore those old days of glory. The emperors and popes would thus pursue the same goal in different ways, but each with the same futile results. Still, the empire would fall not with fading glory but in the drama of the Napoleonic wars.

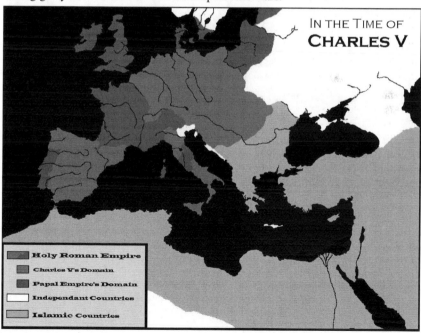

435

Titian – Charles V – 1548

26

—

The Counter–Reformation

When an institution becomes corrupt, those in power are not wont to surrender it, even when the people who make up that institution demand it. Such is the case in history. Loyal Catholics as well as Protestants desired a reformation, although they each had different ideas about what comprised a reformation. The Protestants demanded not only political reform within the Church but also theological reform, calling the Church back to the teachings of the early church. The loyal Catholics believed that only political reform was needed, insisting that, as the Council of Trent declared, tradition was equal in value to the Bible and the early church. In the end, the theological reform was never to take place. Political reform for still centuries away, for the powers that be did not want to surrender it.

The Counter–Reformation was really a war. It was a reprisal against Protestantism which was to leave countless thousands dead. Sir Robert Anderson, a Chief Inspector at Scotland Yard during the time of Jack the Ripper, was also a historian and theologian who estimated that thirty million Christians suffered and died at the hands of the various medieval and post–Reformation Inquisitions and crusades. While modern scholars may scoff at these numbers, the Chief Inspector was not one to leap to illogical conclusions. It is true that Anderson had to estimate the vast number of undocumented tortures and deaths which occurred in these centuries, and not all tortured victims were put to death, but even if his numbers were vastly exaggerated, no honest scholar can doubt that millions of evangelical believers suffered at the hands of the Inquisitions and crusades. Nor would it be incredulous to say that more people died in the hundred years following the Reformation than had died in the three hundred years preceding it.

During the Counter–Reformation the Spanish Inquisition would continue its savage attempt to stamp our heresy, with the assistance of Philip II, Charles' son. In France, Henry II would wage a war against the Huguenots, and in Italy another war to be waged against the Waldenses. Pope Paul IV was to wage a cruel war against all "heretics" and spent much of his time increasing the power of the Roman Inquisition. Even loyal Catholics such as Cardinal Morone were imprisoned for heresy if they dared to criticize the excesses of the pontiff. Paul expanded the Congregation of the Inquisition and revised the Index of Forbidden Books to the extent that few books could realistically be printed with dispensation to do so. Jews were segregated and forced to wear distinctive headgear. He was to lead the Counter–Reformation in Italy while Philip II lead it in Spain and Henry II lead it in France. Only the emperor Ferdinand, whom Paul refused to recognize, left the Protestants in peace.

Europe Before 1560

After the peace of Augsburg Ferdinand was content to remain in peace. Charles V had divided the Hapsburg Dynasty two among his children. There was now the German–imperial Hapsburgs who ruled over the German states, and there was the Spanish–papal Hapsburgs who acted on behalf of the church and ruled over Spain, the Americas, Milan, Naples, Sicily, and the Netherlands. Thus, the Roman empire which had split in two was now divided even further. The Holy Roman Empire remained one in name, but the two co–equal heads of the empire, the emperor and pope, were no longer united. The papacy would support its Spanish princes, hoping that they could restore the popes to medieval glory, while the emperors were to become an increasingly German entity, clinging hopelessly to lost glory.

Germany itself was largely Protestant already. Only Bavaria and Austria, Ferdinand's home, were predominantly Catholic lands. Peace was maintained in accordance with the peace of Augsburg throughout Ferdinand's rule, as he was content to live in peace wherever possible. The same could not be said of Charles V's son, Philip.

Philip II had inherited war with France, but Henry II and Philip were both concerned that Charles had allowed the war to hinder the suppression of Protestant "heresy." Henry had seen this occur in France as well. He had created the Chamber Ardente in the Parliament of Paris for the purpose of rooting out and trying alleged heretics but the Huguenots seemed to grow every day. In 1555 the Huguenots even founded the Huguenot church of Paris showing the incompetence of the Chamber to deal with "heresy." For every Huguenot executed, it seemed as three new ones were appearing. In May 1559, the Huguenots formed a synod in Paris issuing a declaration of faith which was distinctively Calvinistic. Among the signers of the declaration were King Gaspard de Coligny of Navarre, who was also a French Admiral, and his brother Prince Bourbon of Conde.

This so infuriated Henry that he was resolved to make peace with Philip in order to devote his time to the suppression of Protestantism. The peace of Cateau–Camresis was signed within a month, giving Henry's daughter in marriage to Philip, whose wife Mary Tudor had died months earlier. Ironically, Henry died weeks later, on July 10, 1559. His young son, Francis II, became king, but the teenage boy had suffered from illness for years and quickly became a puppet to Cardinal Charles of Lorraine and Duke Francois of Guise. Both men desired more than anything to stamp out Protestantism. The persecutions continued and hundreds of evangelicals were burned at the stake in the months following.

In March 1560, Duke Bourbon conceived the conspiracy of Amboise. He planned to wrest control away from Charles and Francois by kidnapping Francis II. His Huguenot troops surrounded the Chateau of Amboise and attempt to liberate Francis from the hands of Charles and Francois, but the Bourbon's soldiers failed and the reprisals were severe. Duke Bourbon himself was imprisoned to await execution, but Catherine Medici, the mother of Francis II, was fearful of the entire situtation. She did not want to see her son dragged into a crusade and appointed a new chancellor. When Francis, whose illness was terminal, died in December, Charles IX, who but ten years old, became king, and Catherine immediately became regent.

Catherine spared Bourbon and tried to estbalish peace between the Catholics and Protestants. Theodore Beza, the famed Calvinist scholar, met in Paris with officials of both sides, but no true accord was reached. Within two years war was destined to erupt once again.

The Persecutions of the Counter-Reformation

In Italy, the new pope was plotting yet another attempt to exterminate the Waldenses from the Piedmonte Valleys. In 1559 Paul IV had passed away. His death brought celebratory riots to the streets. The headquarters of Paul's Inquisition was destroyed and its prisoners freed. Paul's statue, erected by himself, was torn down and destroyed. Pius IV replaced him four months later.

Pius differed from his predecessors only in that he was politically savy. He did not want to alienate his allies with harsh despotism. He also knew what he wanted. He had two of Paul IV's "nephews" executed and continued Paul's war against evangelicals. The Waldenses had not ceased to be persecuted over the years, but they still existed, and thrived, in the valleys of Piedmont. In 1560 Pius IV passed the Act for the Purgation of the Valley. It was to be the second major war against the Waldenses. Duke Philip of Savoy promised a pardon to all "outlaws" and "convicts" who would join the army for war against the Waldenses. The papal army, under the command of La Trinita, approached from the south. His army consisted of over four thousand men, while the Waldenses army was made up of only about a thousand, but the common man of the Valley had just as much to fear as the rag tag Waldenses army.

The Waldenses employed a hit and run strategy, retreating at each step of the papal armies advance. The result was that the papal army was moving through the valley and occupying territory but their losses numbered in the sixties compared to three of the Waldenses soldiers. La Trinita decided on a new strategy. He declared that if the Waldenses would lay down their arms, pay 20,000 crowns, and make concessions, which he laid out, he would lift the siege and leave them in peace. The conditions were harsh, but agreed upon. Nonetheless, no sooner did the Waldenses lay down their arms than La Trinita unleashed his army on them. The Valley of Lucerna was ravaged, along with its women. The villages laid waste, and the population which had not fled was massacred.

When news of the tragedy reached other areas of the empire, the Protestants were outraged and compassion fell upon them. The Calvinists of Geneva, along with the Protestant Elector of Palatinate Germany and others, sent an army to assist the Waldenses. They swore an oath of allegiance to protect one another, promising also, "to maintain the Bible, whole an without admixture, according to the usage of the true Apostolic Church."

In Rome Pius IV was meeting with the Inquisitor–General Alexandrini to discuss the extermination of "heretics" in Naples when news of the alliance came. Immediately, Alexandrini was sent to Calabria to destroy any undefended evangelical hideaways as he could find. Alexandrini granted pardons to murders, rapists, and cutthroats of all kinds which composed his army, and set off for Calabria where the city of San Sexto became the first victim of the pope's wrath. Over sixteen hundred people were taken prisoner and suffered such indignities as being beating with hot iron rods, having their bowels cut out, thrown of tower tops, and, of course, burned alive.

Meanwhile, in the valleys La Trinita and the Duke of Savoy were now faced with a larger, better organized resistance. The Waldenses went on the offensive and forced several garrisons to surrender. In contrast to the papal armies, the prisoners admitted to be treated with the upmost dignity and without abuse. La Trinita and Duke Philip were discouraged when French reinforcements arrived, but in the end it was of no avail. The Waldenses knew the valleys and had the defensive advantages. Moreover, it was said, even by their enemies, that "God was fighting for the barbets [Waldenses preachers]." The war of extermination failed a second time.

The Italian war against heretics was not the only war of persecution that erupted in the early 1560s. France soon followed. Like his brother, Charles IV suffered ill health and would eventually die of tuberculosis just before his twenty–fourth birthday. He also suffered from emotional problems which have been variously interpreted. In any case, he was dominated by his mother, even long after his adulthood. Although Catherine had advised restraint and peace with the Huguenots, she was not sympathetic to them. Her reasons for making peace with the Huguenots were political, and as the years passed she would increasingly become more hostile to them as she feared they were winning her son over to their cause.

Catherine removed Cardinal Charles of Lorraine and Duke Francois of Guise from the king's court and, in 1562, passed the Edict of St. Germain. That edict granted Huguenots permission to worship as they chose but then forbade them from owning church property, meeting in synods, gathering in large numbers, forming an army, collecting donations, or holding services at nighttime. In short, the "freedom" granted to the Huguenots was repressive. Despite this, Charles of Lorraine and Francois of Guise refused to obey the edict, viewing it as giving the Huguenots too many liberties (such as life). Two months later, several men of Guise surrounded a stable where the Huguenots were worshipping and slaughtered them. This Massacre at Vassy began the War of Religion. Admiral Gaspard de Coligny, the king of Navarre, led the Huguenots forces while Duke Francois of Guise led the Catholic forces. Although the Catholics were winning the battles, they appeared to loose the war when the Catholic general was assassinated exactly one year after the Massacre at Vassy. A truce was declared and the Edict of St. Germain was recognized for the time being.

Maximilian II

Maximilian II was the king of Bohemia and Hungary before succeeding his father to the imperial throne in 1564. He had long had secret sympathies with Protestants, although he himself was a Catholic. As a result granted freedom of worship to the nobility of Austria, which had formerly been enforced Catholicism. Protestantism might have won over the whole of Germany but for the Protestants. Paul IV had alienated the Catholic princes of Germany and the Protestants had, despite their own intollerances, showed themselves to be more tollerant than the Catholic bishops. Protestantism seemed to be everywhere in Germany, but the Lutherans were still men of their time. Like Luther, whom they admired, they inherited the medieval mind which still lingered. In short, they made the most trivial of theological issues into dreaded heresy. Philip Melanchthon had tried to urge restraint and tolerance, but he died in 1560 and with his death the princes of Germany began to show the bigotry for which German history is too often stereotyped.

The Elector of Palatinate had become a Calvinist, and with him, much of the Palatinate was now Reformed in theology, rather than Lutheran. The followers of Melanchthon were called "crypto–Calvinists" and fell under the persecution of the new Saxon Elector. Krakow, the leader of the so called crypto–Calvinists was arrested, imprisoned, tortured, and finally executed. Such internal conflicts allowed the Catholics, and Jesuits in particular, to regain control of many areas in Germany and set the stage for the eventually Thirty Year War.

The Jesuits had formally been established in Paris in 1534 as the Society of Jesus. They were founded by Ignatius of Loyola, whose Spanish blood brought the mentality of the Spanish Inquisition to the east. In 1540 he obtained papal approval for the new order which pledged sole obedience to the pope. They were technically missionary in character, but that task was to be carried out with it the missionary character of the Spanish Conquistadors. The Jesuits came to be known as a very oppressive anti–Protestant religious order which struck fear into many of its enemies. In 1573 Loyola founded the

Collegium Germanicum school in Germany for the expressed purpose of training fighters who would go to war against Protestants.

As for Maximilian himself, he reign was a time of peace in Germany, but his conflict with the Ottoman Turks was a failure. In 1568 he was even forced to pay tribute to the Sultan in exchange for his promise not to invade the empire.

Maximilian's peace in Germany did not extend to Italy, where the pontiff opposed all his measures of tolerance with the Protestants. In 1566 Pius V succeeded Pius IV was pontiff of Rome. The former Inquisitor–general had spent most of his life in the Inquisition but had been removed by Pius IV because of his excesses, and this was from the same pope that had waged war against the Waldenses! Pius V did not repent but took his extreme methods to the Vatican. He built a new palace for the Inquisition, expelled most Jews from Rome, and placed all printing presses directly under the control of the papal office. He excommunicated and "deposed" Queen Elizabeth of England (although no one in England really cared), and fervently denounced the peace of St. Germain in France. His denunciations may well have played a part in the massacre which followed.

St. Bartholomew's Day Massacre

The War of Religion in France had re–erupted twice during this time. The first time was in 1567 but once again the sides were forced to a draw and a peace treaty established tolerance which was to last almost three years. In 1570 the violence again erupted. Catherine Medici, whose sympathy laid with the Catholics, wanted peace. Another short peace was established during which time the Protestants were called to court for discussions in favor of a lasting peace. Admiral Gaspard of Coligny appeared in court in 1571 where he soon found favor with the young King Charles IX. So favorable were these meetings that a marriage alliance was proposed between Margaret of Valois (Charles' sister) and Henry Bourbon (the prince of Conde and Gaspard's brother). A grand marriage was arranged and set for August 24, St. Bartholomew's Day.

The Catholics were fearful of the marriage alliance and began to try to turn Catherine and Charles against the Huguenots. Duke Henry of Guise had recently come to power after the murder of his father. He believed that Gaspard had assassinated his father, although this is doubtful, and in turn tried to assassinate him. The attempt failed, but Gaspard was wounded. Charles was incensed and threw all the princes of Guise out of court, but the Queen Mother had been secretly speaking with Duke Henry. She feared that Gaspard would soon gain control over her son, the way that she had controlled her son. She was convinced that the Protestants would one day seize the throne if allowed to marry into the royal family, or least she would loose all of her influence over

Charles. The king, who was easily manipulated by his mother, apparently gave his consent for the acts which followed.

The royal wedding took place as planned. Bourbon was the king's brother–in–law and Protestants now hoped for freedom and tolerance, but the marriage was to become known as the "scarlet nuptials" for on St. Bartholomew's Day it was to be drenched in blood. Assassins threw broke into Gaspard's bedchamber and threw him out the window. Duke Henry mutilated the body and hung it on a gibbet. The massacre which followed had been carefully planned. With the Huguenot leaders present for the royal wedding, the duke's men laid an ambush and slaughtered thousands Huguenots, but the massacre was not restricted to one city. It was said that the royal palace itself, and the Louvre, were stained with blood. King Henry Bourbon of Navare, the groom, was dragged before Charles who demanded that he renounce his faith or die. He agreed.

The Massacre of St. Bartolomew's Day claimed the lives of over two thousand Huguenots. Duke Henry ordered that they be slain wherever they were to be found, throughout all France. He was making his play to become the next king of France. When the new pope, Gregory XIII, heard the news he threw a celebration in the streets of Rome and Philip II of Spain rejoiced at the news of the massacre which ended Huguenot support of the rebel leader William of Orange who threatened his Netherland possessions.

The Spanish War for Dominance

While the Hapsburgs of Germany were at peace with the Protestants, Philip II was in a protracted war. Since the death of Queen Mary of England, Philip, her husband, had dreamed of conquering England. With the support of Pope Gregory XIII he had even planned an invasion which would hit the island from the west and southeast. Ireland and the Netherlands were to be his staging grounds, but the plan would not work because the Netherlands was in revolt. Philip's dreams of conquering England would have to wait.

The technical name of the Netherlands at the time was the Low Countries or the Seventeen Provinces. Charles V had inherited the rule of these lands and passed it on to Philip. Even before Martin Luther the Brethren of the Common Life, founded by Erasmus of Rotterdam, had began translating the Bible into the common tongue and called men back to the Bible. It is, therefore, not surprising that after the Reformation it became a haven for Anabaptists as well as Calvinists. The evangelical religions began to flourish in the region.

Although Philip lived in Spain he exercised complete dominance of the country through Margaret of Parma, his half–sister and regent. Spanish troops were placed throughout the Netherlands and the Spanish hatred of "heretics" was brutally enforced. Persecutions were severe and constant throughout the years, but did not stem the tide of Protestantism. Soon Philip's excesses began to alienate even the Catholic princes of the Low Countries, who desired independence. Finally, William, prince of Orange, a former confidant of Charles V, led a group of men in revolt.

William's enemies called his army "beggars," which his soldiers eagerly took up as their banner. A flag was made featuring the then stereotypical bag of a beggar. This was to be their banner, and they called themselves the "beggars." Their goal was to abolish the Inquisition in the Low Countries and establish religious liberties. William of Orange was, at the time, a tolerant Catholic, but most of his army was Protestant. In 1573, frustrated with Catholic intolerance and lack of doctrinal integrity, William converted to Calvinism, but most of his years were spent as a Catholic fighting against the excesses of his own Church.

In 1566, when Philip heard the news of the revolt, he sent an ambassador to Rome declaring that he had "no desire to be the ruler of heretics," and promising to stamp out heresy in the Netherlands. With the pope's help Spanish and Italian troops were placed at the disposal of the duke of Alba who organized the "Council of Blood" in 1567. The council declared that not only Protestants but Catholics were culpable because they had not supressed heresy. The call was similar to the old battle cry of the Albigenses Crusade, "kill them all, let God sort them out!" Over a thousand people, including counts and princes, were executed immediately after the council, and Prince William, the son of William of Orange, was captured and send to Philip as a hostage. In the war which followed, the French Huguenots eventually pledged their support to William of Orange, but when the Massacre of St. Bartholomew's Day occured, William's troops were left to themselves.

In 1572 Gregory XIII had been elected pope. He had actively subsidized the French war against the Huguenots and encouraged Philip to mount an invasion of England from Ireland and the Netherlands. However, the plan could not be carried out until William of Orange's rebellion was quelled. The Duke of Alba had ravaged most of the countryside and slaughtered many of its inhabitants. Some historians have called it a reign of terror, and such it was. Only the seas were dominated by William's navy, the "beggar navy." On land, William was loosing the battles, but they would not give in, knowing that death awaited them whether they surrendered or not. So brutal were the Spaniards that in 1576, a treaty called the *Pacification of Ghent* agreed to put aside religious differences and fight Spain for freedom and unity. Along the signers was Don John, governor of Austria and half–brother of Philip II. The Albanese prince had died and the treaty effectively negated Philip's power. The Netherlands was to be at relative peace under William who was recognized as the "Chief and Supreme Authority."

In 1578, Gregory XIII realized that Philip would not get control of the Netherlands. Gregory desperately wanted to crush Queen Elizabeth of England and did not have the patience to wait for Philip so he hatched a plan to assassinate the Queen. When the plan failed to bear fruit, he was again forced to place his hope in Philip.

The *Pacification of Ghent* had ended the war, but it had not truly resolved the problems in the Netherlands. When the horrors of the war abated, the old predudices were renewed. Don John was a Catholic and wanted to make the Low Countries Catholic. In January, 1579, the southern provinces of the Netherlands, under Don John, joined the Union of Arras against the Protestants. William struggled to keep the Netherlands united and sought compromise, even granting sovereignty to some Catholic princes in certain provinces. In 1584 William was assassinated by a man eager to collect a bounty that Philip had placed on his life. William's last words were a prayer for the people of the Low Countries.

Philip, although rejoicing over William's death, reneged on his bounty and refused to pay. Maurice, the son of William, took up the cause of liberty and in the end, many years later, the Netherlands was to be divided into three countries. In the south, modern day Belgium and Luxemburg were Catholic countries whom vigorously persecuted Protestantism, while in the north, the Netherlands was Protestant but with a toleration of the Catholic minority.

Rudolf II

The death of Maximilian II, in 1576, caused a great stir in Germany; not because of Maximilian's death, but rather because of the electorial situation. The archbishop, count, and elector of Cologne, whose name was Truchsess, was a Catholic who fell in love with the countess of Waldburg. As the Council of Trent failed to reverse Hildebrand's unbiblical prohibition against clerical marriage, the elector considered converting to Protestantism. This would have given the Protestants a majority of electors, since three were already Protestant. The Catholics went into panic, fearing that the dreaded heresy might overwhelm Germany. In the end, the archbishop and elector resigned from the clergy and married to live a quiet life away from politics. Rudolf, the son of Maximilian, was elected emperor.

Rudolf had been raised in Madrid under the influence of his anti-Protestant uncle, Philip II. Rudolf sought to reverse many of the liberties that Protestants had been given of the years. However, any fears that Rudolf II would bring the Spanish Inquisition to Germany were allayed by his own incompetence. Rudolf suffered from fits of depression, not to mention paranoia. He became a recluse who did not want to sign either the most trivial nor important of documents.

Meanwhile, the Protestants were to find that peace was their greatest enemy. When the Catholic Church persecuted the Protestants, they united under the banner of the Bible and prevailed, but in the time of truce, the Protestants of Germany were dividing themselves along Lutheran and Reformed (Calvinist) lines. The *Book of Concord* was composed in 1580 in an attempt to unite the Protestants of Germany and was signed by fifty–one princes and thirty–five cities, but its rejection of certain elements of Reformed Theology prevented many other cities and princes from signing it. As a result, German Protestants were effectively two seperated groups; the Lutherans and the Reformed or Calvinists.

During the next twenty years Germany remained largely a peace, but the events surrounding them in Europe were ominous in tone. To the north, the war in the Netherlands was in a period of truce, but the death of Don John of Austria led the Catholics of the south to call Matthias, Rudolf's brother, to be their governor. To the west, France was still embroiled in the War of Religion, which was about to erupt into a civil war over the succession of a Protestant king to the throne. The papacy, likewise, kept pressure on Germany to defend Calvinism against the heretical Protestants and Jesuit "missionaries" were emerging everywhere in Germany.

Although the emperors no longer wielded sovereignty over Europe, the affairs of Europe played manifestly into the politics of the empire. It was not merely the squables of Germany that led to the Thirty Year War but, far more importantly, the wars of France and Spain. Those struggles, more than anything in Germany, contributed to the atmosphere that created the Thirty Year War.

The Spanish Armada

Amid the turbulent times of the Counter–Reformation, the pope was still pressing Philip II for the conquest of heretical England. Sixtus V had become pope in 1585. He had inherited the papal estates in chaos, as the enemies of Gregory XIII had formed bands of bandits who terrorized the countryside. Sixtus, nicknamed the "Iron Pope," finally had these brigands hunted down and executed. He excommunicated Henry of Navarre, the man whose marriage had been the pretext for the St. Bartholomew's Day Massacre, because he believed Henry's repentance of Protestantism to be insincere (it was). Nevertheless, Sixtus major tasks was to pressure Philip into invading England. He promised huge subsidies to pay for the campaign, which he would deliver to the Spanish King as soon as possible.

Philip agreed to this challenge. He still considered himself the rightful king of England, since he had been married to Queen Mary Tudor. Moreover, Queen Elizabeth had given safe haven to the "beggar navy" of William of Orange and lent assistance to the "beggars." When Elizabeth had her Catholic rival, Mary Stuart, Queen of Scots, executed in 1587, Philip used it as a pretext for war. He created an "invincible" Armada with which he would invade and conquer England.

The Spanish were then the dominant power in the world. No country could match Spain on even footing. Even in the seas, Spain saw themselves as the masters of the world. Philip planned to take control of the English Channel and rendevouz with a Spanish army of 30,000 more troops in Parma, near Holland. Everything seemed destined to spell the victory of the Spanish and the fall of England, but providence was not with Spain. The massive Armada was battered from long range cannon fire and bombships.   When the Spanish attempted to flee, the waters themselves fought against Spain as the weather conditions prevented their escape. The Spanish Armada fell.

After the defeat of the Spanish Armada, Pope Sixtus V refused to pay the subsidies he had promised. The result of the defeat of the Spanish Armada brought an end to Spanish dominance, and the beginning of the British Empire. England, under the Protestant Queen Elizabeth, was quickly rising to power as the dominant power of Europe, but her Protestant religion made England peaceful. England would not invade Europe's mainland, as Europe's princes had done so often to England. Therefore, the defeat of the Armada, in 1588, halted the expansion of the Hapsburgs. From this point in history forward, the Holy Roman Empire and the Holy Roman Church were to decrease in size and power. Never again would they dominant the world.

The War for France

The defeat of the Spanish Armada was followed by more devastating news for the pope and Philip. In 1589, France was to have its first Protestant king. Civil war was the result.

Back in 1576 Henry III, the king of Poland, inherited the French throne. King Henry Bourbon of Navarre, who had renounced his Protestant faith in order to save his life after the St. Bartholomew's Day Massacre, was soon released from his prison. It was not long before Henry Bourbon's recantation was proven insincere. After the Catholic's had seized the Chateau de La Reole, Bourbon came to their aid and defeated the invaders in a crushing blow. For the next few years he became the protector of the Huguenots. It was in 1584 that unique circumstances led to Henry Bourbon becoming heir to the throne.

Henry III had no children and when his brother died, Henry Bourbon became the next in line to inherit the crown should Henry die. Anticipating trouble, Pope Sixtus V immediately excommunicated Henry Bourbon and the Catholic Holy League allied itself with Spain in an attempt to prevent Henry Bourbon from ever taking the throne. Henry III, at first, took his mother's advice and began to oppress the Protestants, but the threat of Spanish troops entering France changed his attitude. He saw the pending war as one of France versus Spain, rather than Catholic versus Protestant. Things came to a head when, in 1587, the Catholic Holy League took upon itself to declare Elizabeth of Valois, the daughter of Philip II, as heir to the French throne. Henry saw this as a challenge to French authority itself. How could the Spanish papal alliance choose the next French king without French backing? In 1588, Henry reluctantly had two major leaders of the Catholic Holy League assassinated; the duke of Guise and Henry III's own brother, Cardinal Louis of Lorraine. The pope and the league condemned Henry and threatened war against him if he did not relent. Henry III now felt the pope was his enemy and that he had no choice but to back Henry Bourbon as his heir.

On July 30, 1589, Spanish/papal troops beseiged Paris itself. During the seige Henry III was stabbed by a Jacobin friar. He died; leaving the Protestant heir Henry Bourbon as king.

Henry Bourbon was to be called Henry IV in his lifetime, but Henry the Great after his death. He was to be one of a handful of great kings in France's less than great history. It was a title that Henry would have to earn. His ascension was not an easy. Even though there is no doubt that the assassin of Henry III was a Catholic who supported the Holy League, the Spanish/papal propaganda ministers attempted to promote the belief that Henry Bourbon had assassinated the king so he could take the throne. Rebels were surrounding Henry everywhere. Even the army of Henry III disbanded, forcing Henry Bourbon to flee Paris and prepare for his comeback.

For four years Henry fought the Holy League, making some headway, but it was clear to him that France was still largely Catholic and tolerance was not something that the church had instilled in its population. Protestants had learned tolerance out of the Bible and out of a desire to live, but the papacy saw the very existence of Protestantism as a threat to its survival. Henry, therefore, decided to gain support by renouncing Reform Theology and once again pretending to become Catholic. On July 25, 1593, he formally abjured Calvinism and declared himself a Catholic. He had done this once before to save his life. Now he did it again to save France. The result worked both times.

Even though many French cities continued to resist Henry, other major cities, including Lyon and Orleans, were tired of war and willing to accept Henry's claim. Within less than a year Henry had won, by sword and pen, France. On March 22, 1594, he entered Paris and is alleged to have said, "Paris is worth a mass."

Henry was to spend four more years at war with Philip II. He fought bravely and was praised by all who knew him. His military tactics were second only to his ability to motivate the troops and inspire the French. On April 13, 1598, the Edict of Nantes ended the war and established peace, but more importantly it established freedom of worship in Brittany, which became a haven for the Huguenots. The War of Religion was over and for the next forty years the Protestants and Catholics would live in relative peace.

Philip II died a few months later. Philip had inherited the greatest power on earth at the time. He did not cause it fall, but he lorded over it when it occurred. He had claimed the throne of Portugal in 1580, but Spain would loose it in 1640. The days of Spanish glory were fading along with the Holy Roman Empire. The two were closely related, for both were the domain of the Holy

Roman Church, and their opposition to the Reformation insured their ultimate failure.

Henry IV was to rule for another twelve years, but Catholic hatred for him resulted in many assassination attempts. Some of these were believed to have been at the hands of Jesuit assassins, causing Henry to expel the Jesuits in 1594. However, in 1610 one finally succeeded. Henry died a martyr, for although he professed to Catholicism, all knew he was still a Protestant in his heart. He had provided the Huguenots safe haven and restored France. Although he found little peace in his lifetime, he found it in death and earned the title, "Henry the Great."

Charles–Gustave Housez – The Assassination of Henry IV – 19th Century

The Papacy Before the Thirty Year War

Sixtus V died in August 1590. Roman mobs celebrated and torn down his statue. The tyrany of the popes had become as severe as ever. The Counter–Reformation papacy had been dominated by Inquisitors and warriors who sought to enforce their will upon all. Even the loyal Catholics of Italy felt the wrath of the tyrants.

449

The next year and a half would see four different popes ascend the papal throne. The first was Urban VII. He died of malaria less than two weeks after his election. Gregory XIV lasted less than a year. During that time he supported Spain against the French King Henry Bourbon, dispatching a papal army and reaffirmed Henry's excommunication. The few reforms he attempted to undertake was to outlaw gambling on the outcome of papal elections and to nix an attempt to limit the duration of papal reigns. Innocent IX followed and lived but two months. He too gave financial support to Philip II's war against Henry Bourbon before passing on to final judgment.

In 1592 Clement VIII took the tiara and reigned for over a decade. He continued the papal Counter–Reformation by increasing suppressive measures. He placed all Jewish writings on the Index of Forbidden Books and increased the severity of the Inquisition tactics. During his years on the throne, an average of three people a year were burned at the stake in the Holy City of Rome itself. Many hundreds more suffered unspeakable tortures which included having their genitals ripped off or burned with pinchers. Women might be raped with hot pokers. Such was the state of the post–Renaissance papacy.

In 1593 Clement did feel compelled to lift the excommunication against Henry Bourbon, who was professing to Catholicism at the time. The rest of Clement's deeds were futile attempts to enforce Catholicism upon Sweden and Poland, which were also becoming swept up in the Protestant Reformation. Clement died in 1605.

Leo XI reigned for one months, promising Emperor Rudolf funds to fight the Ottoman Turks, but dying before anything substantial could be done. It was Paul V who would live to see the eruption of the Thirty Year War, which he actively supported. Before that day came, Paul was largely known for an incident which demonstrated the declining power of the papacy. That incident was his failure to force Venice into submission. Using the old medieval tools of the church, Paul attempted to force Venice to release two clerics who had been imprisoned for crimes. Paul insisted that the clergy could only be tried by clerical courts, as was the case in the Middle Ages, but the Venesians refused to release them. Paul them ordered an interdict upon the whole of Venice. No more severe penalty existed in medieval times, for the very salvation of the populous might be threatened by their failure to partake of the sacraments, but the Venesian priests largely ignored the interdict while the Venesians expelled the militant Jesuits and even threatened to become Protestant. Paul was forced to back down. It was a signal that the papal weapons of old were no longer effective in the modern world. It was also a signal to Paul that Protestantism was a far greater danger to his office than any emperor had ever been.

The Emperor Matthias

Rudolf's mental state soon became so severe that the princes of Germany were eagerly seeking a way to remove him from power without a revoultion. They, therefore, turned to his brother Matthias. In 1605 the princes began to press for Matthias to be regent over Hungary, which was still threatened by the Ottoman Empire. In 1608, Rudolf was finally forced to cede control not only of Hungary, but also Austria and Moravia. Moreover, Matthias was made heir to Bohemia.

That same year the Diet of Regensburg was called. At the diet the Protestants and Catholics quarreled as the Protestants demanded the Religious Peace be fully enforced. Two years earlier Duke Maximilian of Bavaria, a disciple of the Jesuits, had gone so far as to take an army into Donauworth and force the Protestants there to convert or die. The Protestants demanded these activities stop and even promised to withdraw their support from the war on the Hungarian border against the Turks if sporatic persecutions and suppression of Protestant freedoms did not stop. So tense were relations between Protestants and Catholics that the Protestants formed the Evangelical Union, similar to the Smalcaldian League in preparation for an attack from the Catholics. The Catholics, in turn, formed the Catholic League, lead by Duke Maximilian of Bavaria.

To add to these troubles the recluse Rudolf came out of hiding in 1611 to attack Bohemia with the aid of Archduke Leopold. Protestant Hussites felt the sting of Leopold and Rudolf, so they turned to Matthias for help. Matthias' troops surrounded Prague and prevented anyone from leaving. Rudolf was forced to cede Bohemia to Matthias as promised, and Matthias granted concessions to the Protestants, but the concessions were only temporary. Bohemia, which had fostered the Hussite War over religious freedom years before the Reformation, was again aflame over the cries of religious liberty.

In 1612 Rudolf died and Matthias became emperor. Under his rule Prussia became a German state, deeded as a fief by Poland. Matthias' reign was relatively short, lasting until 1619, but it was marred by the eruption of the Thirty Year War. Since Matthias was childless, the Catholic archdukes had decided to name Ferdinand of Styria as the heir to Bohemia. The Protestants were well aware of Ferdinand's vehemently anti–Protestant views and refused to accept him as heir. In 1618 the Bohemian Revolt was to begin, signalling the beginning of the Thirty Year War.

The Coming War

The Counter–Reformation was really nothing more than the attempt to suppress the Reformation. It was, therefore, literally *counter* to reform, rather than being a true reform as its advocates claimed. Wars to exterminate

Protestantism engulfed Europe, with the Thirty Year War being the climax of the conflicts. The difference between the Counter–Reformation and the Albigenses Crusade was the people of Europe. Centuries of oppression had awakened the eyes of the common man. No longer were the princes and commoners willing to lay down.

The Counter–Reformation must be said to have failed with the ultimate failure of the Thirty Year War. From a strictly historical point of view (ignoring theological issues) it must be said that the reformation of the Catholic Church did not occur until the Vatican II Council in the 1960s, and even then the Vatican II Council ultimately reaffirmed every single doctrinal stance of the Council of Trent. This is why many Protestants to this very day resist Catholic advances. Doctrinally the Catholic Church of today has reaffirmed all the medieval views that led to the Reformation, even though they have renounced the political tactics of the medieval church. The Vatican II Council can thus be considered a political reform, but not a true theological reform. Nevertheless, these changes would not occur until the Holy Roman Empire itself fell and the papal estates were lost. It was to be a struggle for centuries.

Holy Roman Emperor	_Rival (if any)_	Pope

--- 1555 ---

--- 1556 --- Paul IV

Ferdinand

--- 1555 ---

--- 1564 --- Pius IV

--- 1565 ---

Maximilian II

--- 1566 ---

Pius V

--- 1572 ---

--- 1576 --- Gregory XIII

--- 1585 ---

Sixtus V

--- 1590 ---

Urban VII

--- 1590 ---

Gregory XIV

--- 1591 ---

Rudolf II

Innocent IX

--- 1591 ---

--- 1592 ---

Clement VIII

--- 1605 ---

Leo XI

--- 1605 ---

--- 1612 ---

Matthias Paul V

--- 1619 ---

--- 1621 ---

Ferdinand II Gregory XV

--- 1623 ---

--- 1637 --- Urban VIII

--- 1644 ---

Ferdinand III Innocent X

--- 1655 ---

--- 1657 ---

--- 1658 --- Alexander VII

--- 1667 ---

Leopold Clement IX

--- 1669 ---

453

Philippe Champaigne – Richelieu – 1637

27
—

The Thirty Year War

A hundred years had passed since the nailing of Luther's theses to the church door. Evangelical Christianity had been in Bohemia even longer. At first, the Catholic hierarchy was slow to realize that Luther was just a signal flare to men throughout the empire. "Heresy," so called, was not just the ravings of a few madmen, but the clarion call of a mass of humanity. The Counter–Reformation attempted to stamp out Protestantism, but it was too little, too late. Protestants now had princes and even kings on their side. Switzerland, Sweden, Poland, the nothern Netherlands, and England were Protestant. Even France had threatened to defect to Protestantism under Henry the Great. Now Germany and Bohemia threatened to abandon the mother church for the evangelical call.

The Thirty Year War was not just a German or Bohemian war. It was to engulf the whole of Europe by the time of its completion. The war first broke out in Bohemia and quickly embraced Germany. Spain entered the war, followed by Denmark and other countries. The papacy was naturally involved even from the early days and even France began to dabble in the politics of the war under the famed Cardinal Richelieu.

The Thirty Year War had been in the making for a hundred and one years. The Church of Rome, and its partner the Holy Roman Empire, were to engage in war for dominance. It was to be a final attempt to restore the ancient Roman Empire to its old glory by crushing the elements that were largely responsible for its divisions. There was to be one empire and one church. The future of the empire, and the course of human freedom, would largely depend on the outcome of the war, but the Protestants did not need to win; they only needed a draw, for unlike their Catholic adversaries, the Protestants were content to allow Catholic freedom, so long as they had their own, but if the Catholic Church was to continue to dominate the Holy Roman Empire, then it had to win.

The Bohemian Revolt

Years of oppression from Catholic princes and priests had worn on the now largely Protestant Bohemians. Although they were actually a majority by this time, they were still oppressed and persecuted. When Ferdinand of Styria was named king of Bohemia, and heir to the emperor's throne, the Bohemians became distraught. Ferdinand had tutored under the Jesuits and was a close friend of Duke Maximilian of Bavaria who had, a decade early, invaded Bohemia and forced many of the populous to convert to Catholicism. The

455

breaking point occurred when a Catholic Archbishop tore down a Protestant Church and ordered all people to attend Mass or be fined. The Protestants appealed to the king, but the pleas were ignored.

In 1618 a diet met in Prague where the infighting became bitter. The king's advisors refused to back down and demanded obedience from the Protestants. Finally, the Protestants, in a malicious jest, took two of the kings advisors and threw them out the window into a garbage bin. Their humiliation was just the beginning. The Bohemians then set up a provisional government, created an army for their defense, and finally deposed Ferdinand, electing Elector Frederick V of the Palatinate in his stead. It was a revolution which spread almost instantly to Moravia. Eventually, the whole of Europe would enter into the conflict.

Ferdinand ordered his Spanish troops to invade from the southern Netherland provinces. Frederick, a Calvinist who was married to the daughter of King James I of England (the same James whose name appears on the popular Bible translation), soon gathered his supporters. For the immediate struggle Hungary, Austria, Saxony, the Palitinate, and, of course, Bohemia lined up to support him.

In 1619 Matthias died. Ferdinand was no longer just the deposed king of Bohemia but the emperor of the Holy Roman Empire. The revolt, therefore, took on an international flavor for if they succeeded in challenging the very emperor, the whole of the empire might defect. The Hapsburg emperor had instant support from his cousin, Philip III of Spain and the pope. In 1620, the army of the Catholic League marched into Bohemia and at the Battle of the White Mountain dealt a blow to the armies of Frederick. Frederick became known as the "Winter King" because his rule lasted but a single winter. Ferdinand then wreaked revenge upon the people of Bohemia. All the leaders were executed and their families deprived of their property and inheritance. Protestant freedoms were instantly taken away and over three hundred nobles lost their homes and property which were given to Catholics. Persecution was to increase over the years, leading to much of the population fled the country.

In addition, Ferdinand had promised Duke Maximilian of Bavaria an electorate in exchange for his support. Since Ferdinand did not techincally have the power to create an electorate at the time, he awarded the Palitinate to Maximilian, thus making Maximilian the new elector of the Palitinate in place of the now defeated Frederick V. In fact, Ferdinand had made a secret pact promising to make Bavaria an electorate, which he still intended to do.

The suppression of the Bohemian revolt did not end the strife; it was but the beginning. The Protestant princes who had supported Frederick braced for war, knowing that Ferdinand would use their support as an excuse to conquer their territories and stamp out Protestantism. Indeed, Ferdinand II's grand scheme involved a conquest of Denmark using the armies of the Catholic

Netherlands while his Spanish/papal allies would conquer Italy on behalf of the emperor.

Jaroslav Cermák – After the Battle of White Mountain : The Counter Reformation – 1854

The Valtellina Massacre

The plans of Ferdinand gave justification to papal aggression against the Protestants of Italy, whose destruction had already been planned. Valtellina was a region in Italy often called the "hammer of heretics" because of its Inquisition and persecutions. When Bohemian revolt took place, the Protestants Grisons undertook to execute a number of citizens who were known to be Inquisitorial spies and banished those behind the perseutions. Among those banished as a knight named Jacob Robustelli.

In July 1620, even before the final defeat of the Bohemians, Robustelli returned to Valtellina with a Spanish army. The Valtellina Massacre rivaled that of the St. Bartholomew's Day Massacre. Around midnight the troops slipped into the Valtellina cities unnoticed and began butchering citizens. In one case, a Protestant minister's head was left on the pulpit. In another case a church, where women and children had taken refuge, was burned to the ground. Even the dead were not left in peace, but mutilated and fed to wild beasts. Women were raped and tortured, including an eighty year old former nun. Among the victims was a woman who declared, "you may kill the body, but not the soul."

457

For three long days the massacre continued, and after it was finished Robustelli moved on to other regions to seek out Protestants, burning the town of Brusio to the ground and committing many more outrages.

Gregory XV

Upon hearing that Frederick V had been defeated on White Mountain Paul V rode in a procession as celebration, during which he suffered a stroke and passed away in January 1621. Many believe this was a sign from God of his displeasure. Nevertheless, the hint was not taken for Gregory XV became the next pontiff in February. He was the first Jesuit to become pope. He had founded the Sacred Congregation for the Propogation of the Faith which became the headquarters for the Jesuits and the supreme authority over all missionaries. Hence, the mission field was now to be under the control of the militant Jesuit order.

Gregory, not content with the defeat of Frederick V, pressed Ferdinand to restore Catholicism to all of Germany. He provided huge subsidies to pay for the war and sent Jesuits to Bohemia for the forced conversion of Protestants. He also pressured Philip III to resume his was in the Netherlands against the northern Protestants. Finally, he sent papal troops to Valtellina to occupy the city, which had remained in anarchy since the massacre. Catholicism was now to be enforced there by the sword of the papal army.

Gregory passed away in July, 1623. In August Urban VIII replaced him. Like Gregory, Urban had been trained in a Jesuit school. He was to continue Gregory's policy of military conquest of the Protestants and support Emperor Ferdinand II in his campaign against the Protestant princes.

The Early Campaigns

The armies of the war were to divided into three main groups. Lower Saxony was placed under the command of the king of Denmark, Christian IV. In the north, the Calvinists turned to fellow Calvinist, King Gustavus Adolphus of Sweden. Ferdinand's armies were composed mainly of the Catholic League which he placed under the command of Albreht von Wallenstein. Thus the three main armies of the early campaigns were led by a Denmark king, a Swedish king, and a Catholic Bohemian prince.

Adolphus, in hopes of reclaiming Prussia, invaded Poland which had taken the fief back after Frederick's defeat. Wallenstein and King Christian IV were to meet many times on the battlefield, but the Danes were constantly driven back. Although England sent some assistance, the Denmark king was not able to hold back the advance of Wallenstein. At the peace of Lubeck, Denmark agreed to withdraw from the war in exchange for the promise not to threaten its borders. That left Wallenstein's army to ravage much of lower Saxony with little resistance. Soon they were making their way north.

In 1626 Ferdinand had enough control to begin the forcible conversion of Protestants in captured lands. In Bohemia it is estimated that four fifths of the country fled to escape forced conversion to Catholicism. Bohemia had been reduced from a population of three million people to a country of just over six hundred thousand people. In the Palitinate, a peasant insurrection followed the decree which required all to convert to Catholicism or face exile. Maximilian's troops had also been responsible for many atrocities which outraged the people. Faced with banishment, the Protestants of Germany were looking for help as their remaining armies were ineffective against those of Maximilian and Wallenstein.

Matters worsened in 1629 when the Edict of Restitution (backed by the pope, emperor, and Spain) established Catholicism over conquered territories and required exile for all who failed to convert, save a few Lutherans who were to be deprived of nobility and property. Further, the Edict of Restitution required all church property since 1552 to be returned to the Catholic Church. Protestant churches were then seized and converted into Catholic churches. Finally, the Jesuits entered the territories and began to require that all other Catholic orders submit to them and take a more active, and militant, stance against Protestants.

In response to these actions and the Edict of Restitution, Adolphus made a peace treaty with Poland and entered Germany to defend the Protestants suffering there. Adolphus was to become the hero of the Protestants in the Thirty Year War.

The Rise of Richelieu

France was not yet involved in the Thirty Year War, but it was only a matter of time. The truth is that France felt surrounded by anti–French interest. To the north there was the Protestant English. To the south there was the Spanish Habsburgs. To the east there was the Hapsburg emperor. Armand–Jean du Plessis Richelieu was a Catholic Cardinal who had risen to become an advisor to the queen mother Marie Medici and eventually to the king himself, young Louis XIII, surnamed the Just. Through a series of events, Richelieu soon became the most powerful man in all of France. He came to believe that whatever he wanted to do he could easily convince the king to do. Indeed, rarely did Louis ever fail to take Richelieu's "advise."

The French Cardinal, immortalized in Alexander Dumas' *Three Musketeers*, had fought in wars against the Protestant Huguenots and had no love for the evangelical faith, but he had even less love for the Hapsburgs. It was his love of France, not the Protestants, that led the Catholic Cardinal to begin supporting Protestant interest in the Thirty Year War, in hopes of breaking the Hapsburg's power. He feared that if the emperor was successful in the war, France would be controlled by foreign Hapsburg powers. To that end Richelieu expelled papal troops from France and, in 1629, signed the peace treaty of Ales with the defeated Huguenots which gave them freedom of worship according to their conscience, but forbade them from forming a military.

Now freed from Protestant "threats" in France, Richelieu began to subtly promote Protestant interest in Germany. He even sent subsudies to Adolphus to assist in his war against Wallenstein. To the south, Richelieu fought the Spanish for control of the fortress of Casale near the border of France and Italy. When Louis the Just signed a treaty with the Spanish, Richelieu refused to have the treaty ratified, which led the Spaniards to push Urban to excommunicate the king, but nothing was to come of it. The incident illustrates how Richelieu manipulated political events and even antagonized the pope, who never took measures against him, even when he knew Richelieu was promoting Protestant rebellion in Hapsburg territories. Already Richelieu had become the target of numerous conspiracies and plots. In 1630 the queen mother Maria Medici, fearing that Richelieu had more power over the king than she did, attempted to oust Richelieu, but instead the queen mother was herself exiled. This came to be called the Day of Dupes, because the queen and her supporters believed that Richelieu was to be exiled, when it was, in fact, they who were exiled.

Henri Motte – Richelieu at the Siege of La Rochelle – 1881

The next year, in preparation for France's eventual entry into the war, Richelieu formed a defensive alliance with Bavaria. Later, when two Italian duchies claimed by the French were vacated, Emperor Ferdinand bequeethed them to his Hapsburg relative. Richelieu now felt more intimidated by the Hapsburgs than ever. France's entry into the war only a matter of years away.

The Fall of Magdeburg

Adolphus had entered Germany in defense of the Protestants in 1630. The Swedish king was greatly respected by the people. His troops never abused the citizens nor forced the conversion of the populous. Adolphus was a chivalrous man in an unchivalrous age. By contrast, the troops of Maximilian were brutal and cruel. They had been known to butcher the populous of villages and defile women. Adolphus was, therefore, welcomed as a hero and often found many volunteers eagerly awaiting his arrival in hopes of joining his army. Even the Catholic populous was pleased to have a man of virtue in their city where they could expect dignity.

The change of fortunes favored the Protestants and disturbed the Catholic princes, who blamed Ferdinand and Wallenstein in particular. Wallenstein was mistrusted by the German princes for several reasons. The Jesuits hated him because he was not as brutal as Maximilian. Although a Catholic, Wallenstein's father had been Protestant, so he was suspected of Protestant sympathies. The German princes hated Wallenstein because he was a foreginer (Bohemian). In addition, everyone knew that Wallenstein was ambitious. The Catholic German princes wanted to get rid of Wallenstein.

When the emperor Ferdinand met with the Catholic electors and sought to make his son, Ferdinand III, King of the Romans and heir to the imperial throne, the electors refused unless he agreed to dismiss Wallenstein. Ferdinand reluctantly agreed, but found that the electors were now making additional demands. They even made the emperor to promise not to wage war except where authorized by the Catholic electors. In fact, they were fearful that Ferdinand was not only trying to stamp out Protestantism but to reassert imperial control over all their states; something the princes did not want to happen. They wanted an emperor in name, but not in power.

Wallenstein's army was now led by Count Johan of Tilly. They acted swiftly to prevent the advance of Adolphus and in 1631 moved on Magdeburg, an ancient religous center of Germany. It was also a cultural center, featuring many landmarks and architectural achievements. The city was in many ways symbolic of German Christianity; both Catholic and Protestant. The Count von Tilly beseiged the city, which was now a Protestant stronghold, and hoped to make an example of it. Magdeburg was virtually razed to the ground. Its citizens were massacred and the monuments to German history were set aflame. Fifty women were found bound with their throats cut in the remains of a church.

Most of the other women did not fair as well. Those who were attractive enough were taken away, after being raped, and forced to live as concubines. The rest were raped and murdered before their husbands' or fathers' eyes. The atrocities of the fall of Magdeburg stirred the Protestants to action. Saxony and the elector of Brandenburg now joined Adolphus. The elector of Brandenburg even offered his son in a marriage alliance with Adolphus' daughter. Formerly, the Lutheran princes had been reluctant to assist the northern Calvinists, but the fall of Magdeburg strengthened the Protestants resolve and made them forget trivial differences. Adolphus named the head of the *Corpus Evangelicarum* ("body of evangelicals") and the army of Adolphus marched to meet Count von Tilly and the perpetrators of the atrocities.

The Rally of the Protestants

In 1632 Adolphus met the Count von Tilly in battle at Lech. There Tilly's army was defeated and the count was himself mortally wounded. The Catholic League was in disarray and there was no one to stand in the way of Adolphus' advance to the south.

Some Catholic princes of Germany were now ready to made overtones to peace. They offered religious tolerance, the return of the Palitinate to Frederick V, and the expulsion of all Jesuits, but the emperor would have none of it. In desperation he reinstalled Wallenstein as *generalissimo* of the armies, but Wallenstein would not take the post without first securing more authority for himself. He demanded, and was granted, the power to make treaty with Adolphus and to negotiate peace on his own terms. Wallenstein was thus given the authority of the emperor in regard to ending the war, but he was also given the authority to confiscate property of conquered lands for himself.

Almost immediately, Wallenstein entered into secret negotiations with Adolphus, who offered Wallenstein Bohemia as a viceroyalty, but Wallenstein wanted more. He was constantly negotiating with both sides for a peace which would bestow the most power possible upon himself. What is interesting in the negotiations is that he was conceding the eventual defeat of the Catholic League. Wallenstein was merely trying to delay that until he could get something for himself.

The Deaths of Adolphus and Wallenstein

On November 16, 1632, at Lutzan, Wallenstein and Adolphus met on the battlefield. Adolphus' army again emerged triumphant, but Adolphus himself was slain. It was a hollow victory. The Protestants lost their best general and a national hero. In Rome Pope Urban VIII was instigating thanksgiving masses to celebrate the death of Adolphus. In Protestant countries Adolphus was mourned. The Catholics of Germany had been wanting peace for a year. Now Protestants were desirous of peace, but there were still too many obsticles. For one thing, Wallenstein still wanted as much as he could in exchange for peace. The Swedes also wanted recompense for their defense of Germany. However, the real reason for the continuation of the war was Spain. They wanted to forge out a possession of their own between their Italian possessions and the southern Netherlands, which could only mean cutting out a slice of Protestant Germany for Spain.

The situation seemed to be out of hand. When one enemy was defeated, another arose. Germany, Bohemia, Denmark, Sweden, Italy, England, the Netherlands, and Spain had all entered the war at some point, and France too would enter the mix as well. Ferdinand's advisors did not trust Wallenstein whom they suspected was negotiating with their own titles and lands for his own advancement. In 1634 they successfully convinced Ferdinand to assassinate Wallenstein. So it was, in 1634, that both sides had lost their best generals. Adolphus was to remain a national hero in Sweden, and a great war hero of the Protestants of Germany. Wallenstein was never honored or remembered, but he was the best that the Catholics had. Now Ferdinand took the field personally, commanding the armies of the Catholics by his own hand.

He allied with the Spanish troops and pushed the Protestants back. Soon, alliances were to be forged that broke the religious barriers and took on a nationalistic tone. John George, a Lutheran, agreed to ally with Ferdinand against the Swedes and Calvinists, provided Lutheranism was tolerated as had been the case in decades past. Catholic France, on the other hand, allied itself with the Swedes and Calvinists against their mutual enemies; the Hapsburgs. The resulting Peace of Prague in 1635 was not to be a peace to the war, but rather new alliances. That same year France declared open war on Philip IV of Spain.

France Enters the Conflict

Spain had used the war to advance their own interest. Once the dominant power of the world, Spain had been on the decline since the death of Charles V and had been dealt a major blow with the loss of the Spanish Armada. During the Thirty Year War Spain's ambitious policy was to reclaim the northern Netherlands, increase their domains in Italy (at the expense of France), and carve out a slice of Protestant Germany to forge a path between Italy and the Netherlands. France also laid claims to Italian territory. This was the central background to the hatred between Richelieu and Philip IV. When Spain seized the Archbishop of Trier, under French protection, Richelieu declared war on Spain and allied with Sweden against the Catholic League.

It is important to note that France was careful to argue that they were not in rebellion against the empire (although they were at war with the emperor), but rather that they were protecting the interest of the empire against Spanish aggression. Since the popes had often come into conflict with the emperors in times past, and since Urban VIII secretly desired to weaken Spanish power in Italy (in hopes of one day reestablishing papal authority over it), the pope tactfully maintained a sort of neutrality toward France. Officially, he criticized France' role in the conflict, and yet he refused to censure Richelieu.

In Germany, Bernard of Weimar attempted to replace Adolphus but he was neither the leader, nor the religious figure that Adolphus had been. The war was locked in a stalemate when Ferdinand II died. His son, Ferdinand III, was not like his father. He desired peace but the cruelties perpetrated during the war embittered the Protestants who would accept nothing less than religious freedom while the pope, Maximilian, and the Spaniards (whose native citizens were largely safe in Spain) refused to grant any concessions to the Protestants. Ferdinand felt that his hands were tied for the time being.

In 1639 Bernard of Weimar died and the French personally took command of the troops in conjunction with Sweden. Together they launched the first co–ordinated attack on Bavaria, the home of Maximilian. For all these years, Bavaria had largely been left out of the conflict, but now Maximilian's home was the target. It was an attempt by the French to go on the offensive. Unlike Adolphus‘ armies, the French troops were just as savage as those of the Catholic League. For the French it was not a war of religious freedom but of national pride and territorial expansion. Brutalities raged on both sides.

In 1641 Urban VIII‘s relationship with France and Richelieu was deteriorating. Urban had ousted the lord Farnese of the Castro fief and installed his own "nephews" as sovereigns. Thus Italy now had the pope entering into the struggle for control over Italian territories and France came to Farnese's defense. Richelieu maintained that the pope had no right to deprive Farnese of his fief without proper justification. Soon France allied itself with Venice and Tuscany against the papal armies.

Richelieu died before the war was finished. His puppet king, Louis the Just, died five months later. The queen mother of Louis XIV, Anne of Austria, decided to appoint one of Richelieu's close confidants, Cardinal Jules Mazarin, to run the affairs of state. Mazarin continued Richelieu's policies, including his war against the papal fief of Castro. In 1644, after the papal estates had been ravaged by war, France won back control of the fief. Urban died that same year, causing celebratory riots in the streets of Rome.

Urban's reign was marked by his blind backing of the Thirty Year War and his insistence that no compromise should be made with "heretics." The only other incident of note was the trial of his close friend Galileo Galilei. Galileo was a controversial figure who believed that the earth revolved around the sun, rather than the sun revolving around the earth. He was, however, better known among some circles for his secretive dismissal of the Trinity. In short, the pope's colleague was a heretic. Urban's political enemies wished to use Galileo to humiliate the pope and try Galileo for heresy, but after a series of political negotiation it was decided instead that Galileo would be tried for the "heresy" of his Copernican theory of the earth, and spared being burned at the stake. The outcome was predetermined. Galileo would officially renounce his Copernican theory and the pope would be sufficiently humiliated. This occured in 1633.

Innocent X replaced Urban, although many insisted that his sister–in–law was the real power of the papacy. She lived in his court and dominated his affairs the same way that Richelieu dominated the affairs of Kind Louis.

Back in Germany, French and Swedish forces forced Maximilian to delcare a truce. In 1644 Ferdinand III began to press for peace. The treaty, however, was to be four years in the making, for each side wanted as many concessions as possible, and both Protestant and Catholic alike also sought to diminish the authority of the emperor. Sweden pressed the issue by invading Bohemia, the land in which the revolt had begun and which now languished with a population one fifth of what it had been when the war began.

Despite these factors, the Spanish might not have agreed to the peace treaty had not their own power diminished. Although they had hoped to expand their domains, they in fact were loosing them. In 1640 Portugal (which had become united with Spain under Philip II) revolted. In 1647 Naples also revolted against Spanish rule. Spain had lost the northern Netherlands, Portugal, and now Naples was threatened. Even they were now willing to give backing to Ferdinand's peace plans.

Peace of Westphalia

Four years of debate and negotiation resulted in the Peace of Westphalia in 1648, over the constant objections of Pope Innocent X. The peace was to change the character of the empire and to shape modern Germany.

Territorially France was given the lands as far as the Rhine. Sweden received vast lands in the Baltic and North Sea as well as 5,000,000 gulden as compensation for their troops. Religiously, the treaty gave freedom of conscience and worship to Catholics, Lutherans, and now Calvinists (Reformed). Other religious sects, such as the Anabaptists, were still outlawed. Further, the treaty gave amnesty to all rebels save those directly under the territory of the emperor, who insisted that rebellion against the emperor could not be forgiven. Finally, the princes of Germany were given increased power, at the expense of the once mighty emperor. German princes were given the right to make treaties and alliances with foreign powers so long as they did not threaten the empire, while such a right was actually taken away from the emperor! The emperor now had to get electorial approval for all wars, exiles, and alliances (even though the princes needed no such approval for alliances).

The result of the Peace of Westphalia was two fold. First, Germany was divided along religious lines. Southern Germany, including Austria and Bavaria, remained largely Catholic. Northern Germany, including the Palitinate and Brandenburg, was to be dominated by Protestants. Second, the emperors were now little more than figureheads. Although France, Spain, and Italy would remain nominally a part of the empire, the emperor was really nothing more than a weak German king, and one who had to seek approval from electors for many of his decisions. The papacy too suffered a loss of power. Their "spiritual tools" had been proven ineffective in the modern age. Excommunication and interdicts were no longer sufficient to make kings bow to their will. The Roman Empire was disintigrating before their very eyes.

In November, months after the signing of the treaty, Innocent formally denounced the Peace of Westphalia, but he was urged, possibly by Maidalchini, his sister–in–law, not to release the condemnation until two years later.

Summary of the Thirty Year War

Over a third of the population of Germany died in the Thirty Year War. It was the in reality the last crusade whose aim was to reinstate the medieval church as sovereign over Europe. Its ultimate failure proved to the Catholics that the Protestants were here to stay, yet this fact was something that the papacy did not come to grips with until centuries later. It also spelled the end of the medieval theory of government. During the next hundred and fifty years democracies were to rise to power under the influence of Protestantism. In England the Puritans, under Oliver Cromwell, were already setting to stage for a republic while the Pilgrims were taking those notions to American soil even while the Thirty Year War raged. Monarchies, however, were to decline. Already the great imperial power was restricted to Germany and the once great papal power was now restricted largely to Spain and Italy.

The last hundred and fifty years of the Holy Roman Empire was to be a struggle between the various empire's surviving monarchies and the rising tide of freedom promoted by the Reformation. These last years were to culminate in to failed attempt of Napoleon to restore the Holy Roman Empire under a curious mix of democracy and imperial power. So the Thirty Year War may mark a rubicon in the history of the empire. One where papal/imperial conflicts were replaced with monarchial/democratic ones.

28

The Gallic Power

The past century had seen the quick rise to power of Spain and its even quicker fall. Now it was the French or Gallic power which sought to become a world power to rival Great Britain, which was putting the Catholic countries to shame. The French rivalry with the German emperors is as old as the empire itself, but it was to reach its climax with Napoleon Bonaparte. During the Thirty Year War the French had hoped to break the power of the Hapsburg and make France a role player in the empire. The plan worked in part. With France's continued war on Spain the power of the Hapsburgs would eventually be broken to the west, but the eastern Hapsburg emperors would stubbornly hold on the crown (with one exception) until the Frenchman Napoleon himself took what no Frenchman since Charles the Bald (Louis III was technically from Provence) had claimed. In the meantime, France would play a dominant role in the empire's history; far more than its own emperor.

Despite the increased prominence of France the emperor Leopold did increase the power of the Austrian state and strengthen his monarchy, but this was done at the expense of the imperial power. The eighteenth century was to see almost constant warfare throughout the empire as the various states warred over succession. These wars were only made possible by the absence of imperial authority. From 1701 until the French Revolution there was to be the First and Second Northern Wars, the War of Spanish Succession, the War of Polish Succession, the War of Austrian Succession, the Seven Years' War, and the War of Bavarian Succession. During this time the empire was collapsing under the strife of its petty princes while in England and its colonies in North America the rise of democracy would become the greatest threat that the empire had ever faced. It was a threat which the papacy took seriously.

The English Revolution

While not a part of the Holy Roman Empire, the events in England and in the colonies would profoundly effect the fall of the empire. It was in the 1640s that a Puritan revolution took place in England. Under Oliver Cromwell the entire country of England was to become a short lived democratic republic. Although the Middle Ages had seen cities attempt to employ a republican system, no country since ancient Rome had utilized a true republican democracy.

The rise of republican democracy in history can be traced throughout the history of dissident Christianity. Arnold of Brescia first tried to resurrect the ancient dream but was executed by Frederick Barbarosa. Cola de Rienzo was no Christian but nevertheless revived Arnold's old dream, even if for just a brief moment. Savaronola also attempted to restore democratic ideals, but with a theocratic element. So also John Calvin preferred the mixture of republican and theocratic elements. From Calvin, republican ideals spread to England through Reform preachers and became embedded in the Puritans. England itself had already been the first country to touch upon republican ideas, for the Christian princes of England had long ago forced King John to sign the *Magna Charta* and created Parliament. Even if Parliament was but a shadow of a true Republic, it was a start, and it from that start that the Puritan Oliver Cromwell was able to lead a revolt against King Charles and establish the Cromwell government which, for the first time since antiquity, created a Republican government over not a city, but the whole of a country.

Paul Delaroche – Cromwell Before the Coffin of Charles I – 1831

The revolution, and the establishment of the republic, ended not with the assassination of King Charles but with his summary trial and execution in 1649. This event remains vitally important in history for it was the first time that a king had been *lawfully* executed by the laws of the country. In other words, it was the first time that the king was recognized by the courts as being subject to the laws. The execution of King Charles, however, was to haunt Oliver Cromwell, for the general populous of Britain was not as well educated as the Puritans (who founded both Harvard and Yale in the colonies), and democracies cannot survive without education. Consequently, the people soon began to demand a king, and even offered the crown to Cromwell, but this noble man refused the crown saying no one but Christ is king.

The republic itself would only last until shortly after Cromwell's death. He was to be called a king in all but name, and when the republic fell to Charles' heir, the Puritans took their republic ideals with them to the New World as they fled persecution and retaliation from the king. For the time being, however, Oliver Cromwell and the Puritans were the power of England.

The Piedmonte Massacre

The Thirty Year War had ended but the war between France and Spain would continue for another eleven years. During that struggle it was Italy that suffered the worst for not only did France and Spain claim the former Lombard possessions but the pope also asserted his authority wherever he could. Piedmonte was currently under the sovereignty of the French duchy of Savoy. In 1650 the "Council for the Propogation of the Faith and the Extirpation of Heretics" was established in Turin by Jesuits. Its purpose was clear.

Twice before papal armies had entered into the valleys of Piedmonte in an attempt to destroy the Waldenses. Twice before the papal armies would fail. A third time they would try, but this time they came very near to their goal. The massacre of the Waldenses remains one of the greatest tragedies in history. It surpasses the St. Bartholomew's Day Massacre in its treachery, savagery, and inhumanity. It was said that neither Nero nor the Inquisitors had perpetrated the cruel atrocities on the level that occured in April, 1655.

On January 25, 1655, the order of Gastaldo was sent forth to the Waldenses. It declared that all the Waldenses had three days to move to segregated lands designated by the Marquis de Pianeza and to sell all their current property to Catholics. This was in the heart of winter in the cold mountains of the valley which the Marquis made it impossible for the Waldenses to undertake such a journey had they desired to obey the edict. It was really nothing more than an edict of death.

The Waldenses sent representatives to the Marquis but they were denied a hearing. On April 17, the Marquis de Pianeza led an army of 15,000 men into the valleys but as the Waldenses had done before they utilized the mountain passes and landscape, not to mention their faith and desire for preservation, to beat back the Marquis' troops. After four days of fighting, the morale of the Marquis' men was failing. He, therefore, developed a new plan, or as one historian said, a new weapon. That weapon was deceit. He was, after all, doing the work of the Jesuits whose controversial doctrine of "Probablism" (which Blaise Pascal condemned) made virtually any act, no matter how immoral, justifiable. Essentially, they believed that the ends justified the means.

The Marquis sent a delegation to the Waldenses insisting that the men who had attacked them were bandits that his troops were sent to track down. He asked them the use of their valleys and the courtesy of their homes. In short, he asked the Waldenses to allow his troops to quarter themselves within their very homes as guests, rather than invaders. Too often the innocent fail to suspect the guile of the guilty. Such was the case. Some of the villages took in their own murderers as house guests. The soldiers were ordered to wait until the signal to strike, so that the Marquis could prepare simultaneous attacks elsewhere. After a few days, the Waldenses, if they suspected anything at all, were relieved of their suspicions and hence were taken completely off guard.

At four A.M. on the morning of Saturday, April 24, the attack began. The soldiers began their work with such horrors as have not been equally since the days of the ancient Vikings or Aztecs. That the accounts of these actions are not exaggerations cannot be denied, for an investigation was later to made by a delegation of Lord Cromwell of England to confirm the accuracy of the reports, which shocked the Protestant world and brought England to brink of invasion in defense of the Waldenses.

Sir Samuel Moreland, historian for Cromwell himself, recounts the crimes both reported to him by eyewitnesses and of the evidence found laying in the mountains, for the criminals did not undertake to bury their victims, nor to remove the skin of one man from the window upon which it was hung as a curtain. Women were not only raped by men, but with swords and pikes as well. Some men were sawed in half, while others were roasted alive. Mutilation of victims was common, but only the lucky ones were left to bleed to death. The others had torches placed upon their open wounds to prolong their deaths. Childred were torn limb from limb in front of their mothers. Hearts were cut out. Men were skinned alive new uses for gunpowder were devised on hapless victims. Even cannabalism was practiced as a cruel joke.

The savagery of the massacre remains unrivaled in "civilized" countries. So angry was Cromwell that he contemplated going to war. His secretary, the famous poet John Milton, wrote a poem memorializing the victims of the massacre, which read in part;

> "Avenge, O Lord, they slaughtered saints who bones
> Lie scattered on the Alpine mountains cold;
> Even them who kept the truth so pure of old
> When all our fathers worshiped stocks and stone."

Cromwell sent out dispatches to Louis XIV to plead on behalf of the Waldenses. The result was a peace treaty, but the treaty was little more than politics, for the dirty work had been done and there were few Waldenses left to be saved. Those who remained had peace for thrity years until Louis resumed the persecution of Protestants in France in 1685. For now, they had rest.

Leopold's Ascension and the Gallic Power

Pope Alexander VII took the throne just weeks before the massacre of Piedmonte. He had tried to establish good relations with France and the Cardinal Marazin but when Rome offered protection to the Cardinal de Retz (who had fled France after a conspiracy against Marazin was revealed) France resumed their support of Farnese over his claim to the fief of Castro. Thus, Alexander found most of his reign occupied with Gallic opposition.

Two years later, Ferdinand III died in April 1657. Although it is likely that the French no longer believed they could win the imperial diadem for themselves, as the electorate excluded all Frenchmen, it is obvious that sought to use their muscle to deny the Hapsburgs the title. The Rhenish Confederation, led by France, brought German Protestant princes and other non–electorial voices of the empire, including Sweden, together to counteract the power of the electorate. The confederation's power was negligible and would be dissolved in 1668, but it did succeed in slowing up the election process which dragged out for over a year.

Because the French had conflict with Pope Alexander, he was unsympathetic to their cause and wholeheartedly threw his support to Leopold, the second son of Ferdinand. Nevertheless, even the Germans were leary of the Hapsburgs, whom they viewed largely as Spanish rulers. Ulitmate, in 1658, Leopold was elected but only after swearing an oath not to support Spanish interest against France. This was, in a small way, a victory for the Gallic party. Although the Hapsburg dynasty continued in the east, France could hope to continue its policies against the Spanish Hapsburgs in the west. This allowed Cardinal Marazin to continue his his war Spain in Italy which resulted in Spain conceding some possessions in exchange for the peace of the Pyrenees in 1659. Additionally, in 1660, Louis XIV married the elder daughter of Philip IV of Spain, Marie Therese of Austria.

On March 9, 1661, Marazin died. With him died the last of Cardinal Richelieu's policies. Louis XIV, now of age, decided that he was would take complete control over the affairs of state. The French monarch developed an elevated view of himself which he fostered among the people, earning him the byname "the Sun King." Some even claim that he believed himself a god incarnate. Immediately, Louis began to alienate the nobility by his domination of affairs, but they were, despite several revolts, appeased by the extravagant luxuries and decadence with which he showered upon them.

Although the policies of Richelieu had passed away with Marazin, Louis did not abandon Richelieu's ultimate goals. He wanted France to be the dominant power of the empire. That meant that he considered himself greater than both the emperor and the pope. Using some pretext, he sent troops to occupy Avignon and threatened to invade the papal estates. In 1664 Alexander was forced to sign the treaty of Pisa in order to keep peace. France found itself virtually unopposed in its Italian possessions.

Leopold was at this time largely unconcerned with the struggles of the west, for in 1663 the Ottoman Turks again invaded Hungary, this time reaching its capital. Leopold united many German princes to drive back the Turks, establishing what was to be a twenty year truce at the Peace of Vasvar. However, this conflict was a foreshadowing of the war that would rage in twenty years time. The wars of Europe had prevented the emperors from eliminating the Turkish threat, and the Ottomans were always willing to wait patiently for the weakness of Europe. For now, Leopold was victorius.

In 1665 Philip IV, king of Spain, died. Charles II claimed the throne and gave his younger daughter, Margarita Teresa of Austria, in marriage to Emperor Leopold. That marriage spelled future conflict between Leopold and and his step–brother Louis. Both were now related by marriage to the Spanish royalty. Although Margarita died a few years later, Leopold and Louis would one day enter into a war of succession over the Spanish crown. For the time being, the real power in Spain was a Jesuit confessor to the queen mother. Spain and France were soon to enter yet another conflict; this time over the Spanish Netherlands.

The Netherlands Conflict

Upon the death of Alexander VII, his secretary of state and the Roman governor was elected with the wholehearted backing of the French. Apparently Louis knew something the rest of the world did not. Clement IX was to bow to almost every whim of the French party. That same year, 1667, Louis invaded the Netherlands.

This War of Devolution was short–lived for Louis had not anticipated that the English, Swedes, and Danes would come to the rescue of their Protestant friends in the northern Netherlands. Louis had successfully kept Leopold from entering the fray, but he had not counted on the strong Protestant support, even though much of Louis' objective was aimed at the Spanish south, rather than the north.

In 1668, Clement IX played a role in establishing a peace treaty, but that peace was only temporary. Louis was the cousin of Charles II, who had stayed in France during much of Oliver Cromwell's government. Although it was Charles who had come to the Netherlands' defense, he was won over to Louis' side and in the Secret Treaty of Dover, and on May 1670, Charles not only allied himself with Louis, but converted to Catholicism. The treaty also promised that France would come to Charles' aid if his Catholicism roused the people of England. They also promised to keep this clause in the treaty secret, but that secrecy would allow Louis to blackmail his cousin as Charles' position later became unstable.

In 1672 England and France together invaded the Netherlands and the war was renewed. This time the war would last six years. Louis was constantly playing politics in hopes of keeping Germany from entering the war in the Netherland's defense. Secret alliances with German princes were common, but some of the princes played both sides of the fence. The "Great Elector" of Brandenburg, Frederick William, made an alliance with France to stay out of the war, but then, in 1675, allied himself with Prussia against France. This was to be the beginning of the Prussian rise to power in Germany. It also created allied Prussia, the emperor, Holland, Sweden, Denmark, and Spain against France and England. Louis won moderate support from the new pope Clement X (who ascended in 1670) by professing to liberate Holland and the Netherlands from Protestant heresy.

Louis' demands for peace were the same ones he had sought from the beginning. He wanted all Italy, Sicily, and the Netherlands for himself and promised Leopold that he could have Spain but the demands were too grand. Nonetheless, by making such grand demands, his concessions ultimately left him with the triumph. The Treaty of Nijmegen in 1678 was much more favorable to France and gave him new territories in the north. He had also conquered part of Flanders from Spanish interest. Louis was hailed in France as the "Sun King," "the Grand Monarch," and "the Great." Under his reign France was to become modernized. Louis undertook the building of roads, ports, and canals and structured a police force more closely similar to modern police, but no sooner had Louis' great triumph taken place then his decline began.

Louis' Decline

In 1676, Innocent XI became pope. The French had previously vetoed certain candidates for the papal office, but did not resist Innocent. The last two popes had succumbed to Gallic pressure easily so they may have assumed that Innocent would as well. In fact, Innocent was to resist French domination throughout his relatively long reign. He is considered the greatest of the seventeenth century popes, although his competition among the seventeenth century popes was obviously negligible. Ultimately, although strong in comparison to the weak popes of the century, Innocent really only had one true victory late in his reign when the Turkish threat again reared its head. Before that time Innocent was consumed in a struggle with French power.

So dominant was the French influence in the papal court before Innocent's rise that Clement X had once been forced to back down after a French ambassador threatened violence in May 1675. Innocent would not be so easily deterred. When the French clergy passed the Gallic Articles of 1682, which denied papal authority over the French clergy, the pope and king became enemies. Louis' position was, however, weakened by the events of the past few years.

In 1680 Louis suffered the public humiliation of the Affair of Poisons. Louis' mistress was accused, along with other high ranking nobles, of sorcery and murder. Over four hundred people were suspected resulting in the execution of thirty six. Louis finally halted the procedings and destroyed all evidence which implicated his mistress. The affair debased the high view that the people had once held of Louis, and gave ammunition to Innocent. This may have been one of the reasons for Louis' decision to actively supress "heresy."

Even before the 1680s Louis had taken a strong interest in suppressing Catholic heresy such as the Catholic Jansenists who held to a view of Predestination that the Jesuit power found to be too close to Protestant Calvinism. Louis pressed the pope to condemn the teachings of the Jansenists, which including names such as Blaise Pascal. In 1681, Louis turned to the Huguenots. He issued the abominable order that all Protestant children were to be taken from their parents and to be raised by Catholic families. Four years later he revoked the Edict of Nantes (see pg. 448) which spelled open persecution of the Huguenots, who were forced to either convert or leave France.

So pitiless was his persecution of Protestants that even Innocent, who approved of the revocation of the edict, began to criticize the brutal methods of the king. The Huguenots, in memorial to their fellow victims, changed part of their crest from a dove descending from heaven to a tear drop falling from heaven. Said a high official of the French court, "all was permitted to the soldiers except murder." Rape, torture, and pillaging were common. So severe was the persecution that over 400,000 Protestants fled to the American colonies, England, the Netherlands, or Prussia. Their suffering also stirred up the enemies of France. The Great Elector of Brandenburg, who had allied with France, now broke with the king and responded with the edict of Potsdam which promised to defend the Netherlands against French aggression and extended open hands to the oppressed Huguenots. Twenty thousand Huguenots took up the elector on his offer and fed the state with an influx of intellect and culture which the Huguenots provided. Further, Frederick William now used his electorial power to back the son of Leopold as King of the Romans; which the French had staunchly opposed.

While Louis was preoccupied with his war on Protestants the rest of the empire was uniting against a true enemy. The Ottoman Turks had again taken Belgrade. In 1686 Pope Innocent XI helped form the Holy League to repel the Turks once again. The league was comprised of Poland, Venice, and even the Russians. Two years later the Turks were driven out of Belgrade.

In England, it looked for a time as if the empire might once again regain the lost kingdom. The so-called Popish Plot of 1678, which many believe to be untrue, alleged that the papacy was involved in a conspiracy to assassinate Charles II and install Catholic brother James II on the throne of England. When James II finally assume the throne, in 1685, the Protestants of England were fearful of another tyrant like bloody Mary. They were not entirely misguided. Rebellions were crushed with a ferocity and cruelty which once again called forth criticism from his ally Pope Innocent. Three years of bloody wars ended with his deposition, the establishment of Parliament as the ruling power in England, and the ascension of William III of Orange.

1688 was to be a bad year for King Louis. His conflict with the papacy had grown to such an extent that Innocent XI secretly excommunicated the king and his officials. He then sent notice to the king of the secret excommunication. The fact that the excommunication was secret was doubtless to prevent Louis' humiliation and leave the door open for Louis to negotiate with the pope without loosing face. It also signalled the loss of papal power, for the pope was now very careful in how he approached a powerful king. Nonetheless, a greater problem was to arise for Louis. With the defeat of the Turks in Belgrade, the empire was freed to turn its attention toward its disobedient child. The savage persecution and the expansionistic policy of France ultimately led to the Grand Alliance of the emperor, the English, and the Dutch against France. That same year a new war erupted as the Grand Alliance invaded. Soon Savoy and Spain joined against France.

The war was to last nine long years. Louis tried to patch up relations with the papacy by returning Avignon to the new Pope Alexander VIII, who regined briefly from 1689 to 1691. When he died the French and imperial parties fought over his successor. Innocent XII finally won out, which appeared to be a victory for Louis since Innocent buckled to most every French whim including allowing the doctrine of Gallicism (the view that the French clergy should control themselves without papal interference) to be accepted. Nevertheless, the war was not to be decided in Rome but on the battlefields, where Louis was loosing.

During the later years of the war the emperor was distracted by yet another invasion of Turks. Only with the assistance of the Duke Eugene of Savoy, the hero of the war, was Leopold able to hold off the Turkish menace, but it was clear that Germany could not fight a war on two fronts. Germany had been winning the war against the French, but now Leopold was forced to conclude a peace with France before he wanted. In 1697 the Treaty of Rijswijk was concluded which neither side liked.

The Treaty of Rijswijk reversed many of the victories of the Treaty of Nijmegen. France lost many of its former acquisitions and lost its prestige. Leopold, however, did not consider himself the victor for France was allowed to acquire Strasbourg from Germany, which made Leopold look weak in the eyes of his people. France surrendered claims to the Palatinate and Lorraine. They also returned Luxemburg to the Netherlands. Other indirect results of the conflict included the expansion of the electorate to nine as Leopold sought to increase his alliances. Palsgrave had received an electorate many years ago, and now Hanover received the ninth electorate. France no longer had any of the electors in its pocket.

With France no longer in the picture, the emperor, with the able assistance of Duke Eugene was able to force a treaty with the Turks. In 1699 virtually the whole of Hungary was finally freed from the Ottomoan empire. Additionally, Transylvania and large portions of Croatia and Slavoia were returned to the emperor. The Treaty of Carlowitz brought peace to the war torn country, but their liberty came a price for Leopold had several prominent Hungarian noblemen executed. It was suspected that the Protestant princes were fearful of the Catholic emperor and wished to make Hungary independant of the empire. Their execution signalled Leopold's intollerance of Protestant secessionists. Germany was clearly returning to prominence while the power of France was in decline, but Louis would renew the struggle three years later in the War of Spanish succession.

The War of Spanish Succession

King Charles II of Spain, surnamed "the Mad," was childless and dying. The succession of the Spanish throne was of paramount importance to the empire. Both Leopold and Louis were related to the king by previous marriages, but Louis' grandson, Duke Philip of Anjou, had recently married into the family as well. France wanted the Spanish dominions for itself, although the conflicts it had engaged in over years did not endear France to Spain. Charles, however, did respect his son–in–law. Leopold, on the other hand, was determined that the Hapsburgs maintain control over the Spanish dominions and resisted any more expansion of French authority. For some time before Charles' death discussions raged over the succession. Pope Innocent XII often acted as negotiator. Plans for partitioning the kingdom's possessions seemed to be in place when Innocent, always under French influence, recommended naming Philip heir to all the Spanish domain. Charles, on his deathbed, agreed to this; paving the way for the War of Spanish succession.

Charles the Mad died on November 1, 1700. Innocent, who had influenced the will of Charles, actually preceded Charles to the grave. Clement XI was to replace Innocent, and would spend the dominant portion of his pontificate involved with the War of Spanish Succession. At first, he tried to remain neutral, but Leopold insisted that his youngest son, Charles, should be heir. The battle lines were once again drawn.

Since the Netherlands were still considered a Spanish domain, the war became an excuse for the Netherlands, Sweden, Denmark, and the other northern powers to fight for supremacy. The Second Northern War was, therefore, an extension of the War of Spanish Succession and actually outlasted it. The War of Spanish Succession ended in 1715 but the Second Northern War dragged on until 1721. Denmark, the Netherlands, Poland, and even Russia were to enter the fray. The German states also began to evolve as modern powers. Prussia, in particular, had become a dominant power under the influence of the elector of Brandenburg, who became king of Prussia. Saxony also strengthened itself with an alliance itself with Poland.

The main battlefields for the War of Spanish Succession lay in southern Europe; particularly Italy. Portugal sided with the emperor, putting pressure on the Spanish from the west as well as the east, and Duke Eugene of Savoy, the war hero of the Turkish war, became the leader of the imperial troops.

In 1705 Leopold died. Joseph, his elder son and King of the Romans, now succeeded his father to the throne. He resumed the war on behalf of his brother, but was distracted when Louis helped to stir up a revolt in Hungary. Angry over the execution of the Protestant nobles years earlier by Leopold, the Hungarians under Ferenc II rebelled. Peter the Great of Russia had offered to ally itself with Emperor Joseph against the Hungarians but Joseph feared bringing Russia into the southern war. He respectfully declined.

The French forces were supported by the Spanish and the Hungarians. Philip was also related to the Bavarians in that his mother was the daughter of the old Bavarian elector Ferdinand. As a result, Philip enjoyed the support of Bavaria, even it is was not military support. Finally, Clement XI recognized Philip as the king of Spain. Joseph had his revenge.

In 1709 Joseph sent Austrian and Prussian troops into Italy. They conquered the papal estates, occupied Naples and threatened the city of Rome itself if Clement did not reverse his position. The pope backed down and endorsed Charles as king of Spain in Philip's place.

The German victories were wearing on Louis. He began to push for peace, even offering to surrender Strassburg to the emperor if he would agree to let Philip be king of Naples and Sicily. Joseph was willing to accept but Philip steadfastly refused. Joseph suggested that France combine their forces with his to defeat Philip, but Louis would not betray his own grandson, so he withdrew the offer and the war continued.

In 1711, Joseph died without an heir. His brother, Charles, was the next in line. This was the same Charles who claimed the Spanish throne, so when he became emperor, he found even much of his German support diminishing. No one, including the German princes, wanted a truly universal emperor again. If Charles acquired all the estates for Charles V, he would be the most powerful emperor in over a hundred years. Sentiment was turning against Emperor Charles VI. After the Battle of Denain, where French forces, defeated the imperial troops, Charles realized that it was time for peace.

The Treaty of Utrecht was a modest victory for both sides. Philip V retained the Spanish crown, which he had desired above all else, but he agreed to surrender the Spanish Netherlands to his Bavarians relatives. He also abandoned his claims to both Naples and Sicily, which became united under a single king. Only Spain and the American possessions remained for Philip, but it was enough. The treaty was signed in 1713.

The War of Polish Succession

Louis had seen the height of French power in the eighteenth century, but its decline had begun with his as well. He was, however, to be spared the sight of the French monarchy's moral and political collapse. He died on September 1, 1715, lamenting, "I have loved war too much." In his will he left his kingdom to the Duke of Maine, instead of the Duke of Orleans, as was expected. Parliament then met and quickly nullified the will, leaving the kingdom to Louis' five year old great–grandson, and making Philip II of Orleans his regent.

In 1721 the Second Northern War was finally over, but like many other wars, the treaty had not solved the heart of the matter. Instead it created many new powers who sought supremacy in the north. Prussia and the Saxon–Polish alliance were now two of the most powerful German states. The German elector of Hanover, James III, even dared to claim the throne of England, where he became known as the "Great Pretender." He set himself up as the rival king of England to George I but never gained recognition, in part because he insisted on the restoration of Catholicism and the Holy Roman Empire. To the east, the Polish throne was vacated by Stanislaw I, whose daughter was married to King Louis XV. In Stanislaw's place the Elector Augustus the Strong of Saxony was made king. A new war was already brewing.

This same year saw the death of Clement XI. The new election again saw one party or the other veto potential candidates whom they feared might not be symphatetic to their cause. France had done this many times. This time it was the emperor who vetoed a candidate. The resulting compromise made Innocent XIII pope. He rewarded the emperor by giving him the united kingdom of Naples and Sicily, restoring the kingdom to the emperor for the first time since Charles V. He also promised 10,000 ducats to James III, the "Great Pretender," if he would re–establish Catholicism in England, but the plan came to naught. Innocent died in 1724 and was replaced by Benedict XIII who, anecdotally, had to be informed that he was the XIII, not XIV, as he had originally requested (since the last Benedict XIII was an antipope and not officially recognized). Benedict's reign was largely inconsequential. The only footnote that might be said in regard to his brief rule is the reaction of the empire to his attempt to make feast commemorating Gregory VII international. Gregory VII (Hildebrand) is universally seen as the father of the medieval papacy, and the kings of Europe had not forgotten. The feast received many protests, and some governors censored all references to Gregory's deposition of Emperor Henry IV. Benedict died in 1730.

Clement XII was a seventy–nine year old man who became bedridden with gout and blind. In the War of Polish Succession, which broke in 1733, he constantly wavered from one side to the other; desiring only to be on the winner's side. He was the epitomy of the eighteenth century papacy which had lost all power and respect among the kings of Europe. He was incompetent to do anything about the wars which erupted in Europe.

From 1733 to 1738 the Polish throne was the subject of the war which made Prussia one of the dominant powers of Germany. Peter the Great of Russia also forged territory for himself. France, whose king was related to the deposed king of Poland, also entered the war. Although the resolution of the Polish succession was not truly decided until many years after the war, that ultimate end was the partitioning of the Polish kingdom among the powers of the east. By the late eighteenth century, the duchy of Warsaw was all that was officially left of Poland. Saxony took in part of Old Warsaw, as did Russia, but it was probably Prussia which benefitted the most, forming a large state in the north which touched Denmark in the west and Russia in the east. The immediate end, in 1738, was the appeasement of the various powers. Duke Francis surrendered Lorraine to the former king Stanislaw, but the Polish crown remained in the hands of the Saxon elector.

The War of Polish Succession also gave Spain another excuse to invade and occupy the papal estates in 1736. Clement was incapable of doing anything to stop the Spanish occupation. When the Spaniards attempted to draft Romans into their armies, the populous revolted and Clement was blamed for the problems in Italy. Both Spain and Naples cut off diplomatic relations to the papacy, until Clement agreed to invest Naples and Sicily to Don Carlos. The pope agreed, thus stripping the "Two Sicilies" of the emperor. Had Emperor Charles VI not been preoccupied with another Turkish conflict, he might have objected more strongly, but by the time his conflict with Turkey was over, in 1739, the War of Austrian Succession was ready to break out. Clement finally died in 1740.

The War of Austrian Succession

The War of Austrian Succession was a war that pitted the very survival of the Hapsburg Dynasty itself. France, a long time enemy of the Hapsburg, would be pulled into the war along with many others. What was at stake was not only the Austrian succession, but the succession of the imperial throne as well. As Charles VI had no sons, he bequeathed his inheritance to his daughter, Maria Theresa, who was the wife of Duke Francis of Tuscany and former duke of Lorraine. However, since daughters were not allowed to inherit estates, Charles first drafted the royal act of the Pragmatic Sanction which allowed women to inherit. It was to be a controversial act, as Charles Albert, the elector of Bavaria, claimed the Hapsburg domains by virtue of the fact that his wife was the daughter of Emperor Joseph. Nonetheless, Maria Theresa declared Austria for her husband and sought the imperial diadem for him as well.

Less than two months before Charles VI died, Pope Benedict XIV was elected. Considered a weak pope, he was, nevertheless, a respected pope, not only among Catholics but among Protestants and secularists as well. One philosopher of the day said in a satirical complement that he was a "pope without nephews." Still, he did not begin his reign on the right foot, for he resisted recognizing Maria Theresa until two months after the fact. This allowed Maria's rivals to stir up dissension and created antipathy between herself and the pope.

Charles of Bavaria and Maria Theresa were not the only ones who had a stake in the succession issue. France, a long time enemy of the Hapsburgs, was very interested in seeing them fall from power, even though Maria's husband, Francis, had been Duke of Lorraine. One reason for Louis' alliance with Bavaria was the fact that his mistress had close ties to Prussia and urged him to take their side. So Louis abandoned Duke Francis of Lorraine, and allied with Bavaria. Saxony also had interest in some parts of Austria, and Prussia laid claims to a section of territory called Silesia, near Bohemia. Austria's main ally in the beginning was Holland who did not want to see Prussia or France expand their horizons. England also supported the Hapsburgs and King George II personally led her armies in many battles. In 1740 Frederick II of Prussia officially began the war by invading Silesia.

The war dragged out the election of a new emperor, as did the rivals' claims, to almost a year but the outcome was in Charles' favor. Charles VII was crowned in February 1742. He was recognized by Benedict XIV which earned the wrath of Maria Theresa who sent Austrian troops to invade the papal states and Bavaria itself, Charles' homeland, was overrun by Austrian armies. Later that year, Prussia withdrew from the war on the condition that it be allowed to keep Silesia, although it was granted only as a Bohemian fief.

After King George defeated the French at Dettingen Saxony changed sides and allied itself with Maria. Charles seemed to be seeing his allies fall when Prussia again entered the war. He invaded Bohemia and assisted the French in driving Austrian troops out of Bavaria. This was accomplished by 1744, but only three months after the victory, on January 20, 1745, Charles VII died.

The death of Charles eliminated Francis' rival to the throne and the main claimant to Austria outside of Maria. Louis' Prussian mistress had also died, leaving the French king with little interest in the outcome of the war in Germany, although he still had interest in Flanders and the Italian possessions. Louis, therefore, turned his attention toward those lands and, having abandoned his interest in Protestant Prussia, he renewed the persecution of the surviving Huguenots.

With the elimination of the threats of Bavaria and France, Maria Theresa agreed recognize the return the Bavarian lands in exchange for peace, the abandonment of Bohemia by Prussia, and, most importantly, the election of Francis as Holy Roman Emperor. He was crowned on September 13 ending the war in Germany, but not the war of succession, for Italy and Flanders continued the struggle.

The French, English, and Spanish continued to fight over Flanders and the Italian possessions. It was almost three years before the Peace of Aachen ended the war. Sardina was given to Francis and his recognition was made universal throughout the empire. Austria had emerged as one of the dominant powers of Germany, rivaled only by Prussia.

The Seven Years' War

There was to be a period of eight years between the War of Austrian Succession and the Seven Years' War during which the country rebuilt itself and strengthened its various states. This very fact, however, disturbed the Hapsburg Empress. Prince Kaunitz of Austria, one of her trusted allies, assured Maria that Prussia was a far greater threat to her power than the declining power of France. He, therefore, spent years trying to break Prussia's alliances by poisoning them against him. Russia was the easist ally to win over, for King Frederick II of Austria had slandered the Czarina Elizabeth and this became known to her. France was not as easy an alliance to break, however. Even though Louis' Prussian mistress had passed away, he thought it would be beneficial to maintain the alliance with the Hapsburg's greatest enemy. That would change when Frederick II made the mistake of creating an alliance with England. France quickly changed policy and signed a defensive pact with Austria.

Austria was eager to crush the rival power of Prussia and their Protestant faith also rallied the Austrians who had sporatically continued to persecute Protestants and Jews under Maria Theresa's hand. Their ulimate goal was to partition Prussia among Russia, France, Sxony, Poland, and Austria. Frederick II was well aware of this and believed that his best chance for victory was to commence a first strike against Austria's allies and break their power before they could launch a united attack on him. In 1756 Frederick invaded Saxony, beginning the Seven Years' War.

The Seven Years' War encompassed not only Germany, but the Americas as well, for France and Great Britain, Prussia's ally, engaged in a war over the North American possessions. In Europe Frederick's invasion of Bohemia failed, but Prussia was able to hold off the assaults of overwhelming numbers. It seemed that, despite the resolve of Prussia (who was fighting for her very survival) it was only a matter of time before her destruction. In fact, it only *seemed* that way, for when the Czarina Elizabeth died, Czar Peter III had no desire to continue the conflict and signed a peace treaty. This reduced the number of fronts that Prussia had to fight and allowed her to disperse those troops to the southern and western fronts. Soon Saxony followed in seeking peace, and France (which was in danger of loosing her American possessions) also made peace with Prussia.

Austria was now isolated and without any real allies. Austria was also financially broke. The years of war were taking its toll. She was forced to make peace. Prussia had not been forced to cede any territory whatsoever. Her king, affectionately called "Old Fritz," now became Frederick the Great. Prussia had won.

Summary of the Gallic Power

France had risen to the height of European power under Louis XIV, but her decline began under the same king. She had entered into many wars with the princes of Germany, but never successfully. In the Seven Years' War France had lost the majority of her possession in America to Great Britain. Canada, as well as the thirteen colonies, now belonged to England. The kings of France had become decadent and the subject of ridicule. Soon the French people were themselves to hate their very kings and France would become the graveyard of anarchists.

Out of the anarchy which would reign in France emerged a man whose destiny was to be one with the Holy Roman Empire. He sought to liberate France and to restore the Imperial Crown to its "French" ancestors. This little Corsican man dreamed of liberating his island from French oppression, but soon became the most recognized Frenchman in history. His rise to power was to coincide with the dawn of a new age.

Holy Roman Emperor	Rival (if any)	Pope
		——— 1670 ———
		Clement X
		——— 1676 ———
		Innocent XI
Leopold		——— 1689 ———
		Alexander VIII
		——— 1691 ———
		Innocent XII
		——— 1700 ———
——— 1705 ———		Clement XI
Joseph		
——— 1711 ———		
		——— 1721 ———
		Innocent XIII
Charles VI		——— 1724 ———
		Benedict XIII
		——— 1730 ———
		Clement XII
——— 1740 ———		——— 1740 ———
War of Succession		
——— 1742 ———		
Charles VII		Benedict XIV
——— 1745 ———		
Francis		——— 1758 ———
——— 1765 ———		Clement XIII
		——— 1769 ———
Joseph II		Clement XIV
		——— 1774 ———
——— 1790 ———		
Leopold II		Pius VI
——— 1792 ———		
		——— 1799 ———
Francis II		——— 1800 ———
	——— 1804 ———	
	Napoleon Bonaparte	
	——— 1806 ———	Pius VII
Napoleon Bonaparte		
——— 1814 ———		
		——— 1823 ———

The American Revolution spawned several failed attempts at overthrowing monarchies.

29

The Dawn of an Age

The last half of the eighteenth century promised what it could not deliver. Liberty, justice, equality, and democracy were the battle cries heard throughout America and Europe, but only in America would the cry be heeded. In Europe, the cries of freedom were drowned by the cries of the dead. Emperor Joseph II came far closer to the dreams than did the French Revolution, whose anarchy threatened the whole of Europe, and the empire. Only through the actions of one man was the empire to be saved from complete destruction, but that man would actually become the very instrument through which the empire would fall.

The Abolition of the Jesuits

The Jesuit order had been created with the Counter–Reformation and its purpose was closely related to that war. The Jesuits sought to enhance the power of the papacy, to crush Protestantism, and to spread Catholic missions to the Americas and the east. In the first two respects they not only failed, but earned the antagonism of Europe and the princes thereof. The Jesuits had come to viewed with mistrust and suspicion everywhere. They had adopted a theology which sanctioned teachings similar to "the end justifies the means." In 1759 things were to come to head.

The previous year, Benedict XIV had passed away. The French, still eager for dominant influence in the papal court, vetoed the first choice for pope, eventually settling on Clement XIII. It was Clement who first had to deal with the reaction against the Jesuits. Portugal had accused the Jesuits of complicity in a plot to assassinate the king and expelled all Jesuits from their country. France soon followed. On December 1, 1764, France abolished the Jesuit order by royal decree. Clement objected and issued a bull the next month praising the Jesuits. The papacy, however, had lost its power to influence international affairs and other states soon emulated the French, expelling the Jesuits from their countries. In February 1767 Spain expelled the Jesuits. In November, Naples and Sicily did the same. Finally, four months later, Parma followed their example. When Clement pressured France and others to lift their sanctions, France occupied Avignon.

In January 1769 the powers of Europe now dared to demand that the pope formally dissolve the Jesuit order. Clement was shocked. His death the following month spared him further humiliation. For months the election of the new pope dragged on as the royalists sought a pope who would bow to their will and disolve the Jesuits. Clement XIV was finally agreed upon, based on his statement that the Jesuit order might be disolved, but it seemed a ruse for Clement had himself devoted one of his books to Loyola, the founder of the Jesuits and made constant excuses for delaying the abolition of the order. It appears that he believed the commotion would one day die down, but by 1773 it was obvious that it would not die. France, Spain, and the Two Sicilies even threatened to break with Rome; effectively making them Protestant states. Maria Theresa, a strong supporter of the Jesuits, gave her consent to Clement and on August 16, 1773, Clement formally disolved the Jesuit order. The order would eventually be restored in 1814, but their power was, for now, abolished.

Ironically, the only two lands who refused to recognize the order were Protestant Prussia and Orthodox Russia. In Prussia, where freedom of religion was practiced, the anti–Protestant Jesuits found refuge among the Protestants. In all Catholic lands the Jesuits were forced to disband. The order had existed for just over two hundred years and co–incided with the Counter–Reformation. They also died with the Counter–Reformation. Protestantism had spawned the democratic ideals that were in full blossom in America. There, in America, a religious revival known as the Great Awakening had been in full swing a few decades earlier. Even men such as Benjamin Franklin served as interns to the religious preachers of that movement. The Jesuits represented the old medieval theology. The American colonies represented the new.

Joseph II and the Enlightenment

In 1765 Emperor Francis died. His son, Joseph II, was elected emperor. As with Francis, the real power resided in Maria Theresa, but Joseph, after her death, would one day prove to be, like Louis the Bavarian before him, a man ahead of his time. Had he lived in a different time or place, he might have been called great, but in Germany during the eighteenth century he was to be opposed by the nobles who sought desperately to hold to what power they still had.

It would not be until 1780 that Joseph became ruler of the empire in fact, as well as in name. It was during the interim that he developed many of the ideas that he would attempt to institute when that day came. These ideas came from a variety of sources. Although many historians attribute his views to the French Enlightenment, that is an oversimplification. He did have a love for the Enlightenment views, but he also rejected some of their notions for the more serene views of the colonies. In order to understand these influences, in both Joseph and the French Revolution , it is necessary to examine the philosophies that were predominant at this time.

Due to political biases of this day an age, too many historians have attempted to blur the differences between the views of the American Revolution and those of the French Revolution. The mere fact that the one created the longest lasting democracy in history whereas the second led to anarchy, is sufficient to prove that there was something intrinsically different about the American Revolution. The difference was in the philosophical presumptions behind democracy. The French historian Alexis DeTocqueville came to America to discover for himself what those different philiosphical presumptions were. To his surprise, the answer was religion. In America, religion was the basis for democracy. It was fashioned after the Presbyterian style of Church government. In the French Enlightenment, it was the alleged inate goodness of man. Democracy was secular in France, but religiously motivated in America.

DeTocqueville admits that "Puritanism was almost as much a political theory as a religious doctrine."[3] In reading our founding fathers he says "one seems to breathe the atmosphere of antiquity and to inhale a sort of Biblical fragrance."[4] The earliest laws in the American colonies, up until the American Revolution (and even after) quote the Bible verbatum and refer to both Satan and Christ. Biblical injuctions in favor of the death penalty were also common. DeTocqueville notes that "the death penalty has never been more frequently prescribed by the laws or more seldom carried out."[5] He was forced to conclude with the American forefathers that "freedom sees religion as the companion of its struggles and triumphs, the cradle of its infancy, and the divine source of its rights."[6] This was startling testimony from a Frenchman.

It is important to understand that the papal see saw Democracy not as a secular threat, but as a Protestant threat. Of all those who experimented with republican democracies, only Cola de Rienzo represented a secular democratic idea. Arnold of Brescia, Savoranola, John Calvin, and Oliver Cromwell all saw democracy as the ideal government for sinful men, since it kept power away from a select few and distributed it among many. From Cromwell the Puritans brought democratic ideals to America where it found fruition in the religious revival known as the Great Awakening, led by Jonathan Edwards and George Whitefield. Even the "secular puritan," Benjamin Franklin, had served as an intern for one of the great preachers. Washington retired from the presidency to become a church vestryman and John Adams constantly spoke of the Bible and God. The list of American forefathers whose ties to Protestantism and the "Puritian ethic" is innumerable.

The Enlightenment had not yet reached fruition in France when the American Revolution was brewing in the minds of our forefathers. Thomas Paine's famed pamphlet *Common Sense* was not even *written* until the year the Declaration of Independence was drafted, and certainly did not find wide circulation in America until after the Revolution had come to the colonies. Paine was a member of the French Revolutionary Convention during the Reign of Terror and a forefather of the French Revolution, not the American as so many revisionists have insisted. The great names of the American Revolution were Washington, Adams, Henry, Madison, Jefferson, and Franklin. The great names of the Enlightenment were Rousseau, Kant, Paine, Voltaire, and Goethe.

The fact is that the French Revolution was based on alternate views of man and declared religion the enemy of man, as Jules Michelet readily admitted. Man, so the Enlightenment authors said, was was innately good. James Madison, the author of the Constitution, responded to the Enlightenment saying, "if men were angels, no government would be necessary." This was what the Enlightenment failed to understand. They held that man was good, but that he was corrupted by religion and government. The problem with that logic is that if religion is the invention of man, and man is good, then how does good man invent something so evil? How can good men form governments that produce evil? If men were angels then Madison would have been correct; "no government would be necessary." That men are not angels is why power corrupts and why the French Revolution would result in anarchy. The French hated religion. The Americans practiced it religiously.

This was something that neither the deists of the French Revolution understood nor the papists of Rome. The one saw democracy was a threat to its existence. The other agreed and backed that threat, but neither one understood Puritanism or the Founding Fathers of America until after the French Revolution deteriorated into anarchy.

Joseph was influenced by both views. He was a great respecter of the Enlightenment, to the disgust of his mother, but he opposed their anti–religious views. In that sense Joseph was far more influenced by the Protestants, with whom he was friends. Prussia, for example, won the affection of the Austrian emperor. He sought to establish religious freedom on the one hand, but on the other he sought to liberate his own church, the Catholic Church, from the hands of Rome. He staunchly supported the Febronianists, who were the German equivalent of Gallicism, asserting the independence of the German Church from the papal see. To this he added the monarch's right to enforce his will for the good of the people. Joseph's philosophy was, therefore, a mixture of Enlightenment views, Protestantism, monarchy, and Catholicism. When he came to power he would seek to reform the government in the manner he saw fit. His actions were clearly reformatory in nature, but they were done with an autocrats tact, against the power of the nobility, and in the face of papal opposition.

The Last Days of Maria Theresa

During the early years of Joseph's reign he spent most of his time voraciously reading and learning. Politically, Maria Theresa ran the country except on occasion when Joseph used his influence to change policy, much to the chagrin of his mother. Joseph's studies, and his friends, all distressed Maria. She was a woman of the old monarchy. Joseph was a man of the new world. His friendship with Protestants, his books by Rousseau and other Enlightenment authors, his sympathy for the American Revolution, and his opposition to papal authority all disturbed his mother, but their relationship remained on good terms and Joseph did not exert his authority until after her death.

If Maria was disappointed in Joseph's interests, she was not in those of her daughter, Marie Antoinette. In 1770 Marie was married to King Louis XVI. Her destiny was to be tied to his. It is perhaps providence that did not permit Joseph to live to see her demise at the hands of those he loved so much.

In 1772, Joseph exerted his political influence against his mother's wishes. Poland had a civil war and was caught in strife. The people despised the decadent King Stanislaw II and he faced revolt after his love affair with Catherine the Great of Russia became public. Joseph met with Maria's dreaded enemy, Frederick the Great of Prussia. Together they discussed a partition plan that would divide Poland among its neighbors and end the civil war. It seemed the best way to avoid further bloodshed, not to mention expanding Austrian and Prussian interest. In the partition the Ukraine went to Russia, Lithuania was given to Prussia, and Austria took Galicia. The civil war was ended, but at the cost of Poland's independence.

In 1775 Clement XIV died. During his last years, he had slipped into a melancholy paranoia and lived with an obssession that people wanted to assassinate him. When he finally died, rumors spread that he had indeed been assassinated, although an autopsy showed his death to be by natural causes.

The new Pope Pius VI was to begin a crusade against democratic ideals and modern theories. Rousseau had already been placed on the Index of Forbidden Books by Clement XIII, but Pius made sure of its enforcement. He was to spend his life fighting against the rise of democracy which he saw as the greatest threat to the Church of Rome. Pius said that "monarchy is the most natural form of government" and condemned the teaching that commeners, whom he said have "no understanding of things," could govern themselves. The hostility of Pius to the American Revolution was such that John Adams opposed even sending a minister to the Vatican because he believed that even if the papacy did send a legate to the congress, "the United States will be too wise ever to admit into their territories."

Pius also reinstituted the old laws against Jews, outlawing Talmudic writings. He was to spend his life fighting a loosing cause. He would condemn virtually every act and legislation of either Joseph II, the American colonies, or the French Revolution that bestowed rights upon the common man. He would also spend much of his early years in conflict with Joseph over the aforementioned Febronianism.

Maria's last years saw the War of Bavaria Succession. The bizarre outcome of the war showed that the long years of petty princes fighting over possessions had taken its toll. When the Bavarian elector died without heir, the elector of the Palitinate claimed the Bavarian possessions, but he was challenged by Maria Theresa for her son. However, it seemed as if a mutual decision could be reached when Joseph and the Elector Charles Theodore of Palitinate agreed to exchange Bavaria for part of the Netherlands (modern Belgium). Charles Theodore would take Belgium and Austria would receive Bavaria. Prussia immediately objected, fearing Austria's expansion. Saxony united with Prussia and invaded Bohemia in July, 1778.

In the strange course of this war no battles were fought. No sooner had the troops gathered than their supplies ran short. Decades of warfare had taken their toll. Negotiations, rather than battles, decided the outcome. In May of the following year a treaty was made that basically kept the status quo although Austria was allowed to keep small territorial gains. The next year, Maria Theresa died, leaving Joseph the sole ruler of the empire.

The Reforms of Joseph II

Now that Joseph was the sole ruler, and emperor, of the Holy Roman Empire, he began his policy of reform, called "Josephinism." That policy earned him the respect of the peasants, and of future historians, but it led to many conflicts with both the nobility of the empire and the papacy. In the end, Joseph's reforms were only partially instituted and he would die without having acheived his dreams or receiving the honor which was his due.

Under Joseph mandotary primary education was established throughout Germany. This had actually begun when Maria still reigned, but Joseph now took his education policy even further. He sought out the best scholars and scientists for the University of Vienna. He also found the best doctors, making the General Hospital of Vienna the best in Europe. In October 1781 he passed the Edict of Toleration which banned the oppressive laws against Jews and Protestants, granted freedom of the press, and declared religious equality before the law. This brought the quick condemnation of Pius VI.

The edict not only established freedom of religion but it also employed the seperatist doctrine of Febronianism which placed monasteries under the jurisdiction of the state, rather than Rome. It also restricted the anti-Protestant activities of some Catholic orders. Moreover, Joseph, although promoting freedom of religion, sought to reform the Catholic Church in Germany in his own image. He, therefore, sought to convert many monasteries into modern parishes, since he despised the hermit like practices of the monks. Many monks were forced to either leave or begin more useful missionary or charitable activities. Pius, therefore, saw the edict as a direct attack upon Catholic sovereignty. So distressed was he over the emperor's desire to create independence for the Catholic churches of Germany that he journeyed to Vienna. There he was greeted by the advisor Kaunite, but when the pope extended his hand that Kaunite might kiss the ring, he instead took his hand and shook it. The act seemed a fitting prelude to the loss of dignity when the papacy was to endure over the next few decades. He received no concessions from Joseph, save a promise that Joseph would visit him in Rome.

490

When Joseph kept that promise and arrived in Rome he was hailed by the people of Rome who shouted and praised him as their emperor. He was treated as Charlemagne and Otto the Great had been. It was a fitting contrast to the treatment of the papacy, and showed the attitudes of the people toward the emperor and pope. Once again, the pope gained no concessions from Joseph.

In 1786 the pope was dealt another blow by the Agreement of Ems in which Church bishops and officials endorsed Febronianism. The power of the papacy over European affairs was quickly fading. Josephinism was prevailing.

In foreign relations Joseph had mixed results. He supported the American Revolution, where hundreds of thousands of Germans had immigrated in the previous three decades, and immediately recognized their Republic. He met Catherine the Great in Russia where they discussed plans for Catherine's reconquest of Constantinople, for she had hoped to re–establish the line of eastern Roman emperors with herself as the first new empress. Joseph also traveled to France where he was greeted with honors by the Enlightment thinkers of the day. In his own country, Joseph was less successful.

One of the most noble efforts of Josephinism was Joseph's desire to abolish serfdom. He had outlawed the practice and attempted to make former serfs hereditary tenants, but in the enforcement of this he was strongly opposed by the nobility. Austria itself resisted the reform and the other states also proved less than willing to comply. Matters were complicated when Joseph and Bavaria once against took up the idea of swapping Bavaria for the Austrian Netherlands.

Upon hearing news of Bavaria's plans Frederick the Great formed a League of Princes in 1785 to prevent the land swap from occuring. Many princes, already upset at the freedom of the serfs, joined. Frederick was seeking nothing less than liberty from imperial authority. His death a year later ended the hopes of the League. Frederick is considered the greatest of Prussian kings. He had a friendly rivalry with Joseph II but an enmity with his mother and father.

When Joseph died in 1790 he felt he had failed to acheive his goals, but he had gone further than any emperor in disolving the tired old facade of medievalism which still gripped much of Europe. Joseph would not be appreciated for what he was until after his death. He is today considered the "enlightened despot" who struggled against the nobility in favor of the common man. He had lived to see the American Revolution and the outbreak of the French Revolution, but it is perhaps fortunate that he did not live to see its end, for the failure of the French Revolution and the death of his sister at the hands of the revolutionaries would have destroyed his illusions. Joseph, like Louis the Bavarian before him, was a man who did not fit in the age in which he lived, but deserves to be remembered for his noble goals, if not his achievements.

The Coming Revolution

In Joseph's last few years, events were occuring in France that would change the course of the empire's history; events which his brother–in–law, Charles XVI, was not only incompetent to handle, but in fact spurred through his wavering inaction and folly.

The French monarchy had assisted the colonies in their revolution against Great Britain for no better reason than that he wished to further damage his rival England, from whom France had already won the Canadian provinces and other territories. If the monarch was satisfied with the result of the revolution, he was naïve to fail to understand that French peoples' support was for a far different reason. They had no concern for the international politics of England and France, but for their own families. The corrupted French monarchy had done little for the common man, and had done much to antagonize it. The persecution of the surviving Huguenots had also resumed in recent years, causing many people to witness the crimes of Louis' soldiers. In the Court of Toulouse it is documented that more than thirty percent of those called before it were executed, and most tortured.

Another problem in France was the lack of food. France was a country of an estimated 28,000,000 people. It was the largest country in Europe, thanks to the expansionists policy of the past. The old feudal system could not support that population and the monarchy. Food riots erupted on several occasions as local rural communities fought to keep food from being shipped out of their town to cities like Paris which had no farmers.

Although an estimated 93% of the population was officially Catholic, the deism of the Enlightenment was the real religion of many of the people of France. The oppression of the Catholic Church for the last centuries left a bitter taste in the mouth of the populous. Most understood nothing of Protestantism, which is why they failed to understand the difference in the American Revolution and their own. To the common man Protestants were merely victims of Catholic oppression, as they viewed themselves. The Church owned one quarter of the property in France although the clergy only made up less than one percent of the population. The high clergy were especially wealthy, earning as much as 450,000 livres a year, while the commoner not only lived on meager rations, but was forced to pay a mandatory 10% tithe to the Church in addition to their regular taxes. With the coming revolution was to come a brutal backlash against the Catholic Church. Its barbaric cruelties shocked the world. It may also have shocked the Vatican into reality. For three centuries they had refused to recognize that the Middle Ages had passed.

While all these problems doubtless combined to make the French malcontent, the problem which led to the conflict was that of the deficit and taxation. France had spent billions of livres on wars and the full brunt of that was laid directly on the commoner. The nobility were exempt from taxation and the Church paid only 3% of their income to the state. Commoners had to surrender part of their crops to their noble landowners, pay mandatory tithes to the Church, and then pay taxes on what was left.

It was obvious that the commoners, who already bore the brunt of taxation, could not afford to pay off the rising deficit of the French court. In February, 1787, the Assembly of Notables was called to Versailles in hopes of reaching an agreement which would lift the tax exempt status of the nobility. Not surprisingly the nobles were dramatically opposed to the idea and the assembly was dismissed in May. Unable to convince the nobles to accept taxation, a law was passed requiring uniform land–taxes but the *parlement* (court officials whose job was to enforce the king's edicts) refused to enforce the law. In response, *parlement* was exiled to Troyes.

The exile of the *parlement* court officials did nothing to enforce the ruling. Short of military force, there seemed to be no way the king's officials could enforce taxation on the nobility without compromise. The nobles were defying the king's officials and supporting *parlement*. In September the assembly and *parlement* were recalled in hopes of achieving a compromise. Instead, they called for the Estates–General. The Estates–General was a grand assembly of representatives of all France from the Church to the nobility to the commoner. It had not convened since 1614. The king's officials were outraged and warned that the king shares power "with no one." *Parlement* was reminded that their job was to "maintain the edicts of the kingdom, and not to build up in their bodies a power to rival royal authority."

In May, 1788, *parlement* was again exiled causing rioting to break out in the streets of Paris. The "revolt of the aristocratic bodies" forced the king's official to recall *parlement* the very same month. Finally, an assembly of the Estates–General was agreed upon and set for May 1789. Further, censorship of the press was lifted so that all the parties could freely present their arguments. Over the next year thousands of tracts were released. Many of the tracts began to debate how the Estates–General would take shape and whether or not the commoner's voice would be heard.

The Estates–General was composed of three bodies. The "First Estate" was made up of representatives of the clergy. The "Second Estate" made up the nobility. Together these two estates represented less than three percent of the populous of France. The "Third Estate" represented all the other members of French society from bankers to serfs. Eighty percent of France were peasants who made up the majority of this body, but the "Third Estate" had generally had no power, and they wanted it. Tracts spread out demanding that the "Third Estate" provide fair representation and power before the king. The First and Second Estates responded that the rabble should have no real voice. In December Louis XVI agreed to let the Third Estate have twice as many representatives as the other estatess, making the Third Estate was large as the First and Second combined. The state was set for a confrontation.

At this time the king might still have found favor with the people. Had he shown a consistent policy or acted fairly in the ensuing months and years, he might have become a great king, for it was he who called the Third Estate and he who agreed to doubling its number of representatives, but it was also he who antagonized it repeatedly in the months to come.

Bastille Day

The Estates–General met on May 5, 1789. No sooner did it convene than the "Third Estate" (or commoner's representatives) was insulting by being required to wear black cloaks. Further, although they had twice as many representatives as the other two estates, the votes of the estates counted as one, thus the commoners were outnumbered by the clergy and nobles, despite their vastly fewer numbers. Finally, the Estates–General decided that all votes of the estates would meet separately; effectively making debate between the estates null and the actual votes (as opposed to the results) secret. These issues were debated and argued for over a month.

On June 17, the Third Estate declared that since they represented nearly 95% of the populous, their votes should not be silenced. They declared that they were forming the "National Assembly" and they wisely invited any and all representatives of the First and Second Estates to join their National Assembly, although they would not have more voting power than the members of the Third Estate. They were setting themselves up as rivals to the Estates–General, which they saw as being monopolized by the first two estates. Louis responded to this act by locking them out of the meeting hall on June 20. The "National Assembly" then moved to a tennis court where took an oath to meet anywhere possible until as such time a constitution was written and approved.

The king was furious, yet he could not act openly as one hundred and fifty members of the clergy defected from the Estates–General to the National Assembly. The nobility objected and Louis was eager to appease them, but he feared the National Assembly and their supporters. When several nobles defected to the National Assembly, including Louis cousin, the Duke of Orleans, he decided to feign support. 20,000 troops were called into Paris on the pretext of protection for the Assembly, but the members saw it differently. Fear and apprehension among the people and members became acute. The nobles were suspected of hoarding food and plotting against the assembly. A month later, the king dismissed his only minister from the Third Estate, Jacques Necker. This was the call to arms for the peasants, or parisians, as they were called in France.

Days of rioting followed culminating the storming of the fortess Bastille. Soldiers had not done much to quell the violence in those days, and some soldiers joined with the rebels. Most simply turned a blind eye to the rioting. The peasant army even entered a compound and seized hundreds of weapons without opposition from the soldiers. However, at the fortress Bastille, this was not to be the case. An estimated 8,000 peasants laid seige to the fortress and its commander, outnumbered by almost a hundred to one, ordered his troops to open fire. The prison fortress Bastille could not hold out against the overwhelming odds. Nearly a hundred peasants died but the fortress was taken and horrible revenge was wreaked upon its commander. His head was cut off and placed on a pike where it was paraded around in a victory march.

The commander of the Bastille was not the only victim. The mayor of Paris caught trying to flee the city and was butchered. He heart was pulled out even while he still lived. Other atrocities were common as well. Anarchy was ruling the city.

Paul Delaroche – The Conquerors of the Bastille – 1839

The storming of the Bastille was as much a symbolic victory as anything. The peasants had seized a major fortress of the king, which had symbolized the nobility's oppression. As news of the Bastille spread throughout France, so also did immitators. The "Great Fear" as it came to be called led to riots and murder. In some communities Jews were slaughtered, but the nobility were the usual victims. Twenty six of the thirty largest cities in France saw similar uprisings and many rural communities stormed their local castles, catching them off guard, and destroyed all documents that were used to collect tithes, taxes, and the like. It was an uncoordinated uprising on a national scale. Everywhere in France there seemed to be lawlessness and disorder. It was a foreshadowing of the anarchy to come.

Although the long term consequences of the storming of the Bastille and the Great Fear were to be disasterous, the short term results were quite effective. The nobility was terrorized by the peasant rabble and August 4 the National Assembly, with the support of its noble members, declared the abolition of serfdom and feudalism. However, when calm was finally achieved, the assembly "clarified" that the landowners were still the legal property holders and could still charge rent for their lands.

The National Assembly appeared to have won. The "revolution" was really nothing more than a simultaneous uprising by peasants and commoners throughout France, but the results was the same. The National Assembly was now a recognized force which the king could not dismiss without a war. National Assembly was to work toward a constitution, but the next move still belonged to King Louis. France was still a monarchy. Would he let it become a constitutional monarchy or would he wait for an opportune time to eliminate the assembly and its members? A good king could have avoided Bastille Day. A mediocre king could have avoided the terror to come. A bad king only invited what was to come.

The Legislative Assembly

On August 27, 1789, created the Declaration of the Rights of Man and of the Citizen. The document is often compared to the Bill of Rights in the U. S. Constitution inasmuch as it outlines the rights of man. However, there are stark differences which highlight the distinction between the American forefathers and the French Revolutionaries. The Bill of Rights specifically identify those "inalienable" rights, given by God Almighty, which government may not infringe upon without due process of law, including a trial by jury. The Declaration of the Rights of Man rather vaguely defined that which "does not harm another" and then allows that the limits of those rights "can only be determined by the law." In other words, the U. S. Constitution placed limits on the government. For example, the First Amendment saws that no law may be made "prohibiting the free exercise of religion," but in the French declaration "limits" to freedom of religion are ambiguously assigned to "the law," and, therefore, to lawmakers, which in this case was still the king. In short, the Declaration of the Rights of Man was little more than an acknowledgement of the concept of rights with no real limitations upon government's abridgement of the freedoms thereof. To this day France can take away religious freedoms which it does not like as was evidenced recently when Jacques Chirac outlawed the wearing of Muslim Headscarfs, Jewish Yamakas, and Christian Crosses in public schools.

Despite the obvious flaws of the Declaration, it was the first attempt, however unsuccessful, to establish rights for the commoner. King Louis refused to sanction it. In response a large march of peasant or *parisian* women, numbering about 7000, came to Versailles, where the royal family had fled. General Lafayette, who had assisted the colonies in their war against Britain, had been placed at the head of the new National Guard and was ordered to lead these women, who then helped save the royal family's lives and brought them back to Paris, where they were kept under house arrest until their death. There Louis, obviously intimidated by the people and the National Assembly, began to nominally cooperate with the assembly; all the while secert corresponding with foreign leaders including his brother–in–law the emperor, the future emperor Leopold II.

National Assembly declared that a Legislative Assembly would be elected and convened for the creation of a new constitution. For the next two years the Legislative Assembly began to frame that new constitution, but they soon found that the task was far more than they had anticipated and the people of France soon found that Legislative Assembly was just another despotic ruling party dressed in the guise of democracy.

In theory the assembly sought to create a constitutional monarchy that would share power with the king, but while the king had power to appoint ministers, the assembly gave itself the powers of lawmaking, declaring war, and forming treaties. The separation of powers employed in the U. S. Constitution was not utilized in a consistent manner in France, and often not at all. Even jury trials were denied in civil cases and the veto power of the king was challenged. A compromise gave the king the right of "suspensive veto" which would delay the enactment of a law for three sessions, but if the assembly still favored the law by the end of that time, it would pass without the king's approval.

The assmebly also sought to make public executions more humane and to that end Dr. Joseph Guillotine, the assembly's chairman of the health committee, invented the now infamous device which allowed for quick and easy decapitations. It would also, in the years to come, allow for mass executions in a fast and "efficient" manner. Still other legistlation portended the anarchy to come. The people soon found that the tithes they no longer had to pay to the Church were now diverted to the state via increased taxation. In fact, many peasants were now paying more than they had in the old monarchy. Further, they soon found their rents increased as the landowners also sought to compensate for their new taxes.

On March 8, 1790, the Legislative Assembly passed legistlation that deliberately ignored the issue of slavery, thus maintaining the legality of slavery. Only after large scale riots by former slaves did the assembly, in April 1792, grant equality to "free" Africans. Even then, slavery remained legal. Women too found that they were not to receive the same rights as their counterparts. In response to the apparent rights denied to women some splinter groups prepared the Declaration of the Rights of Woman and of the Citizeness which was largely ignored.

The greatest error of the Legislative Assembly was its failure to understand the proper meaning of the separation of church and state. Like liberal activist judges of today, they believed it was their responsibility to control church activities as it related to the general public. They first began to infringe upon religious freedom by nationalizing church property. In other words, they siezed land from the church and gave it to the state, which it then auctioned off for money. They went even further with the Civil Constitution of the Clergy which was passed in July 1790. This brought the church under state regulation, absolving many monastic orders and requiring an oath of loyalty to the state. When the church objected, the assembly openly declared their own authority in church matters over that of church councils or parishes or especially the pope, who condemned not only the Civil Constitution of the Clergy but also the Declaration of the Rights of Man.

The matter grew worse as the church and people became divided as time to take the oath of loyalty approached. Only seven bishops agreed to take the oath, while the rest of the clergy were roughly divided in half. Some peasants reviled priests who took the oath. Some priests were threatened. Others harassed. Angry mobs gathered to prevent such oaths. Finally, the national guard was employed to forcibly install the new state approved bishops and priests.

Those who opposed the state's interference with religion were not the only mobs or demonstators that were dealth with in those days. In August 1790 the assembly approved of the slaughter of many demonstrators in the streets of Nancy. Other demonstrations and insurrections were also crushed in the following month. The demonstrators came from all spheres of life and all sides of the political spectrum. Counter–revolutionaries were apparent, but so were the radicals. The Jacobin Club was one such radical group whose leading member, Maximilian Robespierre, would become dominant in the anarchy to come. Another agitator was Jean–Paul Marat whose radical newspaper called openly for violence against counter–revolutionaries.

The Legislative Assembly found themselves under attack from the left and right. The radicals wanted the king's head. The moderates felt that the Assembly had already gone too far by attempting to control church government and curbing too many liberties of the nobility. Finally, on June 20, things went from bad to worse as King Louis was discovered missing. Papers were discovered in which the king condemned the revolution and the new constitution. It begged the people to return to him and to cast off the revolutionary rabble. King Louis was fleeing the country.

King Louis' attempt to flee, with the help of his brother–in–law (the new emperor) proved futile. He was recognized before he could make it to the border of the Netherlands. He was then siezed and forced to return to Paris. The Assembly was in a panic. They were already under attack from both the left and right. If they executed the king, as the radicals wanted, they would alienate the nobility and moderates from whom they needed support. On the other hand, it was obvious that the king had been plotting against the Legislative Assembly from the beginning. They decided to allay the peoples' fear by claiming that the king had been kidnapped. They then issued an order declaring that if anyone applauded the king he would be beaten and that if anyone insulted the king he "will be hanged." They were trying desperately to play both sides of the fence.

On July 17 unarmed demonstrators demanded Louis' abdication as they marched down the Champ de Mars. General Lafayette was ordered to squelch the demonstrators and after a warning to disperse, he ordered his men to open fire, killing an estimated fifty demonstrators. More violence followed in the months to come. The constitution was not even finished and already France seemed to be on the brink of civil war. In September, 1791, the constitution was completed and the assembly dissolved its session, but the Constitution was not to last even a year.

Francis II and Louis' Execution

Germany, and the rest of Europe, kept a watchful eye on the events in France. The emperor, in particular, had an acute interest in the revolution. Joseph II had died before many of these events passed. He had lived to see Bastille Day but passed on just after the Legislative Assembly had opened its session. If the assmebly might have found sympathy with Joseph, it was to find no sympathy with Leopold who revoked most of Joseph II's reforms. He undertook the reconquest of the Austrian Netherlands and organized a secert police force to keep a watchful eye. A secret correspondence with Louis XVI was begun from the beginning of his reign in 1790. Finally, Leopold passed an imperial edict declaring the acts of the assemblies to be illegal and invalid, urging his subjects to reject them. When it was apparent that his edict fell on deaf ears, he helped to arrange for Louis' failed flight from France. When Louis was captured, Leopold joined with the Prussians in the Declaration of Pillnitz, August 1791, which emplored the people of France to use force, if necessary, in defense of their king against the rebel assembly.

The Legislative Assembly now began to take seriously the fear of intervention from foreign countries. Because of their oppressive measures, *emigres* (or defectors) fled to Germany and other neighboring countries. The nobility made up the predominant percentage of these *emigres* as they were the ones who seemed to have the most to loose if they stayed in France. The defections bolstered anti–revolutionary sentiment in those neighboring countries and also effected the French military. As many as two thirds of the royal guards defected, leaving the French armies without military officers. Promotions of unqualified men was common, but even this left the ranks of the armies depleted as there was a mounting resistance to the military draft. So concerned was the Legislative Assembly that a certain Lieutenant Napoleon soon found himself a Captain despite being delcared AWOL a month earlier and having been brought up on charges of suspected treason. This Napoleon had long sought the independence of his native homeland, Corsica, and was believed to have participated in several assaults on French garrisons. He had come to Paris in Jaunary, 1792, where he corresponded with the assembly. They dropped all charges against him and elevated him to Captain.

Their leniency was probably because of their need for good soliders in the coming days. War seemed imminent. Two months earlier, the assembly gave until January 1 for all *emigres* to return to France or be declared traitors pubishable by death. Louis used his suspensive veto to prevent this, but the message was clear. The *emigres* were believed to be stirring up dissension in neighboring countries, particularly Prussia and Austria.

In February Leopold made a defensive alliance with Prussia against any French aggression. He died less than a month later. His son, Francis II, proved equal in his hatred of the revolution. He was quick to take up the alliance his father had made.

France was already on the verge of anarchy. The people were discontent with their new rulers and the assembly was quick to blame all dissention, directly or indirectly, on counter–revolutionaries. Some of the revolutionary camp believed that it was their duty to take the revolution to all of Europe. Others believed that course would prove fatal. In either case, the assembly became convinced that they should strike first. It was not the emperor who invaded France, but France who rushed to war. On April 20, 1792 France declared war on Prussia and Austira.

In the early stages of the war, the commander of the Imperial armies, Duke Charles William Ferdinand of Brunswick, issued the Brunswick Manifesto in which he warned the people of Paris that if the royal family was harmed Paris itself would be destroyed in retaliation. That threat stirred the revolutionaries to anger and further antagonized them against Louis. Louis remained officially the king of France and the head of the Legislative Assembly, but he was obviously an unwilling participant.

Sentiment against Louis by the radicals led to rhe creation of the Paris Commune which created a national guard made up of 20,000 men. On August 10 armed peasants, assisted by the national guard, stormed the royal palace and occupied Tuileries. Six hundred royal guards were either killed in the fighting or butchered after surrendering. The king fled to the Legislative Assembly but the assembly, which had tried to protect the king in hopes of keeping France together, was now forced to reluctantly suspend the king. He was taken back to his prison. The mobs then found the princess de Lamballe, a close friend of Marie Antoinnette, and tore her to pieces. They put her head, breasts, and genitalia on a pike and paraded it outside the royal family's prison window. These events were witnessed by the young Napoleon Bonaparte who was in Paris that week.

This was the beginning of the end for the Legislative Assembly. They were now little more than puppets to the mobs and the Paris Commune. A few weeks later they were pressured into passing a new edict. All clergy members who had not taken the oath of allegiance were given seven days to leave France or face trial for treason. Finally, Legislative Assembly was dissolved and a National Convention was declared which would write a new constitution.

With the coming of a National Convention, the radicals were already making a play for power. Jean–Paul Marat stirred up the mobs by suggesting that one only need open the doors of the prisons to have the counter-revolutionaries spill out, overthrow the Paris Commune, and welcome the imperial armies. The mobs believed they had to act first. In early September the September Massacres began. Mobs broke into the prisons and set up mock trials. Over half of the 2,800 prison populous were hacked to death and mutilated. The massacre continued for four days as the Paris Commune turned a blind eye to the events. Marat even advocated the massacre.

While exonerating the mob Maximilian Robespierre used the massacre as an excuse to push for martial law in order to prevent such anarchy. The truth is that Robespierre and the Men of the Mountain (members of the Jacobin Club) were already making a play for power. Both Robespierre and Marat were among the deputies elected by Paris for the National Convention.

The war had not been going good for France. Enemy troops were moving toward Paris when France achieved its first real victory on September 20, 1794, at Valmy, just over a hundred miles from Paris. The next day news arrived of the victory. It was hailed as good omen for a day later, September 22, was officially the first day of the First French Republic.

No sooner was the National Convention to begin than omens of its tyrrany were to begin. Robespierre and Marat declared Louis had been judged by the people (by which he was referring to the mobs) and needed no trial. They demanded his execution. However, the Convention refused to execute him without a trial. During the trial he was even blamed for the crimes which had been perpetrated by Natioanl Assembly such as the massacre at the Champs de Mars. It seems that his guilty was predetermined. What was not as clear was his punishment. Initially the death penalty was favored by a single vote, atlhough twenty six members later changed in favor of the execution. In vain were appeals and motions for a reprieve or a national referendum. Louis was taken to the place of execution on execution Jan. 21, 1793. There he showed courage in the face of death and declared that he pardoned all those who were guilty of this crime.

The Jacobins Reign of Terror

The execution of Louis backfired. France had finally begun to make some gains, taking Belgium, the Rhineland, and Savoy but when news of Louis' execution spread abroad, the whole of Europe seemed to rise up against France. Great Britain, Spain, and Piedmonte joined the Imerpial armies in the First Coalition against France. By spring the Austrian Netherlands and the Rhineland were reclaimed. Other uprisings were to take place as well.

The new government gave orders to begin to confiscation of the property of all *emirges*. They then sent out spies to try accuse those who were suspected of sympathy with the enemy and allowed for the arrest of anyone who had been accused by a neighbor. Finally, the Convention ordered 300,000 conscripts to be drafted for the army. The result of these actions was an open rebellion in parts of France. The west had rebelled in early March, beginning the Wars of the Vendees.

The civil wars alone would claim over 200,000 lives. Another 200,000 were killed in the war with the empire. 117,000 people are estimated to have died in the towns ravaged by the French army. It was reported to the Convention that no prisoners were taken since they did not want to spare the food to feed them. "Pity is not revolutionary," they said. The "Catholic and Royalist Army," as the rebels were erroneously referred to, were to be utterly destroyed and an example was to be made of all the rebellious cities. Some historians have called the result of these War of the Vendees genocide.

In April the Committee of Public Safety became virtually merged with the Committee on General Security. They were given police powers which they were to use to squelch an demonstrations, uprisings, or threats to the new republic. The framework was set for a dictatorship, and Robespierre was waiting in the wings. He and Marat were the most notable radicals at the Convention. Their hated enemies were the Girondins who opposed the Jacobins' extemism. They became fearful of the increasing power and influence of Marat, Roebspierre, and the Paris Commune, denouncing one and all. Robespierre then called upon the people to "rise in insurrection." The Commune responded with mass demonstrations on May 31. Two days later the Commune's National Guards appeared at the convention hall along with many armed peasants.

The Jacobins were staging a coup. The Girondins were forced to resign as deputies of the Convention and fled. Robespierre and the Jacobins were now the undisputed leaders of the Convention. Everything was going to change; for the worse.

Jacques–Louis David – The Death of Marat – 1793

Fearful of the Jacobins' rise to power a number of assassinations took place. On July 13, Marat was killed in his bathtub by a woman. Two other Jacobin leaders were also killed in the following week. This became an excuse for Robespierre to justify the extermination of the Girondins. On July 27 Robespierre became the head of the Committee of Public Safety. On October 10, the provisional government was placed under the care of the Committee of Public Safety whose only restriction was its requirement to report to the Convention every week. Robespierre had gained dictatorial control over France. He was to instigate the Reign of Terror in hopes of terrifying all detractors into submission. Not only were royalists a target but so also were Girdonins, Federalists, Catholic sympathizers, and many others. In short, all who opposed the views of the Jacobins could expect to be arrested and charged with treason.

No sooner was the new constitution finished than Robespierre suspended it until as such time as peace was established. Elections were suspended as well as the individual liberties promised in the Declaration of the Rights of Man. Even protests, through which the Jacobins had risen to power, were now outlawed and protesters subject to arrest.

That same month, the government ordered the execution of the leading Girondins under the charge of treason. Additionally, the last symbol of royalism, Marie Antoinette, was executed on October 16, 1793. She had been hated beyond belief among the revolutionaries. A fake autobiography was circulated in which Marie allegedly called herself a prostitute and rumors of the famed comment "let them eat cake" circulated freely, although many historians doubt it was ever uttered. Her death, like that of her husband, was dignified.

The next month Robespierre and the Jacobins made numerous changes. The changes were all to be largely symbolic. They wanted to cast off everything "old," which they equated with superstition and ignorance. The "new" was to begin with the calendar. The names of the months were changed and instead of dating history from the time of Christ, the new calendar was to date history for the establishment of the First French Republic. Hence, September 22, 1792 became Vendermiaire 1, Year 1. The seven day week was also seen as a remnant of the Bible. It was replaced by a ten day week and worship every seven days was forbidden. Additionally, all the old systems of measurement were based on common things. A foot was supposedly the length of a man's foot. An inch, the length of a knuckle. A yard, the length of a man's arm. These measurements, however, were "royal" measurements, and therefore a symbol of the old. The Convention therefore decided to follow the metric system, still utilized today in many parts of the world, which was based on a system of ten. Finally, even the clock was changed from twelve hour days to ten hour days made up of a hundred minutes which in turn were made up of a hundred seconds.

These changes were frivolous but symbolic changes. Other changes were more dramatic, including the virtual establishment of deism as the state religion. The Jacobin radicals called for a de–Christianization of France. Over 20,000 priests were forced to abandon their calling and resign the priesthood. Cities names after saints were renamed after the "heroes" of the Revolution including men such as Marat and Rousseau. Catholics and Protestants were mutually faced with persecution. Thousands of priests were murdered or executed. The new deistic religion even came to have its own festivals and cults; many based on the old pagan religions, and some pornographic in nature. Additionally, some Cathedrals were forcibly converted into "temples of reason" which were now adorned with images of men like Rousseau. Although Robespierre spoke out against the atheistic and anti–Christian extremists, he did not seriously attempt to hinder them. By the time of Robespierre's fall, only 150 of the 40,000 parishes were saying mass.

Other changes to the law worthy of note include the easing of restrictions on divorce. Like modern day America, men or women could file for divorce on almost any basis. However, all women's clubs were shut down. Public education became both free and mandatory except that the government did not have the money to hire teachers or establish schools. Consequently, there were actually fewer children attending schools over this period than had been the case previous. Out of a city of 20,000 people only a hundred and twenty five actually attended school. The only money which seemed to be diverted to this noble enterprise was the appropriation of propaganda text books on the "heroic" acts of the "French Republicans."

The only good which the Jacobins seemed to have done was to abolish slavery and to resume the law against prostitution, which had been previously lifted by the Revolution. This, however, did nothing to change the attitudes of many of the French people. The "Federalists" were in open rebellion. Normandy, Provence, Lyon, Toulouse, and Bordeaux had risen up in arms. France was faced with the War of the Vendees in the west, invasion from the east by Prussia and Austria, rebellion in the south by the Federalists, and further invasions by Britain and Spain. These facts were sufficient for Robespierre to justify his extreme measures. The "Reign of Terror" was just beginning.

Over the next year an estimated 300,000 suspects were arrested. Over 17,000 executions by guillotine took place, but this does not count the hundred thousand or more victims of the French army who were killed or executed in the suppression of the revolts. Nor does this number count those who perished in prison. "The Incorruptible Robespierre," as he was called, sentenced over a hundred thousand men to die either directly or indirectly through his actions. Before the modern age, when Hitler literally made killing an assembly line process, there are few, if any, incidents to compare to the mass slaughter of victims as that which occured under Robespierre. He belived that "terror is nothing other than justice." He said that virtue is fatal without terror and terror is powerless without virtue. For Robespierre terror was a means to an end. He saw the end as virtue and terror as the means to accomplish it. Such perverted thinking is the end product of the Enlightenment's view of democracy. It is "the end justifies the means" in poetic language. Nowhere in history, save the Russian Revolution of 1917, can a similar comparison be made where lofty ideals of equality became the justification of mass murder. Indeed, the Russian Revolution was in many ways a repeat of the French Revolution, with the same end; a dictatorship.

One of the first major cities to be suppressed was Lyons. The French army captured Lyons, a symbol of rebellion, and made an example of it. Houses of the wealthy were demolished and over 2,000 civic leaders and civilians were massacred. The city's name was even changed from Lyons to "Liberated City."

More atrocities followed in the coming months. At Nantes 1,800 Vendean rebels were drowned. One by one the rebellious cities fell and its populous made to suffer for their choice. Tens of thousands died at the hands of the victorious French armies, not counting those who fell in battle before their victory. At Toulon, however, the British had attempted to establish a base of operations. The city was considered crucial to any attempt to keep the British at bay. On December 19, 1793, a certain Major Napoleon Bonaparte took the city, and drove the British from the city. He then turned his cannons on the helpless victims who were gathered togethered in the town square to await their punishment. Hundreds were massacred and the young Major became a national hero. Napoleon was praised in the Convention by a close friend of his named Augustin Robespierre, the brother of Maximilian Robespierre. Three days later

Napoleon Bonaparte was promoted to General. He had risen from a lieutenant to a General in two years time by ridding the wave of the Reign of Terror and befriending men in high places, but his future was still waiting for him.

Despite the victories, the Reign of Terror increased. In the next two months nearly seven thousand people went to the guillotine. Soon voices were heard in the Convention dissenting and asking for an end to the Reign of Terror. Georges Danton cried out against the folly saying, "you want to remove all your enemies by means of the guillotine! Has there ever been such great folly? Could you make a single man perish ... without making ten enemies for yourself from his family or friends?" His dissention did not last long, because in March, 1794, Danton was executed, along with many of his supporters.

With most of his dissenters guillotined, or so he believed, Robespierre was elected president of the Convention on June 4. Four days later led the "festival of the Supreme Being" as head of the new religion. Choreographed by the famed Revolutionary artists, and member of the Committee of Public Safety, Jacques–Louis David, the festival was fashioned after the old Greek pagan festivals. It symbolized not only the new deist religion of the government, but it also made Robespierre look the fool to many who still clung to Catholicism or Protestantism. The image of Robespierre prancing around become fodder for his critics.

On June 10 Robespierre helped pass a new law which denied the accused a right to defend themselves and establish the death penalty as the *only* punishment for the accused. This was called the Law of 22 Prairial and once again stirred up silent dissent. Even many of Robespierre's former supporters believed he was now going to excess. Nearly a half a million people had died in France from the Terror or its related wars.

On June 26, 1794, the French army achieved their greatest success to date. At the battle of Fleurus France defeated the Imperial troops of Austria. The immediate dangers to France had passed. The Federalists were largely in submission, the War of Vendees was victorious, and the Imperial armies were no longer threatening French cities, but Robespierre still refused to halt the Reign of Terror. This was the signal for yet another revolution. The Convention was ready to turn against Robespierre.

On July 27 the Convention ordered the arrest of Robespierre and his brother Augustin. During a skrimish at City Hall Robespierre shot himself in the jaw, apparently preferring suicide to the guillotine, but he lived long enough to make it to the guillotine. The ironic justice of Robespierre's death by guillotine was not lost on his enemies. He was guillotined on July 28 along with a hundred of his followers. In addition many of his known associates and allies were arrested throughout France, including a certain General Napoleon Bonaparte.

30

The Rise of Napoleon

The end of the Reign of Terror did not bring peace or democracy to France. In fact, more revolutions were to follow. France was still in a state of anarchy. It had no leader who could hold them together. The people were divided in politics. They were divided in religion. They were divided in social classes. They were, in fact, divided in almost every way. There was no real unity that could hold the country together and without a leader, the country could not expect to hold out forever against the emperor of Rome and the combined forces of Europe. It is usually under these circumstances that dictators rise to power, promising order out of chaos. Such was the case with Napoleon who would one day rise to claim nothing less than the Imperial diadem itself. Debate upon whether or not this crown was truly that of the Roman Empire, or some new French empire, will be reserved for later. How he rose to such lofty heights from a prison cell following the execution of his close associate Augustin Robespierre is in itself a grand story.

The Thermidorian Reaction

Napoleon had been suspect as a close associate of Robespierre. He had even published an article in which he declared that his "saints" were Marat and Robespierre. He was, therefore, fortunate that Augustin Robespierre was not his only friend in the National Convention. Paul Francois Barras was another close associate of Napoleon. In fact, it was Barras who would first introduce Napoleon to one of his lovers; a certain Josephine. As a "liberated" Enlightenment man Barras did not mind sharing his lovers and Napoleon would soon fall in love with the woman, although she is said to have hated him. Barras was also one of the leaders of the coup against Robespierre. He, therefore, argued on behalf of Napoleon who soon released, with his full rank reinstated. France was still at war and needed all the good generals it could get.

The execution of Robespierre had occured in the French calendar date of the 9th of Thermidor. The new rulers were, therefore, called the Thermidorians and the time of transition became known as the Thermidorian Reaction for the Reign of Terror was to be replaced by the "White Terror" in which the surviving victims of Robespierre took out their vengeance on the Jacobins. An estimated two thousand victims were killed by lynchings, gang murders, and even some prison massacres. It would be several months before the White Terror died down and some semblance of order was acheived. In the meantime a third constitution was drawn up by the Thermidorians.

While the Convention was drawing up a new constitution the war was still continuing against the Holy Roman Empire and the royal family was now making an attempt to return to power. Louis XVII, the son of Louis XVI and Marie Antoinette, had died a child of ten while rotting in prison. Only months later, in June 1795, the uncle of Louis XVI claimed the rights to the throne and issued a proclamation from his safety in Verona calling for a return to the monarchy and an end to the anarchy. Given the horrors that the French Revolution had brought, including the deaths of over a half million people, it is not surprising that Louis found many sympathizers who were calling for a return to the first constitutional monarchy. The royalists party and the neo–Jacobins were polar opposites, save in their hatred for the Thermidorians.

That same year, before the constitution had been completed, Prussia made peace with France at the Peace of Basel. Prussia promised to withdraw from war, officially leaving the decision of who controled the now French occupied portion of the Rhine to the emperor but in a secret pact Prussia acknowledged France as the true sovereign of the Rhine. One reason Prussia had made peace was so that Prussia could concentrate on a new dispute over Poland. Another partition was to result in Warsaw, Masouin, Bialystok, and part of Podlachin becoming part of Prussia. The real consequence of the peace was the realization that France was no longer merely in a war of defense, but rather a war of expansionism.

By the end of September, the new constitution was almost complete. It would create a Council of Five Hundred along with a Directorate of five men who would be elected by the legislature. Under the newest constitution petitions, political clubs, and unarmed demonstrations were outlawed. Many demonstrators were already objecting and on October 4, just after midnight of that morning, thousands of protesters and royalists began to march on Paris. A new revolution seemed to be in the making. Generals Barras and Napoleon were both in Paris and were given orders to crush the insurgency. Barras attempted to secure the suburbs while Napoleon placed artillery in the streets of Paris, including large cannons near the Church of St. Roch which provided a large open area where the cannons could do their work. Fighting carried on throughout the day until the mobs reached St. Roch where the artillery was unleashed on the crowds. 1,400 people died in the shelling. Napoleon reported, "I could not be happier." He had saved the new constitution and become an instant hero.

The next day a general amnesty was proclaimed for political prisoners and the new constitution was put into effect. Napoleon was celebrated as the hero who saved the Republic and was introduced to the mistress of Barras, Josephine whom he met at a *bacchanalia*, or "filthy orgy." Originally called Rose, Napoleon took her middle name, Josephine, and called her by that name. She did not love him, but she was ever the forture hunter and Barras assured her than Napoleon was moving on to bigger and better things. Napoleon, for his part, was deeply in love with her. She once said, in a terrified manner, that he did not lover her, but worshipped her. In either case, he wanted to marry her. She resisted at first until persuaded by Barras. Among other things, he promised her that Napoleon would soon be leaving for an invasion of Italy, whose conquest he had himself suggested and whose plans he had presented to the Council.

The prohibition against civil marriage ceremonies, which had been effect for a time, was temporarily lifted and on March 9 Napoleon and Josephine were married, although the officiator of the ceremony was not legally licensed. Two days later Napoleon left for his conquest of Italy.

Conquest of Italy

It was Napoleon who had first presented plans for a conquest of Italy. The war against the emperor largely preoccupied the French to the east, but the Hapsburgs controlled northern Italy and Lombardy. By attacking Francis' interest in Italy it was hoped that the Austrian army would be diverted to the south. The Council viewed Napoleon's invasion as a diversionary tactic and little else. Napoleon had other plans.

Napoleon was given the least of the armies to complete his invasion. The Army of Italy was poorly fed and its morale low. They had not been paid in months and desertion were probably on their minds. Napoleon promised them the riches of Italy. From the very beginning looting and pillaging was a part of Napoleon's plans, although he officially wrote to the Directory that he would rather resign that have looters in his army. The troops morale was increased by promises of the rewards they would find among their vanquished. Napoleon also knew that he could not expect financing from Paris, so what they stole in Italy would finance his army, as well as increase his own personal wealth.

His army had only 37,000 men compared with the combined total of 52,000 men from the Austrian and Piedmonte armies. Napoleon believed it essential to keep the two enemy armies from uniting. He, therefore, pressed attacks against the Austrians to keep them on the run. He marched his troops around the Alps and on April 28 the king of Sardina made a treaty with Napoleon, promising to break his alliance with Francis II. He then moved on toward Milan. Despite this relative early success, the Directory believed that Napoleon needed help and they sent a general to serve as joint commander. Napoleon was furious and decided to take Milan before the new commander could arrive. Napoleon wanted to share his victories with no one.

On May 15 Napoleon arrived at Milan and was please to find they had opened their gates to him; accepting him as a liberator. They were soon to regret their decision. Rape, murder, pillaging, and looting ensued. Napoleon feigned regret and even executed a few men who had gone to excess, but this was only to cover up himself for the Directory. When the Milanese revolted days after Napoleon's troops left, he returned with a vengeance. More raping and murding occurred, but worse yet was how Napoleon sought to make an example of them. All the male children from a neighboring town were taken and executed, and the town burned to the ground afterwards. Napoleon would not rule as a liberator by as a tyrant to be feared.

That same month Paris was the objective of more conspiracies. The Babeuf plot was exposed in which by neo–Jacobins were plotting to sieze power. Resistance to conscriptions, or the military draft, increased including burning of town records buildings so that the government would not have any records of who should be conscripted. Militarily, the French were advancing into southern Germany and Saxony made peace until emperor objected, eventually abandoning the peace they had made. When part of Napoleon's captured treasures arrived at Paris the wealth was not only welcome to a country in financial desperation, but the Directory soon began to see the usefulness of Napoleon. Using the pope's refusal to lift this condemnation of the Civil Constitution as an excuse, they now ordered Napoleon to invade the Papal States.

In June Napoleon advanced into Tuscany and the Papal States. By June 23 the pope was making an armistice in which he promised to turn over many of the riches of the Vatican itself to Napoleon. He paid 21,000,000 francs and turned over some of the famous paintings and other works of art found in the Vatican. Napoleon's conquest of Italy was rapid and overwhelming, but if Naples came to the pope's defense Napoleon would face a war on two fronts as the Austrians were coming to his aid as well. On October 10 Naples signed a treaty which freed Napoleon up to concentrate on the Austrians who sent fresh troops into Italy in early November. Before then, Napoleon wanted to set up some form of government that would make the Italians feel that they were being liberated. Three artifical Republics were declared and established by Napoleon. In fact they were little different from the "Banana Republics" of today. French troops remained and Napoleon was the real power. Eventually, even the mayors of the respective cities were appointed by Napoleon, rather than being elected.

The irony of Napoleon's "liberations" is nowhere more obvious than in his conquest of his native Corsica. He had once dreamed of liberating Corsica from French occupation, but when Corsica finally rebelled it was Napoleon who undertook the reconquest of his native home on behalf of the French.

The Austrians proved a capable threat to Napoleon's army. Famine and plague became Napoleon's allies and began to take a toll on both armies, but particularly the Austrians. In January the Austrians were defeated at the Battle of Rivoli which again led to Napoleon's presige as his victories mounted. This was followed by the surrender of two more Austrian garrisons who were already starving and ill. Napoleon did not let up but immediately turned south to invade the Papal States again. He declared that the Austrians had come at the pope's request and weeks later, in the middle of February, papal emissaries signed the Treaty of Tolentino in which the pope agreed to pay another 30,000,000 francs and surrender all claims to Bologna, Ferrara, and the Romagna. Napoleon then turned to Vienna.

Spain, fearing the power of Napoleon, made peace in 1797. He was now free to threaten the Austrian borders near Italy. Although he had not been given any authority, Napoleon took it upon himself to threaten Austria. In fact, he was bluffing. Napoleon's army had been hit as hard by disease and famine as any. It was a bluff that paid off. In April the Austrians acknowledged their willingness to negotiate with Napoleon. He demanded nothing less than Belgium, Holland, and the west bank of the Rhine. Many months later, in October, the Treaty of Campo Formio was signed, ceding to France all that Napoleon had requested. Napoleon, who had acted without authorization, was again the hero of France.

Belgium and the Rhine, as part of the French conquest, became "sister republics." In addition the sham republics of Italy and the Batavian Republic of the northern Netherlands made the French look like liberators. Although the republics were no different than if the French had instigated puppet kings, it did lay the groundwork for future democracies and showed that the age of kings was coming to a close. Napoleon was a national hero at twenty–seven years of age.

The Egyptian Campaign

In Paris the new constitutional government was undergoing a crisis. They believed they needed to "safeguard" the new constitution from royalists and neo–Jacobins, so after the elections of 1797, the "coup of Fructidor" saw the government arrest two royalist leaning directors and nullify all elections in areas where the results favored the royalists. Even the Directory itself was considered suspect. A return to the Reign of Terror was not imminent, but the same paranoia and suspicions which had created it began to surface again. Supporters of Louis XVIII were sought out and anti–Catholic reactions resumed once again. Although the new calendar had fallen out of usage for a time it was resumed and all worship on Sundays was again outlawed. Renewed persecutions of both Catholics and Protestants saw the arrest of hundreds for saying mass or even refusing to work on Sundays. The public display of the cross, such as a necklace, was outlawed as well.

Despite these ominous warnings of trouble France appeared externally to be the leader of free Europe. In January 1798 the Switzerland Republic joined as a sister republic to France. It was followed by the Roman Republic in February and the Parthenopean Republic of Naples. The image for France was that they were liberating Europe and establishing democracies throughout the old empire. In reality, it was occupation under the guise of democratic freedom, but Napoleon himself said of Republics that they were a "fad" which would pass "like all the others." He disdainfully spoke of the common man saying, "give them baubles, that suffices them; they will be amused and let themselves be led, so long as the end towards which they are heading is skillfully concealed from them." Already Napoleon was giving hints of his master plan. The signing of the Treaty of Campo Formio had taken many months because Napoleon himself felt that "peace is not in my best interest." He said to his friends, "do you really think that I triumphed in Italy in order to aggrandize that pack of lawyers who form the Directory, men like Carnot and Barras?" No, he was himself after a seat on the Directory but he was rebuffed by them, noting, among other reasons, that the minimum age for sitting on the Directory was forty. Napoleon was still in his late twenties.

The truth is that the Directory was itself aware of the threat that Napoleon posed them. Once, when Napoleon threatened to resign, one of the Directors quickly grabbed a piece of paper and asked Napoleon to sign his resignation. Napoleon, of course, was bluffing. The Directory initially decided that Napoleon would best be used for an invasion of England, but that plan was soon abandoned. Napoleon pressed for another plan. He wanted to invade Egypt. This invasion plan was officially tied to the war with England, who had not yet signed a peace treaty. In reality Egypt had nothing to do with England. The excuse was that France needed a gateway to the east in order to compete with the British Indies (India). The reality is that Napoleon, and France, wanted glory. Conquering a European state was nothing. Conquering the glory of Egypt would win Napoleon all the praise he craved. The riches of Egypt itself would be looted. To that end Napoleon not only prepared an invasion army but also took with him astronomers, geometricians, naturalists, geologists, archaeologists, and even a chemist. It was as much a historical and scientific expedition as a conquest.

While Napoleon was preparing his fleet to sail for Egypt, the Directory was insuring that it remained in power. Royalists and neo–Jacobins were each striving for power and as they gained more supporters among the people, the legislature and the Directory once again "safeguarded" the new constitution by annulling more unfavorable elections.

At the end of May 1798 Napoleon set out for Egypt. Earlier that month the famed English Admiral Sir Horatio Nelson arrived in the Mediterrean with orders to hunt down and destroy Napoleon's fleet. Over the next month Admiral Nelson would come within eighty miles of Napoleon's fleet but would never see them. The two fleets simply missed each other time and time again.

Before reaching Egypt Napoleon had planned to take Malta. The tiny island was under the protection of the Czar of Russia and controlled by the ancient Malta Knights, otherwise known as the Order of the Knights Hospitalers of Saint John of Jerusalem. The fortress of Malta was considered impregnable, but that was when it was fully manned and Napoleon's spies had told him that there were now no more than a few hundred knights who were available to man the guns and defend the vast walls. When Napoleon arrived he requested to enter with his entire fleet to collect provisions of water. Malta saw through his lies and refused. After several days of fighting, Malta surrendered. The ancient Hospitaler Knights ceased to exist and the new "republic" of Malta was formed under French control. When the pillaging and looting was over, Napoleon resumed his course for Egypt.

Napoleon's fleet arrived near the coast of Alexandria just days after Admiral Nelson's fleet had left. Unable to find Napoleon, Nelson ordered the fleet to move up the coast toward Crete. Crushing Napoleon, France's best general, was Nelson's most urgent duty. Had he been more patient, Napoleon's fleet would have sailed directly into Nelson's waiting Armada. However, as Nelson had left, Napoleon landed his fleet amid turbulent waters and storms.

Napoleon had studied the conquest of Cortez. He knew that Cortez had conquered a vast empire with only a handful of men by befriending the people. Napoleon had orders to avoid provoking the Ottoman Empire, which was the official sovereign of Egypt. Therefore, Napoleon planned to present his conquest as a war against the Mamlukes, rather than against the Egyptians. He assured the Alexandrians that he respected Muhammad and the Koran. He promised there would be no rape or pillage and threatened to execute anyone who committed such crimes. In the end, Alexandria surrendered, but Napoleon's promises were only partially kept. His undisciplined troops continued raping and pillaging. Even some of Napoleon's generals were involved. The troops had never been used to disciple and Napoleon had usually promised them loot and women as a reward for their services. Consequently, Napoleon did little to prevent the atrocities even though he would continue to insist that only Mamlukes were fair prey.

Having secured Alexandria Napoleon began the long march down to Cairo, via Rosetta, where the famous Rosetta Stone was to found a year later. The Rosetta Stone provided archaeologists a way of translating Egyptian hieroglyphics since it had three languages presented side by side. It was the "key" to ancient Egyptian hieroglyphics and remains one of the most famous archaeological finds in history.

On the long march Napoleon had brought little provisions. He expected to "live off the land." The hot desert and lack of water alone killed hundreds of Napoleon's soldiers. In addition, the Mamlukes were following Napoleon imploring a hit and run tactic. Some soldiers were even kidnapped and sodomized by the Mamlukes for entertainment. When told of these occurrences, Napoleon merely laughed. His undisciplined soldiers continued to terrorize the villages they encountered and they sometimes burned the fields to the ground when they left. Finally, in late July, they arrived near Cairo.

Murad Bey was the Mamluke leader. The citizens of Cairo had heard of Napoleon and his troops' actions. Anarchy siezed the city as mobs killed every Jew and Christian they could find. Refuges fled Cairo only to be raped, robbed, and/or murdered by their neighbors. Outside the city Murad Beys' soldiers prepared for battle. The "Battle of the Pyramids" took place on July 21, 1798. There on the battlefield a couple thousand Mamlukes were slain compared to a few hundred of Napoleon's men. Murad Bey retreated to Giza and Cairo, already victimized by Murad Bey, surrendered. Cairo was in Napoleon's hands.

Jean Leon Gerome – Napoleon and His General Staff in Egypt – 1867

He set up a nine man Egyptian council called the divan, whose members were naturally appointed by himself. They were told to propagate that Napoleon had himself been prophesied in the Koran, but the people never believed it. In addition, the scientific Egyptian Institute was set up. Napoleon convinced himself that he was the master of Egypt. In fact, he controlled only two major cities, and was soon to be completely cut off from France. The victory of Napoleon was shortlived.

Napoleon had ordered his Admiral to wait for his troops in Abukir Bay, east of Alexandria. The Admiral had warned Napoleon that his fleet would be vulnerable to Nelson's armada if they remained, but Napoleon refused to listen. On August 1 Admiral Nelson returned and seeing the French fleet, he ordered an immediate attack. Many of the French sailors were ashore and unable to get back to their ships. The Battle of the Nile resulted in the destruction of Napoleon's fleet. The flagship itself was literally blown up, sending shockwaves throughout the remaining French sailors. In the end, nearly two thousand Frenchmen were killed, and three thousand captured. The English now controlled the Mediterrean and cut off Napoleon's troops from France and any supplies or reinforcements that it might have provided him.

514

Napoleon was trapped in Egypt with no way to get home. He blamed the Admiral, claiming to the Directory that he had ordered them not to remain in Abukir Bay. The lie was not unusual. When Napoleon was victorious, he exaggerated his victory to heap even more praise on himself. When he lost, he blamed his subordinates, even making up outrageous lies. Fortunes had drastically changed. Russia had now declared war on France following the capture of Malta and the French had broken the treaty with Austria on the excuse that the mobs who had burned a French flag were acting as officials of the emperor. The Second Coalition of 1798 now unified Britain, Austria, and Russia against France. On September 9, the Ottoman Empire entered the fray, declaring war on France for invading Egypt. The expedition to Egypt was to be a disaster for France and for Napoleon. He had to find a way back to France.

For a while it seemed that Napoleon refused to accept reality. He saw himself as the master of Egypt and refused to see things otherwise. On October 21, an insurrection erupted in Cairo. Thousands of Egyptians were slaughtered in the battles which followed and Napoleon demolished a grand mosque, which only angered the people more. Executions began to take place daily. Despite this, it was not until the end of the year that Napoleon came to the realization that no help could get through the British blockade of the Mediterranean. Always seeking glory for himself, he found a way to return to France and gain more glory. He would march his army, now depleted by almost half, up through the Holy Land to Damascus and Constantinople; conquering all. Then he would merely march on foot home to France and sieze control of the Directory itself. The plan was naïve.

On January 31, Napoleon set out for Damascus. They were able to take the Gaza and other relatively undefended areas, but the real battles lie ahead. En route Napoleon not only lifted the restrictions that he had unsuccessfully placed on his troops against rape and murder, but he wanted to subject the Arabs "to all the horrors of war in their most hideous form." In one case, two thousand Arabs soldiers surrendered after being promised that their lives would be spared. Instead, Napoleon had all of them executed; many by bayonet to save ammunition.

In March 1799, Pope Pius VII replaced Pius VI who had died a prisoner of the new Roman "Republic." No longer powerful, the papacy had to play a careful game. They wanted to restore the Catholic Church to France, to regain authority over the Papal Estates, and ultimately to restore their own once mighty position in the empire. Pius was to play a dangerous game with the dictator Napoleon in the years to come. They both needed one another, but it was Napoleon who was to get the final laugh.

The next month Napoleon arrived before Acre. For nearly a month he would fight against the undermanned Acre without avail. On May 20, he abandoned the siege and returned to Egypt. He had seen newspapers telling of the changing fortunes of France. The French were loosing ground. Italy was again in rebellion and the people were furious at the Directory over its increasing suppression of dissent and its nullification of unfavorable elections. Napoleon believed that it was the opportune time to return to France and sieze power. He sent back reports full of outrageous lies, including the allegation that he had razed Acre's ramparts to the ground. Napoleon must have known that such absurd lies would soon or later be discovered, but he was probably counting on being in control before that ever happened. Beside, the commoners believed the news reports, and that was all Napoleon really needed.

On his journey back to Cairo, foot supplies were short and disease was rampant among the men. Napoleon gave orders that fifty hospital patients be poisoned in order that they might devote their attentions and supplies elsewhere. The doctor refused, but others carried out some of the poisonings, while still others protected the wounded. On June 14 Napoleon had finally reached Cairo; a city once again on the verge of rebellion. Banners accompanied him into the city, as he pretended to have conquered all the Holy Land.

Four days later, on June 18, 1799, the Prairial coup in France resulted in the ouster of two Directory members who were replaced by Neo–Jacobins. A certain Sieyes had also been elected to the Directory a month earlier. The Jacobins were making a play to return to power.

Before this news could reach Napoleon, news of a more imminent nature arrived. The British and Ottomans had landed in Abukir Bay and were sending troops to vanquish Napoleon. Napoleon mustered what few troops he had left and went to meet them. There, on July 25, Napoleon experienced his first *real* victory. It would not insure that the British navy did not continue to control the Mediterranean, but it gave Napoleon back his port, halted the ground invasion, and gave him enough fast ships to be able to slip by the British blockade unnoticed. On October 9, 1799, Napoleon left Egypt, leaving with a third of the troops he had arrived with; the other two thirds dead. He had left Egypt in failure, but returned to France hailed as a hero and conqueror. The people of France were none the wiser, even if the Directory suspected that his reports were falsified.

Napoleon Siezes Power

Napoleon returned to France to find it on the verge of another revolution. The conditions were ripe for Napoleon's play. In May 16, Emmanuel "Abbe" Sieyes was elected to the Directory. He was to become the main rival to Barras, to whom Napoleon owed so much. Unlike others, Sieyes was sly and not brazen. Even while Barras was struggling to hold power, Sieyes sat by quitely, neither antagonizing Barras, nor openly supporting his overthrow.

The problems had begun some time ago. The war was no longer going France's way and the government was increasingly becoming repressive. The "Law of Hostages" allowed the government to sieze the relatives of suspected traitors and royalists, neo–Jacobin clubs were shut down, and the "Executioner of Lyons" was named head of the Police Ministry. Fear was growing that the Reign of Terror was about to return.

The Council of the Five Hundred demanded that the Directory give an accounting of itself and its actions, but the Directory ignored the council. In return, the Council declared that it would remain permanently in session until the Directory complied. In September Barras ordered troops to "defend" the Directory. On the 4th the Directory ordered the arrest of General Pichegru who was a royalist sympathizer. He warned the Directory that Napoleon, not he, was the true enemy of France and the Directory. They did not believe him (although some were very concerned that his unauthorized return to France, amounting legally to desertion, was for some sinister purpose). The resulting "coup of Fructidor" saw the arrest of hundreds of Jacobin "conspirators" and kept Barras' position secure from both royalists and Jacobins. However, Sieyes, like Barras, had his own plans.

Sieyes believed he needed a "sword" to sieze power. He wanted to take control, but had seen too many come and go. He approached Napoleon and offered him a seat of power next to him in exchange for his military support. Unknown to Sieyes, Barras had made a similar request. Napoleon could choose whomever he wanted and Napoleon had no loyalty. Barras had been one of the major reasons for Napoleon's rise to power, but Barras had scoffed at Napoleon's request to sit on the Directory years earlier. Napoleon was a vengeful man. He was also angry with his wife, Josephine, whom Barras had introduced to him. She was a notorious vixen and adultress. Napoleon consoled himself with his own mistresses, although he continued to love Josephine.

In any case, Napoleon through his lot with Sieyes. He was to get assistance from his brother Lucien, who was elected president of the Council of the Five Hundred on October 25. Three days later the Directory called Napoleon to a hearing where he was charged with desertion and embezzlement. It is likely that Barras knew Napoleon was planning a coup and tried, unsuccessfully, to head it off. Napoleon argued that the money he received was bonified booty and loot which soldiers were permitted in those days. The charge of desertion was also dropped, probably on account of Napoleon's popularity among the general populous. The trial, however, did indicate that Napoleon needed to act fast; Barras may have had plans of his own.

On November 9, 1799 (the 18th of Brumaire according to the new French calendar) Napoleon's coup was pulled off. Napoleon's fellow consipirators had successfully convinced the council that Jacobin mobs were advancing and moved the council to places where they would be "safe" from "Jacobin conspirators." Napoleon was appointed general by the Council of the Ancients with the duty to protect the Republic. Other conspirators confronted Barras and forced him to tender a prewritten resignation which included a reference to the "glory" of the "illustrious warrior" Napeolon. This was followed by the appearance of troops which surrounded the councils.

Napoleon appeared before the Council of the Five Hundred, of which his brother was president, but the Council was defiant and shouted "down with dictators" and "no dictators." Napoleon had hoped that the Council would hail him as a hero rather than a dictator, but he was blinded by his own ego. The defiant Council even threatened to "outlaw the tyrant" and Napoleon was even forced to be escorted to safety. Lucien left the Council and urged Napoleon to act. Troops began to pour into the halls and the Council members fled for their lives.

A handful of loyal council members convened and created a "temporary executive committee" which established the triumvirate consulship of Napoleon, Sieyes, and Roger–Ducas, a fellow conspirator. The old constitution was nullified and a new one was promised. For the third time in ten years, the government of France had fallen and a new one was set up. This one was to be ruled by the First Consul Napoleon Bonaparte with as much power as any king had ever wielded.

The New Government

Napoleon had pulled off the coup successfully in large part due to the efforts of his brother Lucien. Napoleon had not anticipated that the Council would have defied him as they did. Only through Lucien was he able to use the military forces while still maintaining the illusion of protecting the Republic. Now came the illusion of making Napoleon look like a savior of the Republic ideals, rather than its executioner. Once again Lucien was to prove invaluable. He was an expert forger whose skills Napoleon made good use of in the coming months. Lucien helped forge necessary documents and embezzle funds, but his most notorious achievement was in the Constitutional election of January, 1800. The people were asked to approve the new constitution which would place virtually all power in the hands of one man; Napoleon. The "results" of the election was an astounding 99.99% favorable vote out of nine million eligible voters. Only 1562 voted against the new constitution. Of course, based on extant evidence modern scholars believe that the true results were actually closer to 70% *against* the new constitution and 30% for it.

The triconsulship gave Napoleon, as First Consul, such vast powers that he soon pushed Sieyes and Roger–Ducos out, making himself the sole and supreme authority over France. Sieyes, who had planned the coup, was double–crossed by the ambitious general. The rest of govenment was also made to be subordinate to the First Consul. The senate was hand–picked, the one hundred member Tribunate was given no real authority other than to debate issues presented to it, and the legislative body itself could vote on those laws presented to it, but was not even permitted to even debate the matter. The

Council of State was created by, and for, Napoleon. On February 16, 1800, Napoleon finalized his control over government with an administrative decree which made local governments, like the senate and legistlature, a "rubber stamp." It gave Napoleon the authority to appoint all mayors, prefects, and judges in towns of more than 5000 people. The man who had once called Republican Democracies a "fad" had successfully created a sham Republic which was really nothing more than a thinly veiled dictatorship.

As dictator of France, Napoleon now had a challenging task before him. The war with the Holy Roman Emperor and Second Coalition was still ongoing, as was another civil war with the Vendees. Worse yet was the threat that President John Adams of the United States of America might join the war against France. French interest in America had, after all, been harassing and attacking the colonists in an unofficial war. However, the rise of a new leader in France gave John Adams pause. He sent two ambassadors to speak to Napoleon.

Napoleon's hands were full. He had a desire, from the very beginning, to conquer Europe, and even North America, but he knew that he could not successfully fight a war on three or four different fronts. "Divide and conquer" has always been the dictators best strategy and "the Little Corporal" knew it well. Before he could hope to conquer the Holy Roman Empire and claim its throne, he had to break the coalition and end the civil wars and strife in France. He generously offered the Vendees to lift religious persecution and other oppressive laws but when they refused the offer he ordered the uprising brutally suppressed. Towns were burned to the ground on Napoleon's orders and the rebels killed. However, when the Vendees were subjugated, Napoleon saw the wisdom in making them content so that they would not rise in rebellion again. A combination of fear and justice became Napoleon's policy toward them. He allowed royalists to return to their lands, even giving back confiscated lands. Further, he ordered freedom of religion and the restoration of the Catholic Church in the Vendees, which served to pacify many of the residents, and harmed the royalists who had been counting on Catholic support against Napoleon. Napoleon had said that as he had (allegedly) conquered Egypt by making himself a Muslim, he would subject the Vendees by making himself a Catholic. Religion for him was merely a means to an end and freedom of religion was essential to maintaining peace and stability in France; a fact lost on many dictators and leaders.

At the same time Napoleon reconquered Italy which had been lost while he was in Egypt. Using the same tactics he had employed in the Vendees, Italy was subjugated easily and Napoleon began to open friendly negotiations with the pope, who was eager to see Catholicism restored to larger France.

In the meantime, long negotiations with both the emperor and the U. S. Ambassadors were continuing. Finally, the U. S. Ambassadors came back to America with a new treaty which had been presented to them on October 1,

1800. What the ambassadors did not known was that Napoleon was also in secret negotiations with Spain. Three days after coming to terms with the United States Spain ceded the vast Louisiana lands and Hispaniola to France at Second Treaty of Ildefonso. John Adams honored the treaty, but was very leary of Napoleon's new domains which cut off the colonies from the west and left the U. S. virtually surrounded.

Next on Napoleon's agenda was the emperor's armies in Austria. Peace negotiations began from the time that Napoleon had taken office, but they dragged on until Dec. 3, 1800, when General Moreau defeated the Imerpial Archduke John, killing 17,000 Austrian soldiers. The emperor was now forced to make peace. The Treaty of Luneville was signed on February 9, 1801. It bascially maintained the status quo but the result was that the emperor permanently lost all claims to Italian lands.

Five months later Napoleon made another significant move to bring peace to France. A concordat with the pope was signed on July 15, 1801. The concordat agreed to restore Catholicism to France but *Napoleon* would nominate all bishops who would in turn be paid by the state. Napoleon was thus making himself the master of the French church, as well as of the state. One critic even warned that the "tyrant" would soon have 40,000 priests at his beckon call. The pope, eager to see Catholicism restored to France, reluctantly agreed to these conditions, severely reducing Catholic opposition to Napoleon.

The final task of the First Consul was to end the war with England and Russia. After England took control of Malta, Napoleon was able to turn Russia against England, convincing them that England was only concerned with advancing their own interest. Russia abandoned the Coalition, isolating England who then eventually signed Treaty of Amiens on March 25, 1802. England was to return Malta to the Knights of St. John and Egypt (which they had taken from the French after Napoleon's departure) was returned to the Ottoman Empire.

These victories of the Consul were tremendous and inspired confidence among the people. His power was such that in August, 1802, the constitution was amended to make Napoleon made Consul for life. This time the vote was given as 99.8% of the votes in favor of the amendment! Fraud was a staple of Napoleon's "republic" but such absurdities were new to fledgling democracies although even then it astounds historians how Napoleon, or anyone else, could really have believed such numbers.

Lucien, who was behind some of these fraudulent elections, had been useful in forging and embezzling for Napoleon, but his ambitions made Napoleon turn on his brother, who was tried privately for treason on November 1. The trial was kept private. Lucien was sent away as an ambassador to Madrid. The trial was doubtless to show what would happen to Lucien if he ever tried to return to power in France.

Thus in less than three years Napoleon had brought peace to a France which had been constantly at war with itself or its neighbors. Anarchy was brought to an end, freedom of religion was established for the first time, the borders of France were secure, and Napoleon was Consul for life. Now Napoleon could begin his policy of expansion and conquest anew.

The new Czar Alexander of Russia and Napoleon began talks which included keeping Germany at bay and even hinted at the division of German lands. This was an ominous foreboding of the Consul's plans to conquer the Holy Roman Empire and claim its crown for himself. In order to keep the empire weak Napoleon made seperate treaties with Prussia and Bavaria, thus implying that Prussia and Bavaria were not bound by the Imperial treaty. This strategy successfully led to a German diet in which the Principal Decree of the Imperial Deputation was presented on Feb. 25, 1803. The decree atttmped to restructure Germany and redifine the borders of each state and elector. The emperor's Austria domains would have been reduced and it would have given Protestants more electorial votes than Catholics. Not surprisingly Francis II vetoed the decree but did not push his own agenda, perhaps fearing that the electors might depose him for another emperor. The status quo remained in effect with the result that Prussia, Bavaria, and Austria were effectively seperated although they all remained nominally under the emperor's control. Truly the days of imperial glory were fading for Germany; but not for France. Shortly after the diet ended France cut off diplomatic relations with the emperor. Francis II would have to deal with Napoleon virtually by himself.

All these events freed Napoleon up for his master plans, but he needed still one more thing; money. One could not finance such vast conquest without money and France had for years relied on Napoleon's loot to finance their otherwise bankrupt country. Napoleon was forced to sacrifice his plans for conquering the United States and sold the Louisiana Purchase to Thomas Jefferson. The sale freed America from the threat of possible invasion and opened the west up for the fledgling democracy. For Napoleon, it provided large coffers of money which Napoleon spent to prepare a massive invasion fleet of England. His dream of conquering England was set into play.

The Road to Self Coronation

Just over a year after signing a peace treaty with England, Napoleon announced his plans to invade and conquer England. Sir William Cornwallis of England's fleet was alerted to watch for any French ships and sink as many as he found. The war had officially begun anew but Napoleon had not yet even completed his vast fleet and the weather conditions delayed any actual invasion for many months. Napoleon had started a war he was not even ready to fight. Not until the fall would Napoleon's naval fleet even put a dent in the English navy, and it never did conquer England.

In January 1804 Napoleon's most monumental acheivement became law. It was the Civil Code or Napoleonic Code. The code remains largely in effect to this very day with all its flaws and corruptions. Nevertheless, it was an outstanding acheivement for a country which had been in anarchy for over a decade. It established true law and order for the first time in France and provided a comprehensive, if flawed, code of law that courts could follow.

The Code itself was a mixture of good and bad. On the one hand it promoted morality by curtailing the laws which had formerly favored the ease of divorce. On the other hand Napoleon gave fathers the right to imprison their children for up to a month. Another section of the Code was very lax on homosexual conduct which was now basically legal. In regard to slavery the Code was again inconsistent. Although slavery had officially been outlawed by the Jacobins, the code provided that, as Christopher Herold put it, "all blacks not specifically declared free were subject to the Black Code as it existed in 1789 – that is, they were slaves."[7] Slavery was thus legalized again. Not until Napoleon's successor, Louis XVIII, would slavery finally be abolished once and for all from France.

The Napoleonic Code also provided for the establishment of public schools, but those schools were, in fact, to be schools of propaganda. Students were literally made to march into class to a drum beat. Discipline and propaganda were the order of the day. Adolph Hitler's later youth camps are believed to have been inspired by these Napoleonic schools. Of course, the textbooks used were those commissioned by the government and censored by Napoleon. As one historian remarked, "Napoleon alone knew what was acceptable."[8] The press and publishers were under the thumb of the Consul and if anyone said anything he did not like, they could expect to flee the country, never to return. History classes portrayed the French as saints, with narry a bad comment. Napoleon was, of course, portrayed as the glorious successor to Charlemagne. Even plays were regulated by the government. Historical dramas, for example, were banned by Napoleon.

One month after the Napoleonic Code became law, two of France's most famous generals, behind Napoleon, were arrested. Generals Moreau and Pichegru were arrested on charges related to an assassination attempt which had been made against Napoleon years earlier. The secret police had been watching carefully for any and all conspirators and the private words and meetings of Moreau and Pichegru made them suspect in Napoleon's eyes. Most historians believe that neither they, nor the duke who was arrested with them, were guilty, but Napoleon would tollerate no opposition. Pichegru was found strangled to death in his jail cell and the duke was tried and executed in less than two hours. Only Moreau seemed to escape unscathed, in large part because of public outcry both from abroad and from within France. The publicity did Napoleon little good, so Moreau, the hero of the war with Austria, was sentenced to several years in prison and thereafter banished to the United States.

Soon even Napoleon's family members were speaking out against him. On April 4, 1804, Lucien was exiled to Italy for life. No one could criticize Napoleon and expect to go unpunished.

One month after banishing his brother, a Tribune, on orders from Napoleon, proposed making Napoleon Emperor. The vote was carried by the Tribunate and the Senate (whose members were hand picked by Napoleon) and on May 18 a public vote on the proposal resulted "officially" in a 99.99% favorable decree. Only 2,569 of the seven million or eight million votes cast were against the proposal. Of course, about half of votes seemed to have dissappeared, leaving the official vote at 3,572,329 votes for and 2,569 votes against. Even without Lucien, it was easy enough to fix elections.

Even from the beginning Napoleon's France had revived the ancient Roman titles. Counsul and tribunes had not been seen in France for centuries. Now the French would reclaim the title that they believed Otto the Great had stolen from them eight hundred years before. There was only one thing that Napoleon needed. Before the Reformation the papacy had crowned, or least recognized, every emperor since Charlemagne. No one could claim to have been emperor without the blessings of the Church. Napoleon did not believe that he *needed* the pope's blessings, but he did know that he needed the recognition that would come with it. Although he had no love for the pope or the Catholic Church, he feigned love for the Church and began long negotiations with Pope Pius VII to officiate over the coronation. The curia opposed the measure and Pius resisted for many months. The coronation was set for December but the pope still had not given his consent when September arrived.

Napoleon tried a mixture of threats and empty promises. The problem for the papacy was that it could not hope to regain its long lost power unless Europe itself were restored under a strong emperor. Had they believed in Napoleon's sincerity as a Catholic, the pope might have leaped at the change of installing a rival to Francis II, but everyone knew what sort of man Napoleon was. On the other hand, he had restored the Catholic Church to the Vendees and even to France, albeit under his authority. Pius threw his lot with Napoleon. By the end of September he had agreed to officiate the coronation, unaware that Napoleon would not allow the pope to place the crown on his head, but would actually coronate himself! It was the last gambit for the papacy, and for the Holy Roman Empire itself.

The Coronation

The Coronation was fashioned after the ancient Roman coronations. Jacques–Louis David was commissioned to do paintings of the ceremony and designed some of the ornaments and costumes. Ancient Roman banners and the golden eagles were displayed throughout Paris. Napoleon also wore the ancient garland of laurel. No expense was spared to make the ceremony as grand as had ever existed, even since the time of antiquity. It is estimated that the coronation ceremony cost the French people 8,500,000 francs, roughly equivalent to fifty million dollars today.

Jacques–Louis David – The Coronation of Napoleon I – 1806

The pope, whose long and arduous journey across the Alps had been tiresome to say the least, was greeted with a mixture of honor and contempt. Some jeered and mocked the pope. One pair, upon seeing the pope riding his traditional donkey, called out, "is that the pope's ass?" to which the other replied, "Yes, that is what you must kiss!" On the other hand, Napoleon gave the pope the gift of a gold tiara which was adorned with 4000 diamonds, rubies, and emeralds. The gift, however, merely compensated for a shock which Napoleon's men now delivered to the aged pope. He *would not* crown the emperor. Napoleon would coronate himself and his wife. The gesture was utilized once before by the last Catholic king of Jerusalem, Guy. Ironically, it would now be employed by the last emperor. The symbolic value was that Napoleon was claiming to be emperor by his own authority, and not the church's. The pope could scarcely turn and around and go home, especially since he found himself surrounded by Napoleon's supporters. He instead responded by objecting that Napoleon and Josephine had not been legally married in the eyes of the church. It was, therefore, agreed that Napoleon and Josephine were to be married by the pope himself just days before the ceremony.

On December 2, 1804 the coronation ceremony began. The pope administered triple unction on the emperor and empress. Napoleon then turned his back to the pope, before an astonished audience, and lifted Charlemagne's crown which he placed on his own head. He then crowned his wife, Josephine as empress. Next, the pope handed the emperor the consecrated imperial signet ring declaring that the ring signifies "the strength and solidity of the empire." The emperor was said to be approved by none other than "Jesus the Christ, the King of Kings and Lord of Lords." The pope then turned to the crowd and shouted, "long live the eternal emperor!"

As Napoleon left the altar crowds cheered the "most august emperor Napoleon" and hundreds of church bells rang out alongside cannon blasts and fireworks. Such a grand ceremony had never been seen before in Paris and probably never will again. Napoleon had become the last emperor.

Jean Ingres – Napoleon I on His Imperial Throne – 1806

31

The Last Emperor

Some say that the Holy Roman Empire ended with a whimper rather than a bang, but no one denies that it ended with Napoleon. The question is whether Napoleon destroyed the empire from without or from within.

Some believe that Francis II was the last emperor and either treat Napoleon as a usurper or claim that his empire was an entirely different empire from that of the Holy Roman Empire. Others grant that Napoleon was the last emperor, as he claimed. In either case, they are the same, for whether Francis II or Napolon was the last emperor, it was with Napoleon that the empire fell. No emperor has ever claim that throne since. Nevertheless, this begs the questions, that must now be answered.

Was Napoleon the Last Emperor?

The arguments for and against Napoleon as the last emperor should be examined briefly before the history of his fall is recorded. That he was truly the last emperor has become a minority view in recent years, and perhaps it has been a minority view even since Napoleon's day, but it is clearly the correct view, for Francis himself was forced to abdicate in his favor, as shall be discussed forthwith.

In order to become emperor of the Holy Roman Empire there are four traditional requirements, all of which have rarely been met even by the greatest of emperors. First, he must be approved by the papacy as per the charter of the Holy Roman Empire. Second, he must be elected by the Electors. Third, he must be acknowledged by the kings of Europe. Forth, he must be able to excercise that power. Of these four, Francis had only one sure claim; that he was elected by the Electors. Two others, acknowledgement by kings and the excercising of his authority, were suspect, even from the beginning. Francis had never been officially approved by the papacy. Napoleon, on the other hand, had all but the Electors approval and that, as will be discussed later, could easily have been his as well.

That Napoleon claimed to be the successor of Charlemagne, and not the founded of some new empire, is attested by himself. He openly called himself the successor of both Charlemagne and Augustus Caesar. The ceremony itself was fashioned after the ancient Roman coronations and the crown he bestowed on himself was that of Charlemagne. The French, not Germans, so said Napoleon, were the true successors of Charlemagne. This sentiment, echoed back to the time of Otto the Great, was never forgotten. Napoleon was simply reclaiming the crown that the French had always believed rightly belonged to them.

Second, if Napoleon's empire was not that of Charlemagne's then one is bewildered at his attitude toward the titles of "emperor of Austria" or "emperor of Prussia." Not only did he never object to those titles, but he had actually urged the king of Prussia to adopt the title. It was not "emperor of Austria" or "emperor of Prussia" which bothered him, but "emperor of the Romans." *That* was the title that Napoleon demanded Francis drop. *That* was the title which Napoleon could not allow Francis to hold, because *that* was the title which Napoleon was claiming for himself. For a year and a half Napoleon sought to break Austria's power. For a year and a half Napoleon sought to win the German Electors to his side, by conquest if necessary. The "emperor of the Romans" was the title Napoleon wanted.

Third, whether Napoleon was a usurper or not, he became universal emperor when Francis abdicated his title. Francis' feeble attempt to "retire" the empire and the title was an attempt to save face for himself and for the German people and is one reason that Napoleon is often not treated as the last emperor, but it was a matter of semantics. The empire was transferred to Napoleon. Francis could not dissolve what was not his to dissolve. More importantly, the Electors, although never electing Napoleon, had signed a treaty with him, accepting him as their "protector" and emperor. Francis could not dissolve the empire, for the empire was far more than Francis II.

Forth, the pope was by charter co–ruler with the emperor and Pius VII had cast his lot with Napoleon. The emperor and pope together comprise the leadership of the Holy Roman Empire, which was centuries synonymous with the Holy Roman Church. The support of the papacy was not a question of religion for Napoleon, who recognized no god but himself, but rather by gaining the support of the papacy, Napoleon was claiming the legal right to Charlemagne's throne; something that Francis II had never obtained.

Fifth, the German Electors threw their support to Napoleon. While it is true that they never elected Napoleon, this was by *his* choice. He had at one time considered forcing his election by the Electors, but feared that such a vote would minimize his self coronation, implying that the will of the Electors was dominant over his own. Therefore, he decided to crush Francis' authority by making himself master of the Electors who accepted him, without vote, as their emperor. The Electors were then forced to submit by Napoleon's will, not by their own. Nevertheless, they did submit.

Finally, Napoleon exercised the authority of an emperor. He was, in fact, the first emperor to exercise any *real* authority since Charles V, who himself was challenged in many areas. In terms of absolute authority Napoleon wielded more than any emperor since antiquity. Only Charlemagne and Otto the Great wield close as much power as Napoleon who had made himself master of both Europe and the French Church.

Objections to Napoleon's rightful claim to the throne usually follow standard arguments; most of which were created by German historians, eager to deny the French any claim to "their" empire. It is noted that Napoleon referred to the empire more often than not, the "Empire of the French." Nonetheless, "he called himself 'Emperor of the French,' not 'of France'"[9] There is a difference. Napoleon marked "a distinction between 'la France' and 'l'Empire francais'"[10] because the empire was not intended to refer to an empire restricted to France but to the dominance of the French over the empire. This stemmed from the ancient argument between the heirs of Otto the Great and the lingering heirs of the Carolingian Dynasty. The French never did openly accept the Germanic emperors and sought for hundreds of years to "reclaim" the title for a Frenchman. Philip the Fair came to dominate the papacy in hopes of creating a counter–balance to the Germanic emperors, or more accurately the dominance of the German electors (since the emperors still came from across the empire). Now Napoleon was claiming the empire for the French. That empire being Charlemagne's.

Finally, critics claim that Francis disolved the empire by Napoleon's own will. This is, however, a semantic argument. As will be discussed in the ensuing pages, Napoleon debated whether to have himself elected emperor or whether or not to merely break Francis' authority and dissolve *his* "empire." In other words, Napoleon did not want to give the German Electors any say in choosing the emperor since that might take away from Napoleon the right to determine his own heir to the throne or, even worse, risk returning the empire to the Germans some day in the distant future. He therefore resolved to crush the old administration and structure of the empire as it had existed in Germany. Francis claimed that he was retiring the crown, but he knew full well, that his abdication was an admission that Napoleon was the new emperor. Usurper or not, Napoleon won the throne of Charlemagne and no one dared to deny publicly. Napoleon Bonaparte was the last emperor.

War Renewed

No sooner had peace come to Europe than Napoelon was beginning plans for war anew. He had already began construction of a vast fleet for the invasion of Britain but announced his plans too soon. The weather and other factors prevented his launching the fleet at the planned time and alerted the British Navy to the French threat. Admiral Nelson patrolled the Mediterrean while Admiral Cornwallis patrolled the English Channel. Time and time again, weather, circumstances, or the English Navy put a halt to Napoleon's plans. No fewer than nine different invasion plans were present by Napoleon over the next two years; one included an attempt to draw the English Navy away from the channel by attacking their American interest. In that case, the plans were intercepted by English ships. Napoleon became furious with his Admirals, blaming them for his problems.

In January 1805 it looked as if things were finally going Napoleon's way. The British had attacked and destroyed several Spanish ships and after prodding from Napoleon, the Spanish signed an alliance against Britain on the fourth of January. The alliance, however, did precious little good. Britain was the dominant power of the seas and Napoleon's own impatience and his unwillingness to listen to his naval commanders, not to mention providence, ultimately led to the failure of the entire expedition. In one instance Napoleon, against the advice of his Admiral, ordered the launch of his fleet during turbulent weather conditions. The result was hundreds of French soldiers dead and dozens of ships lost.

Frustrated and tired of the naval misadventures, Napoleon turned to his greater plans for Europe. Even while the plans for the invasion of England were still ongoing, Napoleon marched into Italy and was crowned the King of Italy. All the northern kingdoms of Italy became united into the Kingdom of Italy, under Napoleon. It was the first step toward the reunification of Italy, which had been divided since the invasion of the Lombards during the times of ancient Rome. It was also a wake up call to the rest of Europe. Russia almost immediately signed a treaty with Britain beginning the Third Coalition in April, 1805. Months later, August, Sweden and Austria joined that coalition.

By that time the invasion fleet which had been destined for England had dwindled from 2350 vessels to a mere 675 seaworthy vessels. Two months later, Napoleon's dreams of invading England were dashed. On October 21 Admiral Nelson met the combined fleets of the French and Spanish at the Battle of Trafalgar. There, on the southern tip of Spain, the English dealt a crushing blow to the French and Spanish. Over 5500 French and Spanish sailors were among the casualties. The Franco–Spanish fleet was finished. The cost to the English was aproximately 1700 casualties, including the great Lord Admiral Horatio Nelson.

The Subjugation of Germany

Napoleon had been deliberately pushing Austria toward war so that he could tell the French people that he was acting only in self defense, but he was determined to crush his imperial rival who had refused to abdicate his crown even after numerous threats. The French Emperor had, however, underestimated his opponents. All the years of bringing peace to France had been designed to isolate his future targets, but they were now uniting under the Third Coalition. Napoleon knew that his armies would be hopelessly outnumbered. The demands of the Third Coalition were simply and fair. If Napoleon would withdraw all his troops from Holland, Switzerland, Germany, and Italy, there would be peace. Napoleon would either have to sacrifice his plans for conquest or gamble on a swift offensive that would leave France open to invasion.

On September 24 he began the march to the Rhine with virtually every French soldier that could be spared. France itself was left virtually defenseless. Less than 30,000 troops remained behind to defend the whole of France. Had England, or even Italy, prepared even a small invasion force France would have fallen, but Napoleon was counting on surprise. No one would have expected a sane man to leave France so open to attack, but no sane man would have used so many human lives as fodder for his own personal ambitions. Indeed, Napoleon, like Hitler after him and Caesar before him, was subject to what some historians call "epileptic" fits. Uncontrollable fits of rage would consume him, sometimes resulting in uncontrollable convulsions in which he would vomit, gag, and froth at the mouth like a mad dog. This was one of the times. Before invading the Rhine his generals had, for the first time, seen one of these fits that they had heard about.

Napoleon's plans worked perfectly. The Germans never expected such a swift and massive offensive from Napoleon. Within a month several German princes had already surrendered and signed treaties with Napoleon. The Duke of Baden was the first, followed by the Elector of Wurttemberg and the Elector of Bavaria. In the south Napoleon's generals had even taken the captial of Austria; Vienna, but this was done at a terrible price. October 17, 1805, saw Vienna fall to France, but the general in question had failed to pursue the fleeing armies of Austria which united with Russian troops and returned to threaten the capital. Napoleon was furious. Matters worsened when Russia signed the Treaty of Potsdam on November 3 with Prussia who now threatened to enter into the war.

The capture of Vienna was a hollow victory and the city was abandoned as Napoleon and his army retreated back to Austerlitz where the terrain allowed Napoleon to make a defensive stand against the vastly superior armies of Austria and Russia. There, at Austerlitz, Napoleon won his greatest military victory. On December 2, 1805, the "Battle of the Three Emperors" (Napoleon, Francis II, and Czar Alexander) resulted in the defeat of the Austrian allies. As Napoleon had ordered no prisoners to be taken alive thousands of soldiers were massacred in their retreat. Now all Germany seemed to have been subjugated to Napoleon. Less than a month later Francis II was forced to signed the Treaty of Pressburg, which had been called the most severe treaty ever imposed on a subjugated country. It gave to Napoleon everything he demanded and allowed for the reoganization of Germany which would take place over the next seven months. It also required Francis II to pay 40,000,000 francs to the French emperor.

Over the next few months Napoleon consolidated his victories. After quietly returning the Gregorian Calendar to France, Napoleon forced Spain to sign a new agreement which would pay 6,000,000 francs a year to France. He then appointed his brother Joseph as King of Naples. When Pius objected to the intrusion into Italy, Napoleon sternly warned him, saying, "you are the sovereign of Rome, but *I* am its emperor!"

In regard to Germany Napoleon created the Franco–Prussian treaty of February 15, 1806, but neither he nor Prussia really had any intensions of keeping the treaty. Napoleon's reorganization of Germany was designed to create a rival German power to Prussia's and to break the authority of Francis II.

Napoleon debated with himself about how to go about this and to best gain the indisputed imperial crown. He had considered forcing his own election as "emperor of the Romans" but realized that such an election might do two things. First, it might cast doubt on his previous coronation by implying that the will of the electors was needed. The second problem with this idea was that it would have conferred the right to imperial elections back on the German electors, which Napoleon could not have. He alone would decide his successor and that successor would be a Frenchman, not a German. Napoleon, therefore, decided the best course of action was to create a new German Confederation of States in the Rhine which owed its allegiance to himself.

On July 17, 1806, the Act of the Confederation of the Rhine was signed. Napoleon was declared their protector. On August 1, Napoleon issued a further declaration that the Rhine should no longer recognize their allegiance to Francis. Napoleon was their emperor. Francis was now isolated. He reluctantly abdicated his crown on August 6, 1806, but politically he still tried to deny Napoleon what he had already claimed. In renouncing his crown, Francis declared that he was retiring the crown and dissolving the empire. He declared that the Holy Roman Empire was at an end. In fact, Francis had no authority to dissolve the empire, which he had lost authority over years ago. The Holy Roman Empire was under the domination of Napoleon.

After daring to declare the Holy Roman Empire dissolved Francis named himself "emperor of Austria." The title, an oxymoron, did not bother Napoleon one bit. In fact, Napoleon urged the king of Prussia to adopt the title of emperor as well. The only imperial title which Napoleon wanted was that of the "emperor of the Romans" and that title was now his, and his alone.

Nevertheless, the while the creation of the Confederation of the Rhine forced the abdication of Napoleon's only rival for the imperial crown, his military rival was still Prussia and they objected to the creation of a such a large state south of their borders. The king send a letter to Napoleon demanding that the Confederation be dissolved. Napoleon responded by drafting another 50,000 men (Napoleon had already drafted hundreds of thousands of French citizens, which made him increasingly unpopular) and marching toward Prussia with his army. The result was the same as previous campaigns. On October 14, the Battles of Jena and Auerstadt resulted in the defeat of the Prussian army. Cities were looted, its women raped, and the people subjected to the torments of war, which Napoleon always made as severe as possible. By the end of 1806, all Germany had fallen to Napoleon.

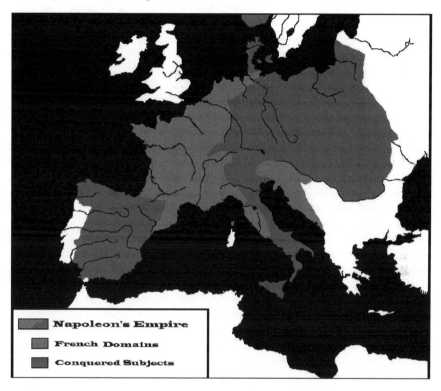

At War with the World

Napoleon could not be content as master of Europe. He quite literally had long term plans for the conquest of the world itself. He had once dreamed of conquering the New World. He had substantive plans to conquer north Africa and the Ottoman Empire. He had long sought to conquer England, which alluded him. He even dreamt of conquering Asia, or at least western Asia and Russia. Since he had failed so miserably at invading England he revenged himself by requiring all countries to blockade Britain and forbade trade with them. He hoped to damage England's economy, although he did far more damage to his allies.

Next on Napoleon's agenda was Poland. In November, 1806, he began his march to Poland, proclaiming himself Poland's deliverer. He reminded them that they had been partitioned by Prussia, Austria, and Russia several times. He hoped to win Poland without a fight. He almost did. In December Warsaw was occupied without a battle. The people of Poland cautiously admitted the French, fearing the consequences. There Napoleon met a beautiful countess whom he had to have. He sent notice to her that if she did not submit to him all Poland would pay the consequences. Her husband had no say in the matter. Russia did.

The Czar Alexander feared that the invasion of Poland was a prelude to the invasion of Russia. Poland might not fight, but Russia would. They assaulted Napoleon's armies in February, 1807, in a terrible battle that claimed casualties of over 40,000 men; most of them French casualties. This war would not be won easily.

In April France signed a new defense pact with Prussia, but Prussia really wanted little part of Napoleon. They were merely playing the field. It was not until June 23 that the French "victory" could be claimed at the Battle of Friedland. 20,000 Russian soldiers died in the battle, but the Czar's greater problem was war with the Ottoman Empire. He did not want to fight a war on two fronts and the south was gearing up for trouble. Over a 150,000 men, both Russian and French, had died in the war and the Czar could not afford more losses if he was to maintain his southern borders. For nearly a month negotiations continued ending with the Treaty of Tilsit on July 9. There Russia and France effectively divided the whole of Europe between them, with Russia maintaining her borders, and France taking the rest. Poland was also forced to pay 26,000,000 francs to the emperor who refused to grant them the independence they requested. He was sickened by their refusal to fight for their freedom, yet he would have crushed them if they had. He simply argued that they were not ready for independence.

The treaty so angered Napoleon's foreign minister, Talleyrand, that he turned in his resignation, declaring "I no longer wish to be the executioner of Europe." As astonishing as it may seem, most historians believe the Talleyrand had been a moderating influence on Napoleon. That became most obvious by Napoleon's course of action after his retirement. Napoleon no longer conquered foreign nations that were of no threat to him, like Poland, but he now began to conquer allies so that he could appoint his own relatives as kings of those countries. In his megalomania, he would go to war with the Papal States, Spain, and Portugal. Soon Austria would rise in rebellion again and a renewed war with Russia would lead to Napoleon's fall. All of this could have been avoided by even the slightest restraint and/or common sense, but Napoleon's ego knew no bounds. He had once openly declared that he wanted to create a "world dictatorship" and nothing was going to stop him.

Napoleon's initial excuse for turning on his allies was their unwillingness to support his embargo of England. Pope Pius VII had English ambassadors in Rome, which continued to trade with Britain (so did Joseph Bonaparte in Naples). Portugal had also continued trade with Britain. In October, 1807, Napoleon sent French armies through Spain, without asking their permission, and quickly took effective control of Portugal. They were ordered to pay 100,000,000 francs to the emperor. Spain, whose country was now occupied by "allied" French armies had no say in the matter.

The emperor also wasted no time warning the pope of the consequences of disobedience. By November he was in Milan, already with plans to conquer the Papal States and to place them under his control. On April 2, French troops entered Rome and siezed the city. Pius remained silent for fear of Napoleon's wrath. A month later the situation in Spain was aggravated when Napoleon named his brother Joseph King of Spain on May 6, 1808.

In less than a month Napoleon's plans began to unravel. Spain was in revolt. French adminstrators were assassinated and Spanish armies were driving French troops into retreat. Worse yet was the appearance of British troops on Portugese soil. The one time allies of Napoleon were now allied with Great Britain. Portugal was lost virtually overnight. The war in Spain would continue for many years to come. In fact, the war would never really be resolved until Napoleon's defeat in Russia. Over a quarter million people would become casualties of a war that need never have happened.

By August Napoleon decided to take personal command of the armies in Spain. He sent an order for another 140,000 men to be drafted into the army, furthering discontent among the French, and entered Spain in October with a force which now totaled over 300,000 men. By contrast Spain had only 200,000 soldiers, many of whom were reserves. However, these numbers did not take into account what then men were fighting for. Spain was fighting for their liberty. Napoleon's men were tired, exhausted from years of war, and maltreated. It is estimated that as many as 20% of the French troops deserted including one of Napoleon's own generals! By January, 1809, Napoleon had lost over 75,000 casualties. Even worse, Napoleon received news of two disturbing events. He was told that Talleyrand and his the head of the French Police were plotting against him. He was further informed that Austria was mustering an army in preparation for the invasion of France.

Portugal was lost. The British were landing troops on Portugese soil. Spain was in rebellion. Napoleon's soldiers had lost all morale. Even his own French officials were beginning to turn against him. Now Napoleon had to leave to protect his borders against the former emperor, Francis II. He quickly returned to Paris where he surprisingly spared Talleyrand and the head of the Police. Apparently, he still needed them since he had no time to find effective replacements for him. In any case, he set off for Austria after drafting an additional 270,000 men!

In February, 1809, Francis II was on the move. Although he proclaimed to his soldiers, "your victories will break Europe's chains!" he had underestimated the power of fear over the populous of Germany. Upon entering Bavaria he had hoped to find thousands of allies willing to support his cause, but it was not to be so. Napoleon's armies were split in two. One proceeded north to confront the Austrian army while Napoleon himself headed the second army to Vienna. The northen army was less than successful. The Austrians escaped and were headed to join up with the armies defending Vienna. On May 10, Napoleon arrived at Vienna and occupied it by the 13th. The retreating army of Vienna burned all the bridges on the Danube so that Napoleon could not pursue them. That gave time for the army of Archduke Karl to join up with them.

Even while the Ausrtia war was continuing, Napoleon had sent orders on May 17, 1809, to have all of the Papal States annexed. A month later, on June 10, 1809, French soldiers took down the papal flag in Rome. Pius, formerly fearful of the emperor, now responded by excommunicating the tyrant. He knew that Napoleon's wars were not going well and hoped that his excommunication would hasten the fall of the man he had helped install, but Napoleon's response was severe. Soldiers invaded the palace and arrested the pontiff. He was taken way to prison where he would remain until Napoleon's defeat.

During this time Napoleon was at work making pontoon bridges so he could cross the Danube and crush Karl's army. On May 21, the first major battle began. It was a victory for the Austrians. The Battle of Aspern–Essling ended with almost 50,000 French casulaties, compared to 23,000 for the Austrians. The French army was forced to retreat back onto a small island in the middle of the Danube. Karl believed the French were trapped. Instead of crushing Napoleon while he had the chance, his army merely waited ... and waited. Napoleon was not idle. Over the next month and a half his army began construction of numerous additional bridges which would allow them to sent their forces across in great numbers.

The Battle of Wagram began on July 5, 1809. Casualties on both sides were high, but Napoleon did not care how many of his own soldiers died. That was his strength in battle. Even though the French lost as many soldiers as the Austrians, and even though the French lost an amazing 1,800 officers, they would not retreat. It was Archduke Karl asked for an armistice. Napoleon had won again.

The actual terms of the treaty were negotiated for many more months. Napoleon may not have pressed the issue sooner because news reports were reaching him that on July 29 an Enlish armada had landed soldiers in the Netherlands to invade France. The expedition failed but put pressure on Napoleon to return to France. In the meantime, he demanded that Francis abdicate his Austrian throne. Francis refused. Finally, on October 13, the Treaty of Schonbrunn was signed. The terms of the treaty took vast land from the Austrians and gave them other princes. Francis was also required to pay 85,000,000 francs as a war indemnity.

The Autumn of Napoleon's Reign

Throughout Napoleon's reign France never knew peace. Despite his conquests, and in fact because of them, war continued. Spain and Britain did not cease the fight. Napoleon, however, felt due for a rest. He left the war in Spain to his generals and returned to France to deal with marital issues.

Laslett John Pott – Napoleon's Farewell To Josephine – 19th

The first item on his agenda was the divorce of his long time wife Josephine. Neither had been faithful to one another and there had been no love in their marriage. More importantly to Napoleon; she had born him no children and he despised the thought of one of his relatives succeeding him to the throne. Since his own laws restricted divorce, Napoleon instead had the marriage annuled on the grounds that the marriage had not been officiated by the church (ignoring that the pope officially married them just before their coronation). On December 15 the annulment was complete.

Next was the decision on who Napoleon's next wife would be. He was not interested in love; just a political union. It was to be an old fashioned marriage alliance. Ealier Napoleon had asked the Czar for the hand of his sister in marriage but the Czar tactfully ignored the letters. By January Napoleon decided on the former emperor Francis II's daughter, Marie Louise. It was politically a perfect union. Francis would not dare against defy France, with his own daughter as empress. Moreover, their offspring would be unchallenged as emperors of the Holy Roman Empire. His son would be the son of Emperor Napoleon and grandson of Emperor Francis II. No one would dare to deny his legitimacy to the imperial throne.

On April 1, appropriately April Fool's Day, they were married. Shortly after his Honeymoon he discovered that the chief of police and Talleyrand, whose lives he had spared earlier, were negotiating a peace settlement with England. Napoleon was furious and again threatened them with execution. Conquest, not peace, was the solution to Great Britain. This same year he officially annexed Holland and Switzerland. Nothing would make Napoleon back down from his plans for world conquest and the very thought of England's defiance made his furious. This obsession would invariably lead to his downfall.

In December the emperor received word that Russia had broken the embargo against England and was engaging in trade. The embargo was hurting Europe more than England, but Napoleon didn't care. No one would trade with his enemies and just as he had invaded Portugal and the Papal States for breaking the embargo he now began plans to invade Russia. To help pay for the troops Napoleon demanded that French taxes again be raised to help support his military endeavors. By the time he left for Russia, Napoleon had more than tripled the taxes that had existed under Louis XVI. Although he had wanted to depart for Russia in May, 1811, his departure would be delayed for a full year due to financial problems and the time required to assemble another large army; especially with war in Spain continuing daily. Nevertheless, by November Napoleon boasted that he had 800,000 soldiers at his disposal. In May, 1812, Napoleon finally departed on his final campaign.

The Master Folly

Napoleon left Paris on May 9, 1812 to invade Russia. He had successfully assembled the largest army in the history of Europe up to that time; over 600,000 soldiers were to accompany him to Russia. Another 275,000 remained behind to portect France and deal with Spain, Portugal, and England. Russia, by comparison had a vast army of 400,000, which would have sent shivers up anyone else's spine; but Napoleon outnumbered them by 200,000. Of course, half of his soldiers were foreigners from conquered nations, whose loyalty to Napoleon was solely based on fear.

Since Napoleon had been preparing for war for over a year, Czar Alexander had time to made a treaty with the Turks and rally his forces to prepare for the defense of Russia. As Napoleon marched through Prussia and Poland, he left them with defensive treaties, promising to protect Napoleon's rear, but little could he realize in his megalomania, that they were secretly hoping for Russia's victory.

As the emperor progressed into Lithuania the soldiers were surprised to see deserted cities. Towns and cities were evacuated and most of their supplies taken. Napoleon's generals saw almost immediately what the Czar Alexander's plan was. It was a long road to Moscow. Over 700 miles lay between Warsaw and Moscow and Napoleon had an army of 600,000 mouths to feed. Nonetheless, the emperor was too arrogant to care about the lives of his men. He ignored the advise of his generals and proceeded to drag his cannons and artillery through the rainy season and along 700 miles of land.

On June 24, Napoleon's army crossed the Niemens river against the advise of his generals. Their supply lines to France were being cut off by the vastness of space, and by small Russian forces left to watch the border. Since there were not enough cultivated fields or crops to feed such a vast army, Napoleon's soldiers began to starve. As many as 20% began to desert. Soon disease began to rip through the army. It was not until July 28 that Napoleon reached Vitebsk, about 300 miles west of Moscow. Once again, it was deserted.

Napoleon dispatched messages to Czar Alexander. He was willing to negotiate a treaty. The Czar ignored the emperor. Napoleon was becoming furious. He wanted war. He wanted a great battle. He was getting neither, nor would Alexander negotiate. Perhaps the real reason Napoleon began to fly into rages was that he did not know what to expect. He must have suspected that he was being suckered in to Moscow, but his ego would never allow him to admit it. Nor would he accept the idea of a strategic retreat. That would tantamount to admitting failure, and Napoleon *never* failed! So he thought.

It was another couple of weeks, in mid August, when the army reached Smolensk, still 250 miles from Moscow. There, south of Smolensk, Napoleon was to be satisfied with his first battle. Although both sides suffered equal losses, it was Russia who made the strategic defeat. Napoleon, as usual, did not care how many of his soldiers died, so long as he got the victory. The negative effects, however, were obvious. In addition to the over 100,000 deaths and desertions since entering Russia, Napoleon now had to deal with the additional casulaties. He also received disturbing news from Spain. General Wellington of England had dealt a severe blow to French interest in Spain. Napoleon knew that if he did not return soon, his "victory" in Russia would be negated by the loss of Spain and the occupation of British troops just south of the French border. He was determined to press onward to Moscow as soon as possible.

As the troops continued their long march the health of the troops worsened, as did that of Napoleon himself. He developed a gastic ulcer, which led to his constant holding of his side, made famous by several paintins of Napoleon with his hand inside his vest.

Finally, in early September, the army had reached Borodino, just south of Moscow. On September 7 Napoleon fought what he thought would be a decisive battle. Over fifty thousand casulaties were claimed by each side respectively before the Russians made another strategic retreat. As was the case earlier, Napoleon would claim the victory at the Battle of Borodino, but in fact he was again put in far worse shape than his Russian opponents. Although each side had 50,000 casualties, the entire nursing corp had deserted long ago. There were only forty–five doctors available to treat the thousands of wounded soldiers. Add to this the health problems and disease of Napoleon's army and it was hardly an effecient fighting force.

Vasily Vereshchagin – Napoleon I on the Borodino – 1897

On September 15 Napoleon made his "triumphant" entry into Moscow, but it was more than a hollow victory. It was an eerie experience. The great vast city of Moscow was deserted. The streets were barren, and even the Czar's palace was vacant. Moscow was a ghost city. Or was it?

Unknown to the Napoleon, several soldiers remained hidden. A Russian general encouraged his troops by burning down his own mansion. The soldiers were then sent out to set fires throughout the city. The water pumps had been sabotaged. Moscow was caught aflame. Napoleon, at 4:30 in the morning, was forced to retreat from Moscow, just hours after his triumphant entry. Not until September 18 was Moscow safe to reenter.

Napoleon's army was now reduced to less than half its initial size. Only about 250,000 soldiers, of the original 600,000 remained, yet he had only fought two battles! The emperor again sent messages to the the Czar promising a favorable peace, but Alexander continued to ignore him. Had they wanted to negotiate peace, they would not have burned Moscow. Alexander wanted one thing : the destruction of Napoleon and his army.

Napoleon decided to wait out the cold Russian winter in the safety of Moscow, but his generals continued to pressure him to return to France. Napoleon began to blame them for his troubles and constantly ranted. He declared he would never retreat. Whatever changed his mind appeared to coincide with a failed coup in Paris.

In late October the former general Malet attempted to seize the government of France. He prepared forged documents declaring that Napoleon had died and that he was the successor. Interestingly enough, the people of Paris did not seem to care. One dictator was as good as another, but when Malet began to arrest Napoleon's cabinet members he was challenged and the feeble coup attempt was thrwarted.

On October 19 Napoleon left Moscow for France. He had left orders that the Kremlim be blown up, but the soldiers did not carry out the orders. They may have known that they would never see Paris again, and hoped for mercy from Russia. In any case, Napoleon's troops made a hasty retreat across the vast 700 miles of land that lay between Poland and Russia. All the way they were harassed and hit by Russian soldiers. The emperor's revenge was to rape and ravage every city or town they encounted. The revenge of the land was the death of over 60,000 men in less than a month. Not until January, 1813, did Napoleon again cross the Niemen river. All that was left of Napoleon's massive army, the largest ever assembled up to that time, was 43,000 men.

The Fall of Napoleon

The failure of Napoleon's Russian campaign was a signal to the oppressed victims of his empire. Judgment day was coming for the last emperor of the Holy Roman Empire. Prussia was the leader of the newest rebellion, but Napoleon was oblivious to their preparations. He knew that Prussia was assembling an army, but believed that it was for defense against Russia. He was not aware that Prussia and Russia were already in negotiations for an alliance against France. Everything seemed as if Russia was preparing to invade Prussia. Thus Napoleon, upon his return to France, resumed his quest to establish his son as heir to the throne.

On January 24, 1813, the imprisoned Pope Pius VII was forced to sign a Concordat in which he would coronate the new Empress Marie Louise, Francis II's daughter, and his son. In exchange the pope would be transferred to a Chateau in Avignon where he would be kept under house arrest, rather than in the dreary prison where he now resided. The tide of events, however, would soon make the pope again change his mind. Nevertheless, all seemed well with the dictator.

One month later the Treaty of Kalisch was presented to Czar Alexander by Friedrich Wilhelm of Prussia. It was the beginning of a new Grand Alliance against France. Russia had captured Warsaw in February. The French were forced to flee Berlin on March 4 and Hamburg on the twelfth. On March 13, Prussia officially declared war on France. On March 17 the Russo–Prussian Alliance summoned all Germany to rise up against the emperor and King Friedrich Wilhelm created the Iron Cross to be awarded to those who fought in the war. Things were rapidly changing for Napoleon. The pope too saw that fortunes were changing and on March 24, the pope reversed his position on the former Concordat and refused to coronate either Marie Louise or Napoleon's son.

Once again Napoleon ordered more men to be drafted but by now there was a backlash. As many as 40,000 draft dodgers had formed gangs and were terrorizing recruiters and government officials. It seemed that everyone was tired of their sons being drafted into Napoleon's senseless wars, never to be seen again. Nevertheless, in April the emperor entered Saxony with a substantial army in an attempt to reclaim and protect Dresden, Erfurt, and Leipzig. On May 1, he was taken by surprise as the Russians unexpectantly hit the army at the Battle of Lutzen. Despite these setbacks, Napoleon was still a master general and the Russians and Prussians both excercised extreme caution, prefering strategic retreats to defeats. As a result, Napoleon occupied Dresden on May 8 and Leipzig soon followed.

On June 2 a ceasefire was agreed upon and the Armistice of Pleiswitz was signed on June 4, which arranged for a temporary truce. Napoleon needed time to nurse his wounds, while the Russo–Prussian Alliance sought to use the time to strengthen their allies. They succeeded when, on June 15, Great Britain joined the alliance despite being bogged down in a losing war with the United States (the War of 1812). Less than a month later, on July 8, the British signed the Treaty of Trachtenberg which promised large subsidies to help Russian and Prussia pay for the war. The Alliance was demanding that France withdraw to the borders it had formerly held before the emperor's conquests. When Napoleon received word of this and of the Treaty of Trachtenberg he became enraged. He declared "I will sacrifice a million men if necessary!" Indeed, more than million of his own Frenchmen had already died in his petty wars. He did not care if another million died. On August 10, the war was renewed.

On September 19, when it appeared obvious that Napoleon would fail, Austria joined the Grand Alliance against Napoleon. Sweden had also joined in against the emperor. Every day it seemed as if the Grand Alliance was getting new recruits while Napoleon was loosing his. He was finally forced to withdraw most of the troops to unite with those of Leipzig. There, beginning on October 16, the Battle of Leipzig, also called the Battle of the Nations, began. Leipzig was completely surrounded by the Allies and the battle could not be won by the French. Finally, on October 18, Napoleon decided to retreat, but the city was surrounded. They would literally have to fight their way out of Leipzig. On the nineteenth most of the French were able to fight through the lines to make good their escape, but some were lost when some of Napoleon's men prematurely destroyed the bridge upon which they were crossing. Hundreds of their own soldiers were killed and many others left behind were forced to surrender. Nearly 75,000 French died in the Battle of the Nations. All Germany was lost. Only France remained.

It was now obvious that Napoleon's empire was finished, and so was he. Nonetheless, Napoleon declared "if worse comes to worse we will bury ourselves under the ruins [of Paris]." If Napoleon was to fall, he would take Paris with him. He attempted to draft 300,000 more men, making over a million draftees in a single year, but the people were no longer heeding his call. Mobs and rioters inhibited further drafts. Finally, on December 28, Napoleon's own hand–picked Senate voted to demand peace. The emperor, enraged, outlawed the assembly. People began to flee Paris.

In January Denmark and Naples defected to the Grand Alliance. Napoleon was alone. He had already left Paris himself but left orders to defend Paris at all cost. "I have decided to win or perish." He was becoming unhinged. He even threatened to have anyone who petitioned him for peace tried for mutiny. On March 25, the Allies began their attack on Paris which surrended without a real fight. Napoleon was now loosing his faculties. One day he would threatened to march on Paris with his meager army and crush the alliance. The next he would quietly agree to abdicate. Then the following day he would again change his mind. When his own army refused to fight Napoleon declared, "the imbeciles simply cannot see that the health and safety of France depends on me alone." He said, "France cannot get along without me."

On April 11, Napoleon signed his abdication papers. He was to be exiled to Elba and made sovereign of that tiny island. King Louis XVIII was then brought to Paris where a constitutional monarchy was established. The Holy Roman Empire had fallen. Francis II did not reclaim the crown, for the Prussians had not fought simply to replace one emperor with another. No emperor would ever again claim to rule over the whole of Europe. No one has yet replaced Napoleon, but if Napoleon was to be the last emperor then he would make his exit as grand as possible. Napoleon was not yet finished.

Jean–Louis–Ernest Meissonier – Napoleon I in 1814 – 1862

The Hundred Days

Before he was sent into exile on Elba, Napoleon had attempted to kill himself rather than loose his empire. He had swallowed a vial of poison, but the vial was years old and the poison had lost its potency. The wiser of the Allies regretted that his suicide attempt failed and warned the victors that Napoleon should not be treated leniently. Nevertheless, Napoleon arrived at Elba on May 4. There he consoled himself with his sister, who most believe was also his lover. There he plotted his escape.

Several factors made Napoleon's escape possible; even probable. First, although Napoleon's letters were examined for secret messages, several of Napoleon's friends were allowed to come and go from Elba. There was nothing to prevent them from carrying messages to Europe. Second, two decades of anti–royalists sentiment and power left France with no royalists capable of administrating the country or governing the armies. Nor could Louis XVIII draft new soldiers for Napoleon had conscripted millions of Frenchmen during his reign and Louis would not dare conscript new recruits. He had to make do with those who had formerly served the emperor. In other words, Louis XVIII was surrounded by men loyal to Bonaparte. The allies would soon come to regret their leniency.

On February 26, 1815, seven ships sailed for Elba under the command of some of Napoleon's former generals. Napoleon was rescued from his island prison and landed on the shore of France less than one year after loosing his empire. He declared "I have come with six hundred men to attack the King of France and his six hundred thousand soliders. I shall conquer this kingdom!"

On March 1 he began to march up to Paris, ignoring all fortified cities en route. Obviously, the king heard the news almost immediately and sent out troops to intercept them, but those soldiers, when confronted with their former commander either let him pass unobstructed or defected to his cause. Within a week Napoleon's six hundred men grew to eight thousand and within another week, after passing peaceably through Lyons, Bonaparte had twenty thousand men. On March 20 he entered Paris unopposed.

Already news had reached all Europe of Napoleon's return. The Grand Alliance rallied quickly together and at the Treat of Vienna on March 25, agreed to spare no expense in defeating, permanently, the emperor. Additionally, the people of France were in a state of rebellion. Napoleon's administrators and soldiers might follow him to hell, but the people resisted. The Vendees, once again, rose up and allowed the British to land freely on the western borders of France. Napoleon seemed largely unconcerned. Perhaps, like Satan, his wrath was great because he knew his time was short (c.f. Revelation 12:12).

Nonetheless, Bonaparte immediately took to restoring the old Napoleonic Code in many forms. Almost exactly one year after Louis XVIII had again abolished slavery, Napoleon again legalized it. He also issued warrants for the arrest of those "traitors," like Talleyrand, who had not returned to his side. Of course, in order to show the "support" of the French people, another "election" was held in which Napoleon won a 99.99% favorable victory. This even while uprisings and rebellions were beginning to crop up across the country.

With the Allies moving in Napoleon's most urgent need was to create another grand army. This was nearly impossible given the state of virtual rebellion in many parts of France but mid–June he had assembled an army of some 300,000, including soldiers who were already quelling the civil strife in the country. Bonaparte had roughly over 175,000 soldiers with which to take on the 700,000 allied armies which were even then converging on France. However, those armies were currently all divided. The Prussians, Russians, British, and other armies were coming from different directions. If Napoleon could take them on one at a time, he believed he might have a change. General Wellington of England had just under 100,000 men, giving Napoleon a strong advantage. He, therefore, moved his troops up north to meet Wellington and to crush him before he could united with the Prussians. He left Paris with his army on June 12.

Wellington knew that time was on his side and after a brief encounter, made a strategic retreat toward Waterloo. Napoleon was then bogged down attempting to cut off 40,000 Prussians who were coming to merge with Wellington's forces. Then, on June 16, the Battle of Waterloo began. For three days the battle raged but Napoleon's combined forces, although outnumbering Wellington, could not prevail. Two days after the battle, Napoleon left his army and fled. Over 80,000 soldiers lay dead or dying on the battlefield. Bonaparte's last battle ended in tragic defeat. He was now fleeing to Laon.

The Allies informed France that "it is against Napoleon alone that Europe has declared war" and demanded that he be turned over to them. On June 22, 1815 Napoleon abdicated his throne to his son, Emperor Napoleon II. Of course, his son never took the throne. Louis XVIII returned to power and Napoleon Bonaparte was again exiled under heavy English guard at St. Helena.

After his defeat Napoleon openly admitted that "I wanted to rule the world." He said, "I could not attain this goal except by means of *world* dictatorship. I tried it. Can it be held against me?" The man who had dared to compare himself to Christ on several occasions was finally defeated for all time. On May 5, 1821, Napoleon Bonaparte died. The official reports declared that he had died of cancer, but recent scientific studies prove that Napoleon was, in fact, poisoned. The usual suspect was Napoleon's closest friend and ally during his imprisonment. The man who had betrayed all Europe was betrayed by his most trusted friend. The last emperor had fallen.

32

After the Fall

The fall of the Holy Roman Empire left a vacuum from which Europe is still trying to recover. What was once a single empire was now dozens of individual states. Germany had been divided into more than a dozen tiny countries, Italy was also divided into different states, France was still teetering on the brink, and other countries like Spain, Hungary, Poland, Denmark, the Netherlands, Bohemia, Switzerland, and others would remain prey to aggressive neighbors.

Over the next hundred and fifty years successive attempts to restore the Roman Empire would result in a half dozen dictatorships and wars. From Napoleon III to Bismark to Kaiser Wilhelm to Adolf Hitler, Europe still dreamed of restoring the ancient glory of Rome. It still tries to this very day. It is little wonder than the ancient theologians and philosophers prophesied, from the Bible, that "when Rome falls, so shall the world."

Europe's Vacuum

The fall of Napoleon led to the reorganization of Europe. The congress of Vienna met to decide her ultimate fate. Louis XVIII returned once again to France but her boundaries were reduced back to the pre–Revolutionary war days. All the territories she had acquired since 1789 were lost while Italy and Germany were further divided.

In Italy the former emperor Francis II took possession of Lombardy and Ventia, which lost its ancient Republic, for the Hapsburgs. These became a part of Austria. Tuscany and Piedmont became virtually independant. Parma was given to Napoleon's second wife, and Francis II's daughter, Maire–Louise. The Papal States were returned to the pope. Naples and Sicily remained united under a single king.

In Germany the situation became even more confusing. The Confederation of the Rhine was dissolved and replaced with the German Confederation. In essence Germany was divided into dozens of tiny kingdoms ranging from Hanover to Bavaria to Hungary. Prussia and Austria remained the dominant powers of Germany and Prussia remained at the head of the Confederation in the north while Austria's interest seemed to focus more in Italy and the southern regions of Germany.

Such divisions granted independence to the many peoples of Europe but utterly destroyed the unity that Europe once held. Moreover, it did not resolve the major issue of the day; that of democracy versus monarchy. The

"American experiment" was *still* considered just that; an experiment. Constitutional Monarchies were becoming common, as they gave a voice to the people, but the French Revolution had left a bad taste in Europe's mouth. Napoleon's banana Republics also did nothing to promote democracy on the continent. The result was a lingering disatisfaction which was aggravated by the poor economic conditions which followed the decades of European war under Napoleon.

A rebellion had been fostering for some time. It seemed to have begun in Italy, although it would spread across the whole of Europe in little time. Under the pope the Papal States began to centralize government, attempting to restore the power of the pope over the whole of the estates. Murat, a former general under Napoleon, siezed power in Naples and established a powerful monarchy there. The Venetians, who had held a Republic of sorts even throughout much of the Middle Ages, now found themselves under Austrian control. Revolutionaries began to crop up in Italy, and spread to France where the Charbonnerie (and Italian name) formed a secret society whose aim was to overthrow the monarchy. In 1820 an assassin even attempted to kill Louis XVIII. Under his successor, Charles X, the monarchy reacted strongly against the radicals and began to argue once again for the divine right of kings. Soon a French party, the Orleanists, began to support the Duke of Orleans, Louis–Phillippe, over Charles X. They were openly calling for the establishment of a more progressive constitutional monarchy with Charles deposed.

In July 1830, the dam broke. Charles had attempted to nullify elections which did not favor him and the massive protests soon turned to rebellion. Louis–Phillippe won the support of the aged veteran hero Lafayette and became the "citizen king." However, the results of the rebellion were not local. In Germany demands for a more representative government arose, along with an increasing desire for unification. In Italy revolutions followed. "Young Italy" was a movement which had been founded by Giuseppe Mazzini. Its purpose was to found a unified Republic in Italy through insurrection. By this time it had 60,000 members. The revolts, however, were unsuccessful and Mazzini was forced to flee to England for many years.

The monarchs of Europe reacted strongly against the rebels. Even Louis–Phillippe soon fell out of favor with the French people and in 1848 another European revolutionary movement began. This one would end with similar results. As the French Revolution had ended in the dictatorship of Napoleon, so also this revolution ended with the rise of Napoleon III and his feeble dream of restoring the empire.

Napoleon III

Louis–Napoleon was the cousin of Napoleon Bonaparte. He had spent many years in exile, along with the rest of Napoleon's family. The death of

Napoleon's son, who had born the title Napoleon II for a few days, left Louis–Napoleon as the professed heir to Bonaparte. When a new revolution, in February 1848, overthrew Louis–Phillippe, Louis–Napoleon was able to secure for himself the Presidency of the "Second Republic" (in fact, France had undergone no fewer than five constitutions and two or three "republics" since the French Revolution).

In Italy the revolution of 1848 signaled revolt through the Italian provinces. The Italian Kings were forced to recon with the uprisings. Piedmont and Milan bowed to the wishes of the people and created more democratic constitutional monarchies, and Charles Albert of Milan soon came to believe that the revolutionary Republicans were the key to unifying Italy and casting off Austrian rule. Soon he openly declared war on Austria. Venice, Milan, Piedmont, and Lombardy rose up against the Austrians.

Germany had to deal with the revolutionary movement, not only because of its effects on Austria, but because of the sentiment in Germany. In May a Frankfurt National Assembly met to discuss the reunification of Germany and the establishment of a new constitution. There was, however, no final agreement as the Grossdeutsch party demanded Austrian sovereignty over any new Germany while the Prussians wanted supremacy themselves.

In June, Napoleon III was still attempting to consolidate his power. No sooner had he become president than he sought to overturn unfavorable election results and oust political enemies. The June Days was a brief but bloody civil war which resulted in the death of 1500 rebels and more than 12,000 arrest.

In the meantime Italy was still convulsing from the revolutions. Charles Albert had at first driven the Austrians out of Italy, but a new wave of troops entered Lombardy and defeated Charles Albert in August. The Austrians resumed their control of northern Italy while Rome now rose in rebellion against Pius IX who fled Rome in disguise. Rome re–established a Republic and invited Mazzini (who had "prophesied" that imperial and papal Rome would be followed by "a third Rome") to come to head it. Pius then turned to Louis–Napoleon for aid. The situation was perfect for Napoleon who had designs on re–establishing the empire of Napoleon. Even as Charlemagne had liberated Pope Leo, Louis–Napoleon would liberate Pius. Rome was "freed" and Mazzini again sent into exile; this time for good.

Although the campaign enhanced Louis–Napoleon's prestige and garnered the support of the papacy, it did not achieve any long lasting results. When, in 1851, Louis–Napoleon realized that he was in danger of losing his power (for the constitution did not allow presidents to run for a second term) he staged a coup and arrested seventy of his political enemies. Protests were greeted with violence over 27,000 arrest made. Louis–Napoleon then created yet another constitution (the seventh since 1789) which established the "Second Empire." Louis–Napoleon took the name Napoleon III and became its first, and only, emperor. Of course, more was needed than a name if the empire were truly to be restored. One thing Napoleon needed was universal prestige, not to mention military conquests. To that end he united with Britain against the expanding power of Russia and came to the defense of the Turks in the Crimean War. The result, however, was not favorable. Napoleon would have to look elsewhere if he were to expand French influence in Europe. This time he found the key in Italy; the home of Rome.

It was an assassination attempt by a member of the famed Orisini family of Italy that led Napoleon to proclaim himself the liberator of northern Italy from their Austrian oppressors. France allied itself with Piedmonte and Lombardy who fought to overthrow Austrian rule. Nevertheless, Napoleon III was no Napoleon. Only Piedmonte remained free from Austria and they were rewarded by the emperor's annexation of Savoy and Nice. It was only a matter of time before Napoleon was in a war with the Italians themselves. The Italian fortunes were changing. In 1860 a new revolution broke out in Parma between Lombardy and Piedmonte and on March 17, 1861, the Kingdom of Italy was proclaimed which began the unification of Italy including Naples. Parma, Tuscany, Naples, Sicily, and a large portion of the papal states became a part of the Kingdom of Italy. Only Rome, Lombardy, and Piedmonte remained outside the kingdom.

Attempting to make peace with Austria, Napoleon launched plan for expansion in the Americas. He offered the Austrian archduke the crown of a new "kingdom of the Andes" but he was unsuccessful here as well for when the U. S. civil war ended, they exerted pressure to keep the expansionistic French out of the Americas. Moreover, Germany was making a play for power which would not only rival Napoleon's "empire" but ultimately break his feeble attempt at restoring French sovereignty.

It was in 1862 when the Prussian ambassador to France, a certain Otto von Bismark, was recalled to Prussia and made both prime minister and foreign minsiter. Bismark's new empire was to eclipse Napoleon III's empire and lead to the ultimate failure of Napoleon III's dreams. It was also to lay the foundations for two future world wars while showing the seeming futility of every attempt to restore the Holy Roman Empire.

Bismark

Bismark was neither a king nor an emperor, but he was the man who made the German Empire on behalf of the Kaisers (the German word for Caesar). He may not have envisioned the reunification of all of Europe, but he did envision, and largely accomplish, the reunification of Germany. It was the first major step toward the restoration of the once great Roman Empire.

Bismark believed that the greatest obstacle to the reunification of Germany was Austria. Austria and Prussia both wanted supremacy over any new Germanic empire and neither would yield to the other. Moreover, the thought of another Hapsburg dynasty disturbed many Germans who remembered only the great failures of the Hapsburgs. Bismark, therefore, concluded an alliance with Italy and promised to give Italy Venetia, which was still a part of Austria. Napoleon III deliberately remained neutral in the coming conflict, hoping that Austria and Prussia would be severely weakened in the civil war, leaving them open to invasion from France. He was to be disappointed again.

On June 9, 1866, the Seven Weeks' War began as Prussia invaded Austria. On July 26 the victory was complete with the Peace of Nikolsburg. Prussia had swept a clean victory but Bismark was too wise to embitter the Austrians. He knew that subjugated kingdoms rise in rebellion years later if not treated favorably so on August 23 the Treaty of Prague allowed Austria to keep all its possessions except for Venetia. Austria was simply made to accept the annexation of Hanover, Nassau, Hesse–Kassel, Schleswwig, Holstein, and Franfurt by the new North German Confederation with Prussia as its head.

Next on Bismark's agenda was the pacification of France and Napoleon III. He did not want to openly start a war, for Bismark, whatever one may think of his personal ambitions and ethics, was no fool. Prussia did not want to look like an invader or conqueror, but if France began the war Bismark could be a hero for disarming France. That would allow Prussia to become the dominant power of Europe and assist in the creation of the German Empire.

In 1870 Napoleon III obligued. The Prussian king's brother had been named king of Spain and Napoleon III insisted that they were trying to "surround" France. He declared war on July 19, 1870. By September 2 Napoleon realized he had made a mistake. He surrendered and was captured in battle. The fall of Napoleon III would profoundly change events in France, Italy, and Germany. For Prussia it eliminated the only real rival power to Prussia. For France it would signal yet another bloody revolution. For Italy it signaled the end of the pope's protector and the seizure of Rome.

On September 20, 1870, just weeks after Napoleon's capture Italian troops from the Kingdom of Italy entered Rome. The papal army could offer no real resistence and the pope fled to the confines of Vatican City. Rome, center of the old Roman Empire, was now a part of the Kingdom of Italy. On May 13, 1871, the Law of Guarantees permitted the papacy full religious freedom and granted Vatican City rights as an independant state. The pope could have ambassadors, just as foreign nations could, but the temporal power of the papacy over Italy was finished. The emperors had fallen under Napoleon. Now, in 1871, Pius IX was sealed up in the tiny Vatican State. One might declare that the once vast Roman Empire now resided solely within the confines of the 100 acres, or .16 square mile, of Vatican City. Ancient Rome had divided the power of the emperor between the emperor and pope. If the popes had not yet fallen, the emperors had fallen under Napoleon, although Bismark sought to restore that dignity on behalf of the Prussia king.

In France the fall of Napoleon III had more drastic consequences. The empire was dissolved and a "Third Republic" was proclaimed. The eighth constitution in eighty–six years was about to be written. That made for an average of ten years per constitution. The United States, by contrast, was close to celebrating its hundredth anniversary. The Paris Commune, however, was now far more influenced by the popularity of Marxism, or Communism, than the failed democratic experiments of the past century. Communism, rather than democracy, was what many Frenchmen were calling for and revolution was what Marxism demanded. The result was a new civil war. The "Bloody Week" of May 21–28, 1871, led to the death of over 20,000 Communards (as they Communist party was called).

If France was caught in chaos, Germany was about to enter a new imperial age. Prussia, and Bismark, were hailed by north and south Germany. On January 18, 1870, the new German Empire was proclaimed. The North German Confederation was absorbed into the empire along with Bavaria, Baden, Hesse, and Wurttemberg from the south. Additionally, Alsace and Lorraine were annexed from the vanguished French. Bismark became its first chancellor of the new German Empire and William (Wilhelm) I became its first Kaiser or emperor. It was hardly the glory of ancient Rome but it was the first step. Germany, for the first time since Francis II, was an empire again.

The Kaiser and World War I

For twenty years Germany enjoyed peace. Bismark is generally accepted by historians as the strongest leader Germany had seen since the fall of the Holy Roman Empire. Certainly he was a stronger and better leader than many of its last German emperors, but that did not mean that he enjoyed the affections of the people. Communism was rising in popularity. Bismark despised the communists. He had many enemies in the Reichstag (German congress). When Kaiser Wilhelm I died in 1888, he was replaced by a sick Frederick III. His son seemed to be urging the old man to die. Three months later, he got his wish. Wilhem II (or William II) rose to the throne in June 1888 at age twenty–nine. Although the empire's constitution restricted the power of the emperor, Wilhelm sought to enforce his authoritarian rule by finding a chancellor who would be his puppet. In 1890, when the Social Democrats (a Marxist party), won a large percentage of the seats, Bismark felt surrounded and handed his resignation to the Kaiser. He would not be the cause of a revolution. He had ruled in the name of Wilhem I (or William I) for almost thirty years. Now Kaiser Wilhem II was the true power of the German Empire. He would seek to restore the great European empire under the banner of the German Empire. He would lead the world into the unnecessary "War To End All Wars."

Kaiser Wilhelm would never truly replace Bismark. In the twenty–four years before the outbreak of World War I the Kaiser cycled through no fewer than four chancellors. Europe was currently undergoing the Industrial Revolution. Kaiser was eager to use that revolution to make Germany a powerful military. New technology was rapidly developing that would change the face of war. Machine guns, tanks, bi–planes, larger bombs, and even submarines would come into play during the next major war. All initially served to the advantage of the Kaiser.

In order to truly become a great power Germany felt it had to rival Britain for control of the seas. He thus set out to build up a great navy which often came into political conflict with England. Tensions between England and Germany grew constantly over the next two decades, helped in part by the Kaiser's foreign policy. The famed German sociologist Max Weber spoke to the German's sense of nation pride, declaring that while Germany was struggling internally the other great powers of Europe were expanding into Africa and Asia. Both France and Britain now occupied most of the African continent as well as interest in America and Asia. Germany was being left out in the cold. Kaiser Wilhelm believed he needed to confront and hamper such expansionism by his rival powers.

In 1904 Germany supported Morocco's bid for independence against France. German troops arrived to help them cast of French rule but with the alliance of France and England the Kaiser was forced to back down. Only after Germany restored more favorable diplomacy with Britain did the Kaiser once again turn to Morocco in 1911. War seemed imminent when the Kaiser decided that the time was not yet ripe. France, England, and Russia were allied with one another. Germany did not want to start a war it could not win. Once again Germany backed down. It was not until 1914 that Kaiser Wilhelm saw what he believed was his opportunity.

The Austrian Archduke Francis Ferdinand was assassinated in June 1914 by Serbian radicals. Although Serbia was not involved and had no conflict with Austria, the incident soon became an international incident. Russia and France were both allied with Serbia while the German Empire was allied with Austria–Hungary. All historians agree that the war was unnecessary. Serbia was a small country south of Austria whose leaders and people were clearly innocent of the conspiracy. Nevertheless, the Kaiser saw this as an opportunity to expand the empire's influence, and possibly absorb Austria as natural allies, in the process. Germany invaded Serbia and World War I began.

Kaiser Wilhelm feared a two front war so he had hoped to take out France in a swift attack, but his troops became bogged down near the outskirts of Paris. For years each side dug in trenches and the boundaries moved no more than a few miles throughout most of these years. On the eastern front Russia proved a formitable opponent. In January 1915, Germany introduced its most terrifying new weapon; gas weapons. Various forms of gas were used to suffocate, kill, and maim allied soldiers. Never before in history had such horrifying weapons been used. In the years following World War I the world outlawed chemical weapons. Even Hitler never used them in battle (although he made use of them in the concentration camps).

On May 7, 1915, Germany sank the Lusitania, an ocean liner carrying thousands of civilian passangers. Although the ship had been secretly carrying weapons as well, the death of over a thousand civilians, including over a hundred U. S. citizens threatened to bring the United States into the conflict, but Woodrow Wilson was a pacifist by nature and chose to remain out of the war. Meanwhile, the Ottoman empire allied itself with Germany in hopes of throwing off Russian and British power. Despite being outnumbered more than two to one, the "Central Powers" of the German alliance kept the allies at bay for years. When, in 1917, the Communist Russian Revolution appeared to take Russia out of the picture the outcome of the war began to favor the Kaiser, but his refusal to even discuss terms of surrender or a peaceful treaty brokered by the United States finally led Woodrow Wilson to enter the conflict after German submarines destroyed three U. S. merchant ships. On March 20, 1917, the United States declared war. Moreover, the new Soviet Russians resumed the war against Germany. Within a year Palestine and the Middle East were within allied hands and the Ottoman empire fell.

The loss of the Kaiser's Turkish allies left the outcome of the war inevitable. Kaiser Wilhelm's refusal to negotiate a favorable peace when it was offered was one of the ultimate reasons for his own downfall. He believed that Germany was destined to ruled Europe. He believed that the Holy Roman Empire was a *German* empire (as many revisionist historians also claim). He refused to even back down or deny Germany its "destiny." When the end came, he fled to the Netherlands where he remained in exile until his death, two years after the outbreak of World War II.

World War I had cost over 8,500,000 lives and over 37,000,000 casualties, including millions who would be forever scarred by the advent of gas weapons. The embittered allies took their revenge on the arrogant German nation by requiring $32,000,000,000 in war reparations or the equivalent of $300,000,000,000 in modern funds. Further all of Germany's foreign interest in America and elsewhere were stripped from them. The result was an economic depression which, when compounded with the world depression of 1929, resulted in the rise of Adolf Hitler.

The Rise of Fascism

If we are to understand the rise of fascism in Europe than we must recognize the forces that led to its rise rather than catering to the rhetoric of some historians. Fascism and its counterpart Nazism were *not* "right wing" movements, but socialistic movements made in reaction against the extreme left wing communists and Marxists. There were only "right wing" in that they were to the right of the extreme revolutionaries. They were, in fact, far to the left of both America and Great Britain. Socialism was at the cornerstone of virtual every political movement in Europe since the end of the nineteenth century. The first arose in Italy following World War I.

Many Bolshevic Communists had hoped that the Russian Revolution would set off a world revolution of workers. As a result the Bolshevics threatened democracy and even the most liberal republics throughout Europe. In Italy the popularity of socialism left the Roman Republic in fear for its very survival. In Milan, Mussolini, began a fascist party which combined socialistic elements with a national emphasis. Italy could not fall prey to some international Bolshevic revolution but must institute socialistic ideals within the confines of national interest. This form of socialism was in reaction against the fears of Communism, which became the great enemy of fascism, and won great favor in Italy. In 1922, Mussolini marched on Rome, seized power, and began to transform the Roman Republic into a modern dictatorship.

In Germany the path took longer but followed a similar course. After World War I the "accidental republic" was formed before the allied powers helped to establish the more permanent Weimar Republic. Bavaria broke off from the former German Empire and formed its own socialist republic while the "Sparticists" party, or German revolutionary Communists, pushed to abolish democracy in any form and carry the Russian Revolution to Germany. By the time the Allies had created the ill–fated League of Nations and established the Weimer Republic in Germany the socialistic elements of Germany were already pushing the country in another direction. The depression caused by the harsh conditions of the Treaty of Versailles further spawned various socialistic parties which all began to vie for power. In 1923, a certain Adolf Hitler of the National Socialist Workers Party (or Nazi party) attempted a failed coup which placed Hitler in prison, but did not end his political career.

Back in Italy Mussolini had managed to completely turn Italy's former republic into a dictatorship. Political prisoners could legally be shot without trial and the Chamber (or congress) became a mere rubber stamp. On February 11, 1929, Mussolini signed the Lateran Treaty in which Pope Pius XI formally recognized, for the first time, the legitimacy of the Kingdom of Italy. In return the Sovereign State of Vatican City was granted more freedom and Italy was declared a Catholic nation. Pius XI was making a futile play to return the papacy to international power.

That same year the American stock market crashed, causing a world wide depression which impacted Germany more than any other industrialized nation. Already suffering from an economic depression the crash now made Germany's fears more pronounced and increased fears that the Communists would use the depression to seize power in Germany. In 1932 a new presidential election was held. The Nazi party, under the now released Adolf Hitler, had come to outnumber the the Democratic Socialists and Christian Socialists in the Riechstadt. In the presidential election, Hitler finished with just

30% of the vote. Current President Hindenburg, however, did not get enough votes to win a majority so a run–off election was delcared, and Hitler captured 37% of the vote but lost to Hinderburg. Nevertheless, Hinderburg need a coalition government, which he did not have. Hitler was eventually offered the Vice–Chancellory which he accepted. A few months later, Hitler decided to make his play for power. Vice–Chancellor Hitler's famed SS soldiers confronted the aged Hindenburg and ordered him, at gun point, to resign. Hitler was then made Chancellor, without having been elected. The Wiemer Republic was dissolved and a new banana republic was established; the Third Reich. Hitler declared that just as the First Reich, the Holy Roman Empire, had lasted a thousand years, so would the Third Reich.

Adolph Hitler

After seizing power Hitler sought to establish papal recognition, even as Napoleon had done before him. On July 20, 1933, Pius XI signed a concordat with Adolf Hitler granting legitimacy to the Nazi government. Despite the concordat, Hitler, although raised as a Catholic, had no love for an Judeao–Christian religion. He despised Jews, whom he considered an inferior race, and hated Christianity. However, he knew that Germany was still nominally Christian so he began to imitate Napoleon's educational policies. All Churches and schools were required to recited Nazi propaganda. Those churches, predominantly Protestant, which refused to comply were persecuted. Jews were forced into Ghettos.

Over the next decade Hitler began to form the German military into the strongest in the world. By 1939, six years later, Germany had four times as many military planes as did Great Britain. Hitler began to unify the German countries into his new empire; sometimes through democratic means, sometimes through coups, but always through whatever means necessary. He was determined to restore the Holy Roman Empire under the German banner. That meant that every country which had ever been a part of the Holy Roman Empire could expect Hitler to conquer it, but Europe at large was naïve. Hitler was appeased repeatedly. Before his invasion of Poland in 1939, Germany had taken in the Rhineland, Austria, Bavaria, and Bohemia. Winston Churchill had warned Europe of Hitler's intentions but the world remained blissfully ignorant. When, in August 31, 1939, Germany invaded Poland, World War II officially began, but even then not a single shot was fired. The Allies were hoping that the Nazis would back down. Not until a terrible Blitzkreig demolished Paris and German troops occupied France did the Allies realize that they had another World War on their hands.

The war, which would last for six long years, resulted in more deaths than World War I. In addition, Adolf Hitler attempted the genocide of the Jewish race, calling for the execution of over 6,000,000 Jews in the gas chambers. When the war was finally over the survivors of the Holocaust would find a home in the newly established State of Israel where many Arab nations promised to finish the job Hitler left incomplete. Thus, the world of today, from the Middle East to Europe, is the product of the fall of the Holy Roman Empire and the ill–fated attempts to restore that empire to its former glory.

Conclusion : Europe After the Fall

After the fall of Hitler Europe has continued to suffer from the same problems which created Hitler, and Napoleon, and Kaiser. The United Nations ultimately replaced the League of Nations but has proven just as inept. It has consistently been unable to handle the problems that Europe has faced or to deal with threats to Europe's peace. The European Economic Union has made the reunification of Europe more feasible from an economic point of view by creating a single currency and allowing Europe economy to become more unified, but ultimately Europe remains divided.

The effect of the Roman Empire remains to this very day. It has never been replaced, nor has it been supplanted. The Roman Empire had lasted in its imperial form for over two thousand years. It had 232 emperors from Augustus to Napoleon. 112 of those emperors were from ancient Rome before Charlemagne. 51 were emperors of the eastern empire who ruled in Constantinople. Another seven were the Latin emperors of Constantinople. 62 emperors ruled the west from Charlemagne to Napoleon. This list includes some, but not all, of the usurpers and pretenders to the throne.

It it little wonder that the famed secular poet Lord Byron, echoing ancient prophetic thought, declared, "when Rome falls, so shall the world." The ancient view to which Lord Byron referred was passed down from the ancient Jewish interpreters to Church Fathers to the medieval theologians and down to modern evangelicals. It taught that the Messianic Kingdom alone would supplant the Roman Empire. Only after the Roman Empire fell could the Messianic Kingdom expect to come. That is why many Jews rejected Jesus, for He did not claim to come to crush Rome. That is also why many shiver at the thought of Europe reuniting under a single banner. According to the evangelical view, there is but one more emperor to come. Napoleon is not the last. It is the anti–Christ who is last. This is an ominous allusion to the greatest empire known to history. It is an empire whose history is integrally tied to the fate of the world itself. Is its fall complete? If not, will it revive in one last imperial coup as the prophetic theologians say? That is future history. Past history is grand enough. The future still awaits.

Appendix A : A Historical Atlas of the Holy Roman Empire

The Empire of Charlemagne

The empire of Charlemagne stretched across almost the whole of the European mainland. It reached the Atlantic in the west and as far as the Rhein, and beyond, in the east. In the South it bordered the Pyrenees Mountains of Spain and cut through central Italy. To the north it bordered the English Channel and the North Sea. In relation to the territory of ancient Rome it was but a fraction of the once great empire, but in relation to the Western Empire, as divided from the time of Constantine on, it was far more grand and great. The Empire of Charlemagne was truly the succession of the western Roman Empire and took in what is today France, Germany, Switzerland, Belgium, the Netherlands, Austria, and most of Italy.

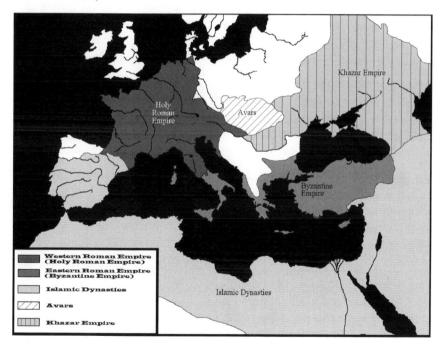

The Empire of Otto

Was the empire of Otto larger or smaller than that of Charlemagne? As aforementioned throughout this book, most historians have a hard time relating to the Holy Roman Empire, for it was dramatically different from all others. In both political and religious authority it often defies attempts to define and circumscribe its borders. Some kings openly acknowledged fealty to the empire while others ignored it, but few great kingdoms rebelled against it. The kings of Europe wanted to be united under the Roman banner, but they did not want to relinquish their authority. Otto's empire is universally recognized to take in Germany, Burgundy, Poland, Denmark, Hungary, and most of Italy. The problem is primarily defining the role of France and England at this time.

In regard to England, the marriage of Otto to the granddaughter of Alfred the Great probably created more of an alliance than the creation of a new realm. Certainly there appear to be no extant admissions of fealty to Holy Rome and no clear indication that England was anything more than newfound allies. This marriage, and the Christian heritage left behind by Alfred the Great, paved the way for England's eventually acceptance into the Empire but it may be agreed here, with most other historians, that England was but an ally.

France, however, creates a far more controversial debate. From the time of Charlemagne there was no doubt that France was not only a part of the empire, but a substantial and influential part. Charlemagne was as much the father of France as of Germany. Indeed, the very name "France" comes from "Frankland," the land of the Franks, and yet the Franks were a *German* tribe. When the lands were divided among Charlemagne's grandsons the seeds of division were immediately planted by the new countries. The Germans and the French both considered themselves the legitimate heirs to Charlemagne and when the Carolingian Dynasty died out the French kings and German kings remained largely independent of one another. The recognition of Otto as Holy Roman Emperor sat well with Germany, after the initial tribal struggles, but France was unwilling to accept a German as the successor of Charlemagne whom they considered French. They, therefore, *ignored* the new emperor. It has been noted that before the reign of King Hugh Capet in 987 the French never *formally* recognized any of the emperors of the empire, but they also never formally renounced the emperor, nor especially the empire. They did not deny being a part of the empire, they merely denied that Germans were the heirs of Charlemagne. Indeed, nearly a thousand years later the Frenchman Napoleon hoped to restore the Holy Roman Empire under a *French* Emperor. Later French Kings like Philip Augustus clearly indicate that France was a part of the empire and its fealty to the papacy is undeniable. There can be no doubt that the French considered themselves not only a part of the Holy Roman Empire but the *true* successors thereof.

560

It is somewhat amusing to see modern maps of the Holy Roman Empire that exclude France but have a large prominent star pointing to the spiritual capitol of the "German Empire" *in France*. I refer to Avignon, where the papacy would reside for almost a hundred years. At this point it is not necessary to indulge in a long defense of this position. It merely needs be said that the empire extended beyond the practiced authority of the emperor and encompassed the domain of the papacy and all those kings who heeded the temporal commands thereof. France, although rebellious against outside authority, *always* considered themselves a part of the Kingdom of Charlemagne.

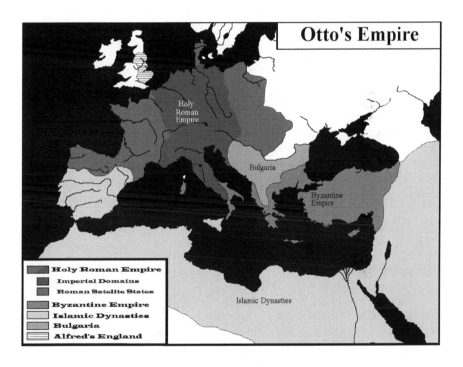

The Empire at the Time of the Crusades

By the time the Ottonian dynasty fell it was obvious that the Holy Roman Empire, though still one empire, had effectively divided into two halves. The western empire, as well as Sicily and other areas, nominally continued to accept the emperor and swore fealty to the pope, but the kings ruled as they saw fit without interference from the emperor. In time it would become clear that the concept of power sharing between emperor and pope was failing. The "papal empire," as the western areas might be called, was clearly under the dominion of the pope, many even paying a form of tribute to their suzerain overlord, but to the emperor they gave nothing except nominal obedience. Nevertheless, what the west had lacked were strong kings to make up for the lack of an emperor. William the Conqueror would fill one of these voids. As the strongest of western kings he would eclipse even the emperor in power and authority, but his kingdom must still be considered a part of the Holy Roman Empire. When the Crusades were called not long after his death, it was his kingdom, and the west, that heeded the call with as much enthusiasm as any in the eastern Holy Roman Empire.

The rise of England had occurred many years earlier. Canute, ally and friend of the emperor, had controlled not only England but also Denmark and Sweden. Spain, though still without real authority, sometimes turned to the Church for help. They are considered a nation within the empire at this time only because of their king's allegiance to the papacy, but in practical terms they were still a struggling country separated from it by civil war with Muslims and other Catholic kings.

In 1068 the Kingdom of Aragon was bequeathed to the pope. The emperor too had involvement in Spanish affairs, but the Spanish, like the French, were independent minded and some even claimed the title emperor for themselves. By the time of King Sancho X all Christian Spain was a part of the empire and Sancho himself even received electoral votes for Holy Roman Emperor, a title he claimed in opposition to the German king. A few hundred years later the German electors would even vote for Alfonso X of Castile to become emperor. However, for the time being, only Aragon can clearly be said to be under the temporal domain of the papacy, but the emperor's involvement was limited.

By the time of the first Crusade the west was made up of France, Normandy, Britain, Sweden, Denmark, and Aragon of Spain. Sicily may be considered a part of this coalition as well, although technically it would not claim fealty to the pope until a few years later. The east consisted of Arles (or Burgundy), Italy (Lombardy & Tuscany), Germany, Hungary, Bohemia, Moravia, and Poland. The Palestinian land taken during the Crusades was clearly a part of the empire as well, although it never formally acknowledged fealty to either emperor or pope. They desired to be independent of these authorities, but the lands were conquered by vassals of the empire in the name of the Church. Indeed, when Saint Louis was asked to surrender Damietta by the Muslims, he responded that only the emperor could order such a surrender. It would, therefore, be hard to consider it a separate kingdom since its finances, kings, soldiers, and appointments all came from the Holy Roman Empire.

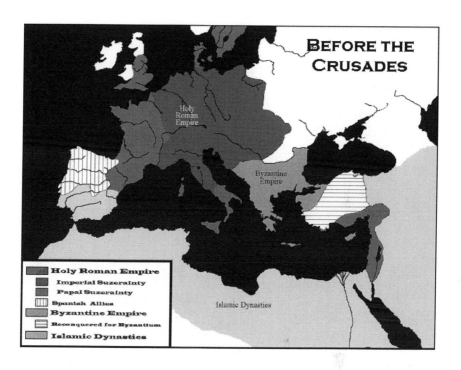

The Empire of Frederick Barbarossa

By the time of Barbarossa the empire had reached it grandest size, but only if one justly counts the lands of papal suzerainty, for Frederick's lands, and those of the emperors, were being reduced year by year. As kingdoms realized that the emperors authority did not exceed the papacy's they chose what they believed was the lesser of two evils. The kingdoms of Europe did not truly want complete independence from one another, but they did want independent rule of their countries. To the kings of Europe papal interference was less troublesome that imperial interference. The weapons of the pope were excommunication and interdiction. The weapons of the emperor were sword and execution. It is not, therefore, surprising that kingdoms willingly offered their kingdoms to the pope as a fief. They did not seek to withdraw from the empire and risk invasion, but they sought to secure freedom from imperial intrusion by accepting papal ones.

The papal suzerain lands of the empire, or "papal empire," now spread out over England, France, Ireland, Denmark, Sicily, Poland, and most of modern Hungary and Spain. The imperial lands were now confined largely to Germany, Italy, Bohemia, and the kingdom of Arles, or Burgundy. Venice themselves eluded the empire although it is possible they *officially* accepted the suzerainty of the pope.

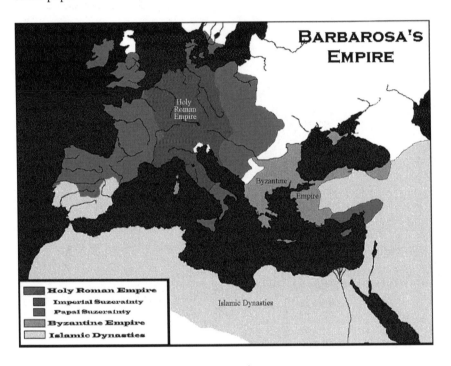

The Empire in the day of Frederick II

After the reign of Frederick II the empire began to disintegrate. Without a strong emperor the void created could never be filled by the corrupt papacy. Wars between neighboring countries would threaten to devour the empire ever so slowly. Nevertheless, Frederick II's reign might be considered the pinacle of

564

the Holy Roman Empire in terms of its medieval dominions. Never did the empire stretch so far and wide, at least nominally, as it did in Frederick's day.

The papal empire covered France, England, Ireland, Scotland, most of Spain, Poland, Hungary, Denmark, Venice, Crete, most of Greece, part of Sweden, part of modern day Turkey, and the Palestinian kingdom of Acre and Jerusalem. The emperor ruled Germany, Arles, Bohemia, and Sicily.

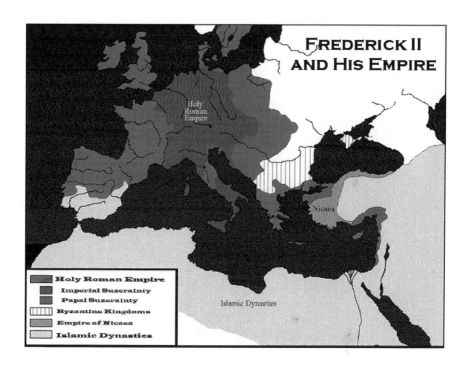

The Empire Before the Reformation

Charles V, in terms of his domain, held more possessions than any emperor since Frederick II, and, in fact, possessed in name far more than Frederick. However, his many titles (emperor, King of Spain, King of Naples, King of Sicily, ruler of the Netherlands, and master of Milan) did little to enforce true authority. He dreamed of restoring the glory of the ancient emperors, but his lack of vision actually caused many defections from the empire during the Reformation years.

Before the Reformation the empire could be said to be composed of the German states, Italy, Naples, Sicily, France, England, Scotland, Ireland, the Netherlands, Spain, Portugal, New Spain (in America), Switzerland, Bohemia, and Hungary. Under the Reformation Switzerland and England would openly defect from the Holy Roman Empire, and France would maintain virtual independence, while still clinging to the empire in name. In addition, the Reformation challenged the authority of the pope even in countries which remained in the alliance of nations. Kings, not emperor or popes, were the new rulers of the empire, and the rise of democracy would eventually spell an end to the empire altogether.

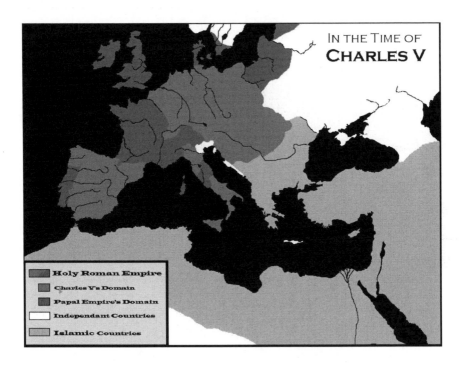

IN THE TIME OF
CHARLES V

Holy Roman Empire
Charles V's Domain
Papal Empire's Domain
Independant Countries
Islamic Countries

The Empire Of Napoleon

The empire of Napoleon stretched across the whole of Europe's mainland encompassing Spain, Italy, Naples, France, Austria, Hungary, Prussia, Poland, Denmark, Norway, Holland, and Switzerland. Portugal was captured by Napoleon as well, although it was freed from his dominion quickly with British assistance. Only England was spared conquest by Napoleon. It was one brief revival of ancient Rome in all her glory under the foot of a tyrant.

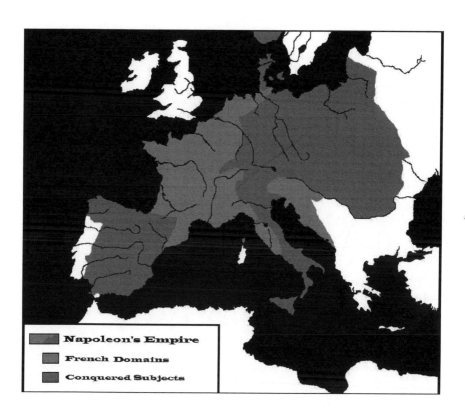

567

Appendix B : Chronology of the Emperors and Popes

Holy Roman Emperor	Pope	AntiPope (if any)
——— 800 ———		
Charlemagne (Charles I)	Leo III	
——— 814 ———		
	——— 816 ———	
	Stephen IV (V)	
	——— 817 ———	
	Paschal I	
Louis the Pious (Louis I)	——— 824 ———	
	Eugenius II	
	——— 827 ———	
	Valentine	
	——— 827 ———	
——— 840 ———	Gregory IV	
Civil War		
——— 843 ———	——— 844 ———	
	Sergius II	*John*
Lothair I	——— 847 ———	− 844 −
	Leo IV	
——— 855 ———	——— 855 ———	
	Benedict III	*Anastasius*
		− 855 −
	——— 858 ———	
Louis II	Nicholas I	
	——— 867 ———	
	Adrian II	
	——— 872 ———	
——— 875 ———		
Charles the Bald (Charles II)		
——— 877 ———		
Interregnum	John VIII	
(Charles the Stammerer – 878 – rejected crown)		
——— 881 ———		
	——— 882 ———	
	Marinus I	
Charles the Fat (Charles III)	——— 884 ———	
	Adrian III	
	——— 885 ———	
——— 887 ———		

Holy Roman Emperor	Pope	AntiPope (if any)
	——— 885 ———	
——— 887 ———	Stephen V (VI)	
Second Interregnum (Arnulf – not anointed until 896)		
——— 891 ———	——— 891 ———	
Guy of Spoleto (Usurper)		
——— 894 ———	Formosus	
Lambert (Usurper)		
——— 896 ———	——— 896 ———	
	Boniface VI	
	——— 896 ———	
	Stephen VI (VII)	
	——— 896 ———	
Arnulf	Romanus	
	——— 897 ———	
	Theodore II	
	——— 897 ———	
	——— 898 ———	
——— 899 ———	John IX	
	——— 900 ———	
Louis the Child	Benedict IV	
(was too young to be anointed)	——— 900 ———	
——— 901 ———	*Interregnum*	
	——— 903 ———	
Louis the Blind (Louis III)	Leo V	*Christopher*
	——— 904 ———	
——— 905 ———	Sergius III	
	——— 911 ———	
Third Interregnum	Anastasius III	
(Louis remained Emperor in name)	——— 913 ———	
	Lando	
	——— 914 ———	
——— 915 ———		
Berengar	John X	
——— 924 ———		
	——— 928 ———	

Holy Roman Emperor	Pope	AntiPope (if any)
——————— 924 ———————		
	——————— 928 ———————	
	Leo VI	
	——————— 928 ———————	
	——————— 929 ———————	
	Stephen VII (VIII)	
	——————— 931 ———————	
	John XI	
Fourth Interregnum	——————— 935 ———————	
(Otto began reigning in 936 but was not	——————— 936 ———————	
anointed Holy Roman Emperor until 962)	Leo VII	
	——————— 939 ———————	
	Stephen VIII (IX)	
	——————— 942 ———————	
	Marinus II	
	——————— 946 ———————	
	Agapetus II	
	——————— 955 ———————	
——————— 962 ———————	John XII	
	——————— 964 ———————	
	Leo VIII	*Benedict V*
	——————— 865 ———————	
Otto the Great (Otto or Otho I)	John XIII	*— 866 —*
	——————— 972 ———————	
——————— 973 ———————	——————— 973 ———————	
	Benedict VI	
	——————— 974 ———————	
Otto II		*Boniface VII*
	Benedict VII	*— 974 —*
——————— 983 ———————	——————— 983 ———————	
	John XIV	
	——————— 984 ———————	
		Boniface VII (2nd time)
	——————— 985 ———————	
Otto III	John XV	
	——————— 996 ———————	
		— 997 —
	Gregory V	*John XVI (XVII)*
		— 998 —
	——————— 999 ———————	
——————— 1002 ———————		

Holy Roman Emperor	Pope	AntiPope (if any)
	——————— 999 ———————	
——————— 1002 ———————	Sylvester II	
	——————— 1003 ———————	
	John XVII	
	——————— 1003 ———————	
	John XVIII	
Saint Henry II of Bavaria	——————— 1009 ———————	
	Sergius IV	
	——————— 1012 ———————	
	Benedict VIII	*Gregory (VI)*
		—1012 —
——————— 1024 ———————	——————— 1024 ———————	
	John XIX	
Conrad II	——————— 1032 ———————	
	Benedict IX	
——————— 1039 ———————		
	——————— 1045 ———————	
	Sylvester III	*Benedict IX*
	——————— 1045 ———————	
	Gregory VI	
	——————— 1046 ———————	
	Clement II	
Henry III	——————— 1047 ———————	
	Benedict IX	
	——————— 1048 ———————	
	Damasus II	
	——————— 1048 ———————	
	Leo IX	
	——————— 1054 ———————	
	——————— 1055 ———————	
——————— 1056 ———————	Victor II	
	——————— 1057 ———————	
	Stephen IX (X)	
	——————— 1058 ———————	
	Benedict X	
Henry IV	——————— 1059 ———————	
(Early regents were Agnes & Anno)	Nicholas II	
	——————— 1061 ———————	
	Alexander II	*Honorius (II)*
		—1072 —
	——————— 1073 ———————	

Holy Roman Emperor	Pope	AntiPope (if any)
——— 1056 ———		
	——— 1073 ———	
	Gregory VII	
		−1080 −
	——— 1085 ———	
	——— 1085 ———	
Henry IV	Victor III	
	——— 1087 ———	*Clement (III)*
	Urban II	
	——— 1099 ———	
		−1100 −
		Theodoric
		−1102 −
	Paschal II	*Albert*
		−1102 −
		−1105 −
——— 1106 ———		*Sylvester (IV)*
		−1111 −
	——— 1118 ———	
Henry V	Gelasius II	*Gregory (VIII)*
	——— 1119 ———	
	Calistus II	*−1121 −*
	——— 1124 ———	
——— 1125 ———		*Celestine (II)*
	Honorius II	*−1124 −*
Lothair II	——— 1130 ———	
		Anacletus (II)
——— 1137 ———		*−1138 −*
——— 1138 ———	Innocent II	*Victor (IV)*
		−1138 −
	——— 1143 ———	
	Celestine II	
Conrad III	——— 1144 ———	
	Lucius II	
	——— 1145 ———	
	Eugenius III	
——— 1152 ———		
	——— 1153 ———	

Holy Roman Emperor	Pope	AntiPope (if any)

——————— 1152 ———————

——————— 1153 ———————

Anastasius IV

——————— 1154 ———————

Hadrian IV

——————— 1159 ———————

Victor (IV)
—1164 —
Pascal (III)
—1168 —

Alexander III   *Callistus (III)*

Frederick Barbarosa   *—1178 —*
—1179 —
Innocent (III)
—1180 —

——————— 1181 ———————

Lucius III

——————— 1185 ———————

Urban III

——————— 1187 ———————

Gregory VIII

——————— 1187 ———————

——————— 1190 ———————   Clement III

——————— 1191 ———————

Henry VI

Celestine III

——————— 1197 ———————

——————— 1198 ———————   ——————— 1198 ———————

Dispute over legitimate emperor was not settled
Until 1208 by Innocent III

——————— 1208 ———————

Philip

——————— 1208 ———————   Innocent III

Otto IV

——————— 1214 ———————

——————— 1215 ———————

——————— 1216 ———————

Honorius III

Frederick II   ——————— 1227 ———————

<u>Holy Roman Emperor</u>	*Rival (if any)*	<u>Pope</u>	*AntiPope (if any)*

* – Italicized means claimant was never coronated

——————————— 1215 ———————————

——————— 1216 ———————

Honorius III

Frederick II

——————— 1227 ———————

Gregory IX

——————— 1241 ———————

Celestine IV

——————— 1241 ———————

——————— 1243 ———————

——— *1245* ———

Frederick II deposed

——— *1246* ———

Henry Raspe   Innocent IV

——— *1247* ———

——— 1250 –

Conrad IV   *William of Holland*

——— 1254 –

——————— 1254 ———————

——— *1256* ———   Alexander IV

— 1257 ———

——————— 1261 ———————

Urban IV

The double election of

——————— 1264 ———————

Richard of Cornwall &

——————— 1265 ———————

Alfonso X of Castile   Clement IV

——————— 1268 ———————

——————— 1271 ———————

——— 1272 –

Gregory X

——————— 1276 ———————

Innocent V

——————— 1276 ———————

Hadrian V

——————— 1276 ———————

Rudolf   John XXII

——————— 1277 ———————

Nicholas III

——————— 1280 ———————

Holy Roman Emperor	Rival (if any)	Pope	AntiPope (if any)

<u>Holy Roman Emperor</u>   *Rival (if any)*   <u>Pope</u>   *AntiPope (if any)*
*– Means the pope ruled from Avignon

——————— 1272 ———————

——————— 1280 ———————

Martin IV

——————— 1285 ———————

Rudolf   Honorius IV

——————— 1287 ———————

Nicholas IV

——————— 1291 ———————
——————— 1292 ———————   ——————— 1292 ———————
——————— 1294 ———————

Adolf   Celestine V

——————— 1294 ———————

——————— 1298 ———————

Boniface VIII

Albert

——————— 1303 ———————

Benedict XI

——————— 1304 ———————

——————— 1308 ———————

Henry VII   Clement V*

——————— 1313 ———————

——————— 1314 ———————
——————— 1316 ———————

John XXII*   *−1328−*

Louis the Bavarian   *Nicholas (V)*
    −1330−

——————— 1334 ———————

Benedict XII*

——————— 1342 ———————

——————— 1347 ———————   Clement VI*

——————— 1352 ———————

Charles IV   Innocent VI*

——————— 1362 ———————

576

Holy Roman Emperor	Rival (if any)	Pope	AntiPope (if any)

* – Italicized means claimant was never recognized
* – Means the pope ruled from Avignon

——————— 1347 ———————

——————— 1352 ———————

Innocent VI*

Charles IV

——————— 1362 ———————

Urban V*

——————— 1370 ———————

Gregory XI*

——————— 1378 ———————   ——————— 1378 ———————

Urban VI   *Clement (VII)**

Wencelas

——————— 1389 ———

Boniface IX   *−1394 −*

——————— 1400 −

——————— 1404 −

Rupert

Innocent VII

——————— 1406 −

Gregory XII   *Benedict (XIII)**

— 1409 —

——————— 1410 ———————

Alexander V

Robst

— 1410 —

——————— 1411 ———————

John XXIII

— 1415 — *−1415 −*

—1417 —   *−1417 −*

−1423 −

Sigismund

Martin V   *Clement (VIII)*

— 1425 —

Benedict (XIV)

−1429 −

——————— 1431 ———————

——————— 1437 ———————

577

Holy Roman Emperor	Rival (if any)	Pope	AntiPope (if any)
		——— 1431 ———	
——— 1437 ———			
Albert II		Eugene IV	−1439−
——— 1440 ———			Felix V
		——— 1447 −	
		Nicholas V	−1449−
		——— 1455 ———	
		Callistus III	
		——— 1458 ———	
		Pius II	
Frederick III		——— 1464 ———	
		Paul II	
		——— 1471 ———	
		Sixtus IV	
		——— 1484 ———	
		Innocent VIII	
		——— 1492 ———	
——— 1493 ———		Alexander VI	
		——— 1503 ———	
		Pius III	
Maximillian		——— 1503 ———	
		Julius II	
		——— 1513 ———	
		Leo X	
——— 1519 ———			
		——— 1521 ———	
		——— 1522 ———	
		Hadrian VI	
		——— 1523 ———	
		Clement VII	
		——— 1534 ———	
Charles V		Paul III	
		——— 1549 ———	
		——— 1550 ———	
		Julius III	
		——— 1555 ———	
		Marcellus II	
		——— 1555 ———	
——— 1556 ———		Paul IV	

Holy Roman Emperor	*Rival (if any)*	Pope
		————— 1555 —————
————— 1556 —————		Paul IV
Ferdinand		————— 1555 —————
————— 1564 —————		Pius IV
		————— 1565 —————
Maximilian II		————— 1566 —————
		Pius V
		————— 1572 —————
————— 1576 —————		Gregory XIII
		————— 1585 —————
		Sixtus V
		————— 1590 —————
		Urban VII
		————— 1590 —————
		Gregory XIV
Rudolf II		————— 1591 —————
		Innocent IX
		————— 1591 —————
		————— 1592 —————
		Clement VIII
		————— 1605 —————
		Leo XI
		————— 1605 —————
————— 1612 —————		
Matthias		Paul V
————— 1619 —————		
		————— 1621 —————
Ferdinand II		Gregory XV
		————— 1623 —————
————— 1637 —————		Urban VIII
		————— 1644 —————
Ferdinand III		Innocent X
		————— 1655 —————
————— 1657 —————		
————— 1658 —————		Alexander VII
		————— 1667 —————
Leopold		Clement IX
		————— 1669 —————

Holy Roman Emperor	*Rival (if any)*	Pope
		——— 1670 ———
		Clement X
		——— 1676 ———
		Innocent XI
Leopold		——— 1689 ———
		Alexander VIII
		——— 1691 ———
		Innocent XII
		——— 1700 ———
——— 1705 ———		
Joseph		Clement XI
——— 1711 ———		
		——— 1721 ———
		Innocent XIII
Charles VI		——— 1724 ———
		Benedict XIII
		——— 1730 ———
		Clement XII
——— 1740 ———		——— 1740 ———
War of Succession		
——— 1742 ———		
Charles VII		Benedict XIV
——— 1745 ———		
Francis		——— 1758 ———
——— 1765 ———		Clement XIII
		——— 1769 ———
Joseph II		Clement XIV
		——— 1774 ———
——— 1790 ———		
Leopold II		Pius VI
——— 1792 ———		
		——— 1799 ———
		——— 1800 ———
Francis II		
	——— 1804 ———	
	Napoleon Bonaparte	
——— 1806 ———		Pius VII
Napoleon Bonaparte		
——— 1814 ———		
		——— 1823 ———

SELECTED BIBLIOGRAPHY

Primary Sources (Only those primary sources readily available in English are listed)

Catechism of the Catholic Church United States Catholic Conference (USA) 1994

John Foxe, Acts and Monuments of the Christian Church Vol. 1 Religious Tract Society (Picadilly, England) 1841 ed.

John Foxe, Acts and Monuments of the Christian Church Vol. 2 Religious Tract Society (Picadilly, England) 1841 ed.

John Foxe, Acts and Monuments of the Christian Church Vol. 3 Religious Tract Society (Picadilly, England) 1841 ed.

John Foxe, Acts and Monuments of the Christian Church Vol. 4 Religious Tract Society (Picadilly, England) 1841 ed.

John Foxe, Acts and Monuments of the Christian Church Vol. 5 Religious Tract Society (Picadilly, England) 1841 ed.

John Foxe, Acts and Monuments of the Christian Church Vol. 6 Religious Tract Society (Picadilly, England) 1841 ed.

John Foxe, Acts and Monuments of the Christian Church Vol. 7 Religious Tract Society (Picadilly, England) 1841 ed.

John Foxe, Acts and Monuments of the Christian Church Vol. 8 Religious Tract Society (Picadilly, England) 1841 ed.

Samuel Moreland, The History of the Evangelical Churches of the Valleys of Piedmont Henry Hills Printers (London, England) 1658

Philip Schaff, ed., Nicene and Post–Nicene Fathers Series I Vol. I   William B. Eerdmans Publishers (Grand Rapids, Mich.) 1989

Philip Schaff, ed., Nicene and Post–Nicene Fathers Series I Vol. II   William B. Eerdmans Publishers (Grand Rapids, Mich.) 1989

Philip Schaff, ed., Nicene and Post–Nicene Fathers Series I Vol. III William B. Eerdmans Publishers (Grand Rapids, Mich.) 1989

Philip Schaff, ed., Nicene and Post–Nicene Fathers Series I Vol. IV William B. Eerdmans Publishers (Grand Rapids, Mich.) 1989

Philip Schaff, ed., Nicene and Post–Nicene Fathers Series I Vol. V   William B. Eerdmans Publishers (Grand Rapids, Mich.) 1989

Philip Schaff, ed., Nicene and Post–Nicene Fathers Series I Vol. VI William B. Eerdmans Publishers (Grand Rapids, Mich.) 1989

Philip Schaff, ed., <u>Nicene and Post–Nicene Fathers</u> Series I   Vol. VII William B. Eerdmans Publishers (Grand Rapids, Mich.) 1989

Philip Schaff, ed., <u>Nicene and Post–Nicene Fathers</u> Series I   Vol. VIII William B. Eerdmans Publishers (Grand Rapids, Mich.) 1989

Philip Schaff, ed., <u>Nicene and Post–Nicene Fathers</u> Series I   Vol. IX William B. Eerdmans Publishers (Grand Rapids, Mich.) 1989

Philip Schaff, ed., <u>Nicene and Post–Nicene Fathers</u> Series I   Vol. X   William B. Eerdmans Publishers (Grand Rapids, Mich.) 1989

Philip Schaff, ed., <u>Nicene and Post–Nicene Fathers</u> Series I   Vol. XI William B. Eerdmans Publishers (Grand Rapids, Mich.) 1989

Philip Schaff, ed., <u>Nicene and Post–Nicene Fathers</u> Series I   Vol. XII William B. Eerdmans Publishers (Grand Rapids, Mich.) 1989

Philip Schaff, ed., <u>Nicene and Post–Nicene Fathers</u> Series I   Vol. XIII William B. Eerdmans Publishers (Grand Rapids, Mich.) 1989

Secondary Sources

David Abulafia, <u>Frederick II : A Medieval Emperor</u> Oxford University Press (Oxford, England) 1988

Dante Alighieri, <u>Divine Comedy</u> Mark Musa, ed. Penguin Press (New York, NY) 1995 ed.

Augustine, <u>City of God</u> Modern Library (New York, NY) 1993 ed.

Anne Berthelot, <u>King Arthur and the Knights of the Round Table</u> Discoveries (New York, NY) 1997

Morris Bishop, <u>The Middle Ages</u> Houghton Mifflin Co. (Boston, Mass.) 1968

Loraine Boettner, <u>Roman Catholicism</u> Presbyterian & Reformed Publ. (Philipsburg, NJ) 1962

James Viscount Bryce, <u>Holy Roman Empire</u> MacMillan & Co. (London, England) 1950

J. B. Bury, <u>The Invasion of Europe by the Barbarians</u> W. W. Norton & Co. (New York, NY) 1967

Earle E. Cairns, <u>Christianity Through the Centuries</u> Zondervan Publishers (Grand Rapids, Mich.) 1981

Norman F. Cantor, ed., <u>The Encyclopedia of the Middle Ages</u> Viking Books (New York, NY) 1999

Carlo Cipolla, <u>Faith, Reason, and the Plague</u> W. W. Norton & Co. (New York, NY) 1979

Roger Collins, <u>Charlemagne</u> University of Toronto Press (Toronto, Buffalo) 1998

Peter de Rosa, <u>Vicars of Christ</u> Poolpeg Press (Dublin, Ireland) 1988

Alexis de Tocqueville, <u>Democracy in America</u> Perennial Library (New York, NY) 1966 ed.

Eusebius, The Church History Paul Maier, ed. Kregel Publishers (Grand Rapids, Mich.) 1999

John Ferguson, The Religions of the Roman Empire Cornell University Press (Ithaca, NY) 1970

H. P. R. Finberg, Formation of England : 500–1042 Granada Publishing (London, England) 1974

W. Warde Fowler, The Religious Experience of the Roman People Cooper Square Pub. (New York, NY) 1971

John Foxe, Foxe's Books of Martyrs William Byron Forbush, ed. Zondervan Publishers (Grand Rapids, Mich.) 1967 ed.

Leroy Edwin Froom, Prophetic Faith of Our Fathers   Vol. 1 Review & Herald (Washington, DC) 1950

LeRoy Edwin Froom, Prophetic Faith of Our Fathers Vol. 2 Review and Herald (Washington, DC) 1948

Peter Gaunt, Oliver Cromwell Blackwell Press (Oxford, England) 1996

Patrick J. Geary, Before France and Germany Oxford University Press (Oxford, England) 1988

Edward Gibbon, The Decline & Fall of the Roman Empire : Vol. 1 Alfred A. Knopf (New York, NY) 1994 ed.

Edward Gibbon, The Decline and Fall of the Roman Empire : Vol. 2   Alfred A. Knopf (New York, NY) 1993 ed.

Edward Gibbon, The Decline & Fall of the Roman Empire : Vol. 3 Alfred A. Knopf (New York, NY) 1994 ed.

Edward Gibbon, The Decline & Fall of the Roman Empire : Vol. 4 Alfred A. Knopf (New York, NY) 1994 ed.

Edward Gibbon, The Decline & Fall of the Roman Empire : Vol. 5 Alfred A. Knopf (New York, NY) 1994 ed.

Edward Gibbon, The Decline & Fall of the Roman Empire : Vol. 6 Alfred A. Knopf (New York, NY) 1994 ed.

Martin Gilbert, ed., The Illustrated Atlas of Jewish Civilization MacMillian (New York, NY) 1990

Michael Grant, Constantine the Great Barnes & Noble Books (New York, NY) 1999

Serge Gruzinski, The Aztecs : Rise and Fall of an Empire Abrams (New York, NY) 1987

William Reginald Halliday, Lectures on the History of Roman Religion   University Press of Liverpool Ltd. (Liverpool, England) 1972

J. Christopher Herold, Age of Napoleon Houghton Mifflin (Boston, Mass.) 1963

Alexander Hislop, The Two Babylons Loizeaux Brothers (Neptune, NJ) 1916

Hammond Innes, The Conquistadors Alfred–Knoff (New York, NY) 1969

J.N.D. Kelly, <u>Oxford Dictionary of Popes</u> Oxford Press (Oxford, England) 1986

Angus Konstam, <u>Atlas of Medieval Europe</u> Checkmark Books (New York, NY) 2000

Gordon J. Laing, <u>Survivals of the Roman Religion : Our Debt to Greece and Rome</u> Cooper Square Publishers (New York, NY) 1963

Kenneth Scott Latourette, <u>A History of Christianity Vol. 1</u> Harper & Row (New York, NY) 1953

Kenneth Scott Latourette, <u>A History of Christianity Vol. 2</u> Harper & Row (New York, NY) 1953

Hugh M'Neile, <u>The Character of the Church of Rome</u> George Smith (Liverpool, England) 1836

James G. McCarthy, <u>The Gospel According to Rome</u> Harvest House (Eugene, Or.) 1995

Peter McPhee, <u>The French Revolution 1789–1799</u> Oxford Press (Oxford, England) 2002

Charles Maitland, <u>The Apostles' School of Prophetic Interpretation</u> Longman, Brown, Green & Longmans (London, England) 1849

S.L.A. Marshall, <u>World War I</u> Houghton Mifflin (Boston, Mass.) 1964

Andrew Miller, <u>Miller's Church History</u> Pickering & Inglis (London, England) 1963 ed.

Kenneth Morgan, ed., <u>The Oxford Illustrated History of Britain</u> Oxford Press (Oxford, England) 1986 ed.

Samuel Elliot Morrison, <u>The Oxford History of the American People Vol. 1</u> Oxford Press (Oxford, England) 1965

James Julius Norwich, <u>A Short History of Byzantium</u> Vintage Press (New York, NY) 1997

Robert E. A. Palmer, <u>Roman Religion and the Roman Empire</u> University of Penn. Press (Philadelphia, Penn.) 1874

Robert Payne, <u>The Dream and the Tomb</u> Cooper Square Press (New York, NY) 2000

Steven Runciman, <u>A History of Christianity Vol. 1</u> Cambridge University Press (New York, NY) 1951

Steven Runciman, <u>A History of Christianity Vol. 2</u> Cambridge University Press (New York, NY) 1951

Steven Runciman, <u>A History of the Crusades Vol. 1</u> Cambridge University Press (New York, NY) 1951

Steven Runciman, <u>A History of the Crusades Vol. 2</u> Cambridge University Press (New York, NY) 1951

Steven Runciman, <u>A History of the Crusades Vol. 3</u> Cambridge University Press (New York, NY) 1951

J.J. Saunders, <u>A History of Medieval Islam</u> Routledge Press (New York, NY) 1965

Philip Schaff, <u>History of the Christian Church Vol. 2</u> Hendrickson Publishers (Peabody, Mass.) 1996 ed.

Philip Schaff, <u>History of the Christian Church Vol. 3</u> Hendrickson Publishers (Peabody, Mass.) 1996 ed.

Philip Schaff, <u>History of the Christian Church Vol. 4</u> Hendrickson Publishers (Peabody, Mass.) 1996 ed.

Philip Schaff, <u>History of the Christian Church Vol. 5</u> Hendrickson Publishers (Peabody, Mass.) 1996 ed.

Philip Schaff, <u>History of the Christian Church Vol. 6</u> Hendrickson Publishers (Peabody, Mass.) 1996 ed.

Philip Schaff, <u>History of the Christian Church Vol. 7</u> Hendrickson Publishers (Peabody, Mass.) 1996 ed.

Philip Schaff, <u>History of the Christian Church Vol. 8</u> Hendrickson Publishers (Peabody, Mass.) 1996 ed.

Alan Schom, <u>Napoleon Bonaparte</u> HarperPerennial (New York, NY) 1997

William Shirer, <u>The Rise and Fall of the Third Reich</u> Fawcett Press (New York, NY) 1950

Pauline Strafford, <u>Unification and Conquest</u> Edward Arnold Publishers (New York, NY) 1989

Jonathan Sumpton, <u>The Albigensian Crusade</u> Faber and Faber (New York, NY) 1978

Georges Tate, <u>The Crusaders : Warriors of God</u> Discoveries (New York, NY) 1991

Keith Thomas, <u>Religion and the Decline of Magic</u> Penguin Books (London, England) 1971

Robert Turcan, <u>The Cults of the Roman Empire</u> Blackwell (Cambridge, Mass.) 1992

Thieleman J. van Braght, <u>Martyrs Mirror</u> Herald Press (Scottdale, Penn.) 1999 ed. (1886 orig.)

Veit Valentin, <u>The German People</u> Alfred A. Knopf (New York, NY) 1946

Michael Wood, <u>The Conquistadors</u> Unviersity of Berkley (Berkley, CA) 2000

J.A. Wylie, <u>History of the Waldenses</u> Cassell & Co. (New York, NY) 1996

Reference Works

<u>Catechism of the Catholic Church</u> United States Catholic Conference (USA) 1994

<u>The New Encyclopaedia Britannica : Vol. 1</u> Encyclopaedia Britannica Inc. (Chicago, Ill.) 1992

<u>The New Encyclopaedia Britannica : Vol. 2</u> Encyclopaedia Britannica Inc. (Chicago, Ill.) 1992

<u>The New Encyclopaedia Britannica : Vol. 3</u> Encyclopaedia Britannica Inc. (Chicago, Ill.) 1992

The New Encyclopaedia Britannica : Vol. 4 Encyclopaedia Britannica Inc. (Chicago, Ill.) 1992

The New Encyclopaedia Britannica : Vol. 5 Encyclopaedia Britannica Inc. (Chicago, Ill.) 1992

The New Encyclopaedia Britannica : Vol. 6 Encyclopaedia Britannica Inc. (Chicago, Ill.) 1992

The New Encyclopaedia Britannica : Vol. 7 Encyclopaedia Britannica Inc. (Chicago, Ill.) 1992

The New Encyclopaedia Britannica : Vol. 8 Encyclopaedia Britannica Inc. (Chicago, Ill.) 1992

The New Encyclopaedia Britannica : Vol. 9 Encyclopaedia Britannica Inc. (Chicago, Ill.) 1992

The New Encyclopaedia Britannica : Vol. 10 Encyclopaedia Britannica Inc. (Chicago, Ill.) 1992

The New Encyclopaedia Britannica : Vol. 11 Encyclopaedia Britannica Inc. (Chicago, Ill.) 1992

The New Encyclopaedia Britannica : Vol. 12 Encyclopaedia Britannica Inc. (Chicago, Ill.) 1992

Index

Cadaver Synod, vi, 56, 57, 59, 60, 65, 315
Caesar, xvi, 4, 12, 24, 41, 48, 193, 262, 297, 306, 307, 527, 531
Caesaropapism, 12
Cajetan, 406
Callistus, 154, 155, 161, 247, 388, 574, 578
Callistus (III), 192
Callistus III, 375
Calo-John, 250
Calvinism, 413, 444, 446, 448, 474
Canute, 96, 98, 562
Cappel War, 421
Cardinal Charles of Lorraine, 438; Charles of Lorraine, 440
Cardinal de Retz, 471
Cardinal Fieschi, 292
Cardinal Morone, 437
Carloman, 18, 22, 23, 52, 53
Carolingian Renaissance, 26
Carolingians, 18, 54, 61, 79
Cataneo, 382, 383
Cathari, 90, 187, 188, 193, 224, 225, 227, 228, 231, 232, 236
Catherine Medici, 442
Catherine of Siena, 343
Catherine of Thou, 366
Catholic Holy League, 447
Celestine (II), 145, 161, 573
Celestine II, 145, 168, 171, 573
Celestine III, 211, 213, 214, 215, 217, 247, 574
Celestine IV, 248, 268, 575
Celestine V, 300, 303, 305, 313, 576; Peter (or Pierre) of Morone, 300
Cencius, 117
Charlemagne, 3, 4, 6, 7, 8, 9, 10, 15, 16, 18, 19, 20, 21, 22, 23, 24, 25, 26, 27, 28, 29, 30, 32, 33, 34, 35, 36, 37, 38, 39, 40, 41, 42, 43, 58, 62, 66, 67, 72, 73, 76, 78, 79,

80, 90, 91, 95, 108, 121, 129, 132, 136, 161, 177, 183, 213, 215, 217, 218, 232, 243, 244, 260, 319, 425, 427, 491, 522, 523, 525, 527, 528, 529, 557, 559, 560, 561, 569, 583
Charles Albert, 549
Charles II, 62, 297, 298, 300, 339, 472, 475, 569
Charles IV, 313, 324, 327, 332, 335, 338, 339, 340, 342, 346, 357, 360, 440, 576, 577
Charles IX, 439, 442
Charles Martel, 16, 17, 18, 46
Charles of Anjou, ix, 279, 285, 288, 289, 296
Charles of Durazzo, 349, 352; Charles III, 62, 349, 569
Charles of Moravia, 330
Charles of Valois, 305, 319
Charles the Bald, 43, 45, 47, 48, 50, 51, 52, 62, 467, 569
Charles the Bold, 380, 381
Charles the Fat, 52, 53, 54, 62, 569
Charles the Mad, 476; Charles II of Spain, 476
Charles Theodore, 489
Charles V, 24, 341, 344, 346, 348, 388, 392, 393, 394, 396, 397, 399, 401, 403, 408, 409, 410, 412, 416, 418, 421, 422, 434, 435, 438, 443, 444, 463, 477, 478, 528, 565, 578; Charles the Wise, 342, 350
Charles VI, 347, 350, 352, 353, 366, 367, 477, 479, 480, 483, 580
Charles VII, 366, 367, 368, 369, 371, 372, 375, 480, 483, 580; Dauphin Charles, 366, 367
Charles VIII, 385, 386, 392
Charles William Ferdinand, 500
Charles X, 548

434, 438, 451, 453, 456, 457,
458, 459, 461, 463, 465, 471,
477, 579
Ferdinand II, 377, 453, 456, 458,
464, 579
Ferdinand III, 461, 464
Ferdinand of Styria, 455
Ferenc II, 477
First Council of Lyons, 270
First Saxon Capitulary, 29
Formosus, 52, 53, 55, 56, 57, 58,
59, 60, 63, 570
Fourth Lateran Council, ix, 242,
243, 254, 255
Fra Domenico, 387
France, 4, 6, 8, 11, 30, 39, 46, 47,
50, 51, 53, 58, 61, 66, 68, 72, 76,
78, 79, 82, 83, 85, 87, 89, 95, 98,
101, 102, 108, 109, 112, 128,
135, 148, 151, 153, 163, 164,
166, 167, 172, 174, 181, 183,
184, 186, 187, 188, 191, 193,
197, 198, 203, 204, 206, 213,
214, 215, 218, 219, 226, 231,
237, 238, 240, 242, 256, 257,
262, 264, 266, 267, 273, 275,
276, 279, 282, 283, 287, 288,
294, 295, 296, 298, 301, 303,
304, 305, 309, 315, 316, 317,
321, 324, 326, 328, 329, 335,
336, 337, 339, 340, 341, 342,
344, 345, 346, 347, 348, 350,
352, 353, 355, 356, 361, 366,
367, 372, 374, 375, 380, 381,
386, 392, 393, 408, 412, 416,
420, 421, 424, 428, 430, 431,
433, 434, 437, 438, 440, 442,
443, 446, 447, 448, 449, 455,
459, 460, 461, 463, 464, 465,
466, 467, 469, 471, 472, 473,
474, 475, 476, 477, 478, 479,
480, 481, 482, 485, 486, 487,
491, 492, 493, 494, 495, 496,

497, 499, 500, 501, 502, 503,
504, 505, 506, 507, 508, 511,
512, 513, 514, 515, 516, 517,
518, 519, 520, 521, 522, 523,
529, 530, 531, 534, 559, 560,
561, 562, 564, 565, 566, 567,
584
Francis I, 393, 408, 412, 416, 423,
430, 431
Francis II, 3, 4, 438, 439, 483, 499,
500, 509, 521, 523, 527, 528,
531, 532, 535, 538, 542, 543,
547, 552, 580
Franciscan Spirituals, 280, 315,
321, 324, 325, 328, 332, 338,
344, 347
Franciscans, 226, 227, 279, 289,
300, 324, 339
Francisco Orellana, 401
Francisco Ornella, 403
Franco, 75, 530, 532
Francois of Guise, 438, 440, 441
Franconian Dynasty, vii, 95, 159
Frankish Kingdom, v, 11, 12, 16,
17, 25, 28
Franks, 12, 15, 16, 17, 18, 19, 21,
22, 23, 30, 54, 59, 67, 169, 170,
171, 182, 190, 194, 259, 264,
269, 335, 560
Frederick Barbarosa, 147, 172, 175,
211, 247, 468, 574
Frederick II, 214, 218, 241, 242,
243, 245, 247, 248, 249, 250,
251, 252, 253, 254, 270, 271,
272, 273, 276, 277, 279, 280,
281, 282, 287, 288, 290, 291,
319, 323, 409, 480, 481, 564,
565, 574, 575, 583
Frederick III, 336, 371, 372, 375,
381, 385, 388, 392, 552, 578
Frederick of Baden, 286
Frederick of Swabia, 206

595

Isabella, 317, 377, 378, 389, 391, 392, 394, 408

Isabelle, 254, 259

Italy, 4, 6, 7, 8, 10, 11, 12, 13, 14, 15, 17, 18, 19, 21, 23, 26, 30, 32, 43, 45, 46, 47, 48, 50, 51, 52, 53, 54, 55, 56, 58, 59, 60, 61, 65, 66, 68, 69, 70, 71, 72, 75, 76, 77, 78, 80, 82, 83, 84, 85, 86, 87, 88, 89, 95, 97, 98, 99, 100, 102, 103, 106, 107, 117, 119, 120, 121, 125, 126, 127, 128, 147, 150, 152, 153, 154, 162, 163, 164, 165, 166, 167, 177, 180, 181, 182, 183, 184, 188, 192, 193, 196, 197, 198, 206, 211, 212, 214, 215, 217, 218, 219, 220, 223, 224, 225, 226, 231, 241, 243, 257, 261, 262, 264, 265, 269, 271, 272, 276, 280, 281, 282, 285, 286, 287, 290, 292, 295, 297, 318, 319, 322, 324, 326, 327, 328, 329, 332, 333, 336, 339, 341, 343, 347, 348, 349, 352, 356, 371, 375, 377, 384, 385, 386, 389, 392, 393, 408, 416, 417, 434, 437, 439, 442, 449, 457, 460, 463, 464, 466, 469, 471, 473, 477, 479, 481, 509, 510, 511, 512, 515, 519, 523, 530, 531, 532, 559, 560, 562, 564, 566, 567

Jacobin Club, 498, 501

Jacques de Molay, 318, 321

Jacques Necker, 494

Jacques-Louis David, 506, 523

James I of Aragon, 295

James I of England, 456

James II, 298, 300, 475

James II of Aragon, 300

James III, 478

Jerome, xi, 359, 360, 361, 362, 363, 364, 369, 381, 429, 431

Jerome of Prague, xi, 359, 360, 361, 362, 363

Jerome Riario, 381

Jerusalem, 8, 91, 130, 136, 141, 142, 143, 144, 147, 148, 149, 150, 151, 155, 156, 157, 158, 169, 170, 171, 173, 189, 190, 194, 195, 196, 197, 198, 201, 202, 204, 206, 207, 209, 214, 219, 221, 240, 244, 251, 252, 254, 255, 258, 259, 260, 261, 264, 265, 269, 270, 273, 276, 282, 283, 289, 295, 298, 316, 386, 391, 512, 565

Jesuits, 441, 449, 450, 451, 455, 458, 459, 461, 462, 469, 470, 485, 486

Jews, 9, 25, 29, 72, 130, 132, 133, 143, 172, 232, 233, 236, 243, 245, 254, 262, 280, 315, 316, 317, 337, 340, 347, 378, 379, 380, 390, 415, 427, 437, 442, 481, 489, 490, 495, 557

Joachim, 204, 224, 242, 243, 300, 303, 389

Joachimites, 205, 266, 280

Joan of Arc, xi, 112, 152, 366, 367, 368, 371, 375

Joan of Naples, 349

Joan (Pope), 293

John VIII, 52, 53, 55, 62, 569

John IX, 56, 57, 58, 59, 63, 570

John X, 60, 61, 63, 65, 570

John XI, 65, 66, 93, 571

John XII, 69, 70, 71, 77, 93, 326, 329, 571

John XIII, 71

John XIV, 77, 93, 571

John XV, 78, 79, 80, 83, 93, 571

John XVI, 82, 93, 571

John XVII, 78, 86, 87, 124, 572

John XVII (XVIII), 78

John XVIII, 87, 124, 572

John XIX, 95, 96, 124, 572
John XX, 293
John XXI, 293
John XXII, x, 248, 313, 322, 323,
    324, 325, 326, 327, 328, 333,
    575, 576
John (XXIII), 356, 360, 363
John Adams, 487, 489, 519, 520
John Aston, 359
John Calvin, 32, 421, 424, 427,
    428, 468, 487
John Comnenus, 171
John Comyn, 317
John Crescentius II, 86, 87
John de Grey, 238
John Foxe, 362, 418, 429, 433, 582,
    584
John Frederick, 420, 431
John Gaunt, 350
John George, 463
John Gratian, 99
John Huss, 333, 351, 356, 359, 363,
    387
John II of Aragon, 377
John Knox, 433
John Milicz, 344
John Milton, 470
John of Bohemia, 330
John of Brienne, 254, 255, 257,
    259, 261, 269
John of Comminges, 329
John of Gaunt, 345
John of Ibelin, 258, 259, 260
John of Swabia, 319
John Philagathos, 81, 82
John Philagathus, 78
John Pupper: John of Goch, 383
John the Fearless, 366
John the Good, 340, 341
John the Postumous, 327
John the Steadfast, 417, 420; John
    the Constant, 420
John V Palaeologus, 342

John von Wesel, 384
John Wessel, 383
John Wycliff, 333, 338, 343, 344,
    345, 350, 359, 362, 363
John Zizka, 363
Jordan of Capua, 125
Joscelin, 156, 157, 158, 169, 170,
    171
Joseph, 477, 480, 483, 486, 488,
    489, 490, 491, 492, 532, 534,
    535, 580
Joseph Guillotine, 497
Joseph II, 485, 489, 499
Josephine, 507, 508, 509, 517, 524,
    525, 537
Josephinism, 490, 491
Jules Michelet, 488
Julian Medici, 377
Julius, 24, 41, 306, 388, 391, 392,
    393, 417, 433, 578, 585
Julius II, 388, 391, 417, 578
Julius III, 434
Justinian, 10, 12, 13, 14, 15
Kaiser Wilhelm, 3, 547, 552, 553,
    554
Kant, 487
Karlstadt, 414, 415, 416
Kaunite, 490
Kerbogha, 139, 140
Khazar, 17, 46
Kiev, 83, 122, 128
King Stephen, 83, 181
Kingdom of Acre, 201, 206, 209,
    210, 251, 273, 279, 298
Kingdom of Jerusalem, 148, 169,
    189, 194, 201, 202, 269
Kingdom of Naples, 180, 297
Knights Hospitalers, 512
Knights of St. John, 149, 150, 157,
    319, 520
Konrad of Marburg, 263
Krakow, 441
Kubla Khan, 299

Lucius III, 196, 226, 247, 574
Luther, 6, 24, 32, 73, 163, 188,
    244, 270, 325, 333, 370, 383,
    385, 405, 406, 407, 408, 409,
    410, 411, 412, 413, 414, 415,
    416, 419, 420, 421, 423, 426,
    427, 428, 429, 430, 441, 443,
    455
Lutheranism, 412, 413, 419, 426,
    463
Luxemburg, 324, 330, 445, 475
Magna Charta, 98, 105, 238, 239,
    240, 245, 249, 270, 277, 294,
    468
Magyars, 48, 58, 67, 68, 70, 90
Maire-Louise, 547
Malet, 541
Malinche, 397
Mamlukes, 513, 514
Manco, 402, 403
Manfred, 276, 280, 281, 282, 285,
    286
Mansio, 404
Manuel Comnenus, 190
Marat, 498, 501, 502, 503, 504, 507
Marazin, 471
Marcellus II, 388, 434, 578
Marco Polo, 299, 307, 308, 382,
    389
Margaret of Parma, 443
Margaret, the Queen of
    Luxemburg, 330
Margarita Teresa, 472
Maria Theresa, 479, 480, 481, 486,
    488, 489, 490
Marie Antoinette, 489, 503, 508
Marie Antoinnette, 501
Marie Louise, 538, 542
Marie Medici, 459
Marie Therese, 471
Marinus I, 53, 62, 296, 569
Markward, 218

Marozia, 60, 61, 65, 66, 71, 75, 81,
    99
Marquis de Pianeza, 469
Martin II, 53, 296
Martin IV, 295, 296, 297, 313, 576
Martin V, 356, 357, 360, 362, 363,
    364, 368, 369, 577
Martyrs, 90, 99, 101, 189, 245,
    347, 354, 356, 359, 360, 361,
    362, 366, 372, 374, 380, 384,
    410, 413, 418, 429
Mary Stuart, 446
Massacre at the Champs de Mars,
    501
Mateo Visounti, 320
Matteo Orsini, 267
Matthias, 419, 446, 451, 453, 456,
    579
Maurice, 15, 154, 174, 431, 432,
    445
Maximilian, 381, 385, 388, 392,
    393, 394, 407, 408, 441, 442,
    445, 451, 453, 455, 456, 459,
    461, 464, 465, 578, 579
Maximilian I, 392
Maximilian II, 441, 445, 453, 579
Mazarin, 464
Mazzini, 548, 549
Medici, 376, 377, 386, 405, 416,
    439, 460
Melanchthon, 412, 419, 423, 426,
    427, 441
Melisende, 170, 171, 189, 191
Melus of Bari, 89
Merovig, 12
Michael Cerularius, 102
Michael III, 48, 50
Michael of Cesena, 324, 326, 328,
    330
Michael Pelaeologus, 292
Michael Servetus, 428
Michael VII, 120
Michael VIII Palaeologos, 296

Ponce de Leon, 394, 401
Poor Men of Lyon, 225
Pope Joan, 293
Pornocracy, 59, 77
Portugal, 173, 218, 318, 355, 377,
378, 380, 391, 392, 448, 465,
477, 485, 534, 535, 538, 539,
566, 567
Prince John, 210, 212; King John,
232, 238, 240, 242, 256, 258,
266, 270, 282, 338, 339, 340,
341, 349, 432, 468
Prince Thoros, 139
Prince William, 444
Procopius, 364, 370
Procopius Rosa, 364
Protestants, 29, 32, 90, 168, 188,
224, 225, 226, 227, 263, 326,
373, 383, 411, 412, 418, 419,
420, 421, 424, 425, 426, 427,
428, 429, 430, 431, 433, 434,
437, 438, 439, 440, 441, 442,
443, 444, 445, 446, 447, 448,
451, 452, 455, 456, 457, 458,
459, 461, 462, 463, 464, 465,
466, 471, 474, 475, 480, 481,
486, 488, 490, 492, 504, 511,
521
Provence, 58, 65, 256, 336, 345,
416, 467, 505
Prussia, 356, 417, 451, 458, 473,
474, 477, 478, 479, 480, 481,
482, 486, 488, 489, 490, 500,
505, 508, 521, 528, 531, 532,
533, 534, 539, 541, 542, 547,
550, 551, 552, 567
Pseudo-Isidorian Decretals, 123
Puritans, 2, 466, 468, 469, 487
Queen Elizabeth, 422, 434, 442,
444, 446, 447
Queen Joan, 318, 336, 348, 349
Queen Margaret, 374
Rainald, 134, 261

Ratbod, 17
Raymond IV, 137
Raymond of Poitiers, 170
Raymond of Toulouse, 135, 174
Raymond of Tripoli, 174, 196, 201,
202
Raymond VI, 231, 233, 235, 236,
238, 243, 256
Raymond VII, 255, 256
Raymond-Roger, 233, 234, 235,
251
Reginald Pole, 433
Reign of Terror, 8, 487, 502, 503,
505, 506, 507, 511, 517
Renaissance, xi, 2, 42, 73, 105,
276, 283, 285, 335, 338, 372,
373, 374, 375, 450
Reynald, 190
Rhineland, 272, 280, 282, 502, 556
Richard Grosseteste, 280;
Grosthead, 280
Richard II, 347, 349, 351, 353, 359,
361
Richard III, 381
Richard Neville, 380
Richard of Cornwall, 248, 279,
282, 287, 288, 290, 292, 575
Richard of Gloucester, 381
Richard of York, 374
Richard the Lion-Hearted, 4, 202,
203, 207, 209212, 213, 214, 219,
225
Richelieu, 455, 459, 460, 461, 463,
464, 465, 471
Robert Anderson, 437
Robert Guiscard, 102, 107, 120,
125, 126, 135, 136, 139, 163
Robert II, 82, 87, 90, 95
Robert of Anjou, 320
Robert of Courtenay, 255
Robert of Geneva, 343, 346, 348
Robert of Glouchester, 166

Vikings, 39, 47, 71, 90, 102, 109, 151, 470

Viscount Bernabo, 343; Bernabo Viscounti, 346

Vladislav, 392

Volkmar, 132, 133

Voltaire, 5, 36, 487

Waldenses, 32, 90, 160, 187, 188, 224, 225, 226, 227, 257, 264, 266, 285, 319, 321, 324, 325, 332, 337, 343, 344, 345, 347, 350, 354, 356, 359, 366, 382, 383, 409, 419, 424, 429, 434, 437, 439, 440, 442, 469, 470, 586

Waldo, 188, 225, 226

Wallenstein, 458, 459, 460, 461, 462, 463

Walter Brute, 353

Walter the Penniless, 131, 134

War of Austrian Succession, 467, 479, 481

War of Bavarian Succession, 467

War of Devolution, 472

War of Polish Succession, xiii, 467, 478, 479

War of Religion, 441, 442, 446, 448

War of Spanish Succession, 467, 476, 477

War of the Roses, 374, 380, 381

Wars of the Vendees, 502

Waterloo, 4, 546

Wellington, 539, 546

Wencelas, 86, 346, 347, 350, 351, 353, 355, 356, 357, 360, 361, 363, 577

Western Franconia, 46

Western Frankonia, 68

Widukind, 28, 30

William Cornwallis, 521

William Courtenay, 345

William Farel, 421, 425

William II, 127, 137, 151, 191, 192, 211

William III, 212

William III of Orange, 475

William of Aquitaine, 95

William of Holland, 248, 272, 276, 279, 281, 575

William of Nogaret, 310

William of Occam, 326, 328, 330

William of Orange, 443, 444, 446

William Swinderby, 353

William the Bad, 180, 191

William the Conqueror, 89, 103, 105, 107, 108, 110, 111, 112, 113, 118, 122, 123, 127, 135, 137, 151, 304, 562

William the Good, 197

William Thorpe, 359

William V, 98

William Wallace, 294, 317

William, Duke of Normandy, 101, 107

Winston Churchill, 556

Woodrow Wilson, 554

Wulf, 165, 166

Zacharias, 18, 182

Zengi, 169, 170, 171, 173

Zeno, 11, 339

Zwingli, 412, 413, 418, 419, 420, 421, 423

609

Endnotes

1 James Viscount Bryce, *The Holy Roman Empire* MacMillan & Co. Lmt. (London, England) 1950 ed. pg. 50

2 Veit Velentin, *The German People* Alfred A. Knoff (New York, NY) 1946 pg. 153

3 Alexis DeTocqueville, *Democracy in America* Perennial Library (New York, NY) 1966 ed. pg. 38

4 Ibid. pg. 37

5 Ibid. pg. 42

6 Ibid. pg. 47

7 J. Christopher Herold, *The Age of Napoleon* American Heritage Press (New York, New York) 1963 pg. 147

8 Alan Schom, *Napoleon Bonaparte* HarperCollins (New York, New York) 1997 pg. 295

9 Bryce, op. cit. pg. 405

10 Bryce, op. cit. pg. 407

Printed in Great Britain
by Amazon.co.uk, Ltd.,
Marston Gate.